Please remember that this is a library book,
and that it belongs only temporarily to each
person who uses it. Be considerate. Do
not write in this, or any, library book.

# TRUSTED CRIMINALS

## White Collar Crime in Contemporary Society

## David O. Friedrichs

University of Scranton

 Wadsworth Publishing Company
I(T)P™   An International Thomson Publishing Company

Belmont • Albany • Bonn • Boston • Cincinnati • Detroit • London • Madrid • Melbourne
Mexico City • New York • Paris • San Francisco • Singapore • Tokyo • Toronto • Washington

Criminal Justice Editor: Sabra Horne
Editorial Assistant: Jessica Monday
Production: Vicki Moran
Print Buyer: Karen Hunt
Copy Editor: Alan Titche
Interior Design: Wendy LaChance
Cover Design: William Reuter
Cover Photograph: Mark Tomalty/Masterfile
Composition: Publishing Support Services
Printer: Quebecor Printing Book Group/Fairfield

Printed in the United States of America
3 4 5 6 7 8 9 10—02 01 00

For more information, contact Wadsworth Publishing Company:

Wadsworth Publishing Company
10 Davis Drive
Belmont, California 94002, USA

International Thomson Publishing Europe
Berkshire House 168-173
High Holborn
London, WC1V 7AA, England

Thomas Nelson Australia
102 Dodds Street
South Melbourne 3205
Victoria, Australia

Nelson Canada
1120 Birchmount Road
Scarborough, Ontario
Canada M1K 5G4

International Thomson Editores
Campos Eliseos 385, Piso 7
Col. Polanco
11560 México D.F. México

International Thomson Publishing GmbH
Königswinterer Strasse 418
53227 Bonn, Germany

International Thomson Publishing Asia
221 Henderson Road
#05-10 Henderson Building
Singapore 0315

International Thomson Publishing Japan
Hirakawacho Kyowa Building, 3F
2-2-1 Hirakawacho
Chiyoda-ku, Tokyo 102, Japan

**Library of Congress Cataloging-in-Publication Data**
Friedrichs, David O.
    Trusted criminals : white collar crime in contemporary society /
  David O. Friedrichs.
      p.   cm.
  Includes bibliographical references and indexes.
  ISBN 0–534–50517–1 (pbk.)
    1. White collar crimes.  2. White collar crimes--United States.
I. Title.
HV6768.F75   1995                            95-22353
                                                   CIP

*For Jeanne*

Davɪd O. Frɪedrɪchs is professor of Sociology/Criminal Justice at the University of Scranton. He was educated at New York University and taught for nine years at City University of New York (Staten Island). He has published some 50 articles and essays on such topics as the legitimation of legal order, radical criminology, victimology, violence, narrative jurisprudence, postmodernism, and white collar crime. His articles have been published in such journals as *Criminology, Justice Quarterly, Crime & Delinquency, Criminal Justice Review, International Journal of Comparative and Applied Criminal Justice, Journal of Human Justice, Social Justice, Humanity & Society, Social Research, Social Problems, Qualitative Sociology, Journal of Legal Education, Journal of Criminal Justice Education,* and *Teaching Sociology,* as well as in various books. He was editor of the *Legal Studies Forum* between 1985 and 1989. He has also been active with numerous professional associations and has chaired or served on committees of the American Society of Criminology, the Academy of Criminal Justice Sciences, the Society for the Study of Social Problems, and the Association for Humanist Sociology. He has been a visiting professor or guest lecturer at a number of colleges and universities, including the University of South Africa and Ohio University (as Rufus Putnam Visiting Professor). This text is his first book.

# BRIEF CONTENTS

# CHAPTER 4 Occupational Crime                96

# CHAPTER 5 Governmental Crime: State Crime and Political White Collar Crime        122

## CHAPTER 6 State-Corporate Crime, Finance Crime, and Technocrime     153

## CHAPTER 7 Enterprise Crime, Contrepreneurial Crime, and Avocational Crime     183

## CHAPTER 10  Policing and Regulating
White Collar Crime                                                         271

**T**HIS BOOK WAS principally inspired by several considerations. The first is the conviction that white collar crime is an immensely important issue for our society. Second, white collar crime has been relatively neglected—certainly in comparison with conventional or street crime—in criminological and criminal justice scholarship and curricula. Third, an especially large measure of confusion surrounds the whole topic of white collar crime, including a lack of consensus on what the term itself means. Fourth, currently a small handful of books at most could be described as general texts on white collar crime; in the present author's view there was clearly room for a text with another approach to understanding such crime. This book seeks to survey the whole realm of white collar crime more exhaustively than any other text.

Among the topics covered here that tend to be either slighted or wholly excluded in other general surveys of white collar crime are the following: the historical development of the concept of white collar crime; crucial elements of white collar crime: trust, respectability, and risk; the role of the media and other agents in shaping our image of white collar crime; those who expose white collar crime, from whistle-blowers to investigative reporters to criminologists; the challenges involved and the specific methods used in studying white collar crime; perceptions of white collar crime relative to other types of crime; the measurement of the costs and extent of white collar crime; and the victims of white collar crime.

Five chapters (3–7) are devoted to systematic surveys of what we know not only about high-consensus forms of white collar crime such as corporate crime and occupational crime, but also about often-neglected cognate, hybrid, and marginal forms of white collar crime, including governmental crime, state-corporate crime, finance crime, technocrime, enterprise crime, contrepreneurial crime, and avocational crime. Two typically neglected (and sensitive) topics—universities and colleges as corporate criminals, and academics as white collar offenders—are covered in two of these chapters.

Chapter 8 offers a comprehensive survey and evaluation of the whole range of theoretical explanations for white collar crime, from demonological to postmodernist, and from individualist to structuralist. The next three chapters (9–11) provide a very full treatment of the law and other forms of social control of white collar crime; the justice system response to such crime by many different entities, ranging from the local police to federal agencies, including the regulatory agencies; and the adjudication of white collar crime, including the roles of grand juries, trial juries, prosecutors, defense attorneys, and judges, and a discussion of sentencing guidelines. Finally, Chapter 12 offers a fairly exhaustive survey of the many possible responses to white collar crime, from the imposition of fines to the structural transformation of the social order.

In sum, this book explores the conceptual, metaphysical, and methodological issues involved in the study of white collar crime; it delves into the character, causes, and consequences of this type of crime; it explores the relationship of white collar crime and elite deviance to other types of illegal and deviant activity; it examines the response of the law and of the justice system to white collar crime; and it considers the prospects for deterring, preventing, and obliterating white collar crime.

This book is intended primarily as a text for advanced undergraduate and graduate-level courses on white collar crime and closely related matters. However, it should also be useful to scholars and other parties interested in white collar crime, because it endeavors to clarify various conceptual and theoretical issues and to survey critically a large and unwieldy literature. It also attempts to provide a relatively balanced presentation of the many controversies involved in the whole issue of white collar crime.

That considerable dissensus exists on matters pertaining to white collar crime is reflected by the fact that there is even disagreement over the usage of the text's central term: Should it be "white collar crime" or "white-collar crime"? The more common (and, from a strictly grammatical point of view, more correct) usage is "white-collar crime," but we have omitted the dash here because it suggests too literal a reading of the term, when in fact it is better thought of as a metaphor. Interestingly enough, the seminal work in the field, E. H. Sutherland's *White Collar Crime*, did not use this dash (although even Sutherland wasn't completely clear on this matter and used a dash in his original 1940 article on white collar crime).

White collar crime is a problem in all contemporary societies. This text uses examples from the United States for most illustrative purposes. Obviously, the specific character of the white collar crime problem, and the response to it, varies somewhat among different countries, but many parallel patterns exist in all these countries. References to other countries and societies are made, and at least some of the foreign literature on the subject is drawn upon and cited, but as a practical matter it was simply not possible to make a systematic, crosscultural comparison. To date, white collar crime and the justice system response to it are far more fully documented for the American experience than for other countries, although the literature for such countries as Great Britain, Australia, and Canada is clearly growing.

## Rationales for Studying White Collar Crime

WHITE COLLAR CRIME—and more generally, the illegal, unethical, or deviant activity of respectable institutions and individuals—has been relatively neglected in the study of crime and deviance. Traditionally, criminology has focused on "street crime," not "suite crime." The sociology of deviance has emphasized the activities of "nuts, sluts, and perverts," not of corporate executives, physicians, and retail store owners, and this relative neglect has been generally reflected in the media. But one of the guiding premises of this book is that the range of activities that can fall under the heading of white collar crime is more pervasive and is more costly to society than is conventional crime and deviance.

The study of white collar crime should obviously be of interest to students planning criminal justice careers, and to people already employed in the criminal justice system as well. In recent years white collar crime has received more attention from the criminal justice system, and there is reason to believe that this attention will increase in the years to come. As the investigation and prosecution of white collar crime increases, career opportunities for individuals well-informed about this type of activity should expand. The prevention of some forms of white collar crime is also a major concern in the so-called private sector, and thus there are career opportunities in this realm as well. One of the many paradoxical characteristics of white collar crime that will be further explored here is this: Even though much white collar crime is committed within the context of legitimate governmental and business activities, careers combating such crime can be pursued in either the public or private sector.

The study of white collar crime is likely to be of interest to students of the social and behavioral sciences because white collar criminality, as it is defined here, often involves human behavior in its most devious and diabolical forms. This type of activity raises fundamental questions about human nature and responsibility. It forces us to confront the harsh realization that the distinctions between crime and order are not as great as we like to imagine, and that those who benefit most from a stable social system often do the most to threaten its well-being. Few areas of human activity reveal more starkly the complex relationship between the creative and the destructive aspects of human nature than does white collar crime. We cannot fully understand our political, economic, and social institutions without attending to white collar crime, and our understanding of human psychology is deepened through the study of white collar criminals.

The law in the white collar realm that confronts pre-law and law students is especially dynamic and complex. The problem of corporate liability poses special difficulties, and the subtle and sometimes arbitrary lines of demarcation between the criminal law and the civil law are crucial aspects of the study of white collar crime.

But a strong argument can also be made that a deeper understanding of white collar crime should prove useful and relevant to students in any major. As citizens, employees, employers, and professionals, most of us are likely to be affected more by white collar crime than by any other type of criminal activity. And if we or the people with whom we have the most regular contact become involved in illegalities, such activities are likely to be some form of white collar crime.

Finally, if the problem of white collar crime is to be effectively addressed, many ordinary citizens will have to be aware of the nature of the problem and willing to engage with the forces that promote it. Certainly one objective of this book is to promote this consciousness and engagement.

## A Note to Instructors

WHITE COLLAR CRIME courses are relatively new additions to the curriculum in most criminology and criminal justice programs, and they are offered under various titles and with a variety of approaches. Some instructors are especially concerned with identifying the broad varieties of white collar crime and the different theoretical explanations for them; other instructors are far more concerned with white collar crime as a problem of social control and with the justice system response to it. This text was developed to accommodate the considerable diversity of perspectives on making sense of white collar crime. The order of the chapters is reasonably consistent with a conventional criminological approach to crime and criminal justice, but this arrangement inevitably has a certain arbitrariness to it. Each chapter was written to stand alone, and thus instructors can arrange the chapters to suit different approaches. For example, Chapter 9, on law and social control, and Chapter 10, on policing and regulating white collar crime, and Chapter 11, on adjudicating white collar crime cases, can be assigned up front and followed by the substantive chapters on different types of white collar crime. A variety of rearrangements are clearly possible.

A test bank, compiled by the author, is available to all instructors who adopt this text.

## A Note to Readers

ALL AUTHORS WELCOME responses to their work, and I'm no exception. I have attempted to produce a book that is clear, accurate, informative, and thorough, but I recognize that at least some readers may find the book deficient on one or more of these grounds. Any comments—positive or negative—and suggestions can be sent to me at the following address:

David O. Friedrichs
Department of Sociology/Criminal Justice
University of Scranton
Scranton, PA 18510-4605

Comments and suggestions will be especially helpful for future editions of this book. Substantial comments and suggestions will be properly acknowledged in any new edition.

**M**ANY DIFFERENT INDIVIDUALS, in diverse ways, contributed to the making of this book over the course of more than five years. Perhaps my most basic debt is due to the numerous scholars and journalists whose work is cited throughout this text. I have learned a great deal from their prodigious labors and can only hope I have done justice to their efforts in my discussions of and references to their work.

An invitation to give a series of lectures at the University of South Africa in 1988 turned out to be one of the early sources of inspiration for this book, because I chose to give one of these lectures on white collar crime. I am grateful to Professors Jan Pretorius and Cornie Alant of the Department of Sociology, University of South Africa, for extending the invitation to present these lectures.

A number of professional acquaintances and friends provided encouragement early on, sent me useful material, or gave me some good advice. They include Harold Barnett (University of Rhode Island), John Braithwaite (Australian National University), Kitty Calavita (University of California, Irvine), Frank Cullen (University of Cincinnati), Rob Elias (University of San Francisco), Nancy Frank (University of Wisconsin–Milwaukee), Frank Hagan and Peter Benekos (Mercyhurst College), Paul Jesilow (University of California, Irvine), David Kauzlarich (St. Joseph's University), Ronald Kramer (Western Michigan University), Gary Marx (University of Colorado–Boulder), Marilyn McShane and Frank Williams (California State University–San Bernardino), Dragan Milovanovic (Northeastern Illinois University), Larry Nichols (West Virginia University), Nikos Passas (Temple University), Hal Pepinsky (Indiana University–Bloomington), David Shichor (California State University–San Bernardino), David Simon (San Diego State University), Roman Tomasic (Canberra College, Australia), and Peter Yeager (Boston University). The late Al Lee of Brooklyn College–CUNY, and Richard Quinney, presently at Northern Illinois University, offered instrumental encouragement earlier in my career. Stuart Hills, recently retired from St. Lawrence University, has been on my case for years about finishing up this book, and he will be relieved to see it in print. I am especially indebted to my great friend Martin D. Schwartz of Ohio University for constant encouragement, sound advice, and overall inspiration. Some of the material in this book was refined when I prepared my Rufus Putnam Visiting Professor lectures at Ohio University in 1991, and this opportunity was arranged and coordinated by Marty Schwartz. In addition, even though authors typically follow a long-standing convention of accepting responsibility for errors that may surface in their book, in this case Marty Schwartz has generously offered to accept responsibility for any such errors.

At the University of Scranton, the Faculty Research Committee, the Faculty Development Committee, and the University Travel Committee provided absolutely crucial support in several forms: annual faculty research grants, which enabled me to visit research libraries, acquire essential research materials, and defray numerous production costs; a sabbatical leave for Fall 1991; two summer grants at critical stages in the project; and travel grants that allowed me to attend and participate in professional meetings, where much current work is discussed and useful exchanges with professional colleagues occur. The provost of the university, Richard Passon; the graduate dean and director of research, Tom Hogan; and the dean of my college, Paul Fahey, have all been supportive of this project in various ways. Within my own department several colleagues, especially John Pryle, Tom Baker, and Richard Wright, have also provided encouragement. Richard and I collaborated on a journal article on white collar crime, and he has provided me with very helpful responses to parts of the manuscript and some useful research materials over the years. I am also indebted to various reference librarians at the university's Weinberg Memorial Library—especially Bonnie Strohl, Katie Duke, and Kevin Norris—for their assistance. A number of individuals associated with the university's Computer Service and PC Maintenance Center—including Vince Merkel, Aileen McHale, Deanne Loftus, Karl Johns, Joe Kitcho, and Glen Pace—have bailed me out of a number of hardware and software near-catastrophes. My department secretary, Judith Lestansky, has provided efficient assistance on many aspects of this project. I have also benefited from feedback from some of the numerous students I have had in my white collar crime course over the years, especially students in a January 1995 intersession course, who first used this text; Josianne Aboutanous, Ingrid Farally, and Marius Stan were especially noteworthy in this regard. And for their helpful service and good cheer during my long days and nights working in my office, I want to thank two members of the maintenance staff, Joe Rankosky and Stanley Janus.

I visited many libraries over the course of this research. I am grateful to the late Professor Diana Vincent-Daviss of the NYU Law Library for making that collection accessible to me, and especially to the remarkable Phyllis Schultze of the Criminal Justice/NCCD Library at Rutgers University-Newark for numerous forms of assistance on this project.

Several editors have been involved with this project. Cindy Stormer initiated this book at Brooks/Cole, and Peggy Adams, Brian Gore, and Sabra Horne worked on it after criminal justice titles were shifted to Wadsworth. I am grateful to them for encouragement and suggestions, and would also like to thank Jason Moore, Jennifer Dunning, Diane Honigberg, and Jessica Monday for their work on the book. I am indebted to Vicki Moran and other individuals who have efficiently shepsarded this project through the production process. Alan Titche, the copy editor, has made an outstanding contribution toward enhancing the clarity and accuracy of this text.

A number of external reviewers for Brooks/Cole and subsequently for Wadsworth provided me with some helpful advice, and I was much heartened by their very favorable and encouraging assessment of my prospectus and manuscript. Those known to me are William Clements (Norwich University), Lee Colwell (University of Arkansas, Little Rock), Jurg Gerber (San Houston State University), Richard Janikowski (University of Memphis), Sally Simpson (University of Maryland), and Kip Schlegel (Indiana University–Bloomington). Quite a number of the specific suggestions of these reviewers were adopted in the course of revising the manuscript.

Finally, various members of my fairly large extended family have been supportive over the years. My father and mother, both now deceased, were always extraordinarily supportive and encouraging, and an important source of inspiration for my professional work. My two children, Jessica and Bryan, have been uncommonly understanding of a father who has too often been occupied, or preoccupied, with his work. As for my wife Jeanne, she has probably not read more than two lines of the manuscript because she has been very busy with the demands of her own career in occupational therapy, her dedication to the happiness of our children, her magnificent gardening, and her uncompromising insistence on having fun (lately, in the form of country line dancing). Nevertheless, this book would never have been written without her loving support. For that reason, and because she makes our life together so wonderful, this book is dedicated to Jeanne, with much love.

# The Discovery of White Collar Crime

**C**ONSIDER THE FOLLOWING list of activities:

- A huge multinational corporation is charged with criminal negligence when one of its ships spills millions of gallons of oil into Alaska's Prince William Sound.
- A butcher's shop is accused of short-weighting customers, of giving them less meat than they have paid for.
- A billionaire financier is fined $600 million and sent to prison for illegal manipulation of the securities market.
- A bank clerk embezzles several thousand dollars from her employer to cover family-related debts.
- A physician is found to have defrauded Medicare out of more than a million dollars using misbilling and phony bills.
- A major automobile corporation is indicted and tried in connection with deaths arising from accidents involving one of its cars, the Pinto.
- An auto repair shop charges customers for false or unnecessary repairs.
- A manufacturer of asbestos declares bankruptcy in the face of billions of dollars of liabilities to employees and others harmed through exposure to its product.
- A group of young computer hackers are alleged to have used their computer expertise to steal confidential credit information, which they then sell.
- Three executives of a film processing plant are convicted of homicide in the death of an employee exposed to poisonous chemicals in the plant.

- A defense contractor agrees to pay millions to settle charges of defrauding U.S. taxpayers.
- A famous New York City hotel owner, worth billions, goes to prison on tax evasion charges.
- The manufacturer of an immensely popular video game admits to price-fixing.
- A lawyer embezzles a large sum of money from clients' escrow accounts.
- A powerful member of Congress is indicted on allegations of defrauding taxpayers through various corrupt practices.

The activities in this list might seem to have little in common. They involve the very powerful and the relatively powerless, large-scale organizations and isolated individuals, enormous sums of money and relatively modest sums, the loss of numerous lives and incremental, less-apparent threats to long-term health. But all these activities have several things in common. First, they do not include the forms of crime that typically come to mind most readily when people think of crime: murder, rape, aggravated assault, burglary, car theft, larceny, and the like. Second, the offenders or offending organizations enjoy a relatively high level of trust and respectability, at least when compared with organized crime and street criminals. Third, these activities have not been a traditional focus of the law and the justice system, and these institutions have responded to them in quite different ways. Fourth, they have all been considered forms of white collar crime according to at least someone's conception of that complex term. Indeed, although the term *white collar crime* is by now quite familiar to many people, it is also a source of considerable confusion. A brief history of the "discovery" of white collar crime, and a consideration of the problem of defining this term, follows.

## Edwin H. Sutherland and the Discovery of White Collar Crime

ALTHOUGH CRIMINOLOGIST EDWIN H. Sutherland is generally given credit for introducing the term *white collar crime* into the literature in 1939, recognition of this type of crime extends well back in history. Europeans have long recognized (as is evident in the works of Marx and Engels) that the powerful and the privileged commit "crimes," loosely defined as consequences of the character of the capitalist economic system and the special status of the priviledged within it. The American muckrakers of the early 20th century inveighed, as well, against the exploitative crimes of the "robber barons" and their confederates.

Sutherland was apparently most directly inspired by E. A. Ross's (1907) *Sin and Society: An Analysis of Latter Day Iniquity* (Geis and Goff 1987: 3). Writing shortly after the turn of the century, Ross, a prominent sociologist of his time, promoted the notion of "the criminaloid": the businessman who committed exploitative (if not necessarily illegal) acts out of an uninhibited desire to maximize profit, all the while hiding behind a facade of respectability and piety (1907: 17). Ross regarded these criminaloids as guilty of moral insensibility and held them directly responsible for unnecessary deaths of consumers and workers. At the very outset of his book Ross (1907: 7) observed that:

> [t]he man who picks pockets with a railway rebate, murders with an adulterant instead of a bludgeon, burglarizes with a "rake-off" instead of a jimmy, cheats with a company prospectus instead of a deck of cards, or scuttles his town instead of his ship, does not feel on his brow the brand of a malefactor.

For Ross, the actions of criminaloids were threatening to a just and decent capitalist society, which Ross supported. Although his book enjoyed popular acclaim, it did not persuade the sociologists of the day to attend more fully to either criminaloids or white collar crime.

E. H. Sutherland (1883–1950) is quite commonly regarded as "the most important contributor to American criminology to have appeared to date" (Gibbons 1979: 65). In addition to his seminal contributions to the study of white collar crime, he produced an influential textbook, formulated a major criminological theory (differential association), and published important works on professional crime and laws concerning sexual psychopaths. When Sutherland began publishing in the 1920s and 1930s, American sociology was especially concerned with promoting its status as a legitimate social science, and it consciously distanced itself from the passionate moral exhortations of Ross and his contemporaries (Geis and Meier 1977: 24). Despite Sutherland's claim that his work on white collar crime was theoretical and scientific in purpose, his personal sense of outrage at corporate criminality was clearly a strong motivating factor for his work. Sutherland did not quarrel with the virtues of an openly competitive entrepreneurial form of capitalism as originally envisioned by Adam Smith. Rather, he was deeply angered by those behaviors and actions of "Big Business" that corrupted and threatened the laudable aspects of the American economic system (Sutherland 1949, 1983: 90–93). Sutherland's value system combined a quintessentially American synthesis of entrepreneurial and progressive beliefs with his professional commitment to detached social scientific inquiry.

Sutherland's interest in white collar crime has been traced back to the 1920s, when he produced the first edition of his celebrated textbook entitled *Criminology* (1924). His interest appears to have been motivated, in part, by his realization that the conventional criminological theories of his time focused almost exclusively on explaining lower class criminality, and provided little if any guidance for understanding the criminality of middle- and upper-class people (Cohen, Lindesmith, and Schuessler 1956: 3). He came to believe that his theory of differential association, which attributed criminality to a learning process, was precisely the type of general theory that could usefully explain both lower-class and upper-class crime. Then in 1929, with the crash of the stock market, the country entered a long period of economic distress. With so many Americans barely surviving, the crimes of the rich may well have appeared to be especially insidious. Throughout the 1930s Sutherland collected data on crime by respectable individuals, especially embezzlers, and refined an emerging conception of white collar crime with his graduate students at Indiana University (Geis and Goff 1987: 6–9). His election as president of the American Sociological Society offered him a unique opportunity to introduce and publicize the concept of white collar crime.

Sutherland's presidential address in Philadelphia in December, 1939, was entitled "The White Collar Criminal." In this initial characterization of white collar crime, published the following year in the *American Sociological Review*, Sutherland (1940: 1) alluded to "crime in the upper or white-collar class, composed of respectable or at least respected business and professional men...." A principal attribute of this type of crime is that it consists of "violation of delegated or implied trust..." (Sutherland 1940: 3). Examples of white collar criminality in business included various forms of misrepresentation, manipulation, embezzlement, and bribery (Sutherland 1940: 2). Sutherland suggested that white collar crime was a long-established American tradition, and he provided some evidence of its prevalence, its staggering financial costs, and the special vulnerability of its victims. Sutherland argued for the recognition of white collar crime as "real," even if convictions by criminal courts weren't necessarily involved. He pointed out that the white collar classes have both special influence on the formulation of criminal laws and various means of minimizing the chances of criminal conviction.

During the 1940s Sutherland undertook a major study that culminated in the publication of *White Collar Crime* (1949), his last major contribution before his death in 1950. In this book Sutherland focused on the 70 largest U.S. manufacturing, mining, and mercantile corporations with respect to the legal decisions (by criminal, civil, or administrative tribunals) against them concerning allegations of wrongdoing (Sutherland 1949: 19). Each of these corporations had one or more decisions against it, with an average of 14 decisions against each corporation during the course of its existence. (However, no more than 16 percent of the decisions against the corporations emanated from the criminal courts.) These decisions, in descending order of frequency, included restraint-of-trade violations, infringement of patent and other rights, unfair labor practices, fraudulent advertising, and illegal rebates. These findings led Sutherland (1949: 227) to conclude that some 97 percent of the corporations, each with two or more adverse decisions, were criminal recidivists.

The main body of Sutherland's *White Collar Crime* consists of a systematic exploration of the specific forms of white collar crime as committed by major corporations. Sutherland was especially venomous in his characterization of corporate profiteering, fraud, and evasion of taxes during war (specifically, during World War II); he characterized white collar crime as a form of organized crime. The crimes committed by corporations are rational, deliberate, persistent, and much more extensive than prosecution of them indicates (Sutherland 1949: 228). Victims are often quite impotent to respond effectively to corporate crimes, which are difficult to prove, and corporations are well-positioned to "fix" cases against them (Sutherland 1949: 236–38). Businessmen caught violating the law did not generally suffer a loss of peer status; in fact, businessmen as a group were commonly contemptuous of law (Sutherland 1949: 230–33). In their view, if they were technically in violation of certain laws, it was not because they were criminals but because the laws themselves were bad.

Although the significance of Sutherland's contribution can hardly be overstated, the slow pace of development of white collar crime research in his wake is somewhat mystifying. On the one hand, criminologists have generally acknowledged that Sutherland's *White Collar Crime* was one of the most important contributions to the field of criminology. On the other hand, for a long time this work was little cited and rarely emulated (Geis and Goff 1982: 16–17). In addition to the ongoing conceptual confusion regarding the term *white collar crime* (for which Sutherland must assume some responsibility), this work can be faulted on other grounds. Even his admirers concede that Sutherland overemphasized an individualistic framework (and social-psychological factors) and largely ignored social structural factors (for example, capitalism, profit rates, and business cycles). He failed to make clear-cut distinctions among white collar crimes, and he did not adequately appreciate the influence of corporations over the legislative and regulatory processes (Geis and Goff 1987: 27–28). Still, when all is said and done, it is difficult to imagine the study of white collar crime without Sutherland's contribution. The oft-cited accolade by the prominent criminologist Hermann Mannheim (1965: 470) is worth repeating here: If a Nobel Prize were awarded in criminology, Edwin Sutherland would surely have been a deserving recipient for his work on white collar crime.

## Defining White Collar Crime

MORE THAN HALF a century, then, has passed since Sutherland formally introduced the concept of white collar crime. Despite this extended passage of time, there is today more confusion than ever about the meaning and most appropriate application of this concept. The problem of defining white collar crime has been characterized as "an intellectual nightmare" (Geis and Meier 1977: 25) and "a lion's den from which no tracks return" (Hirschi and Gottfredson 1989: 363). Meier (1986: 415) observed that "every student of white-collar crime since Sutherland has…failed to propose an acceptable definition," and Wheeler (1983: 1655) wrote that "the concept of white-collar crime is in a state of disarray." Geis (1974: 283) bluntly called the concept of white collar crime "a mess." Why is this so?

First, it must be recognized that a wide variety of terms have been used to characterize activities that could either be classified under the broad rubric of "white collar crime" or are closely linked with white collar crime. Some of these terms include *economic crime, commercial crime, business crime, marketplace crime, consumer crime, respectable crime, "crime at the top," "suite" crime, elite crime and deviance, official crime and deviance, political crime, governmental crime, state (or state-organized) crime, corporate crime, occupational crime, employee crime, avocational crime, technocrime, computer crime,* and *folk crime.*

In some cases different terms refer to the same activity; in other cases the terms refer to very different types of activity. Obviously the invocation of so many different terms, interrelated in such a bewildering variety of ways, contributes to the general confusion about white collar crime. Each term is likely to have some unique connotations, and each tends to emphasize a particular dimension of white collar crime.

The term *crime* itself can have many meanings: *legalistic crime*—that is, activities prohibited by criminal law (statutory) or by the finding of a criminal court (adjudicated); *humanistic* and *moralistic crime*—that is, those activities that involve demonstrable harm to human beings or are at odds with a "higher" eternal law; and *political* and *popular crimes*—that is, acts offensive to those in power or at the focal point of public interest. When the term *white collar crime* is invoked it may be premised on one or the other of these different understandings of "crime."

The term *deviance*, which is preferred by some students of white collar "crime," also raises problems of meaning. Deviance has been defined in *absolutist terms* (as a violation of an eternal law or standard), in *normative terms* (as a violation of prevailing norms), and in *reactive terms* (in which a stigmatizing label is imposed on some actions or actors)(Goode 1994). Deviance is most readily associated with the mentally ill, homosexuals, drug addicts, rapists, muggers, and others who engage in any "disvalued" activity, whether or not they are breaking the law. Sociologists have long criticized the inherent conservatism of focusing on such "pathological," individualistic, and sensational forms of deviance while neglecting the aberrant, harmful practices of elites (Liazos 1972; Mills 1943; Thio 1973). Some writers discussing activities that most people would describe as white collar crime have preferred to use terms such as *elite deviance* (Simon and Eitzen 1993), *corporate deviance* (Ermann and Lundman 1982), and *official deviance* (Douglas and Johnson 1977). The principal rationale for favoring *deviance* over *crime* is that the former term emphasizes that governmental and corporate elites in particular undertake a great deal of harmful activity that is not specifically classified as criminal.

In sum, both *crime* and *deviance* have been used to describe many of the activities discussed in this book. The choice has been made to emphasize the term *crime*, because this term is more closely associated with doing harm to others than is *deviance*. Second, quite a bit of white collar crime unfortunately does not deviate from typical patterns of behavior (e.g., deception in the marketplace). Third, many white collar offenders avoid the stigma that is so central to the notion of deviance; they do not have a deviant self-identity or lifestyle.

Definitional clarity is, however, a precondition for any coherent theorizing about white collar crime. The original debate on the concept, initiated by Tappan (1947), attacked Sutherland on the grounds that white collar crime should refer to acts defined by the criminal law and adjudicated in a criminal proceeding. This issue continues to be debated in some form today, and in the intervening years other conceptual controversies arose: whether white collar crime should refer to acts committed by higher-status individuals or institutions, or those committed in the context of a legitimate occupation, regardless of socioeconomic status; whether it should refer to acts involving economic and financial activities only, or other acts involving physical harm as well; and whether it should refer to acts of people only, or organizations only, or both.

More recent attempts to define white collar crime and closely related concepts have emphasized a range of attributes, including commission in a legitimate occupational context, respectable social status of perpetrators, presence of calculation and rationality (with economic gain or occupational success a primary goal), absence of direct violence, offenders' noncriminal self-image, deterrence of, and a limited criminal justice system response (Coleman 1987; Edelhertz 1970; Geis 1974; Katz 1979; Shapiro 1980). Students of white collar crime disagree about which of these attributes should be emphasized (and about other matters as well). This "war among the white collar criminologists" includes debates over whether we should favor narrow, operational definitions, or deliberately ambiguous and inclusive definitions of white collar crime; whether we should limit our understanding of white collar crime to acts defined as criminal by the state, or formulate independent definitions based on criteria of exploitation and harm; whether our approach to defining white collar crime should be solely to seek the advancement of scientific understanding, or be directed toward elevating political consciousness; and whether our definitions should focus on the nature of offenders or of acts (Aubert 1952; Biderman and Reiss 1980; Braithwaite 1989g; Edelhertz 1970; Friedrichs 1992; Geis 1992; Goff and Reasons 1978; Hirschi and Gottfredson 1989; Meier 1986; Michalowski 1985; Michalowski and Kramer 1987; Pepinsky 1974; Reed and Yeager 1991; Reichman 1986; Schlegel 1988b; Shapiro 1980, 1983, 1990; Simon and Eitzen 1993; Snider 1993; Varette et al. 1985; Yeager 1991b). It is not our goal here to sort through all these issues (see Friedrichs 1992 for an attempt at doing so); instead, this text adopts a generally inclusive approach that recognizes that the term *white collar crime* can be used in many different ways. In the following section some general guidance toward understanding these different meanings is provided.

## A Multistage Approach to Defining White Collar Crime

A coherent and meaningful understanding of white collar crime must be approached in stages. The first (most general) definitional stage is *polemical* or presentational, the second stage is *typological* or taxonomic, and the third stage is *operational* or heuristic.

The traditional, "popular" conception of white collar crime—the illegal and harmful actions of elites and respectable members of society carried out for economic gain in the context of legitimate organizational or occupational activity—has an important *polemical* and pedagogical purpose (as even such critics as Shapiro [1990: 346] concede). This generalized conception, for all its operational deficiencies and logical contradictions, challenges a popular tendency to associate criminality with inner-city residents, minorities, young men, and conventional illegal activities such as homicide, robbery, and burglary. The more complex and qualified the concept, the less potent it is likely to be for challenging conventional crime consciousness. It is not clear whether any of the many previously mentioned terms, all with somewhat more restricted connotations, can hope to achieve the easy recognition accorded *white collar crime,* which has been quite widely invoked for many decades.

Some white collar offenses have more of the defining attributes of such crime than do other offenses (Katz 1979). We even find some recognition of this among politicians concerned with white collar crime (U.S. Senate 1987: 17). Thus corporate illegalities and employee theft are two activities that are widely recognized as forms of white collar crime, although ideological bias would seem to play a role in which is emphasized. Political corruption and bribery are sometimes defined as white collar crimes, and at other times as forms of political crime. In contrast, including welfare cheats or professionals who sexually exploit their clients in a discussion of white collar crime is controversial and a matter of low consensus.

The second stage of conceptual development of white collar crime is *typological*, but there has been some skepticism concerning whether criminological typologies correspond with reality. They may well put a disproportionate emphasis on more dramatic forms of criminality (Hartjen 1974: 69). The patterns of actual lawbreakers are so varied that a taxonomic classification (typology) may distort reality rather than clarify it (Clarke 1990: 3; Gibbons 1979: 92; Hagan 1986: 92). Such criticisms are certainly significant, but what are the realistic alternatives to typologies of some sort? Nontypological generalizations about crime and criminals must necessarily distort realities even more dramatically than the most rudimentary typology, as long as the basic limitations of any criminological typology are borne in mind.

The concept of "occupational crime" was first clearly identified by Quinney (1964) and was specifically defined by Clinard and Quinney (1967: 131) as "violation of the legal codes in the course of activity in a legitimate occupation." They considered this formulation more useful than Sutherland's conception of white collar crime, which is restricted to high-status offenders. Following Newman (1958a), among others, they recognized that crimes can be committed by farmers illegally watering down milk, by repairmen undertaking and charging for unnecessary repairs, and by a host of other non-white-collar workers who commit crimes within the context of their occupations. Following Bloch and Geis (1970: 307) they differentiated among occupational crimes committed by individuals as individuals (e.g., doctors against patients), by employees against employers (e.g., embezzlers), and by merchants against customers (e.g., consumer fraud). Typically, occupational crime has been applied to acts in which financial gain or status is sought (or prevention of its loss is involved).

Clinard and Quinney (1973), in the second edition of their influential book, *Criminal Behavior Systems*, designated corporate crime as but one form of occupational crime. This distinction has been the single most influential typological scheme of white collar crime. It has been widely adopted not only within the field, but in the more sophisticated media as well. Corporate crime was defined as "offenses committed by corporate officials for their corporation and the offenses of the corporation itself" (Clinard and Quinney 1973: 188). It has been recognized that this was in fact the type of crime Sutherland was concerned with in *White Collar Crime* (1949). Subsequent, more elaborate definitions of corporate crime have put special emphasis on its character (Kramer 1984: 18). It is widely accepted, then, that corporate crime has characteristics and consequences that make it fundamentally different from the range of activities subsumed under the heading of occupational crime.

A somewhat parallel but hardly synonymous conceptual differentiation that was refined during the 1970s distinguishes between *organizational* and *individualistic* white collar crime (see, for example, Schrager and Short 1977). The complex mixture of motives and objectives in organizational white collar crime is not easily conveyed by such a dichotomy (Reichman 1986). Indeed, various more fully differentiated typologies of white collar crime developed over the years have incorporated offender-victim relationships, offender attributes, offense context, offense form and objectives, nature of harm perpetrated, or some combination of these variables (Bloch and Geis 1970; Edelhertz 1970; Hagan 1986; Michalowski 1985; Shapiro 1980).

We see, then, that quite different approaches can be applied to the challenge of formulating a typology of white collar crime. Despite the inevitably arbitrary and limited attributes of any classification scheme, typologies provide a necessary point of departure for any meaningful discussion of (and theorizing about) white collar crime. The synthetic typology offered in this text is adapted from some of the existing typologies but also encompasses the wide range of activities labeled as white collar crime. The principal criteria for differentiating between the types of white collar crime, broadly defined, are:

- Context in which illegal activity occurs, including the setting (e.g., corporation; government agency; professional service; etc.) and the level within the setting (e.g., individual; workgroup; organization)
- Status or position of offender (e.g., wealthy or middle class; chief executive officer or employee)
- Primary victims (e.g., general public or individual clients)
- Principal form of harm (e.g., economic loss or physical injury)
- Legal classification (e.g., antitrust; fraud; etc.)

The typology that follows includes activities that some students of white collar crime would exclude, but at a minimum these activities have a close generic relationship with white collar crime:

1 **Corporate Crime**: Illegal and harmful acts committed by officers and employees of corporations to promote corporate (and personal) interests. Forms include corporate violence, corporate theft, corporate financial manipulation, and corporate political corruption or meddling.

2 **Occupational Crime**: Illegal or harmful financially driven activity committed within the context of a legitimate, respectable occupation. Forms include retail crime, service crime, crimes of professionals, and employee crime.

3 **Governmental Crime**: A cognate form of white collar crime; a range of activities wherein government itself, government agencies, government office, or the aspiration to serve in a government office generates illegal or demonstrably harmful acts. Forms include the criminal state, state-organized crime, and political white collar crime.

4 **State-Corporate Crime, Finance Crime** and **Technocrime**: Major hybrid forms of white collar crime that involve a synthesis of governmental and corporate crime, or of corporate and occupational crime. *Finance crime* specifically refers to criminal activity in the realm of high-level finance, from banking to the securities markets. *Technocrime* involves the intersection of computers and other forms of "high technology" with white collar crime.

5 **Enterprise Crime, Contrepreneurial Crime** and **Avocational Crime**: "Residual" forms of white collar crime, or a variety of miscellaneous illegal activities that include more marginal forms of white collar crime. *Enterprise crime* refers

to cooperative enterprises involving syndicated (organized) crime and legitimate businesses; *contrepreneurial crime* refers to swindles, scams, and frauds that assume the guise of legitimate businesses; *avocational crimes* are illegal but nonconventional criminal acts committed by "white collar" workers outside a specifically organizational or occupational context, including income tax evasion, insurance fraud, loan/credit fraud, customs evasion, and the purchase of stolen goods.

The third stage for defining white collar crime can be called *operational* or heuristic. On this level the objective of the definition is to provide a point of departure for focused empirical research or comparative critical analysis. In the positivist tradition, Wheeler and his associates (1988) provide us with one approach to an "operational" definition of white collar crime. For purposes of systematically comparing white collar criminals and "common" criminals, they define white collar crime as violations of eight federal crime categories: securities fraud, antitrust violations, bribery, tax offenses, bank embezzlement, postal and wire fraud, false claims and statements, and credit and lending-institution fraud. Although they recognize that such an operational definition does not encompass a representative sampling of the total body of white collar crime, they consider it to reflect quite accurately federally prosecuted white collar crime (Wheeler et al. 1988: 334). If such an operational definition allows these researchers to make quantitative comparisons, then obviously any resulting generalizations must be qualified relative to the definition. Many positivistically oriented studies of white collar crime adopt much narrower definitions of very specific types of white collar crime for purposes of quantitative analysis.

Such definitions, however, are not simply the purview of mainstream positivistic white collar criminologists. Critical criminologists have also formulated white collar crime definitions that are intended to facilitate comparative analysis. Michalowski and Kramer (1987: 47), for example, have defined "corporate transgressions" as violations of international standards of conduct (developed by the United Nations, for example) by transnational corporations that result in identifiable social injury. It could be argued that such a definition raises some formidable interpretive questions, but its intent and thrust is to facilitate systematic, comparative analysis. Again, critical white collar criminologists have developed comparable but much more narrowly focused definitions for elite and corporate activities they consider criminal.

The concept of white collar crime is, in the final analysis, somewhat like a Chinese puzzle: Whichever way one turns with it, new difficulties and conundrums are encountered. Perhaps its least problematic or controversial definition is negative: It refers to illegal or harmful activity that is neither street crime nor conventional crime. More generally, *white collar crime* is a generic term for the whole range of illegal, prohibited, and demonstrably harmful activities involving a violation of a private or public trust, committed by institutions and individuals occupying a legitimate, respectable status, and directed toward financial advantage or the maintenance and extension of power and privilege. But we should give up the illusion that *white collar crime* can—or even should—have a single meaning or definition. Ideally, whenever a definition of white collar crime or cognate activities is advanced, it should be done so in conjunction with a clear indication of its purpose.

White collar crime, then, has many different dimensions. In the sections that follow, several important dimensions will be explored in somewhat greater depth.

## Trust and White Collar Crime

The notion of trust is a central one in contemporary social existence, but until quite recently it has been somewhat neglected by social theorists (Luhmann 1979; Barber 1983; Gambetta 1988). There is no single meaning of the term *trust*. It has referred both to a property of individuals and organizations and to expectations defining various types of relationships (Barber 1983; Shapiro 1987).

In the traditional world of our ancestors, life was largely confined to a small circle of people, primarily one's family, with whom one had long-standing, mutually interdependent relations. One of the central features of the modern world, however, is that people typically spend much more time interacting with or dependent on many individuals and organizations with whom they have narrower and more instrumental relationships. This applies to corporations that employ us, banks where we deposit money, stockbrokers with whom we invest, retail businesses from which we purchase goods, physicians from whom we seek treatment, and so forth. Trust—the confidence that the other party in such transactions or relationships will act with honor and integrity—has become much more problematic in the modern world.

The diffusion of impersonal trust into a broad range of relationships and transactions creates countless opportunities for corruption, misrepresentation, and fraud. Of course, in a complex society we develop many forms of monitoring and surveillance directed at overseeing these trust-based relationships and transactions. The broad extension of trust thus appears to be both unavoidable and necessary in a modern society, although a great deal of variability exists in the degree of trust involved in relationships and transactions. Donald Cressey (1980), the distinguished early student of white collar crime, argued that we must confront a fundamental paradox: If we attempt to curtail sharply the extension of trust in business relationships in the interest of reducing opportunities for white collar crime, we will also severely jeopardize legitimate business relationships and other interpersonal transactions.

Trust and its violation are certainly key elements of white collar crime. Sutherland (1940: 3; 1949: 152–58) characterized white collar crime as involving a "violation of delegated or implied trust." Susan Shapiro (1990: 350) has argued forcefully that *the* central attribute of white collar crime is the violation of trust, which then takes the form of misrepresentation, stealing, misappropriation, self-dealing, corruption, and role conflict. It is especially difficult to prosecute successfully the violations of trust that occur behind the closed doors of "suites," and the parties involved can often manipulate the organizational structure to conceal their misconduct (Shapiro 1990: 355). For lack of any other term that better captures the common links among the broad range of white collar crimes, this book adopts the notion of "trusted criminals," even though focusing on the nature of their offenses may be more important than making sense of the offenders themselves.

The adoption of the term *trusted criminals* and the recognition of the central role of trust in white collar crime should not be interpreted as an unqualified endorsement of the thesis that "violations of trust" differentiate white collar crime from other forms of crime, for trust is very much a relative phenomenon. Trust and its violation are elements of other crimes, from confidence games to domestic violence. Conversely, the level of trust in white collar relationships and transactions is hardly absolute, although it is typically higher than in many other realms, and this tends to broaden both the scope and the scale of possible crimes. Nevertheless, from a critical or progressive perspective, the essence of white collar crime resides in the harm done, not simply in the violation of trust.

The violation of trust has some significant consequences beyond the immediate losses suffered by victims of misrepresentations, embezzlements, and other specific crimes. One of the most pernicious consequences of violations of trust—especially when committed by people in high places in government and in the corporate world—is the potential for an increase in *distrust*. To the extent that people become distrustful and cynical, the likelihood of cooperative and productive relationships is diminished. The long-term consequences of violations of trust, and the difficulties involved in restoring trusting relations once such violations occur, are relatively understudied. Still, the harmful consequences of the erosion of trust are surely diffuse and many.

## Respectability and White Collar Crime

The idea of respectability has traditionally been closely associated with white collar crime. As noted earlier, Sutherland's (1940: 1) initial characterization of white collar crime identified it as "crime in the upper or white-collar class, composed of respectable or at least respected business and professional men...." This identification of white collar crime with respectability has been criticized because "respectability" is not so easily defined, can be faked, and is not linked with specific norms for acceptable behavior (Shapiro 1990). Admittedly, the term *respectable* can be used in quite different ways, which causes some confusion. Dictionary definitions of *respectable* include worthy of esteem, of good standing, proper or decent, of moderate excellence, and of considerable size.

For our purposes, however, three different meanings of *respectable* must be distinguished: first, a normative meaning, or an assessment of moral integrity; second, a status-related meaning, that is to say a legitimate position or occupation; and third, a symptomatic meaning, or the outward appearance of acceptable or superior status. Obviously these different meanings are not synonymous; there are dishonest (or morally unrespectable) stockbrokers and honest (but low-status) streetpeople. The successful con artist projects an appearance of respectability but lacks either the required moral qualities or sufficient status. In the present context, the latter two meanings of *respectable* are invoked. No implication of moral integrity is intended, and in fact its absence among people who enjoy both the appearance and status of respectability is one of the core characteristics of white collar crime. When people object to the notion of "respectable criminals," they are, of course, focusing on the moral meaning. From this point of view, people who commit crimes and perpetrate harms are never respectable. Even if those who are exposed as criminals may indeed lose their respectable status, it is important to recognize that often it is precisely this status that enabled them to commit their crimes in the first place.

Most of us like to think of ourselves as respectable, or "worthy of esteem." The desire to achieve or retain a respectable status—that is, a "good social standing"—is a powerful force in our society. The appearance of respectability is often a virtually essential commodity; in fact, it has been suggested that the appearance of respectability may be literally a life-or-death matter. Studies of emergency room operations have shown that the quality and quantity of medical care given patients is influenced by the degree of perceived respectability of the patients (Ball 1970). Cab drivers often attend carefully to the appearance of respectability of prospective riders as a means of minimizing their chances of being robbed, or even killed, by a passenger (Henslin 1968). And we can identify numerous illustrations of the ways in which most of us attempt to convey in our everyday lives the appearance of respectability. For example, people in professional and social circumstances typically wear practical and appropriate clothing that conveys a respectable status.

Respectability is always a situational and contextual matter (Ball 1970). A variety of personal and impersonal attributes signify one's degree of respectability. Because many who enjoy a respectable status also have one or more obvious attributes more commonly associated with a nonrespectable status, what matters is the overall configuration or balance of attributes. Those who are manifestly respectable enjoy many benefits: People will cash their checks, admit them to fine restaurants, employ them, and so on. The more respectable a person appears to be, the *more* likely (other things being equal) they are to be trusted. The more respectable a person appears to be, the *less* likely (other things being equal) that they will be suspected of committing serious crimes. In a parallel vein, organizations (e.g., corporations) typically strive to be regarded as legitimate and respectable, with the view that such a perception will contribute significantly to their ability to compete effectively and maximize their profits. There may be many exceptions to these propositions, but they are at least valid generalizations.

Societies have ceremonies or rituals wherein respectable status is publicly acknowledged. Club inductions, commencement exercises, baptisms, and weddings are but a few of many ceremonies that confer a new or heightened status of respectability on the primary parties involved. Other ceremonies—Garfinkel (1956) has called them "degradation ceremonies"—strip people of their respectable status. The criminal trial is perhaps the most obvious example; even though many who are brought to trial did not enjoy a truly respectable status to begin with, a criminal trial resulting in a conviction and a prison sentence formally transforms someone from a free citizen into an incarcerated felon. Commitment proceedings, formal expulsion processes, and other such rituals strip people of at least some measure of respectability. Some evidence of the advantages of a respectable status for those who are processed by the criminal justice system will be offered in subsequent chapters.

## Risk and White Collar Crime

The term *risk* has had a variety of meanings. Originally it was associated with a wager, or the probability of an event occurring; more recently it has come to mean great danger and alludes to negative outcomes exclusively (Douglas 1990). In the context of white collar crime, *risk* can refer to either meaning.

Risk applies to white collar crime in the original sense insofar as a calculated gamble is taken; the chances of being caught and punished are quite remote compared with the benefits that accrue from committing the crime. Although of course such calculation can play a role in most forms of crime, it is especially likely to be a central feature of much white collar crime. Much evidence cited elsewhere in this book strongly suggests that in most cases the risk strongly favors the offender because the probability of detection, prosecution, and sanctioning is typically very low.

Risk is also involved in an important class of white collar crimes in the second, more recent sense: as the assessment of chances of dangerous (even catastrophic) consequences of corporate and professional decision making. One distinctive element of much white collar crime is the absence of the *specific* intent to cause harm. Rather, the harm of much white collar crime is a function of making the pursuit of profit or economic efficiency paramount over all other objectives. More to the point, corporations and professionals have often been prepared to put their workers, customers, and the general public at higher risk of harm if their course of action is seen to enhance profit or result in lower risk of loss.

Meier and Short (1985: 390), in a seminal article on crime and risk, argued that certain white collar crimes are more similar to natural disasters than to ordinary crime, and thus are a subset of a broader category of hazards endangering human safety. The media play an important role in shaping perceptions of hazards and tend to portray them as natural rather than human-made (Spencer and Triche 1994). With respect to the celebrated Buffalo Creek, West Virginia, catastrophe, in which the collapse of a mining company's dam led to the destruction of a community and the loss of many lives in 1972, debate persists about whether it was a crime or a technological failure, or some combination of the two. This problem applies as well to many other such incidents, from the explosion of the space shuttle *Challenger* in 1986 to the emission of poisonous gases from Union Carbide's Bhopal (India) plant in 1984. No credible analysis of these events suggests that it was the intention of the decision makers involved that people should die as a consequence of their decisions. Rather, decisions were made to realize some organizational objective, and considerations of risks to human life were at best not adequately attended to, and at worst were disposed of with criminal irresponsibility.

Charles Perrow (1984) coined the term *normal accident* to refer to the accidents that complex modern technological systems inevitably produce. Perrow insisted, however, that we recognize that the choices underlying high-risk systems are knowingly made in deference to organizational goals. The costs of such choices should not be simply dismissed as accidents dictated by the technology itself, or as human error. Rather, the nature of the risky choices built into these complex systems must be confronted.

In recent years interest in risk analysis has increased exponentially (Clarke 1989; Freudenburg and Pastor 1992; Short 1984; Short 1990). The rubric "risk analysis" incorporates risk assessment and risk management. Although today we live in an environment in which many of the risks that once faced people have either been eliminated or reduced, we are also confronted with new, dramatic forms of risks in addition to ongoing threats, including conventional violent crime. Modern technology, as just suggested, has produced some terrifying risks; the possibility of nuclear war presents perhaps the most extreme risk of loss of human life, indeed of all life. It is widely conceded that no form of modern technology can be made entirely risk-free, and the myth of "secure" high-risk technology has been exposed (Perrow 1984). It is also widely accepted that virtually all modern technology has beneficial consequences, such that if it were possible to eliminate modern technology because of the risks it imposes, the drawbacks and losses from such a policy would be likely to outweigh any benefits. Clearly, then, risk avoidance has costs as well as benefits (Short 1989). But it is far from clear, at least when corporations are involved, that a justifiable balance concerning risk has been realized.

Perceptions of risk are a significant function of cultural differences; some types of cultural outlooks entail greater acceptance of risk, whereas other cultural outlooks are more risk-aversive (Wildavsky and Dake 1990). Americans have often insisted on the right to make risky choices (e.g., to smoke cigarettes) but are increasingly less tolerant of having risks imposed upon them (Brandt 1990; Teuber 1990). The media play an important role in shaping specific perceptions of risk, as they tend to highlight some types of risks and not others, rather than providing a dispassionate assessment of actual risk (Short 1984; Stallings 1990). Special interest groups are also seen by some as exploiting fears and exaggerating minor risks, as is the case for asbestos removal contractors with respect to exposure to asbestos in homes and schools (Sapolsky 1990). The things we fear will harm us most often pose the least actual risk, and vice versa (Lewis 1990). Most people, for example, tend to overestimate the likelihood of major nuclear power plant accidents and underestimate the hazards of lawn mowing (Clarke 1988: 23). The study by Meier and Short (1985) previously cited produced some evidence, however, that citizens are increasingly conscious of the risks of becoming a white collar crime victim, recognizing that, on the average, the likelihood of such victimization is greater than for ordinary crimes or natural disasters. The perceived likelihood of white collar crime victimization among the respondents in this study varied substantially.

In any case, recognition of the inherent risks of modern technology in particular has stimulated a number of questions. First, to what extent can science make reliable calculations of risk for a whole range of potential hazards? Second, what are "acceptable" levels of risk, and who should make these determinations? Third, who should be held responsible for the harmful consequences—which may include the loss of human life—that result from decisions about risky technology, and, specifically, how should charges in these cases be processed? As Short (1989) observed, science and law are increasingly required to interact with one another and have become quite interdependent in this respect. Serious efforts to impose legal controls on many important sources of societal risk date only from the mid-1960s and led to the establishment of federal regulatory agencies such as the Environmental Protection Agency and the Occupational, Safety and Health Administration (Priest 1990). Product liability, which focuses intensely on acceptable and unacceptable risk, has expanded greatly only in recent years and has now been identified as the largest subfield of civil law (Priest 1990: 210). The enormous growth of public and private law concerning risk assessment and the apportionment of blame for accidents has been vigorously criticized from many quarters as being economically inefficient and fundamentally unjust.

Although the use of risk analysis for various purposes has become a minor industry, the whole enterprise has been criticized on a number of grounds. From a methodological perspective, risk analysis has been criticized as excessively quantitative, technical, and psychological, and as failing to consider qualitative aspects of risk (i.e., how it is experienced), the social construction of risk (i.e., the social process of giving meaning to risk), and the organizational and interorganizational processes involved in making decisions about risk (Clarke 1988; Draper 1984; Freudenberg and Pastor 1992; Jacobs and Dopkeen 1990). Perrow (1984) bluntly characterized risk assessment as a pseudoscience that legitimates the status quo by persuading us to accept "normal accidents." Huber (1990) is similarly blunt in his critique of pathological or "junk" science associated with risk assessment, but his concern is with the inflated costs of products and lower levels of production that he considers a consequence of the testimony of risk assessors on behalf of tort case plaintiffs.

Conversely, the cost-benefit analysis that plays such a central role in much risk assessment undertaken on behalf of corporations is seen by some as fundamentally immoral, especially when it dispassionately attempts to impose a monetary value on human lives and accepts the loss of a certain number of lives as an economic necessity (Teuber 1990). The claims of some students of risk (see, for example, Viscusi 1983)—that workers make rational choices to engage in some risky occupations, and that in a capitalist system the state should minimize its involvement—has been criticized on the reasonable grounds that workers typically lack both the knowledge and power to make alternative choices or to modify dangerous working conditions (Draper 1984; Nelkin and Brown 1984). Employees who work in high-risk workplaces, when given the opportunity to express themselves, display considerable anxiety and anger over their circumstances (Nelkin and Brown 1984). Decision making about risks does not occur on a level playing field.

Some evidence suggests that corporations are more likely to take certain types of risks if they have reason to believe they can get away with it. For example, their concern for short-term financial gain means that they are more likely to reduce risks involving worker safety than those involving workers' long-term health (Felstiner and Siegelman 1989). Workers and regulatory inspectors alike tend to respond more readily to hazards that pose immediate risks of direct injury than to the uncertainties of long-term or latent injuries (Hawkins 1990). The short-term interests of corporations are not necessarily compatible with the months or years of trial and error often needed to reduce such risks (Short 1990: 185). Furthermore, corporations tend to accept higher levels of risk to employees than to the general public, because accidents involving the public are more likely to get media attention (Hutter and Lloyd-Bostock 1990).

Such decision making about risks is not, of course, restricted to corporations, although the scope of potential harm is especially broad in that realm. Physicians, for example, may impose unnecessary risks on patients either to maintain their control over a situation or for economic advantage. Other professionals (e.g., stockbrokers) may expose their clients to excessive financial risks to increase their own income from commissions. A basic issue in such cases is whether the patients or clients were made fully aware of the risks involved and gave their consent for a riskier course of action. Criminal charges are quite uncommon in such cases due to the often formidable difficulty of demonstrating criminal intent.

Some level of risk may be an inevitable feature of modern existence. Certainly no reasonable person imagines that all risk of harm (physical or financial) can be eliminated from modern corporate and professional activities, and it has been acknowledged that an excessive aversion to risks carries costs of its own. But a substantial amount of evidence also demonstrates that corporations (and professionals) have too often imposed excessive risks on vulnerable parties, such that the costs outweigh any possible benefits. Taking risks in the political and social realm (as opposed to corporate risk) that led to unsafe conditions and environmental damage is part of what made America great (Perrow 1984: 311). The risks created by corporations (and professionals) today are exceptionally harmful in many instances. Clearly, making decisions involving risk can cross a line and become a form of criminal conduct: white collar crime.

## The Social Movement Against White Collar Crime

EVEN THOUGH WHITE collar crime continued to be relatively neglected for several decades after Sutherland's famous call for more attention to it, the situation began to change in the early 1970s. Sociologist Jack Katz (1980b) has argued that a social movement against white collar crime that emerged during this period was the most substantial attack on such crime since the early 20th-century Progressive Movement, which brought together rural populists, muckraking journalists, and organizations of civic-minded businessmen concerned about the excesses and outrages of big business.

The movement against white collar crime today is rooted in an evolving legitimation crisis and crisis of confidence, both of which are products of the tumultuous 1960s (Friedrichs 1980a). A *crisis of confidence* refers to a precipitous erosion of confidence or trust in major institutions and their leadership, including government, business, and the professions; a *legitimation crisis* more properly refers to a loss of faith in the system itself (Friedrichs 1981). Any system of authority depends for its efficient functioning, and ultimately its very survival, on its ability to maintain both a reasonable level of confidence in its leadership and legitimation of its core values. In complex modern democracies the involvement of the state in an ever-expanding range of activities, as well as expanded media coverage of these governmental activities, heightens public expectations and makes it increasingly difficult to generate high levels of confidence and legitimation (Cullen, Maakestad, and Cavender 1987).

In the United States at the end of the 20th century, the problem has been more a crisis of confidence than a full-fledged legitimation crisis, but certainly elements of both are in evidence.

One manifestation of this crisis, then, was a growing recognition of the harmful and specifically illegal actions of individuals and organizations within government, business, and the professions. The profound and diffuse disillusionment with the U.S. military campaign in Vietnam, followed by exposure of the various crimes of Watergate, helped create fertile soil for a social movement against white collar crime (Simon and Eitzen 1993). During this period of time both a growing recognition of the central role of the corporation and a number of highly publicized corporate crime cases occurred (Clinard and Yeager 1980).

Emerging movements on behalf of minorities, consumers, and the environment in particular highlighted social inequities and injustices and fed into increasing attention to white collar crime. Within the social sciences, conflict theory (and more specifically a neo-Marxist critique) directed much more attention to the crimes of the state and the economic elites, and to the disproportionate role of the rich and the powerful in the law-making process. Katz (1980b) argued that a variety of "moral entrepreneurs"—including investigative reporters, legislators reacting to scandals, and federal prosecutors—both responded to and measurably raised public consciousness about white collar crime. The motivations on the part of politicians and prosecutors in particular were hardly fueled by moral outrage alone, although in some cases such outrage may have played a role. To the extent that public concern with at least some forms of white collar crime increased, politicians and prosecutors could enjoy some career advantages by pursuing it (Cullen et al. 1987: 113). But the need to reinforce confidence in the leadership and established institutions, and the need to reinforce the legitimation of the system itself, clearly played an important role in the institutional response to white collar crime.

If there is in any meaningful sense a social movement against white collar crime today, it has not developed with any consistent momentum. Commentators are somewhat divided on whether an intensified response to white collar crime has become entrenched and institutionalized or has been highly selective and limited (Katz 1980b; Kramer 1989; Levi 1992). In the more conservative 1980s in the United States some curtailing of federal investigative resources and budgets of regulatory agencies occurred, and a dip in white collar crime convictions resulted (Caringella-MacDonald 1990; Poveda 1990). A number of large-scale white collar crime cases, from insider trading cases to the S & L frauds, received a good deal of attention.

In the early 1990s federal prosecutors appointed by the Clinton administration expressed commitments to intensified efforts against white collar crime. At the same time, stimulating a healthy economy and reducing unemployment was prominent among the major challenges facing the new administration. In the past, concern over the economy and jobs has often taken precedence over, and even derailed, vigorous pursuit of white collar crime. If broad popular support for such vigorous pursuit is to be generated in such a social climate, it is imperative to demonstrate that white collar crime (e.g., health care fraud) is a significant contributor to economic distress. In the sections that follow, important aspects of how we become conscious of white collar crime, and specifically how it is exposed, will be explored in some depth.

## Images of White Collar Crime: The Role of the Media

PRESUMABLY WE ARE not born with an image of crime and criminality, but such images develop quite early in life. Surprisingly, we still know relatively little about the specific process of such image formation (Graber 1980). It is quite clear, however, that early images are significantly shaped by exposure to television programs, films, video games, music tapes, comics, and other elements of the culture of young children. Some evidence indicates that these early images favor certain stereotypes and are distorted and simplistic. They heavily reinforce the image of criminals as offenders who commit interpersonal, conventional types of crime, and such images probably remain a significant (if not always conscious) influence on our way of thinking about criminals. The term *crime* is primarily associated with murder, rape, robbery, burglary, theft, and other such conventional offenses.

### The Media Image of Crime

The media are a pervasive element of contemporary life. Television, in particular, plays a dominant role, especially for children, and the average American spends several hours a day watching television (Lichter, Lichter, and Rothman 1991). The media are a crucial source of our understanding of crime because few people experience a wide variety of crime firsthand (Surette 1992). The role of the media in providing us with images of crime, although intensified in more recent years, is hardly new.

The media have traditionally portrayed crime mainly in conventional terms, with an emphasis on sensational (especially violent) crimes (Marsh 1991). Americans' fascination with crime goes back to the earliest colonial period. In the 17th and 18th centuries, crime was discussed mainly in sermons, conversion narratives, and criminal autobiographies, originally intended to promote Protestant piety, provide entertainment, or offer tips on crime prevention (D. A. Cohen 1988; Rawlings 1992). Crime stories have been a staple of the American press since the early part of the 19th century (Dominick 1978: 107). In recent times crime has been the third largest news category in newspapers, after sports and government-related news (Sherizen 1978: 208). Crime stories occupy some 5–10 percent of the copy space in newspapers and are prominent in the broadcast media as well (Dominick 1978). Many studies have documented the conventional, melodramatic, and sensationalistic biases of this coverage, which serves the ideological function of deflecting attention from the structural and political sources of crime (Altheide 1976; Altheide and Snow 1991; Barlow, Barlow, and Chiricos 1995; Marsh 1991; Gitlin 1980; Humphries 1981; Roshier 1973; Sherizen 1978; Tuchman 1978).

The news media have always devoted at least some space to the crimes of the rich and powerful, especially when scandalous circumstances are involved (Papke 1987). According to one study conducted in the 1970s, some 20–33 percent of the space devoted to crime news focused on white collar crime, principally business-related and political corruption (Graber 1980). Following the Watergate Affair, coverage of white collar crime increased (Gans 1979); consumer fraud and bribery ranked third and sixth, respectively, among the most frequently reported crimes

(Graber 1980). But any increase in reporting on white collar crime was spotty. A study of newspaper coverage in 1976 of a major price fixing case involving the folding carton industry found that large-circulation newspapers did not report any more frequently or extensively on this episode than they did on a 1961 heavy-electrical-equipment price-fixing case (Evans and Lundman 1983). To the extent that this case was covered, the coverage focused on individual defendants and their sentences, rather than on the culpability of the corporations involved (a finding replicated by other studies; see, for example, Morash and Hale 1987). When 25 employees of a chicken processing plant died in a fire in North Carolina in 1991, the media attributed the tragedy to violations of safety regulations, but they did not characterize it as a crime despite the manslaughter conviction of the owner (Wright, Cullen, and Blankenship 1995). The coverage of corporate crime on news telecasts has followed a pattern similar to that in the print media, with parallel inconsistencies (Randall 1987). Such coverage apparently increased following Watergate until 1978 and then dropped, increasing again somewhat in 1983.

One study examined random samples of network television coverage of corporate crimes between 1974 and 1984 (Randall 1987: 151). Of the 1,093 corporate crime stories surveyed in this study, 93 percent dealt with legitimate businesses engaged in illegal acts. The crimes covered were categorized as manufacturing (34 percent), financial (30 percent), environmental (14 percent), labor-related (12 percent), administrative (9 percent), and unfair trade (9 percent). The great majority of the corporate crime stories were not aired at the beginning of the news telecast, but tended to be relegated to a later segment. Television coverage of these crimes concentrated mainly on the stories' early stages (initial revelation) and final stages (legal resolution). According to a follow-up study, coverage of white collar crime was not a consistent interest of the media during the 1980s (Randall, Lee-Sammons, and Hagner 1988); conventional crime and the "drug wars" were accorded more generous coverage. Among the major white collar crime stories of the 1980s—one that the media generally was very slow to pick up on and then failed to cover in a manner commensurate with its importance—was the looting of the S & Ls, which will cost U.S. taxpayers billions of dollars when all is said and done (Martz 1990b; Hume 1990). Of course, the corrupt and illegal doings of various Reagan administration members and their associates received some attention during the 1980s, as did the crimes of insider traders. Overall, more dramatic crime stories (e.g., common over elite; personal over property; and corporate over occupational) received greater coverage, even if they were less objectively consequential. Furthermore, even when members of the public are exposed to media coverage of white collar crime, they continue to be far more concerned with conventional, interpersonal violent crimes (Graber 1980). The reporting of white collar crime seems to have a smaller impact on the audience than does the reporting of conventional violence.

The somewhat more limited media coverage of white collar crime may have several explanations, including the more indirect harm experienced by individual victims, public resistance to viewing corporations as criminal, and the fact that large and wealthy media organizations may not be inclined to link other large and wealthy organizations with criminality (Evans and Lundman 1983). On a more practical level, media organizations may be intimidated by corporations that threaten directly or indirectly to withdraw advertising or institute defamation suits (Grabosky and Wilson 1989: 96–97). Further, the reporting of corporate crime is far less likely to produce the striking visual images (with oil spills a possible exception) on which the media (and television in particular) thrive. The S & L frauds, for example, produced few vivid images for television coverage and were "boring" in the sense that complex financial transactions and federal regulations were involved.

White collar crime trials are especially likely to be drawn out and dull, and typically do not make especially lively copy (Grabosky and Wilson 1989). Because corporate crimes in particular are often highly complex, their coverage requires exceptionally knowledgeable journalists (Grabosky and Wilson 1989), but even skillful journalists do not always have the backing of their superiors to report on corporate fraud. Some further dimensions of such constraints on reporting this type of crime will be considered in more depth in a subsequent section on investigative reporting.

## The Media as Entertainment

The media are not simply sources of news, but also are major sources of entertainment. In the case of television in particular, entertainment programs take up considerably more of the schedule than do news shows. This dimension of the medium influences our perception of crime; it has also been accused of promoting criminal behavior (Surette 1992). The many studies of this alleged association have focused mainly on violent, interpersonal crimes, but it seems logical that involvement in white collar crime can also be influenced by television dramatizations.

It has been commonly assumed that television portrayals of crime concentrate very disproportionately on conventional, predatory offenders. When upperclass people are portrayed as criminals, the activity involved is more likely to be murder than corporate misdeeds (Box 1983: 16–17). But increasingly on television, businessmen have become popular villains, arguably even television's favorite villains (Basler 1987; Lichter, Lichter, and Rothman 1991: 20). J. R. Ewing, of the long-running "Dallas" show, was an especially prominent example of an increasingly common portrayal of businessmen. One study found that the ratio of "good" businessmen to "bad" was only 2 to 1, whereas for the police this ratio was 12 to 1, for doctors 16 to 1 (Gitlin 1983: 268). Still another study found that businessmen were five times more likely than those in other occupations to be represented as greedy (Lichter, Lichter, and Rothman 1991: 144).

The evil businessmen portrayed in television dramatizations are typically no less stereotypical than are the portrayals of conventional offenders (Braithwaite 1987: 57). Businessmen are often portrayed as engaging not only in murder, but in stealing, lying, and cheating as well. We are told that the "typical exploits of a television bad guy make the worst robber baron seem like a candidate for canonization" (Lichter, Lichter, and Rothman 1991: 132). More recently, television dramatizations have featured businessmen engaging in such practices as committing bribery, dumping toxic wastes, defrauding the public, subjecting employees to dangerous working conditions, and stealing ideas (Basler 1987; Lichter, Lichter, and Rothman 1991: 139). Such portrayals may reflect both the liberal biases of creative people in television and a growing public suspicion of businessmen (Basler 1987; Gitlin 1983; Lichter, Lichter, and Rothman 1991). Businessmen are in a position of power, and a corrupt businessman locked in a struggle with another individual is an ideal conflict for a television drama (Gitlin 1983: 269). It may also be less controversial to portray businessmen as "heavies" than to do so with members of minorities.

A traditional American ambivalence about businessmen, who are both admired and reviled, is reflected in media portrayals. Businessmen may be shown committing heinous deeds, but they are also portrayed as enjoying the "spoils" of their success: fancy cars and clothes, luxurious homes, glamorous parties, exciting recreational activities, and the like. Television conveys contradictory messages: It suggests that cheating and lying may "pay off" materially, but it also panders to the audience's appetite for seeing elites get their just deserts.

One recent study argued that if television initially tended to serve the status quo, on balance it has increasingly become an agent of social change, fostering public suspicions of businessmen and other elites (Lichter, Lichter, and Rothman 1991). The apparent increasing attention of television dramatizations to white collar crime, then, both reflects and contributes to the social movement against it. The portrayal of businessmen involved in crime remains quite distorted; the frequency of their commission of murder is exaggerated. Television's portrayal of the processing of these cases by the criminal justice system is especially unrealistic. Even if the television audience is entertained by villainous businessmen and finds them a satisfying vicarious target for their own hostility toward business generally, it is far from clear that this audience feels directly threatened by businessmen-villains in the same way that it fears conventional predatory criminals. The specific influence of television's attention to the crimes of businessmen on public perceptions of white collar crime, however, has yet to be fully investigated.

## Exposing White Collar Crime

WHITE COLLAR CRIME, as a rule, is less visible than conventional crime. Although most conventional crime does not literally occur in that most public of places, the street, it does frequently come to the attention of the police because victims and witnesses report it, and the police even observe some of it directly. White collar crime is generally far less visible—much of it, after all, takes place in suites, not streets—and many of its victims are not clearly aware that a crime has been perpetrated against them. "Witnesses" of white collar crime, who often don't realize that a crime has occurred, are often intimidated or confused about what to do in response to it. And our traditional, frontline enforcement agencies (e.g., the urban police) have not been organized to monitor and respond to white collar crime. Accordingly, other "agents" play an especially important role in exposing white collar crime.

### Informers and Whistleblowers

When people think about crime detection, their initial thoughts may focus on police (or private detectives) "tracking down" criminals. The stereotypical image of the detective with the magnifying glass and the scent-detecting dog has been promoted in the public imagination, and fictional detectives from Sherlock Holmes to Lt. Columbo have entranced generations of crime story fans. Much attention has been devoted in recent decades to a long string of increasingly sophisticated crime detection technologies, from fingerprint analysis to DNA analysis. But aside from reports by victims, the resolution of major crimes relies heavily on cooperation from *informers*, or *informants* (Webster, in Reinertsen and Bronson 1990: 100).

**Informers** Informers provide criminal justice system personnel with crucial information that can lead to the investigation, arrest, indictment, and conviction of law violators. It is quite inevitable that those who have the most specific and most incriminating information about illegal activity are themselves in varying degrees involved in illegal activity.

The use of informers goes far back in history. Jonathan Wild (1682–1725), was a legendary English thief, fence, and informer who sent some 100 thieves to the gallows, and ended up there himself (Marx l988: 19). At least since the time of Wild, informers have provided information in exchange for either payment or some favorable arrangement concerning criminal charges against themselves, or both. Because white collar crime cases are relatively invisible, sophisticated, and complex, the use of informers is often indispensable.

Informers played a central role in exposing Vice President Spiro Agnew's acceptance of bribes; in revealing the involvement of White House officials in the Watergate Affair; and in the series of Wall Street insider trading cases of the 1980s, with each cornered insider trader providing evidence against another wealthier and more powerful offender (Cohen and Witcover 1974; Stewart 1991; Woodward and Bernstein 1976). All these informers were criminally implicated themselves and received some form of "consideration" from the criminal justice system in return for revealing what they knew about illegal activity.

The use of informers in any criminal cases, including white collar criminal cases, raises complex ethical questions (Marx l988: 152–58; Reinertsen and Bronson l990). On the one hand, inappropriate lenience may be extended to informers who themselves have committed serious crimes, and informers may use their status as informers to commit additional crimes with some sense of immunity; on the other hand, viable criminal cases against major offenders often cannot be made without the assistance of informers, and the exposure of white collar crime is vitally dependent upon them.

**Whistleblowers** A related crucial source of information needed for the detection, and ultimately the prosecution, of white collar crime (especially the governmental and corporate varieties) is the *whistleblower.* Although whistleblowers have in common with informers an insider's perspective on the illegal activity, they are not criminally implicated.

White collar crime differs from many forms of conventional, organized, and professional crime insofar as the context within which it occurs has not, typically, been organized specifically, publicly, and consciously to carry out an illegal or manifestly criminal operation. White collar criminals—whether in a government agency, a corporation, a retail business, or a professional service enterprise—may work with colleagues and associates who are not committed to the illegal activity or are directly opposed to it. Most of these associates, once they become aware of illegal activity, will not necessarily "blow the whistle" on it, for many reasons. Probably foremost among these reasons is the widely diffused self-preservation ethos: It is not generally in one's rational best interest to blow the whistle on illegal activity occurring within one's organization, agency, corporation, or community. This is the lesson learned by the protagonist of Henrik Ibsen's late 19th-century play, *The Enemy of the People* (1882), who is persecuted by his fellow townsmen for exposing the dangerous pollution of their resort's "therapeutic baths" (MacNamara 1991). A fear of social ocstracism, loyalty to one's organization and associates, belief in the company's rationales for unethical or illegal activity, denial that one knows enough or has the appropriate responsibility, and in some cases even fear for one's physical safety deter most people from becoming whistleblowers.

One study (Glazer and Glazer 1989) adopted the alternative term *ethical resisters* to distinguish those who "blow the whistle" for principled reasons from those who may do so for less than pure reasons—and in some cases for blatantly self-interested or instrumental reasons (e.g., to settle a personal score, to get rid of one or more personal competitors, or to attempt to deflect attention from the whistleblower's own wrongdoing or liability). But authentic whistleblowers are motivated by moral outrage at illegal and often dangerous (or potentially dangerous) corporate policies and practices (Glazer and Glazer 1989: 4). Rather than being ideological heretics and professional misfits, these whistleblowers tend to be conservative people who are dedicated to their work and genuinely committed to professional codes of ethics to which many others merely give lip-service (Glazer and Glazer 1989: 69).

Even though there have always been isolated individuals who have played the whistleblower's role, the Glazers (1989: 11) argued that whistleblowers (or the ethical resister type) are a historically new group that emerged during the 1960s and 1970s in response to increasing concern over abuses of power and environmental threats. Three widely shown films of the 1970s and 1980s had whistleblowers as heroes: *Serpico* (1973), *Silkwood* (1983), and *Marie* (1985), about police corruption, nuclear power plant safety, and pardon board corruption, respectively. Although these films largely adopted the image of the whistleblower as a loner, certain organizational and work-related conditions have been found to promote whistleblowing, including good access to information, relative autonomy from direct supervision, and norms supporting professional expertise on technological matters (Miethe and Rothschild 1994; Perrucci et al. 1980).

Whistleblowing has been characterized as a thoroughly social activity involving a network of relationships (Ling 1991). In some cases an organization or agency may blow the whistle on another entity. For example, Mylan Laboratories Inc., a small Pittsburgh-based generic-drug company, hired private detectives in 1987 to investigate its suspicion that the Food and Drug Administration was not acting favorably on its applications to produce new generic drugs because agency officials were accepting bribes from competitors (Freudenheim 1989). Typically, however, whistleblowing is most likely to occur when there is no appropriate organizational channel for responding to concerns about illegal or unethical activity, and when there is a perception of broadening collegial support for challenging such activity.

Although at least some whistleblowers have acted heroically, the response to them has hardly been uniformly positive. In ancient times, as MacNamara (1991: 122) reminds us, messengers who were the bearers of bad tidings were often put to death. Today a fundamental ambivalence in cultural norms exists, especially prescriptive norms concerning loyalty and proscriptive norms concerning "tattletales," "stool pigeons," "squealers," "snitches," "turncoats," and "rats" (MacNamara 1991: 122). In the context of a congressional investigation, a "debate" may ensue on the question of whether someone who has come forward to report corrupt or wasteful practices in a branch of the government is a whistleblower (in the positive sense) or a renegade (Nichols 1991). Reactions to whistleblowers who seem to be motivated by greed and self-interest are likely to be negative in comparison with responses to whistleblowers who seem to be altruistic and concerned with the well-being of others (Miethe and Rothschild 1994: 337). Again, the superficially respectable attributes of the organization, executives, or bureaucracies who are the target of the whistleblowing, and the general absence of direct or immediate forms of economic and physical harm that can unambigously be linked with the intentional actions of the organization's executives or bureaucrats, also play a role in fostering this ambivalence. Workers tend to support whistleblowers when direct threats to their health and well-being have been exposed, but when the dangers are less direct or imminent and the whistleblowing may jeopardize jobs or the local economy, workers are much less likely to be supportive (Glazer and Glazer 1989: 124).

As a rule, whistleblowers pay a very substantial price for their courageous actions. According to one study, some 50 percent of a sample of whistleblowers suffered retaliation, and a significant percentage (between 10 and 20 percent) suffered traumatic personal consequences such as suicide, divorce, and the loss of a home, all of which were attributed to fallout from whistleblowing (MacNamara 1991). The literature contains many accounts of personal devastation experienced by whistleblowers, as well as retaliation from management in the form of blacklisting, dismissal, transfer, personal harassment, and even sexual harassment (Eichenwald 1994b; Glazer and Glazer 1989; Greenwald 1993; Mintz 1993; Soeken and Soeken 1987). In some cases whistleblowers have allegedly been shot at or even murdered (Maas 1973; Rashke 1987). Some of the whistleblowers who have been dismissed from their jobs have successfully sued for multimillion-dollar damages or reinstatement, and in rare cases they have even been formally vindicated by their company, complete with high-level apologies for their suffering (Eichenwald 1994b; Gerth 1988; Glazer and Glazer 1989). But more often they must move on to new jobs and careers, and at least a small minority remain unemployed (and embittered) following the whistleblowing episode.

Traditionally, federal agencies and the courts have done rather little to intervene on behalf of whistleblowers (MacNamara 1991: 130). Recently, some steps have been taken on both the federal and state levels to offer whistleblowers at least a measure of protection. The False Claims Amendment Act of 1986, which revitalized an 1860s law offering whistleblowers a monetary reward in the form of a percentage (15–30 percent) of funds recovered through a successful prosecution, has enabled a small number of whistleblowers to receive millions of dollars, a result that has proven controversial (Stevenson 1992c). Of course, the existence of such laws cannot be said to offer whistleblowers any absolute guarantees of protection, insofar as a retaliatory dismissal (as opposed to a rationally justifiable dismissal) or some other such action may be difficult or impossible to prove. The whistleblower protection laws are examined somewhat more fully elsewhere in this text.

As long as corruption persists in government agencies and private corporations, the financial and physical well-being of the general public can be significantly affected by whistleblowers. The likelihood that whistleblowers will come forward is enhanced to the extent that public concern about corrupt and harmful conditions remains high, media attention is persistent, public interest groups are supportive, protective legislation is implemented, and the singular courage of whistleblowers is rewarded and celebrated.

## Muckrakers and Investigative Reporters

Journalists historically have been a thorn in the side of the establishment because of their periodic exposures of wrongdoing by the powerful and privileged. The emergence in America of the so-called "muckrakers" in the early 20th century was an important development, for they firmly established the revelation of high-level wrongdoing as a legitimate journalistic enterprise.

Lincoln Steffens's *The Shame of the Cities* (1904), a powerful exposé of municipal political corruption, has been credited with ushering in the muckraking era (Weir and Noyes 1983: 3). Steffens refuted the then-commonplace notion that urban corruption could be blamed on the new waves of European immigrants, and he revealed the central role of established American businessmen in this form of corrupt activity (Palermo 1978: 42). At about the same time, Ida Tarbell's landmark *The History of the Standard Oil Company* (1904) recounted the range of illegal and unethical actions that were integral to the formation of the richest and most powerful trust monopoly of its time (Brady 1984). Very shortly after this came Upton Sinclair's *The Jungle* (1906), which exposed the shocking—literally sickening—practices in the meat-processing industry and was instrumental in promoting new regulatory laws (to be discussed elsewhere). Even some of the films of this period engaged in muckraking. *Children Who Labor* (1912) exposed the exploitation of young children; other films, such as *The Reform Candidate* (1911), *The Grafters* (1913), and *The Land Swindlers* (1913), exposed corrupt politicians and businessmen (White and Averson, 1979: 5).

The period 1902–1912 has been referred to as the "golden age" of muckraking. During World War I and in the decades following it, the energy and visibility of muckraking seemed to go into decline, even though journalistic exposés of major forms of high-level crime and corruption were produced (especially in the 1930s). This decline has been attributed to the changing economics of journalism, some pressure from target corporations, growing public boredom with shrill social criticism, and a certain sense of disillusionment because adequate reforms had failed to result from the muckraking enterprise (Downie 1976: 255; Geis 1993: 14; Weir and Noyes 1983: 3).

During the mid-20th century a relatively few journalists exposed governmental and corporate wrongdoing. Columnists Drew Pearson and his protégé, Jack Anderson, produced exposés of governmental wrongdoing over a period of several decades. The independent journalist I. F. Stone, who for many years produced a weekly that uncovered all manner of scandalous and illegal practices buried in government documents and obscure periodicals, was perhaps the most remarkable of the mid-century muckrakers.

In the 1970s muckraking experienced a formidable revival, although it became more commonly known as *investigative reporting*. The political activism and anti-establishment rhetoric so conspicuous on the university campuses in the late 1960s and early 1970s helped produce a generation of younger journalists who were either skeptical of or openly antagonistic toward establishment institutions. The unraveling Watergate Affair (1972–1974) and the enormous attention directed at two investigative reporters for *The Washington Post*, Bob Woodward and Carl Bernstein, played a role in inspiring a new wave of interest in investigative journalism.

The realities of investigative reporting are not as glamorous as popular public perception would have it. Rather, investigative journalism is likely to be lonely, frustrating, tedious, expensive, time-consuming, sometimes hazardous, often controversial, and emotionally draining work; it can also be intensely satisfying and sometimes prestigious (Downie 1976: 10; Behrens 1977; Weir and Noyes 1983: 1). Two reporters for *The Philadelphia Inquirer* won the Pulitzer Prize in 1989 after spending months examining a mass of complicated tax documents that revealed a special class of exemptions for privileged, well-connected individuals, estimated to cost the Treasury Department $10 billion a year (Alter 1989). Insofar as these exemptions were incorporated into the tax law, they were not, strictly speaking, criminal, but "the biggest scams in life are often legal" (Alter 1989).

Americans have displayed some ambivalence toward muckrakers and investigative journalists. Many citizens see them as biased and unpatriotic and as contributors to excessive disillusionment and cynicism (Downie 1976: 233–36). Investigative reporters for Tucson's *Arizona Daily Star* who exposed illegal practices in the popular University of Arizona football program in 1980 were the target of much hostility and prompted significant retaliation by advertisers (Patterson and Russell 1986). Such news stories will inevitably offend some people in positions of power (Weir and Noyes 1983: 323).

Investigative journalism remains a fairly limited enterprise today; only a very small proportion of the nations' newspaper reporters could be accurately characterized as investigative reporters. The traditional focus of muckraking and investigative journalism has been political corruption; it has been much less active in examining private business (Downie 1976: 237; Gans 1979: 56). It is not immune to the pervasive media bias that favors sensational stories about individual wrongdoing (which sell more papers and receive the most attention) over the unraveling of complex, involved forms of institutional wrongdoing that may be much more harmful (Downie 1976: 257; Patterson and Russell 1986: 1; Levi 1987: 12). If investigative reporting has become more common since the 1970s, it has also confronted an expanding range of constraints, including expanding government concern with secrecy, fear of libel suits, increasing concentration of the ownership of media outlets, and the growth of increasingly complex corporations (e.g., multinationals) (Weir and Noyes 1983). Due to the considerable resources often needed to support investigative journalism, it has been undertaken mainly by major newspapers such as *The Washington Post* and *The New York Times*.

Newspapers in small cities and towns are limited mainly to exposing local political corruption, consumer fraud, and sometimes illegal or unethical practices of local public institutions and corporations. Some progressive or liberal publications of fairly limited circulation have promoted investigative journalism; these publications include *Mother Jones, Multinational Monitor,* and *The Progressive.* And of course the tradition of book-length exposés has continued. Books such as Rachel Carson's *The Silent Spring* (1962), about the destruction of the environment, Ralph Nader's *Unsafe at Any Speed* (1965), about unsafe automobiles, and Mary Adelaide Mendelson's *Tender Loving Greed* (1974), about scandalous nursing-home practices, have contributed significantly to inspiring investigations and new laws. Many discussions in this text draw on these books, and on many others like them.

Historically, investigative reporting on television has been a very limited undertaking. Periodically, and with considerable fanfare, the networks have produced documentaries such as "The Selling of the Pentagon," which exposed questionable Pentagon public relations practices (Gans 1979: 57). Some regular network "magazine" shows—"60 Minutes" is the best-known example—have also exposed various white collar crime practices. Many newer shows, such as "20/20," "PrimeTime Live," and "Day One," have followed the lead of "60 Minutes." In one season, for example, "60 Minutes" aired segments exploring questionable loan practices of the Farmers Home Administration; medical fraud; exploitation of illegal immigrant workers; toxic waste dumping by the Hooker Chemical Company; the criminal case against a prominent politician, former Treasury Secretary John Connally; the underground economy; the policies of the Federal Trade Commission; frauds relating to wills; phony auto repairs; and the misuse of church money (Wallace et al. 1980). Whenever "60 Minutes" has gone after federal agencies—not only the Federal Trade Commission, but the Federal Drug Administration, the Environmental Protection Agency, and the IRS, among others—it has typically encountered formidable resistance. The Defense Department even had a long-standing policy of noncooperation with "60 Minutes" (Madsen 1984: 113–15). In some cases "60 Minutes" has exposed major forms of corporate crime, including Kepone pollution of the James River by Allied Chemicals; the story resulted in a criminal indictment and a $13 million fine against the company. In other cases it has exposed harmful or illegal practices of major corporate sponsors, such as the Ford Company's defective Pintos (Madsen 1984: 118–38).

But most of the segments on "magazine" shows like "60 Minutes" are devoted to celebrity interviews and a range of rather prosaic foreign and domestic stories. Television networks have not made investigative reporting focusing on a range of white collar crimes a staple, or anything more than a quite marginal offering, for several reasons. One reason is a significant degree of self-censorship: Networks are anxious about offending either a government whose regulatory agencies exercise considerable power over them, or the traditionally conservative owners of their affiliate stations (who are unlikely to be enthusiastic about anti-establishment journalism), or the corporate advertisers upon whom they are so dependent (Hickey 1981).

Beyond these basic inhibitions, many additional factors make investigative reporting of white collar crime typically unappealing to television network executives. Most white collar crimes (oil spills excepted) don't provide vivid visual images; investigating white collar crimes is time-consuming, and many white collar crime stories cannot be covered in the brief TV segments typically available; the fairness doctrine requires equal time for editorial rebuttals; TV executives fear lawsuits; undercover reporting with the very conspicuous paraphernalia normally used in TV production is difficult; and finally, most importantly, the popular appeal and ratings potential intrinsic to most such stories are low (Hickey 1981). As one TV executive has commented: "People get bored to tears with corruption stories unless they relate either to the White House or to some sex bomb in a Congressman's office" (Hickey 1981: 170).

Some local television stations conduct a certain amount of investigative reporting, often focusing on municipal corruption and consumer fraud, but local stations also face constraints similar to those of the networks and typically have more limited economic resources. In competitive local television markets there is a strong temptation to go with "sensationalistic" exposés rather than in-depth investigations of complex white collar crimes. TV personality Geraldo Rivera made a name for himself with a controversial and sensationalistic exposé of Willowbrook, an antiquated institution for the retarded (Madsen 1984: 107). It is easier for TV to capitalize on such visibly disgraceful conditions than on convoluted elite financial crimes.

Investigative reporting has also been represented in television series that feature the news business, such as "Lou Grant" and "Capital News." Because the scripts for these shows are often directly inspired by real cases and the audiences for these shows can be very large, they are probably not insignificant vehicles for raising consciousness about certain forms of white collar crime.

Finally, no discussion of the role of journalism in exposing white collar crime would be complete without some discussion of the historical role of political cartoonists, especially in the realm of exposing political corruption. The authentic political cartoon seeks to do more than amuse. It attempts to produce a picture of reality that captures the essence of truth in a particular situation; it conveys a message, and it seeks to create a mood (Press 1981: 62). Insofar as cartoons are surely among the most widely read and easily understood parts of newspapers, they are clearly significant and potentially influential.

The earliest such cartoons were broadsides, flyers produced and posted for public consumption in the 16th century, and political cartoons have appeared in some form since then. In the latter half of the 19th century, Thomas Nast became the most celebrated American political cartoonist of his time. His brilliant cartoons of New York City's corrupt political boss, William Marcy ("Boss") Tweed of Tammany Hall, and his circle, were widely credited with contributing to the fall of this political machine in the 1870s (Press 1981: 246). In the late 19th century, Homer Davenport and Frederick Opper produced cartoons that attacked the large capitalist trusts of the time; their images of the trusts were widely reproduced (Press 1981: 268).

Throughout the 20th century, political and editorial cartoonists have continued to produce memorable, powerful images of corruption in high places. Since the late 1940s, Herbert Block's (Herblock's) cartoons have been especially influential, exposing the dark deeds of Senator Joseph McCarthy and President Richard Nixon (Press 1981: 302–11). In the 1970s and 1980s, editorial cartoonists had an endless series of targets, from Watergate to the "sleazy" doings of members of the Reagan administration. Garry Trudeau's comic strip "Doonesbury" has been an especially widely circulated and discussed satirical critique of wrongdoing in high places.

Despite the much vaunted First Amendment rights enjoyed by American political cartoonists, it does not follow that such cartoonists operate entirely free of constraints. Publishers and their contacts in high places can exert direct or indirect pressures, and of course cartoonists often are forced to produce in the face of tight deadlines (Press 1981: 184–94). There can be little question, however, that political cartoons can create powerful and enduring images of crime in high places.

## The Consumer Movement and Public Interest Groups

An earlier section touched on the common claim that traditionally the general public has been relatively indifferent to white collar crime, and discussed significant recent evidence indicating that the public perceives many forms of white collar crime as quite serious. Some exposure of white collar crime has resulted from the efforts of both individuals claiming to act on behalf of the public (or consumers) and public interest groups making parallel claims.

The exposure of frauds perpetrated on consumers is hardly a new enterprise. In 1880, for example, Anthony Comstock, a former special agent of the Post Office best known for his campaign to suppress vice, published *Frauds Exposed*. A book published in 1927, Stuart Chase and F. J. Schlink's *Your Money's Worth*, dealt with deceptive advertising and high-pressure sales and led to the publication of *Consumer's Bulletin* (Coleman 1989: 139–40).

In 1911 the advertising industry had created Vigilance Committees "to rid itself of false claims, snake-oil salesmen, and fly-by-night operations" (Logan 1988: 29). One result is the establishment of the Better Business Bureaus, which today have some 174 local branches. The BBBs, which claim to act on behalf of consumers, have distributed various publications exposing business frauds; mainly they have served as a complaint bureau for dissatisfied consumers. In 1985 more than 9 million Americans reportedly turned to the BBBs for information and assistance. Because the BBBs are sponsored by businesses, however, they have often been seen as an instrument acting more on the behalf of business than of consumers, deflecting substantial consumer actions and focusing mainly on the most flagrant, small-scale business frauds. They have not played a significant role in exposing the wrongdoing of major corporations.

The environmental movement can trace its ancestry, to some extent at least, to the conservation movement that emerged in the late 19th and early 20th centuries. For much of the 20th century this movement was a limited enterprise, hardly a vigorous campaigner against corporate practices contributing to the destruction of the environment. In the final decades of the 20th century, however, grassroots environmental organizations began to play a significant role in raising consciousness about corporate environmental crime and in mobilizing responses to it (Cable and Benson 1993).

The emergence during the late 1960s and the 1970s of a public interest movement and of civil activism has been attributed to a number of factors. First, the relative prosperity of the period helped generate a perception that corporations could now afford to behave far more responsibly in producing safe products, improving working conditions, and limiting harm to the environment. On the other hand, an escalating rate of inflation promoted consumer anxiety and mistrust of business. The enormous increase in the number of young, well-educated people emerging from colleges during this period, after a sustained period of campus-based campaigns against a host of abuses of power and social injustices, created a large constituency receptive to critiques of big business (Vogel 1989: 95–100).

Common Cause, a public interest group founded in 1970 and having a membership mainly composed of upper-middle-class whites, was concerned with combating undue power of special interests; it campaigned for federal election campaign reform and against the oil depletion allowance, among other issues (McFarland 1984). Other public interest organizations—supported by private contributions and dues, foundations, and tax benefits or government subsidies—promoted a range of environmental and consumer-related causes, not all of them pertinent to white collar crime (Vogel 1989: 104). But one man in particular, and the public interest groups he established, played an especially significant role in the "movement" against such crime.

Ralph Nader is generally acknowledged to be the founder of the consumer rights movement. Nader was born in 1934 to a Lebanese-American family that championed a strong political consciousness (*Current Biography Yearbook* 1986). As a teenager he read the muckrakers, and as a hitchhiking college student he became alarmed by the auto accidents he observed. At Princeton he led a campaign against spraying campus trees with DDT. After acquiring a law degree from Harvard and serving in the army, he went into private practice for a brief time. Then, as a government staff lawyer in the mid-1960s, he undertook the research that led to the publication of his landmark study, *Unsafe at Any Speed* (1965). This book exposed long-standing automotive-industry practices of knowingly producing and selling structurally defective automobiles, the result of placing profit-maximizing objectives over concern for consumer safety. The book led to congressional hearings and played an important role in the passage of the Traffic and Motor Vehicle Safety Act of 1966. The revelation that General Motors had engaged in a secret probe of Nader, in the hopes of discrediting him with compromising information about his private life or past political ties, only served to enhance Nader's status as an authentic hero to American consumers (Whiteside 1972).

In the years since he acquired his early fame, Nader has been a central figure in the revelation of a wide range of unethical and illegal corporate practices, and he has established various investigatory and advocacy organizations to promote consumer interests and safety. Nader's success has been somewhat mixed and his influence uneven during this period, as public interests and values have shifted, but he and his associates are credited with important roles in the establishment of the Environmental Protection Agency and the Occupational Safety and Health Administration, among other accomplishments.

## The Role of Politicians and Political Institutions

Political institutions are both the locus of major forms of corruption and illegal activity, and a principal instrument for the exposure (and prosecution) of such activity. Politicians and government officeholders are most typically the products of the same broad segment of society that produces white collar criminals. More narrowly, politicians often have a complex of close ties with corporations and businessmen whose improper and illegal activities they are sometimes compelled to expose. Thus the role of politicians and political institutions in exposing white collar crime must be understood in light of these complex ties among the constituencies involved.

Illegal practices of marginal, quasi-respectable businesses and professionals that elicit much public indignation can be quite easily condemned by politicians; however, the improper activities of major corporations, established professions, and government agencies themselves—to say nothing of fellow politicians—is more complicated. Some such condemnation may indeed be idealistic, inspired by nothing more than the authentic outrage of the investigating politician; in other cases partisan motives, calculated and cynical political ploys, or pragmatic responses to powerful interest groups may be involved. Obviously, a mixture of motives may be involved in any particular case of political exposure, but these motives must always be carefully evaluated. And of course legion are the instances of rank hypocrisy of politicians' accusations of corrupt and illegal activities, in which the accusers themselves are revealed in time to have engaged in similar or worse practices.

Politicians have generally found it more attractive to attack street crime and call for "law and order" than to attack the crimes of powerful corporations, which sometimes requires them to bite the hand that is feeding them. In the late 1980s the savings and loan debacle was much less a political issue than it should have been, in part due to its inherent complexity, muted public interest, and the fact that politicians in both major parties were implicated in some way. Historically, Americans have had a love/hate relationship with business generally that has gone through cycles of public popularity and antagonism (Vogel 1989). If the 1980s was largely characterized as a celebration of business, in the first half of the 1990s the pendulum swung back somewhat in the other direction in response to the excesses of the earlier decade.

The legislative branch has played a role in exposing white collar crime primarily through congressional investigative committees. The first such committee was established in 1792 to investigate the defeat of General Arthur St. Clair at the hands of Ohio Indians (Schlesinger and Bruns 1975: v). Since then such committees have investigated a range of issues at such times that a legislative response is deemed potentially appropriate. Committees investigated the corrupt dealings of congressmen in the Credit Mobilier affair in the 1870s and of cabinet officials in the Teapot Dome scandal of the 1920s. Other such committees looked into the monopolistic power of the trusts early in the 20th century, and into the Wall Street financial manipulations that helped bring about the stock market crash in 1929.

In the latter part of the 20th century the congressional committees that received the most public attention were those that exposed alleged wrongdoing in the White House, notably during the Watergate hearings of the 1970s and the Iran/Contra arms hearings of the 1980s. Other congressional hearings during this period have explored specific white collar crimes such as oil company price-fixing and investment banking check-kiting, but these investigations have not inspired public interest that is even remotely equivalent to that directed at the political cases (Nichols 1990; U.S. Congress 1979; U.S. House 1986, 1987; U.S. Senate 1987). Such committees can potentially raise public consciousness about particular forms of white collar crime and lead to useful new legislation; they have also been accused of being occasions for political grandstanding and of violating the rights of some witnesses. Investigative committees, whatever their abuses and objectives, are likely to continue playing a role in the exposure of white collar crime.

## Criminal Justice Professionals and Criminologists

The preceding sections have identified some significant agents in exposing white collar crime. Other parties also play important roles in the exposure of such crime. Some zealous prosecutors, for example, have put a high priority on bringing white collar crime to the attention of the public, although most prosecutors do not (Benson, Cullen, and Maakestad l990b). The role of prosecutors and other criminal justice personnel is explored more fully in Chapter 11.

Social scientists, and academic scholars generally, have also played a role in exposing white collar crime, a role that has sometimes been downplayed (Cullen, Maakestad, and Cavender l987: 9). On the other hand, it has been suggested that the growing number of academics who have studied white collar crime have not been entirely successful in generating a public response, perhaps because they do not yet know enough and are not effectively communicating what they do know (Kramer l989: 162). Of course, a book such as this one draws very heavily on the role of social scientists and academics generally in exposing white collar crime, and this contribution is more systematically explored in Chapter 2.

## Discovering White Collar Crime, In Sum

THIS CHAPTER HAS thoroughly explored the "discovery" of white collar crime. Any serious study of white collar crime must be rooted in the recognition that there is still a great deal of confusion and dissensus on how it should be defined. The "movement" against white collar crime, such as it is, has emerged more slowly and less vigorously than the long-standing social movement against conventional crime. We have seen that the media, which is such a pervasive element of contemporary life, have portrayed conventional crime and white collar crime quite differently, although growing attention has been accorded to at least some forms of white collar crime in more recent years. Finally, it is a premise of this chapter that the exposure of white collar crime tends to take a different form than the exposure of conventional crime, and it is worthwhile to systematically identify some of the agents who expose it.

# Studying White Collar Crime and Assessing Its Costs

**M**ORE THAN A half-century has passed since E. H. Sutherland issued his celebrated call for more attention to white collar crime. Some 35 years after Sutherland's appeal, criminologist Stanton Wheeler (1976), making a presidential address to the Society for the Study of Social Problems, called attention to the almost total scholarly neglect of corporate illegality, technocrime, and governmental or entrepreneurial bribery and fraud.

Considerable evidence indicates that until the 1970s, criminology, criminal justice, and related areas of inquiry devoted very little systematic attention to white collar crime and its most significant manifestations. There were, of course, a number of important exceptions to this pattern of neglect, including Marshall Clinard's *The Black Market* (1952), Donald Cressey's *Other People's Money* (1953), studies of illegal practices in the meat industry (Hartung 1950), labor relations regulatory violations among small industrial manufacturers (Lane 1953), prescription violations among retail pharmacists (Quinney 1963), and price-fixing in the electrical equipment industry (Geis 1967). A major review of the criminological literature reveals that fewer than 45 (or 1.2 percent) of 3,700 books and articles on crime and justice published through the mid-1970s were devoted to white collar crime, and a survey of *Sociological Abstracts* for 1945 through 1972 established that an average of fewer than one article per year was published on white collar crime during this period (Geis and Goff 1982; Wolfgang, Figlio, and Thornberry 1978).

The "social movement" against white collar crime, discussed in Chapter 1, both contributed to and reflected the growth of attention to white collar crime in criminology from the 1970s on. By the 1980s attention to white collar crime (especially in the form of corporate crime) had increased substantially.

Through the 1970s the bulk of white collar crime scholarship was a "criminology" of white collar crime concerned principally with its causes and patterns of behavior. Since 1980 a growing literature on the justice system's responses to and processing of white collar crime cases has developed; a vigorous literature on the development of white collar crime law has also emerged. The scholars who produced this literature are principally law professors, criminologists, and sociolegal scholars; criminal justicians have played a more limited role to date.

On the whole, criminology has continued to be more attentive to white collar crime than has the field of criminal justice. Criminology textbooks, for example, tend to devote considerably more space to white collar crime than do criminal justice textbooks (Wright and Friedrichs 1991). Claims are made that the boundaries between criminology and criminal justice have blurred or have largely eroded (see, for example, Langworthy and Latessa 1989; Pepinsky 1986), but these two disciplinary traditions can still be differentiated. Criminologists tend to be more concerned with theory and explanation, criminal justicians with description and application.

## Studying White Collar Crime

### Underlying Assumptions and Different Perspectives

In the course of learning about white collar crime, students are exposed to many assertions, claims, and characterizations. Upon what are these assertions, claims, and characterizations of white collar crime based? How can we best study and understand the many different dimensions of white collar crime?

We can begin by recognizing that all studies of white collar crime explicitly or implicitly adopt assumptions about such matters as the nature of reality, human nature, the basis of morality, and the character of society. Although these enduring philosophical issues cannot be adequately explored here, we can make a few brief observations specifically pertinent to the study of white collar crime.

First, to the extent that "reality" is a human production, we should recognize that the white collar classes have more influence over defining this reality than do less privileged members of society. Second, the social response to white collar crime has tended to adopt the view that humans are fundamentally rational but self-interested creatures, capable of making free choices for which they can be held accountable, although much social science acknowledges the central role of deterministic influences on individual and organizational behavior. Third, much moral hypocrisy permeates the realm of white collar crime, insofar as elites in particular have often given lip service to moral absolutes but have rationalized their own unethical, illegal, and harmful activities. And fourth, the conventional view that law and social order are based on a democratic consensus is confounded by much evidence of the roles of power and conflict in shaping law (traditionally favoring white collar over conventional offenders) and in maintaining social order. Some of these assumptions, which are worth bearing in mind at the outset of one's formal study of white collar crime, are explored more fully in other sections of this text.

It is also necessary here to differentiate at least briefly between positivistic and humanistic approaches to the study of white collar crime. A *positivistic approach*, which draws on the tradition of the natural and physical sciences, generally assumes that white collar crime can be studied "scientifically." Positivistic students of white collar crime tend to adopt a conception of such crime as a violation of law, and they believe that we can best study white collar crime through systematic observation and measurement and through dispassionate, quantitative analysis. A *humanistic approach* generally rejects traditional scientific methods as inappropriate for the study of the human realm, and looks instead to the tradition of the humanities. Humanistic students of white collar crime tend to focus on the social construction of the meaning of white collar crime, and they believe we can best study such crime through interpretive observation and qualitative methods.

Finally, no one academic discipline allows us to acquire a deep and broad understanding of something as complex as white collar crime. Many different disciplines have something to contribute. Philosophy aids us in thinking more clearly about our assumptions and presuppositions and can deepen our understanding of ethical conundrums involved in white collar crime (see, for example, French 1979). Historical investigations can trace the evolving character of the white collar crime problem and identify the forces that promote new laws and prosecutorial initiatives against it (see, for example, Robb 1992). Economics is obviously relevant to the study of crime, which is driven largely by economic considerations and has many economic consequences (see, for example, Barnett 1986). Political science examines the law-making processes relating to white collar crime, as well as the relationship between governmental agencies and businesses (see, for example, Lane 1953). Psychology helps us make sense of the rationalization processes involved in white collar crime, and of individual decision making in an organizational context (see, for example, Milgram 1963). Sociology has been especially well-represented in white collar crime studies, and such sociological concepts as subculture, organization, socialization, social structure, social status, and social conflict are all crucial elements in the analysis of white collar crime (see, for example, Gross 1980). Finally, a true mastery of this subject requires some familiarity with jurisprudence and legal writing generally, the business-related disciplines (e.g., management and accounting), communications studies, and many other disciplines as well. In the final analysis, white collar crime is so complex and multifaceted that it can be understood only by invoking the concepts and insights of a wide range of disciplines.

## Specific Challenges in the Study of White Collar Crime

The study of crime in a number of ways confronts researchers with difficulties not typical of many other areas of social and behavioral research. The contradictory complex of criminogenic influences and proscriptive or deterrent forces makes it more difficult to explain crime than, say, educational choices. The physical, financial, and emotional devastation crime causes makes it more difficult to be dispassionate about it than, for example, about dating patterns. The illegal or shameful character of criminal activities, and frequent extralegal responses of criminal justice agents to it, makes it more difficult to obtain valid (and accurate) data on crime than, for example, on household consumer practices. The study of white collar crime involves special difficulties within the broader category of criminological study.

**The Complex Nature of White Collar Crime**   We can begin by referring to the considerable lack of consensus on definitions and core concepts pertaining to white collar crime, as discussed in Chapter 1. This conceptual confusion is greater than in many other areas of criminological research and makes the formulation of testable hypotheses more difficult (Dinitz 1982: 144). It also makes more questionable various types of comparison of studies conducted in different times and places.

Since the 1970s, the unit of analysis in white collar crime studies has increasingly shifted from the individual to the organization (Clark and Hollinger 1977: 150; Vaughan 1981: 141). White collar crime is often unusually complex, insofar as it may involve a large organization acting in concert with one or more organizations, numerous individuals occupying very different positions in these organizations, and a series of complicated transactions—some of ambiguous legal status—carried out over a long period of time (Clinard and Yeager 1978: 265–66). Given this complexity, researchers may need to understand aspects of many different fields, including economics, management, law, sociology, psychology, and organizational theory (Clark and Hollinger 1977: 151; Geis 1984: 138; Dinitz 1982: 143). Students of white collar crime sometimes contend with such matters as bidding awards, auditing mechanisms, interlocking ownership arrangements, codes of regulation, and the like (Clark and Hollinger 1977). By comparison, juvenile auto theft and most homicides are far more straightforward.

A much broader range of social control agencies—for example, criminal justice, regulatory, and professional agencies—may respond to white collar crime than is typically the case for conventional street crime. Problems of objectivity are arguably intensified in the realm of white collar crime if disputes over its very definition and the most appropriate legal responses to it are especially pronounced, and if researchers are especially likely to be drawn to the field by moral outrage (Clinard and Yeager 1978: 268–69). At least some students of white collar crime become advocates of specific white collar crime policies, whereas others feel that such advocacy is inappropriate for scholars.

Finally, conventional street offenders are typically more accessible (especially in detention) and perhaps more open about their illegal activities than are white collar offenders, the vast majority of whom are never processed by the system and in any case are more likely to feel shame about and deny criminality (Geis 1984: 138; Katz 1988: 319; Dinitz 1982: 144). Accordingly, it is more difficult, if not impossible, to compel powerful people and institutions to cooperate with a white collar crime research project.

**Gaining Access in White Collar Crime Research**   To obtain the cooperation of an organization such as a corporation in a research project on some aspect of corporate crime, the research proposal must be presented in a nonthreatening way, must incorporate a framework and use terminology familiar to the organization, and must be seen as having some potential benefit or "payoff" for the organization (Yeager and Kram 1990: 133). In his study of corporate morality, Jackall (1988) was turned down by 36 corporations before four large corporations gave him access for his research. If the powerful consider the research findings distressing, they are more likely to be in a position to retaliate against the researcher (Williams 1989: 254). Interviews of powerful people require special techniques that take into account accommodating time constraints, alleviating concerns about confidentiality, establishing empathy and credibility, and framing questions in forms most likely to elicit candid responses (Dexter 1970; Williams 1989).

It stands to reason that sophisticated people may be especially adept at providing misleading, self-serving responses to researchers' inquiries.

**Obtaining White Collar Crime Statistics**  Because there is no real white collar crime equivalent to uniform crime report data, which exist for conventional crime, data with various limitations must be extracted from a wide range of sources, including governmental agency and annual financial reports, newspapers, and journals (Clinard and Yeager 1978; Dinitz 1982). In official police crime statistical reports, corporate and occupational crimes are often lumped together, and white collar crime statistics in federal and state agency reports are divided among criminal, civil, and administrative agencies (Simpson, Harris, and Mattson 1993). Furthermore, especially in the case of corporate crime, the data tend to be recorded only during an advanced stage of the proceedings, rather than immediately following the incident itself. Direct observation is the least effective method of monitoring control of corporate illegality because of the large number of actors involved and their dispersal over time and place (Shapiro 1984). Conventional police agencies have been much more fully researched, and are more easily observable, than the various other agencies that investigate white collar offenses (Dinitz 1982).

**Obtaining Research Support**  On a practical level it has traditionally been easier to obtain research support for projects that explore conventional forms of juvenile delinquency and crime than for research on white collar crime, especially elite forms. Galliher (1979) has produced evidence that peer review panels for government research funding are establishment-connected and biased, that individualistic-focused, quantitative studies relevant to conventional crime and its control are most likely to receive funding, and that studies of major corporations or government organizations themselves have been funded less commonly. Longmire's (1982) research provides some unsurprising indications that criminologists with a leftist orientation are less likely to receive research funds.

The state and corporations that sponsor research can display some understandable discomfort with research that hits too close to home (Dinitz 1982: 145; Katz 1988: 320; Levi 1987: xxii–xxiii; Williams 1989: 254). In more recent years in the United States, however, the government has funded studies of corporate crime and other forms of white collar crime. A division of the U.S. Department of Justice, for example, provided major funding support for Clinard and Yeager's (1980) massive study of corporate crime. A critic of their study, T. R. Young (1981), has suggested that their inquiry on corporate crime was too narrow in scope and was not linked with the capitalist system; another reviewer, Paul Ruschmann (1981), accused them of having a pro-government bias. Whenever the government or corporations fund research on white collar crime, it seems relevant to ask whether such funders measure the researchers by some ideological standard, and whether the researchers consciously or subconsciously adapt their research to accommodate the sponsor's perspective or interests.

**A Case Study: The Revco Medicaid Fraud Case**   A clearer idea of the challenges confronting the white collar crime researcher can be acquired by looking at one specific example of such research. Diane Vaughan's *Controlling Unlawful Organizational Behavior* (1983) studied the Revco Medicaid fraud case in which a large drugstore chain in Ohio initiated a computer-generated double billing scheme that cost the government half a million dollars in Medicaid funds. Company officials, however, believed they were entitled to these funds because of perceived inequities they attributed to inefficient or unfair reimbursement practices.

Vaughan first developed a file on this case by "snowballing" bits and pieces of information, which led in turn to further leads, and so forth. But Vaughan, trained as a sociologist, was confronted with an early obstacle posed by the need to master the many specialized languages involved in the case: the computer language of the Welfare Department's Division of Data Services, that department's "Medicaid language," and the financial language of the corporation (Vaughan 1983: 113). Conversely, Vaughan's tendency to use sociological language had to be "translated" to become comprehensible to the personnel of these different organizations.

A second challenge involved the Revco Corporation's concerns about revealing secrets that would be useful to its competitors, as well as affecting employee morale and generating undesirable publicity. Thus it resisted Vaughan's requests for access (despite the fact that Revco was essentially claiming to be the victim in the case). Means of gaining cooperation from the various investigatory and prosecutorial agencies involved in the case also had to be negotiated; individual bureaucrats were reluctant to assume responsibility for providing access.

This led to a third basic challenge. The involvement of eight large, complex organizations in this single case required Vaughan to face difficult strategic and ethical choices: how to gain the trust and confidence of the various parties involved without revealing confidences, becoming intrusive, or becoming an advocate for any particular party. In analyzing the mass of often-conflicting information collected, researchers must be conscious of, and resistant to, different possible biases. Despite all these obstacles, Vaughan was able to produce an informative study of one corporation's encounter with and control of criminal conduct.

## Research Methods for Studying White Collar Crime

EVERY MATURE, REASONABLY intelligent member of our society knows something about white collar crime. We are all exposed to reports of various types of white collar crime activities through the media, especially newspapers, magazines, radio, and television. These reports are largely a product of what we can call *journalistic research.* The quality and credibility of such reports vary greatly, as was discussed in Chapter 1. There is an intrinsic bias in much of the media toward the sensational;

, getting a good story often takes precedence over a balanced and thoroughly accurate representation of the facts. And even though journalists are trained to use sound methods for collecting and analyzing data, they must often contend with time and space constraints that preclude a full-fledged report of their findings.

Having said all this, we must also acknowledge the crucial role journalists play in facilitating our understanding of white collar crime. The journalistic role here is perhaps proportionally more important than in other types of crime. Major media enterprises have both the formidable resources and the access that is often required for effective investigations of the illegal activities of high-level governmental or corporate officials. Journalistic reports are drawn on and cited throughout this book. Mark Dowie's "Pinto Madness," originally published in *Mother Jones* in 1977, is but one outstanding (and award-winning) journalistic report that exposed a significant example of corporate misconduct and played a role in the response to this misconduct (Cullen, Maakestad, and Cavender 1987: 160–63). Not only can such reports provide us with a vivid image of illegal activity; they can also generate hypotheses for further, more systematic study.

## Scholarly Research and White Collar Crime

The formal study of white collar crime has used a variety of research methods. *Case studies*—in-depth examinations of a particular case of white collar crime—have been more conspicuous in this field than in the study of conventional crime. In addition, surveys and interviews have been widely used. Many studies, especially of corporate crime, have used official data to examine financial and structural correlates of lawbreaking (Yeager and Kram 1990: 128). At least a limited number of fieldwork and observational studies have been conducted as well. Historical accounts, legal doctrines, and other existing "data" (e.g., media accounts) have been subjected to systematic analysis.

Many studies have used a combination of several different methods to explore some facet of white collar crime, or to test a particular hypothesis. This is especially true of case studies, such as Geis's (1967) study of the heavy-electrical-equipment antitrust cases, Vaughan's (1983) study of the Revco Medicaid fraud case, and Cullen, Maakestad and Cavender's (1987) study of the Ford Pinto case, to mention but three examples. The use of multiple methods applies, as well, to studies of regulatory agencies (see, for example, Shapiro 1984 on the SEC), white collar crime defense lawyers (see, for example, Mann 1985), and federal judges in white collar cases (see, for example, Wheeler, Mann, and Sarat 1988). Researchers, then, might use a mixture of surveys, interviews, direct observations, examination of case records, and analysis of secondary data. These and other specific methods merit some further discussion.

## Experiments

The experiment, a method of study exemplifying a positivistic or scientific approach, has to date seldom been used in the study of white collar crime. Still, it is worth exploring whether this quintessentially positivistic method has any application to such study.

The classic experiment calls for an examination of the effects, if any, of an independent variable on a dependent variable. In its traditional form, a randomly selected experimental group and a virtually identical control group are tested before and after the experimental group alone has been exposed to the independent variable. This method has been used quite extensively in the behavioral sciences and has proven to be especially useful in the study of learning, memory, perception, and related matters.

The *laboratory experiment* has been used rarely, if at all, in studying white collar crime; most of what we want to learn about white collar crime does not lend itself to such a highly controlled, specific setting. Nevertheless, the experiment has at least a limited potential usefulness in this field. It could be used to examine, for example, how the personal attributes of defendants in white collar crime cases affect the perceptions and judgments of jurors. We could produce videotapes of simulated portions of white collar crime trials; the tapes shown to both experimental and control groups would present identical evidence but the tape the experimental group views would feature defendant attributes (e.g., respectability) that are absent from the control group tape. Our objective here would be to measure the effects of various defendant attributes on the jury's verdict (the dependent variable). If we replicate modified versions of this experiment over a period of time, we may be able to identify which specific defendant attributes in white collar crime cases work in the favor of, or against, the defendant.

In Milgram's (1963) famous experiment on authority and obedience, large numbers of subjects (ordinary people) complied with the experimenter's instruction that they should administer electrical shocks to other subjects when the latter apparently failed to accomplish a specific task. This experiment at least suggests that ordinary and even "good" people will often engage in "dirty work" if such specific actions are legitimated by some authority figure or occur in a particular context (Hughes 1964). The discussion of Milgram's experiment has centered on its relevance or irrelevance for understanding participation in the Holocaust and parallel events (Miller 1986), but it is clear that one of the persistent themes in the study of white collar crime (especially its organizational or corporate form) is the involvement of "good" (or at least ordinary) people in "dirty" (or at least clearly illegal) activities.

The *field experiment* differs from the laboratory experiment insofar as it is carried out in a real-life setting rather than in a laboratory. One of the overriding limitations of laboratory experiments is the problem of *external validity;* that is, can we validly generalize from what has been observed in the laboratory to statements about how people in real-life situations (e.g., on an actual jury) will behave? The field experiment sacrifices some of the control achieved in the laboratory setting for some degree of external validity.

Consider the following field experiment involving occupational crime. A car that has been declared in perfect running order is brought into a service station with the coil wire disconnected. Because the car won't restart after being shut off and refueled, it is left there for any necessary repairs. Will the problem be correctly diagnosed and properly repaired, and will the charges be appropriate for the repair? In a famous

1941 study sponsored by *Reader's Digest*, 63 percent of the 347 repair shops visited in 48 states overcharged or did unnecessary work (Blumberg 1989: 65). When this experiment was repeated (with minor variations) in 1987, the results were essentially the same.

A similar field experiment on fraudulent claims to insurance companies submitted by auto body repair shops was conducted by Paul Tracy and James Alan Fox (1989). Drivers were engaged to take damaged rental vehicles to 91 randomly selected auto body shops in Massachusetts to obtain repair estimates. At each body shop, estimates of repair costs were obtained for two cars, one of which was said to be covered by insurance and the other of which was not. Although a number of variables were manipulated (including the driver's sex), "the key experimental variable was whether the damage was covered or not covered by insurance" (Tracy and Fox 1989: 596). The hypothesis—that repair cost estimates for vehicles covered by insurance would be inflated because drivers would have little (if any) incentive to go to the trouble of shopping around if the repair cost wasn't coming out of their pocket—was confirmed.

A well-known study by Schwartz and Skolnick (1964) also incorporated a field experiment. They compared the effects (as measured by employability) of legal stigma on lower-class convicted assaulters and on physicians convicted of malpractice. The field experiment aspect involved the preparation of parallel resumés with and without mention of criminal convictions. Unsurprisingly, the assaulters' chances of employment were greatly diminished when this legal stigma was included. On the other hand, physicians found guilty of malpractice did not report parallel negative consequences from this "legal stigma." Although the data on physicians in this study were gathered by a survey rather than a field experiment (and even though malpractice is not uniformly regarded as white collar crime), it is obvious that such "experiments" can be used to study the consequences of white collar crime convictions.

In a more recent study, McGraw and Scholz (1991) compared levels of taxpayer compliance. One sample of taxpayers received an appeal (via videotape) to comply (pay their taxes) due to civic virtue, another group received an appeal based on self-interest, and a control group received no appeal at all. This study did not find clear support for the claim of Schwartz and Orleans's (1967) article that appeals to one's ethics would produce greater taxpayer compliance than would appeals emphasizing deterrence and self-interest.

A third form of experiment, the *natural experiment*, allows the researcher to observe (but not manipulate) a real-world situation in order to identify the effect of some relevant independent variable. For example, a series of studies that compare annual injury rates in manufacturing plants subjected to regulatory inspections with those that were not constitutes a natural experiment to ascertain whether such inspections help reduce worker injuries (Gray and Sholz 1993). Of course, very formidable methodological and measurement problems are involved in any such comparison.

Although they characterized their method as "event history analysis" because it did not follow the classic experimental model, Simpson and Koper (1992) have provided us with a useful analytical tool. They studied a sample of 38 corporations charged with serious antitrust violations (between 1928 and 1981) to determine whether sanctions deterred corporations from recidivism, and if so, which type of sanctions (e.g., civil, criminal, or administrative) were most effective. They found at least an indication of some deterrent effect of convictions and the imposition of sanctions.

## Surveys

A second major research method is the *survey*, which is perhaps most readily associated with the study of opinions, attitudes, and beliefs but can also be used to explore experiences. The major challenge in survey research is obtaining a sample that is representative of the population about which one wants to generalize. A related challenge is obtaining a response rate high enough for the survey to be meaningful. Surveys may be carried out in person, over the telephone, or by mail; each approach has both strengths and drawbacks. A third set of challenges centers on the problems of formulating questions that aren't loaded, administering the survey in a way that minimizes problems of bias, and coding or interpreting the data in a valid way. Choices must be made about the benefits and drawbacks of using forced-choice and open-ended questions.

Surveys may investigate relative levels of fear of crime, attitudes toward punishment, perceptions of the fairness and effectiveness of the criminal justice system, personal patterns of involvement in illegal activity, experiences of crime victimization, and rationales for justice system responses to white collar crime. Surveys can contribute greatly to our understanding of white collar crime because we still have much to learn about patterns of involvement, rationalizations, and attitudes pertaining to white collar crime issues. As discussed elsewhere in this chapter, some recent survey studies have challenged the traditional claim that the general public regards white collar crime as far less serious than conventional street crime.

Many other types of relevant surveys can be identified. For example, Braithwaite and Makkai (1991) surveyed nursing home administrators to attempt a measurement of the deterrent effect of sanctions. Benson (1984) surveyed convicted white collar offenders to assess the consequences of their criminal status on their occupational status. Wheeler, Mann, and Sarat (1988) surveyed a sample of federal judges to uncover the reasoning behind their sentencing practices for white collar offenders.

Surveys of attitude—for example, assessments of the relative seriousness of various types of white collar crime—always raise the question of whether the professed attitudes in fact translate into equivalent choices and actions in real-life situations. Does, for example, a recognition of harmfulness of corporate illegality (e.g., producing unsafe products or polluting the environment) translate into a willingness to campaign for tougher laws or to send actual corporate executives to prison? Responses to surveys are typically somewhat removed from actual decision-making processes. People's visceral reactions (and biases) may still put conventional offenders at a disadvantage relative to white collar offenders, even if the crimes they commit are rated as less serious than certain white collar crimes.

## Observational Research

*Observational,* or *participant observer, research,* which involves direct observation of individuals, a group, or an organization over a period of time, has been quite useful in social science. To date it has been applied only to white collar crime in a somewhat limited way because gaining access to either criminal enterprises or social control agencies is difficult. Blumberg (1989) analyzed the accounts of some 600 students who reported their experiences with deceptive practices in a range of retail businesses. Jackall's (1988) study of corporate morality and Vaughan's (1983) use of observation in the Revco Medicaid fraud case were mentioned earlier.

Observational fieldwork has probably been most widely used in studies of regulatory agencies. Examples include studies of environmental regulatory agencies by Hawkins (1984) and by Yeager (1987), and of regulatory agencies focusing on working conditions by Braithwaite (1985b) and by Shover, Clelland, and Lynwiler (1986). Although Shapiro (1984) was able to observe the operation of the Securities and Exchange Commission from within, she also found that she had to overcome a rather high level of suspicion and distrust, and that in any case much about SEC enforcement practices cannot be efficiently discovered by direct observation. To Shapiro it became quite evident that observational methods work much more successfully when applied to the social control of street crime than when applied to the social control of white collar crime.

## Secondary Data Analysis

Much white collar crime research has involved the analysis of secondary data: data that were not directly generated or collected by the researcher. Such secondary data often take the form of statistical information collected by various official agencies. Clinard and Yeager's (1980) major study of corporate crime relied heavily on such data, and Wheeler, Mann, and Sarat (1988) analyzed data on sentencing patterns for white collar offenders.

Hagan and Palloni (1986) extracted data from the files of the Probation Department of the federal Southern District in New York (among the most active of jurisdictions in the pursuit of white collar crime) to test the proposition that sentences given white collar criminals were more severe after Watergate. The probation department data enabled the researchers to compare sentences before and after Watergate for both white collar and common crimes; educational level and additional variables (e.g., prior convictions, race, sex, etc.) were also taken into account. Although the substantive findings of this and other sentencing studies are discussed in a subsequent section of this book, it can be pointed out here that the validity of any analysis of statistical data is limited by the quality and accuracy of the data. And if such an analysis finds—as at least one study (Wheeler, Weisburd, and Bode 1982) did—that high-status offenders are sentenced more harshly than low-status offenders, then we have to ask what this means. One possible meaning is that a far smaller proportion of high- as opposed to low-status offenders reach the sentencing stage, but that those relatively few who do receive especially tough sentences. It is quite widely recognized today that statistical data are open to a variety of interpretation. In evaluating any statistical analysis, researchers should ask themselves whether the appropriate statistical tests have been applied and applied correctly, and whether all relevant variables have been incorporated into the analysis.

## Archival Data Analysis

The more complex a crime, the more likely it is to generate a large file of written documents. Even if much white collar crime (and the justice system responses to it) is difficult to observe directly, often a mass of records is available.

Donald Scott (1989), in his study of the policing of corporate collusion, was able to reconstruct antitrust cases by systematically reviewing investigative files of the Antitrust Division of the Department of Justice (available through the Freedom of Information Act). Much of the evidence in such cases is documentary. As Barnett (1982) observed, corporate offenders have a bureaucratic need to maintain records, and this need may conflict with their desire to destroy incriminating evidence. Much the same can be said of various forms of governmental crime. The crimes of the Nazi regime were significantly reconstructed (and continue to be investigated a half century later) through examination of documentation produced by the Nazi bureaucracy. The White House tapes, which played a central role in the impeachment and resignation of President Richard Nixon, can be cited as classic proof of the fact that the desire to maintain a historical record can produce a fascinating record of elite crime in the making.

Since the Watergate Affair in particular, the paper shredder has become an important instrument for destroying potentially incriminating documentary evidence. Among the principal limitations of archival data analysis, then, are the selective nature of what is recorded in the first place, and the incompleteness (through deliberate destruction or accidental circumstances) of the existing documentary record. Still, because for many white collar crimes documentation is the single most credible and complete source of information, archival data analysis is an important method for studying white collar crime.

## Content Analysis

Content analysis is a method that systematically analyzes the representation of something in the media "to find underlying forms and structures in social communication" (Sanders 1974: 12). Given the pervasive role of the media in our lives, it is important to analyze their treatment of white collar crime. In Chapter 1 quite a number of studies using content analysis were discussed. In one study, Evans and Lundman (1983) compared 29 leading U.S. newspapers' coverage of a major 1976 antitrust case with newspaper coverage of a similar 1961 antitrust case, to determine whether the level of newspaper coverage of corporate crime had increased in the post-Watergate period. In another study, Lynch and associates (1989) compared the reporting of the Bhopal disaster (the emission of poisonous gases from a Union Carbide plant in India in 1984, killing and injuring thousands of individuals) in Indian and American periodicals to determine whether the media in the two different countries were more likely to treat the incident as a "crime" or as an "accident." This type of analysis, at least on an elementary level, is especially accessible to undergraduate students.

## Methods of Studying White Collar Crime, In Sum

It is important to realize that to date far less basic data on white collar crime have been collected in comparison with the vast amount of data available on conventional crime and conventional offenders. Jurg Gerber and Eric Fritsch (1993) have suggested that students in white collar crime courses be assigned the project of collecting relevant data on white collar crime from such sources as *The Wall Street Journal; Standard & Poor's Register of Corporations, Directors, and Executives; Who's Who in America;* the *Standard Directory of Advertisers;* and the *Statistical Abstract of the United States.* Students, then, have a role to play in advancing our understanding of white collar crime.

The preceding review makes no claim of exhaustively identifying the range of methods applied to the study of white collar crime. Rather, it is an attempt to introduce the diversity of possible research strategies and some of the problems associated with them. These difficulties are further explored in the next two sections of this text.

## Public Perception of White Collar Crime: How Serious Is It?

MEDIA COVERAGE AND some agents of exposure of white collar crime were reviewed in Chapter 1. How serious a problem is white collar crime in the public view?

The traditional view has been that white collar crime is perceived as less serious than conventional crime. This view was first advanced by pioneering students of white collar crime—for example, E. A. Ross (1907: 467) and Edwin Sutherland (1949: 224)—and it has endured in more recent times. The President's Commission on Law Enforcement and Administration of Justice (1967a: 48) observed in 1967 that "the public tends to be indifferent to business crime or even to sympathize with the offenders when they have been caught." Such assertions, however, have not been based on empirical research, and they have been quite strongly challenged by various studies in the past several decades.

The traditional view has inspired a number of questions: If it ever was the case that the general public regarded white collar crimes as less serious, is it still the case today? What kinds of white collar crime are considered most serious, and how do these perceptions compare with perceptions of conventional forms of crime? If at least some forms of white collar crime are indeed perceived as less serious, why is this the case? How valid are measurements of public perceptions of the seriousness of crime, and what implications can we derive from such findings?

Some empirical studies that explored perceptions of crime in the 1950s found some evidence of condemnation of white collar crime generally, indentified disapproval of some specific white collar crimes (such as advertising misrepresentation and maintaining detrimental work conditions), and called for harsher sentences for at least some of these offenses (Aubert 1952; Newman 1957; Rettig and Passamanick 1959). Other illegal actions of businessmen were defended, however. The systematic study of the seriousness of crime perceptions is commonly thought to originate with Sellin and Wolfgang's *The Measurement of Delinquency* (1964), but this study did not include white collar crime.

Many of the studies examining perceptions of the seriousness of crime that have been conducted since the 1950s suggest relatively high levels of consensus in the ratings, especially among Americans (Wolfgang et al. 1985; Grabosky, Braithwaite, and Wilson 1987; Hauber, Toonvliet, and Willemse 1988; Newman 1976; Scott and Al-Thakeb 1977; Warr 1989). However, this consensus tends to be lower for white collar crime than for conventional violent crime and narcotics offenses (Hauber, Toonvliet, and Willemse 1988; Miethe 1984). Some studies have suggested that women, older people, and people of lower socioeconomic status view white collar crime as somewhat more serious (Grabosky, Braithwaite, and Wilson 1987; Hauber, Toonvliet, and Willemse 1988). According to one study, blacks regarded white collar crimes directed at consumers as somewhat more serious than did whites, who expressed more concern with crimes directed at businesses (Miethe 1984). Perhaps unsurprisingly, some studies have found that business executives, managers, criminal justice bureaucrats, and lawyers tend to view white collar crimes as more complex and varied, and as less appropriately dealt with by harsh penal sanctions, than does the general public (Cole 1983; Frank et al. 1989; Hartung 1953; McCleary et al. 1981). Another study found some equivalence in the perception of police chiefs and the public on the seriousness of white collar crime, but it also concluded that federal investigators regarded white collar crime as more serious than conventional crime (Pontell et al. 1985).

Several studies from the late 1960s through the 1980s found that members of the general public regarded such white collar crimes as manufacturing unsafe products (e.g., pharmaceuticals or automobiles) and selling contaminated food as worse in some cases than armed robbery and arson, and majorities favored imprisonment for antitrust violators and embezzlers more often than for burglars or prostitutes (Cullen, Link, and Polanzi 1982; Cullen et al. 1985; Grabosky, Braithwaite, and Wilson 1987; Hauber, Toonvliet, and Willemse 1988; Meier and Short 1982; Rossi et al. 1974; Wolfgang et al. 1985). White collar crimes involving fraud, illegal price fixing, or other purely financial losses tended to be regarded as less serious than those actually causing physical harm, although such a crime as obtaining money under false pretenses might be rated as more serious than housebreaking if a significant amount of money was involved (Levi 1987: 61–63).

It is something of a paradox that crimes directed at a single individual (a typical attribute of conventional predatory crimes) tend to elicit greater anger than do crimes that have a large number of victims (a more typical attribute of white collar crime), provided the physical harm or financial loss is less direct and less extreme in any particular case (Hauber, Toonvliet, and Willemse 1988). It has long been established that the public views white collar (and other) crimes directed at large business organizations as less serious than those directed at small businesses (Smigel 1970), and certain white collar offenses (e.g., tax evasion) are generally rated very low in seriousness. All of these studies, then, have produced evidence suggesting that perceptions of white collar crime are significantly influenced both by one's status and vantage point and by the victim's attributes.

Some studies have revealed a measurable increase in ratings of the seriousness of white collar crime following the massive publicity about elite abuse of power in the Watergate Affair of the early 1970s (Carroll et al. 1974; Reed 1979). Many (but not all) studies support the claim that the perception of the seriousness of white collar crime has increased; for white collar crime without physical consequences, considerable public indifference is still apparent (Goff and Nason-Clark 1989). Any generalizations about an increasing perception of the seriousness of white collar crime must be rejected, then, both because of the variable nature of such crime and the somewhat inconsistent findings in a limited number of studies.

Ultimately, perception of white collar crime is complex, and not only because the term *white collar crime* covers such a broad range of activities. Studies of perceptions of the seriousness of crime generally are plagued with methodological difficulties. Some studies call for normative (i.e., wrongfulness) evaluations, whereas others call for factual (i.e., harmfulness) evaluations; some studies have focused on individual offenders, whereas others have addressed corporate entities; some studies have used categorical (fixed) scales (i.e., 1 to 9) for seriousness ratings, whereas others have used magnitude (relative) scales; some studies have simply listed types of offenses, whereas others have used situational vignettes (Frank et al. 1989; Green 1990; Meier and Short 1982; Warr 1980). It has also been suggested that a high rating for the seriousness of corporate crime could vary with the context in which the questionnaire was disseminated (e.g., higher during a period when a celebrated corporate crime case is in the public eye) (Goff and Nason-Clark 1989). Respondents are often asked to make the proverbial comparison between apples and oranges—that is, to compare activities that may be more or less serious in very different terms (financial loss; physical harm; psychological trauma; loss of trust; etc.). And we must always be sensitive to the possibility that the findings of "seriousness of crime" studies are distorted by methodological artifacts, such as nonrandom samples of citizens, inappropriate use of statistical measures, overrepresentation of certain types of acts, variations in the number of individuals rating different criminal acts, and biases in the administration of such surveys (Miethe 1982). In some cases these studies are also flawed by the adoption of narrow or conventional conceptions of white collar crime.

Despite such limitations, the research on perceptions of crime is significant because it challenges the traditional assumption that the public generally does not regard white collar crime as especially serious. Even though the full meaning of the findings of these studies is still open to interpretation, they do not dispute the traditional claim that the crimes people fear most, and those that arouse their strongest visceral reactions, tend to be violent personal crimes involving direct physical injury or death. And it is not entirely clear that the perception of at least some white collar crime as very serious will translate into a willingness to impose harsh penalties on specific white collar offenders who appear highly respectable, express remorse, or have various plausible rationalizations for their actions (Grabosky, Braithwaite, and Wilson 1987: 42). Nor is it clear under what circumstances perceptions of seriousness translate into willingness to actively support legislation that takes a tougher stance on white collar crime. In the final analysis, the measure of how seriously citizens regard white collar crime is provided not by what they think about it, but by what they are willing to do about it.

## Measuring White Collar Crime: How Prevalent Is It?

THERE IS NO simple or especially accurate answer to the question of how much white collar crime occurs. Quantifying all forms of crime is difficult, and in the case of white collar crime many of the difficulties are compounded.

Since the early 19th century the analysis of crime statistics has served as an important basis for understanding and explaining crime. In the conventional view, the crime statistics collected by official agencies are regarded as quantitative measurements of crime and criminal justice system outcomes. A critical view today, however, contends that crime statistics are products of particular agencies and entities, each with ideological biases, strategic purposes, and finite resources (Selke and Pepinsky 1984).

In this view, understanding the process by which statistics are produced is more important than the resulting statistical data. In any case, statistics about criminal activity obviously should not be confused with statistics on criminal justice system responses to such activity (Reiss and Biderman 1980). Furthermore, there is considerable reason to believe that the statistics of official agencies direct much more attention to conventional crime than to white collar crime (Eitzen and Timmer 1989: 39). All general and comparative claims about the incidence and distribution of different types of crime must be approached with great caution and considerable skepticism.

Crimes are neither uniformly defined, reported, or recorded, and the integrity and efficiency of criminal justice agencies varies. These problems are intensified in the case of white collar crime because legal definitions are especially likely to be variable or ambiguous and because victims of white collar crime are often unaware of their victimization. Once they become aware of having been victimized, they are much more likely to report their victimization to some public or private agency other than the police.

A number of studies of victims of consumer fraud, for example, have documented that such victims are unlikely to report the crime to the police (Jesilow, Klempner, and Chiao 1992; Titus, Heinzelmann, and Boyle 1995). They often have a sense of futility about the police response, and they are often quite unaware of the existence of special fraud units set up to investigate these crimes. Many organizational victims of fraud (e.g., corporations) are especially reluctant to file reports because they fear negative publicity and a public loss of confidence in the organization (Levi 1992). Thus if victims of fraud and many other white collar offenses report an offense at all, they often report it to some entity other than the police. Accordingly, such data as exists on white collar crime victimization is dispersed among numerous different agencies, each with different forms of record-keeping.

The best-known source of national crime statistics in the United States has been the FBI's *Uniform Crime Report*. More recently, the National Institute of Justice has issued reports that constitute an important source of crime data. So-called "index" crimes (i.e., conventional crimes such as homicide, forcible rape, aggravated assault, burglary, and the like) are the principal focus of the *Uniform Crime Report*. Although some forms of fraud and embezzlement are incorporated into the index crime categories, these crimes tend to be the less significant, smaller-scale white collar crimes or activities such as welfare fraud and passing bad checks that are not typically regarded as white collar crime at all.

In addition to the fact that much crime of all types is not ever reported to the police, the *UCR* has many other limitations, including flawed operational definitions, lack of clarity, and unstandardized data collection policies (Schneider and Wiersema 1990). Since the early 1970s an annual *Sourcebook of Criminal Justice Statistics,* which collates data from the FBI and other federal sources, has served as an important reference work for statistical information about crime. It is worth noting that according to this source, arrests on fraud charges have increased more dramatically (by almost 90 percent since the early 1980s) than did any other category of crime (Levi 1987: 7). One analysis by the Bureau of Justice produced figures suggesting that prosecution and conviction rates for white collar offenders were comparable to or even higher than those for property crime offenders, that incarceration rates were slightly lower, and that the percentage incarcerated for over a year was much lower (Manson 1986). An unknown but significant proportion of crimes defined as white collar cases in these statistics are in fact very-low-level frauds, and such data simply do not tell us what percentage of the whole class of white collar offenders is arrested relative to the percentage of conventional property offenders arrested.

A large amount of statistical data on civil and administrative cases has also been collected, especially by the various regulatory agencies. Those who favor restricting the definition of white collar crime to activities violating the criminal law argue that inclusion of civil and administrative data leads to overcounting of white collar crime. On the other hand, sole reliance on data from criminal agencies vastly undercounts by any reasonable criteria the incidence and prevalence of white collar crime.

There are numerous problems with regulatory agency data. These agencies have considerable discretionary leeway in defining (and responding to) offenses. Of the offenses that in fact come to their attention—and many do not—various factors can affect how the offenses are classified and recorded. Because these agencies often focus their enforcement activities on corporations rather than individuals, they are not likely to be reliable sources of data on individual offenders, and they are not organized to track either organizational or individual offenders over time (Reiss and Biderman 1980). Some of the statistics generated by regulatory agencies are cited at appropriate points in this book, but the limitations of such data should be kept in mind.

## Victimization Surveys and Self-Report Studies

The limitations of official enforcement agency data for measuring white collar crime had become quite widely recognized by the 1960s. Many criminologists adopted the notion that crime data collected from sources less removed from the criminal event, rather than data processed by official agencies, was likely to be more accurate (Jackson 1980), and thus victimization surveys were undertaken as one alternative to official data. The National Crime Survey (NCS), under the auspices of the Bureau of Justice Statistics, has annually surveyed a large sample of American individuals and households to determine whether they have been victims of crime over the preceding year. Not surprisingly, the NCS has revealed a much higher level of crime victimization than is indicated by the *Uniform Crime Report* (although some criminologists regard the *UCR* as more reliable for certain types of offenses) (Jackson 1980). In the case of white collar crime, however, the usefulness of the survey is severely limited.

As we noted earlier, one of the defining attributes of white collar crime is that victims (e.g., of price fixing) are much more likely to be unaware of their victimization than are victims of conventional offenses (e.g., robbery). The greater ambiguity of the laws also makes it more difficult for victims to be clear about whether they have been victimized. Indeed, in the case of fraud it is possible for victimization to be overreported if survey respondents mistakenly interpret all instances of consumer-related dissatisfaction to be cases of criminal victimization. In privately conducted surveys in 1992 and 1994, between one-third and three-quarters of the respondents reported having been deceived or defrauded by telemarketing or other personal marketing schemes (Titus, Heinzelmann, and Boyle 1995: 55).

*Self-report surveys,* yet another alternative to the statistics of official agencies, have revealed much higher levels of illegal activity than are suggested by official data. However, for the most part these surveys have focused on the activities of juveniles (assault, theft, vandalism, illicit drug use, and the like) rather than on white collar offenses (Chambliss 1988c: 43–45). Any such surveys directed at the population of white collar criminals would also encounter the problem that such offenders are especially likely to rationalize their conduct and may well deny even to themselves that they have violated laws.

Still, at least some self-report studies are pertinent to white collar crime. For example, surveys of self-reported noncompliance with income tax laws have been undertaken (Long and Swingen 1991). In a survey of middle managers who were retired and thus perhaps more candid about their activities, Clinard (1983) attempted to explore patterns of corporate lawbreaking, although he did not generate statistical data. Corporations may be required by regulatory agencies to file formal self-reports on selected offenses (Simpson, Harris, and Mattson 1993: 121). On the other hand Zimring (1987) has suggested that we might produce some useful data by surveying white collar personnel and businesses not about their own offenses, but rather about those of their competitors.

In principle, we could attempt to measure white collar crime through *direct observation* of it (Green 1990), as we noted earlier. Although such studies (e.g., of retailers and repair services) can provide estimates of the incidence or prevalence of white collar crime within certain spheres, most white collar crime simply cannot be observed directly.

## Measuring Specific Forms of White Collar Crime

There is no truly reliable way to measure the incidence of the many diverse forms of white collar crime, from antitrust violations to violations of environmental law to Medicaid fraud to employee embezzlement. Various "ballpark estimates" exist and will be referred to in this text where appropriate, but we must always try to identify the basis of these estimates.

Simpson, Harris, and Mattson (1993) have suggested that we can more reliably measure corporate crime by developing a model that takes into account such factors as opportunities to commit offenses, interconnections among actors, and numbers of transactions. This is, admittedly, a complex challenge. Zimring (1987) has made an innovative proposal for measuring the incidence of insider trading, one form of white collar crime that is surely underreported. He has suggested sampling corporations that have made major announcements (e.g., about takeovers), using computers to construct baseline data on the volume of the corporations' stocks traded under normal circumstances, and then scanning for significant deviations from baseline trading figures in the period preceding such public announcements. Such an approach, he believes, could be applied to other forms of white collar crime, including the performance of unnecessary surgery. The resulting information might not identify individual offenders, but it could hypothetically provide us reliable indicators about the distribution of white collar crime.

## Measuring White Collar Crime, In Sum

Reliable statistical data on white collar crime can serve many useful purposes. They can broaden awareness of the true scope of the problem and can provide a basis for obtaining more support for investigating and prosecuting white collar crime. Ideally, demonstrating that white collar offenders can be identified, successfully prosecuted, and punished can have some deterrent effect. To that end, various statistics are cited throughout this text.

Much still needs to be done to improve the quality of this statistical data. To date the most exhaustive study of problems involved in the measurement of white collar crime is Reiss and Biderman's *Data Sources on White-Collar Law-Breaking* (1980). Among other recommendations, they called for greater standardization of definitions and recording practices, more reliable characterizations of the universe of offenders, and better coordination among the criminal, civil, and administrative agencies that collect statistics. At the same time, from a critical perspective it is essential that we not rely exclusively on official statistics, but instead exploit many alternative ways of measuring the true scope of white collar crime.

## The Costs and Consequences of White Collar Crime

THE NOTION OF the "cost of crime" is most readily associated with economic costs, which can only be quite roughly estimated.

Many difficult questions are involved in measuring the economic cost of crime (Shenk and Klaus 1984), and for white collar crime it is substantially more difficult to measure than for conventional and many other forms of crime.

First, the ongoing disputes about defining and identifying white collar crime, discussed in Chapter 1, complicate the process. Even though there is considerable agreement that billions of dollars were lost in the savings and loan crisis, for example, and government estimates in 1988 and 1989 suggested that criminal activity was involved in 70–80 percent of the insolvencies (Calavita and Pontell 1990), years of litigation will likely be needed to grapple with the question of what proportion of the losses can be attributed to criminal fraud, and which proportion to poor judgment, bad luck, or even (as one prominent S & L bank director, Charles Keating, claims) to the ill-advised intervention of federal regulators (Carlson 1990a).

Second, as noted earlier, a much higher percentage of white collar crime is neither reported nor officially identified compared to conventional crime generally, and the costs of unreported crime are more difficult to measure. For example, major frauds against businesses may not be reported because they are embarrassing to the business (Levi 1987, 1992).

Third, there is no uniform way to measure costs even when a crime is identified and reported. If employees steal goods from a retail store, should the loss be calculated as the wholesale cost of the stolen goods, the retail value, or possibly different costs involved in their replacement? As Levi (1987: 29) noted, it is especially difficult to assess the economic cost of bribe-related activity. For example, a relatively small bribe to a building inspector might ultimately lead to the immense costs associated with the collapse of a building.

## Direct Costs

Some economic costs of white collar crime are clearly direct costs. Arson committed to defraud an insurance company may result in destruction of property of measurable value (again, however, we must differentiate among the original cost of the building, its current market value, and its replacement cost). Much conventional crime, and most white collar crime, involves the illegal transfer of assets from one party to another—fraud, by definition, increases the material well-being of one party at the expense of the other—and in these cases costs are typically defined in terms of the victims' losses.

Almost all crimes, white collar crimes in particular, have winners or beneficiaries. For example, many stockholders benefit, however unwittingly, from corporate and securities-related crimes that enhance corporate profit and the value of stock. Corporations may benefit from the crimes of their employees, and employees may benefit from the crimes of their employers. Even legitimate businesses and professionals may profit from white collar crimes. Among the many profiteers are those who insure against such crime, sell security services, conduct investigations, repair or replace damage done by white collar crime (e.g., asbestos removal firms), treat victims of such crime, provide legal representation—and even those who write and teach about white collar crime.

Certainly, many parties benefited from the savings and loan frauds of the 1980s. A whole class of very wealthy investors were able to buy up some of the bankrupted savings and loans (or their assets, principally real estate) at bargain prices and with little financial risk (Thomas 1990). Indeed, some of those responsible for the fraudulent losses in the first place may well profit from picking up the pieces of the financial mess they created (Gerth 1990d; Pontell and Calavita 1992). Over the long run, of course, the losers rather substantially outweigh the winners. Although the original depositors (often older people with significant savings) should at least recover their deposits, for decades to come taxpayers (many of them younger people, with limited or nonexistent savings) will have to bear much of the cost of the immense frauds involved, which alone should conservatively cost billions of the total bailout cost of up to a trillion dollars or more.

A conservative argument contends that the direct costs of promulgating and enforcing laws prohibiting a wide range of improper, harmful, or instrinsically corrupt activities by corporations and politicians may outweigh the benefits (Machan and Johnson 1983). For example, if U.S. corporations are prohibited from bribing public officials in foreign countries to obtain lucrative contracts but corporations of other countries are not so constrained, U.S. corporations may well suffer from a competitive disadvantage. The results would include a reduction in foreign contracts, loss of American jobs, and possibly loss of foreign influence.

Similarly, some conservatives claim that the costs of regulating environmental pollution, worker safety, and consumer products too often outweigh the benefits. Some corrupt acts—for example, telling a contractor the amount of the lowest competing bid so that he or she can underbid it—may actually save taxpayers money (Levi 1987: 29). And the claim has been made that stringent restrictions on campaign fund-raising and private-sector careers following regulatory agency service deter some of the most qualified people from running for election or re-election, or from accepting governmental appointments.

In the final analysis, however, the direct economic losses from all forms of white collar crime are immense and dwarf those of conventional crime. In the mid-1970s it was estimated that annual losses in the United States due to conventional property crime (i.e., robbery, theft, larceny, and auto theft) generated losses of no more than $4 billion, whereas economic losses due to white collar offenses (i.e., consumer fraud, illegal competition, and deceptive practices) totaled at least $40 billion (Conklin 1977). These frequently cited statistics suggest that economic losses from white collar crime were at least 10 times greater than such losses from conventional crime.

In view of the vast scope of white collar crime in more recent years, such estimates of the differential cost might be considered to be conservative. In one small state, Rhode Island, the annual estimated costs for white collar crime were pegged at $250 million (Moran, Parella, and Dakake 1988). Price-fixing losses in many individual industries total tens of millions; defense contract overcharges cost hundreds of millions; the losses in the Equity Funding case (a massive insurance fraud of the 1970s) totaled some $2 billion; some $10 billion was involved in the E. F. Hutton check-kiting case of the 1980s; the cost of treating diseases related to toxic exposure in the workplace adds up to tens of billions; the annual cost of antitrust or trade violations has been estimated at $250 billion in recent years; and so on (Cullen, Maakestad, and Cavender 1987). The annual cost of credit card fraud in the United

States is several billion dollars. (Levi 1987: 43). In the United States the average felony robbery involves several hundred dollars, whereas the average white collar felony involves several hundred thousand dollars (Levi 1987: 35; Cullen, Maakestad, and Cavender 1987: 54–55). According to *UCR* data, the total take from some 6,000 bank robberies in 1985 was $46 million dollars; the fraudulent losses from the failure of a single savings and loan, the Centennial, have been estimated to be $165 million (Benekos and Hagan 1990). Losses from some 20 years of street property crime have been estimated to total less than half of the hundreds of billions of dollars in losses of the savings and loan failures (Benekos and Hagan 1990). Estimates of tax evasion costs in the United States have ranged from less than 4 percent to over 30 percent of the gross national product, which amounts to hundreds of billions of dollars (Levi 1987: 33). Still more such statistics could be cited.

## Indirect Costs

Beyond the direct economic costs of crime are many significant *indirect costs*, although these costs are especially difficult to measure accurately. Among these indirect costs are higher taxes, increased cost of goods and services, and higher insurance rates (Shenk and Klaus 1984). Furthermore, substantial sums must be spent in efforts to prevent or offer protection against crime. In the case of conventional crime these expenses include the costs of locks, gates, burglar alarms, and the like. In the case of white collar crime, corporations and businesses with significant numbers of employees must typically spend money to screen out high-risk applicants from being employed in the first place, to purchase technology and internal personnel to maintain surveillance of employees, and to establish cumbersome procedures to minimize employee crime. On the other hand, because employees, customers, clients, and taxpayers are not especially well-positioned to protect themselves against white collar crime victimization, these parties may expend some money to minimize their chances of being employed by or patronizing of businesses and professionals who will subject them to illegal or fraudulent actions.

The costs of maintaining regulatory and justice systems to respond to white collar crime can also be included in the cost of this type of crime. The conventional criminal justice system expends proportionally less on white collar crime than on conventional crime, despite the much greater cost of white collar crime. The average per-crime cost of responding to white collar crime is higher than the average per-crime cost of responding to conventional crime, both because of the greater complexity of white collar crimes and the greater defensive resources available to the perpetrators (especially if they are organizations). Of course, any attempt to gauge the costs of responding to white collar crime must take into account the many different agencies (civil, administrative, private) other than criminal justice agencies that investigate and process this activity. Again, we must remind ourselves that many employees of these various agencies benefit from the existence of this type of crime.

In calculating the economic costs of white collar crimes we could subtract from the total the amount of fines collected by the government, principally from organizations convicted in white collar crime cases (Levi 1987: 48). In the insider trading cases of the 1980s, record fines were levied: $100 million against Ivan Boesky and

$600 million against Michael Milken (Stewart 1991). But these widely publicized figures, and other large fines levied against corporate offenders, may be somewhat misleading because tax write-offs can reduce substantially the final cost to the convicted party. In the savings and loan fraud cases, many of the guilty parties were ordered to repay hundreds of thousands, or even millions, of dollars. Because in many cases little if any of this money was actually collected (Pizzo and Muolo 1993), the gap between fines levied and restitution demanded (i.e., the net amount of money actually collected by the government) must always be taken into account.

Significant *residual economic costs* are also a consequence of white collar crime. In the case of conventional street crime, the loss of business for retail stores in high-crime areas is an example of a residual economic cost; in the case of white collar crime, a loss of investor confidence following revelations of insider trading or other manipulations, with consequent declines in stock values or increases in bond interest rates, is another example. The long-term consequences of declines in investor confidence are not really known, but they are surely formidable (Levi 1987: 48). Overall, a whole range of economic transactions are likely to become more costly to the extent that white collar crime precipitates diminishing trust.

## Physical Costs

Even though the *physical costs* of crime—personal injury and loss of life—are most immediately associated with conventional predatory crime, the physical costs of white collar crime are very substantial, and by one interpretation exceed such costs for violent personal crime. The physical costs of white collar crime include death and injury from polluting the environment, from unsafe working conditions, and from marketing unsafe products. Even crimes ordinarily thought of as exclusively economic, such as fraud, may lead to substantial physical harm to people. For example, fraud involving governmental or nongovernmental aid agencies in third-world countries may lead to thousands of deaths from malnutrition. Those who argue for a more expansive definition of white collar crime would include the physical costs of illness and death from smoking. And if governmental crimes are included as well, the largest losses of life and physical injury result from acts of war and genocide.

The physical costs of conventional violent crimes in the United States, as measured by the *Uniform Crime Report*, add up to over 24,000 deaths and 1,000,000 serious injuries a year (Reiman 1995: 70). Figures from the U.S. Bureau of Labor Statistics and other sources suggest that some 34,600 Americans die annually from work-related diseases and accidents, and nearly 1,850,000 workers are seriously injured in the workplace (Reiman 1995: 74). Because the entire population is vulnerable to conventional-crime violence, and because only less than half of the population in the labor force is vulnerable to work-related death or injury, the risks in the work context are much greater than from conventional violent crime. Approximately 15,000 deaths each year in the United States have been attributed to unnecessary medical operations alone (Reiman 1995: 77). Although it is obviously possible to question how many such deaths can be attributed to white collar crime specifically, it is also quite clear that the cost of white collar crime in lives and injuries is real and extensive.

## Other Costs

Other types of "costs" and consequences of white collar crime are even more difficult to measure, even though they are also real and substantial. They include the cost of the psychological trauma of victimization (which is discussed in the section on victims of white collar crime).

The cost of crime to what has sometimes been called "the social fabric" is arguably the most difficult cost to measure. In the case of conventional crime, one such cost is the intensification of intergroup hostility and conflict. Various commentators have suggested that in the long run the most pernicious cost of white collar crime lies in the alienation it generates, and in the distrust and erosion of confidence in major institutions it promotes (Meier and Short 1982). The President's Commission on Law Enforcement and Administration of Justice (1967a) claimed that pervasive white collar crime, and the failure of the justice system to respond effectively to it, was harming the moral legitimacy of the justice system. But Levi (1987: 51) noted that it is not entirely clear whether white collar crime—especially in its elite form—is a cause or a consequence of widespread cynicism. It seems likely that there are reciprocal effects—that is, that some level of cynicism promotes elite crime, and that elite crime then promotes even greater cynicism. Regardless, alienation, delegitimation, and cynicism are very significant costs of white collar crime.

## Victims of White Collar Crime

THE MOST COMMON image of a crime victim is surely the victim of murder, rape, robbery, burglary, or some other conventional crime. There can be little question that most people are likely to fear being victimized by such crime. Even though people who have not been victims of some form of direct, predatory crime do not typically think of themselves as crime victims, all of us, without exception, are victims of various white collar crimes, often without being aware of it.

The concept of "victim" does not have a single, fixed meaning. Traditionally it has been most commonly applied to those harmed by deliberate acts of predation. More recently it has been much more broadly invoked for large classes of people, including minorities and women, who are alleged to be exploited, abused, or persecuted in some way. In the broadest definitions of white collar crime or elite deviance, people who suffer from racism, imperialism, sexism, and the like are victims. An obvious drawback to such an inclusive meaning of victimization—that "we are all victims"—is that it strips the term of any coherent meaning (Karmen 1990: 7). Even though the difficulties generated by broader applications of the concept of "victim" must be duly noted, official conceptions of "crime victim" reflect a middle-class bias emphasizing the victimization of innocent people by irrational and dangerous conventional offenders (McShane and Williams 1992: 261). This narrowly restrictive conception of crime victims tends to reinforce the false notion that only this type of victimization is truly significant.

The victims of crime have been relatively neglected by the modern criminal justice system and by criminologists alike. The criminal offender and the criminal justice agencies that respond to crime have been the principal focus of criminological theory and research. In more recent times, however, this has begun to change. In the 1970s victimology emerged as a recognized specialization within criminology, although its roots can be traced to a number of earlier articles and books (from the 1940s on) that focused on crime victims. A victim's rights movement was a parallel development that also emerged during essentially this same period of time.

Both victimology and the victim's rights movement have been almost exclusively directed toward victims of conventional, predatory crimes (Karmen 1990). Both have been dominated by a conservative ideological outlook, and they have been more successful in promoting harsh penalties for conventional offenders than in truly helping crime victims to recover from their experiences. They have largely ignored (or even deflected attention from) white collar crime victimization (Friedrichs 1983; Fattah 1986; Moore and Mills 1990; McShane and Williams 1992). Robert Elias (1986) has called for linking victimology with a conception of human rights, and for attending to victims of consumer fraud, pollution, and other forms of suffering generated by social inequality and abuses of power. There is a need, then, for a more expansive conception of victims of crime.

All of us are victimized, in many capacities, by white collar crime.White collar crime victimization is especially diffuse, and victims' attributes are especially heterogeneous (McShane and Williams 1992: 262). We are generally less likely to be conscious of this victimization than of conventional crime victimization. As workers or employees we are victimized by hazardous and illegal conditions in the workplace, or by managerial practices that illegally deprive us of our just compensation and other labor-related rights. As consumers we are victimized by such corporate crimes as price-fixing and the sale of unsafe products. As customers, clients, and patients we are victimized by fraudulent and unethical practices of small businesses, entrepreneurs, and professionals. As citizens and residents of particular areas we are victimized by corporate pollution. As taxpayers we are victimized by defense contract frauds· and by frauds involving thrift institutions with government-insured deposits. Among the many other classes of victims of white collar crime are business competitors, business partners, shareholders, investors, and pension holders. Of course, governmental entities and organizations (including corporations) are victims of certain forms of white collar crime as well (Shichor 1989).

Many forms of white collar crime victimization, especially those involving the environment or the workplace, are defined as accidents or "disasters" and thus as beyond human control (Walklate 1989: 97). Victims themselves often accept this misleading notion, although much evidence suggests that many of these accidents and disasters are avoidable. Shichor (1989: 73–74) differentiates among primary (personal) victims, secondary (organizational) victims, and tertiary victims (abstractions such as the community at large or the public order). Vaughan (1980: 93) has noted that direct victims of white collar crime are often surrogate victims for real (but indirect) victims who are in a position to recognize their victimization. As an example she cites a state welfare department that is defrauded by a private corporation; the welfare clients who lose services and the taxpayers whose tax bills are inflated are the ultimate but less visible victims.

For some forms of white collar crime—for example, hazardous substances in the workplace or illegal pollution—it is especially difficult to establish three crucial parameters: (1) either intent to do harm or willful negligence that caused harm; (2) a direct causal link between health problems of workers or area residents and the hazardous conditions in the workplace or the illegal pollution; and (3) the time frame of harmful activity.

For at least some classes of white collar crime, each of a large number of victims suffers relatively minor losses. For example, a defense contract fraud or a price-fixing scheme may involve millions of dollars of losses, but each individual taxpayer or customer may lose only a few dollars or less. Of course, in these cases the cumulative losses are very substantial and the physical harm over time can be considerable, and in some cases economic losses and physical harm are very direct and very great.

Even when victims of white collar crime are fully aware of their victimization, they are often more likely to be both confused about how to report it and pessimistic about receiving meaningful assistance from the criminal justice system. In one study of older defrauded consumers, many of the victims claimed that their reported complaints remained unresolved (McGuire and Edelhertz 1980). Victims of conventional crimes often have discouraging—sometimes rather traumatic—experiences with this system, but the structure of mainstream criminal justice agencies makes them even less able to respond effectively to complex white collar crimes, and jurisdiction for white collar crimes is spread among many different types of government agencies.

When white collar crime cases are successfully prosecuted, the victims are not necessarily satisfied with the outcome. In one study of white collar fraud cases, about half the victims thought the sentences were too lenient (Levi 1992). This study concluded that when victims pursue cases, they are principally motivated by a desire to promote general deterrence and adhere to their company's policy, rather than by a desire to seek compensation or retribution. But to date there has been very little serious study of white collar crime victims who pursue cases, and accordingly broad generalizations aren't warranted.

## The Roles of Victims

Victims of conventional crime have traditionally been thought of as passive and innocent elements of the crime. During the past two decades or so, research on victim proneness and provocation (or precipitation) has demonstrated that victims' attributes and actions can play a significant role in victimization, and for certain classes of offenses it can be difficult to draw sharp lines of demarcation between perpetrators and victims.

Although many crime victims may be wholly innocent, and although a significant number clearly precipitate the crime, these extremes can distort the complex realities of the situation. The "victim blaming" tendency associated with at least one form of conventional crime, rape, has been strongly criticized by feminist commentators. Walsh and Schram (1980) argue that both white collar crime and rape cases provoke ambivalent responses; attention is shifted from exclusive focus on offenders to the circumstances in the cases. In both white collar crime and rape cases, victims may be stigmatized. Victims of rape may be blamed for sexually provocative behavior, whereas victims of white collar crime may be blamed for being greedy and self-interested.

Such motivations clearly play a role in some classes of white collar crime victimization, as when people invest money in highly speculative ventures that turn out to be fraudulent. In other kinds of cases—for example, employee injuries in hazardous workplace situations—corporations have often offered the defense that the employee's own reckless and freely chosen actions caused the injury. Conversely, corporations and other types of organizations can play a role in inspiring their own victimization by their exploitative and unethical policies, as when corporations are defrauded by disgruntled employees.

Organizations accused of fraudulent activity may claim in response that they are exploited victims whose illegal actions were only undertaken defensively. In her study of a case in which the Revco Pharmaceutical Company was charged with defrauding the Ohio Department of Public Welfare with a computer-generated double-billing scheme involving prescription charges for welfare beneficiaries, Vaughan (1980) shows us that from Revco's point of view, it was the victim of the welfare department's failure to make the timely reimbursements to which it was entitled. Small businesses engaged in illegal schemes may also view themselves or be seen more as victims of structural pressures imposed on them by large organizations (corporate suppliers and government regulatory agencies) than as victimizers (Sutton and Wild 1985). The complex character of many white collar crimes, especially those involving organizations, makes it possible to contest accusations of being the victimizer and claim victim status instead. Further, the very nature of white collar crime dictates that a somewhat disproportionate percentage of its victims are wealthy individuals or organizations, and such victims are somewhat less likely to generate sympathy than do many other classes of victims. According to Levi (1991), the police are less sympathetic to corporate victims of fraud than to individual victims of fraud. Because most of the victims of white collar crime are not privileged members of society and are unfairly blamed for their victimization (Walklate 1989), notions of victim precipitation and victim proneness are not readily applicable to the great majority of victims of white collar crime, especially corporate crime.

## Organizations as Victims of White Collar Crime

If organizations are important white collar crime victimizers, they are also more likely to be victims of white collar crime than of conventional crime. Whereas most victims of conventional crimes are individuals, white collar crimes such as embezzlement or employee theft are often directed toward an organization rather than an individual, and such crimes as tax evasion are by definition directed at organizations. The very size and impersonality of large organizations often makes it easier to commit crimes against them. Smigel (1970) produced evidence that people feel less guilty about stealing from large, private organizations than from small businesses and government agencies. Smigel attributed these attitudes to the size of the businesses, as well as to such factors as anonymity, impersonality, and bureaucratic efficiency. Other attributes of large organizations—the delegation of authority, specialization of functions, and dependence on complex technology—render them especially vulnerable to victimization (Vaughan 1980).

Organizational victimization is particularly likely to occur over a long period of time, and rather than being overt it may be buried in a complex series of transactions. Thus not only is it easier to rationalize stealing from larger organizations; it is also easier to get away with it. On the other hand, due to their superior resources, organizations are better postioned than individuals to publicize their victimization, and they may be able to exert special pressure on the criminal justice system to get a response to their victimization.

A number of studies (see, for example, Hagan 1983; Kruttschnitt 1987 Levi 1991) have established that the victims of prosecuted white collar crime cases are more likely to be organizations than individuals, and that organizational victims have more clout in court. Hagan (1983) attributes the greater success of organizational victims in achieving satisfactory outcomes for their cases more to their structural compatibility with criminal justice organizations than to their superior resources. Levi (1992), however, cautions that organizations' greater satisfaction with the outcome of their cases—relative to cases brought by individuals—may reflect differences in the types of cases pursued by organizations and individuals rather than a bias favoring corporations. But whatever accounts for this success, the victimization of organizations has received a disproportionate amount of attention, and possibly a disproportionate measure of justice.

Organizations may experience various harmful consequences when they are victims of white collar crime. At a minimum, profits are likely to be diminished; losses may be incurred. In a certain percentage of cases, private corporations, businesses, and professional partnerships will be bankrupted, and possibly dissolved, as a consequence of being victimized. An organization that survives its victimization may be demoralized, and working conditions may undergo a considerable transformation. Individual victims of white collar crime, by contrast, may experience their losses very directly and very painfully.

## Specific Forms of Suffering of White Collar Crime Victims

The various costs of white collar crime were identified in a previous section. Here we consider the specific impact of these costs on victims. Although the economic costs of white collar crime have been pegged at billions of dollars, the losses to any individual victim of a specific white collar crime can range from the trivial (often spread among millions of victims) to financial devastation. Even within the framework of a particular white collar crime, the effect on individuals is not necessarily uniform. An investment fraud may wipe out one individual's life savings while another individual may lose a nominal amount of money.

In a parallel vein, physical white collar crime victimization takes many forms, including the development of painful, ultimately fatal conditions; physical maladies ranging from birth defects to sterility to cancer; and rather minor injuries and illnesses. Hills (1987) and Mokhiber (1988) provide accounts of some of the numerous cases of victimization from corporate violence, including those involving Agent

Orange, coal and cotton dust, asbestos, the Dalkon shield, DES, thalidomide, the Ford Pinto, and other unsafe corporate practices and products. There is no special reason to believe that the physical suffering associated with white collar crime (especially in its corporate form) is less intensely experienced than is conventional crime violence. In fact, the physical suffering is often more enduring in corporate crime cases (e.g., asbestosis).

The psychological trauma of victimization in conventional crimes such as rape, robbery, and burglary can be formidable, and sometimes it outweighs economic loss or physical injury. An enormous psychic cost is also involved in the *anticipation* of possible conventional crime victimization. Millions of Americans, especially residents of big cities, live with a pervasive fear of being victimized, and this fear substantially influences their lifestyles (Furstenberg 1972; Jensen and Brownfield 1986).

The psychological suffering of white collar crime victims is likely to take a somewhat different course than that of conventional crime. First, the realization of victimization is likely to be more gradual, in some cases occurring years after the illegal event or process. Second, because direct physical confrontation is less likely, the white collar crime victim is somewhat less likely to have a sharply defined target for his or her anger. Third, a common psychological response to either the anticipation of or the experience of white collar crime victimization (of the more common economic type) is distrust or cynicism. In the case of victims of corporate or occupational violence—for example, individuals injured or made ill by unsafe products, dangerous working conditions, and environmental harm—severe psychological trauma often accompanies the physical injury.

Most of us probably have a stronger visceral fear of personal crime victimization and find the prospect of such sudden, direct, and extreme victimization more terrifying than corporate violence. Reiman (1990: 52–53) suggests that a defender of the present legal order might explain this not only in terms of differences of directness, but also by viewing corporate violence as a by-product of a legitimate pursuit in which victims have some choice in whether or not they are exposed to the violence. In response to this position, Reiman (1990: 52–56) cites the many constraints on the choices of victims of white collar crime (e.g., workers frequently do not have realistic choices about where they work). Numerous accounts and experiences of victims of environmental pollution (e.g., the Love Canal case), unsafe working conditions (e.g., the Manville asbestos case), and unsafe products (e.g., the Ford Pinto case) fully convey the intense psychological suffering of these victims. If a victim attributes the harm to, for example, a trusted employer, the sense of betrayal may well intensify the psychological damage incurred.

Such trauma is not limited to victims of physically injurious white collar crimes. It also occurs in conjunction with white collar crimes involving financial loss, although the degree of psychological trauma varies. In a study of victims of the failure of the Southern Industrial Banking Corporation (SIBC) due to gross mismanagement and fraud, Shover, Fox, and Mills (1994) found that the impact varied enormously, with victims fitting into three broad categories: the inconvenienced, the sobered, and the devastated. Those in the third category, the devastated, reported that the emotional and psychological damage was even worse than the financial loss (which often involved entire life savings), and these victims made such comments as: "Really, it destroyed our life. We're not happy people anymore.... I don't feel like a free human being anymore.... It's destroying us..." (Shover, Fox, and Mills 1991: 13–14). Many of the victims were disheartened by the feeble governmental response to their victimization, although this study found no evidence of significant, enduring delegitimation of political institutions that could be traced to the victim's experience with SIBC. But clearly the effects of white collar crime victimization, in this case, parallel those of conventional crime.

In one of the very few studies of the psychological consequences of white collar crime victimization, Ganzini, McFarland, and Bloom (1990) found that 29 percent of the 77 victims of a white collar crime (fraud) suffered a major depressive episode in the 20 months following their loss, compared to only 2 percent of a control sample. The victim of a bank failure caused by fraud wrote of losing her job, her home, and her husband (due to premature death) as a consequence of a white collar crime (Halbrooks 1990).

Even though the principal victims of the massive failure of the S & L thrifts in the 1980s are taxpayers who experienced little if any psychological trauma, there were also some direct victims. Some 23,000 individuals, many of them retired people with limited incomes, lost millions of dollars after being induced to purchase bonds from the Lincoln Savings & Loan Association, one of the more notorious failures (Mayer 1990). Charles Keating, the chairman of that bank's holding company, was confronted at his trial for securities fraud by a 90-year-old woman screaming, "You took all my money. Give me my money back" (Stevenson 1991a). Keating was ultimately convicted in the case.

## White Collar Crime Victimization, In Sum

White collar crime victimization, then, is significant and may be enduring. To date it has not been subjected to extensive and systematic study. We still have much to learn about the nature of the victim-offender relationship and the full range of consequences of white collar crime victimization. There is a need, in particular, to understand more fully the reasons that this type of crime victimization does not evince the same level of concern as conventional crime victimization. It is far from clear that the general public wants a greater proportion of policing resources directed at preventing white collar crime victimization (Levi 1991). One of the key questions is whether public priorities concerning crime victimization are based on objective measures of harm or are fundamentally distorted by pervasive misrepresentations of such victimization.

# Corporate Crime

IN HIS LANDMARK book *White Collar Crime,* Edwin Sutherland (1949: 9) defined such crime "as a crime committed by a person of respectability and high social status in the course of his occupation." But because the principal focus of his book was violations (of different branches of law) by 70 major corporations, it has subsequently been argued that Sutherland should have entitled his book "Corporate Crime" (Clinard and Yeager 1980: 13).

In the second edition of their influential *Criminal Behavior Systems* (1973), Marshall Clinard and Richard Quinney first clearly differentiated between corporate crime and the other major form of white collar crime, occupational crime. They defined corporate crime as "offenses committed by corporate officials for their corporation and the offenses of the corporation itself" (Clinard and Quinney 1973: 188). Since the mid-1970s the term *corporate crime* has been widely invoked. It is seen as both a major form of white collar crime and a specific form of organizational crime, a term that encompasses governmental organizations and their abuses (Kramer 1984: 17).

Some of the implications of the concept of corporate crime—for example, whether corporations per se can be said to commit crimes, and whether harmful acts involving corporations are crimes even if they are not prohibited by the criminal law—are considered elsewhere in this text. But because corporate crime was the focus of Sutherland's (1949) pioneering work on white collar crime, remains a principal concern of students of such crime, and is arguably the most consequential type of such crime, it seems appropriate here to begin our review of the varieties of white collar crime with a discussion of corporate crime.

Before we explore corporate crime specifically, a brief review of the historical development of the corporation and its character today is in order.

## The Historical Development of the Corporation and Corporate Crime

THE LEGAL IDEA of a corporation can be traced back to Roman times (Geis 1988: 16). In the Anglo-American tradition, the earliest corporations—or "proto-corporations"—were churches, towns, guilds, and universities, which over time came to be recognized as "trusts" with legal control over certain property (Coleman 1974; Stone 1975). The great trading corporations began to emerge in the 16th century, and in the 17th century the modern corporation, with specific corporate powers, can be recognized in the East India Company, founded in 1612 (Stone 1975: 13).

The trading corporations of the 17th and 18th centuries played a central role in massively harmful acts; the devastation of Native Americans and the slave trading of Africans are two primary examples (Sale 1990; Williams 1966). Early corporations were also involved in specifically fraudulent and illegal activity. The so-called "South Sea Bubble" case in the early 18th century is a famous example. The South Sea Company was chartered in London in 1711 to engage in slave trade and commerce in South America. Over a period of about 10 years, investors lost large fortunes because the whole enterprise was quite fraudulent, driven by bribery, false financial statements, and stock manipulation (Geis 1993; Robb 1990; Stone 1975). The legislative response to the scandal (the South Sea Bubble Act of 1720) was an early form of recognition of the need for some legal controls on corporations, although such early laws were exceptionally clumsy and may have done more harm than good.

The Industrial Revolution of the late 18th and 19th centuries eventually gave rise to immensely powerful and wealthy capitalist corporations, although during this period and into the 20th century relatively little regulation of these enterprises was effective (Clinard and Yeager 1980). The corporate empires of the "robber barons" (e.g., Rockefeller, Vanderbilt, Gould, Carnegie, and Frick) of the second half of the 19th century were involved in every manner of bribery, fraud, stock manipulation, predation against competitors, price gouging, exploitation of labor, and maintenance of unsafe working conditions, but these corporations were largely invulnerable to legal controls (Myers 1907; Josephson 1934).

In the late 19th century the monopolistic practices of huge "trusts" (holding companies for a chain of corporations), such as Standard Oil, helped inspire the Sherman Antitrust Act. Through the early part of the 20th century, major corporations became increasingly national in character; since World War II in particular mergers, the formation of conglomerates, corporate takeovers, and the growth of transnational or multinational corporations have been characteristics of corporate development (Clinard and Yeager 1980). If corporations no longer operate with the almost complete freedom of the 19th-century corporations of the robber barons, they are nevertheless very powerful, and the notion of corporate crime is still very real.

## The Corporation in Society Today

CORPORATIONS ARE A conspicuous feature of contemporary societies, and in American society in particular, and in many respects corporations are viewed in a positive way. They are widely regarded as the centerpiece of a free-market capitalist economy and as a powerful manifestation of entrepreneurial initiative and creativity. They are a major factor in the generally high standard of living Americans typically enjoy.

Many people hold corporations in high esteem. Millions of people are employed by corporations and regard them as their providers. Many young people aspire to become corporate employees. Corporations produce the seemingly endless range of products we purchase and consume, and they sponsor many of the forms of entertainment (especially television) we enjoy. They are also principal sponsors of pioneering research in many fields and a crucial element in national defense. Corporations are important benefactors of a large number of charities, public events, institutions of higher learning, and scientific enterprises. And of course the major corporations in particular, with their large resources, are quite adept at reminding us of their positive contributions to our way of life. Thus the very notion of "corporate crime" is jarring and disconcerting to many people, for it challenges a widely projected image of beneficence.

The dark side of corporations has long been recognized. Karl Marx (1867) regarded the corporation (or "joint-stock company") as one of the instruments of a capitalist system that exploits and dehumanizes workers and deprives them of a fair return on their labor. Marx and Friedrich Engels held capitalist corporations responsible for willful homicide and assault through the operation of industrialized enterprises that maximized the pursuit of profit and minimized the preservation of human life (Harris 1974).

With the great growth of the joint-stock corporation in the 19th century, Marx came to recognize that corporations were no longer fully controlled by those who "owned" them (i.e., the stockholders); in the Marxist view, the stockholder is a small-scale capitalist who has lost much control over his capital to those who actually manage the corporations (Mandel 1983). The corporate managers, who are often large stockholders as well, are in a position to advance their own interests and enrich themselves at the expense of workers and ordinary stockholders alike. But because in the Marxist view both managers and stockholders have a common interest in maximizing profit, they inevitably exploit workers and others as well. Many non-Marxists also recognize that the pursuit of profit is the principal rationale for the corporation, and that it often takes precedence over all other considerations.

Major corporations are immensely large and wealthy. The combined sales of the top 10 corporations have exceeded the gross national product of most nations today, with annual sales of the Fortune 500 corporations of approximately $2 trillion dollars (Currie and Skolnick 1988: 250). Corporate wealth is highly concentrated and is becoming even more so; by the late 1980s the largest 100 manufacturing corporations controlled over 70 percent of all business assets (Curran and Renzetti 1990: 40; Evans and Schneider 1981; Kolko 1962; Mintz and Cohen 1971).

Corporate ownership and corporate-generated wealth has traditionally been concentrated in the hands of relatively few people, with about 0.5 percent of the population owning about 80 percent of the corporate stock (Michalowski 1985: 323). Although millions of Americans belong to pension plans that own large blocks of stock, the influence of these Americans over corporate affairs is essentially nonexistent. *Oligopolies* of a relatively few corporations dominating their market have replaced classical monopolies, which were outlawed in the United States by the Sherman Antitrust Act in 1890. In many industries (e.g., auto, tire, aircraft) a small number of corporations control up to two-thirds of the market (Simon and Eitzen 1993: 15). *Conglomerates* (a combination of centrally owned and controlled firms operating in different markets) have also become far more common, especially because of multibillion dollar mergers in the 1980s (Curran and Renzetti 1990: 44). Many of these conglomerates today are *transnational* (*multinational* or *global*) *corporations*, which produce goods outside of their home country (Currie and Skolnick 1988: 93; Michalowski and Kramer 1987). Although in a broad sense such corporations have existed for hundreds of years, their number, importance, and influence increased greatly in the final decades of the 20th century; their annual revenues exceed $100 billion (Barnet and Muller 1974; Clinard and Yeager 1980; Heilbroner 1975; Michalowski and Kramer 1987: 35).

These corporations, by their very nature, are especially well-positioned to take advantage of political corruption, the absence or paucity of regulatory controls, and the desperation for economic enterprise characteristic of many third-world nations. Some of the "corporate transgressions" (harmful although not necessarily illegal actions) associated with transnationals operating in third-world countries include highly hazardous and dangerous working conditions at industrial facilities; exportation of unsafe products (often banned in developed countries); dumping of toxic wastes, and other forms of environmental pollution; bribing and corrupting politicians; massive tax evasion by shifting profits to subsidiaries in countries with favorable corporate tax policies; and complicity in a range of human rights violations, including torture and assassinations, undertaken by repressive third-world governments and military or intelligence entities of developed governments (Michalowski and Kramer 1987; Simon and Eitzen 1993).

Even though desperately poor third-world countries and their citizens may well derive some economic benefits from transnational economic activity in their countries, they are also clearly exploited and pay a high price, especially in terms of harm to health, for these benefits. These "corporate transgressions" have been condemned by United Nations codes (despite the efforts of transnational corporations to influence those codes) and are clearly injurious by any reasonable standard (Michalowski and Kramer 1987: 41). In view of the constant expansion of the "global marketplace," the transgressions of transnational corporations are likely to become increasingly significant in the future.

Their enormous resources give corporations (national and transnational) great influence over politicians on all levels (explored more fully elsewhere) and play a major role in shaping public policy. A "power elite" of the top people in the corporate world, government, and the military have "interlocks" (a complex network of ties) that enable them to advance their interrelated interests and move quite easily between high-level private- and public-sector positions (Freitag 1975; Kolko 1962; Mills 1956; Reasons and Perdue 1981; Simon and Eitzen 1993; Useem 1983). The corporate elite in particular dominate the state through active pursuit of their own interests, coordinated corporate activities outside the government, and exploitation of economic conditions (Schwartz 1987). Despite the formidable political power of corporations, they have been relatively free of accountability and traditionally have been able to conceal much of their power-wielding activity (Mintz and Cohen 1976). On all levels of government, then, powerful corporations play an important if not always fully visible role.

The large corporations so dominant in today's economic environment have transformed capitalism into something very different from the economic system envisioned by its principal philosopher, Adam Smith. In fact, in *The Wealth of Nations* Smith (1776, 1937: 460) condemned "the mean rapacity, the monopolizing spirit of merchants and manufacturers, who neither are nor ought be the rulers of mankind." Smith's conception of freely competing individual entrepreneurs has given way to a world dominated by huge, vastly powerful corporations, and the prevalence of authentic entrepreneurs has declined dramatically (Michalowski 1985: 323).

Corporations are increasingly controlled by "paper entrepreneurs," or investors who are principally concerned with short-term profit rather than long-term commitments either to product development or to the local communities in which corporate operations are based (Reich 1983). Paper entrepreneurs were the driving force behind the intensified wave of corporate takeovers in the 1980s, which had devastating personal consequences for millions of middle managers and ordinary workers who lost jobs, benefits, or better salaries, and indirectly for taxpayers and consumers, who absorbed lost revenue from vast debt service payments or paid higher prices for products (Brooks 1987; Cooper 1987; Faludi 1990). Even though such corporate takeovers are not illegal—some parties have even defended them as beneficial—others argue that they are too often harmful and should be discouraged or prohibited (Galbraith 1986; Henriques 1990b; Icahn 1986; Iseman 1986; Newport 1989; Reich 1989; Samuelson 1987). In general, corporations in the United States today want to be left alone when business conditions are favorable and they are making money, but they want the government to bail them out when they get into trouble (Mintz and Cohen 1971; Mintz and Cohen 1976). This has been called the "socialization of risk": Leave profit to the private sector and let the public sector absorb the risks.

## A Typology of Corporate Crime

HOW CAN WE best categorize the many different activities that can be encompassed by the term *corporate crime*? One approach is to adopt a typology emphasizing the primary victims: for example, the general public, consumers, employees, or a corporation's competitors. A second approach is to focus on the nature of the harmful activity: for example, corporate violence, corporate corruption, corporate stealing, or corporate deceptions. A third approach emphasizes the size or scope of the corporate entity: for example, crimes of transnational corporations; crimes of major domestic corporations; crimes of small, locally based corporations; or crimes of incorporated individual enterprises. A fourth approach has classified corporate crime according to the type of product or service involved: for example, crimes of the automotive industry, crimes of the pharmaceutical industry, crimes of the banking industry, or crimes of health care providers.

Other criteria can be taken into account in differentiating among corporate crimes. One criterion is the primary corporate agent of the criminal activity: for example, the chief executive officer or principal executives, the middle managers, the corporate foremen, or employees. Even though corporate crime typically involves corporate personnel on all levels and is closely linked with conditions prevailing in the corporation as a whole, it may be instructive to determine who initiates and implements the corporate transgression. Furthermore, one can ask which instrument or mechanism is used to initiate and commit the crime. In this context we can consider the interrelationships of and relative importance of oral policy directives, computer programs, product handling practices, and the like. Other criteria for classifying corporate transgressions emphasize the type of law that is invoked (criminal, civil, or administrative) or the specific legal class involved (e.g., antitrust law, consumer protection law, environmental law).

There is, then, no one way to classify or approach corporate crime, and the typology or classification we use is likely to be dictated by what we are seeking to explain or understand in a particular context. For purposes of this chapter, the major distinction is the type of activity; thus we will examine *corporate violence* and *corporate abuse of power, fraud, or economic exploitation*. Within these two broad categories a further differentiation is made by type of victim. Accordingly, for corporate violence, we have corporate violence against the public, corporate violence against consumers, and corporate violence against workers. Within the category of corporate abuse of power, fraud, or economic exploitation, we have crimes against citizens, against consumers, against employees, against competitors, and against owners or creditors. Other criteria, such as the type of product or service involved, are then incorporated into discussions of these types. The rationale for this scheme is not that these categories require separate and distinct theories—indeed, explanations tend to cut across the types—but rather that it enables us to organize and discuss the bewildering range of corporate crime activities with some coherence.

## Corporate Violence

WE HAVE SEEN that violent crime is most readily associated with conventional predatory offenders, serial killers, mafiosi, and terrorists. Despite some reluctance to regard corporations as violent offenders, they are engaged in activities with violent consequences.

Corporate violence differs from conventional interpersonal violence in several ways. First, it is *indirect* in the sense that victims are not assaulted by another person. Corporate violence results from policies and actions, undertaken on behalf of the corporation, that result in the exposure of people to harmful conditions, products, or substances  Second, the effects of corporate violence are typically quite removed in time from the implementation of the corporate policy or action that caused the harm, and the causal relationship between the corporate action and the injury to health (or death) cannot always be clearly and definitively established. Third, typically in corporate violence a large number of individuals acting collectively, rather than a single or very few individuals, are responsible for the actions that result in physical injury or death. Fourth, corporate violence, virtually by definition, is motivated by the desire to maximize corporate profits (or survival) and minimize corporate overhead, and the violence is a consequence rather than a specifically intended outcome of such motivations. Finally, corporate violence has traditionally inspired a far more limited legal and justice system response than has conventional interpersonal violence.

## Corporate Violence Against the Public: Unsafe Environmental Practices

Corporations' contributions to the polluting and poisoning of the environment may well be the most common form of corporate violence. In the view of one commentator (Bellini 1986), the situation is so serious that we are confronting a "high-tech holocaust." There are, of course, many different sources of pollution, and corporations are hardly responsible for all of it. Ordinary citizens as well as government operations on many levels can contribute to pollution. In New York State, two leading assembly members contended that the state government itself was the worst polluter, citing 450 violations of environmental laws at 267 state sites (Gold 1990). Still, corporations account for a disproportionately large share of the most dangerous pollution, and corporations have been especially flagrant violators of environmental laws.

Through most of human history the disposal of wastes of all kinds was little regulated or controlled. Obviously the lack of proper disposal of wastes contributed to highly unsanitary living conditions, the prolific spreading of disease, and premature death. But it is not the case, as some might imagine, that concern over pollution is entirely modern. In 1290, for example, King Edward I of England prohibited the burning of coal while Parliament was sitting because it filled the London air with acrid smoke, and in 1470 a German scholar, Ulrich Ellenbog, identified some adverse effects of exposure to carbon monoxide, lead, mercury, and other metals or substances (Bellini 1986: 6). Similar and increasingly sophisticated observations of this type were made in subsequent centuries.

The modern problem of pollution, in contrast, is characterized in part by the dramatic increase in the production of toxic wastes, especially since World War II. In the United States an exponential increase in the production of synthetic organic chemicals has occurred (over 300 billion pounds annually in the last quarter of the 20th century); the same is true for hazardous or toxic wastes (some 125 billion pounds annually, or 600 pounds per U.S. citizen) (Brownstein 1981: 5; Regenstein 1986: 17). Improper disposal of deadly wastes occurs an estimated 90 percent of the time.

The overall harmful consequences of such practices for the health of Americans seem evident to many observers. An estimated one-quarter of the U.S. population (56 million people) will develop cancer, and by some (admittedly controversial) estimates 80–90 percent of all cancers may be environmentally related (Brownstein 1981: 10–11; Regenstein 1986: 15). Cancer is the only major cause of death that increased in prevalence in the 20th century: In 1900 it accounted for approximately 3 percent of all deaths; by 1975 it accounted for 20 percent of all deaths (Brownstein 1981: 11). In addition to cancer, however, environmental pollution is associated with a range of other maladies and serious health problems, including heart and lung diseases, birth defects and genetic disorders, and sterility (Regenstein 1986: 16; Brownstein 1981: 12–16). Polluted air alone may jeopardize the health of some 35 million Americans, and it contributes to 200,000 premature deaths annually (Regenstein 1986: 16). By any measure, then, corporate polluting of the environment is a serious crime.

Much evidence indicates that corporations either knew, or should have known, the inherent risks arising out of their practices of dumping toxic wastes. Corporations have often opted for highly dangerous, low-cost methods of getting rid of such wastes. They have not been forthcoming with information available to them on dangers concerning wastes and pollution, and they have not infrequently engaged in deliberate deception. Corporations have typically denied responsibility for the harmful consequences attributed to their polluting practices and have resisted changing these practices until forced to do so (Brownstein 1981). And they have actively lobbied against environmental legislation.

Some specific forms of corporate polluting include release of toxic chemicals (including pesticides, herbicides, and oil) and air pollution. We examine these types of corporate pollution next.

**Toxic Waste**  Some of the most notorious releases of toxic chemicals have occurred outside the United States. In one of these cases a Japanese petrochemical corporation, Chisso, had for years been dumping a huge volume of poisons into the sea. In the 1950s hundreds of residents of a small, nearby village, Minamata, developed severe brain and body dysfunctions, including birth defects, paralysis, blindness, and other horrendous consequences (Mokhiber 1988). In the Bhopal case in India, a massive poisonous chemical cloud was emitted from a Union Carbide plant in December 1984. Although estimates vary, it is generally believed that at least 5,000 people in the area died as a consequence; some 200,000 others were injured, 60,000 of them seriously and some 20,000 of them permanently (Everest 1985; Mokhiber 1988; Pearce and Tombs 1989). In both of these cases, subsequent investigation revealed that the corporations involved had been negligent or had cut corners on safety, had attempted to conceal or minimize their responsibility, and had avoided criminal prosecution (cases were being resolved through civil lawsuits or settlements).

Within the United States, the Love Canal case is among the best-known cases of corporate pollution. In the 1940s the Hooker Chemical Corporation bought the canal (near Niagara Falls), drained it, and began dumping into it a huge number of 55-gallon metal drums filled with highly toxic chemical wastes (Mokhiber 1988). Eventually the property was acquired by a local school board, and both a school and residential neighborhood were built in the area. Over a period of decades school children and residents were exposed to noxious fumes and surfacing chemicals, allegedly resulting in a disproportionately high number of miscarriages, birth defects, liver ailments, and emotional disorders among this population. (A causal link to the Love Canal chemicals was never conclusively established.) The corporation's initial response was to attempt to suppress pertinent evidence and to limit its own legal liability, but eventually several hundred families were evacuated from the area and Hooker Chemical was compelled to pay $20 million to former Love Canal residents.

One of the worst cases of aquatic pollution occurred on March 24, 1989, when the oil tanker *Exxon Valdez* ran into a reef in Prince William Sound, Alaska, and dumped 11 million gallons of oil into the sea, with devastating consequences for wildlife, the environment, and the economy of the region (Davidson 1990; Egan 1990; Labaton 1989a; Schneider 1991a). Complex questions of responsibility arose out of this incident, but evidence emerged that the Exxon Corporation was aware that the ship's captain had a drinking problem, and had also reduced the size of the tanker's crew, leaving them fatigued. In 1991 the Exxon Corporation agreed to plead guilty to a criminal charge and to pay a $100 million fine, part of a civil and criminal settlement totaling over $1 billion (Schneider 1991a). In September 1994, a federal grand jury in Anchorage ordered Exxon to pay $5 billion in punitive damages to Alaskans harmed by the Valdez oil spill; additional trials are anticipated (Schneider 1994). Remarkably, these outcomes had no significant negative effect on the corporation's earning prospects or stock price (Schneider 1991b; Schneider 1994).

**Air Pollution**   It is well known today that automobile emissions constitute a significant proportion of the air pollution problem, and that some cities—Los Angeles is a notable example—have generally unhealthful air conditions much of the year. What is less well known is that the automobile companies deliberately promoted a situation in which nonpolluting public transportation systems were largely displaced by automobiles and buses in some areas (Mokhiber 1988).

In the 1930s General Motors formed a subsidiary, United Cities Motor Transportation Co., to buy out the electric street car system in Los Angeles and replace it with buses. In 1949 General Motors and several other companies with a vested interest in gasoline-fueled transportation—for example, Standard Oil of California and Firestone—were convicted of violating antitrust law by criminally conspiring to eliminate electric transportation and monopolize the sale of buses. The companies received only token fines of $5,000 apiece, and no one went to jail. When by 1970 the harmful environmental consequences of emissions from internal combustion engines were becoming more evident and the Clean Air Act was passed, another major auto manufacturer, Ford, spent a great deal of money lobbying against such initiatives, and engaged in deceptive practices to avoid complying with emissions standards required by clean air legislation. In 1973 Ford pleaded no contest to 350 counts of criminal and civil charges pertaining to violations of the Clean Air Act, and paid a combined $7 million fine.

**Corporate Polluting of the Environment, In Sum**   Neither the environmental movement nor the implementation and enforcement of environmental protection laws has deterred major corporations from attempting to save money by illegal polluting. In 1990, for example, the Lockheed Corporation was fined a record $1 million by a Southern California pollution control agency, for illegal paint-spraying activity

(Stevenson 1990a). In New York State another major corporation, Bethlehem Steel, was fined a record $1 million for emissions of benzene, a carcinogen, in violation of state air pollution laws (Associated Press 1990).

For the most part such cases have been settled in civil court. In 1988, in the first felony indictment of a corporation under the Clean Water Act, Ocean Spray Cranberries Inc. was charged with polluting the sewer system of Middleboro, Massachusetts, over a five-year period (Gold 1988). In 1990 Eastman Kodak admitted to two criminal violations of state antipollution laws and was fined $1.15 million (Hanley 1990). The corporation was found responsible for chemical spills and groundwater pollution in Kodak Park and failing to notify state authorities.

Only a handful of businessmen have ever been sent to prison in pollution cases. In one such case Russell Mahler, president of Hudson Oil Refining Company, was sentenced to one year in prison (and fined $750,000) for violations of 22 counts of the Clean Streams Act (Chavez 1982). Mahler, a distinguished-looking Cornell graduate and to all external appearances a successful businessman, ran various companies in the oil reclamation business. But instead of legally and properly disposing of the toxic chemicals separated from oil wastes produced by various major corporations, Mahler's operation illegally dumped those wastes in city landfills, sewers, and other such locations. In one case truck drivers for his company arranged to dump toxic wastes in a bore hole behind a garage near Wilkes-Barre, Pennsylvania. The carcinogenic waste spilled into the Susquehanna River and contaminated the water supply of various northeastern Pennsylvania communities. When Mahler was confronted with the evidence of this illegal dumping, he initially attempted to arrange a cleanup in the hope—or expectation—that criminal prosecution could be avoided. In this particular case the ploy was unsuccessful; Mahler actually went to prison.

**Corporate Destruction of a Community**  One final form of "polluting" by corporations requires attention here, even though it differs from the conventional conception of such offenses.

When the Buffalo Creek dam burst in February 1972, the town of Saunders, West Virginia, was completely demolished (Erikson 1976; Stern 1976). The dam's rupture left 125 members of the community dead, and some 4,000 Buffalo Creek residents lost their homes. The dam had been used to contain mining wastes dumped over a period of many years by Buffalo Mining, which was owned by the large and powerful Pittston Mining Corporation. Even though for years citizens has expressed concern about the company's dumping practices, and despite a partial collapse of the dam that foreshadowed what was to come, Pittston Mining attempted to absolve itself of basic legal responsibility by claiming that the rupture was "an act of God."

An inquiry after the disaster established that for many decades mining companies had been aware of the dangers of their dumping practices, and that Pittston had specifically violated federal safety standards and ignored warnings about this particular dam's vulnerability. Despite this evidence, no grand jury indictment was directed at the corporation, and it eventually made a $13.5 million out-of-court civil settlement. The entire affair contained echoes of a similar famous disaster in 1889:

the Johnstown (Pa.) Flood, which caused the loss of over 2,000 lives and was also attributed to the negligence of powerful corporate magnates.

## Corporate Violence Against Consumers: Unsafe Products

Although corporations hardly wish to inflict harm on consumers, they have in fact all too often done so when the drive to maximize profit or survive in the marketplace has taken precedence over a concern with consumer safety. An enormous range of consumer products—including many foods, drugs and medical devices, motor vehicles, household products, and cosmetics—have been identified as hazardous to various degrees (Brobeck and Averyt 1983). Some 70,000 Americans are alleged to die annually from product-related accidents, and millions more suffer disabling injuries at a cost of over $100 billion in property damage, lost wages, insurance, litigation, and medical expenses (Brobeck and Averyt 1983: v). Even though certain products (e.g., lawnmowers) are intrinsically dangerous, much evidence suggests that corporations, in their almost single-minded pursuit of profit, have been negligent—sometimes criminally negligent—in their disregard for consumer safety. A brief review of a few specific products or services that harm consumers follows.

**Food Products**  In his influential novel *The Jungle* (1906), Upton Sinclair exposed the grossly unsanitary conditions in the Chicago meat markets of the time. References in this novel to rats and even workers falling into the meat vats and becoming part of the final product inspired revulsion and helped bring into existence the Meat Inspection Act of 1906. Since that time the public has come to assume that meat (as well as other food products) is inspected according to government standards to protect consumers, but much evidence indicates that throughout the century bribery of government meat inspectors and deception (through use of dyes and by other means) has resulted in the foisting of much unhealthy meat on the American public (Swanson and Schultz 1982; Kwitny 1979). In the final decades of the 20th century, reports of unsanitary conditions in meatpacking plants, marketing of unsafe meat, and paid-off inspectors were still forthcoming, and millions of Americans were suffering from food poisoning as a result of such practices (Associated Press 1987; Frank and Lynch 1992; Halpin 1988; National Heart Savers Association 1990).

Of course, meat is hardly the only unsafe food product. Corporations entice millions of Americans, especially children, to consume misleadingly labeled foods with an unhealthfully high sugar or fat content, and the widespread practice of processing foods with additives or irradiation may also increase the incidence of cancer among consumers (Curra 1994; Mindell 1987; Simon and Eitzen 1993). Because the consumption of food is an unavoidable activity, the questionable—and sometimes illegal—consequences of corporate practices in food production are especially far-reaching.

**Pharmaceutical Products and Medical Devices**  Even though "drug pushing" is most readily associated with sleazy inner-city dealers catering to the needs of vulnerable (often poor) people, pharmaceutical corporations can also be characterized as "pushers" insofar as they spend millions of dollars advertising the use of psychoactive drugs and encourage their sales representatives ("detail men") to use various inducements to persuade physicians to prescribe new drugs and other pharmaceutical products (Braithwaite 1984). At the core of this activity is a high (if arguably eroding) level of trust, for there are few commonplace products about which the typical consumer is less capable of making independent judgments.

The pharmaceutical industry has been accused of unsafe or unsanitary practices in the production and distribution of some of its products; the promotion of such overprescribed drugs as Valium and Darvon have had a variety of adverse consequences for users, including tens of thousands of emergency room admissions and hundreds of deaths (Braithwaite 1984). Thalidomide, DES, and the Dalkon shield were especially notorious products.

In the case of thalidomide, some 8,000 babies whose mothers had taken this prescribed tranquilizer during their pregnancies were born grossly deformed in the early 1960s, mainly in Europe (Knightly et al., 1979; Mokhiber 1988). Much evidence suggests that the principal pharmaceutical company involved, Chemie Grunenthal, had early indications of the drug's dangers (as well as its limited effectiveness), but the company continued to promote it as an over-the-counter drug until the enormous scope of harm being done had been widely publicized and they were forced to withdraw it from the market (Mokhiber 1988: 408–15). A criminal indictment filed against Chemie Grunenthal in Germany in 1967 was dropped after the company agreed to pay a $31 million fine, and other pharmaceutical companies also eventually made civil settlements (Braithwaite 1984).

DES, a drug discovered in the 1930s, was subsequently marketed by the pharmaceutical firm Eli Lilly as an effective agent in preventing miscarriages (Mokhiber 1988: 173). Many thousands of daughters of women who took DES in the 1950s developed sometimes-fatal vaginal and cervical cancer and often experienced infertility or other serious reproductive problems; even some DES sons developed testicular abnormalities and fertility problems. Thousands of civil suits resulted, although no criminal indictment was ever produced in this matter.

Considerable evidence exists concerning early corporate awareness of both the carcinogenic properties of DES and the danger it posed to fetuses (Mokhiber 1988: 174). The Federal Drug Administration (FDA) had relied on the pharmaceutical company's evaluations rather than on its own tests, and the FDA Drug Division Chief who approved the marketing of DES took a highly-paid position with a drug company shortly thereafter (Mokhiber 1988: 176–77). Ironically, it has never been established that DES is in fact effective in preventing miscarriage; it has been very fully established, however, that DES has caused (and continues to cause) enormous psychological anguish, profound reproductive abnormalities, cancer, and premature death.

The Dalkon shield was an intrauterine birth control device sold in the 1960s by the A. H. Robins Company (Mintz 1985; Mokhiber 1988). Millions of these shields were distributed all over the world. Because the device was defective (bacteria were able to travel up the device's wick and into the womb), thousands of women were rendered sterile, gave birth to stillborn or deformed children, or suffered other reproductive system problems. Despite the fact that Robins had early indications of these problems, it neither voluntarily warned women nor withdrew the Dalkon shield from the market because the product was highly profitable. After much stonewalling by the company, the FDA halted distribution of this product in 1974. Thousands of users sued, many lawsuits were settled with a long-term payout of approximately $1 billion, the corporation declared bankruptcy in 1985, and two top executives were found guilty of criminal contempt.

Many other dangerous drugs and pharmaceutical products have been inflicted on an unwitting public. Drugs such as Clioquinol, MER/29, Oraflex, and Selacryn, all developed since the 1930s for the treatment of such conditions as diarrhea, excessive cholesterol, arthritis, and mild blood pressure, were widely marketed, and in each case thousands of people suffered devastating side effects, from blindness and paralysis to death (Mokhiber 1988).

In the early 1990s claims surfaced that silicone-gel breast implants (used by up to 2 million American women) might rupture and increase the risks of cancer (Hilts 1992a; Hilts 1992b). There were allegations that the Dow Corning Corporation, the primary producer of these implants, had not conducted adequate testing and had not been forthcoming about its own scientists' concerns over the risks involved. In 1993 six executives of the C.R. Bard Co., the world's largest medical device manufacturer, were indicted in connection with the selling of untested heart catheters (Hilts 1993a). The company agreed to pay over $60 million in fines; at least one death and 22 emergency heart surgeries were attributed to their untested device.

The common element in all of these pharmaceutical product cases was that the corporations put the pursuit of profits ahead of scrupulous concern for the health and safety of the users of their products. Despite the fines, civil damages, and negative publicity experienced by the pharmaceutical companies, they have typically suffered no lasting damage and have continued to operate profitably.

Whenever pharmaceutical corporations run into marketing problems in developed Western nations or seek new markets, they turn to third-world countries, where safety standards are lax or nonexistent (Braithwaite 1984; Silverman, Ree, and Lydecker 1982). The Nestle Corporation's marketing of infant formula in less-developed countries is one of the better publicized cases of these practices (Gerber and Short 1986). It has been claimed that millions of babies in these countries suffer or even die because their mothers are enticed into using infant formula without the knowledge, means, or conditions to use it safely (e.g., only contaminated water is available). The protests and boycotts directed at Nestle were ultimately successful in compelling the company to abandon its aggressive marketing of infant formula in third-world countries.

**Transportation Products and Services** Americans have been described as having a long-standing "love affair" with the automobile, but there has also been a dark side to this relationship. Each year some 50,000 people are killed in automobile accidents that are typically blamed on driver recklessness or error, or on weather and road conditions. Recently it has become more widely recognized that design defects in automotive products contribute to accidents and to fatalities as well. The automotive industry has put profits ahead of consumer safety for a long time. In the 1920s, when the Dupont Corporation tried to interest General Motors in installing safer glass in their cars, the president of GM, Alfred P. Sloan, wrote back that he was not interested because such glass would not contribute to profit on the cars (Mintz and Cohen 1971: 321). Another GM executive, John Z. De Lorean, speaking of his experience with the company several decades later, observed that "at General Motors the concern for the effect of our products on our many publics was never discussed except in terms of cost or sales potential" (Wright 1979: 6). When a colleague raised questions about the safety of one of GM's cars, the Corvair, he was chastised for not being a "team player." De Lorean put this outlook into perspective in the following way:

> These were not immoral men who were bringing out this car. These were warm, breathing men with families and children who as private individuals would never have approved this project for a minute if they were told, "You are going to kill and injure people with this car." But those same men, in a business atmosphere, where everything is reduced to terms of costs, profit goals and production deadlines, were able as a group to approve a product most of them wouldn't have considered approving as individuals. (Wright 1979: 6)

After its introduction in 1959 as a new sports car, it quite quickly became evident that the Corvair had "oversteering" and engine-exhaust problems, and it was involved in a disproportionate number of accidents (Mokhiber 1988: 130–38). GM was soon aware of the problems and chose not to address them. Inspired by this case, a young lawyer named Ralph Nader wrote *Unsafe at Any Speed* (1965), which succeeded in focusing public attention on the issue of auto safety. Some years later General Motors admitted that it had hired private investigators to shadow and investigate Nader in the hopes of uncovering damaging personal or professional information that would discredit him (Whiteside 1972).

In the years since Nader's book first appeared, many other cases of unsafe automobiles have surfaced, and automobile companies have been compelled to recall hundreds of thousands of defective cars. The Ford Pinto case was the single most famous such case, and it ultimately led to a criminal prosecution (Cullen, Maakestad, and Cavender 1987; Dowie 1977; Mokhiber 1988).

Facing increasing competition from foreign imports in the late 1960s, Lee Iacocca, then president of the Ford Motor Company, called for the production of a car weighing less than 2,000 pounds and costing less than $2,000. In order to meet these requirements, the designers of the new car, the Pinto, placed the gas tank in the rear of the car.

In the early 1970s, after the car had been widely marketed, several Pintos were involved in rear-end collisions in which the gas tank exploded, burning some people to death. One such case, involving three Midwestern schoolgirls, led to the criminal prosecution of Ford. Investigation of the company in conjunction with this case revealed that Ford had made a calculated decision: It would be cheaper to pay any civil damages arising out of these accidents than to recall the car and make it safe. Further, installation of a rubber bladder (cost: about $5) would have prevented the gas tank explosions.

Ultimately Ford had to pay millions of dollars of judgments in civil lawsuits and had to recall the Pinto at great expense, at a total cost estimated at some $100 million. Although Ford was acquitted in the criminal case—perhaps at least in part because the presiding judge ruled certain crucial pieces of evidence inadmissible—this case is commonly cited as evidence of the relative indifference of automobile manufacturers to the safety of drivers and their passengers; safety features such as seatbelts and airbags are adopted only when the companies have been compelled to do so or it has become sufficiently profitable to do so.

Despite greater attention to safety features in more recent years, unsafe vehicles still reach the market. In a case involving a 1988 accident in which a Ford-built school bus burst into flames, killing 24 children and three adults, it came out that Ford was aware that the bus's design was unsafe (Kunen 1994). In the early 1990s Ford was accused of legal responsibility for fatalities resulting when some of their Bronco II's rolled over, and General Motors was found liable for gas tank defects in some of its pickup trucks (Applebome 1993a; Meier 1992b; Meier 1992e; Meier 1993). In both cases the companies were alleged to have concealed safety problems of which they were aware. In October 1994, Transportation Secretary Federico Pena ruled that GM pickup trucks produced between 1973 and 1987 were dangerous and had led to some 150 unnessary deaths (Thomas 1994).

Over the years many other components of the transportation industry have been accused of selling products or engaging in practices that put the lives of consumers in jeopardy. In the 1970s the Firestone Company was alleged to have sold defective radial tires that played a role in thousands of accidents (Mokhiber 1988). The company was ultimately compelled to recall millions of tires and was fined $50,000. The airline industry has been accused of flying planes with safety defects and falsifying airplane maintenance records (Cushman 1990; Mokhiber 1988; Weiner 1990). A 1990 incident involving Eastern Airlines led to the first criminal indictment concerning airline maintenance. In all such cases consumers have little real choice but to trust the transportation company, but it is clear that such trust is not always warranted.

**Corporate Violence Against Consumers, In Sum** The preceding review is highly selective; a legion of other unsafe, even deadly, products have been foisted on consumers by corporations. In the final years of the 20th century the production, promotion, and sale of tobacco products is increasingly considered a "crime" in the broad sense of the term, even though in a strictly legal sense tobacco products involve "victims without crime" (Brown 1982). Reputable scientists estimate that smoking causes the premature death of over 400,000 Americans annually (Cowley 1988, 1989, 1990; Rosenblatt 1994). In addition to the direct harm to smokers, exposure of nonsmokers to "passive smoke" has been implicated as a cause of birth defects and other health problems (Brownlee and Roberts 1994; Cowley 1990). Smoking exacts a staggering economic toll—in the billions of dollars—in the form of medical costs, lost productivity, and the like (Wald 1988). At the same time, the enormous economic (and political) clout of the tobacco industry has been a major factor in perpetuating the on-going legal status of this dangerous product.

A basic sequence of events can be applied quite uniformly to corporate cases involving unsafe products. First, in the interest of realizing a competitive advantage and enhancing its profit, a corporation seeks to develop a new, appealing product. The desire to get the product on the market as quickly as possible takes precedence over exhaustive testing of the product and the dispassionate evaluation of any findings that raise safety considerations. Precautionary measures and devices, where applicable, are typically rejected unless and until they are forced upon the corporation, even if only very modest expenditures are involved. Data concerning dangers inherent in the product, which the corporation's own research often uncovers, is likely to be deliberately concealed. When confronted with potent evidence of the dangers of its product, the corporation denies that the harmful outcomes are attributable to the product itself and instead blames consumers for misuse of the product. The corporation may continue marketing the dangerous product as long as possible or find new markets in which it can "dump" the product. If litigation arises, the corporation either contests it with expensive, vigorous defenses or attempts to settle cases individually, without assuming liability. The product is discontinued or modified only when the corporation is confronted with massive negative publicity and experiences crippling economic losses due to ongoing lawsuits and prosecutions. Despite the very large loss of life and the serious physical injuries clearly caused by some unsafe products, corporate executives have very rarely been subjected to criminal prosecutions in these cases, and no corporate executive has been sentenced to prison for producing such products.

## Corporate Violence Against Workers: Unsafe Working Conditions

Throughout human history employers (and "masters") have often demonstrated a willful indifference to the health and safety of their employees (or servants and slaves). Friedrich Engels (1845: 108–109), alleged that employers were guilty of murder because they knew perfectly well that the conditions to which workers were subjected would result in premature deaths. But for most of history employers were not held liable for deaths, injuries, and illnesses suffered by workers as a consequence of workplace conditions; until very recently these deaths, injuries, and illnesses did not elicit a response from the criminal justice system. Workers (to say nothing of servants and slaves) who have assaulted their employers have historically been punished in the harshest terms. Still, much evidence supports the contention that far more employees have been maimed and killed as a consequence of employers' actions than the reverse. According to various sources, work-related accidents and diseases are the single greatest cause of disability and premature death in the United States today (Cullen, Maakestad, and Cavender 1987; Michalowski 1985: 325; Reiman 1990). Various recent studies by the government and private organizations have estimated the annual deaths from work-related diseases at up to 100,000; deaths from job-related diseases ranged from 136,800 to 390,000; and work-related accidents have been estimated to cause 10,700 deaths and 1.8 million disabling injuries annually (Reiman 1990: 58–61; White 1983).

No single reliable way to compile death and disease statistics exists. Job-related deaths may be either underreported or overreported, depending on the definition of "job-related"; some such deaths may be due to worker negligence or freak accidents. But by some estimates, work-related deaths are twice as frequent as automobile accidents, and very much more frequent than homicides (i.e., 9 murders per 100,000 people per year compared to 115 work-related deaths per 100,000 workers per year) (Michalowski 1985: 325–38). Many of these deaths and diseases are preventable; even if they have not traditionally been classified as crimes, they clearly are crimes in the humanistic sense.

The evidence of workers' dramatically increased consciousness of health hazards in the workplace is striking. One study reported that between 1969 and 1977, workers who said they were exposed to hazardous conditions in the workplace rose from 38 percent to 78 percent (Nelkin and Brown 1984: xvi). If workers are increasingly anxious about workplace hazards and embittered about the failure of management to protect them adequately, it is also true that they are frequently too intimidated to file formal complaints (Nelkin and Brown 1984: 25). Workers recognize that management is mainly concerned with external appearances and with the efficiency rather than the safety of the production process.

**Asbestos and the Manville Corporation**   One of the most widely publicized cases of a corporate employer knowingly exposing employees to unsafe working conditions involved the Manville Corporation (originally Johns-Manville), a producer of asbestos products. The term *asbestos* refers to any of several silicate minerals that are extremely heat-resistant and unusually pliable, qualities that led to its widespread use as insulation and for other purposes since ancient times. As early as the first century A.D. the Greek geographer Strabo and the Roman naturalist Pliny noted that slaves who worked with asbestos suffered from a lung disease; in the 20th century the term *asbestosis* was applied to the crippling and ultimately fatal lung disease resulting from exposure to asbestos (Brodeur 1985: 10–11). From at least the 1930s on, the Manville Corporation had internal medical reports of asbestosis among its workers, but on the basis of cost-benefit analysis it continued to produce and market this highly profitable product for several decades thereafter, concealing information about the health hazards even from its own workers (Brodeur 1985; Mokhiber 1988). By the mid-1970s and into the 1980s, thousands of asbestos workers were dying of abestosis. Some 25,000 personal injury lawsuits had been filed against the company, and in 1982 the Manville Corporation went into bankruptcy in anticipation of potential liabilities of some $2 billion from such suits (Delaney 1992; Feder 1982; Mokhiber 1988).

Many asbestos workers and their families and friends were deeply embittered toward the Manville Corporation, both for the original crime of knowingly exposing workers to dangerous asbestos dust and then for trying to evade responsibility; other workers, concerned about their jobs and perhaps engaging in psychological denial, disparaged the dangers of exposure and denounced the lawsuits (Freedman 1982). Many of the civil lawsuits remain unsettled today, and neither the corporation nor any of its officers have been criminally indicted (Labaton 1990c). The physical, emotional, and economic consequences of the asbestos tragedy are clearly going to persist for some time to come.

**Other Cases of Corporate Violence Against Workers** If the asbestos exposure of Manville Corporation workers is an especially well-known case, it is far from unique. The workers of many other industries, especially the mining, textiles, and chemical industries, are routinely exposed to dangerous conditions.

In the coal mining industry an estimated 100,000 deaths and 1.5 million injuries have occurred since 1930; mining and quarry workers have the highest mortality rate due to "occupational trauma": 55 fatalities per 100,000 workers (Cullen, Maakestad, and Cavender 1987: 68). The most dramatic of these deaths result from a mine collapse or fire. The death of 78 coal miners in 1968 in an explosion in a West Virginia mine helped to expose routine neglect of safety rules by mining corporations (Mokhiber 1988: 97). Although this tragedy helped stimulate the passage of the Federal Coal Mine and Safety Act (1969), miners still die in fires and collapses and because of ventilation failures in which companies have flagrantly disregarded safety standards (Cullen, Maakestad, and Cavender 1987: 68). Hundreds of thousands of miners have also died or been permanently disabled by "black lung" resulting from exposure to dangerous mine dust (Mokhiber 1988: 98).

In the textile industry as well, tens of thousands of workers have developed "brown lung" (byssinosis) from inhalation of dust, and in the chemical industry millions of workers are routinely exposed to toxic and dangerous chemicals (Mokhiber 1988; Nelkin and Brown 1984). Typically there is evidence both of a longstanding awareness of dangers on the part of the corporations involved and of active resistance to regulatory and worker-compensation laws. The relatively few criminal and civil penalties imposed on corporations in these industries for safety violations of federal standards have most typically been token fines.

**The Film Recovery Systems Case** Even though federal workplace safety laws have been in place since 1970, criminal prosecutions have been exceedingly rare; as of 1988, only 14 employers had been prosecuted for exposing workers to unacceptable risks, and none had been sentenced to jail (Glaberson 1990). The Film Recovery Systems Case, originating in 1985, was the first case in which an employer was specifically charged with murder in connection with a work-related death (Frank and Lynch 1992).

A Polish immigrant, Stefan Golab, died after being exposed to a cyanide solution used in the Film Recovery Systems factory (in Illinois) to recover silver from used photographic plates. The indictment of several company executives for murder (the company itself was charged with manslaughter) was based on the fact that conditions in the factory were obviously unsafe, and that these executives were aware of this fact. Three of the executives were convicted of murder and sentenced to 25 years in prison, and the company was fined $10,000, but the convicted executives successfully appealed the verdict; to date no new trial has occurred. By 1990 at least three state high courts had upheld the principle that employers can be criminally prosecuted for unsafe working conditions, and the conviction of two factory owners (and their corporation) in Brooklyn, New York, for exposing workers to unsafe conditions had been upheld (Glaberson 1990). Such criminal prosecutions are controversial, however, and it remains unclear whether they will become more common and continue to be upheld by the courts.

**Corporate Violence Against Workers, In Sum**　The issue of culpability can be complex in work-related accidents. It is hardly in the self-interest of corporations to seek to harm their workers deliberately. But workers are inevitably harmed—sometimes fatally—when corporate management limits or disregards safety precautions, or imposes on workers production pressures that lead them to disregard such precautions, all in the interest of maximixing profit and minimizing costs. The absence of direct intent to do harm, the difficulty of pinpointing the specific cause of harm, the diffusion of responsibility for harm-producing corporate decisions, and the economic and political clout of corporations have all tended to shield corporate employers from full-fledged liability for work-related injuries and deaths.

## Corporate Abuse of Power, Fraud, and Economic Exploitation

MUCH CORPORATE CRIME has no violent consequences, but rather vast political and economic consequences. In his landmark study of white collar crime, Sutherland (1949) focused almost entirely on corporate offenses that had economic as opposed to violent consequences. These offenses included restraints of trade; rebates; patent, trademark, and copyright violations; misrepresentations in advertising; unfair labor practices; financial manipulations; and war crimes. With respect to the last offense, Sutherland (writing during and immediately after World War II) examined illegal profiteering and violations of other laws (such as embargoes and restraints on trade of war materials) committed by corporations during the war. He concluded that for large corporations, profits took precedence over patriotism.

Corporate abuse of power in the form of corruption of the political process has economic consequences for ordinary citizens insofar as corporations obtain favorable treatment on such matters as reducing their tax liability and increasing their freedom to raise prices or underpay workers. Corporations also use their immense economic clout to distort the political process in a system that claims to be democratic, and as a consequence much policy ends up favoring the interests of corporations over those of ordinary citizens.

Direct bribery of governmental officials (of legislators in particular) has long been a common practice of corporations (Miller 1992; Noonan 1984). A great deal of corruption is less blatant; some takes the form of political campaign contributions (today, through corporate political action committees, or PACs) and aggressive lobbying, and as such is firmly rooted in the whole structure of the relationship between corporate interests and public officials (Etzioni 1988a; Jackson 1988; Rose-Ackerman 1978). When these various forms of influence compromise the state's control over harmful activities of corporations, or when military interventions are undertaken on behalf of corporate interests, physical and economic harm may result. The whole topic of corporate corruption of the governmental process is explored more fully in Chapters 5 and 6.

Our discussion of the many different forms of corporate fraud and economic exploitation will consider these activities in terms of the primary victims. First we examine corporate crimes against the average citizen, who loses far more money over the long term to the illegal activities of corporations (e.g., from price-fixing conspiracies) than to conventional offenders.

## Corporate Crimes Against Citizens and Taxpayers: Defrauding the Government and Corporate Tax Evasion

Government, whether at the federal, state, or local level, is a major purchaser of corporate products and services, expending billions of dollars annually on such purchases. Corporations with contracts to provide goods and services to the government have defrauded the government of billions of dollars; citizens and taxpayers ultimately foot the bill for these frauds. Defense and health-care–related expenditures are among the largest items on the federal budget.

**Defense Contract Fraud** Defense contract frauds have been especially numerous and costly. By the late 1980s the Department of Defense was spending over $600 million a day for all expenditures; a significant proportion of its budget was allotted to some 60,000 prime contractors (U.S. Department of Justice 1989). The Lockheed Corporation alone was collecting some 85 percent of its $10 billion-a-year income from the Defense Department (Perez-Pena 1993).

The whole system of awarding defense contracts has traditionally provided rich opportunities for fraud. A high percentage of new weapons-systems contracts, for example, have been awarded without competitive bidding. Corporate contractors have charged unreasonable prices, collected tens of millions on cost overruns, falsified test data, double-billed the government and billed it for costs related to commercial contracts, and then have often delivered defective products or systems (Simon and Eitzen 1993; U.S. Department of Justice 1989). Literally billions of dollars were wasted on "gold-plated" (i.e., unnecessarily sophisticated) weapons systems and other military hardware that failed (Isaacson 1983).

In the early 1980s the media widely publicized the Defense Department's gross overpayments for spare parts and tools—for example, $110 for a diode available elsewhere for 4 cents; $1,118 for a navigator's stool cap, which was subsequently priced at $10; $2,043 for a nut worth 13 cents; $9,606 for an Allen wrench available for 12 cents at hardware stores; and so forth (Mohr 1983; Tolchin 1984). A nationwide investigation later that decade uncovered "rampant bribery" in military contracts (Magnuson 1988b). Since then many specific cases involving major defense contractors have come to light, including incidents in which Lockheed, Rockwell International, Boeing, Unisys, and General Electric overcharged, double-billed, and defrauded the Defense Department of hundreds of millons of dollars on contracts for transport planes, jet engines, battlefield computer systems, and the like (Adelson

1988; Cushman 1986; Engelberg 1989; Feder 1990; Fried 1991; Stevenson 1991b; Stevenson 1992b; Stevenson 1992d). Several aspects of the defense fraud cases are striking: The amount of money involved is large; the offenders are major corporations; these corporations do not seem to be deterred by publicized prosecutions; and the resolution of the cases typically involves a financial settlement rather than disqualification of the corporation from future government contracts. Defense contractors, not "national security," were the primary beneficiaries of the trillion-dollar defense-spending buildup of the Reagan era.

Defrauding of the government—that is to say, the taxpayers—is hardly limited to defense contracts. Businesses that provide the government with goods and services in virtually all sectors of the economy have perpetuated fraud.

**Health Care Providers Fraud**   Hospitals, including mental hospitals, rehabilitation centers, testing laboratories, and other medical facilities, are believed to defraud the government of billions of dollars annually through Medicaid and Medicare programs (Anderson and Robinson 1992; Freudenheim 1993; Kerr 1991b; Kerr 1992b). In 1993 federal officials estimated that medical fraud accounted for up to $100 billion of the $900 billion annual health care bill in the United States; taxpayers footed a significant proportion of this bill (Freudenheim 1993). Working under severe economic pressure in the 1990s, hospitals have manipulated numerical codes for services rendered and demanded kickbacks from physicians for referrals; these illegal costs are ultimately included in the fraudulent, inflated bills submitted to federal health-insurance programs (Pear 1991c; Pear 1992b). Although criminal prosecutions for corporate health care provider fraud are complicated and relatively uncommon, they do occur. In 1992, for example, National Health Laboratories, Inc., a large clinical diagnostic testing corporation, pleaded guilty to defrauding government health-insurance programs and agreed to pay over $100 million to settle the case (Sims 1992b). Such fraudulent activities have contributed to the alarming rise in the national health bill in recent years and figured prominently in the Clinton administrations's major effort to reform the health care system.

**Corporate Tax Evasion**   Major corporations also cost U.S. taxpayers huge amounts by evading their fair share of the tax burden. Sutherland (1949: 170–72) identified a number of corporate tax evasion schemes, especially in conjunction with war profiteering, including padding cost figures (to reduce apparent profits), juggling financial data, and making fraudulent claims to the government on war-related expenditures.

Corporations' total share of the tax burden declined from about 25 percent of all federal revenues in the 1950s to only 7 percent by the early 1990s (*Multinational Monitor* 1993). Major corporations with net incomes of hundreds of millions of dollars were paying virtually nothing in taxes, at least in part because of the success of corporate lobbyists in persuading legislators to adopt tax laws (with devices such as depletion allowances, asset depreciation tables, and investment tax credits) that favor corporations. During the Reagan era (1981–1988), the top corporate tax rate was reduced from 46 percent to 34 percent, and the oil industry successfully lobbied for repeal of a windfall profits tax that had originally been directed at them (Castro 1986;

Simon and Eitzen 1993: 27). The official tax rate means relatively little, however, because corporations also have highly paid, creative lawyers and accountants who enable them to maximize their liabilities and minimize their profits for the purposes of calculating their taxes. The General Dynamics Corporation, the nation's largest military contractor, did not pay any federal income tax in the 13 years from 1972 to 1985, despite profits of some $2 billion during this period (Gerth 1985). In 1990 the IRS sought $7 billion from the nation's largest oil company, Exxon, for taxes involving pricing manipulations during the years 1979 through 1982 (Wald 1990b). Such cases abound.

Foreign-owned and -based corporations are often especially well-positioned to evade taxes. A 1990 IRS report noted that more than half of almost 37,000 foreign-owned companies filing returns in 1986 reported no income, and one IRS official estimated that these corporations were underpaying taxes by some $12 billion (Pear 1990). One of the principal means of reducing tax liability was to pay artificially high prices to the foreign-based parent company for goods, services, and technology; such costs could then be written off against profits.

Although some critics of corporate taxes have complained that such taxes impose an unjust burden on investors and consumers and inhibit economic development, the fact is that many corporations have accumulated vast profits during a period when millions of ordinary taxpayers are struggling to pay their bills. Clearly, corporate tax evasion has contributed substantially to the national deficit.

## Corporate Crimes Against Consumers: Price-Fixing, Price Gouging, False Advertising, and Misrepresentation of Products

Obtaining the highest-quality product at the lowest possible price was one of the principal rationales advanced by Adam Smith on behalf of a free-market economy. The idea was that freely competing entrepreneurs would have to enhance quality and reduce price to stay in business, and consumers (whose welfare was Smith's primary concern) would benefit. Accordingly, when competing corporations join together and agree to fix prices at a certain level, this activity, known as *price-fixing*, negates any such benefit to consumers.

**Price-Fixing**  Much of the "fixing" of prices does not involve a specific conspiracy, but rather takes the form of "parallel pricing" wherein industry "leaders" set inflated prices and supposed competitors adjust their own prices accordingly (Currie and Skolnick 1988: 86). Parallel pricing, which is virtually beyond the reach of law, has been estimated to cost consumers over $100 million annually.

Explicit price-fixing was prohibited by the Sherman Act of 1890 as a form of "restraint of trade" (Clinard and Yeager 1980: 134). Despite this legal prohibition, much evidence suggests that price-fixing has been extremely common—even the norm—across a broad range of industries (Jamieson 1994; Nader and Green 1972). Sutherland (1949) identified at least six different methods for fixing prices and found evidence of numerous suits alleging this activity. By the early 1980s this specifically illegal activity was costing U.S. consumers an estimated $60 billion annually (Simon and Eitzen 1993: 9). In 1991, in recognition of the widespread violation of the price-fixing prohibition, Congress moved to reform the law to make the practice more difficult (Labaton 1991). For example, "vertical" price-fixing, in which some manufacturers attempt to dictate retail price levels and lock out discounters, became vulnerable to lawsuits as a result of this reform.

Over the years, price-fixing conspiracies have been uncovered for virtually every imaginable product or service, including oil, sugar, milk, infant formula, cardboard cartons, long-distance phone companies, and airlines (Simon and Eitzen 1993: 100). The most celebrated price-fixing conspiracy involved heavy-electrical-equipment manufacturers, including General Electric and Westinghouse, who conspired over a period of decades to fix prices on their products (Geis 1967; Herling 1962). Fairly substantial fines (tax-deductible, however, as business expenses) were imposed on the companies, and a number of middle-level executives, who denied that their actions constituted a crime, went to jail briefly (for less than a month). Price-fixing cases that came to light in the 1990s include an illegal scheme by major telephone companies to inflate prices on long-distance calls; price-fixing of video games involving Nintendo, the leading manufacturer; the limiting of oil supplies and price-fixing by oil companies in Western states; and the conviction of 43 dairy companies for fixing prices on milk contracts with schools and the military (Associated Press 1991; Henriques 1993; Sims 1990b; Tomasson 1991). These and other such cases, which were typically resolved with fines rather than prison sentences, surely cost consumers billions of dollars.

**Price Gouging** Charges of price gouging, or systematic overcharging, have also been directed at various industries and corporations when they take advantage of especially vulnerable classes of consumers or circumstances such as shortages (Simon and Eitzen 1993: 104). For example, the Burroughs Wellcome Company was widely accused of price gouging in connection with AZT, a drug used by AIDS patients at a cost of some $10,000 a year (Nussbaum 1990). Markups as high as 7,000 percent are not unknown in the pharmaceutical industry, and various criminal prosecutions for price-fixing have also been directed against companies in this industry (Braithwaite 1984: 162, 182). President Clinton himself made a claim of price gouging against the pharmaceutical industry in 1993 (N.A. Lewis 1994); the chair of a congressional subcommittee further alleged that this overcharging even applied to drugs developed largely at the taxpayer's expense (Leary 1993). Even though the pharmaceutical industry claimed that the high prices were justified by the enormous costs and risks of research, independent studies suggested that these companies were spending more on promotion than on research (Rosenthal 1993). This industry has a long history of promoting much-more-expensive brand name drugs over less expensive, equivalent generic drugs (Simon and Eitzen 1993). Consumers are obviously more vulnerable to price gouging on prescription drugs than on, say, soda and snacks.

Price gouging clearly occurs in other industries as well. For example, the Hertz Company conceded in 1988 that it had overcharged its car rental customers for repairs and agreed to make refunds (Levine 1988). During that same year, oil companies paid $7.4 billion—Exxon alone paid over $2 billion—to settle cases alleging that they overcharged for crude and refined oil products between 1973 and 1981, in violation of federal price controls then in effect (Wald 1988; Clinard 1990). Major producers of infant formula (a market overwhelmingly dominated by two corporations) were charged in 1992 with illegally overcharging for their product, in a market with sales exceeding $1.5 billion in the United States alone (Noble 1991; Pear 1992). Such price gouging contributes to inflationary tendencies and costs consumers a great deal of money.

**False Advertising and Product Misrepresentation**  In his chapter on misrepresentations in advertising, Sutherland (1949) noted that prosecutions of false advertising cases had proven difficult under the fraud laws due to the absence of major, highly motivated victims and problems of proving intent and damage. But with the passage of special laws such as the Pure Food and Drug Law (1906) and the establishment of the Federal Trade Commission (FTC), action against false advertising was somewhat facilitated. Many major corporations have been charged with false advertising for products with such "household names" as Wheaties, Morton's Salt, Palmolive Soap, Bayer's Aspirin, Elizabeth Arden cosmetics, *Encyclopedia Britannica*, Goodyear tires, and Quaker State Oil (Sutherland 1949: 116).

The history of corporations' blatantly false advertising claims, as well as exaggerated claims, or puffery, is a long one (Fox 1984). False nutritional claims and falsified demonstrations are just two illegal aspects of advertising and product promotion, which is a $100 billion a year business in the United States (Simon and Eitzen 1993: 109). The FTC began to call for a more substantial response to this activity in the 1960s, but little change resulted.

The basic response to false advertising has been to require a modification or discontinuation of a misleading advertising campaign (Fox 1984: 306). Altogether, U.S. consumers have been misled over the years into buying billions of dollars worth of products and services that fail to live up to advertisers' claims, and that in some instances actively harm consumers. Several cases of misrepresented or mislabeled products have occurred in recent years. The Chrysler Corporation was accused in 1987 of selling as new cars that had actually been driven hundreds of miles by executives; some had even been in accidents (Holuba 1987). The Beech-Nut Nutrition Corporation, a major producer of baby foods, pleaded guilty in 1988 to mislabeling as apple juice a cheap mixture of beet sugar, cane sugar, and corn syrup that contained little real apple juice, and marketing this product for babies (Traub 1988). The company was fined $2 million, and two corporate executives received jail terms. The FDA took action in 1989 to address false claims regarding alleged health foods such as high-fiber breakfast cereals (Hilts 1989). Even when clear economic or physical harm to consumers cannot be demonstrated, such cases are nevertheless a form of fraud.

## Corporate Crimes Against Employees: Economic Exploitation, Corporate Theft, Unfair Labor Practices, and Surveillance of Employees

It is widely recognized that employees steal from their employers (as discussed in Chapter 4), but it is less obvious to many people that employers can steal from their employees. In Karl Marx's (1867) view of a capitalist system, all employers (or own-ers of the means of production) were stealing from their employees, because instead of the worker getting a full return on the value of his labor, the owner expropriated a part of this value in the name of profit. This theory of surplus value—the idea that the labor that goes into a product is what gives it value—has been widely dispar-aged by economists, but there can be little question historically that capitalist owners have exploited workers, and in many instances underpaid them by any reasonable standard.

**Economic Exploitation of Employees**   Various corporate efforts to drive down employee wages and benefits have been evident since the early 1970s, and real wages in fact declined during this period (Sheak 1990). The driving down of wages was accom-plished by decreasing the number of high-wage union jobs and reducing wages of U.S. workers using such strategies as exporting capital, using more foreign compo-nents in domestic products, setting up offshore plants, extracting wage and benefits concessions from unions, hiring more part-time or lower-wage workers, and union-busting. These activities can be regarded as "criminal" in the broader sense of the term.

Plant closings, which are especially pronounced in the auto and steel indus-tries, are not crimes in the legal sense, but they have devastating consequences for employees (Perrucci et al. 1988). In some cases corporations have closed plants even when they were profitable; apparently they were not regarded as sufficiently profitable (Logue 1994). It has been well documented that the resulting unemploy-ment has profoundly damaging psychological consequences in addition to the obvi-ous economic hardship it causes (Cottle 1994). In the United States, the decision to lay off workers and close down plants has been regarded as quite exclusively the pre-rogative of management, but most western European countries, Canada, and Japan require prior notice of plant closings (Clinard 1990: 8). Laws can either facilitate, or impose restraints on and penalize, plant closings.

**Corporate Stealing from Employees**   In some cases, thefts from employees clearly vio-late existing laws. For example, in 1988 the federal government accused a major meatpacker, IBP Inc., of cheating workers out of millions of dollars in overtime pay by violating federal laws requiring hourly workers to be paid time and a half for work beyond 40 hours a week (Associated Press 1988). In a somewhat bizarre case in 1990, Cumberland Farms, a corporation with a chain of convenience stores, was accused of extorting money from employees after falsely accusing them of employee theft (Hammer 1990). In 1991 the Continental Can Company was required to pay a $415-million settlement to the United Steelworkers of America for an elaborate, ille-gal scheme to deny steelworkers their pensions by laying off workers before they qualified for retirement payments (Berg 1991).

Many other cases of corporations stealing from their employees involve viola-tions of minimum wage laws, failure to make legally ordained social security pay-ments on behalf of their employees, or improper use of employee pension funds. When corporations have been found guilty of having caused physical (and concomi-tant economic) harm to their employees, they have sometimes found ways to delay, minimize, or entirely avoid payments to the affected workers. Thus to protect itself from personal injury lawsuits alleging damage from exposure to asbestos, the Manville Corporation filed for Chapter 11 bankruptcy protection (Delaney 1989, 1992).

**Unfair Labor Practices**  Throughout much of the 19th century and well into the 20th century, corporate management has resisted, sometimes quite violently, the right of labor to organize, to strike, and to bargain collectively (Brecher 1974). Even though this right was recognized by the courts as early as 1842, a serious means of implementation of the law did not come into being until the National Labor Relations Act of 1935 (Sutherland 1949: 128–29). In addition to suffering physical harm at the hands of corporate private security forces and enforcers, workers collectively have also lost countless millions of dollars by being deprived of adequate and effective representation in negotiations with management. Corporations' discriminatory practices on the basis of race, ethnicity, gender, or age have caused equally massive, ultimately unmeasurable losses to employees and potential employees. Of course, in more recent years a series of laws have rendered such discrimination less common and more vulnerable to legal action.

**Corporate Surveillance of Employees**  Yet another form of corporate crime against employees, the increasing use of intrusive technologies for surveillance, deserves mention here, although typically it would not be considered a form of corporate crime or violence. Einstadter (1992) has argued, however, that this activity is indeed a form of corporate theft insofar as it is an infringement on a traditional and important right to privacy. Furthermore, such corporate intrusiveness is said to contribute to a sense of alienation and estrangement in the workplace. Of course, from the perspective of corporate management this surveillance is necessary to combat another form of white collar crime, namely employee theft. At some point, however, the harms and injustices of such surveillance may exceed any legitimate purpose.

## Corporate Crimes Against Competitors: Monopolistic Practices and Theft of Trade Secrets

Competitors, especially smaller corporations, have historically been victims of unethical and illegal acts by large corporations. In the free-wheeling capitalist economic environment of the 19th century, the "robber barons" used virtually every imaginable means to destroy their competitors, and they were often successful (Myers 1907; Josephson 1934). The Standard Oil Corporation, presided over by John D. Rockefeller, was perhaps the single most famous example of a corporation that ruthlessly undercut virtually all competitors; by the end of the 19th century it had obtained a virtual monopoly, controlling some 95 percent of the market. The Sherman Antitrust Act of 1890 (which is discussed in Chapter 9) was at least in part inspired by anger over the monopolistic practices of the large corporate trusts. Although full-scale private-sector monopolies like Standard Oil disappeared, monopolistic practices endured, in part because of weak enforcement of the Sherman Act and successive antitrust laws.

Sutherland (1949: 76) identified two principal methods 19th-century corporations used to annihilate competitors: reducing their sales and increasing their costs. Competitors' sales could be reduced by undercutting them on price (predatory pricing) and by pressuring dealers, sales agents, unions, and other parties not to work with competitors. Competitors' costs could be raised by forcing up purchase prices on raw materials, making special deals with suppliers of such materials, pressuring lending institutions not to extend credit, and sponsoring direct sabotage of competitors. In the 19th century in particular, large corporations achieved an advantage over smaller competitors by obtaining rebates from railroad companies and other middlemen, who depended on the good graces of these larger corporations.

More recent studies of corporate crime (see, for example, Clinard and Yeager 1980) have found that anticompetitive practices are still quite common. One recent major antitrust case was directed at IBM, although the suit was eventually abandoned (DeLamarter 1976). Still more recently, competitors of Microsoft have complained of its anticompetitive practices, and the video-game maker Nintendo has been the target of similar charges (Manes and Andrews 1994; Sheff 1994). Wal-Mart, the nation's largest retailing corporation, was found guilty of engaging in predatory pricing to undercut competing retailers (Jones 1993). In all such cases, the economic philosophy of the federal or state administration in power is an important factor in determining the form and intensity of the justice system response.

As Sutherland (1949) observed, corporate illegalities directed at competitors can take a number of different forms, including patent, trademark, and copyright infringements. In the current "information age," the theft of ideas and technology has probably become more important than ever. In one case in the 1980s, representatives of the Hitachi Corporation, after an investigation by the FBI, ultimately pleaded guilty to the theft of corporate secrets from IBM (Stewart 1987). (Thus IBM has been both an accused perpetrator of anticompetitive practices and a victim of corporate theft by a competitor.)

Still another form of anticompetitive practice involves interference with contractual agreements. In a well-publicized case in the 1980s, Texaco was accused of improperly undercutting a competitor, Pennzoil, in the acquisition of Getty Oil; specifically, Texaco was found to have fraudulently induced Getty Oil to break a contract with Pennzoil, thereby stripping Pennzoil of rights to a billion barrels of oil reserves (Petzinger 1987). The civil court proceeding resulted in a judgment against Texaco of $11 billion (the largest such judgment in U.S. history), although Texaco ultimately settled with Pennzoil for $3 billion.

Finally, it is clear that in addition to defrauding consumers, false advertising and misrepresentation of products can harm competitors to the extent that the offender gets away with such false claims. Altogether, then, crimes against competitors can take many forms, and at least some of the resulting losses are passed along to consumers.

## Corporate Crimes Against Owners and Creditors:
## Managerial Fraud, Self-Dealing, and Strategic Bankruptcy

In this section we examine how the owners of corporations can themselves be victimized by corporate crime. Adolph Berle and Gardiner Means's *The Modern Corporation and Private Property* (1932) is commonly given credit for advancing the thesis that ownership in the modern corporation is separated from management or from direct control (although this point was hardly original, as Karl Marx made it in 1867 in *Das Kapital*). The owners, of course, are the stockholders, whereas managemnt consists of the executives who run the corporation (and also typically own some of its stock).

The interests of a corporation's managers may not coincide entirely with those of its other stockholders. Research has shown that executive pay levels are highly correlated with company size, which suggests that corporate *growth*, not profit maximization, may be the highest priority of corporate CEOs (chief executive officers) (Powell 1986b). Thus corporate executives may be less concerned with maximizing share values than with maintaining their job security and extending their power; obtaining lucrative compensation, expense accounts, and other perks (e.g., corporate cars and jets, club memberships, vacation homes, etc.); and taking advantage of their inside knowledge to purchase or unload company stock (Altheide et al. 1978: 92). In some cases (e.g., expense-account padding) the perks are clearly illegal; in other cases they are made possible by control of the compensation system. But even when bonuses and perks are not necessarily technically illegal, they can reduce stockholders' returns on their holdings.

Even though managers may not have complete freedom of action, they do have significant opportunities for self-dealing. In principle, corporate boards of directors exercise some oversight and control over managers, but board members are often allies of or beholden to the corporate CEO, and in any case they are not especially well positioned to police the managers (Ermann and Lundman 1982; Powell 1986b; Stone 1975). Recently some corporate boards have become somewhat more actively vigilant, especially in response to an increase in civil judgments against boards concerning mismanagement (Solomon 1993). But as they are presently constituted, boards cannot be depended on to ensure that corporations neither engage in illegal activity nor defraud their owners, the stockholders.

From the earliest stages of corporate history, insiders have often defrauded investors and would-be owners through false financial statements, stock price manipulations, and other such strategies. The previously mentioned, 18th-century case of the "South Sea Bubble" is one example. More recently, the Equity Funding case was one of the most notorious and widely reported cases of corporate crime in which the owners (or stockholders) were the primary victims of managerial fraud. Equity Funding, an insurance company developed from modest origins in the 1960s, attracted large numbers of investors with greatly inflated claims of assets (Dirks and Gross 1974; Soble and Dallos 1974). Ultimately over 50,000 completely bogus insurance policies were created (with the aid of computers), and some $200 million in nonexistent assets were claimed as a means of inflating stock prices and attracting additional investors. When the whole fraud was exposed in 1973, the company went into bankruptcy; thousands of investors suffered losses totaling millions of dollars. A large number of the company's executives, from the president on down, were indicted in this case.

Corporate executives and managers who either manipulate stock values (e.g., by first making false disclosures to drive up the price of the stock and then selling off their own stock at the top of the market) or engage in trading on the basis of their insider knowledge (e.g., by arranging for the buying up of their company's stock in advance of a public announcement that will drive the price up) are effectively "stealing" from other investors or stockholders. In one example of stock manipulation, Eddie Antar, the founder and CEO of a chain of New York-based consumer electronic stores known as Crazy Eddie's, was arrested and charged in 1992 with having made over $60 million through sales of company stock after the stock's value had been grossly inflated by fraudulent statements about inventory and other financial assets (Meier 1992c). In another case, which may be the biggest corporate fraud of the century, the founder and president of the $3 billion Phar-Mor discount drug chain was accused of defrauding investors and creditors of some $350 million, in part by selling stock whose value was inflated by phony financial data (Solomon 1992).

Testimony for the increasing frequency of such corporate crimes was presented in a 1992 front-page story in *The New York Times* entitled "Falsifying Corporate Data Becomes Fraud of the 90's" (Henriques 1992b). The executives involved may be seeking self-preservation in response to pressures to meet optimistic projections and maintain inflated stock prices, or they may be setting up the type of stock-related swindle just noted. Insider trading is discussed more fully in Chapter 6.

Finally, corporations may commit crimes against their creditors by using various strategies to evade payment of debts and obligations. Whereas historically bankruptcy was regarded as a desperate, stigmatized last resort for businesses (and individuals), recently some major corporations have pursued what Delaney (1992) labeled "strategic bankruptcy" to avoid meeting certain burdensome financial obligations, including in some cases obligations to creditors. Texaco, for example, took advantage of bankruptcy laws to force a settlement with a major creditor, Pennzoil. In some instances, corporate managers use various strategies to manipulate the data representing the corporation's financial status (Delaney 1994). Creditors might also be considered victims of some of the many corporate takeovers in the 1980s, insofar as the parties who profited from these takeovers pulled so much capital out of these corporations that some of them went bankrupt (Eichenwald 1991). Of course, employees and shareholders are also victims of corporate bankruptcies.

## Are Universities and Colleges Corporate Criminals?

BECAUSE MUCH STUDY of corporate crime has emanated out of universities, it seems only fair to ask whether universities and colleges themselves are guilty of corporate crime. Many large universities in particular are organized in ways that are not too dissimilar from major corporations, although they are not focused on making a profit. But because universities often have huge financial commitments and are engaged in vigorous competition with comparable institutions, they have been accused of some forms of corporate crime.

In the early 1990s, for example, Stanford University and a number of other prestigious research institutions were accused of charging numerous improper items and activities (e.g., parties, trips, furniture, etc.) to federal research grants (DePalma 1992a; Pear 1992a). Institutions of higher learning have also been accused of cheating the government (and taxpayers) by making fraudulent claims in connection with federal student aid programs (Deloughry 1991; DePalma 1991; Lueck 1993). The most blatant cases of such fraud are associated with proprietary trade schools and religious schools, but other types of educational institutions have sometimes been involved. Winerip (1994) has reported that altogether the federal government loses up to $4 billion annually from waste, fraud, and loan defaults in college and university student aid programs.

Some critics of higher education (see, for example, Anderson 1992; Sykes 1988) claim that universities and colleges are defrauding their consumers—students—by not providing the quality of education promised; instead, undergraduate students in many institutions are taught by overworked, underpaid, and poorly supervised graduate students or teaching assistants. Some institutions of higher learning— for example, the Savannah College of Art and Design in Georgia—have been accused of being inherently fraudulent enterprises.

Universities and colleges have also been investigated for alleged price-fixing in connection with tuition (Jaschik 1990; Leslie 1989). In the early 1990s a controversial Justice Department investigation focused on the claim that MIT and seven other Ivy League colleges engaged in price-fixing in connection with financial aid offers to admittees (Fendrich 1992). Only MIT chose to fight these charges—unsuccessfully— although this antitrust action was criticized as misguided on the premise that bright, financially needy students actually benefited from the agreements among the colleges (DePalma 1992a; DePalma 1992b; *New York Times* 1993a). Universities and colleges have also been accused of engaging in price-fixing of faculty salaries and exploiting part-time faculty (Mundy 1992; Kean 1994).

College and university athletic programs, in particular Division I programs, have been accused of exploiting student athletes by using them for economic gain without really attending to their educational needs (McMillen 1992; Monaghan 1991; Sperber 1990). Of course, college athletic programs, in which millions of dollars are often at stake, have periodically been accused of various violations of NCAA rules (e.g., recruiting enticements) and of being generally corrupt.

All colleges and universities, especially private ones, depend to a significant degree on donations from individual benefactors. Many prominent institutions of higher education have been accused of accepting large donations from notorious white collar criminals, including war criminals, international arms dealers, corporate offenders, insider traders, tax evaders, and the like (Mundy 1993). And even if universities are not readily associated with corporate violence, they have been charged with inadequately protecting students against violent crime and exposing them to hazardous conditions in university laboratories (Colino 1990; Kalette 1990).

None of the preceding discussion is intended to suggest that the corporate crimes of universities and colleges are likely to approximate the scope of other corporate crime reviewed in this chapter. Surely the singular mission of institutions of higher education provides them with less incentive and less opportunity for corporate crime. Still, the common tendency to wholly overlook these institutions in discussions of corporate crime is not warranted.

## Corporate Crime, In Sum

THE BASIC THESIS of this chapter is that corporate crime both represents a substantial threat to the physical well-being of citizens, consumers, and workers and is the cause of enormous financial losses. It takes many different forms and occurs in many different contexts. Corporate crime today continues to exemplify the classic attributes of white collar crime and remains a major social problem.

# Occupational Crime

INHERENT IN OUR society is a conventional expectation that mature adults, for the larger part of their lives, will have a legitimate occupation—that is, some legal way of earning a living (Hodson and Sullivan 1990). An official U.S. government publication recognizes over 20,000 occupational titles, each reflecting some degree of prestige and power (Hodson and Sullivan 1990: 48). Legitimate occupations also provide different sorts of opportunities for engaging in fraudulent conduct and include occupational subcultures that either promote or constrain illegal activity.

The concept of "occupational crime" was first clearly defined by Clinard and Quinney (1967: 131) as a "violation of the legal codes in the course of activity in a legitimate occupation." Typically, the concept of occupational crime has been applied to acts in which financial gain or status is sought (or their loss prevented) in the context of performing one's job. Green (1990: 12–13) recently extended the definition of occupational crime to include "any act punishable by law which is committed through opportunity created in the course of an occupation that is legal." As examples he cites a range of activities, from chambermaids stealing from hotel guests' luggage, to railroad engineers causing a fatal crash due to intoxication, to physicans who sexually abuse their patients. None of these acts, however, are forms of *white collar crime* in any meaningful sense. Even though the boundaries between white collar crime and other forms of illegality committed in an occupational context are often blurred, this chapter focuses on the financially oriented illegalities committed primarily by middle- and upper-class individuals within the context of a legal occupation.

Chapter 3 was devoted to corporate crime, which has indeed been the primary focus of white collar crime scholarship. Some commentators argue that small business crime has been relatively neglected and should receive more attention (Sutton and Wild 1985; Barlow 1993); others have noted that those actually charged and convicted of white collar crimes are disproportionately ordinary members of the middle class with relatively modest incomes, such as small business owners, shopkeepers, restaurateurs, market traders, used-car salesmen, and employees (Croall 1989; Shapiro 1990; Weisburd et al. 1991).

The reasons for this apparent contradiction are explored in other chapters, and Chapter 8 considers ways in which large corporations may create a "criminogenic environment" that facilitates crimes by smaller businesses and enterprises. Large businesses are often in a position to take advantage of smaller businesses, sometimes in illegal ways. In an example noted in Chapter 3, Wal-Mart, the nation's largest retailer, was found guilty in Arkansas in 1993 of "predatory pricing"—that is, of selling certain items at below cost to destroy smaller competitors (Jones 1993).

Clearly, the vast amount of occupationally based illegality committed by small businesses (for example, retail and service businesses), professionals, and employees of a broad range of enterprises is significant, and the incremental financial (and physical) harm caused by occupational crime is substantial. Most of us encounter such forms of white collar crime quite directly. Indeed, if readers of this book ever contend with temptations and pressures to engage in white collar crime, it is especially likely to be associated with the pursuit of a conventional, legitimate occupation. Accordingly, we will review some forms of occupational crime in this chapter, beginning with small business crime.

## Crimes by Small Businesses: Retail Crime and Service Fraud

RETAIL BUSINESSES ARE often thought of as victims of crime, whether by pilfering or embezzling employees, by shoplifters, or by robbers and burglars. But retail businesses of all sizes, from large department stores to "Mom & Pop" neighborhood stores, may themselves engage in a wide range of deceptive and illegal activities, including deceptive and fraudulent advertising, illegal pricing practices, sale of fraudulently represented merchandise, purchase and resale of stolen goods, exploitation of employees (e.g., exposure to hazardous conditions or nonpayment of social security taxes), evasion of sales taxes, and payoffs to inspectors and other public officials. Even though relations between buyers and sellers have traditionally been guided by the maxim "caveat emptor" (let the buyer beware) it is not the case, as some people assume, that the law has always uniformly upheld this doctrine (Hamilton 1931; Geis 1988; Scheppele 1988). Although consumer movements and other forces have recently been quite successful in challenging the caveat emptor doctrine (to the extent that it was part of law at all), sellers continue to be in a position to take advantage of consumers in a variety of ways.

### Retail Crime

The pervasiveness of deceptive business practices—often illegal, always unethical—has been documented by Paul Blumberg in *The Predatory Society* (1989). Over a

15-year period (1972–1987) Blumberg collected essays on the work experiences of over 700 City University of New York (CUNY) students. Among the 638 respondents whose essays were analyzed, 71 percent reported that the business they worked for engaged in some form of deception. Although some of these deceptions were rather minor and commonplace (e.g., misleading advertisements), about 25 percent involved serious deceptions, such as misrepresenting an inferior product as a more expensive one. For example, some gas stations inflate the octane rating for lower-octane gas they sell, cheating U.S. drivers out of millions of dollars nationwide, and nonkosher food is sometimes labeled as kosher and sold at higher prices.

Blumberg identified other deceptive practices. Adulteration of products (e.g., tap water sold as spring water) is an ancient and still a common practice. "Short-weighting" (e.g., providing less meat than the customer pays for) is not only common, but apparently the norm. Other forms of retail deception include "bait and switch" tactics, in which consumers are lured by sale prices for items that are not available and then are sold higher-priced items; bar-code prices that do not reflect advertised sales prices; and the collection of "taxes" for nontaxable items.

Some deceptive practices are especially disturbing because they not only cost consumers money, but impinge directly on their physical well-being. Many of Blumberg's students found themselves in work situations in which a variety of techniques and practices had been developed to conceal food spoilage (e.g., soaking meat in salt and vinegar and using "cosmetic surgery" to conceal mold). Unhygienic food-handling practices were also widely reported, and restaurant owners often paid off health inspectors to avoid fines or closures.

If the responses of Blumberg's students can be taken as representative, they would strongly suggest that at least some level of deception is the norm for small business and entrepreneurial practices. Of course, it may be the case that students selectively recounted memorable work experiences that involved deception and disregarded other jobs in which no deception was involved. There is also reason to believe that conditions in a very large city such as New York may be more conducive to deceptive retail practices than are certain other retail settings. Regardless, Blumberg's study suggests the pervasiveness of deception among small businesses.

## Defrauding Vulnerable People

An especially disturbing form of consumer fraud victimizes the most vulnerable people. In a landmark study conducted in New York City in the early 1960s, David Caplowitz established that *The Poor Pay More* (1967). The poor were overcharged (especially on days that welfare checks were received), were sold inferior or shoddy goods, and were victimized by deceptive credit practices, complicated consumer contracts, and lawsuits threatening wage garnishment. Despite new laws and consumer affairs initiatives, these fraudulent practices (always unethical, sometimes criminal) are hardly extinct. A 1991 Department of Consumer Affairs report in New York City found that shoppers in poor areas of the city were paying almost 9 percent more for food than shoppers in middle-class neighborhoods; a poor family of four spent some $350 a year more than an equivalent middle-class family for the same groceries

(Landa 1991). Retail merchants are undeniably victims of many crimes in poor neighborhoods, including looting during riots, but the daily exploitation of poor consumers in such neighborhoods generally receives less attention.

The recently bereaved and the seriously afflicted or dependent elderly are also among the most vulnerable of consumers. In her best-selling *The American Way of Death*, originally published in 1963, Jessica Mitford shocked the American public by exposing the unscrupulous practices of the funeral industry. Although many of these practices, which often involved subtly persuading bereaved survivors to contract for much more elaborate funeral and burial arrangements than they could afford, were not necessarily illegal, they were highly unethical. Some 10 years later Mary Adelaide Mendelson's *Tender Loving Greed* (1974) exposed scandalous practices in the nursing home industry. Mendelson's investigation uncovered many blatantly illegal practices whereby nursing home operators maximized their revenue (much of it coming from Medicaid and Medicare programs) while minimizing costs by inadequately feeding, clothing, and sheltering nursing home residents. In addition to these fraudulent practices, forgery, embezzlement, and bribery were found to be quite widespread in this industry.

## Service Business Fraud

Repair service businesses have an especially notorious reputation for cheating customers outright, and they are often well-positioned to do so. In an oft-cited study conducted in 1941 under the sponsorship of the *Reader's Digest*, a car in perfect mechanical condition (except for a detached coil wire) was taken to 347 different auto repair shops across the country; some 63 percent of the shops overcharged, inventing unnecessary work and lying about the mechanical condition of the car. A 1987 replication of this study found that most shops overcharged from $2 to $500 (Blumberg 1989: 64). Another study, conducted in 1976, found that only 42 percent of the auto repair shops visited performed the repair at a fair market price (McCaghy and Cernkovich 1987: 380). Such auto repair frauds are hardly restricted to small, independent service stations. In 1992 the California Department of Consumer Affairs charged the chain of Sears Roebuck auto repair centers with systematically defrauding customers by performing unnecessary service and repairs (Fisher 1992). Consumer Affairs investigators made 38 visits to 27 Sears auto repair centers, and on 34 of these visits unnecessary services or repairs were recommended. Sears employees were under pressure from their supervisors to sell a certain amount of such services and repairs during each working day.

A parallel problem exists in the auto body repair business. A study cited in Chapter 2 established that auto body repair estimates were significantly influenced by the car owner's insurance coverage status rather than simply by the actual cost of the repair (Tracy and Fox 1989).

In fairness to the auto repair business, however, it should be noted that not all studies have confirmed high rates of dishonesty. Jesilow (1982b) found that only 10 percent of over 300 auto repair shops he visited claimed that a battery that simply needed recharging had to be replaced, and a 1992 New York State Department of Motor Vehicles investigation of Goodyear and Sears repair shops found abuses in only a few of them (Fisher 1992a). But in the late 1980s U.S. consumers were spending some $65 billion annually on auto repairs, of which an estimated $21 billion involved fraudulent or unnecessary work (Blumberg 1989: 66).

Service fraud problems are hardly restricted to auto repairs. High rates of unnecessary repairs (up to 70 percent) have been found in investigations of television, typewriter, and watch-repair shops (Anonymous 1971; Blumberg 1989). Consumer affairs investigations and insider accounts alike suggest that in at least some of these businesses, making unnecessary repairs or overcharging is the norm, not the exception.

## Small Business Crime, In Sum

By any measure, then, U.S. consumers expend billions of dollars annually as a consequence of retail and service-related frauds. Of course, a great many small businesses are honest. The extent to which small businesses engage in fraudulent conduct is not simply a function of the integrity of the owner, but also depends on the owner's self-perception (as a professional or businessperson), the nature of the community within which the business operates, the importance of a "good reputation," and the type of product or service. Richard Quinney (1963), for example, found that pharmacists who regarded themselves primarily as businesspeople were more likely to commit prescription violations than were pharmacists whose primary self-identification was as professionals. Furthermore, it is obviously easier to cheat people on prescription drugs than on vegetables. A 1993 survey in New York City found vast differences among pharmacies on prescription prices; for example, a heart medication sold for $5.37 in one pharmacy and for $39.95 in another (Steier 1993).

Although sober, rational, and well-informed consumers can be a considerable deterrent to deceptive practices, at least one study found that such attributes hardly guarantee that consumers will be able to respond effectively to attempts to defraud them (McGuire and Edelhertz 1980). Many consumers are unaware that they have been victimized, and even when they have such an awareness they are quite justifiably skeptical that reporting the abuse will lead to effective action. All consumers, regardless of how vigilant they are, will periodically be "robbed" by unscrupulous retailers and entrepreneurs.

## Crimes by Professionals: Medical, Legal, Academic, and Religious Crime

THE PROFESSIONS GENERALLY enjoy great prestige in our society. Doctors, lawyers and scientists, for example, are typically looked up to in their communities. Use of the term *profession* in several different ways has created some semantic confusion (Freidson, 1986: 21).

In the broader sense, *profession* is virtually a synonym for a full-time occupation, as in "professional waitress," "professional wrestler," and "professional criminal." In the narrower sense, which is adopted here, the term *profession* refers to occupations characterized by higher (graduate-level) education and training; specialized technical knowledge and skills; a high degree of autonomy; monopolistic, or near-monopolistic control over services offered to clients and patients; substantial authority over clients and subordinates; legal responsibilities and professional codes of ethics; licensure and accreditation requirements; a fundamental claim to the attributes of a "calling," with altruistic and public service goals; a professional subculture with its own language and generalized value system; and professional associations that promote the interests of the profession and are charged with policing it (Miller 1981; Freidson 1986; Hodson and Sullivan 1990). The classic "liberal professions" were medicine, law, and the ministry, and college professors and scientists are widely regarded as members of this professional elite.

Many other occupational groups, including accountants, engineers, pharmacists, nurses, social workers, and at least some categories of administrators and managers, claim professional status; they also share some important attributes and enjoy at least some of the privileges of the traditional professions (Freidson 1986: 49, 59). Indeed, the relatively high level of prestige, autonomy, trust, and income enjoyed by those accorded the status of professional has led an even wider range of occupations to pursue "professionalization" in the hopes of sharing in these advantages.

On another plane, many who claim professional status (e.g., accountants, engineers, and architects) actually have little real autonomy but must instead respond to the demands of powerful clients upon whom they are financially dependent (Freidson 1986: 218). Indeed, many physicians, lawyers, and scientists are increasingly constrained in their decision making by the fact that they work for large corporations or are funded by powerful governmental and private agencies (Derber, Schwartz, and Magrass 1990). The truly autonomous solo practioner is rather a rarity today.

In our discussion here our principal focus is on the so-called liberal professions, historically the most prestigious. Despite widely publicized criticisms, expressions of distrust, complaints about arrogance, and challenges from consumer groups and other occupations, the evidence suggests that these professions continue to enjoy relatively high degrees of public confidence and prestige (Freidson 1986: 112; Jennings, Callahan, and Wolf 1987: 5). At the same time, the conventional claims of these professions—that they have a "calling" to use their specialized, objective knowledge on behalf of the long-term public interest and common good—have been challenged in fundamental ways. In this context, "public interest" refers to the provision of services to needy individuals and the provision of expertise to policy makers; "common good" refers to the promotion of values and priorities that benefit society as a whole (Jennings, Callahan, and Wolf 1987).

Despite this rhetoric, the professions have often placed self-interest over either public interest or common good considerations. The paternalism of doctors, lawyers, and professors has been challenged by patients, clients, and students, who, especially since the late 1960s, have sometimes demanded greater control over decisions supposedly made on their behalf (Betz and O'Connell 1983; Thompson 1987: 161–69).

A sociopolitical view of the professions regards them as a new class (a "mandarin order") that attempts to exercise domination, and such a view specifically challenges professionals' claims that they have knowledge that entitles them to the power they demand (Derber, Schwartz, and Magrass 1990; Rossides 1990). In this view, the professions seek to profit from a market-based society without being subject to market forces; far from being disinterested appliers of specialized knowledge to social problems, professionals are seen as self-interested entities who promote perceptions of problems that create an artificial demand for their services. This view emphasizes the irresponsibility, incompetence, and outright fraud of the professions.

On balance, members of the medical, legal, academic, and clerical professions have enjoyed a privileged status. The specialized knowledge that is so central to the definition of "profession" puts professionals in a different position from that of entrepreneurs, retailers, and salespeople. As patients, clients, and students, people typically defer to the judgments of professionals much more readily than they do as consumers or customers because they perceive that they have less reason to be confident in their own judgment. The "grey area" encompassed by the notion of "professional opinion" is especially broad and ambiguous; professionals can be guilty of providing either too little of their service or too much. The interests of their patients, clients, or students are all too often at odds with their self-interest. The gap between the sometimes sanctimonious claims about "a calling" and disinterested service to public welfare renders the unethical, fraudulent, and illegal practices of some proportion of the liberal professions especially disturbing. Coleman (1989: 112) has called the crimes of professionals "the least researched and least understood of all white collar crimes." We examine some of what is known about this form of crime next.

## Medical Crime

In the 20th century the medical profession has generally enjoyed great prestige in the United States; indeed, it has sometimes been identified as the most prestigious conventional occupation. Physicians enjoy an image of ultrarespectability and professional self-assurance (Rothman 1978: 71). Physicians are not only well-compensated; they are typically accorded a high level of trust and exercise unusual power or "professional dominance" over patients (Freidson 1970).

Not everyone agrees that such trust is warranted. One professor of medicine who was harshly critical of his own profession suggested that doctors should be no more trusted than used-car salesmen (Mendelsohn 1979). On the one hand, physicians are expected to use their power to benefit their patients, and perhaps the larger community as well; on the other hand, physicians in a capitalist society are seen as profit-seeking entrepreneurs. This is part of the "structural contradiction" in the physician's role (Jesilow, Pontell, and Geis 1992). Even so, the popular images of "physician" and "criminal" would appear to be polar opposites. Even though E.H. Sutherland (1949: 12) noted a number of illegal acts committed by the medical profession, he stated that it was "probably less criminal than other professions." Still, much evidence suggests that many physicians engage in activities that are (or ought to be) defined as criminal.

The recognition that physicians should be held accountable for any grievous harm they cause to their patients extends back to ancient times, and specific diatribes against physician fraud date from the 1600s (Jesilow, Pontell, and Geis 1985). Even though the medical profession has been given substantial powers to police itself, it has traditionally done a poor job of it, being far more concerned instead with promoting and protecting its own interests than with protecting the public from incompetent, unethical, and fraudulent physicians (Pontell, Jesilow, and Geis 1982; Harmer 1975). Historically, in fact, the American Medical Association has been quite indifferent to such medically harmful activities as cigarette smoking and dangerous environmental pollution, has actually opposed legislation that might produce less expensive prescription drugs, and has been extraordinarily timid in encouraging the reporting, investigation, and prosecution of physician crime (Harmer 1975; Geis, Pontell, and Jesilow 1988). The long-standing position of the medical profession is that medical crime is a minor problem.

Among the specifically illegal and unethical activities engaged in by physicians, psychiatrists, and dentists are fee-splitting or taking and offering kickbacks; price-fixing; conflicts of interest arising through ownership of clinics and pharmacies; co-optation by corporate employers; unnecessary operations, tests, and other medical services; conducting controversial and often harmful forms of experimental surgery without patients' consent; false and fraudulent billing (especially Medicaid and Medicare fraud and abuse); filling of illegal prescriptions; false testimony in court cases; the production of iatrogenic diseases (i.e., diseases inadvertently induced by medical intervention); fraudulent activity relating to medical license exams, diplomas, and scholarships; medical research fraud; tax evasion; and outright medical quackery. A selective review of some of the more significant forms of medical crime follows.

**Medical Crime as Violent Crime**   The performance of unnecessary operations is arguably the single most disturbing form of medical crime, insofar as it can be considered violent occupational crime. Most operations (perhaps 80 percent) are elective (not emergency) procedures. Recent studies suggest that up to 15 or 20 percent of the several million operations performed annually in the United States may be unnecessary, and the percentage of such unnecessary operations is actually increasing (Lanza-Kaduce 1980: 344; Jesilow, Pontell, and Geis 1985: 153; Leape 1989: 351). An estimated minimum of 10,000 patients die annually in the United States from unnecessary operations (Barron 1989: 45).

The most common forms of unnecessary surgery have involved removal of tonsils, hemorrhoids, appendixes, and uteruses; heart-related surgery (e.g., coronary bypasses, pacemaker implants); and caesarean section deliveries—all at an annual cost of billions of dollars and many lives (Harmer 1975; Mendelsohn 1979; Lanza-Kaduce 1980; Barron 1989; Grisanti 1989). In at least some cases, surgeons performing clearly unnecessary operations have caused paralysis, blindness, or other forms of permanent injury (Rapoport 1975; Jesilow, Pontell, and Geis 1985). Although admittedly it is not always easy to identify "unnecessary surgery," various studies indicate that the amount of surgery is more a function of an oversupply of surgeons, the availability of reimbursement for particular classes of surgical patients, and the type of hospital, than of the "objective" needs of a patient population (Lanza-Kaduce 1980; Nash 1987). For example, Americans are several times more likely to have certain kinds of surgery than are their British counterparts; Medicaid patients are twice as likely as the general population to have operations.

The traditional American fee-for-service reimbursement system and the absence of effective peer review procedures are among the "criminogenic conditions" promoting unnecessary surgery. In extreme cases, harmful (and nonconsensual) forms of psychosurgery (e.g., lobotomies), sterilizations of retarded women, and experimental surgery on women's sex organs have been performed out of an apparently sincere belief in the benefits of the surgery (Harmer 1975; Wachsman 1989). Surgeons may often be "true believers" in surgery, but the harm they can do is quite well established and rarely subject to formal legal action.

**Medical Crime as Fraud**  Medicaid and Medicare fraud by physicians has been characterized as an especially "pure" form of white collar crime because it occurs within the context of routine occupational activity, is not easily discovered, and can often be covered up and denied (Pontell, Jesilow, and Geis 1982: 117).

The losses from Medicaid and Medicare fraud are enormous. By the late 1980s it was estimated that between 10 and 25 percent of the money disbursed annually by these programs, up to $25 billion, was being lost to fraud, but no truly reliable way to measure the specific level of fraud currently exists (Jesilow, Pontell, and Geis 1987: 8; Geis, Pontell, and Jesilow 1988: 25; Jesilow, Pontell, and Geis 1992). Whatever the actual amount, Medicaid and Medicare fraud clearly drains off medical resources, deprives patients of needed care, and in some cases leads to direct injury of patients through unnecessary and harmful operations (Pontell et al.1985: 1029). In 1990, insurance companies estimated that private and government insurers paid $60 billion in 1989 for claims that were fraudulent or abusive; some 3 percent of the nation's physicians routinely committed outright fraud, with a much larger percentage engaging in improper, ambiguous billing (Rosenthal 1990).

"Overutilization," or billing for superfluous and unnecessary tests and other services, is perhaps the most common form of medical fraud, and it is especially difficult to prove and prosecute successfully (Jesilow, Pontell, and Geis 1987: 8). Some evidence suggests that many physicians do not regard Medicaid fraud as criminal behavior; rather, they see it as an understandable, even justifiable response to the perceived low payment schedule of Medicaid (and similar programs). Some of the specific techniques used in this type of fraud, especially by "Medicaid mills" in poor neighborhoods, include "ping-ponging" (referring patients to several different practioners when their symptoms do not warrant such referral), "family ganging" (extending several unnecessary services to all members of a patient's family), "steering" (directing patients to the clinic's pharmacy to fill unneeded prescriptions), and "upgrading" (billing for services more extensive than were actually performed)(Birenbaum 1977; Pontell, Jesilow, and Geis 1982).

A study of such Medicaid practices in the 1970s found that patients in New York City were being overtreated 70 percent of the time (Birenbaum 1977). More recently, physicians have become especially creative in the use of "code games"—that is, "unbundling" interrelated medical procedures—to run up overcharges estimated to total billions of dollars (Knight-Ridder Newspapers 1990b). By the early 1990s concern had intensified over the inherent conflict of interest in the many circumstances in which physicians were also owners of the laboratories, diagnostic imaging centers, and physical therapy clinics to which they referred their patients; in such cases the cost of services was often higher as a consequence (Pear and Eckholm 1991; Pear 1991b).

Altogether, then, very substantial economic losses result from this form of medical crime. For all kinds of reasons, enforcement efforts have been remarkably lax, and many practical or ideological problems have hindered successful investigation, prosecution, and punishment of Medicaid fraud (Jesilow, Pontell, and Geis 1992). Success in dealing with medical fraud may require a fundamental transformation of the health care system.

**Medical Crime, In Sum** There is much evidence of a broad range of illegal and unethical activities by physicians. In addition to the offenses discussed above, physicians have been accused of various other occupationally related crimes, ranging from narcotics addiction to sexual abuse of patients. Clearly a great many physicians are dedicated and honorable professionals. Still, physicians have abundant opportunities for various abuses because of the generally high level of trust patients extend to them, and they have also enjoyed a substantial degree of immunity from being called to account for these abuses.

## Legal Crime

Lawyers, too, may engage in criminal conduct in the course of discharging their professional duties. Lawyers are officers of the court, and as such are sworn to uphold the law; because they may be intimately associated with lawbreakers, they may confront unique opportunities and pressures to break laws.

The legal profession has attempted to project an altruistic image, and lawyers tend to claim that the ethical standards of their profession are high; their critics, in contrast, have long claimed that the nature of legal education and the conditions of legal practice promote an attenuation of conscience and much unscrupulous, unethical, and illegal activity (Bloom 1970; Jack and Jack 1992; Reasons, Bray, and Chappell 1989; Stern 1980). If lawyers have often been the champions of the innocent, the injured, and the oppressed, they have also been accused of promoting harmful litigation out of self-interest, of taking too large a share of settlements in class-action suits, or of consuming a disproportionate percentage of federal funds intended for environmental cleanup (Eichenwald 1993c; Olson 1991; Van Voorst 1993). The general public is sometimes skeptical of the motives and trustworthiness of lawyers, and public awareness of unethical conduct by lawyers appears to be increasing.

People have long had a relatively high level of hostility toward lawyers and suspicion of their motives, despite the general prestige of the legal profession. This hostility toward lawyers can be attributed to the fact that they may represent highly unpopular clients, may carry out unpopular governmental edicts, and are associated with the highly disagreeable business of litigation. Furthermore, the general public sometimes has difficulty discriminating between the vigorous representation inherent to the legal system's adversarial nature on the one hand, and direct involvement with or personal approval of the criminal conduct of clients on the other.

In some cases lawyers have clearly crossed the line between representation of those charged with illegal acts and participation in illegal activity (Taylor 1985). But even though purely crooked lawyers dedicated to illegal enterprises certainly exist, they are not the norm. It is far more common for lawyers to become involved with, facilitate, or help cover up illegal enterprises while maintaining their primary commitment to the conventional and legitimate tasks of a lawyer.

**Legal Crime as Fraud**   Lawyers may victimize their clients in a variety of ways. Lawyers have periodically been accused of stealing money—sometimes very substantial amounts of it—from clients or colleagues (Bloom 1970). The "power of attorney" granted to lawyers, their control over escrow accounts, and their frequently intimate knowledge of and access to clients' finances provides them with a host of opportunities to commit this type of theft. The crimes can be sensational: A New York lawyer was sentenced to prison in 1990 after admitting to taking $1.8 million from escrow and other accounts of clients (Hagedorn and Barrett 1990); a Manhattan lawyer fled the country in 1991 in the face of accusations that he had stolen $25 million from clients (Margolick 1991); a top Manhattan divorce lawyer pleaded guilty in 1992 to five felony counts of grand larceny for defrauding clients and associates of millions of dollars (Margolick 1992); another very prominent New York lawyer was accused in 1992 of swindling clients and partners out of $3.5 million (Behar 1992).

The very "intangibility" of a lawyer's work provides special opportunities for misbilling clients (especially those with means), and at least some of this activity crosses the line into criminality. John Grisham's popular novel *The Firm* (1991) features overbilling among other crimes committed by members of a rich and powerful Memphis law firm. In 1994, a close associate of President Clinton's, Webster Hubbell, resigned as associate U.S. attorney general and subsequently admitted that he stole some $394,000 from his law partners and various clients by filing false expense vouchers and by overbilling; he pleaded guilty to two counts of mail fraud and tax evasion (Labaton 1994). It has generally proven difficult to establish criminal intent in such overbilling cases.

Fewer opportunities exist for embezzlement or overbilling of indigent clients, but in such cases misrepresentation may ultimately prove more harmful to the client. In a well-known and provocative critique, Abraham Blumberg (1967) contended that criminal defense lawyers often "con" indigent clients into pleading guilty, rather than exercising their constitutional right to trial, because such a plea both better serves the lawyer's own economic interests and reflects the lawyer's primary commitment to courthouse associates (e.g., prosecutors and judges) rather than to clients.

The potential for lawyers to become involved in unethical or criminal conduct is apparent in the career of Roy Cohn (1927–1986), surely one of the best-known lawyers in recent American history. Cohn became famous in the early 1950s, only a few years after his graduation from Columbia Law School, when he became chief counsel for Senator Joseph McCarthy during the McCarthy-Army hearings, which examined McCarthy's largely discredited claims of communist infiltration of the

U.S. government. Cohn went on to a lucrative, high-profile career as a lawyer in New York City, during which he represented many wealthy and famous people. But by the time of his death in 1986, Cohn had been disbarred from legal practice on the grounds that he had failed to repay a $100,000 loan from a client, had lied on his bar application, and had engaged in fraudulent activity in connection with the will of a wealthy liquor manufacturer (Gottlieb 1986; Von Hoffman 1988). Claims emerged, as well, that Cohn had bribed judges, had submitted false affidavits, had failed to pay numerous debts, and had been involved in a series of illegal business schemes. One of the most "successful" lawyers of our time, then, was a crook, a deadbeat, and a hypocrite.

**Legal Crime as Collusion** Lawyers may also engage in activities that specifically aid and abet the crimes of their clients. The ethics code of the American Bar Association both requires lawyers to keep in strict confidence any knowledge of a client's past crimes and prohibits lawyers from advising or assisting a client in the commission of any illegal or fraudulent act (Taylor 1983). The line between maintaining lawyer/client confidentiality and becoming party to illegal activity can be extremely thin. In a case that emerged in the early 1980s, a prominent New York City law firm, Singer Hutner Levine & Seeman, was accused of complicity in a scheme by a client, O.P.M. Leasing Services, Inc., to defraud banks and other lenders of some $210 million (Taylor 1983). It was ultimately revealed that even after it learned of its client's fraudulent lease closings, the law firm had continued to represent O.P.M. Leasing in fraudulent dealings, resulting in further losses of some $15 million.

A number of major insider trading cases of the 1980s involved criminal charges against lawyers who had passed on privileged information about pending corporate takeovers (Frantz 1987; Stewart 1991). Additionally, several leading law firms implicated in some of the massive savings and loan frauds during the same decade paid fines of over $40 million apiece to settle the government's accusations that they had acted improperly in representing fraudulent savings and loan institutions (Cushman 1993; Hughes 1993; Labaton 1992). It is difficult to imagine that billions of dollars could have been stolen from the S & Ls without the connivance (or negligence) of lawyers and other professionals.

**Lawyers and the Abuse of Political Power** In recent American history there has been no more dramatic illustration of "legal crime"—of lawyers involved in illegal activities—than the Watergate Affair. The break-in at the offices of the Democratic Party in the Watergate complex—as well as a range of other illegal acts carried out by the Committee to Re-Elect the President (CREEP), who was Richard Nixon, and by high-level White House officials—involved lawyers on all levels and at each stage of the enterprise.

President Nixon, who resigned in the face of virtually certain impeachment for alleged obstruction of justice following the arrest of the Watergate burglars, was himself a lawyer. His former attorney general, John Mitchell, and a former assistant district attorney, G. Gordon Liddy, went to prison for their roles in approving or engineering the break-in. Nixon's chief assistant for domestic affairs, John Erlichman;

his counsel to the president, John W. Dean III; his special counsel, Charles Colson; and his personal attorney, Herbert Kalmbach, were among the lawyers convicted of various criminal activities, including perjury, conspiracy, obstruction of justice, and illegal fund-raising (Bernstein and Woodward 1975; Woodward and Bernstein 1977). Earlier, Nixon's vice president, Spiro Agnew—also a lawyer—had been forced to resign and plead nolo contendere to a tax evasion charge in connection with accepting payoffs from Maryland contractors (Cohen and Witcover 1974). As one commentator has observed:

> *Watergate marked the final demolition of credence in legal authority. It revealed that law and order was a mask for illicit repression; that those sworn to uphold the law had conspired to subvert it; that lawyers, including the chief law enforcement officers of the nation, were deeply implicated in lawlessness; that double standards of professional conduct protected the wealthy and powerful while destroying the promise and possibility of equal justice under law. (Auerbach 1976: 264)*

Edwin Meese III, a close political associate of President Ronald Reagan and attorney general during his second term of office, was accused of improprieties in connection with both the investigation of the Iran/Contra arms case and the Wedtech fraudulent defense contract case (Martz 1987; Magnuson 1988a). Under formidable public pressure, Meese ultimately resigned as attorney general.

In 1994 a newly initiated investigation of the Whitewater dealings (involving an Arkansas real estate development) produced allegations of improper or illegal acts, conflicts of interest, and misjudgments by highly placed lawyers, including President Clinton, Hillary Rodham Clinton, and lawyers on the White House staff (Church 1994). Even though the Whitewater matter focused on a land deal completed long before Clinton was elected president and clearly did not involve the gross abuses of political power associated with Watergate, the involvement of such prominent lawyers in questionable (and possibly illegal) conduct is disturbing nevertheless.

**Legal Crime, In Sum**  It is important to examine the criminal activities of highly placed lawyers because such activities are likely to have especially damaging consequences. Lawyers operating in the political arena have substantial power and influence, which sometimes at least are applied corruptly (Green 1975). The highly paid, typically very bright lawyers who help corporations hide their immensely harmful activities and sucessfully defend them when they are criminally charged may be responsible for harm on a very large scale.

Of course, ordinary lawyers also engage in illegal conduct in the course of their work. Empirical studies of violations of ethical standards by lawyers have indicated that disbarred lawyers are most likely to be "marginal," solo practitioners (Carlin 1966; Parker 1982; Reasons and Chappell 1987). According to one study, the offense for which such lawyers are most likely to be punished is misappropriation of client's funds and related activities (Reasons and Chappell 1987: 39). As we previously noted, however, such activity is not restricted to marginal members of the profession, although they may be more vulnerable to exposure and punishment. Lawyers on all levels are especially well-positioned—and perhaps especially tempted—to commit a range of illegalities, from bribery to perjury to conspiracy to theft.

## Academic Crime: Professors and Scientists—and Students

The "ivory tower" of academe is often considered to be removed from the "real world" and is rarely thought of as a significant locus of crime. Professors and research scientists tend to be regarded as rather benign and harmless creatures. Thus two recent cases—one in which a prominent Tufts University biochemist, Dr. William Douglas, was convicted of murdering a prostitute whom he had paid with grant funds, and another case in which the head of New York University's Anthropology Department, Dr. John Buettner-Janusch, was convicted of using university laboratories to manufacture and sell illegal drugs—received a lot of attention precisely because they were so unusual (Carpenter 1989; McFadden 1987). Further, any academic writing about the crimes committed by members of other professions would seem to have a special obligation to consider the crimes of professional academics.

That all the ordinary indicators suggest that professors engage in less occupationally related crime than do doctors and lawyers is probably more a function of fewer opportunities for such activity than a matter of greater personal integrity among professors. The principal types of academic crimes of professors and research scientists include plagiarism; misuse of or embezzlement of university discretionary funds or research grants; forgery, or fraudulent claims about credentials; unresolved conflicts of interest in connection with grants, peer reviews, or evaluations of students; pilfering and unauthorized photocopying; gross negligence in the fulfillment of teaching responsibilities (e.g., failure to teach the course for which students enrolled); exposing students or research subjects to unsafe or harmful conditions or procedures; and fabrication of scholarship, or the use of fraudulent data in research studies (Heeren and Shichor 1993; McCarthy, Ladimer, and Sirefman 1989). Some of this activity is "exogenous" (or pertinent to occupational opportunities) and some is "endogenous" (or a violation of professional norms)(Douglas 1992; Heeren and Shichor 1993). The distinction is clarified by Douglas (1992: 77): "A great scientist who happens to steal money, while continuing to be meticulously honest in his scientific work, is a thief, not a scientific fraud." Of course the converse of this example is also possible.

Many unethical and sometimes blatantly illegal acts have occurred in conjunction with highly competitive, high-stakes intercollegiate athletic programs, but because such activities usually involve athletic directors, coaches, college administrators, and alumni rather than professors, it will not be considered here. Many improper activities of professors, including verbally abusing students, providing them with illicit drugs, and sexually harassing them, are covered up by publicity-shy college administrators or are handled internally. Referral to an outside agency, as when criminal prosecution is warranted, is rare. Sexual harassment of colleagues and students by professors (predominantly males) has received much recognition and attention in recent years (see, for example, Dzeich and Weiner 1984); even though such harassment is a form of occupational crime as defined by Green (1990), it falls outside the scope of what is ordinarily defined as white collar crime.

Plagiarism—the use or misappropriation of the ideas or words of others without giving them credit—may well be the "purest" form of academic white collar crime, insofar as ideas and knowledge are the principal currency of the academic world. Allegations of plagiarism surface periodically, although formal charges are relatively rare (Mallon 1989; Mooney 1992). On the other hand, embezzlement, a more conventional form of white collar crime, is hardly unknown in the academic environment. The newspaper *The Chronicle of Higher Education* periodically reports on cases of professors (or college administrators) charged with misappropriation of college funds and on similar offenses, although other university officials (including college presidents) seem to be involved more often than professors (Nicklin 1991; Nicklin 1993). Such administrators and employees often have better opportunities than professors to embezzle or obtain illegal payments.

**Academic Crime as Fraud**   Fraud by research scientists (who may or may not also be professors) has come to light relatively recently (Davis 1989; LaFollette 1992). Science, which has as its principal raison d'être the search for truth, is typically thought of as self-policing, and fraud has traditionally been considered quite neglible.

Indeed, the scientific establishment has tended to deny that scientific fraud is a significant problem (Dong 1991). It has proven difficult to develop reliable data on the extent of scientific fraud, which principally takes the form of fabricating, manipulating, and suppressing data (Zuckerman 1977: 98; Davis 1989: 23; LaFollette 1992: 196). The first detailed national study (in 1993) on fraud and other forms of misconduct in science revealed that such activities are not especially rare; some 6–9 percent of faculty and students in various disciplines reporting direct knowledge of plagiarism or falsified data (Hilts 1993b). New technologies of information transmission have facilitated scientific plagiarism and fraud, and in an era in which more and more scientists are scrambling for fewer research dollars, the pressures that contribute to data manipulation have intensified (Bell 1992; LaFollette 1992). Among the most celebrated cases of scientific fraud are the Cyril Burt case (falsified data on twins were used to demonstrate the inheritability of intelligence); the William Summerlin case (inked patches were drawn on laboratory mice to falsely convey the impression of successful skin grafts between genetically different animals); the John Darsee case (data on drugs administered to dogs were falsified to indicate a reduction in the risk of heart attacks); the Stephen Breuning case (psychopharmacological data pertinent to controlling the behavior of mentally retarded children were falsified); and the Thereza Imanishi-Kari/David Baltimore case (data on gene transplants and the immune system were allegedly faked in a paper in which a Nobel laureate was listed as co-author)(Zuckerman 1977; Sykes 1988; Davis 1989; Sarasohn 1993).

Some of these cases have been hotly contested. In the case of Cyril Burt, for example, Joynson (1994) and others have argued that the case against him was either flimsy or false. Only one of these scientists, Stephen Breuning, was sentenced to a jail term, apparently the first such sentence for falsifying data (Davis 1989: 27). Because his research involved a federal grant, federal fraud charges were involved. Vulnerable retarded children were actually treated on the basis of Breuning's falsified findings, an especially disturbing aspect of that case. Similarly disturbing is a 1994 case in which a Canadian researcher was accused of falsifying data in a study of breast cancer; the results had influenced treatment strategies for women with cancer (Altman 1994). Such cases justify the classification of scientific fraud as a potentially violent form of white collar crime.

**Student White Collar Crime**  Finally, what of student white collar crime? First, it is important to realize that even though many students may also hold part-time (or even full-time) jobs, such jobs are typically held to make school financially possible; thus a student's primary occupation (principal pursuit) is being a student. Students, of course, commit various illegal acts, including vandalism, drunkenness, illicit drug use and transactions, car theft, petty larceny, assault, and rape. Many of these acts occur on campus, and students may have especially numerous opportunities to engage in acts such as "date rape." Much of this behavior, especially if it occurs on college campuses, has been treated as the "sowing of wild oats" or hushed up by college officials concerned about negative publicity (White 1993). This may be especially true if the students are from higher social classes, are attending an elite school, or are star athletes. Stuart Hills (1982: 258) has speculated that college students' experiences of lawbreaking, which often involve peer-supported rationalizations and lenient reactions from college officials, may facilitate adult white collar crime.

The clearest example of student white collar crime—that is, illegal or harmful conduct committed specifically in an occupational context (in this case, being a student), for gain or advantage—is cheating. Academic cheating is clearly commonplace in primary and secondary schools. A study of elite prep schools, which produce a disproportionate percentage of the nation's business elite, specifically identifies such activities as buying homework and obtaining a copy of an upcoming examination as forms of white collar crime (Cookson and Persell 1985: 161). Depending on the perceived seriousness of the activity, punishment ranges from restriction of privileges to expulsion.

Various studies have indicated that cheating is epidemic on college campuses (LaBeff et al., 1990; Collison 1990; Michaels and Miethe 1989). The frequency of academic cheating is variable; the proportion of students who admit to cheating ranges from 13 percent to 95 percent (Michaels and Miethe 1989: 871). A number of studies suggest that at least 50 percent of college students engage in some academic cheating; a national survey of 6,000 students placed the figure at 67 percent (LaBeff et al. 1990; McCabe 1992). In a study conducted at Rutgers University in 1989–1990 one-third of the students admitted to "hard-core cheating," 45 percent had cheated in one or two courses, and "only about 20 percent said they had never cheated at college" (Collison 1990).

Students have considerable ambivalence about academic cheating; some students brag about it, and others discreetly conceal it from disapproving peers (Labeff et al. 1990: 190; Moffatt 1989: 297). Academic cheating takes different forms, of course, including cheating on exams, homework, and term papers. Students who engage in one such form of cheating do not necessarily engage in all forms of cheating (Michaels and Miethe 1989).

Much academic cheating appears to be a response to situational pressures (e.g., not enough time to write one's own paper) and fortuitous circumstances (e.g., finding oneself in a position to see the answers on another student's exam). Some academic cheating may be virtually inevitable because "grades often mattered more to the students than the substance taught in courses, at least in some of the courses" (Moffatt 1989: 297). For college students, passing grades are essential, and good grades are obviously advantageous in many respects. The opportunities for cheating are often very good, and the likelihood of getting caught or suffering any significant penalty is typically very slim. One study found, perhaps not surprisingly, that academic cheating in college is correlated with parental pressure to raise grades, poor study habits, opportunity to cheat without detection, and the condoning of cheating by significant others (Michaels and Miethe 1989).

Many students who recognize that academic cheating is dishonest are able to either "neutralize" any guilt about it or rationalize it as being dictated by circumstances; as being necessary to assist friends; as being the fault of professors, parents, and the system itself; or as being rather harmless in any case (LaBeff et al. 1990; McCabe 1992). Some students, according to one study, believe that cheating is a prevalent practice in American society generally (Collison 1990: A32). Despite students' ambivalence about and the formal condemnations of academic cheating, much evidence suggests that it has been virtually institutionalized in student life and may be contextually normative (i.e., acceptable or at least condoned)(Michaels and Miethe 1989: 881).

Obviously, academic cheating does discernible injury by distorting and downgrading the achievement of honest students, and possibly by depriving them of grants, awards, and positions they might otherwise receive. The experience of academic cheating may also contribute to the making of adult white collar criminals. Endorsing Hills's thesis, Michaels and Miethe (1989: 880) observed that "cheating to receive institutional rewards also may generalize to other organizational settings after graduation, with cheaters subsequently relying on similar adaptations in carrying out their responsibilities in business, industry, and government." A Rutgers University study found, interestingly enough, that students majoring in economics were more likely to cheat than students in other majors (Collison 1990: A32).

**Student White Collar Crime, In Sum**   Cheating is not the only form of student white collar crime. College students (not infrequently in collusion with their parents) may engage in ethically questionable, even overtly fraudulent, activity to obtain financial aid, and defaults on government-backed student loans exceed 20 percent (Ostling 1992). Because college students are especially likely to be proficient in the use of computers, they are likely to be well-represented in software piracy (P. H. Lewis 1994). Abuses (if not outright embezzlements) of student-government funds by student-government officers are not unknown (J. Gonzalez 1991). Student white collar crime, then, is a significant problem in its own right, and arguably an important breeding ground for adult white collar criminality.

## Religious Crime

For some, the notion of "religious crime" may be the most disturbing of all forms of crimes by professionals. In the eyes of the faithful, religious leaders are primary sources of moral guidance and inspiration. They typically take sacred vows to uphold religious doctrine that uniformly denounces theft, violence, and exploitation. The sacred, as Durkheim (1912) emphasized long ago, occupies a special realm in human affairs, quite removed from profane, conventional objects, activities and rituals. By invoking the name of God or Jesus, religious leaders may generate a bottomless well of trust among gullible believers. Accordingly, those who commit crimes from behind the shield of a religiously ordained status violate a special, sacred form of trust. Religious crime, or clergy fraud (Green 1990: 211), has a long history, and no single faith has a corner on the market.

Ministers, priests, rabbis, and other religious leaders or clergy may commit crimes such as sexual molestation of children partly because of the special opportunities provided by their occupation; they may also commit other illegal and harmful acts that do not directly lead to financial gain. Cases of beating of children, raping of women, and even murder of followers have occurred among more marginal religious groups, or cults. Reverend Jim Jones directed the mass "suicide"—some would say homicide—of some 400 of his followers in Jonestown, Guyana in the 1970s, and David Koresh created conditions that contributed to the fiery death of many of his followers in Waco, Texas, in 1993 (Chidester 1988; Wood 1993). But even if such activities could be classified as a form of occupational crime, they lie outside the boundaries of white collar crime as defined here: as crimes carried out in the context of a legitimate, respectable occupation and involving the violation of trust for financial gain.

Some members of the ministry—of whatever faith—may take on the attributes of professionals, whereas others may lack those attributes. Some of the most financially successful ministers are also the least educated, and their ministries are more a function of personal charisma than of specialized knowledge or skills. Some of these ministers appear to have more in common with entrepreneurs than with professionals in the conventional sense, and even less in common with traditional spiritual leaders.

The widely publicized case of Jim Bakker exemplifies the phenomenon of the minister-as-religious-criminal, although in several respects it was a somewhat extreme case (Shepard 1989; Tidwell 1993). Bakker came from a humble Midwest background; his modest education ended when he dropped out of Bible school. Quite early in his career as an evangelist he became involved with a television ministry. His mastery of this form of ministry occurred at a time when opportunities to reach the faithful through televangelism expanded dramatically (assisted, in part, by the deregulation of the Reagan era).

By 1987 Bakker and his PTL ministry "claimed six hundred thousand supporters and reported revenues of more than $120 million in a year" (Shepard 1989: xiii). PTL's relentless televised appeals for donations claimed that the money would be used to support missionaries and various other church-related causes, and Bakker and his wife Tammy claimed that they gave everything they had to the ministry. In fact, however, the Bakkers were drawing large, six-figure salaries and extravagant bonuses, and the ministry was providing them with fancy cars, two expensive homes, a vacation home, a houseboat, luxurious trips abroad, and even $25,000 worth of plastic surgery (Shepard 1989; Tidwell 1993). The $8,500 cost of a 20th-anniversary party was charged to PTL, as was a $11,400 chartered jet flight to California (Shepard 1989: 185). The Bakkers collected close to $5 million in salary and bonuses between 1985 and 1987 (Schmidt 1989).

Jim Bakker's precipitous fall from grace began in earnest when the *Charlotte Observer,* a newspaper in the home city of Bakker's PTL ministry, revealed that $265,000 had been raised by an associate to buy the silence of a young woman, Jessica Hahn, who alleged that Bakker (and an associate) had seduced and exploited her some years earlier. In 1989, Bakker and an associate, Richard Dortch, were indicted by a federal grand jury for concealing this payoff—and the true financial condition of PTL—from the ministry's board of directors (Shepard 1989: 552).

More seriously still, they were indicted for mail fraud, wire fraud, and conspiring to defraud the public through the sale of "life partnerships." Viewers of the "Jim and Tammy Show" had been induced to donate $1,000 or more apiece—ultimately totaling some $150 million—with assurances that they would be entitled to annual visits to a Christian resort and amusement park, Heritage USA, which Bakker was constructing in South Carolina. A federal investigation had revealed that tens of thousands more partnerships were sold than could possibly be accommodated by the available facilities (Shepard 1989: 552). The whole televised operation had engaged in fundamental violations of FCC codes, and the Bakkers as well as the PTL ministry were also charged by the IRS with serious tax code illegalities.

In October 1989, Jim Bakker was convicted of all 24 fraud and conspiracy charges filed against him and was sentenced to 45 years in prison and a $500,000 fine (Applebome 1989). Several associates of Bakker's also received long prison sentences on various counts of conspiracy, fraud, and tax evasion. Even though reporter Charles E. Shepard (1989), who broke the Jessica Hahn story and wrote the most extensive account of the rise and fall of Jim Bakker, alleged that Bakker was afflicted with a narcissistic personality disorder, it is also clear that the relatively new form of televangelism produced huge opportunities for self-professed spiritual leaders to defraud the faithful.

Many other religious leaders—or those claiming such a status—have defrauded believers and used offerings or donations for corrupt purposes. Some allegedly religious enterprises—for example, Scientology—have been accused of being organized principally to defraud large numbers of people out of millions of dollars by a combination of seductive appeals, illusory treatment programs, and intimidation (Behar 1991). With all due respect for the predominantly good work that clergy of all faiths have done, it is also the case that especially reprehensible frauds have been committed by invoking religious claims.

## Crimes By Professionals, In Sum

In the preceding review we have seen that professionals and quasi-professionals engage in various forms of white collar crime. This type of crime is significant because the unusually high level of trust professionals generally enjoy positions them to cause especially substantial harm to clients and patients; in the case of physicians, in particular, illegal or unethical practices may threaten the very lives of their patients. Professionals have also tended to be quite well-protected from detection, prosecution, and conviction for a number of reasons. First, most of the responsibility for policing their activities has traditionally been left to their respective associations, and these associations have tended to be more concerned with maintaining good public relations and seeking economic benefits for their profession than with identifying and taking action against unethical and criminal members. Further, professionals have traditionally been difficult to prosecute due to the reluctance of their peers to provide critical—and critically important—testimony. Finally, the generally high prestige many professionals enjoy tends to shield them from criminal accusations and convictions in all but the most blatant and egregious cases.

## Employee Crime

AMONG THE MORE common images of white collar crime is employees stealing from their employers. From the perspective of employers, unsurprisingly, such crimes are the heart of the white collar crime problem. The chairman of the board and CEO of a major pharmaceutical corporation, Bristol-Myers, made the following remarks in a speech entitled "White Collar Crime: The Need for a Counteroffensive":

> *Speaking as the head of a large corporation, I want to confine myself today to what is probably the biggest subdivision of white collar crime—workplace crime. By this term, I mean the countless crimes committed by employees against their own companies, the great majority of which fall into the white collar category. (Gelb 1977: 1)*

Even though most of us think of "employees" as lower-level workers, strictly speaking an employee is anyone who is in the employ of (is being paid by) another individual, a group of owners, or a business, and thus this definition can also be applied to high-level executives and managers. Indeed, higher-level employees are best positioned to steal from a company on the largest scale, and by some estimates executives and managers are responsible for the largest proportion of losses businesses suffer at the hands of their employees (Coleman 1989: 81).

Executives and managers are often in a position to award themselves huge bonuses and a wide range of exceedingly expensive "perks" (e.g., country club memberships, a private jet, condominiums, etc.) (Altheide et al. 1978: 92). In some cases (e.g., expense account padding) the perks are clearly illegal; in other cases they are distributed as part of the company's compensation system. In many recent cases, high-level executives were awarded stock options, bonuses, or other perks worth millions of dollars, even while their companies were losing tens of millions of dollars (Byron 1992; Samuelson 1991). Even though outright embezzlements are commonly associated with low-level employees such as bank tellers, the amount of money high-level executives of publicly owned companies embezzle tends to dwarf the embezzlements of ordinary employees. For example, Robert Vesco is alleged to have "misappropriated" some $224 million of other people's (mainly, the stockholders') money from Investors Overseas Services (Dorman 1975). At least part of the massive losses in the savings and loan cases can be attributed to embezzlement on a grand scale by highly placed banking executives.

Clark and Hollinger (1983: 1) define employee theft as "the unauthorized taking, control or transfer of money and/or property of the formal work organization perpetrated by an employee during the course of occupational activity which is related to his or her employment." On the most mundane level this includes cashiers who don't ring up friends' purchases and ticket-takers who don't tear up tickets and then collude with someone in the box office to resell them. At its most extreme, employee theft may involve systematic embezzlement of millions of dollars over an extended period of time by someone occupying a key position in the business.

Even though other forms of white collar crime may ultimately be more harmful and costly than employee theft, it is clearly pervasive. A great deal of employee crime is not readily discovered, and even when discovered it may not be reported to any official agency. Because no agency collects and publishes statistics on the range of activities encompassed by the term *employee crime,* only rough estimates based on diverse sources and statistical extrapolations are available for study.

Estimated annual losses due to employee crime in the United States are as high as $75 billion (although such estimates vary widely, with most in the $5–10 billion range); thus employee crime accounts for about 1 percent of the gross national product and inflates the price of consumer items by 10–15 percent (Adkins 1982; Clark and Hollinger 1983; Horning 1983). By all accounts, employee theft is responsible for the largest percentage—perhaps as high as 75 percent—of inventory shrinkage (inventory that is delivered and paid for but cannot be accounted for by sales or stockroom surveys)(McCaghy and Cernkovich 1987: 318). Employees, then, steal far more from most businesses, on the average, than do shoplifters, burglars, or robbers.

Employee theft is also involved in perhaps a third of all business failures and can lead to lost employee benefits, defaulted loans, and intensified mistrust within business (Green 1990: 204; Sieh 1993). A large-scale study of employee theft found that roughly one-third of the employees surveyed in three basic industries (retail, manufacturing, and service) admitted to having stolen company property, and roughly two-thirds reported other forms of employee misconduct such as abusing sick-leave privileges and falsifying time sheets (Clark and Hollinger 1983). Another source suggested that 50 percent of the nation's workforce steals from their employers (Altheide et al. 1978: 90). Some self-report surveys have indicated that between 75 percent and 92 percent of all workers supplement their legitimate incomes in technically illegal ways, a good proportion of which involves some form of theft from their employers (Mars 1982: 1). Furthermore, a vast amount of fraud exists in the Workers' Compensation system, which is funded by employer premiums; cheating is involved in an estimated 20 percent or more of the claims (Kerr 1991c).

## The Forms of Employee Theft

In the broadest possible sense, sooner or later all employees steal from their employers. They use office supplies and machinery for personal purposes; make personal phone calls on a business phone or use a company car for personal reasons; use company time for personal business or for unauthorized recreation; and so on. In addition to a formal paycheck, then, many employees view such activities as "wages-in-kind" (Ditton 1977). Some such wages-in-kind (e.g., tips) are regarded as perfectly legitimate; others (e.g., letting relatives help themselves to store goods without charging them) cross the line into theft. Employees perceive their acquisitive actions as either theft or something else according to the amount of money or material taken, the method used, and the degree of complicity with other employees (Clarke 1990: 42). Admittedly, quite a lot of ambiguity is involved here, and on the pettiest level neither employees nor employers are likely to characterize such activities as "stealing."

Employee theft occurs, then, on a number of different levels. *Pilfering* refers to petty theft, *larceny* to unauthorized taking of something of value. *Chiseling* refers to cheating or swindling, *fraud* is theft through misrepresentation, and *embezzlement* refers to "the destruction or fraudulent appropriation of another's money or merchandise which has been entrusted to one's care" (Altheide et al. 1978: 91). As a matter of law these crimes incorporate a number of different elements. Larceny involves a trespass, taking, and carrying away of the property of another with the intent of keeping it; embezzlement involves the fraudulent appropriation as one's own of another's property that is in one's lawful possession (Bequai 1978: 86, 88). Although employers may well focus on the criminal aspects of these acts, employees who engage in them may see them differently, describing them as "salvaging," "fringing," "borrowing," "fiddling" and "leveling" (Horning 1983: 699). The various different elements of such acts can introduce ambiguities at any stage.

## Employers' Responses to Employee Theft

Some employee theft is tolerated, perhaps even encouraged, by employers, to compensate for low wages and poor working conditions (Zeitlin 1971; Ditton 1977). Indeed, some evidence suggests that such theft contributes to worker satisfaction and productivity, especially in marginal jobs (Mars 1982). But workers who engage in minor employee theft as a "fringe benefit" are somewhat compromised by their participation, and as a result they are less well-positioned to organize and make militant demands for better wages. In this sense employers may actually profit, or save money, from a certain amount of employee theft.

Many employers tolerate some "petty theft" of their time and resources as long as it remains within reasonable boundaries. Employers who attempt to eliminate such theft completely—for example, by requiring formal requisitioning of all supplies, using telephone locks, requiring passes to go to the bathroom, and so forth—may pay a high price by alienating and embittering employees. Many employers are unlikely to involve the police when they discover significant employee thefts because to do so risks disrupting relationships and productive patterns at work, exposing improper or even illegal practices of the employer, and possibly garnering bad publicity if arrests and criminal trials ensue (Clarke 1990: 39–41). Other employers, on the other hand, may take strong measures to prevent employee theft and may investigate it vigorously and punish it harshly—especially when cheap labor is plentiful, or when employee theft is of a form and level that reduces profits or renders managers vulnerable to claims of incompetence (Mars 1982: 23). Managers and employers, then, may use various forms of surveillance to minimize employee theft and uncover it when it occurs.

## Alternative Forms of Employee Crime

Not all employee crime against the employer takes the form of theft. Another type is sabotage, the deliberate destruction of the employers' product, facilities, machinery, or records. According to Hodson and Sullivan (1990: 109), "the word sabotage originated in the 1400s, in the Netherlands, where workers would throw their sabots (wooden shoes) into the wooden gears of the textile looms to break the gears." Workers may commit sabotage to conceal their own errors, to gain time off or more pay, or to express their contempt and anger with their work and employer. The most extreme forms of sabotage, then, are likely to occur in workplace settings in which workers are especially alienated or believe they have been unfairly exploited and mistreated.

Still another form of employee crime is the growing problem of theft of ideas, designs, and formulas—that is, of trade secrets (Bequai 1978: 89–90). In the long run, the theft of a unique design or formula—if it reaches a competitor—can cost an employer far more than the direct theft of money or material property. Such theft, which may be motivated by hostility to the employer or by financial payoffs from competing companies, can be expected to become an increasingly costly problem in the current "information revolution."

## Some Factors in Employee Theft

Not all employees are equally likely to steal from their employers or commit sabotage. Differences in personal integrity are clearly an important factor. Different forms of employee theft or deviance spring from different motives; workers who steal may do so only for themselves or to "altruistically" facilitate the thefts of relatives and friends (Hollinger, Slora, and Terris 1992). In some rare cases, employees who believe their employer is engaging in dangerous or unethical practices may steal or commit sabotage to expose or hinder the employer's operation. Still, only a small minority of employee theft is motivated by altruistic or idealistic objectives.

The most extensive study of employee theft, sponsored by the National Institute of Justice, found that employees who commit theft are more likely to be young (ages 16–25), male, and unmarried (Clark and Hollinger 1983). According to one study (Boye 1991), workers who expect to leave a job soon are more likely to steal. Such personal attributes, however, appear to be considerably less important than both a range of situational and structural factors characterizing the workplace, and employee responses to and perceptions of these factors.

A well-known study by Horning (1970) of 88 blue-collar employees of a large Midwest electronics assembly plant found that they strongly tended to discriminate among company property, personal property, and "property of uncertain ownership." "Company property" refers mainly to basic, bulky components and tools (e.g., power transformers and electric drills), which are quite closely monitored. "Property of uncertain ownership" refers mainly to small, inexpensive, and expendable components and tools such as nails, bolts, scrap metals, pliers, and drill bits. "Personal property" refers to monogrammed clothing, wallets, jewelry, personally modified tools, and the like. (Some personal property, such as lost money or misplaced, unmarked clothes, falls into the category of property of uncertain ownership.) Not surprisingly, workers were most likely to take property of uncertain ownership, and in this study over 90 percent admitted to having pilfered such property at one time or another. Most of the workers (about 80 percent) felt it was wrong to steal company property, although a significant minority were not necessarily so inhibited. Finally, these blue-collar workers quite uniformly condemned the theft of personal property, and virtually all of them (99 percent) claimed that such theft rarely if ever occurred. Thus the question of whether or not employees steal cannot be answered in simple "yes or no" terms, but rather according to the type of property involved.

Unanticipated personal circumstances and the availability of a wide range of rationalizations can also play an important role in employee theft. In *Other People's Money* (1953), a pioneering study of embezzlement, Donald Cressey interviewed some 133 embezzlers and defrauders and determined that the existence of an unshareable financial problem (e.g., gambling losses, a mistress, etc.) increased the likelihood that individuals in a position of trust would embezzle. Even though they knew perfectly well that embezzlement was illegal, they also strongly tended to rationalize their actions as "borrowing" with the intention of eventually paying the money back. They also tended to find some grounds of "justifying" their actions (e.g., I'm entitled to the money), or they denied being able to help it (e.g., I got in a situation in which I had no other alternative).

A subsequent study by Dorothy Zietz (1981) found that female embezzlers were more likely to be motivated by family-related financial emergencies and problems (as opposed to an individual's financial problems) than were male embezzlers. Zietz's study recognized, in fact, that employees who embezzle can be motivated by a range of circumstances and objectives. Some embezzlers deliberately seek out positions that will provide them with opportunities to embezzle, with the goal of enhancing their lifestyle, making up for childhood deprivations, or attempting to satisfy the demands of a spouse or lover; others may be motivated by altruism (the desire to help others), fantasies, weak character, simple greed, or some combination of these factors. Studies of embezzlers, then, have highlighted the complex interrelationship among opportunistic, situational, and personal factors that can generate some forms of employee crime.

## Conditions in the Workplace and Employee Crime

Perhaps the most important factors influencing the form and level of employee theft involve workplace conditions such as the size of the organization. Smigel (1970), in an oft-cited study, found that his respondents were more prepared to steal from large organizations than from small ones. First, stealing from a large organization could be more easily rationalized on the grounds that such organizations are especially exploitative and are far less likely in any case to suffer measurable harm from conventional levels of theft. Second, the larger the organization, the smaller the risk of being caught.

Other studies (see, for example, Clark and Hollinger 1983) have found, perhaps unsurprisingly, that employees' dissatisfaction with the company or with supervisors was associated with higher rates of employee theft. American workers in particular deeply resent affronts to their dignity and self-respect in the workplace, and significant anecdotal evidence suggests that much employee theft and sabotage is inspired by such resentment (Altheide et al. 1978). Clearly, the more alienated the employees are, the less likely they are to be inhibited from committing theft and sabotage against their employers.

From the Marxist point of view, of course, the real theft is committed by the owners or employers, who don't give their workers a full return on the labor they put into products, in order to obtain the profit the capitalist system promotes. Many employees who are hardly Marxists nevertheless believe that their employers don't pay them what they should be paid, and they justify petty thefts of supplies, equipment use, and time in these terms.

Other structural factors promote or influence employee theft. Gerald Mars (1982), a British social anthropologist, developed a typology, based on the closeness of supervision and the presence or absence of a strong work group, to characterize the variety of workplace thieves. "Donkeys" (e.g., cashiers) are closely supervised and have weak group ties; they are most likely to "steal" time and to engage in creative accounting. "Wolfpack" members (e.g., longshoremen) are closely supervised and have strong group ties; they engage in elaborate, systematic pilferage. "Vultures" (e.g., cab drivers) are weakly supervised and have strong group ties; they often organize stable, ongoing systems of pilferage. "Hawks" (e.g., professionals) are both weakly supervised and typically weakly integrated into work groups; they are especially likely to engage in time and expense-account–related abuses.

The conditions conducive to employee theft vary quite widely among occupations. Bank clerks, for example, generally have greater difficulty"skimming the product" they handle than do low-level employees in many other fields (Mars 1982: 136). In some fields, relatively low-level employees may prefer to pass up promotions if the increased pay and constraints of the higher position will not compensate for reduced opportunities to steal (Mars 1982: 205). Other students of employee deviance and theft (see, for example, Snizek 1974; Altheide et al. 1978) have supported Mars's finding that work-group norms are an especially important factor in determining the scope and form of employee theft.

According to the most ambitious study of employee theft, opportunity to steal is a major determinant of employee theft, and those who have the greatest access to things worth stealing are most likely to do so (Clark and Hollinger 1983). The single most important predictor of employee theft, according to this study, is the perceived likelihood of getting caught (Clark and Hollinger 1983: 34). The vast majority of workers who steal (95–99 percent, depending on the type of business) are in fact not caught, although again most of this theft is occasional and relatively petty. Deterrence of employee theft appears to be less a function of a vigorous security presence than of a clearly articulated policy on employee theft, good inventory control, pre-employment screening, and action taken against identified thieves. An overriding conclusion of Clark and Hollinger's study is that employee theft (and deviance) must be understood principally in terms of factors inherent in the workplace, rather than external factors. Employees' perceptions of the quality of the workplace milieu is a significant factor in whether or not theft occurs, and informal workplace norms tend to govern the type and amount of such theft.

## Employee Crime, In Sum

Clearly, a complex of factors can interact in different ways to encourage or deter employee crime. A high level of opportunity to steal may be offset by a high degree of loyalty and job satisfaction. Conversely, a significant amount of employee theft may occur when levels of hostility to the employer are high, even if opportunities to steal are somewhat limited and risky. Altogether, if we are to understand employee crime, we must understand an entire complex of structural and personal interactions.

## Occupational Crime, In Sum

THE CONCEPT OF occupational crime as used here encompasses a very broad range of harmful, illegal, and unethical activities, from the devious practices of retailers, to frauds committed by professionals, to the embezzlements and thefts of employees. Some students of white collar crime (see, for example, Green 1990) have applied the concept more broadly still, to cover everything from corporate price-fixing to sexual molestation committed by day-care providers. But even in the more restricted application adopted in this chapter, the degree of criminal intent and the level of harm caused can vary widely. The unifying factor, of course, is that the offenses are committed within the context of a legitimate occupational pursuit and are made possible by the opportunities available in this context. Occupational crime, as defined here, is quite uniformly a crime motivated by financial objectives, either increasing compensation or minimizing loss.

Of all the categories of white collar crime examined in this text, occupational crime may well be the form that readers of this book are both most likely to commit and most likely to experience directly and regularly as victims. Those who engage in this type of white collar crime are most like us: They are our neighbors, relatives, and friends, and sometimes ourselves. Occupational crime may be especially insidious because it is so deeply woven into the fabric of conventional, everyday life for people of all socioeconomic levels of society.

# Governmental Crime: State Crime and Political White Collar Crime

"**G**OVERNMENTAL CRIME" IS surely a disquieting notion. Government is, after all, the entity that produces, implements, and administers a society's laws. People generally like to think that the government is there to protect them from crime, and to deter, incapacitate, punish, and rehabilitate criminals. The worst crimes—in terms of physical harm to human beings, abuse of civil liberties, and economic loss—have been committed by individuals and entities acting in the name of the government, or the state. By conservative estimates, during the 20th century alone between 100 and 135 million people have died because of deliberate actions of the state (Glaser and Possony 1979: 44). The far larger proportion of these deaths resulted from genocides, massacres, and mass executions, rather than war (Markusen 1992). In addition, a great deal of nonviolent crime with major consequences is committed by governmental officials, either for political or economic gain.

What we here consider governmental crime in the broad sense is not always crime in the narrower legal sense of the term. We must distinguish among those governmental or political actions prohibited by the state's laws, those defined as criminal by international law, and those regarded as criminal on some other criteria of harmfulness not necessarily recognized by either the state's laws or international law. The conventional restriction of the notion of crime to that so defined by the state is clearly limiting in this context because much governmental crime avoids being formally classified as crime (Kauzlarich, Kramer, and Smith 1992).

In this chapter the term *governmental crime* is used as a broad term for the whole range of crimes committed in a governmental context. The term *state crime* denotes harmful activities carried out by the state or on behalf of some state agency, whereas *political white collar crime* refers to illegal activities carried out by officials and politicians for direct personal benefit.

Crimes committed by (or on behalf) of the government have been classified as a type of political crime (Clinard and Quinney 1973; Roebuck and Weeber 1978).The term *political crime,* which has been labeled a "broad and ill-defined category" (Allen et al. 1981: 201), has most typically been associated with crimes such as treason, sedition, disobedience of mandated service (e.g., draft dodging), and illegal protests (Turk 1982). An important distinction must be made between those who commit crimes against the state from without, and those who do so from within; in this chapter we are concerned with the latter type of offenders, not the former.

Governmental crime goes beyond Sutherland's original conception of white collar crime, but it is often so intimately interrelated with it that no survey of white collar crime can neglect it. Some commentators regard governmental crime as inseparable from corporate crime because it reflects an economic system dominated by corporations (Roebuck and Weeber 1978: iv); others subsume both corporate and high-level governmental offenses under the heading of "elite deviance" (Simon and Eitzen 1993). Still other students of white collar crime (see, for example, Coleman 1994; Green 1990) either classify internal political crime (e.g., corruption) and crimes committed on behalf of the state (or some state entity) as forms of individual occupational or organizational white collar crime, or treat it separately as a form of "state authority" occupational crime, depending on the context in which it occurs. The broad category *governmental crime* is adopted here to clearly differentiate such activity from crime carried out by individuals or ideological groups that lack any governmental status.

Governmental crime and political white collar crime are in fact closely related to white collar crime carried out by corporations, professionals, retailers, and others because the parties involved enjoy a respectable status, occupy a position of trust, most typically have moderate or higher incomes, and do not regard themselves as criminals. Clearly, a symbiotic relationship—a mutual interdependence—exists between much governmental or political white collar crime and traditional white collar crime, a thesis explored more fully in Chapter 6.

Even though political white collar crime is often motivated by the desire for financial gain, the extension or maintenance of power plays a much larger and more central role in state crime. When violence occurs as an element of state crime, it is likely to be much more direct than the violence of corporate crime. Although violation of trust is a key element in white collar crime generally, in the case of state or political white collar crime a public trust is violated, whereas corporate and occupational crime involve a violation of an essentially private trust. Accordingly, some commentators regard governmental crime as worse than corporate and occupational crime precisely because the violation of a public trust is a more serious matter than the violation of a private trust.

Admittedly, we cannot always easily discriminate between those who commit crimes on behalf of the state and those who use their state or governmental position to commit offenses for their own personal benefit, but it still seems useful to differentiate between, for example, genocidal actions and accepting bribes. Michalowski (1985: 380) produced a typology that differentiates between political crimes committed by those in political power and those outside government, between crimes that benefit individuals and organizations (including government), and between crimes committed for economic and political gain.

Prosecution of governmental crime and political white collar crime may involve some unique difficulties, especially when the accused are part of the law-making and enforcement apparatus. Indeed, any claim that governmental crimes have been committed is especially vulnerable to the charge of ideological bias, and at least some governmental actions will be either defended as a desirable policy or castigated as a criminal form of repression. When they are exposed, state crime and political white collar crime become the focus of enormous public interest and outrage because of the conspicuous public profile of governmental and political officials (Geis and Meier 1977). No corporate or occupational crime has ever generated the level of public attention directed at the Nuremberg Trials and the Watergate Hearings.

Traditionally, the study of governmental crime has been relatively neglected by criminologists, perhaps even more neglected than the study of corporate and occupational crime (Barak 1990; 1991; Cohen 1993; Roebuck and Weeber 1978). In part, this relative lack of attention can be attributed to the challenge of gaining access to the politically powerful, to some ideological resistance to regarding governmental actors as criminals, and to the complexity and broad scope of the illegalities involved. The somewhat limited examination of governmental crime in this text is more a reflection of the fact that such crime is less central to what is ordinarily defined as white collar crime than a judgment that it is relatively unimportant. On the contrary, as we noted at the very outset of this chapter, the worst of all crimes have been governmental crimes.

The matter of governmental crime is linked with two of the more enduring and complex issues in political philosophy: the question of the nature of a legitimate political order, and the nature of the obligation to comply with the laws and commands emanating from a political order. Clearly, a political order that is not legitimate—for example, a totalitarian dictatorship established by brute force—may be considered inherently criminal, but even a political order that came into being by fundamentally legitimate means—for example, the Nazi state—may be regarded as illegitimate by some other criteria. On the other hand, the nature of our duty to obedience is a difficult matter. The entire tradition of civil disobedience—including the actions of Henry David Thoreau, Mohandas Gandhi, and Martin Luther King, Jr.—is premised on the idea that one has a moral obligation to *disobey* some laws. In some circumstances state agents are morally and sometimes legally obliged not to comply with commands of higher state authority. Although these very large issues cannot be explored here in any depth, they have a part in any discussion of governmental crime.

## Governmental Crime: Some Basic Terms

SOME OF THE terminology of governmental crime requires definition because these terms are used in quite different ways. Even though *abuse of power* is perhaps the broadest charge associated with governmental crime, it has no fixed meaning. The most obvious, least problematic instances of abuse of power occur when the state or its agents violate laws to accomplish some improper or prohibited objective. In its broader meaning, abuse of power occurs when the state assumes and exercises power it ought not to have. When agents of a U.S. government agency such as the FBI engaged in surveillance or break-ins specifically prohibited by law, abuse of power in the first sense was involved; when the apartheid government of South Africa instituted an Emergency Act that enabled it to arrest and detain dissidents, abuse of power in the second sense was involved. The full range of governmental abuses of power entails many forms of harm and can include violations of universally defined basic human rights (Barak 1991: 274; Cohen 1993). Even though in its broadest sense abuse of power certainly includes acts of economic corruption, limiting the use of the term to acts involving the extension or maintenance of power can avoid some confusion.

A second basic concept associated with governmental crime is *corruption*. In the English language of Shakespeare's time, the expression "to corrupt" had both sexual and political meanings, and today's dictionaries offer many different definitions (Heidenheimer 1977: 20; Noonan 1984: 319). Political corruption most typically involves the misuse of political office for material advantage, although it also encompasses acts undertaken for political advantage; it has been applied both narrowly (as the violation of specific laws, typically for some form of payment, and more loosely as deviation from ideal or expected patterns of behavior) (Alatas 1990: 2; *Corruption and Reform* 1986).

Even though the term *corruption* ordinarily has negative connotations, a degree of political corruption is regarded by some as inevitable and functional (Huntington, 1968; Lieberman 1972: 20). Political corruption in some form can be found in all but the most primitive societies, and we have records of such corruption from the earliest times (e.g., the Code of Hammurabi from Babylon, ca. 1700 B.C., and the book of Exodus in the Old Testament)(Alatas 1990: 13). But standards for defining corruption vary over time and across cultures, and actions that might be considered corrupt by one standard may be regarded as acceptable practices by another (Hope 1987: 127; Medard 1986: 115). Corruption is frequently practiced by the same people who condemn it rhetorically.

Bribery is probably the single activity most closely associated with political corruption. In his magisterial book, *Bribes*, John T. Noonan, Jr. (1984: xi) states that "the core of the concept of a bribe is an inducement improperly influencing the performance of a public function meant to be gratuitously exercised." Even though *bribery* is specifically a legal concept, its various meanings include those defined by moralists, those defined by written law, those defined by law in practice and those defined by commonly accepted practices (Noonan 1984: xii). Although the specific definition of bribery varies among societies, the concept reaches very far back in history and cuts across virtually all existing societies.

Finally, the concept of *political scandal* is important to our understanding of state crime and political white collar crime. In a liberal democratic society, major governmental crime is likely to be exposed in the context of a political scandal, and in one view a political scandal is possible only in such a society (Markovits and Silverstein 1988). Such scandals are most likely to occur when a basic division of power exists in society, when a major external threat to the society is lacking, and when politicians violate widely supported norms about proper conduct in political office (Barker 1994; Neckel 1989). In a democratic society the political opposition and the media play the major roles in creating and sustaining political scandals, although the effects of ongoing scandals on the political system are often modest or limited (Szasz 1986a). Because political scandals tend to focus attention on the people involved, they do not necessarily undercut the legitimacy of a political state; they may even enhance it if the perceived wrongdoers are swiftly and justly punished (Logue 1988: 264). Political scandals are more likely to lead to criminal prosecutions than to fundamental, enduring reforms.

## Governmental Criminality on an Epic Scale

IN THE VIEW of one ideological tradition, anarchism, the state is inherently aggressive and fundamentally unnecessary (Krimerman and Perry 1966; Shatz 1971; Wolff 1976). At its most extreme, the anarchist tradition holds that the state is by its very nature a criminal enterprise. This anarchist perspective has not been widely adopted.

If unjustly depriving people of their property, their way of life, and their very lives is regarded as criminal, then imperialistic conquests and state-sanctioned wars are governmental crimes of extraordinary scope. Indeed, in one interpretation the United States was founded upon a crime, insofar as Columbus's "discovery" in 1492 led to the "conquest of paradise" (Sale 1990). The literature documenting many of the state-sponsored crimes committed by those who came after Columbus is formidable, especially concerning the destruction of Native American peoples and the slavery trade involving African Americans (see, for example, Brown 1971; Davidson 1961; *International Social Science Journal* 1992; Thomas 1993). These historical crimes were once celebrated as triumphs of Western civilization.

The waging of war has been even more destructive than imperialistic endeavors. Over time the state became the largest and most efficient user of violence, a dubious distinction it originally shared with bandits and pirates (Tilly 1985). Since the middle of the 19th century various countries have joined together to ratify agreements prohibiting or outlawing particular acts during times of war, including the imposition of needless suffering, the mistreatment of prisoners of war, and the use of chemical and biological weapons (Falk, Kolko, and Lifton 1971). Inevitably, however, only captured members of the losing side have been brought to account for war crimes.

### The Vietnam War

U.S. involvement in the Vietnam War has been widely condemned as criminal by many people all over the world, including a significant number of Americans themselves during the course of the war (Young 1991). Billions of pounds of bombs were dropped on Vietnam; millions of Vietnamese were killed, wounded, orphaned, or uprooted by the war; hundreds of thousands of U.S. soldiers were wounded and traumatized, and tens of thousands lost their lives.

In one view, the U.S. engagement in the Vietnam War was illegal under U.S. law because Congress never specifically declared war, as required by the Constitution (although it did pass resolutions and appropriate funding for the war). Among the specific accusations of illegality by U.S. forces are the use of napalm during air strikes, chemical warfare, torture of prisoners, the burning of villages, illegal detention of civilians, the bombing of hospitals and dikes, moral corruption, and sabotage of the Vietnamese economy. Some observers consider the destruction of millions of arable acres and hardwood forests to be an ecological crime of immense proportions.

The 1968 massacre of some 100 Vietnamese men, women, and children in the village of My Lai (more correctly, Son My) by Lt. William Calley and his troops is the single most infamous episode of American criminality in Vietnam (Young 1991). The subsequent trial and conviction of Lt. Calley (who served 35 months of house arrest on a military base) was widely criticized as deflecting attention from the far more substantial crimes of those higher in the chain of command, including the president and his associates. No U.S. president, cabinet officer, or other high-level civilian or military official involved in the pursuit of the Vietnam War has ever been required to provide a formal defense for his policy decisions, and of course none has ever stood trial for war crimes.

## U.S. Military Activity in the "New World Order"

More recent U.S. military ventures, including the invasions of Grenada and Panama, the mining of Managua (Nicaragua) harbor, and the Gulf War against Iraq, have been condemned in various quarters as illegal or criminal, even though these actions were supported by many Americans. Despite some history of antiwar mobilization—most conspicuously during the Vietnam War—the more enduring theme in American culture has resisted the imputation of criminality to American acts of war. The political leadership in the United States has traditionally rejected, and is likely to continue to reject, judgments of an international judiciary concerning its military actions, even though such leadership may support an international criminal court with more limited jurisdiction (Cavicchia 1992). The need for a truly effective and widely accepted international court with broad jurisdiction is likely to become increasingly evident in the forseeable future.

## The Threat of Nuclear War as Crime

Waging a nuclear war may well be the penultimate white collar crime. An all-out nuclear war has the potential to create a "nuclear winter" that would utterly destroy the planet's environment, leading to the obliteration of humanity (the "death of death") and the "murder of the future" (Schell 1982). The whole issue involving possession and possible use of nuclear arms has generated an enormous literature exploring a range of complex questions about the objectives of developing and producing nuclear weapons, their impact on international relations, and the best strategy for minimizing the possibility of a nuclear war.

It is quite remarkable that the vast criminal potential in the use of nuclear weapons has been almost wholly neglected by criminologists and criminal justicians (Harding 1983; Friedrichs 1985). Although possession of nuclear weapons has not been prohibited by international law, the threatened and actual use of such weapons is prohibited by international law and by the Charter of the United Nations (Kauzlarich, Kramer, and Smith 1992). The traditional nuclear weapons policy of the United States can certainly be interpreted as a violation of such codes, charters, and historical agreements on the conduct of armed conflict.

At a minimum, students of white collar crime should consider how involvement with the nuclear arms race relates to and is distinctive from governmental crime generally. How are the motivations of those who might initiate a nuclear war similar to and different from the motivations of white collar criminals of all types? Does it even make any sense to raise the issue of nuclear warfare in the context of a survey of white collar crime?

## The Forms of State Criminality

STATE CRIMINALITY (AS a specific subtype of governmental crime) takes many forms and occurs on many different levels. When some form of state criminality becomes a dominant force in the operation of the state, we may be justified in labeling the state a *criminal state.*

In one view, a criminal state is simply any state that's successfully labeled as such by one or more other states that are either victorious over it or have the political power to impose such a label (Jenkins 1988). In modern history, Nazi Germany may be the single most prominent case of a state widely labeled as criminal because its criminality was virtually its defining feature (Luban 1987: 784). But many other states have been candidates for this designation, from the Soviet Union to Saddam Hussein's Iraq. Many have characterized the United States as a criminal state as a consequence of its actions in the Vietnam and Gulf wars.

Any accusations of state criminality are ultimately subjective and likely to incorporate an ideological dimension. The distinctions made here among some idealized types—the criminal state, the repressive state, the corrupt state, and the negligent state—are useful only in capturing the essential dimensions of a state's criminality. Predatory criminality, repressiveness, corruption, and negligence often coexist, in varying degrees, within any given state. We first consider the concept of the criminal state.

### The Criminal State

The controversial notion of a criminal state is most commonly applied to the ultimate criminal enterprise wherein the state is used as an instrument to commit crimes against humanity, such as genocide. Even though the term *genocide* was coined as recently as World War II, such atrocities have taken place, in some form, throughout history and in all parts of the world (Chalk and Jonassohn 1990). Although there is no uniformly adopted definition of genocide—some have applied it so broadly that it encompasses such policies as family planning and language regulation in schools— it most commonly refers to a deliberate state policy of mass killing directed at some identifiable group of people (Chalk and Jonassohn 1990). Among the most prominent cases of genocide in the 20th century are the hundreds of thousands of Armenians massacred in Turkey in 1915 (historically denied by the Turkish); millions of members of various groups liquidated in the Soviet Union during the Stalin regime (1922–1953) and in the People's Republic of China under Mao Tse-tung (1949–1976); up to 200,000 Hutus in the impoverished African country of Burundi killed by the politically dominant Tutsis in 1972 and after; up to 2 million Cambodian urbanites, members of the intelligentsia, and others murdered during the regime of Pol Pot and the Khymer Rouge (1975–1978); and several hundred thousand Rwandans killed by government forces in 1994.

The Holocaust perpetuated by the Nazis during World War II is perhaps the single most dramatic, fully documented, and extreme case of genocide ever, arguably unique in its scope and ambition. It has been credibly estimated that between 5 and 6 million Jews died at the hands of the Nazis, and many others (e.g., the mentally retarded, homosexuals, and gypsies) were also systematically exterminated by them (Hilberg 1980; Levin 1973). In addition to these crimes against humanity, the surviving Nazi leadership put on trial in Nuremberg after the war faced charges of war crimes and crimes against peace (Glaser and Possony 1979: 29). The Nazi regime launched unprovoked attacks on other countries; committed numerous assassinations, acts of plundering, and other such criminal acts; and utterly subverted human rights.

The Nuremberg Trials generated some controversy over the question of whether the Nazi leaders could be tried by the Allies when no fully recognized international criminal law existed, and whether some of the Nazis' alleged war crimes were substantially different from those committed by the Allies (Sklar 1964; Taylor 1970). Although some parties felt that the Nazi leadership should simply be shot without trial, the arguments in favor of a trial prevailed. Most of the Nazis were convicted and sentenced to death; several were sentenced to prison terms ranging from 10 years to life. In the years since the Nuremberg Trials the argument that it made an important symbolic statement by administering justice to the guilty in an orderly way seems to have gained wide acceptance.

On the other hand, the Allies' refusal to try their own war criminals, as well as the subsequent refusal of the United States to subject itself to the judgment of the World Court on charges of illegal acts of war involving the mining of Nicaraguan territorial waters in the 1980s, have been criticized as hypocritical (Luban 1987; Kahn 1987). Indeed, since the post-World War II trials of the defeated German and Japanese leadership, no such trials have been held, despite recurrent charges of criminality against various heads of states or political entities, including Saddam Hussein in Iraq and the Serbs in Bosnia.

What is the relationship between the criminal state (and genocide more generally) and "white collar crime"? John Braithwaite (1992: 100), arguably the most prolific white collar crime scholar today, has written that Adolph Hitler is "the greatest white-collar criminal of our century." In justifying this designation he wrote, "I trust that is it obvious that Hitler's genocide was a crime and fits Sutherland's definition of white-collar crime" (Braithwaite 1992: 107). But Sutherland's work on white collar crime dealt with it almost exclusively as a corporate and entrepreneurial activity for economic gain. Despite the fact that Sutherland's famous 1939 speech was made while Hitler was near the height of his power and his 1949 book was published shortly after the full scope of Hitler's crimes had been revealed to the world, Sutherland made no references to Hitler in his work on white collar crime. His book's chapter on "war crimes" deals exclusively with the violation of wartime regulations and other (e.g., tax-related) laws by businessmen.

Some might argue that classifying Hitler and other tyrants as "white collar criminals" trivializes the enormity of their crimes by giving them membership in a group largely composed of price-fixing executives and embezzling employees. In this sense it is preferable to consider genocide and related monstrous crimes not as white collar crime per se, but rather as a cognate type of crime with a generic relationship to it—as a form of governmental crime that is the ultimate expression of the abuse of power, position, and trust.

## The Repressive State

A second form of state criminality takes the form of a *repressive state*. Although such a state does not go so far as waging a formal campaign of genocide, it systematically deprives its citizens of fundamental human rights.

The idea of human rights is rooted in an ancient tradition; the Bible is but one early source. Our current understanding of human rights is principally a product of the writing of Enlightenment philosophers such as Thomas Hobbes, John Locke, Charles-Louis Montesquieu, and Jean-Jacques Rousseau, who argued in various ways that humans were naturally entitled to what the Declaration of Independence so eloquently called "Life, Liberty and the Pursuit of Happiness." These ideas became increasingly influential in the Western world in the 18th century. In one sense the American Revolution (actually a rebellion) and the French Revolution were precipitated by a perception that a people—the American colonists and the French "Third Estate," respectively—were being "criminally" deprived of fundamental human rights, by the British monarchy in the one case and the French *ancien régime* in the other.

Although efforts to promote human rights as an international concern have been made since the early 19th century, until World War I the matter of human rights was essentially a domestic concern, and many of the world's governments made little if any effort to acknowledge fully and guarantee the range of rights considered an entitlement in most Western democracies today. The widespread condemnation of slavery and the promotion of certain rights of minorities, aliens, and prisoners of war in the 19th and 20th centuries were notable exceptions to this general proposition (Driscoll 1989).

The United Nations was formed after World War II partly in response to the gross and conspicuous abuse of the most fundamental human rights by the totalitarian governments of the time. The United Nations Universal Declaration of Human Rights of 1948 identified a long list of fundamental human rights, from the right to life, liberty, and the security of person to the right to work and to leisure, but the United Nations itself has not been able to impose these standards on any government. The rhetoric of human rights is a major source, then, of current notions of international crime (Cohen 1993). Specific states around the world almost universally deny that they are guilty of any such crimes.

South Africa, dominated for 300 years by the white minority and culminating in the establishment of the apartheid system of formal racial discrimination, is a premier example of a repressive state (Sparks 1990). In the latter half of the 20th century—before the establishment of a democratic system and the election of Nelson Mandela as president in 1994—South Africa was regarded by much of the world as a pariah and was the target of widespread sanctions. Although apartheid South Africa has been called a "criminal state," it differed from Nazi Germany insofar as repression rather than extermination was the central objective of the South African state.

Repression and the deprivation of rights can occur in any type of political system, including a Western democracy, but in the 20th century they are most closely associated with dictatorships. The principal motivating factor in the imposition of a repressive system of government is the extension or retention of power, often for its own sake. Repression of rights has certainly facilitated blatant economic exploitation, but this combination has contributed to the downfall of a number of "traditional" dictatorships, including that of the Shah of Iran, Anastasio Somoza of Nicaragua, Ferdinand Marcos of the Philippines, and François Duvalier of Haiti. To many Westerners the Communist dictatorships of the Soviet Union, the Eastern bloc nations, and the People's Republic of China exemplified the repressive state, and surely the repressive elements of these systems ultimately contributed to their political downfall.

In the second half of the 20th century, numerous "modern" dictatorships have emerged in third-world countries, and many of them have endured for many decades. These modern dictators have often come to power in coups or revolutions conducted against traditional right-wing monarchies or dictatorships in the name of promoting broader social justice, a goal they accomplish at least to some degree, along with promoting some sense of national pride and purpose (Rubin 1987: 47). But modern dictators "most often continue or intensify injustice, fear, torture, discrimination, lack of liberty, pervasive material and spiritual corruption, poisonous propaganda, violent hatred, xenophobia, economic decay and aggression" (Rubin 1987: 263). Fidel Castro in Cuba and Mu'ammar Gadhafi in Libya are widely regarded as two examples of such dictators.

The fundamental hypocrisy of allegations of repression in revolutionary third-world dictatorships by Western democracies (e.g., the United States) that had previously tolerated or actively supported corrupt, repressive right-wing dictatorships in these countries is a recurring theme. After some of the repressive dictatorships supported by the United States were overthrown in the 1970s and 1980s, considerable controversy ensued over whether the governments that replaced them (e.g., the Sandinistas in Nicaragua and the Islamic fundamentalists in Iran) increased or diminished the level of state repression or criminality.

## The Corrupt State

A *corrupt state* refers to a state used as an instrument to enrich its leadership. The case of the Philippines under Ferdinand Marcos provides a well-documented example of a corrupt state in which for some two decades the leadership engaged in the systematic enrichment of the president, his family, and his cronies at the expense of the general welfare.

Marcos, a lawyer, came to power in 1965. For most of his tenure as president (until February 1986) he enjoyed strong support from the U.S. government because he was regarded as anti-Communist, willing to protect the interests of U.S.-based corporations, and cooperatively disposed toward the maintenance of strategic U.S. military bases in the Philippines (Bonner 1987). Despite an official annual income of several thousand dollars, Marcos and his wife Imelda were alleged to have accumulated personal wealth of $5–10 billion (several times the total annual expenditure of the Philippine government) before they were finally driven from power (Carbonell-Catilo 1986). This wealth included vast real estate holdings in numerous countries, including the United States; hundreds of millions of dollars in foreign bank accounts; and millions of dollars of gold bullion. The Marcoses lived a life of luxury in several palaces or mansions they owned, and Imelda Marcos in particular was known to spend as much as $12 million in a single day on jewels and over $10,000 on bedsheets; she acquired millions of dollars worth of Impressionist paintings and left over 1,000 pairs of shoes (originally reported to be 3,000, but still a lot of shoes) in Malacanang Palace when she fled to Hawaii (Watson 1986).

The Marcoses' immense wealth was acquired by putting relatives and cronies in charge of major state agencies and by ensuring that the country's principal private enterprises were also controlled by associates; such an economy has been aptly described as "crony capitalism" (Carbonell-Catilo 1986: 238). State agencies extracted commissions and kickbacks for awarding contracts to corporations, and much of this money ended up in the control of the Marcoses, who received a standard 15–20 percent of the take on many transactions. Private corporations were taken over by the state and put into the hands of Marcos associates, or such associates were granted exclusive franchises on many industries ranging from sugar trading to casino operations. Large sums were simply siphoned off from the resources of government agencies under the control of the Marcoses.

In 1972 Marcos was able to impose martial law—the alleged threat of Communism was one pretext—enabling him to suspend ordinary auditing procedures by decree. The judiciary was also largely under Marcos's control by virtue of his powers of appointment and reorganization, and the mass media, also dominated by Marcos associates, did little to expose the massive plundering of the country's wealth (Carbonell-Catilo 1986). The Marcoses made donations of up to $1 million to U.S. presidential campaigns (of Nixon in 1968 and 1972), and this financial payoff probably played a role in the ongoing support of the Marcoses by the political leadership in the United States (Bonner 1987). Many different elements, then, contributed to the development of this corrupt state.

The thorough plundering of the Philippines took place in a country largely populated by impoverished citizens. When the Marcoses were finally driven from power in 1986, the country was beset by a vastly overblown national debt ($26 billion), rampant inflation, declining real wages, and deteriorating social services (Bonner 1987; Carbonell-Catilo 1986). By the early 1990s Ferdinand Marcos had died in luxurious exile in Hawaii, Imelda Marcos had been acquitted in the United States on charges stemming from corrupt real estate deals, and it was far from clear how much of the stolen wealth would be restored to the Filipino people. Unfortunately, the downfall of the Marcoses did not lead to the extinction of corruption in the Philippines. In 1991 corruption on all levels reportedly remained pervasive in the Philippines, despite the perception that President Corazon Aquino, who succeeded Marcos on an anticorruption platform, was honest (Loeb 1991). The corrupt state is best understood as a symbiotic product of structural factors (e.g., traditional values promoting nepotism and favoritism) and personal greed.

Of course, examples of corrupt states are many. During the 30-year reign of the Somoza family in Nicaragua, for example, family members and allied families were alleged to have accumulated a fortune of some $1 billion, including ownership of much of the country's best land (8,000 square miles) and control of some two dozen large, important industries (Herman 1982: 29; Rubin 1987: 93). After a devastating earthquake in 1972, the Somozas and their associates made the tactical error of stealing a large portion of the relief supplies and funds for their own benefit, and outrage over such blatant, heartless corruption in a poor and beleaguered nation contributed to the downfall of the regime not long after.

Many African nations are widely regarded as pervasively corrupt, and some of the leadership spectacularly corrupt (Williams 1987). Mobutu Sese Seko became president of Zaire and is alleged to have subsequently accumulated assets of some $3 billion and built 11 palaces for himself (Lamb 1987: 43–45). Upon his rise to power in 1977, Jean-Bede Bokassa of the Central African Republic—a country with an annual per capita income of some $250 then—expended $20 million on his coronation as emperor; he was ultimately exiled and then executed when he returned to the country (Lamb 1987: 50–51). Other examples of such corruption abound. In the case of these third-world African countries, various factors contribute to corruption, including the absence of a civil service "work ethic," extreme economic inequality, a lack of disciplined leadership, extensive bureaucratic powers, cultural norms favoring tribal loyalties over integrity, and the absence of countervailing forces such as opposition parties or a free press (Hope 1987). If political corruption is to be diminished (if not eradicated) in these countries, a fundamental transformation of the entire administrative structure and related cultural norms must take place.

## The Negligent State

If a corrupt state is one in which the political leadership proactively loots the country's wealth, a *negligent state* is one in which "crimes of omission" are committed. Thus the state fails to prevent loss of human life, suffering, and deprivation that in fact is in its power to prevent (Barak 1991). The concept could even be extended to apply to circumstances in which the state's finite resources are wasted on a vast scale through gross bureaucratic inefficiencies, negligence, and incompetence.

Of course, it can be difficult to distinguish among malfeasance (doing something you are prohibited from doing), nonfeasance (failing to do something you are required to do), and misfeasance (performing a permissible act in an improper manner)(Gardiner 1986). Surely many people would object to extending the concept of criminality to include negligence and wastefulness, which are never subject to criminal prosecution if no demonstrable fraud is involved. But it may be worthwhile to examine such humanistically defined criminality, and to ask ourselves both how it differs from "proactive" forms of governmental criminality and whether it should and could be formally defined as criminal. Attention to wasteful and negligent governmental practices promotes appreciation of the enormous costs to taxpayers of poor governmental stewardship, incompetence, and inherently distorted priorities and policies.

The most serious form of negligent state criminality involves the unnecessary and premature loss of life that occurs when the government and its agents fail to act affirmatively in certain situations. Although the infant mortality rate in the United States has generally declined during the 20th century, it rose (especially among poor black families) in the early 1980s in conjunction with the Reagan administration's reductions in maternal and infant health care programs (Boone 1989). Although many factors contribute to the relatively high infant mortality rate among poor black families in America, government negligence appears to be one contributing factor.

In a similar vein, the political leadership in the United States has been accused of responding too slowly and ineffectively to the AIDS epidemic as it evolved in the 1980s, as thousands of deaths might have been prevented with a more potent response (Shilts 1987). The derelict actions of the U.S. government, and state and local governments as well, have been attributed to the fact that AIDS first surfaced in America in the gay community, and has continued to afflict disproportionately several disprivileged and stigmatized social groups, including drug addicts and prostitutes. Some AIDS activists have called political leaders "murderers" because they could have implemented more effective preventive policies in response to this new "holocaust" and failed to do so (L. Kramer 1989). This accusation mirrors the contention that during World War II the U.S. leadership knew about the Nazi death-camps and was criminally negligent in failing to act more aggressively against the Nazis' systematic genocidal activities (Wyman 1984). Even though in both cases it is acknowledged that many other parties bear responsibility for these tragedies, governmental negligence is too easily overlooked.

Other crimes of the negligent state can be identified. Barak and Bohm (1989) have argued that the "crime of homelessness"—the state's failure to enact laws and formulate policies that provide all people of limited means with affordable housing—should concern us more than the crimes of the homeless. Stuart Henry (1991) classified the existence of an underground economy as a state crime of omission, charging that the state's failure to control the distribution of wealth at the source forces many people into an underground economy, a predicament that makes them especially vulnerable to illicit drug use and involvement in conventional criminal activity. In addition, the sheer wastefulness of many government programs—amounting by some estimates to hundreds of billions of dollars over a period of only three years—can be regarded as crimes of negligence (Diamond 1986; Hershey 1984). Examples of government wastefulness include pork barrel projects, overly generous federal pensions, lax loan collection procedures, inefficient subsidies, and the maintenance of unnecessary military bases.

The concept of the negligent (or wasteful) state could be extended to include inadequate or inefficient governmental responses to poverty in general, to crime, to environmental degradation, and the like. Governmental negligence is principally a consequence both of ideological commitments to favoring particular programs and constituencies over others (e.g., defense spending over antipoverty programs or businesspeople over homeless people), and of decisions of political expediency (i.e., choosing those policy initiatives most likely to produce political dividends). Accordingly, the concept of the negligent state may be seen by some as too remote and tangential to be linked with white collar crime in any meaningful way. But if harmful (and fatal) consequences and unnecessary economic losses occur because of the negligent or wasteful practices of government officials, such results are certainly criminal in the humanistic sense and should be included in the roster of the principal forms of governmental crime.

## State Criminality, In Sum

The clearly interrelated concepts of the criminal state, the repressive state, the corrupt state, and the negligent state need not be considered synonymous. If economic corruption was hardly unknown in Nazi Germany, it is because that state focused instead on extending its geopolitical boundaries and exterminating its perceived internal enemies. Even though the Marcoses are alleged to have stripped the Philippines of its wealth, they were not accused of engaging in genocide or aggressive warfare. Many of the African nations are allegedly thoroughly corrupt states, but not necessarily criminal states; apartheid South Africa was distinctly more a repressive state rather than a corrupt one; and the United States and the western European nations are especially prone to being characterized as negligent states.

Iraq under Saddam Hussein has been accused of genocidal policies toward the Kurds and aggressive warfare against Kuwait; it has certainly been guilty of practicing various forms of repression and denying people their basic human rights. Further, Saddam Hussein allegedly looted some $10–11 billion dollars from the Iraqi treasury, supposedly hiding the money in secret bank accounts and shell companies in various parts of the world (Byron 1991). Assuming the validity of such allegations, Saddam Hussein's Iraq can be regarded as a criminal, repressive, and corrupt state, and undoubtedly a negligent state as well.

## State-Organized Crime

IN A PRESIDENTIAL address to the American Society of Criminology, William J. Chambliss (1989: 184) defined the concept of "state-organized crime" as "acts defined by law as criminal and committed by state officials in pursuit of their job as representatives of the state." Chambliss specifically excluded criminal acts that benefit individual officeholders. Even though state-organized crime is carried out on behalf of a government entity, the lines between individual and organizational benefit cannot always be so easily drawn.

According to Chambliss (and others), piracy is one of the earliest forms of state-organized crime. There is evidence that corrupt governors cooperated with pirates in Ancient Greece and Rome, and during the Middle Ages the Vikings operated as pirates on behalf of Scandinavian governments (Mueller and Adler 1985: 286; M. J. Peterson 1989: 51). During the 16th and 17th centuries the British, French, and Dutch governments arranged for pirates such as Sir Francis Drake to attack Spanish and Portuguese ships returning from the New World laden with vast mineral riches; the state got a share of the loot in return for protection and sponsorship (Jachcel 1981: 213; Chambliss 1989; M. J. Peterson 1989). During the colonial period in America, corrupt governments in New York City and in Charleston, South Carolina, cultivated and protected pirates (including the notorious Edward Teach, or "Blackbeard") and profited accordingly (Mueller and Adler 1985; Browning and Gerassi 1980). Of course, state policy was not uniformly supportive of piracy, and during certain periods governments were actively hostile toward it (Jachcel 1981: 193). But the overall history of relations between governments and pirates suggests that plundering will be overlooked or actively encouraged by the state when it benefits from such activity.

Chambliss (1989) identified various other forms of state-organized crime, including state complicity in smuggling, assassinations, criminal conspiracies, spying on citizens, diverting funds illegally, selling arms to blacklisted countries, and supporting terrorists. These forms of state-organized crime are hardly new and are still very much with us.

Terrorism (including assassination, torture, and kidnapping), although commonly thought of as crimes of individuals and groups outside of government, has often been carried out by agents of the state, on behalf of the state (Stohl and Lopez 1984). Even though "wholesale" acts of terrorism waged by the state against independence or revolutionary movements may be much more consequential, such acts receive less scholarly attention than do conventional forms of "retail" terrorism (Herman 1982; Barak 1990: 14). In the early 1980s, for example, an estimated 90,000 Latin Americans "disappeared" at the hands of state forces (Herman 1982: 12).

Many countries have sponsored state terrorism, the United States among them. It has sold billions of dollars worth of arms and ammunition to "client states" all over the world; those countries have used these munitions for state terrorist activities and for training hundreds of thousands of military and police personnel (Cottam and Marenin 1989; Herman 1982: 127). In El Salvador in the early 1980s, for example, well over 10,000 people were murdered in a single year by government forces supported by the United States, and as many as 70,000 may have been kidnapped and tortured to death between 1981 and 1988 (Herman 1982: 182; Agee 1988: 11–12). It is far from clear that the countless murders committed by "death squads" in El Salvador and other U.S. "client states" can be attributed to "out of control" security forces. Without in any way minimizing the crimes of "conventional" terrorists (e.g., World Trade Tower bombers), it is clear that much of the worst terrorism—in terms of human suffering—is carried out on behalf of the state (Chomsky and Herman 1979: 85–87; Herman 1982: 84). In one view, then, Western governments use the term *terrorist* as a semantic tool against those engaged in antistate activities.

## The White House and State-Organized Crime

Some of the most significant state-organized crime in the United States emanated directly from the White House. Investigation of the Watergate Affair in the 1970s revealed that the Nixon White House was involved in a range of improper and illegal "political policing" endeavors (Wise 1976). At the specific insistence of President Nixon, secret wiretaps were used against journalists and government officials suspected of being "disloyal" to the White House agenda in Vietnam and elsewhere. This improper wiretapping scheme, which the president and his associates later attempted to justify on "national security" grounds but had never properly authorized, provided a basis for one of the articles of impeachment drawn up against President Nixon. The exposure of a so-called White House Plumbers unit also contributed to Nixon's downfall. Over a period of years a group of special operatives (including former New York City police officers, CIA agents, and anti-Castro fighters) engaged in various highly questionable or blatantly illegal "investigations"; the most notorious was the break-in at the office of the psychiatrist (Dr. Lew Fielding) of Daniel Ellsberg, a former defense analyst who made the Pentagon Papers public (Wise 1976). The White House Plumbers were controlled by high-level Nixon aides operating from within the White House.

In the 1980s the single most celebrated case of state-organized crime was the Iran-Contra Affair, or "Irangate" (Crovitz 1987; Draper 1991; *New York Times* 1987; Pfost 1991; Simon and Eitzen 1993). At the heart of this case was the authorization, emanating from the White House, of the sale of weapons to Iran in exchange for funds to arm and support the Contras, who were fighting to overthrow the Sandinista government in Nicaragua. The principal illegality involved was violation of the Boland Amendment, which had expressly prohibited such covert aid to the Contras. The Iran-Contra enterprise, in fact, violated both Article 1, Section 9, of the U.S. Constitution, which requires that all funds raised by the U.S. government go through the Treasury and be approved by a congressional act, and the 19th-century Neutrality Act, which prohibits military expenditures against governments with which the United States is not at war.

The Reagan administration's involvement in the Iran-Contra scheme was broadly rationalized by invoking the promise of democracy in Nicaragua and a concern with human life. But the United States had supported the Somoza dictatorship—hardly a bastion of democracy—for decades, had boycotted the 1984 Nicaraguan elections (given a stamp of approval by international observers), had sought aid for the Contras from decidedly nondemocratic countries, and had attempted to circumvent constitutional constraints in the United States to provide aid to the Contras. It was far from clear that democracy would prevail if the Contras in fact came to power. (Indeed, the Nicaraguan people chose a democratic alternative to both the Sandinistas and the Contras several years after this whole affair.) Some commentators also questioned the sincerity of the Reagan administration's concern with human lives when its actions in this matter involved selling lethal weapons to a war-oriented nation that supported terrorists, and then directing the profits of those arms sales to people with an established record of killing large numbers of innocent Nicaraguans.

In addition to a conspiracy to violate the Boland Amendment (and the Constitution itself) and effectively defraud the government of money and property (for purposes not approved by Congress), the Iran-Contra case also involved perjury before Congress (by high-level officials who testified falsely about the administration's actions) and obstruction of justice in the form of deliberate destruction of presidential documents and other evidence pertaining to the case. A major congressional investigation and an independent prosecutor's investigation focused on the case.

In January 1994, Lawrence Walsh, the independent prosecutor, published his final report (Johnston 1994). By this time, after seven years of investigation, 11 people had pleaded guilty or had been convicted of charges in the case, although Admiral John Poindexter and Lt. Colonel Oliver North, the key White House personnel involved, had their convictions overturned on appeal on the grounds that their right to a fair trial had been compromised during congressional hearings. The Walsh Report alleged that President Reagan had at a minimum acquiesced in a cover-up, that then-Vice President George Bush had withheld evidence, and that Attorney General Edwin Meese had apparently been party to both illegal shipments of missiles and efforts to conceal the president's knowledge of these transactions. Despite the seriousness of the offenses involved, the violation of constitutional duties, and the deliberate misleading of Congress, the Iran-Contra case never fully generated widespread public indignation.

## State-Organized Crime and Federal Investigative Agencies

Some of the most significant state-organized crime is carried out under the auspices of governmental agencies with investigative powers, including the Central Intelligence Agency (CIA), the Federal Bureau of Investigation (FBI), and the Internal Revenue Service (IRS). The FBI and the IRS are two major federal law enforcement agencies that obviously play an important role in the investigation and prosecution of some of the most significant white collar crime. But the tables can be turned, and in recent years in particular it has been recognized that these agencies have sometimes engaged in forms of governmental crime.

**The Central Intelligence Agency (CIA)**    The CIA was established after World War II to prevent another Pearl Harbor (a surprise attack on U.S. territory) and as a response to the emerging "Cold War" (Jeffreys-Jones 1989). An intelligence agency, by definition, engages in covert operations that, at least sometimes, are of doubtful legality in the context within which they occur.

In 1975 a congressional investigation uncovered clear evidence that the CIA had periodically violated its own charter (Wise 1976: 183–84; Johnson 1985; Prados 1986). The violations included illegal opening of U.S. mail over a period of years; prohibited surveillance of various domestic dissident organizations; assassination plots against foreign leaders; unlawful stockpiling of deadly poisons and conducting dangerous, mind-altering experiments with unwitting subjects; complicity in the Watergate Affair; and assisting in the bribing and blackmailing of foreign leaders.

Over a period of decades the CIA intervened improperly in the affairs of many countries, funneling support to corrupt, totalitarian political leaders (including Panama's notorious Manuel Noriega) it viewed as supportive of U.S. policies while aiding in the downfall of other political leaders regarded as threatening to U.S. corporate interests (Jeffreys-Jones 1989; Kempe 1990; Prados 1986). CIA involvement in overthrowing the democratically elected, leftist government of Salvador Allende in Chile in 1973 is one of the best-documented cases of the latter type of intervention. This type of CIA operation has helped generate anti-American sentiments in many parts of the world.

Former CIA agents have in some cases used their special training and contacts for blatantly illegal enterprises after leaving the agency's employ. Howard Hunt became one of the key figures in the Watergate break-in, and Edwin Wilson sold sensitive information and sophisticated weapons to countries such as Libya (Prados 1986: 369–70). Both went to prison.

The CIA has been accused of having a right-wing bias and of placing its own interests ahead of other considerations, including compliance with the law. Many Americans have supported CIA operations and objectives and have viewed CIA personnel in heroic terms while vilifying their Soviet counterparts in the KGB (Andrew and Gordievsky 1990; Ranelagh 1986).

Some of the past misdeeds of the CIA have been exposed in our relatively open society (Ostovsky and Hoy 1990), but surely some "dirty secrets" remain. The future of intelligence agencies in the post-Cold War era remains an open question.

**The Federal Bureau of Investigation (FBI)**  Throughout most of the legendary reign of J. Edgar Hoover (1924–1972) the FBI generally enjoyed a reputation for integrity and high professional standards. After Hoover's death in 1972, revelations of improper and illegal FBI activities became much more frequent.

While still a young U.S. attorney, Hoover had been appointed FBI director at a time when the small government agency was plagued by charges of corruption. The FBI (originally, the Bureau of Investigation) had participated in controversial dragnet raids on draft dodgers and radicals during World War I, and its highest officials had been charged with hindering the investigations of war contractor fraud and the corrupt Teapot Dome dealings (Poveda 1990: 16). Although the FBI and Hoover were not immune to criticism during the years up to 1972 (and especially during the tumultuous 1960s), Hoover was by any measure enormously skillful in promoting a favorable public image of the agency and in maintaining relationships with powerful politicians.

Following Hoover's death the FBI became much more vulnerable to criticism, in part as a consequence of a Nixon administration initiative to reform government intelligence agencies (Poveda 1990: 70). In the mid-1970s in particular, FBI involvement in various abuses or outright illegalities came to light. From the mid-1950s on, the FBI had engaged in extralegal and illegal disruption and destabilization of dissident political groups through COINTELPRO (various counterintelligence programs). Close to 300 surreptitious entries and burglaries were conducted between 1942 and 1968 against at least 14 domestic organizations. Over a period of many decades, Hoover maintained secret files on public officials, a practice that amounted to an implicit (if not an explicit) blackmailing scheme. Through several different administrations the White House was allowed to use the FBI to gather political intelligence for partisan purposes. Some internal financial corruption occurred; FBI agents accepted kickbacks from an electronics firm, and agency personnel performed personal services for Hoover. Finally, informants were used as agent provocateurs to instigate illegal actions by dissident groups (Poveda 1990; Simon and Eitzen 1993).

One widely publicized activity, which is symptomatic of the pattern of FBI abuse of power, involved efforts to neutralize or undermine Civil Rights leader Martin Luther King, Jr. by exposing his alleged Communist ties and alleged marital infidelities (Wise 1976: 298–309). In what was arguably the lowest point in the history of the modern FBI, its acting director, J. Patrick Gray, revealed in April 1973 that he had destroyed documents pertinent to the Watergate investigation on instructions from John Erlichman, chief domestic affairs advisor to President Nixon (Poveda 1990: 66).

It is not clear whether the abusive and illegal activities of the FBI were restricted to a limited period of time in the past or have been ongoing enterprises over an extended period of time. Some leading students of COINTELPRO, which formally existed between the mid-1950s and 1971, contend that the same strategies used before the mid-1950s were directed against dissident groups such as the American Indian Movement in the 1970s and 1980s (Glick 1990; Churchill and Wall 1990). The original pattern of FBI illegalities may have been products of Hoover's personality and ideological biases, as well as the formidable political pressure imposed on the FBI to address perceived threats to the country's internal security (Poveda 1990). Ongoing abuses of power are probably best explained by an organizational culture that promotes a somewhat paranoid response to domestic dissidence and protest.

Even though the exposure of scandalous FBI practices in the 1970s ultimately reduced the FBI's autonomy and almost certainly imposed some constraints on illegalities and corruption, it is far from clear that such patterns have been wholly eradicated. Between 1981 and 1985 the FBI engaged in extensive investigation of more than 100 individuals and groups opposed to the Reagan administration's Central America policies (Jacoby 1988). On the other hand, the FBI has sometimes mounted undercover operations and used deceitful tactics to produce evidence against powerful and sophisticated white collar and governmental criminals (Marx 1988). Our evaluation of at least some of the FBI's "dirty tricks" may be shaped by our biases regarding the targets of the operations.

**The Internal Revenue Service (IRS)**   The IRS is the largest (some 123,000 employees) and arguably the most widely feared government enforcement agency. Despite its frontline role in the investigation of an important class of white collar offenses, it has also been accused—notably in David Burnham's *A Law Unto Itself—The IRS and the Abuse of Power* (1989)—of various crimes of its own.

Burnham's book alleges that the IRS has awarded organizations tax-exempt or tax-favored status based on ideological considerations, and that it has concentrated too much on pursuing small-fry tax evaders instead of wealthy and powerful individual and institutional tax evaders. Various U.S. presidents have used the IRS as a weapon to intimidate, harass, or incapacitate political enemies; the most fully documented case occurred during the Nixon administration (Wise 1976). The IRS has periodically used illegal wiretapping and other improper methods of surveillance, and it has rarely (if ever) apologized when its wrongfully initiated actions led to a taxpayer's financial (and personal) ruin.

Congress has given the IRS unusually broad powers and has engaged in relatively little oversight of its operations, both because members of Congress rely on taxes to fund the programs constituents want, and perhaps because they are fearful of precipitating an IRS audit of their own finances (Burnham 1989). Nevertheless, in 1989 Congress did undertake a major probe of the IRS and uncovered a "near epidemic of misconduct" by agents, including improperly accepting gratuities, misusing government travel funds, hiring relatives, investing in properties of companies under audit, initiating a criminal investigation against a prospective employer's competitor, and covering up (on the managerial level) misdeeds (Behar 1989; Farnsworth 1989). In 1994 government officials reported that since 1989 more than 1,300 IRS employees had been investigated for improper snooping on taxpayers (Hershey 1994b). Both state-organized and political white collar crime is involved in these offenses. Any form of corruption in the IRS is especially threatening to a tax system that very heavily relies on voluntary compliance, insofar as widespread perception of a corrupt IRS can provide many taxpayers a powerful rationale for not complying with the tax law.

Thus far our examination of state-organized crime has concentrated on the federal and state levels. But "state-organized" crime also occurs at the local level—in the form of police crime, our next topic of discussion.

## Police Crime

Among governmental crimes committed by relatively low-level officials, police crimes tend to be especially consequential. It may be useful to distinguish between police crime as a form of state-organized crime involving the abuse of power, and police crime as occupational crime, primarily corruption (Barker and Carter 1986; J. I. Ross 1992), but it is not always possible to differentiate between organizational and personal motivations or objectives.

The history of police crime is a long and varied one, involving violations of constitutional rights, excessive use of force, and related illegal acts to fulfill state or departmental objectives (Walker 1980, 1983). This abuse of police power has been disproportionately directed toward minorities, the poor, political dissidents, and members of the counterculture (Center for Research on Criminal Justice 1977; Chevigny 1969; Cray 1972; Platt and Cooper 1974; Skolnick 1969). Many of the major urban race riots in the 1960s and since were precipitated by abuse of African Americans by white police officers; the 1991 Rodney King case, in which the brutal beating of a man pulled over for speeding was videotaped, is only one of the more recent and widely publicized of a long line of such incidents (Levy 1968; National Advisory Commission on Civil Disorders 1968; Roberg and Kuykendall 1993).

The most serious form of police brutality is the improper—and sometimes fatal—misuse of deadly force (Fyfe 1988; Sherman and Langworthy 1979). Historically, police brutality has rarely been prosecuted, and only in recent decades has this situation improved with the establishment of civilian review boards, citizen mobilization, and a more attentive press. An ongoing debate focuses on whether the improper use of force is ever justified to control crime. This has been called the "Dirty Harry" problem, a reference to a Clint Eastwood film character called "Dirty Harry" Callahan, a police inspector who uses blatantly illegal actions to force information out of a sadistic kidnapper (Klockars 1980).

Police brutality is not the only form of police abuse of power. The Mollen Commission reported in 1994 that New York City police officers frequently committed perjury, made warrantless searches and false arrests, and tampered with evidence (Sexton 1994). The practice of perjury in court testimony was especially common and was known among the police as "testilying." The officers crossed the line into illegality either to achieve the department's crime-fighting objectives more efficiently or to advance their own careers.

For at least a century commissions formed to investigate charges of police corruption have found evidence of significant levels of such wrongdoing. In this context *corruption* refers to illegal and improper behavior on the part of the police to personally enrich themselves. The Lexow Commission in the 1890s uncovered much police corruption in New York City, as did the Knapp Commission in the 1970s, the Mollen Commission in the 1990s, and other investigations in between (Roberg and Kuykendall 1993). Social scientists have also documented the pervasiveness of police corruption (Reiss 1971; Sherman 1978b).

It is useful to distinguish between police personnel who actively seek bribes and kickbacks, engage in "shakedowns," and even steal for personal gain ("meat eaters"), and those who accept minor gratuities, meals, and the like from businesses and individual entrepreneurs on their beat ("grass eaters")(Knapp Commission 1973). The more serious type of corruption has been most frequently associated with vice, or victimless crimes. Police officers can rationalize that their corrupt activity in this realm does no harm because the laws are largely futile and they are only victimizing criminals. Twelve police officers affiliated with the Harlem precinct were arrested in New York City in April 1994 on charges of forcing drug dealers to pay them protection money and beating up dealers who did not cooperate (Krauss 1994). These arrests followed earlier arrests of officers for drug dealing, and further arrests were anticipated. Such corrupt activity occurred in many precincts. Police in virtually every large city engage in this type of corrupt activity.

Some police abuse of power and corruption is simply wrongdoing by a few "bad apples" on the police force. Police work is likely to attract at least some individuals who enjoy bullying others or join the force with the intention of exploiting special opportunities to enrich themselves. However, police crime may well be more fully explained by systemic factors that promote it and tend to shield it from exposure (Sherman 1978b; Roberg and Kuykendall 1993). Police officers enter police work somewhat idealistically and subsequently undergo a process of socialization to the harsh realities of their jobs; the result is often cynicism. Officers are also likely to internalize powerful norms, especially loyalty to their fellow officers, that tend to discourage cooperation with investigations of corruption. Police work is also especially fraught with unusual opportunities and temptations to abuse power or corruptly benefit financially.

Police crime has received a fair amount of attention, but other low-level criminal justice personnel are hardly immune to the temptations to commit occupationally related crimes (Henderson and Simon 1994). Abuse of authority and various forms of corruption occur within all components of the criminal justice system, including the courts and correctional institutions.

# Political White Collar Crime

RECALL THAT WE defined political white collar crime as governmental or political party officials engaging in illegal and improper activity for personal gain (e.g., economic enrichment or political advantage), rather than to advance some state, governmental, or political (ideological) goal.

We can distingush between crimes committed on behalf of political parties, which might be directed toward gaining office in return for improper influence, and crimes committed on behalf of a particular governmental office.

## Political System Corruption

Free elections and competing political parties are defining elements of Western democracies, and most observers would agree that such systems avoid some of the extreme abuses of power associated with one-party systems. But the electoral process and interparty competition in such societies promote their own forms of corruption. In the progressive view, democracy is something of an illusion in a system in which a small "power elite" controls the decision-making process and the general population is largely indoctrinated with the "official line" by a compliant press (Chomsky 1991; Mills 1959). Nevertheless, at least some differences in policy preferences exist between the two major parties in the United States, and competition is a real element in the electoral process.

Once politicians gain the power of office, they more often than not attempt to hold onto it. Incumbency has advantages: enhanced name recognition, the capacity to implement programs for and grant favors to special interests and constituents, a well-documented record of accomplishments, and frequently voters' tendency to prefer stability over change. It has never been illegal for politicians to propose, endorse, or push through policies and programs that despite questionable value still benefit special interests and constituents, as long as no direct quid pro quo ("this for that") exists.

## The Watergate Affair

The single most famous contemporary case of political crime motivated by the desire to stay in power is the Watergate Affair, which ultimately led to the resignation of President Richard Nixon. The Watergate Affair had two primary aspects: a break-in and burglary in June 1972, and the broad range of abuses of power by the Nixon administration, including illegal surveillance, dirty tricks, cover-ups, and enemies' lists (Emery 1994; Silverstein 1988).

The original incident was a break-in of the Democratic National Party Headquarters in the Watergate complex in Washington, D.C., carried out by individuals affiliated with the Committee to Reelect the President (CREEP) and the White House itself. Initially the Nixon White House tried to dismiss the whole matter as a "third-rate burglary" of which they had no part, but over the course of the next two years a massive cover-up conspiracy—with Nixon directly involved—ensued. Investigative reporters (especially Bob Woodward and Carl Bernstein of *The Washington Post*), a special prosecutor, and congressional investigative committees uncovered this conspiracy, including the direct involvement of numerous highly placed Nixon administration and reelection campaign officials. Impeachment proceedings were initiated against Nixon, who in August 1974 resigned the presidency rather than face virtually certain removal from office. Although Nixon was controversially pardoned and excused from criminal liability by his successor, Gerald Ford, many of his close associates went to prison.

One explanation of the affair is that Nixon and his associates were uniquely corrupt and unprincipled, and that the origins of Watergate can be traced to Nixon's paranoia and flawed personality. An alternative view is that the Watergate crimes were products of a political system that imposes high expectations on presidents but frustrates them with checks and balances; in such a system maintaining, exercising, and extending power takes precedent over integrity and compliance with the law. In this view, most recent U.S. American presidents have authorized similar evasions or violations of law (Silverstein 1988). As is often the case, there is a measure of truth to both views.

One of the remarkable aspects of the Watergate Affair is that direct personal enrichment played almost no role. The Watergate crimes focused on maintaining power and punishing political enemies. From the outset every effort was made to cover up illegal acts and shield higher-level conspirators from criminal liability. The individuals ultimately accused in the Watergate case professed to be motivated by concern for the welfare of the country or by political loyalty; in at least some cases career ambitions or the inability to say no to a superior may have played a role.

Still, financial gain was not entirely absent from the affair. The wealthy corporations and individuals (principally the "new money" rich) who violated campaign-contribution laws by funneling large sums of money to CREEP surely anticipated long-term financial benefits from having a conservative administration indebted to them (Sale 1977). Thus Watergate can also be seen as the concerted effort of businessmen and politicians to profit from the maintenance and extension of Nixon's political power.

## Corruption in the Electoral Financing Process

We tend to view political corruption in individualistic terms because it is both easier and more reassuring to focus on individual wrongdoers. Etzioni (1988a: 18) related this tendency to the misleading personality cult prevalent in the media, Americans' pride in their system of government, and the failure to recognize that the beneficiaries of corruption have managed to legalize most of it. The financing of elections—especially legislative elections—and the related practice of legislative lobbying are two integral parts of the political system that promote corruption.

Until the final few decades of the 20th century, campaigns were generally fairly inexpensive, involving the costs of traveling to give speeches and manufacturing campaign buttons and posters (Jackson 1988: 3). More recently, especially with the advent of television, the cost of campaigning has increased exponentially. Since the federal election financing reforms of the early 1970s, which imposed strict limitations on the amount of money individuals could donate to campaigns, political action committees (PACs) have become a vastly more important element in the financing of elections (Barbrook 1987; Etzioni 1988a; Magleby and Nelson 1990; Makinson 1990; Noonan 1984; Stern 1988).

Although any interest group can put together a PAC, wealthy corporations in particular have used this device to funnel tens of millions of dollars to political candidates, especially incumbents and chairs of powerful legislative committees. This form of "legalized bribery" not only gives incumbents an enormous financial advantage over challengers, it has been demonstrated to influence legislators' voting records as well (Etzioni 1988a; Jackson 1988; Makinson 1990; Noonan 1984; Stern 1988). Defense contractors and owners of thrifts, to name but two examples, have used the political campaign financing system to successfully promote their interests, at a cost to taxpayers in the billions of dollars. Furthermore, until quite recently, members of Congress could transfer any PAC money left over from their campaigns into their personal accounts, or could use it however they chose.

Election financing abuse can be considered a white collar crime issue even when laws are not specifically violated. Clearly, the line between a "bribe" (an illegal payoff for an explicit vote) and a "contribution" (a legal donation with an implicit understanding) is exceptionally thin, and to date no member of Congress has ever been indicted simply for accepting PAC money.

## Political White Collar Crime in the Executive Branch

No U.S. president has been convicted of using this high office for personal enrichment, but many presidents are alleged to have engaged in unethical or specifically illegal conduct for economic gain before, during, and after their term of office. Even George Washington is alleged to have engaged in suspect land deals early in his career (Miller 1992). Various 19th-century presidents, including James Garfield, were linked with bribery scandals, and recent presidents, including Eisenhower, Johnson, Nixon, Ford, Reagan, and Clinton, have allegedly accepted generous gifts (or exorbitant honorariums) from foreign leaders or admirers, evaded taxes, accumulated private fortunes by selling political influence, or appropriated secret funds for personal use (Fineman and Cohn 1994; Garment 1992; Gulley and Reese 1980; Miller 1992). Schuyler Colfax, vice president in Ulysses Grant's first administration (1869–1873), was accused of accepting bribes and was politically ruined, even though he was never formally charged (Kohn 1989; Noonan 1984). One hundred years later Spiro Agnew, Richard Nixon's first vice president, was formally accused of having accepted payoffs from Maryland contractors, whom he had favored as governor of that state (Cohen and Witcover 1974). As part of a complex negotiated deal, Agnew was forced to resign and to plead "no contest" to one charge of tax evasion.

Many other high-level members of various presidential administrations have been charged with specific criminal acts. Samuel Swartout, a New York Port customs collector during Andrew Jackson's two administrations, was charged with having embezzled over $1 million (Miller 1992: 124). The Buchanan administration, which immediately preceded Lincoln's presidency, was compromised by much graft, kickbacks, and overpayments (Hagan 1992). The Grant administrations after the Civil War were notoriously corrupt; specific charges of fraud or accepting bribes were directed at Grant's ambassador to Great Britain; his secretaries of war, the navy, and the interior; and his presidential secretary, among others (Browning and Gerassi 1980; Miller 1992). In the famous Teapot Dome scandal during the Harding administration (1921–1923), the secretary of the interior accepted bribes for turning over leases of government oil fields to private oil companies to exploit for their own profit; Harding's attorney general, Veterans Bureau director, and alien property custodian were also charged with various acts of corruption and fraud (Kohn 1989; Miller 1992). In many subsequent administrations, high-level aides or officials were charged with some form of personal corruption (Miller 1992); for example, Truman's military aide Harry Vaughn was alleged to have accepted a freezer, and Eisenhower's chief of staff Sherman Adams a vicuña coat.

The Nixon administration is notorious with respect to governmental criminality and wrongdoing, and perhaps more close Nixon associates went to prison than did the cronies of any other president. Still, it is rather striking that the numerous serious charges against Nixon's associates, including perjury, burglary, bribery, illegal surveillance, altering evidence, and the like, were almost wholly devoid of elements of personal enrichment. In contrast, the Reagan administration's pervasive "sleaze factor" was characterized by a "cashing in" mentality, and it may have been the most corrupt of all presidential administrations (Hagan 1992).

This "cashing in" mentality is best exemplified by the case of Michael Deaver, Reagan's deputy chief of staff. Deaver left the White House in 1985 and immediately engaged in influence peddling for exorbitant fees, collecting millions of dollars from foreign governments and corporate clients in return for "access"; in one case he allegedly received $250,000 for making a single phone call (Martz 1986). Deaver was ultimately charged with violating laws prohibiting lobbying by recently retired federal officials and was convicted of lying about his activities (Beckwith 1987).

Over 200 members of the Reagan administration—including his first and second attorney generals, his first national security advisor, his schedule maker, his CIA director, his deputy secretary of commerce, his federal aviation administrator, his secretary of the navy, his deputy defense secretary, his secretary of the interior, his director of the U.S. Information Agency, and his head of the Veterans Administration—were investigated for ethical or criminal misconduct; personal enrichment was involved in many of these cases (Brinkley 1988; J. I. Ross 1992: 1). But these cases of alleged personal corruption, which typically received substantial media coverage, are less significant than the more subtle and sophisticated forms of institutionalized corruption carried out from within many executive branch departments.

In the case of one cabinet-level department, Housing and Urban Development (HUD), an estimated $4–8 billion was defrauded or wasted during the 1980s, and the department was riddled with corruption and mismanagement (Waldman 1989). The essence of the HUD scandal was that a large number of lucrative department grants were dispensed to or on behalf of Republican Party benefactors, well-connected political figures, and members of Congress. Several HUD officials who left the department to become consultants and lobbyists received lucrative fees for dealing with their former associates still in the department. By the early 1990s a number of HUD officials had been convicted for such offenses as defrauding the government, taking bribes, and lying to Congress (Labaton 1993). In one case an agent hired to resell houses repossessed by the government siphoned off $5 million—apparently the largest individual theft of U.S. government funds in history—when she realized that no one at HUD was monitoring the receipts from the resold houses (DeParle 1990). The media labeled this individual "Robin HUD" after she claimed to have given much of the money to charity, but an unsympathetic judge sentenced her to four years in prison and a $600,000 fine.

The extraordinary hypocrisy of the HUD scandal is quite obvious: Members of an administration that campaigned against big government and government waste engaged in large-scale waste of taxpayers' money; programs intended to assist poor Americans were milked by wealthy developers, private interests, highly paid consultants, and influential politicians for their own benefit; and homelessness in America increased dramatically during a period when HUD money was being ripped off and wasted (Waldman 1989). In this case a form of state-organized crime was driven by the symbiotic relationship between incumbent politicians concerned with staying in office and special interests determined to profit from their ties to and support for those incumbents

In the mid-1990s corruption was alleged to be widespread in farm-aid programs and in connection with immigration matters (Engelberg 1994; Frantz 1994). The financial dealings of the Clinton administration's secretaries of Agriculture, Housing and Urban Development, Commerce, and Transportaion, were under investigation by an independent counsel or by the Department of Justice (Johnston 1995).

**Corruption in State Government** Corruption at the state level dates from the early history of the American colonies. Benjamin Fletcher, one of the first governors (1692–1698) of New York, was driven from office by charges of pervasive corruption, including giving protection to pirates for payoffs, making huge land grants to friends and associates, and intimidating voters at the polls with armed thugs (Browning and Gerassi 1980: 67). Such a pattern of corruption was present in many colonies and persisted into statehood after the American Revolution.

In the modern era, corruption on the state level has been linked with an ethnic style of governing—"a particular political ethos or style which attaches a relatively low value to probity and impersonal efficiency and relatively high value to favors, personal loyalty, and private gain"—the general absence of substantial journalistic oversight, and the relative autonomy of state agencies (Wilson 1966: 30). As of 1993, eight sitting governors in the 20th century had been indicted on criminal charges, and several former governors—for example, Otto Kerner of Illinois and both Spiro Agnew and Marvin Mandel of Maryland—were prosecuted on such charges as conspiracy, fraud, perjury, bribery, racketeering, and income tax evasion (Applebome 1993b; Cohen and Witcover 1974; Kohn 1989; Noonan 1984). These charges typically involved accepting stocks or taking bribes from contractors and others doing business with the state in return for political favors. In 1993 Governor Guy Hunt of Alabama was convicted of felony charges in connection with converting a $200,000 inauguration fund for personal use and was immediately ousted from office (Applebome 1993b).

Corruption on the state level is hardly restricted to governors. In Pennsylvania, a state with a long history of political corruption, the state treasurer, Budd Dwyer, was convicted in the 1980s of accepting payoffs to steer contracts to Computer Technology Associates, a computer company (Jenkins 1993). In a bizarre ending to this case, Dwyer committed suicide with a revolver during the live telecast of a news conference he called prior to his sentencing. Even if this outcome is unusual, the practice of state officials accepting bribes for political favors is not uncommon.

**Corruption in County and Local Government**   A great deal of corruption has occurred on the county and local level as well. Between 1970 and 1977, some 1,290 county executives, mayors, councilmen, and others were found guilty of some form of official corruption (Noonan 1984: 601). The level of prosecution of such officials has certainly increased recently, although it is not clear whether the overall level of corruption itself has in fact increased as well.

During the colonial period in the 18th century, local governments were often guilty of embezzlement, taking bribes, and reserving for themselves the right to rent out city property and sell liquor for profit (Browning and Gerassi 1980: 81). In the 19th century and into the 20th century, city governments were often largely run by political bosses or party machines, who virtually institutionalized corruption (Steffens 1904; Steinberg 1972). Some commentators have even suggested that at least some of this corruption was an inevitable and functionally positive response to the weaknesses and inadequacies of official city governments (Wilson 1961). Even so, it is clearly true that such corruption costs taxpayers a great deal of money and has generated distrustful and cynical attitudes toward local government.

Ed Crump of Memphis, James Michael Curley of Boston, Tom Pendergast of Kansas City, and Frank Hague of Jersey City are among the more colorful and notorious 20th-century political bosses who enriched themselves through political corruption. Hague was a dominant force in Hudson County, New Jersey, in the first half of the 20th century, but corruption in this county persisted long after his demise. A number of subsequent mayors of Jersey City were convicted of conspiracy, extortion, bribery, or tax evasion, most recently in 1991 (Strum 1991). So many public officials have been indicted for criminal corruption in Hudson County that in the 1980s the *Jersey Journal* once published this headline: "No Hudson Officials Indicted Today."

Perhaps the single most famous example of political machine corruption is New York City's Tammany Hall, established in 1789 and a major force in the city's political life for the next 150 years. One early Tammany Hall leader, George Washington Plunkitt, bluntly called the systematic corruption he and his associates practiced "honest graft." He has been quoted as observing, "I seen my opportunities and I took 'em" (Miller 1992: 239). Although many of the city's bosses got away with accumulating large private fortunes through corrupt dealings, Tammany Hall reached its apex in the 1870s under the leadership of William Marcy ("Boss") Tweed. Primarily by exercising control of the department of public works, over a period of years Tweed and his associates defrauded the City of New York of up to $200 million through vastly inflated purchases and repairs, false vouchers, fictitious bills, and other such devices. They became so greedy and obvious in their theft of the city's assets that public outrage finally led to criminal prosecutions (Browning and Gerassi 1980; Kohn 1989; Miller 1992). Tweed was eventually convicted on 204 criminal counts and died in prison in 1878.

One view holds that urban political corruption has generally declined during the 20th century because of such factors as civil service reforms (which reduce patronage), the welfare state's displacement of the urban machines, the decreasing power of white ethnic groups as new minorities emerged, and the increasing importance of television advertising (which diminishes the role of the party organization)(Tager 1988). But if such factors decreased somewhat the scope of municipal corruption, they hardly eliminated it, and new forces provided new opportunities and incentives for corruption. New York City seems to experience a cycle of corruption scandals every five to seven years (Anechiarico 1990).

During the 1980s, more than a century after the era of the Tweed Ring, a major new corruption scandal surfaced in New York City. A municipal fiscal crisis had led to a considerable expansion of private contracting for goods and services (Tager 1988). Well-connected politicians in Mayor Ed Koch's administration engaged in corrupt dealings with private contractors, either through extortion, by taking bribes, or by making investments in which conflicts of interest were involved (Newfield and Barrett 1988). Major scandals ensued. One involving the Parking Violations Bureau led to the suicide of the Queens Borough president; another involved the Taxi and Limousine Commission; still others involved bribery or conflict of interest with ferry service and cable television franchises (Oreskes 1987; Tager 1988).

In addition to high-level cases involving city administrators or political leaders, more than 100 middle-level city employees (e.g., inspectors, buyers, and agency staffers) were convicted of job-related corruption between January 1985 and June 1988 (Newfield and Barrett 1988: 454). This widely reported scandal, which led to many criminal convictions, did not obliterate the problem of corruption in New York City. Subsequent cases included charges of corruption, bribery, or conflict of interest against taxi inspectors, school officials, and Board of Elections members, among others (Buder 1989; Sullivan 1990; Myers 1992; Berger 1992).

The persistence of such corruption tends to support the primacy of structural or institutional causes over individualistic, "bad apples" explanations. In view of the repeated historical failure of reform movements and criminal prosecutions to eradicate municipal corruption, it is likely to endure on some level in the forseeable future.

## Political White Collar Crime in the Legislative Branch

Members of the legislative branch of the government have always had a broad range of opportunities for corrupt dealings. James Madison, one of the Founding Fathers and the fourth U.S. president, believed that the Congress was less corruptible than the executive branch in part because of its large number of members and diluted power (Noonan 1984: 431). But from the beginning state legislators have often found the temptation to benefit personally from their legislative actions irresistible.

In 1795 several Georgia legislators acquired shares in a company seeking leg-islative action that would transfer to it millions of acres of Indian land. Although the legislators involved were punished at the polls at the next election, they could not be criminally prosecuted because at that time Georgia had no law against bribery (Noonan 1984: 435–37). Until after the Civil War, neither effective federal laws nor adequate means of investigating the whole range of corrupt legislative practices existed, and even such venerated statesmen as Henry Clay and Daniel Webster accepted large loans or retainers from special interests.

The Credit Mobilier affair, which surfaced in 1872, was perhaps the first major public scandal concerning congressional corruption (Noonan 1984). Credit Mobilier was a holding company organized in 1864 to coordinate the westward expansion of the Union Pacific railroad. Shares in the company were made available to many con-gressmen at nominal cost (or were given as a gift) by the company's founders (including Congressman Oakes Ames), and Congress enacted a bond capitalization of the scheme that greatly enriched the shareholders. Although considerable public indignation and a congressional investigation resulted once the scheme was revealed, no congressmen were criminally prosecuted, and only two (including Ames) were even censured.

In the century and more since the Credit Mobilier Affair, major congressional corruption scandals have erupted periodically, and some forms of corruption became virtually institutionalized. Some of the specific ways in which lawmakers become lawbreakers include use of official status to evade arrest (for drunken driving and other such offenses); "junketing" (taking trips to exotic locations, at the taxpayers' expense, often on the superficial pretext of making a legislative study); double billing, in which both a private corporation and the government are billed for the same item; use of the franking (free mailing) privilege for political or personal purposes; use of official congressional staff for purely political or personal purposes; and a broad range of "conflict of interest" offenses (Green 1984). There are many docu-mented instances of legislators promoting legislation that benefits special interests who have paid them off (either directly through low-cost loans or through retainers to law partners). In some cases their own investments are directly affected.

Although congressional corruption has been an enduring phenomenon through-out U.S. history, in the 1970s—perhaps because of heightened journalistic and pub-lic interest following Watergate—prosecutions of members of Congress and their staffs increased fivefold relative to the years 1941 through 1971 (Green 1984). The charges included violations of financial disclosure laws, federal mail fraud, salary kickbacks, bribery, conspiracy, perjury, campaign financing violations, income tax evasions, defrauding of the government, and obstruction of justice. In the so-called

"Koreagate" affair, Korean businessman Tongsun Park spent hundreds of thousands of dollars on campaign contributions, personal gifts, parties, and other favors for as many as 115 members of Congress in return for their support of various South Korean interests (Kohn 1989).

A still more dramatic scandal, the Abscam case, was revealed in 1980. In the late 1970s the FBI had set up a bogus company (Abdul Enterprises) and spread the word that wealthy Arab sheiks were prepared to engage in various shady deals (Noonan 1984: 607). Seven members of Congress ultimately indicted for accepting bribes in some form (e.g., $50,000 cash) from the "Arab sheiks" were expelled from Congress or forced to resign and wer? convicted of various charges; several of them, including Senator Harrison Williams of New Jersey, were sentenced to prison terms. The FBI videotapes of the legislators accepting bribes marked the first time such evidence was available in the long history of congressional bribe-taking. However, the claim that the FBI had engaged in entrapment introduced controversy into the case.

The Abscam affair was hardly the last case of alleged congressional corruption. The House Post Office Scandal of the late 1980s even led to the criminal indictment of the powerful chair of the House Ways and Means Committee in 1994 (Thomma 1994). To some members of Congress, the lure of corruption is apparently more potent than any deterrent effect of the threat of disgrace, conviction, and imprisonment.

## Political White Collar Crime in the Judicial Branch

Of the three branches of government, the judicial branch has probably been the least tainted by claims of corruption, but it has not been entirely free of such claims. Concerns over judicial misconduct date back to the earliest civilizations, and judges are known to have accepted bribes in Ancient Rome and during medieval times (Noonan 1984). One of the most famous cases involved Sir Francis Bacon, who served as lord chancellor during the reign of King James I of England and was charged with accepting bribes in return for favorable decisions in 1621. Bacon was fined but later pardoned. Judges in the United States have been charged with many crimes, including bribery, extortion, obstructing justice, income tax evasion, embezzlement, fraud, and abuse of authority (Ashman 1973). Many of the judges so charged were forced to resign; others were impeached, censured, disbarred, and convicted of crimes. A few went to prison.

Criminal prosecutions of federal judges have been rare, although not totally unknown (Jackson 1974). One federal judge was recently convicted of income tax evasion, sentenced to prison, and impeached, and another was impeached for soliciting a $150,000 bribe (Johnston 1989). State court judges and local judges have far more often been charged with milking estates for personal enrichment, making corrupt arrangements with bail bondsmen, and accepting outright bribes (Jackson 1974).

Judges are obviously in a position to abuse their considerable power. If it is in fact true that outright criminal behavior is rare among judges, it may be that the daily contact with lawbreakers in their courts raises their awareness of the harmful consequences of lawbreaking. Insofar as judges are relatively well-compensated and enjoy considerable prestige, they have relatively less to gain and much more to lose by engaging in criminal conduct. Furthermore, it is tempting to believe that the procedures for selecting judges succeed more often than not in advancing individuals of above-average integrity. But there is also some reason to believe that prosecutors and other criminal justice personnel are reluctant to go after judges, and that judges are reluctant to turn on each other (Jackson 1974: 146). Clearly, cases of judicial crime and corruption are especially disturbing, given a judge's role of passing judgment on others convicted of criminal behavior.

## Governmental Crime, In Sum

GOVERNMENTAL CRIME, THEN, has been defined here as a cognate form of white collar crime. It obviously has many attributes similar to those of corporate crime and occupational crime, and it is driven by similar or identical motivations. There are numerous interrelationships between governmental criminals and corporate white collar criminals as people move back and forth between the public and private sectors. The differences between governmental and private-sector white collar crime are principally differences of emphasis; the enhancement or extension of power is somewhat more important in the former case, whereas the maximization of profit (or the prevention of loss) is relatively more important in the latter case. The ultimate scope of harm may be greater in governmental crime cases.

The existence of governmental crime generates some challenging questions: Does governmental crime produce structural conditions that promote white collar crime? Does it generate a moral ambience that facilitates the rationalization of white collar crime? If the government is committing crime, who polices the government?

# State-Corporate Crime, Finance Crime, and Technocrime

SOME MAJOR FORMS of white collar crime are not easily classified as either corporate crime, occupational crime, or governmental crime, but rather are hybrids that combine attributes of two or more of the established forms of white collar crime. In this chapter we consider two especially significant hybrid types, state-corporate crime and finance crime; we also examine an increasingly conspicuous element of various white collar crimes: technocrime.

## State-Corporate Crime

THE HOLOCAUST, WHICH involved the torture and murder of millions of people (principally European Jews), is by any criteria among the most monstrous crimes in history. Although Hitler and his Nazi henchmen rightly receive most of the blame, some German corporations also played a role.

The I.G. Farben Company, a huge chemical combine, built a slave labor camp adjacent to the notorious Auschwitz concentration camp and controlled a company that produced the poisonous Zyklon B gas used in the death camps (Borkin 1978). Only a handful of I.G. Farben executives were convicted of crimes against humanity (and received relatively light sentences) after World War II, and the corporation once again became an enormously powerful and profitable entity. Even though I.G. Farben's wartime actions occurred under extraordinary political circumstances and may well have involved complex and conflicting motivations (Hayes 1987), its use of slave labor and the production of poisonous gas was nonetheless a criminal enterprise, in this case one involving cooperation between a state and a corporation.

It has long been recognized that much illegal governmental activity has many connections with private enterprise. Many linkages exist among the "power elites," and many "interlocks" occur between public and private entities. Kramer and

Michalowski (1990: 3) called for recognition of "state-corporate crime" that "occurs at the interstices of corporations and governments." They define this type of crime as follows:

> State-corporate crimes are illegal or socially injurious actions that occur when one or more institutions of political governance pursue a goal in direct cooperation with one or more institutions of economic production and distribution. (Kramer and Michalowski, 1990: 3)

The premise for the concept of state-corporate crime is that modern states and corporations are profoundly interdependent. A prominent example of such crime is the space shuttle *Challenger* disaster (Kramer and Michalowski 1990; Kramer 1992).

*Challenger* exploded just minutes after it was launched on January 28, 1986, killing all seven astronauts aboard, including a schoolteacher, Christa McAuliffe. This fatal explosion was officially designated a tragic accident attributed to the failure of O-ring seals. But, as Kramer (and Michalowski) revealed, a complex of governmental and corporate pressures led to an avoidable tragedy.

On the one hand NASA, a government agency, was under continual pressure, during a period of diminished political and economic support for the space program generally, to produce a successful launch of the reusable space shuttle as soon as possible. NASA's response to these external pressures was to approve various compromises in the design of the craft; it was also apparently eager to have the *Challenger* in orbit while President Reagan was delivering his "State of the Union" address, which would have allowed him to say that an ordinary American schoolteacher was in orbit, even as he spoke.

For its part, the Morton Thiokol Corporation, the primary contractor on the project, was eager to meet NASA's tight deadlines (and retain its profitable contracts) and pushed ahead with production of the space shuttle despite tests indicating problems with the O-ring seals. Additional pressures to launch were generated by previous postponements due to bad weather and the great public interest generated by the inclusion of a schoolteacher on the flight, and thus the January 28th launch date became a high priority.

A Presidential Commission investigating the tragedy later uncovered clear evidence that Morton Thiokol engineers had expressed strong reservations about launching in the cold weather anticipated for that day, and a simple experiment performed by a commission member, the eminent physicist Richard Feynman, clearly demonstrated that the O-ring seals lost resilience when subjected to cold temperatures. But the dissenting engineers were overruled by corporate and agency superiors who, in so desperately wanting the launch to proceed, refused to heed the warnings of danger. Although the Presidential Commission had some harsh words for the decision makers involved in this tragedy, none of them were ever criminally indicted.

Other examples of state-corporate crime cited by Kramer and Michalowski (1990) include private contractors' violations of environmental, safety, and health standards at federal nuclear weapons production facilities; the Iran-Contra Affair involving governmental personnel and private arms dealers; and defense contract frauds resulting from a cooperative enterprise between military or political officials and private defense industry contractors. The environmental crimes committed in conjunction with U.S. nuclear weapons production are a form of state-corporate crime because they are a collective product of interaction between a government agency (the U.S. Department of Energy) and private business corporations (Kauzlarich and Kramer 1993). Strictly speaking, state-corporate crime reflects the fulfillment of mutually agreed on objectives of a public agency and a private entity achieved through cooperative illegal activity.

The Wedtech case, which involved defense contract fraud on a major scale, was one of the more widely publicized white collar crime cases of the latter half of the 1980s. In terms of the distinctions made in Chapter 5 between state crime and political white collar crime, the Wedtech case might best be classified as state-political white collar crime because on the governmental side the principal parties were acting more on their own behalf than on behalf of a governmental agency. In a broader sense, however, the case occurred because the Reagan administration's support for the Wedtech Company was consistent with the administration's position that underprivileged citizens were best assisted through private enterprise, not by direct governmental support.

The Wedtech Company, which originated in 1965 as a small machine shop (the Welbilt Electronic Die Co.), was founded in the South Bronx in New York by John Mariotta, a man of Hispanic extraction (Sternberg and Harrison 1989; Thompson 1990; Traub 1990). By the mid-1970s the company began to apply for government contracts through a special Small Business Administration program, the 8(A) Program, intended to set aside some contracts for businesses dominated by deprived minorities. The company, operating in an area widely portrayed as the ultimate in urban wastelands, attracted the attention of Mario Biaggi, a well-known congressman from the Bronx. In return for using his influence to steer lucrative defense contracts to the Welbilt Company, Biaggi began to accept from Welbilt payments filtered through a law firm with which he was affiliated.

Biaggi was only the first of a series of well-placed politicians, government officials, government bureaucrats, and well-connected lawyers who were extravagantly rewarded for ensuring that large sums of government money continued to go to the company, later known as Wedtech. More specifically, these parties enabled Wedtech to receive defense contracts despite being grossly ill-equipped to complete and deliver on the contracts, and despite some clear evidence of fraudulent financial manipulations. E. Robert Wallach, a California attorney and close friend of President Reagan's adviser and attorney general, Edwin Meese, used this connection to seek privileged status for Wedtech in return for very generous compensation from the company; Meese himself promoted the interests of the company. President Reagan expressed admiration for John Mariotta when he made an impromptu speech at the White House extolling the great benefits of a company like Wedtech, which employed people in deprived neighborhoods formerly on welfare and gave them an opportunity to become self-sufficient.

Lower-level government bureaucrats who raised questions about Wedtech's ability to deliver on the multimillion dollar defense projects it pursued were either intimidated by political pressure from above or bought off. Forged or phony invoices and fraudulent financial statements were used to keep the government money coming in. Wedtech's principals were mainly concerned with lining their own pockets by skimming off millions of dollars of the company's assets.

Ultimately the Wedtech fiasco was exposed. The taxpayers lost some $300 million, many investors lost their retirement income, many creditors went bankrupt, and Wedtech workers went back on welfare. The company's principals were convicted of various crimes and given prison sentences, as were some of the government officials (including two congressmen) involved in the case. Although Wedtech was not a major corporation, this case demonstrates the potential for especially large losses when corrupt dealings span the private and public sectors. It illustrates the political influence involved in government contracts, the potential for well-intentioned programs to be corrupted, and the contribution to criminal conduct by lawyers, accountants, and other professionals who put their economic self-interest above other concerns.

Kramer and Michalowski (1990: 4) noted as well that state-corporate crime also occurs both on the international level (e.g., the involvement of ITT with activities in Nazi Germany, Chile, and elsewhere; Sampson 1973) and on the local level (e.g., state involvement with private operators of hazardous waste disposal operations). Above all, the concept of state-corporate crime compels us to recognize that some major forms of organizational crime cannot be easily classified as either corporate or governmental, and that the interorganizational forms of crime that bring together corporations and government entities may be especially potent and pernicious.

## Finance Crime

*"Behind every great fortune is a crime."*
—Balzac (Boone 1992: 199)

**WE USE THE** term *finance crime* here to refer to large-scale illegality that occurs in the world of finance and financial institutions. Even though students of white collar crime (see, for example, Coleman 1989; Green 1990) have typically classified finance crime as a form of occupaticnal crime, it may make more sense to consider finance crime apart from other forms of occupational crime for three reasons: First, vastly larger financial stakes are involved; single individuals or financial organizations may illegally acquire tens of millions of dollars. Second, financial crime is closely entwined with corporations and financial networks; the manipulation of corporate stock values is a typical activity. Finally, financial crime threatens the integrity of the economic system itself.

### Banking/Thrifts Crime: The Savings and Loan Mess

Banks are a special type of corporation and are absolutely central to the functioning of the economic system. (Even though thrifts are not banks in the technical sense of the term, they are conventionally regarded as a special type of bank; banking crime and thrifts crime are thus discussed together here.) The physical structure and ambience of banks is intended to convey ultimate respectability and trust, for literally hundreds of billions of dollars are entrusted to banks and the banking system. The critical importance of the banks to the economy, and the catastrophic financial consequences of bank failures, led to the creation of a large regulatory structure intended to oversee and police banking operations. All too often, however, bank regulators have been closely allied with bank directors in promoting banking interests instead of protecting bank customers (Greenwald 1980).

Even as banks have strived to project a positive image as a symbol of reputable financial activity, they have also sought to portray themselves as targets of criminals. But substantial evidence shows that banks, from their earliest days, have engaged in fraudulent activities and have hardly enjoyed a uniformly positive image. One historian, writing of mid-19th-century British banks, contends that there was much fraud and mismanagement amounting to fraud (Robb 1990: 118). Furthermore, the public perception of bankers was often negative:

> The image of the upright and incorruptible Victorian banker is a recent invention....In Victorian novels, the banker was more often than not a villain...the forecloser of mortgages, the despoiler of widows and orphans. (Robb 1990: 113–14)

This negative image has endured into the 20th century, and especially during times of economic distress the banker has been seen as the enemy. Much evidence supports the contention that banks (and institutions that perform banking-type services) have unethically and illegally deprived customers of far more money than bank robbers and embezzlers have stolen from them. By some estimations, banks have deprived customers of billions of dollars of interest through deceptive policies and practices pertaining to checking accounts and mortgage escrow accounts (Greenwald 1980; Mrkvicka 1989). One critic—a former bank president—addressed the following warning to bank customers: "You will overpay your bank, through mortgages, credit cards, loans, checking and savings accounts, over *one hundred thousand dollars* during your lifetime!" (Mrkvicka 1989: xiv).

Banks have allegedly made billions of dollars, improperly, by requiring mortgage lenders to maintain excessive balances in their escrow accounts. In 1993 the Fleet Mortgage Group, the country's largest servicer of home mortgages, agreed to refund approximately $150 million to some 700,000 homeowners from whom they had collected excessive escrow payments (Sack 1993). A long-standing student of banking, Martin Mayer (1984: 86–87), has alleged that banks annually deny depositors the use of funds from out-of-state checks for periods of up to 10 business days; in the early 1980s some $3 trillion worth of deposited checks were so delayed each year, providing banks with daily use of some $60 billion of their depositors' money. Banks were earning some $1.6 billion annually through charges imposed on bounced checks, including (in some instances) charges to depositors of such checks as well as issuers (Mayer 1984: 88).

Most of these activities are legal, regardless of whether they should be. But banks have also been implicated in a wide range of illegal acts intended to enhance their (or their officers') profitability, including bribery, fraud, money laundering, and violations of the bank secrecy act (Villa 1988). Structural weaknesses inherent in close, corrupt relationships among bankers, politicians, and regulators apparently contributed to the collapse of banks in Rhode Island and Maryland in the 1980s and 1990s (Tillman 1994). Banks have defrauded their customers in various ways, and they also have been the instruments of massive frauds perpetrated by their owners, executives, and boards. One observation by California's Savings and Loan Commissioner Bill Crawford is especially apt: "The best way to rob a bank is to own one" (Calavita and Pontell 1990: 321). In recent years the most blatant and extensive instances of such "bank robbery" occurred in the savings and loan thrifts.

**The S & L Frauds**   The losses incurred by the savings and loan thrifts throughout the 1980s may constitute the largest financial mess in U.S. history; they have been called the "biggest bank robbery" and are arguably the biggest white collar swindle as well (Calavita and Pontell 1990; Benekos and Hagan 1990; Waldman 1990). The failure of the S & Ls can hardly be attributed to criminal conduct alone, but such conduct clearly played an important role. Government estimates suggested that criminal activity or outright fraud was involved in between 50 and 80 percent of the failed S & Ls; fraud or criminal misconduct was the decisive factor in 30–40 percent of these failures (Calavita and Pontell 1990; Kerry 1990; Waldman 1990: 51). Such misconduct was, perhaps unsurprisingly, almost certain to be involved in  the biggest S & L losses.

Total thrift failure losses due to criminal fraud and waste have been estimated at $250 billion, and with interest payments over several decades, the resolution of the crisis may even exceed $1 trillion (Martz 1990a; Bartlett 1990; Silk 1990; Waldman 1990). Estimates of the losses vary greatly and may not be entirely reliable (Zimring and Hawkins 1993). Nevertheless, one estimate suggests that the S & L bailout will cost each U.S. taxpayer some $15,000 (Waldman 1990: 3). The lower total figure of $250 billion greatly exceeds the cost of 20 years of street property crime as reported by the FBI's *Uniform Crime Report* (Hagan and Benekos 1991). The $165 million loss from just one failed S & L (Centennial) is several times greater than the total take of $46 million from some 6,000 bank robberies reported by the FBI in 1985 (Hagan and Benekos 1991).

Thousands of people lost large sums of money directly; in some cases retired people lost their life savings by purchasing from savings & loan banks uninsured bonds that were ultimately declared worthless (Martz 1990a). Beyond such immediate victims and long-term costs to taxpayers, the S & L frauds will add greatly to the deficit, will deflect billions of dollars that might have been spent on education, health care, and environmental projects, and will limit credit available to legitimate borrowers, who will pay higher rates for loans they obtain (Martz 1990a).

Ironically, the Southwestern states, where the largest percentage of S & L bank frauds occurred, should eventually reap an infusion of economic benefits from the "bailout" of the failed banks, whereas the economies of other parts of the country will be drained to pay for the bailout (Rosenbaum 1990b). Some commentators have characterized the bailout of the S & Ls as "transfers" of money from taxpayers to insured depositors. Even though there is no complete consensus on the ultimate economic ramifications, there is agreement that a vast amount of unethical and illegal conduct occurred.

How did all of this come about? The historical background and the specific complex of events that led to the massive S & L losses of the 1980s has been described in a number of books (see, for example, Pizzo, Fricker, and Muolo 1991; Pilzer and Deitz 1989; Kane 1989; Adams 1990; Eichler 1989; Waldman 1990) and various articles. The savings and loan banks originated as voluntary savings associations established in England and Scotland in the early 19th century (Pilzer and Deitz 1989). (Banks as such did not exist in colonial America, which operated on a barter economy (Gordon 1991); commercial banks came into existence at about the time of independence, in 1782.) The first savings and loan associations in the United States, established in 1831, were originally cooperative societies organized to enable members to build houses by loaning out portions of a pooled fund (Gordon 1991). Such enterprises, which appealed to the millions of immigrants coming to America, eventually developed into savings banks that paid depositors reasonable interest and made loans for mortgages to borrowers.

In the 19th century banks proliferated and issued a bewildering variety of "bank notes" in an era preceding the establishment of paper money. At least some of these banks were fraudulent enterprises from the outset (Gordon 1991: 58). Bank failures had occurred throughout the history of American banking, but as a consequence of the extensive bank failures during the Great Depression in the 1930s, Congress passed legislation establishing the Federal Deposit Insurance Corporation (FDIC) and the Federal Savings and Loan Insurance Corporation (FSLIC). The purpose of this legislation was to reestablish confidence in the banking system and encourage deposits in banks through the federal government's insurance of deposits (initially up to $2,500). In the case of commercial banks, the guarantee came directly from the federal government; in the case of the savings and loan institutions, Congress would have to take action to implement the guarantee.

The government's general backing of the banking system, coupled with certain restrictions on the types of financial activities in which the different types of banks could engage, was in fact successful in realizing its stated objective. For decades the savings and loans became popular depositories for small savers and a major means for enabling millions of Americans to become homeowners. In the 1970s, however, the rapid inflationary rise in the cost of living made the low, fixed interest rates paid by the savings and loans increasingly unappealing to depositors, and rendered the higher but still relatively modest interest earned on mortgages increasingly unprofitable. Various other changes in the banking system provided potential depositors with more attractive options than those offered by the thrifts. As a consequence, the management of these institutions, facing large losses, exerted political pressure to deregulate the savings and loans and allow them to compete aggressively in a changing economic environment. A series of congressional actions, including the 1982 Garn-St. Germain Act, raised the federal deposit guarantee from $40,000 to $100,000 and allowed the savings and loans to offer much more competitive interest, attract huge "brokered" packages of deposits, and make a broad range of investments and loans, including unsecured commercial loans.

Because the new guarantee pertained to accounts and not to individuals, wealthy people could protect as much of their savings as they wished. Many S & Ls, eager to attract as much of this money as possible, offered unrealistically high interest rates.

Because they were stuck with many low-paying, fixed-interest mortgages, they were bound to go broke unless their loans to highly speculative development enterprises paid off (Gordon 1991: 66). They didn't.

New regulatory accounting practices encouraged risk, and by some measures the savings & loan industry became unregulated, rather than simply deregulated (Hagan and Benekos 1991). These changes, as well as a new rule allowing a single stockholder (instead of at least 400) to own a federally insured thrift, created an extraordinary range of opportunities for dangerously speculative and outrightly fraudulent activity. As one commentator (Solomon 1989: 27) remarked concerning the crucial Garn-St. Germain Act, "Before the ink was dry on the new act, the staid thrift industry was invaded by all manner of promoter, swindler, land speculator, junk bond player and money launderer." But many thrift executives and their professional associates, who may have previously operated in essentially legitimate ways, could not resist crossing the line into blatant criminality to take advantage of the new opportunities.

Calavita and Pontell (1990) classified the various forms of illegality in the S & L frauds as "unlawful risk-taking," "looting," and "covering up." Unlawful risk-taking refers to exceeding the practices legally available to the S & Ls, even in the deregulated 1980s. Huge loans were made to developers engaged in highly speculative projects; the borrowers did not necessarily put any of their own money into these projects, and they did not even put up the origination fees (Pilzer and Deitz 1989: 92). If the projects succeeded, investors stood to make a great deal of money; if they failed, the developers simply defaulted on the loan, and the taxpayers were stuck with the bill. And in a great many cases such defaults occurred. Making these high-risk loans was attractive to the S & Ls because they could report high short-term profits from such new business, and the bankers could award themselves very large bonuses. At one bank $22 million in bonuses was awarded over a four-year period; at another over $3 million in kickbacks was received for arranging one large loan (Pilzer and Deitz 1989: 95–106). In this sense deregulation produced a criminogenic environment that was bound to escalate the level of illegal activity.

Looting, or "collective embezzlement," was a second form of S & L crime. Calavita and Pontell (1990: 16) regarded collective embezzlement as a relatively new and understudied form of crime by one corporation against another. Quite simply, as deposits began to pour into the S & Ls in huge amounts, executives and directors began to siphon off an extravagant percentage of this money for themselves. Erwin Hansen, head of Centennial Savings and Loan in California, threw a $148,000 Christmas party, circled the globe on private airplanes, purchased antique furniture, renovated a house for $1 million, bought expensive artwork, and maintained a fleet of luxury cars—all at the expense of the bank (Pizzo, Fricker, and Muolo 1991: 25–37). Don Dixon, owner of the Vernon Savings and Loan in Texas, bought a $1 million dollar beach house in California, traveled on two jets costing $200,000 a year to operate, took his wife on a gastronomic tour of Europe at a cost of $22,000, and bought a 112-foot yacht for $2.6 million—all, apparently, at the expense of the bank (Pizzo, Fricker and Muolo 1991; Pilzer and Deitz 1989). And these two cases were hardly unique (Gorman 1990; Hershey 1990a; Nash 1990a). Altogether, many executives looted S & Ls for their own personal benefit, even as those institutions were losing large sums of money.

A complex of ingenious strategies was established to loot the banks, including "special deals" (the use of "straw borrowers" to obtain large, illegal "loans" for S & L bank executives); "land flips" (selling land back and forth between related parties to fraudulently inflate its value); "daisy chains" (depositing money into an S & L in return for a promise of a large loan that was often defaulted on); "cash for trash," in which borrowers were required to borrow more money than they wanted and then purchase a repossessed "trash" property from the S & L with the additional money; "lender participation," in which the borrowers were required to direct a portion of the profits, or transfer their ownership, from their projects to the bank; and "dead horses for dead cows," in which S & Ls would transfer bad assets among themselves whenever thrift examiners were due, to avoid the production of an accurate financial report on their liabilities (Calavita and Pontell 1990; Hagan and Benekos 1990; Waldman 1990). As Calavita and Pontell (1990: 325) noted, this "playful jargon reflects the make-believe, candystore mentality of this new breed of white-collar criminal, and belies the devastating consequences of their actions." The practices briefly defined here were used to commit frauds netting billions of dollars.

Finally, as suggested by the "dead horses for dead cows" scheme, the S & Ls engaged in massive deceptions to conceal their fraudulent activities and insolvency from outside examiners. In addition to trading around bad assets, S & Ls kept separate books, engaged in phony transactions to maintain a fictitious impression of net worth, and set up loans so that they would appear to be current when in fact they were phony (Calavita and Pontell 1990). These deceptions were generally aided by highly paid accountants, lawyers, and appraisers (Waldman 1990: 48), and in many cases political pressure and various forms of bribery were used to deflect accurate examinations of the banks' activities and prevent appropriate actions in response to fraud or irregularities.

**The Charles Keating Case** Arguably the most widely publicized S & L fraud case involved Charles H. Keating, Jr., and Lincoln Savings and Loan. Keating, a lawyer, former Olympic swimmer, and scion of a prominent Cincinnati family, first came to wide public attention as a founder of the conservative watchdog group Citizens for Decency Through Law. He was the sole dissenting member of the Federal Commission on Obscenity and Pornography, and he vigorously denounced its very liberal report issued in 1970 (Nash and Shenon 1989). Most recently he achieved notoriety as chairman of Lincoln Savings & Loan, alleged to be one of the most thoroughly corrupt S & Ls.

Although Lincoln Savings and Loan's recorded assets increased from less than $1 billion to over $5 billion between 1982 and 1988, it reported losses in excess of $800 million in 1989; at that time its total losses exceeded $2 billion (Nash and Shenon 1989; Nash 1989c). In late 1989 the Resolution Trust Corporation filed a $1.1 billion civil racketeering suit against Keating and his associates, alleging fraud, insider dealing, illegal loans, and a pattern of racketeering (Morganthau 1989); the Securities and Exchange Commission and the FBI investigated criminal charges as well. Lincoln was accused, among other things, of "manufacturing profits" from sham land sales to businesses that were bought at inflated prices in return for big loans. Keating was alleged to have paid himself and family members some $34 million from the Lincoln Savings and Loan in the three and a half years before its demise (Nash 1989a: A1). Some 23,000 people bought more than $200 million in bonds in Lincoln's parent company from bank officials who falsely conveyed to them that the bonds were either guaranteed by the government or absolutely safe. Among the investors were older people investing their life savings and an order of nuns investing their retirement fund (Nash 1989b). They all lost their money when the bank failed.

When some federal regulators recommended that strong regulatory action be taken against Keating in 1987, five U.S. Senators—Alan Cranston, Donald Riegle, John Glenn, Dennis DeConcini, and John McCain—to whom Keating had donated a total of some $1.3 million in campaign contributions met with regulatory bureaucrats, who then effectively backed off (Nash 1989a). When asked whether he believed his campaign contributions would influence the senators to act on his behalf, Keating had replied candidly, "I certainly hope so" (Carlson 1989a: 27). One apparent consequence of the senators' intervention was a two-year delay in the closing of the Lincoln Savings and Loan, with an additional staggering $1.3 billion cost to taxpayers.

In 1990 Keating predictably claimed he had done nothing wrong and that incompetent regulator interference was the source of the problems (Carlson 1990a). Others condemned Keating as "a financial pirate" and a "financio-path of obscene proportions" (Morgenthau 1989; Nash 1989b). In 1992 Keating was sentenced in a California proceeding to 10 years in prison for defrauding S & L customers, and in 1993 Keating was convicted of 73 criminal counts in a federal prosecution; he faces the likely prospect of spending the rest of his life behind bars (Stevenson 1992a; Sims 1993).

Keating is strongly reminiscent of some of the 19th-century robber barons. They too exuded piety and professed to be repelled by challenges to traditional morality, and yet they financially ruined vast numbers of people without hesitation.

**The Wide Net of Responsibility for the S & L Failures**  Beyond the S & L bankers who directly engaged in fraudulent and illegal activity, a large number of other parties must be held responsible for facilitating the S & L debacle. Many financial institutions and investment groups took advantage of the deregulation of the thrifts for their own benefit. Michael Milken, the "junk bond king" whose illegal activities are discussed later in this chapter, used the S & L thrifts as a dumping ground for billions of dollars of junk bonds he purchased with federally insured deposits, and which subsequently declined precipitously in value (Pizzo 1990).

Numerous government officials helped create the circumstances that made the S & L-related crimes possible; failed to act against the thrifts as they were being mismanaged and looted, or interfered with those who should have been taking action; minimized the dimensions of the problem for a long time; and failed to take timely and effective action to respond to the crisis (Rosenbaum 1990a). The Reagan administration aggressively promoted deregulation and the "free market" ideology, which vastly expanded the opportunity for fraud, blocked the hiring of S & L examiners, and resisted a bailout (Martz 1990a: 25; Solomon 1989). Vice President Bush chaired a task force on deregulation in 1984 that should have sounded the alarm on what was happening in the S & L industry, but did not (Klein 1990; Pilzer and Deitz 1989: 208). In Congress, Speaker of the House Jim Wright and others pushed through deregulatory legislation, accepted money or favors from S & L owners, and intervened with regulatory agencies to discourage or hinder efforts to investigate or shut down some of the more flagrantly abusive S & Ls (Pilzer and Deitz 1989: 100). As noted earlier, five senators who accepted campaign contributions from Charles Keating intervened with regulators on his behalf.

At least some of the federal regulators who were supposed to be overseeing the operations of the S & Ls were at best "asleep at the switch," at least in part because of close ties with the thrift industry, political commitments to the deregulatory philosophy, and a desire to avoid embarrassing the incumbent administration before an upcoming election (Pilzer and Deitz 1989: 150–52). Regulatory agency supervisors and examiners often lacked the technical sophistication to make sense of the complex new financial dealings of the deregulated S & Ls (Pilzer and Deitz 1989: 150–80). In some cases they were intimidated by powerful politicians or were directly corrupted by thrift executives, and in any event the agencies lacked the personnel to carry out fully their responsibilities.

The accounting profession has also been implicated in the S & L frauds. During the 1980s accounting firms aggressively pursued business from the rapidly growing S & Ls, which had the potential to generate very large fees for a whole range of services (Wayne 1989b). In many cases the accounting firms conducted audits certifying that S & Ls were sound and solvent, when in fact they were engaged in wildly unsound practices and heading toward massive losses. In one case an accountant admitted to taking bribes to prepare false financial statements; in another case an accountant who defended Lincoln Savings and Loan's financial practices subsequently went to work for an affiliated thrift for a very high salary (Berg 1989; Wayne 1989a). Various accounting firms were sued for their role in the S & L frauds, as were many law firms.

The media were very slow to report the full scope of the S & L debacle; the massive front-page coverage it truly merited did not begin until 1989 (Hume 1990). Many of the reasons for limited media coverage of white collar crime generally—and of complex "numbers" stories such as the S & L fraud in particular—are explored in Chapter 1. The media were well-positioned to inform the public about the consequences of the pervasive S & L frauds.

**Fraud and the S & L Bailout**   By the time President Bush took office in 1989, it was widely recognized that a massive bailout of the S & Ls was necessary. A new agency, the Resolution Trust Corporation, was established to sell the assets of the hundreds of failed thrifts (Gorman 1990). By 1990 there was growing concern that millions were being lost daily because of the slow start on the bailout effort. It became clear then that the government's efforts to unload billions of dollars of seized assets—from failed thrifts to vast real estate holdings acquired through default—made the opportunities for corrupt special deals almost unlimited (Labaton 1990b).

Many of the buyers of the failed S & Ls' assets were property developers and speculators who had defaulted on loans on these properties (and who were obviously in a good position to know their real value). In one case, a politically connected Arizona businessman who had been indicted in a securities fraud case was allowed to buy 15 insolvent Texas S & Ls with $70 million he borrowed and only $1,000 of his own money (Gerth 1990a). The profits reported by the reorganized thrift could be attributed solely to almost $2 billion in federal aid obtained in this deal. In fact, many extremely wealthy investors were able to obtain defunct S & Ls in the late 1980s at bargain-basement prices, complete with large government subsidies or tax write-offs, as part of the "Southwest Plan" instituted by the regulatory board (Pilzer and Deitz 1989: 212–32). In the late 1980s and early 1990s, outraged claims of overzealous regulators taking draconian measures in closing down thrifts were competing with equally outraged claims that a whole new wave of crooked deals was affecting the bailout program.

**The Criminal Justice Response to S & L Fraud**   Investigating and successfully prosecuting S & L crimes has been very difficult. The crimes themselves are highly complex, the line separating outright fraud from bad business judgment or mismanagement is not always well defined, and the evidence is often buried in millions of financial documents that require sophisticated special knowledge to decipher (Behar 1990; Johnston 1990). Cases take an average of two years to develop. In some cases in which much of the evidence suggests massive fraud, the government must be content to prosecute on relatively narrow tax-evasion charges because the problems of conclusively proving fraud cannot be overcome (Barrett 1990). As of 1990 the Bush administration had allocated relatively little money for criminal prosecution of S & L fraud cases, creating a backlog of over 20,000 complaints of criminal fraud and some 3,500 major criminal cases that are pending (Behar 1990; Cox News Service 1990).

Most of those convicted in S & L cases were minor players, and in many of the cases involving losses in the millions of dollars, only probation and relatively modest fines were imposed (Webb 1990). By the Justice Department's own guidelines, the appropriate jail time for these crimes was less than that imposed for conventional bank robbery, and the fines imposed were less than the total amount stolen (Pilzer and Deitz 1989: 178; Pizzo, Fricker, and Muolo 1991: 284). Only a relatively few harsh prison sentences were given to S & L fraudsters (Hayes 1990a). In response to both internal and external frauds, many thrifts hired private investigators to sift through the financial records of major borrowers who made fraudulent loans, in the hope of recovering some of the money (Woodbury 1990). One lawyer proposed that the government hire trial lawyers on a contingency basis to attempt to recover defrauded S & L assets from insurers (Wachsman 1990). But clearly most of the defrauded and wasted money—much of it gambled away, expended on extragant living, sunk into worthless developments, and the like—would never be recovered.

**The BCCI Case**   The S & L fraud cases were not the only recent cases of major bank-related fraud. The BCCI (Bank of Commerce and Credit International) case that emerged in the early 1990s has been characterized as "the largest corporate criminal enterprise ever, the biggest Ponzi scheme, the most pervasive money-laundering operation" (Beaty and Gwynne 1991) and "the largest financial fraud in history" (Johnston 1991), with losses estimated in the $15 billion range; the bank itself has been called "the world's most corrupt financial empire" (Truell and Gurwin 1992), "the world's sleaziest bank" (Potts, Kochan, and Whittington 1992), "the dirtiest bank of all" (Beaty and Gwynne 1991), and "the bank of crooks and criminals international" (Adams and Frantz 1992).

BCCI was founded in Luxembourg in 1972 by a charismatic Pakistani, Agha Hasan Abedi. It was the first multinational third-world bank. Operating secretively and with little regulatory oversight, it quickly established branches in over 70 countries around the world, acquired assets of some $20–30 billion, became a major force in world financial centers, and was backed up by the immensely wealthy ruler of Abu Dhai, Sheik al-Nahyan.

In 1991 the bank was shut down after investigations in a number of different countries resulted in charges against the bank of corruption, bribery, money laundering, gun running, drug smuggling, terrorism, and massive outright theft. BCCI apparently catered to notorious dictators (including Saddam Hussein) and to international drug dealers (including the Medellín drug cartel). A complex web of strategies, including phony loans, unrecorded deposits, secret files, illicit share-buying schemes, and shell companies, were used to loot the bank of billions (Lohr 1991). Bribery was one key to BCCI's success in infiltrating or taking over banks in many countries and in escaping accountability for so long.

In the United States, a distinguished lawyer, elder statesman, and former cabinet member, Clark Clifford, and his associate, Robert Altman, were formally accused of accepting large bribes (in the form of bank stock) to facilitate BCCI's illicit takeover of First American Bankshares, Inc. (Washington's largest bank), and of concealing relevant facts of this transaction from the Federal Reserve Board (Lohr 1992b). The initial prosecution originated in New York amidst ongoing claims that the Justice Department in the Bush administration had stalled a fuller investigation because it was fearful of uncovering embarrassing ties among BCCI, the CIA, and highly placed political officials (Baquet 1991).

In 1991, the BCCI pleaded guilty to federal and state charges of racketeering, fraud, larceny, and falsification of business documents, and agreed to forfeit $550 million, the largest such forfeiture in a criminal case to date (Johnston 1991). The chief executive of BCCI, Swaleh Naqvi, pleaded guilty to sweeping federal fraud charges in July 1994, admitting responsibility for losses of $225 million in the United States alone (Labaton 1994). Investors, depositors, and small businesses—disproportionately located in third-world countries—lost some $12 billion due to the criminal and negligent activities of BCCI and its subsequent closure. In the United States a number of banks associated with BCCI collapsed, exacting huge losses on U.S. taxpayers (Truell and Gurwin 1992). Altogether, years will likely be needed to trace all the losses and process the various criminal charges. The BCCI case demonstrates that the distinctions between legitimate and illegitimate enterprises are often slight at best, and that the lines of demarcation among governmental crime, finance crime, and organized crime are often blurred (Passas 1993). This case also highlights both the growing significance of the global financial market and the vast potential for taking criminal advantage in the absence of truly effective, international regulation of financial activity.

## Insider Trading

Insider trading became a major symbol of the excesses of the 1980s, and in one commentator's view it is "the representative white collar crime" of that decade (Coffee 1988a: 121). Even if insider trading has not historically been a focus of students of corporate and occupational crime, it is an especially "pure" form of white collar crime. "Violation of trust" may be a principal attribute of white collar crime, but such a violation virtually defines insider trading. Vast amounts of money—sometimes hundreds of millions of dollars—have been involved in insider trading cases. Those engaged in insider trading are quite often wealthy, in some cases very wealthy. Insider trading is typically inspired by the pursuit of unlimited wealth and of power for its own sake.

Insider trading in a broad sense may be as old as the marketplace; individuals with privileged information have always made investment and trading decisions on the basis of such information. And throughout most of history nothing has prohibited taking advantage of privileged information. Even with the emergence of the modern corporation, the common law generally did not prohibit corporate insiders from trading on the basis of their privileged information (Pitt 1987: 5).

Prohibitions of insider trading originate principally with the advent of federal securities laws. Although no specific statutory definition of insider trading exists, SEC regulations and judicial opinions have generally defined it as trading on the basis of material nonpublic information (Pitt 1987: 5). The current laws against insider trading have their roots in a 1909 U.S. Supreme Court decision, *Strong v. Repide,* 213 U.S. 419, which established a "disclose or abstain" rule (i.e., a company official must disclose his identify and special knowledge when purchasing company stock, or abstain from purchasing such stock) and in the antifraud provisions of the federal securities regulations of the 1930s (Lynch and Missal 1987: 22; Pitt 1987: 6).

The prohibitions on insider trading remain confusing to some and illogical to others. As one commentator has observed:

> In the pretzel logic of inside trading laws, gaining secret information from insiders
> such as lawyers, bankers or arbs is illegal; uncovering it on your own is ingenious.
> The former makes you a criminal; the latter makes you rich. (Stevens, in Reichman
> 1989: 187)

At least some conservative economists adopt the view that insider trading is a legitimate element of a free-market economy and should be legalized instead of being prohibited, although polling data support the view that Americans favor fair markets over marginally more efficient ones (Gilson 1987). The overriding rationale for prohibiting insider trading is that it creates a fundamentally unfair market—that it either defrauds those without access to the information or deters large numbers of potential investors from entering the marketplace in the first place because they believe it is "fixed" (Committee on Federal Regulation of Securities 1987: 216; Giuliani 1990: 13). But it is also obviously true that no market can provide all potential investors with truly equal access to material information, especially in a world of electronic trading connections and 24-hour markets (Makin 1986: 6).

Nevertheless, insider trading laws attempt to neutralize the advantages that violate either a basic trust or specific requirements for confidentiality. In this context, the courts have had to grapple with the question of defining "insider" and clarifying who may and who may not trade on "inside" information. A landmark 1968 U.S. Supreme Court decision, which involved executives of the Texas Gulf Sulphur Company who took advantage of their inside knowledge of a large mineral deposit discovery to acquire company stock in advance of a public announcement, clearly established the illegality of such insider trading (Reichman 1989: 188). In 1987, the Court upheld (by a 4-4 split vote) the conviction of a *Wall Street Journal* columnist, R. Foster Winans—who provided information about upcoming stories on particular companies to stockbroker confederates and to his lover, who then used the information to buy stocks—on the basis that this information was "misappropriated" from Winans's employer and was illegally conveyed to others (Castro 1987). A federal court in 1990 also upheld the conviction of a psychiatrist who engaged in stock purchases on the basis of information revealed to him by a patient, the wife of a financier, during treatment (Reuters 1990). On the other hand, in 1990, the U.S. Second Circuit Court reversed on appeal the conviction of a stockbroker who purchased a large block of stock in the Waldbaum supermarket chain after a client, a member of the Waldbaum family, informed him of an upcoming lucrative tender offer for the stock (*White Collar Crime Reporter* 1990). In this case the court decided that the state had not demonstrated that the stockbroker knew that the information was confidential.

**The Pursuit of Insider Trading Cases**  Through most of the 20th century the practice of passing inside "tips" was probably quite common and was not prosecuted (Clarke 1990: 178). The principal legal developments and prosecutions of insider trading cases occurred during the 1980s, when a number of spectacular and highly publicized cases directed much attention to this form of crime. In the 45-year period from 1934 to 1979, the SEC initiated only 53 insider trading enforcement actions, but then in the seven years between 1980 and 1987 it brought in 177 actions (Szockyj 1990: 6). It is not possible to demonstrate conclusively to what degree this increase can be attributed to either a higher rate of violation or a greater rate of reporting and prosecution.

During the 1980s a number of factors increased the visibility (and ultimately the newsworthiness) of insider trading. The financial markets became more vulnerable to insider trading by virtue of the dramatic growth in both the trading capacity of institutions and corporations and in tender offers or takeover situations (Szockyj 1990). New types of securities, the greater use of options, and a higher level of international trading also facilitated insider trading during this period. Altogether, a broader variety of professionals became directly involved in the securities markets, information networks expanded, and traditional securities market controls broke down (Reichman 1989; Zey 1993). At the same time, President Reagan's new SEC chair, John Shad, and the SEC's enforcement division head, John Fedders, were seeking a way to distinguish their administration of the agency from the previous one, which had focused on international bribery and corporate fraud. They were also eager to enhance the credibility of the SEC and respond to critics who alleged that it did not take a sufficiently tough stand on insider trading cases. Moreover, insider trading was generally unpopular with the business world.

**The Victims of Insider Trading**   Clearly, the primary victims of insider trading cases are institutional and individual investors who bought or sold stock at a loss, failed to realize a profit, or overpaid for stock because of insider trader manipulations. The losses may range from thousands of dollars for individual investors to millions of dollars for institutional investors. Because the pension funds of millions of Americans are heavily invested in the stock market, a very large class of unwitting victims of insider trading exists. Once they learn that a company is targeted for a takeover bid, insiders can buy up large blocks of the company's stock, driving the price up and costing the takeover entity a large amount of money they ordinarily would not have had to pay. Investors that lack insider information may be misled and may accordingly buy or sell at a disadvantage. Of course, some investors inadvertently profit from the market manipulations of insider traders. The substantial direct losses of some investors are but a part of the real cost of insider trading; the loss of confidence in the integrity of the market is another, very real, cost.

**The Corporate Takeover Controversy**   The insider trading cases of the 1980s can be properly understood only in the context of the wave of corporate takeovers occurring at the time. In 1974 the International Nickel Company successfully broke a long-standing taboo against hostile corporate takeovers when it acquired the Electric Storage Company. In 1975 an SEC ruling that commissions on stock transactions were negotiable instead of fixed led to a sharp downturn in Wall Street revenues (Reich 1989: 36). Corporate takeovers, including hostile ones, came to be seen as an important new source of income on Wall Street. Leveraged buyouts—in which a company's management joins with investment bankers to buy out the company's shareholders and take the company private—became especially popular. Between 1978 and 1988 the percentage of Wall Street profit provided by mergers, acquisitions, and leveraged buyouts rose from 5 percent to approximately 50 percent (Reich 1989: 36). During one three-year period in the early 1980s, some 9,000 companies or divisions worth some $480 billion changed hands (Cooper 1987: 78). Because the value of a company's stock invariably rises—sometimes quite dramatically—when the company becomes a takeover target, it is not difficult to understand that there is an enormous temptation to acquire and trade on inside information about a planned takeover.

A new breed of "risk arbitrageurs" played a central role in the takeover activity of the 1970s and 1980s. Traditionally, *arbitrage* refers to the practice of trading on different markets to take advantage of the possibility of buying in one market a stock that can be sold at a profit in another market (Reichman 1989: 191). A risk arbitrageur such as Ivan Boesky, who during the early 1980s was "King of the Arbitrageurs," would buy up stock in companies that were takeover targets in anticipation of the higher stock values if the company were in fact taken over. Clearly, illegally acquired inside information on prospective takeovers provides the arbitrageur with a very large advantage.

Whether the takeovers themselves were on balance beneficial or detrimental to the national economy, and whether or not restrictions should be placed on corporate takeovers, are topics of hot debate (Johnson 1986; Brooks 1987; Adams and Brock 1989). Defenders of hostile takeovers involving corporate raiders argue that raiders identify companies with assets that are undervalued on the stock market (due to bad management); that raiders make these companies more efficient and profitable by buying them out and getting rid of inefficient managers, practices, and divisions; and that accordingly, shareholders gain (Cooper 1987; Icahn 1986; Iseman 1986; Newport 1989; Samuelson 1987).

Critics of hostile takeovers, on the other hand, have argued that nothing economically useful emerges from takeovers, and that they actually damage the system by diverting attention from the hard work of developing and producing better products (Galbraith 1986; Reich 1989). In this view, relatively few people (mainly raiders, insiders, investment bankers, and brokers) benefit from the takeovers, and those few derive grossly excessive profits. The RJR Nabisco leveraged buyout, for example, produced some $1 billion in fees for investment bankers, and Michael Milken alone earned at least $550 million ($750 million, by some accounts) in one year based on activities substantially involving takeovers (Burrough and Helyar 1989; Stewart 1991). Corporate raiders have walked away with tens of millions of dollars, perhaps even hundreds of millions, in "greenmail," which is what a target company pays to a corporate raider to sell off his acquired stock.

Meanwhile, ordinary taxpayers must make up part or all of the tax revenues lost from enormous post-takeover or buyout corporate interest payment deductions. Consumers often end up paying significantly higher prices when companies are under intense new pressure to reduce a heavy debt load. Tens of thousands of employees lose their jobs or take major paycuts; their communities suffer the consequences when divisions are shut down or sold to pay off such debt (Cooper 1987; Faludi 1990; Reich 1989).

In Pennsylvania, a controversial anti-takeover law was implemented in 1990 to protect state-based corporations from hostile takeovers (Henriques 1990b). Defenders of this law have argued that such protection against outsiders seeking quick profits from takeover activities recognizes that workers, suppliers, and communities have a legitimate interest in their companies, and that these interests ought not to be disregarded in the interest of investors alone; critics have contended that the law protects inefficient management and discourages investment in new, innovative companies. But whether or not takeovers should be legally prohibited, it is clear that large numbers of people suffered as a consequence of the wave of takeovers in the 1980s, which indisputably created an environment that promotes illegal insider trading on a large scale.

**The Wall Street Insider Trading Cases of the 1980s**   The most spectacular and widely publicized insider trading cases began to unfold in 1985 with an anonymous letter to the Merrill Lynch firm claiming that one of its traders in Caracas was trading on inside information (Stone 1986). This tip led to an SEC investigation of a small bank in the Bahamas, Bank Leu, through which the trades were executed. The investigation revealed that one of the bank's clients had engaged in a pattern of exceedingly profitable trades correlated with corporate takeovers. This client, further investigation revealed, was Dennis Levine, a 33-year-old investment banker with the Drexel Burnham firm in New York. Levine came from a modest middle-class background in Queens, had attended Baruch College of City University, and with a combination of raw ambition, aggressiveness, and charm had quickly worked his way through a series of executive positions with prestigious investment banking firms, including Smith Barney and Lehman. At age 32 he was appointed a managing director of Drexel Burnham with a high six-figure salary.

But Levine was never quite satisfied with the considerable rewards his legitimate career provided. In 1979 he began to establish a small network of friends, business associates, lawyers, and investment bankers, all of them intimately involved in corporate takeover deals, to trade confidential information on pending takeovers that could be used for highly profitable stock trading. Levine assumed that his trades, executed through the Bahamian bank and transacted with a pseudonym ("Mr. Diamond"), would not be traced back to him as an insider (Frantz 1987). By 1985 Levine's personal account at the Bank Leu, accumulated by using insider information about pending takeovers, had passed the $10-million mark; altogether Levine acquired over $11 million from his illegal investments. But Levine had rather recklessly continued his insider trading activities even after learning of SEC inquiries, arrogantly assuming that he was too shrewd to be caught by government investigators.

After Levine was arrested and confronted with the evidence against him, he began to provide government investigators with information about his confederates and associates in insider trading deals. On June 5, 1986—some three weeks after his arrest—Levine pleaded guilty to one count of securities fraud, two counts of income tax evasions, and one count of perjury (Frantz 1987: 331). He settled SEC charges against him by agreeing to pay $11.6 million (which included his entire Bank Leu account) and by accepting a permanent injunction against working in the securities business. He was allowed to keep his Park Avenue apartment (worth some $1 million), his BMW, and some $100,000 in bank accounts.

In February 1987, Levine was sentenced to a two-year prison term and fined $362,000. Several of his immediate associates in the insider trading ring also pleaded guilty to various criminal charges, turned over illegal profits, and received prison sentences (typically, a year and a day) and fines. More significantly, Levine's cooperation with the SEC following his arrest led to a chain of interrelated insider trading cases.

In February 1987, Martin A. Siegel, a 38-year-old investment banker and takeover strategist, pleaded guilty to tax and securities law violations related to insider trading, and agreed to turn over $9 million to satisfy civil penalties (Glaberson 1987). Siegel, at that time associated with Drexel Burnham, had been earning close to $2 million a year at Kidder, Peabody. He ultimately received a two-month prison sentence, five years probation, and 1,500 hours of community service. This light sentence was attributed to his extensive cooperation with government investigators, which led to charges against various former associates.

Ivan Boesky was the next insider trader to achieve front-page, banner-headline attention in the 1980s (Stewart 1991). Boesky came from a middle-class background in Detroit and had a rather inauspicious academic and professional career until he set up his own risk arbitrage operation in 1975 with some $700,000 of his wealthy wife's money. Over the next 10 years he became an increasingly conspicuous player in the Wall Street arbitrage game, taking in huge profits apparently based on his obsessive study of stock deals and corporate takeovers.

By the mid-1980s Boesky was living in baronial splendor, was alleged to be worth some $200 million dollars, was a celebrity (when invited to speak at Stanford University, he declared that "Greed is good"), and was widely admired and envied by other ambitious Wall Street investors, many of whom attempted to trade in his wake. (Of course, he had his detractors. His sister-in-law described him as "the most avaricious, arrogant piece of sewage I've ever met"; Koepp 1986: 51.) But part of the deal Dennis Levine made with government prosecutors to lessen his prison sentence called for providing information on insider trading deals, and one of those he fingered was Ivan Boesky.

In November 1986, Boesky pleaded guilty to illegal insider trading charges, agreed to pay a $100 million penalty (then easily the largest penalty ever for such crimes), and was barred for life from the securities business (Kilborn 1986a). Boesky subsequently received a three-year prison sentence, at least part of which he served at Lompoc Prison in California. His specific offenses included purchasing from Dennis Levine inside information about corporate takeovers and related activities for such companies as Nabisco Brands, American Natural Resources, Union Carbide, and General Foods. This information enabled Boesky to earn huge profits by purchasing and unloading stocks at the optimum times. For example, in April 1985 Levine informed Boesky of the prospective takeover of Houston Natural Gas (a pipeline company); one day before the takeover, Boesky purchased 301,800 shares of Houston Natural Gas, which he sold two weeks later for a profit of $4.1 million (Russell 1986a). Boesky's relatively light prison sentence reflected his agreement to provide information on still other, even larger-scale insider trading deals.

**The Michael Milken Case** Some of the information provided by Ivan Boesky led to the most spectacular securities market prosecution of them all, that of Michael Milken and the Drexel Burnham Company (Byron 1990; Greenwald 1990; Stewart 1991; Kornbluth 1992). Milken became a key figure in the hyper-inflated financial market of the 1980s as the "Junk Bond King."

In the 1970s Milken had come to recognize that vast amounts of money could be raised through issuing and selling high-yield, high-risk (i.e., "junk") bonds. Such bonds can be issued by smaller, less established companies that do not qualify for blue-chip bonds. They pay higher interest because they are viewed as more prone to default, but during the 1980s the actual rate of default was quite low. These junk bonds were widely used to finance the wave of corporate takeovers during the 1980s, and they were bought up by S & Ls as well as many mutual funds.

Operating out of Drexel Burnham's Beverly Hills office, Milken was extraordinarily successful in developing and selling such bonds, as well as in advising companies seeking to expand or to take over other companies. He and his associates became immensely wealthy; in 1987 he was reputed to have personally earned some $750 million in compensation. Then the Wall Street insider trading cases led to an investigation of the activities of Drexel Burnham and Milken. In 1988 Drexel Burnham pleaded guilty to violation of federal securities laws and agreed to pay a $650-million fine (Labaton 1988). This plea was entered in the face of a prospective federal racketeering (RICO) prosecution that could have resulted in the confiscation of the firm's total assets. In February 1990, Drexel Burnham collapsed anyway—after 152 years of existence and a period during the 1980s when it was the most profitable investment banking house on Wall Street (Greenwald 1990).

Although the criminal investigation of Milken initially included charges of insider trading, it ultimately resulted in his pleading guilty to six felony charges of securities fraud and conspiracy in 1990, including manipulating securities prices, filing of false information and false reporting with the SEC, engaging in overcharging of a mutual fund, and filing a false tax return (Eichenwald 1990b). Milken had long resisted any such settlement, paying lawyers some $1 million a month to fight the charges, and consequently he lost some of the leverage he might have had had he settled earlier.

As part of his agreement Milken paid a $600 million fine and was sentenced by Judge Kimba Woods to 10 years in prison. This seemingly harsh sentence was ultimately reduced in return for Milken's cooperation in related cases, and he actually served only 22 months in a minimum-security prison. Not long after his release Milken was teaching a finance course to admiring M.B.A. students at UCLA (Clines 1993). Despite the huge fine he paid, Milken retained a significant portion of his fortune, which at one point was estimated to easily exceed a billion dollars.

Whether Milken was a greedy villain who caused much harm in the securities markets, or a misunderstood financial genius who helped build the economy and was made a scapegoat for the financial excesses of the 1980s, remains a matter of debate (Stewart 1991; Kornbluth 1992). But there is reason to believe that large numbers of investors and taxpayers suffered significant losses because the various manipulations of Milken and Drexel Burnham, and free competition in the markets was seriously compromised.

**Insider Trading, In Sum**   The prosecution and imprisonment of Levine, Boesky, Milken, and others, and the demise of Drexel Burnham, did not mark the end of the insider trading cases. Another major case surfaced on Wall Street in 1992; in 1994 a high-level official of Time Warner agreed to pay the government close to $1 million to settle insider trading charges (Henriques 1992a; Fabrikant 1994). In the mid-1990s insider trading was less concentrated on Wall Street and was more likely to be widespread in U.S. corporations and brokerage houses (Barrett 1994). Such illegal activity is likely to be an ongoing phenomenon as long as the rewards for insider trading are so great relative to the risk of being caught (which is especially small for "outsiders" who have access to privileged securities-related information)(Kempf, Arshadi, and Eyssell 1992). Although individual greed may play some role in insider trading, there is much reason to believe that various structural and organizational factors—for example, relentless pressures to maximize financial returns, and complex networks of corporations, investment banks, and individual financiers within the financial markets—play a key role in promoting insider trading (Zey 1993). There is no easy resolution of the insider trading problem.

## Finance Crime and Financial Markets

In addition to insider trading, many other unethical and illegal activities occur within financial markets. In the early 1980s the prestigious stock brokerage firm E. F. Hutton ("When E. F. Hutton talks, people listen") was charged with carrying out a major check-kiting scheme that involved systematically bilking millions of dollars out of some 400 banks by depositing large numbers of uncovered checks and then earning money on the credited balance before covering the checks (Carpenter and Feloni 1989; Sterngold 1990). Although E. F. Hutton pleaded guilty to 2,000 felony counts and paid a $2 million fine, the Justice Department failed to charge individual members of the firm, and thus none went to prison. In 1987 E.F. Hutton was accused of laundering money for organized crime (Halloran 1987). This brokerage firm was eventually acquired by another company and E. F. Hutton & Co. ceased to exist.

In 1989 federal authorities indicted 46 Chicago commodities traders for trading fraud (Padgett 1989; B. Peterson 1989). The commodities brokers used various schemes, including falsifying trade records and trading on their own accounts on the basis of advance knowledge of customer orders, to cheat customers out of fair market prices on such commodities as soybeans and Swiss francs.

In 1991 the celebrated Salomon Brothers investment banking firm was accused of submitting billions of dollars of phony bids in the U.S. Treasury Department's bond auctions (Bartlett 1991; Henriques 1991b; Eichenwald 1992). Such bids provided Salomon Brothers with a significant advantage over its competitors and had the potential to alter interest rates in ways that could affect millions of citizens and taxpayers. The ruthless and spectacularly aggressive Salomon subculture that undoubtedly contributed to rule-breaking in the pursuit of profit had been portrayed two years earlier in Michael Lewis's best-seller, *Liar's Poker* (1989). Top executives of Salomon were forced out, and federal civil suits followed.

In a 1994 case also involving the municipal bond market, a leading financial strategist, Mark Ferber, was accused of a serious conflict of interest for secretly taking a large retainer from Merrill Lynch, the nation's largest broker, for steering to that broker hundreds of millions of dollars in bond underwriting business from governmental agencies he was advising (Wayne 1994). In some cases a brokerage firm was a primary victim of improper activities relating to the sale of bonds. In 1994 a Kidder, Peabody broker, Joseph Jett, was dismissed from his position and accused of defrauding the firm by creating phantom profits of $350 million while trading in government bonds (Nasar 1994). The vast sums of money involved in the bond markets create large opportunities—and temptations—for improprieties and illegalities.

The retail aspect of the securities industry—the selling of stocks, bonds, mutual fund shares, and other such investments—has also been plagued with various degrees of fraud, and small investors are especially vulnerable to being misled and losing money on investments (Mayer 1994). On the low end of the scale are periodic cases of fraud in the sale of "penny" stocks, or low-priced shares in tiny, volatile, and often worthless companies (Friday and Hammer 1989; Stein 1994). Large numbers of investors have been lured into purchasing such stocks by false claims or artificial manipulations of values, and they have lost tens of millions of dollars.

Mutual funds have grown exponentially in recent years—by 1994 some $20 billion was invested each month in some 4,500 U.S. mutual funds—and the SEC has been unable to oversee this market adequately (Hass 1994). Both the funds themselves and the contracts spelling out brokers' fees have sometimes been misrepresented by mutual fund salespeople (Anspach 1990). In 1990, for example, fraud charges alleging gross misrepresentations were filed against First Investors Corporation, and sales were halted for two of its "junk bond" funds (Norris 1990). Such activity involving the theft of consumer's property by the corporation and its employees has been characterized as another form of collective corporate theft (Anspach 1990: 28).

In 1993 and 1994 a major brokerage firm, Prudential Securities, Inc., agreed to pay $371 million in restitution and fines to settle a wide range of fraud charges for conduct over a period of at least a decade (Eichenwald 1993a; Eichenwald 1993b; Eichenwald 1994a). Prudential was charged with, among other practices, lying to investors about risks, returns, and losses; inadequate supervision of subsidiaries and employees; and abusing client trust and "churning," a persistent problem in the securities field involving the practice of unauthorized, excessive trading in clients' accounts to increase brokers' commissions. In 1994 federal prosecutors investigated possible systematic defrauding of large institutional investors in connection with the sale of limited real estate partnerships (Eichenwald 1994a). These widely publicized criminal prosecutions and civil lawsuits in securities-related matters seem to have little deterrent effect compared to the temptations of making large, illegal profits.

**Insurance Industry Fraud**   The insurance industry, a multibillion-dollar business, is also at the heart of our financial system in the sense that people rely heavily on insurance as a buffer against catastrophic accidents, illnesses, and fatalities, and also as a source of retirement income. This industry has been the target of recurrent and persistent accusations of self-dealing, unsound investments, unsuitable policies, high-pressure sales techniques, and the like (Quinn 1994). As a consequence of the McCarran-Ferguson Act of 1945 and potent lobbying, the industry has been relatively little regulated. Because the income of agents depends significantly on commissions from selling more insurance to clients or inducing them to switch policies, the problem of "churning" is also a factor in this industry (Quinn 1994). Prime America Financial is but one major insurance company accused of selling insurance by deceptive or phony policy illustrations, and it was also accused of recruiting agents through a pyramid scheme that allows recruiting agents to share in commissions (Quint 1994).

Insurance companies have been accused of jeopardizing the financial well-being of clients by reselling policies to weak (or insolvent) companies, by cheating taxpayers by evading legally mandated responsibilities to elderly workers who are then covered by Medicare, and by using various questionable means to avoid insuring certain vulnerable classes of clients such as potential AIDS patients (Knight-Ridder Newspapers 1990a; Kerr 1992c; Scherzer 1987). Some commentators in the early 1990s were predicting that major insolvencies and bankruptcies in the insurance industry would be the next financial megacrisis, with potential losses equivalent to the S & L failures (Schweitzer 1990; Tobias 1990). Although the insurance industry tends to claim that frauds and problems are the fault of a relatively small group of "bad apples," indications of more deeply rooted structural defects are evident in this industry. Insurance fraud has much in common with everyday frauds committed in many occupations, but the centrality of insurance in the economy and the especially devastating consequences of insurance fraud justify considering this type of activity as more significant than run-of-the-mill frauds.

**Finance Crime, In Sum**   The activities characterized as finance crime have become highly visible forms of white collar crime in recent times. Finance crime is not restricted to the United States, and in an increasingly global economy it cuts across many borders (Henriques 1991a). Within the United States, many interconnections or "fraud networks" tie together different forms of finance crime (Zey 1993). Although much finance crime parallels various corporate and occupational frauds, it is best understood as a hybrid of corporate and occupational crime, for several reasons.

First, finance crime most typically involves the use of a financial corporate entity for personal enrichment; "collective embezzlement" is one form of this activity. Second, it is carried out through financial institutions that tend to enjoy especially high levels of prestige, respectability, trust, power, and affluence. Third, the scale of economic losses involved is very great, perhaps running into the hundreds of millions or billions of dollars. Fourth, it often involves institutions that are at the core of the economic system, and thus illicit activity within these institutions can produce a ripple effect throughout the economy and may compromise faith in basic economic institutions. Finally, several factors make policing and prosecuting financial crime a difficult task, including the generally high level of sophistication of the perpetrators of finance crime, the complexity of the frauds involved, the creation from within of ever-new opportunities and pressures for fraud, the discrepancy between the high potential rewards from fraud and the low likelihood of detection, and the vast economic resources and political connections of those involved.

# Technocrime, Including Computer Crime

COMPUTERS AND OTHER forms of modern technology are likely to play an increasingly central role in state-corporate crimes, finance crimes, and most other types of white collar crime in the future.

It is difficult to overstate the rapidity with which new forms of technology have been introduced and disseminated in our society. In 1962 the computer industry had annual revenues of some $1 billion; in 1985 this figure exceeded $60 billion; revenues are projected to be some $500 billion in 2000 (Bequai 1987: 1; Michalowski and Pfuhl 1991: 266). By 1992 the information technology industry, with revenues of about $360 billion, had become the world's single largest industry (Vohra 1994: C75).

At the close of the 20th century the numbers of computer workers, of American workers using computers at work, of businesses relying on computers, and of American children and adults using computers at school or at home was increasing exponentially, and computer use was becoming the norm (Howard and Zeman 1991; McEwen 1990a; Michalowski and Pfuhl 1991). Distribution and use of other forms of modern technology as well—VCRs, for example—have also experienced exponential growth (Klopfenstein 1989). "High technology," then, is one of the defining elements of the present era, sometimes labeled the "Age of Information."

The influx into our lives of increasingly sophisticated forms of technology—computers, faxes, and telecommunications systems, for example—has been acclaimed by some (technocrats) as a substantial improvement and lamented by others (techno-skeptics) as harmful. Even as modern technology speeds up and facilitates many routine and complex tasks, it also tends to divide society in new ways—into those who have access to a technology and those who do not (and with respect to computers, those who are computer literate and those who are not). It provides greater occupational mobility for some, and unemployment for others. In the realm of crime and criminal justice, it offers new and greater protection and security; it also becomes a formidable instrument for committing new forms and levels of fraud, embezzlement, and other types of crime. Even as it provides the criminal justice system with powerful new tools, it enables those who control such tools to engage in massive invasions of privacy and other abuses.

## Technocrime Defined

The term *technocrime* is somewhat broader than the more familiar term *computer crime,* as it encompasses crime facilitated by any sophisticated form of technology (Bequai 1987). Technocrime has been described as a subset of white collar crime, or alternatively as a distinctly new form of white collar crime (Parker 1980; Wasik 1991).

Of course, not all illegalities committed with such technology are white collar crimes. For example, technocrime committed by spies engaged in espionage activities, and in some instances by terrorists, are not white collar crimes. Computer "hacking" is often a sophisticated form of vandalism committed by "electronic delinquents" or "technopaths" who break into computer programs and systems simply for the challenge, or to cause mischief (Bequai 1987; Nicholson 1990).

Still, it is evident that the cost and sophistication of "high techlology" ensure that such crime is especially well represented in the white collar world. Computers play a central role in insider trading cases by helping to hide illegal profits and market positions, by facilitating transfer of money to offshore bank accounts, by parking stocks, and by concealing stock ownership (Reichman 1993: 73). Today some 80 percent of financial transactions in the United States are conducted electronically (Sessions 1991). Computers clearly create a vast new arena for criminal activity.

## Computer Crime

Computer crime has been most simply defined as an illegal act wherein computers and computer technology are used to commit the offense (Conly and McEwen 1990: 3). Computer hardware is protected by the same laws that protect other forms of physical property, but the electronic information inside a computer represents a new form of "property" less clearly protected by traditional laws (Michalowski and Pfuhl 1991). Accordingly, the introduction of computers has created whole new forms of electronic and magnetic "assets," and a whole new language as well (Parker, 1980). A computer may be the tool of a crime (e.g., embezzlement) or the target of a crime (e.g., theft of services)(Schjolberg and Parker 1983). A more complete breakdown of the categories of computer crime includes the following types: internal computer crimes (i.e., sabotaging of programs); telecommunications crimes (e.g., "hacking" and illegal bulletin boards); computer manipulation crimes (e.g., embezzlements and frauds); computers in support of criminal enterprises (e.g., facilitating illicit drug distribution); and hardware/software thefts (e.g., software piracy, thefts of computers and chips, and thefts of trade secrets)(McEwen, 1990a). Of these categories, computer manipulation is most clearly linked with white collar crime. For example, in a 1992 case, several computer hackers were accused of breaking into and stealing confidential credit records (Tabor and Ramirez 1992). This type of theft occurs predominantly within either an occupational or avocational white collar context.

Computer crime has a relatively recent history. The first recorded computer crime case occurred in 1958, and the first federal prosecution occurred in 1966 (Bequai 1987: 52). Despite the increasing publicity about computer crimes, actual prosecutions for such crimes are few. In a 1986 national survey of county prosecutors, Michalowski and Pfuhl (1991) found that computer crime cases accounted for a very small fraction of their case-loads—less than 0.5 percent on average—and that computer crime prosecutions were heavily concentrated in states such as California and Rhode Island with large computer industries. However, many offenses involving computers are prosecuted through ordinary common law statutes, and there is no centralized bank of computer crime statistics.

Recent estimates of the annual losses due to computer crime and technocrime have generally ranged from $100 million (U.S. Chamber of Commerce) to as high as $5 billion, according to a 1990 study by a major accounting firm (Conly and McEwen 1990; Michalowski and Pfuhl 1991). Further, one study estimated that only 1 percent of computer thefts are detected, and perhaps as few as 15 percent of these are reported (McEwen 1990a). When computer crimes are reported and prosecuted, most are settled by some form of bargaining; only about 24 percent go to trial, and about two-thirds of these trials result in acquittals (Shriver 1989: 4).

Most cases of computer crime are discovered by accident because people who use computers to commit crimes are more likely than not to be bright enough and skillful enough to cover their tracks. In one study, a third of those committing computer crimes were managers (Schjolberg and Parker 1983); even if they lost their jobs and were imprisoned as a result of their crimes, they have the skill and intelligence to find subsequent employment much more easily than do most convicts.

The use of computers greatly increases the potential size and scope of thefts. In the 1980s, for example, the FBI estimated that the average computer heist took in between $400,000 and $560,000, whereas the average bank robbery netted between $4,000 and $19,000; other estimates of average computer crime losses during this period were lower, between $10,000 and $93,000 (Bequai 1987: 46; Shriver 1989: 2; Michalowski and Pfuhl 1991: 260). The higher estimates may have been inflated because only the most spectactular computer crimes are likely to be reported and tabulated (Parker 1980).

The largest losses inevitably occur when computer crime is committed as a matter of corporate policy. One of the largest corporate frauds in U.S. history occurred in the 1970s, when officials of the Equity Funding Insurance Co. created billions of dollars of phony policies and assets with the assistance of computers (Bequai 1987: 52–53). In another case in the 1970s, the Revco Corporation developed a computer-generated double billing scheme (for Medicaid prescriptions) that cost the Ohio state government over half a million dollars (Vaughan 1983). However, most of the white collar computer crime that has surfaced to date is best classified as occupational crime.

The use of computers enables people working in certain occupations to use a "salami technique"—that is, to steal small amounts of assets from a very large number of sources; the total stolen is often quite substantial, and detection minimized, because such a small amount (sometimes pennies) is stolen from so many individual accounts (Schjolberg and Parker 1983). Opportunity is an important factor, and both computer-related skills and access are essential.

According to one expert on the computer crime problem, such occupational theft is more likely to be motivated by pressing financial problems than by naked greed (Stuller 1989). As is true of much white collar crime, these offenders tend to deny that they are criminals and may alternatively see themselves as "problem solvers." Such rationalization is more likely when the victim of computer crime is an organization and the spoils of the crime are somewhat intangible and accessed electronically (Parker 1980). A small proportion of computer crime committed by employees is motivated by a desire to avenge perceived mistreatment by the employer. In a similar situation, a provider of computer software was charged in 1993 with attempting to destroy a client's program by introducing a virus into it in the aftermath of a billing dispute (Schemo 1993). Such novel usages of computer programming knowledge are likely to increase.

Other examples of computer crimes committed by employees include programming a bank computer to ignore an overdraft in the programmer's account; stealing merchandise by manipulating a computerized inventory bank; stealing computer time to run one's own business; using computers to extract a business's trade secrets and then selling them to competitors; and manipulating computer records to embezzle funds from employers or customers.

In a celebrated 1980 case, two employees of the Wells Fargo Bank cooperated with a group of sports promoters to defraud the bank of more than $21 million by taking advantage of a flaw in the computerized system of recording deposits and withdrawals (Gerth 1981: B5). In a 1988 case, an $18,000-a-year clerk employed at First National Bank of Chicago, working with outside conspirators, almost succeeded in embezzling $68.7 million from the bank (Bock 1988). This clerk had access to codes used by major corporations in fund wire-transfers—which banks use to transfer some $1 trillion weekly—and was able to arrange the transfers by faking confirmation calls to fellow conspirators. Because checks written on the corporate accounts involved began to bounce immediately, the scheme was uncovered before the transferred money could be withdrawn.

In a 1989 case, an accountant employed by New York City used a loophole in the city's computerized accounting system to divert $1 million to his own bank account (Lubasch 1989). This embezzlement was achieved by arranging full payment to city contractors who extended large discounts to the city; the discounts were diverted to a fictitious company created by the accountant. The computer system was set up to verify the payments but not to identify the discounts. The rapid increase in the use of computers on all levels of government suggests that computer crimes against the government by its own employees are likely to increase greatly (Bennett 1987). The enormous size of many government financial programs renders such programs especially vulnerable to computer crime.

Computers also play a role in tax fraud and evasion, either within a business context or on the part of individual taxpayers. In a 1993 case, Stew Leonard, owner of a large dairy store in Connecticut, pleaded guilty to defrauding the government of $17.5 million in taxes, with the store's computer playing a central role in hiding cash discrepancies (Levy 1993). Now that the IRS has come to encourage the expanded use of electronic filing of federal income tax forms, it must also confront a growing problem of fraudulently filed electronic returns, which can be more difficult to verify than returns with hard-copy documentation (Hershey 1994a). Although computer programs have long been used to check returns more efficiently, it is clear that electronic filing also enhances some opportunities for fraud.

It has proven quite difficult to respond effectively to computer crime. As previously noted, only a small proportion of it is discovered, let alone reported. Because it is carried out electronically, not "directly," evidence is often hidden deep within the bowels of a computer system, and in some case it may be quickly erased. In many cases victims of computer crime are reluctant to report their victimization. Banks and other businesses do not want the vulnerability of their computerized systems publicized, and in any case they may have little confidence in the ability of the criminal justice system to respond effectively to this type of crime (McEwen 1990a; Conly 1990). Finally, public consciousness of and concern with computer crime are relatively small because of its novelty and lack of directness.

## The Law Concerning Computer Crime

Laws specifically prohibiting computer crime are quite recent and not easily enforced. Traditional criminal laws—for example, those pertaining to burglary and larceny—are not always applicable to crimes committed by manipulation of electronic software. Most state and federal laws specifically applicable to computer crime came into being in the 1980s; by the end of that decade all 50 states had passed some form of computer crime laws (Schjolberg and Parker 1983; Shriver 1989; Conly 1990; Nicholson 1990). In 1986 Congress passed a Computer Fraud and Abuse Act, intended to make the use of computers for fraud and theft a felony in cases not covered by state laws (Greenhouse 1986). These laws were enacted either because legislators recognized a rational need for them, or because lawmakers were responding to a perceived threat to established property and authority relations posed by illicit access to a new and ambiguous form of information (Hollinger and Lanza-Kaduce 1988; Michalowski and Pfuhl 1991). No public outcry called for such laws, but introducing them provided legislators with some media exposure at little risk. It is quite clear that the thrust of existing computer crime laws is directed toward computer crime that victimizes corporations, rather than such crime which could potentially be committed on behalf of corporations (Pfuhl 1987). To date the practical impact of computer crime laws has been limited at best, and their symbolic and ideological importance may indeed be more substantial.

## The Pursuit of Computer Crime Cases

Investigation and prosecution of computer crime require specially trained personnel and tend to be quite time-consuming (McEwen 1990b; Sieber 1986; Shriver 1989). In recent years the FBI has expressed some concern over these crimes and has introduced computer crime training classes (Sessions 1991). In local jurisdictions in which special computer crime investigative units have been established, they must compete for finite resources with other units (such as a drug enforcement unit) that have a higher priority (McEwen 1990b).

The prevention and detection of computer crime is principally the responsibility of accountants and other investigators in the private sector (Wagner 1979; Wold and Shriver 1989). It is often necessary to resolve computer crimes privately and informally, in part because special complications arise if cases are pursued through the criminal justice system. Defense lawyers, for example, often challenge the admissibility of computer-related evidence (Schjolberg and Parker 1983). But because there is every reason to suppose that computers and other forms of sophisticated technology will become an increasingly ubiquitous feature of society, it becomes obvious that far more attention and resources will have to be directed toward computer crime. In 1995 "cybercrime"—illegal or harmful actions committed on the rapidly expanding Internet—was characterized as "probably the fastest growing brand of wrongdoing in America" (Meyer 1995); as much as $2 billion in software was illegally copied off the Internet in 1994. However, in the wake of a major federal investigation of computer bulletin boards in 1990, some computer buffs contend that the prosecution of computer "hackers" has gone too far and infringes on First and Fourth Amendment rights (Bromberg 1990; Sulski 1990), engendering concern that the increasing use of computers and sophisticated technology will enable the government to engage in increasingly abusive invasions of citizen privacy and civil liberties.

## Other Types of Technocrime

Automatic teller machines, telecommunications systems, fascimile machines, and other new forms of technology also provide a range of opportunities for misappropriation or theft.

A significant proportion of such technocrime is committed by people who cannot be classified as white collar criminals; thus, losses in excess of $100 million from frauds committed against automatic teller machines is not for the most part considered white collar crime (Bureau of Justice Statistics 1985). Advances in all forms of copying technology have provided new opportunities for organized and professional crime, counterfeiting and distribution of video and audiotapes in particular. Of course such copying, and unauthorized copying of computer software as well, is so widely engaged in by private parties that it hardly requires documentation (Francis 1987: 64). Millions of Americans also engage in airwave piracy through the use of satellite dishes, illegal chips, and the simple expedient of wiring onto a cable line (Bennett 1987; Green 1985). Further, the theft of telephone service—through the use of "blue boxes" simulating telephone system beeps, altered cellular phone chips, and unauthorized use of corporate switchboards—costs the telephone companies and other victimized parties millions of dollars (Andrews 1991c; Buder 1987; Kleinfeld 1978; Ramirez 1992; Sims 1989). Much of this activity is regarded as relatively harmless "folk crime."

At least some proportion of these forms of technocrime either occur in an occupational context or are committed on behalf of corporations. In a 1980 report, for example, the Justice Department identified copyright violations as the third most troublesome area of white collar crime (Mutterperl and McGovern 1991). Rapid, sophisticated photocopying machines facilitate the theft of trade secrets both on behalf of corporations and by corporate employees seeking financial benefit from the use of such information (Bennett 1987). The unauthorized copying of computer programs by U.S. businesses deprived software publishers of some $1.6 billion in 1993; worldwide losses totaled $7.5 billion (Elmer-Dewitt 1994: 62). Businesses of all sizes can be victimized by some technocrimes, but they also commit some of it as well.

The use of technology as an instrument in the commission of a wide range of white collar crimes will become far more common in a future increasingly dominated by highly sophisticated technology. The distinguished University of Pennsylvania criminologist Marvin Wolfgang has been quoted as predicting that "by the turn of the century, the main concern of criminal justice will be information crime" (Bennett 1987: 109). It will be a formidable challenge to generate any meaningfully normative consensus concerning much of this activity, to inhibit commission of it, and to implement effective technological countermeasures and efficient penal responses to deter it. Still, it is important to recognize that technocrime arises out of and is shaped by an ongoing contest between the powerful and the powerless over access to information, one of the premier currencies of our environment today.

## Hybrid White Collar Crimes, In Sum

STATE-CORPORATE CRIME, finance crime, and technocrime do not easily fit into the most commonly recognized categories of white collar crime, namely corporate crime and occupational crime. But these forms of white collar crime became more significant at the end of the 20th century, and they illustrate the increasingly hybrid character of much white collar crime. It is reasonable to infer that *networks* connecting governments, corporations, and various elements of the financial markets will be major features of white collar crime in the 21st century. It is virtually certain that technocrime and white collar crime will become increasingly interrelated as we move into the future.

# Enterprise Crime, Contrepreneurial Crime, and Avocational Crime

T RADITIONALLY, WHITE COLLAR crime has been most readily associated with corporate crime and occupational crime, the foci of Chapters 3 and 4. Governmental crime was explored in Chapter 5 as a cognate form of white collar crime, or as a public-sector parallel of corporate crime and occupational crime. State-corporate crime, finance crime, and technocrime were discussed in Chapter 6 as significant hybrid forms of white collar crime, or as critical new elements of corporate, occupational, and governmental crimes.

This chapter is concerned with what might be called "residual white collar crime"—that is, what is left over ("the residue") once we move beyond relatively high-consensus forms of white collar crime and begin to consider illegal activity on the margins of such forms of crime. The terms *enterprise crime, contrepreneurial crime,* and *avocational crime* refer, then, to hybrids of white collar crime and organized crime, professional crime, and occasional property crime, respectively. These types of crime are either ranged along a continuum connecting white collar crime with these other forms of criminal activity, or are interrelated in some way with such activity.

Considering enterprise crime, contrepreneurial crime, and avocational crime to be separate types of criminal behavior may seem arbitrary and paradoxical in certain respects, and it is always possible that we are distorting reality by making such distinctions (Clarke 1990; Hagan 1986; Zerubavel 1991). The premise here is that for purposes of attempting both to explain crime and to control it, knowing the specific form of and context within which the crime occurs is helpful. For example, the term "enterprise crime" is adopted here to provide a framework within which more familiar, related terms—i.e., organized crime and syndicated crime—can be discussed. Ultimately the interrelated dealings of legitimate businessmen, political officials, and syndicated racketeers take the form of an "enterprise."

## Enterprise Crime: Organized Crime and White Collar Crime

THE TERM *ORGANIZED* crime is familiar enough, but there is considerable confusion about its meaning. In the broadest use, the term could refer to any organized illegal activity, including organized professional theft, business theft, terrorist groups, motorcycle gangs, and "racketeers" who extort money by intimidation and violence (Abadinsky 1985; Fijnaut 1990; Pace 1991). It can easily be confused with the concept of *organizational crime,* an umbrella term for crimes of corporations and government agencies (Coleman 1985). The term *organized crime* is most commonly associated with the "Mafia" (or La Cosa Nostra), an alleged national syndicate of criminals of Italian descent engaged in systematic illegal enterprises centered around the sale and distribution of illicit drugs, gambling, prostitution, loan-sharking, labor racketeering, and other such activities (President's Commission on Law Enforcement and Administration of Justice 1967b; Cressey 1969; President's Commission on Organized Crime 1987). In this view organized crime operates as a "criminal corporation."

Whether or not a unified national syndicate exists has been vigorously debated in the organized crime literature for the past quarter of a century or more; most students of the issue express skepticism (Albanese 1991; Beirne and Messerschmidt 1991). Some students of organized crime contend that it is more accurately characterized as relatively autonomous local syndicates or families engaged in systematic illegal enterprises, possibly with informal ties (Abadinsky 1985; Albini 1971). Perhaps the easiest solution is to refer to the popular image of Mafia-type syndicates (whether local or national) as "syndicated crime" and use the term *organized crime* more broadly (Beirne and Messerschmidt 1991), especially to refer to certain alliances to be discussed shortly.

Several features are commonly associated with syndicated crime. It is a self-perpetuating organization with a hierarchy, a limited membership, specialized roles, and particular obligations, especially a vow of secrecy (*omerta*); it conspires to gain monopolistic control over certain illegal enterprises in a particular geographical area; it uses the threat of or actual use of force. violence, and intimidation as a primary instrument for achieving its aims; it commonly protects itself from investigation and prosecution by corrupting the political and legal system; its primary objective is the acquisition of large-scale financial gain at relatively modest risk; and its success results from providing goods and services for which there is a demand but no legal supply.

The celebrated syndicated crime leader Meyer Lansky once boasted, "We're bigger than U.S. Steel"; indeed, the annual gross income of syndicated crime has been estimated in recent years to exceed $50 billion (or 1 percent of the GNP), and some estimates run as high as $250 billion (Rowan 1986; Beirne and Messerschmidt 1991). There is no really reliable way to measure the total income and profits of syndicated crime.

Other students of organized crime downplay the ethnic and family-related dimensions, and adopt instead the concept of an illicit business enterprise that differs from legitimate businesses principally in terms of its degree of involvement with illegality and the perception of its illegitimacy (Smith 1978; Albanese 1991). This view of organized crime is especially relevant for exploring its relationship to white collar crime. Dwight Smith (1978) argued that businesses are conducted across a "spectrum" of behaviors that are shaped by market dynamics. Both business (or white collar) crime and organized crime can be seen as ways of conducting business illegally, and both reflect political processes that dictate that certain forms of entrepreneurship must be constrained and prohibited. In this view, ethnicity and conspiracy can play a role in both white collar and organized crime.

Legitimate businesses and organized crime engage in many of the same activities (e.g., lending out money) but do so in ways that are somewhat arbitrarily defined as legal or illegal (e.g., the amount of interest charged). When businesses such as savings and loan institutions become a vehicle for engaging in "collective embezzlement," the line between white collar crime and organized crime becomes virtually obliterated. Calavita and Pontell (1993) suggested that if we focus on the nature of the offenses rather than on the people involved, it becomes evident that a good deal of the thrifts crime in the 1980s was a form of organized crime.

Chambliss (1988b) advanced a related view of organized crime, defining it as a coalition of politicians, law-enforcement people, businessmen, union leaders, and racketeers (see also Block and Chambliss 1981). For Chambliss, the essential attribute of organized crime is a network of alliances operating a range of corrupt and illegal enterprises; people often become involved with the network through a somewhat serendipitous pattern of casual contacts in pursuit of money-making opportunities (Chambliss 1988b: 84). Chambliss discovered such a network in an investigation in Seattle, and he believes that similar networks exist in other U.S. cities.

This way of thinking about organized crime, widely adopted by progressive criminologists, views it as both a product of and an important ongoing element of a capitalist political economy (Vold 1958; Quinney 1979; Simon and Eitzen 1993). The contradictions of the capitalist economy—countervailing pressures to acquire and consume and make a profit, to legitimize the system, and to maintain order—generate circumstances in which racketeers, businesspeople, and government officials all benefit from cooperating in carrying out or tolerating criminal schemes (Chambliss, 1988b).

Organized crime performs important functions for corporate enterprises and the capitalist political economy. On the one hand, it consumes many services and goods, invests in many legitimate businesses, and deposits a huge amount of laundered money in mainstream banks; on the other hand, it suppresses dissatisfied workers via labor racketeering, oppresses the restless unemployed with a parallel opportunity structure, and represses impoverished inner-city residents through the distribution of illegal drugs (Simon and Eitzen 1993). The "sweetheart contracts" that organized crime-directed unions negotiate with businesses—guaranteeing labor peace while cheating workers out of wages and other benefits—are an especially good example of the mutually beneficial crimes perpetrated by legitimate businesses and organized crime against relatively powerless workers (Hills 1980). Altogether, organized crime and capitalist institutions coexist quite profitably.

This way of characterizing the economic role of organized crime is obviously controversial and very much at odds with a mainstream conservative perspective. An analysis prepared by Wharton Econometric Forecasting Associates for the President's Crime Commission in the 1980s claimed that "the mob's hold on the economy stifles competition and siphons off capital, resulting in a loss of some 400,000 jobs, an increase in consumer prices of 0.3 percent, a reduction in total output of $18 billion, and a decrease in per capita disposable income of $77 a year" (Rowan 1986: 24). The same analysis contended that tax evasion by "the mob" costs other taxpayers some $6.5 billion, and that the flooding of inner-city areas with drugs can be interpreted as working against the capitalist consumer ethic and fostering property crime against businesses (Inciardi 1980b). Perhaps the most accurate assessment of the economic impact of organized crime acknowledges that it cuts both ways; it benefits some elements of the capitalist political economy while harming others.

## The Relation Between Governmental Crime and Syndicated Crime

Important networks and interrelationships exist among politicians, government employees, and syndicated crime figures, and organized crime may be dependent for its very survival on the cooperation or connivance of some governmental officials (Beirne and Messerschmidt 1991; Chambliss 1988b; Hills 1980; Pearce 1976; Simon and Eitzen 1993).

Corruption in many U.S. cities, from police officers taking payoffs to high-level city officials awarding lucrative contracts for bribes, involves a strong syndicated crime element. The Knapp Commission, which investigated police corruption in New York City in the early 1970s, uncovered evidence of syndicated crime involvement; a study of Reading, Pennsylvania, during the same period established the existence of ties between syndicated crime and the city government (Michalowski 1985; Beirne and Messerschmidt 1991).

Many other investigations have uncovered evidence linking governors, state legislators, judges, and various other government officials with syndicated crime. Some commentators place special emphasis on the increasingly global character of such networks (Van Duyne 1993; Vitiello 1992).

On the national level, ties between government agencies and syndicated crime go back at least a half a century. During World War II Charles "Lucky" Luciano, one of the most powerful syndicated crime figures of his time, apparently assisted U.S. Naval Intelligence in preventing sabotage and unrest on the New York docks, and during the 1960s the CIA enlisted the cooperation of syndicated crime in its attempt to overthrow Fidel Castro (Rhodes 1984; Simon and Eitzen 1993). (If conspiracy theorists are to be believed, these entities also arranged the assassination of President John F. Kennedy.) CIA-syndicated crime cooperative ventures apparently continued during the Vietnam War period and after.

In the realm of politics, syndicated crime has both played a role in corrupting the electoral process via bribes, delivery of votes, fixes, and the like, and provided campaign contributions and other services to candidates in return for cooperation or immunity in criminal enterprises (Hills 1980). Recent presidents, including Richard Nixon and Ronald Reagan, have had close associations with people with alleged syndicated crime ties (Michalowski 1985; Beirne and Messerschmidt 1991). To the extent that such ties exist, one significant form of governmental white collar crime is the fostering of and tolerance of much syndicated crime activity. On the other hand, in one interpretation the prosecution of racketeers—from Al Capone in the 1930s to today—occurs primarily when their activities directly threaten the interests of the corporate and governmental elites (Pearce 1976). In this view, government officials' response to syndicated crime is significantly influenced by their own political agenda.

In the critical or progressive view, then, organized crime must be understood both as a product of a capitalist economy and as the illegal activity of a network of interdependent businesspeople, government officials, and racketeers. It is quite often intimately intertwined with white collar crime.

## Historical Roots of Organized Crime

Organized crime is hardly a new phenomenon. Piracy, which dates from the ancient Greeks and Romans at least, might be regarded as the first form of organized crime (Mueller and Adler 1985; Browning and Gerassi 1980). Significant networks of organized criminals were operating in 16th- and 17th-century London (if not earlier), and in the Massachusetts Bay Colony by the end of the 17th century as well (McMullan 1982; Browning and Gerassi 1980). John Hancock, the celebrated first signer of the Declaration of Independence, apparently operated an organized crime cartel that engaged in large-scale smuggling in the pre-Revolutionary colonies (Lupsha 1986).

The syndicated form of organized crime is often considered to have its roots in various criminal organizations such as the Mafia, which emerged in southern Italy no later than the 16th century; these crime cabals—also known as la Camorro, L'Unione Siciliana, the Black Hand, the Honored Society, and La Cosa Nostra—began to surface in New Orleans, New York, and other U.S. cities by the end of the 19th century (Abadinsky 1985; Inciardi 1975; Ianni and Reuss-Ianni 1972). Through much of the 20th century, Italian-American syndicated crime was widely regarded as the dominant form of authentic organized crime in the United States, although clearly syndicated crime entities developed among other ethnic groups as well.

Prohibition, which occurred between 1919 and 1933, provided an ideal opportunity for the dramatic growth and expansion of syndicated crime because it created enormous demand for a product—alcoholic beverages—in the absence of a legal supply (Lupsha 1986; Abadinsky 1981). In one commentator's view, Prohibition largely turned the alcoholic beverage industry over to criminals (Schelling 1973). It also led to much more systematic contact between the underworld and the upperworld, and in this respect it established a much firmer and more enduring basis for the intermixture of syndicated and white collar crime. Founders of some of the great 20th-century North American fortunes, including Samuel Bronfman of Seagrams, Moe Annenberg of the Nationwide News publishing dynasty, and Kennedy family patriarch Joseph P. Kennedy, are alleged to have greatly enhanced their fortunes during this period, partly through involvement with bootlegging, bookmaking, and other syndicated crime activities (Fox 1989).

The repeal of Prohibition hardly diminished the potency of syndicated crime. In subsequent decades a vast range of opportunities for making money illegally—gambling, drugs, loan-sharking, and labor racketeering—evolved in subsequent decades with newer areas of opportunity, including arson for hire, credit card and real estate frauds, the pornography business, the theft and sale of securities, and cigarette bootlegging (Nelli 1986). The World War II blackmarket also generated a new set of opportunities for syndicated crime. Despite persistent investigations of and campaigns against syndicated crime during much of this period, it has continued to thrive into the final decade of the 20th century.

The presence in syndicated crime of certain 19th-century ethnic groups (e.g., the Irish and Eastern European Jews) has become less visible as others, including African Americans, Jamaicans, Hispanics (especially Cubans and Colombians), and various groups of Asians, have become more conspicuous (Abadinsky 1985). As Daniel Bell (1962) argued in a frequently cited article, syndicated crime was an important (if unorthodox) ladder of mobility for immigrant and minority groups for whom legitimate ladders of mobility were restricted or closed off. This view recognizes very direct parallels between the large-scale legitimate gambling enterprise known as the stock market and the gambling ventures run by syndicated crime (Schelling 1973). The objectives of those involved in syndicated crime thus parallel those of individuals in legitimate occupations, and syndicated crime is simply seen as an unorthodox form of white collar crime.

Even though organized crime has been identified in Canada, Australia, Great Britain, the Netherlands, Poland, Israel, Japan, the Caribbean, and parts of Africa (Kelly 1986; Van Duyne 1993), it is not clear that organized crime in many of these countries is specifically analogous to syndicated crime in the United States (Fijnaut 1990). The specific attributes of organized crime in different parts of the world vary, as does the extent of involvement of organized crime with legitimate businesses and institutions.

## The Relation Between Organized Crime and White Collar Crime

One thesis concerning the connections between syndicated crime and white collar crime suggests that the methods used to establish the great industrial empires and sprawling Western ranches of the 19th century were fundamentally no different from the methods used by 20th century mafiosi and syndicated crime members. As Gus Tyler (1981: 277) observed:

> Original accumulations of capital were amassed in tripartite deals among pirates, governors, and brokers. Fur fortunes were piled up alongside the drunk and dead bodies of our noble savages, the Indians. Small settlers were driven from their lands or turned into tenants by big ranchers employing rustlers, guns, outlaws—and the law. In the great railroad and shipping wars, enterprising capitalists used extortion, blackmail, violence, bribery, and private armies with muskets and cannons to wreck a competitor and to become the sole boss of the trade.

In this view, the 19th-century "robber barons" and cattle barons were the forerunners of 20th-century organized crime. For much of this century the descendants of the robber barons have occupied the pinnacle of the social hierarchy, and prestigious universities and foundations have been named after such robber barons as Vanderbilt and Rockefeller; is it possible, one commentator asks, that one day similar tributes will be paid to syndicated crime figures (Abadinsky 1981: 29)? Such recognition seems unlikely, but the analogy is provocative.

The parallels between syndicated crime and white collar organizational (corporate) crime continue today. Jay Albanese (1982) compared two separate testimonies before Senate investigative committees: in the 1960s, testimony by Joseph Valachi, reputed member of La Cosa Nostra, and in the 1970s, testimony by Carl Kotchian, president of the Lockheed Corporation. Valachi was the first "insider" to confirm (truthfully or otherwise) the existence of a national organized crime network; Kotchian was the first high-level insider to testify openly about secret corporate payments or bribes to foreign governments to secure major contracts. Applying the framework of Smith's "spectrum-based theory of enterprise," Albanese has argued that the Valachi and Kotchian testimonies revealed parallel concerns between organized crime entities and corporations in conspiring to make bribes: Both seek to create a favorable climate (or protection) for their business and to maintain their dominance over competitors in the marketplace.

Ferdinand Lundberg (1968: 131), a prominent student of the crimes of the rich, has argued that corporate criminals "make Mafias and Crime Syndicates look like pushcart operations." It has also been suggested that La Cosa Nostra, whether or not it is a national syndicate, performs functions similar to those of a Rotary Club or other such association for white-collar businesspeople: It facilitates business contacts and promotes the interests of business generally (Haller 1990). That syndicated crime may elicit a harsher legal response than white collar crime and have a more negative image may be attributable to ethnic and class biases.

The general public perception of syndicated crime has in fact been somewhat ambivalent. An enduring fascination with the Mafia, "the mob," "wiseguys," and the like is evident from the public's response to such films as The *Godfather, Goodfellas,* and other films. As a rule, "mobsters" seem to inspire less visceral fear and hatred than do predatory street criminals. Despite such ambivalence, syndicated crime mobsters do not enjoy the same status of respectability that white collar offenders do, and they are more vulnerable to suspicion, investigation, and conviction on that score alone.

Although students of organized crime are divided on many issues, they uniformly agree that syndicated crime infiltration of and interrelationships with legitimate corporations and businesses has increased over the decades (Hills 1980; Nelli 1986; Rowan 1986), for various reasons. Legitimate businesses provide both a front and an important tax cover for illegal activities; they provide employment for associates and relatives who are on probation and parole; they can be transferred more easily to dependents and heirs; and they can provide a more secure source of income and profit (Anderson 1979). Altogether, increasing involvement with legitimate businesses can reduce the exposure of syndicated crime figures to prosecution and may also reflect an aspiration for greater respectability. Although such infiltration is often denounced by politicians and journalists, it isn't entirely clear that society as a whole is better off when syndicated crime reinvests in illicit enterprises alone.

The infiltration of legitimate businesses is often accompanied by the introduction of a higher level of intimidation, corruption, and outright fraud by these businesses

(Cressey 1969). In some cases businesses are stripped of their assets after they are taken over and forced into a planned bankruptcy (Hills 1980; Michalowski 1985). At least some legitimate businesses are taken over when the business has borrowed money from syndicated crime and is then unable to repay it (Hills 1980; Pace 1991: 134). But to the extent that syndicated crime is increasingly involved with legitimate business—through takeovers, partnerships, or alliances—the image of syndicated crime as merely exploiting such businesses is simplistic and distorted (Hills 1980). Often a mutually beneficial relationship develops, and legitimate businesses may initiate contacts with syndicated crime to control its labor force or to acquire loans on short notice.

The involvement of syndicated crime with certain classes of legitimate and quasi-legitimate businesses, including vending machines, construction, nightclubs, casinos, and pornography, has long been recognized. An investigation of New York City's building trades and construction industry in the 1980s uncovered evidence of pervasive syndicated crime involvement, including extortion, bribery, theft, fraud and bid-rigging, and other forms of corruption and violence (New York State Organized Crime Task Force 1988). The syndicate's infiltration and takeover of the meat industry, cheese-processing plants, garment factories, banks, stockbrokerages, and various unions have come to light (Kwitny 1979). The consequences of such infiltration include the dumping of unhealthy food products into ordinary supermarkets, inflated prices for consumers, and lower wages and benefits for workers. The range of businesses with an alleged syndicated crime presence, then, is very broad.

A Senate committee chaired by Estes Kefauver in the 1950s identified some 50 types of business, from advertising and appliances to theaters and transportation, with a syndicated crime presence; a congressional investigation in 1970 identified some 70 areas of economic activity with syndicated crime involvement (Nelli 1986: 5). The character of such involvement, however, has been open to interpretation, and various degrees of association with white collar crime specifically have been identified. An investigation by the Pennsylvania Crime Commission (1980) uncovered evidence that syndicated crime, through its control of various unions, infiltrated a number of health care plan companies, which then overreported services provided to union members and engaged in various other fraudulent practices. More than 20 years after the Pennsylvania Crime Commission (1991: 325) first began investigating organized crime in that state, it concluded that "there is a prevailing influence of organized crime in certain legitimate industries and unions in Pennsylvania." Various studies of organized crime emphasize the interdependence between mobsters and legitimate businesses, and their mutual culpability. Next we examine two examples of this interdependence: arson and hazardous waste disposal.

**Arson**  Arson-for-profit is an especially harmful crime, each year causing over $2 billion in direct losses of commercial property and some $10 billion in indirect losses (e.g., jobs, business income, taxes, municipal costs)(Rhodes 1984). Arson also traumatizes nearby residents and results in the deaths of hundreds of citizens and firefighters annually (Brady 1983).

In a study of the epidemic of commercial arson cases in Boston in the 1970s, Brady (1983) found evidence of mutual involvement of legitimate businesses and syndicated crime racketeers. When banks began to engage in discriminatory "redlining" of mortgages in inner-city neighborhoods, about half of the city's arson fires occurred in the growing numbers of abandoned buildings in these neighborhoods (Brady 1983: 9). Organized crime racketeers would secure mortgages for these buildings by agreeing to buy them at inflated prices; they would then insure them and arrange for the buildings to be "torched." The bank would profit by collecting from the insurance company; the insurance company would pay the claims, raise its premiums, and discourage further investigation because it feared greater state regulation and the perception that it resisted paying claims. Because most insurance companies don't have enough arson investigators to pursue cases effectively and can face possible lawsuits when they deny claims (Rhodes 1984), government officials (such as inspectors) would often be paid off. In this sense, then, arson-for-profit can be regarded as a form of organized crime activity that has a devastating effect on some urban communities. Because arson emanates out of a symbiosis of corporate profiteering, gangster racketeering, and government corruption or ineptitude (Brady 1983), it is more a hybrid form of white collar and organized crime than an activity of mafiosi and lone arsonists-for-hire.

**Hazardous Waste Disposal** The business of disposing of toxic wastes has been heavily infiltrated by syndicated crime because of its long-standing domination of the garbage carting and disposal business (Block and Scarpitti 1985; Reuter 1993; Szasz 1986b). The illegal disposal of hazardous wastes costs only a fraction (perhaps 5 percent) of the cost of safe and legal disposal, and less than 20 percent of these wastes are disposed of properly (Szasz 1986b). Corporations that generate hazardous waste strongly lobbied against laws that would impose substantial liability on them for the effects of improper or illegal disposal; they also contracted with hazardous waste haulers whom they likely knew would not dispose of the wastes legally and properly. (Corporations knew perfectly well that there was a great shortage of adequate waste disposal sites—they had emphasized this in lobbying for an extended transition period to meet new standards—and so they should have been aware that the contracted haulers were not disposing of their waste properly; Szasz 1986b: 17.) The pervasive illegal disposal of hazardous wastes lends especially strong support to the network model of organized crime because it comes about through interdependent ties, corruption, and ineptitude of corporations, politicians, regulatory bureaucrats, and traditional syndicated crime entrepreneurs (Szasz 1986b; Block and Scarpitti 1985). This activity, which may well cause more harm than such syndicated crime enterprises as gambling and prostitution, is an especially clear example of a hybrid type of white collar/organized crime.

## The Relation Between Syndicated Crime and Finance Crime

A fairly long history of ties exist between syndicated crime and finance-related institutions. First, the theft and manipulation of stocks and bonds by syndicated crime has been a major problem since the early 1970s (Pace 1991). Obtaining and then selling these stocks and bonds requires a certain level of cooperation from brokerages, investors, and other legitimate parties. Further, the long-standing practice of "laundering" the huge sums of money generated by illegal enterprises obviously requires some complicity on the part of banks, which benefit from such large deposits (Beaty and Hornik 1989; Hills 1980; Thornburgh 1990).

The looting of the savings & loans thrifts in the 1980s was arguably the most costly of all white collar crimes. In an especially widely read exposé of the S & L frauds, Pizzo, Fricker, and Muolo (1991) claimed to have found evidence that individuals associated with syndicated crime were directly or peripherally involved with a significant number of the defrauded thrifts. The S & L frauds can be characterized either as a form of organized crime, or as an illustration of the blurred lines between syndicated crime and white collar crime, carried out by a network that included businesspeople, confidence men, government officials, and (among others) individuals with syndicated crime ties (Brewton 1992; Calavita and Pontell 1993; Pizzo, Fricker, and Muolo 1991). Taking advantage of opportunities to get in on business-related frauds is certainly quite consistent with the recent history of syndicated crime.

## Enterprise Crime, In Sum

Despite claims that by the early 1990s syndicated crime had been rendered less powerful by the conviction of some of its important leaders, it remains clear that organized crime is likely to be an enduring presence for some time to come, perhaps because it is so deeply interwoven with legitimate American institutions and norms (Hills 1980: 112).

Many people today would argue that they can distinguish between white collar crime and syndicated crime. No one is likely to confuse corporate executives, retailers, or physicians who engage in white collar crime with John Gotti, the most notorious syndicated crime figure of this era. There is a difference in style, in the degree of involvement in illegal enterprises, in the typical character of these enterprises (e.g., illicit narcotics, gambling, and labor racketeering, as opposed to environmental safety law violations, deceptive advertising, and Medicaid frauds), and in the level of direct intimidation or violence. It is likely that these differences will persist for some time to come.

Clearly, many interconnections and interrelationships exist between organized crime and white collar crime, and the boundary lines between them have blurred considerably. In a 1983 interview (Laub 1983: 153–54), criminologist Donald Cressey speculated that at some point early in the 21st century we would no longer be able to tell the difference between white collar crime and organized crime. It remains to be seen whether this prediction will come true.

## Contrepreneurial Crime: Professional Crime and White Collar Crime

LIKE THE TERM *organized crime,* the term *professional criminal* is familiar but vague. It does not, for example, refer to crimes committed by professionals such as doctors and lawyers, which we discussed in Chapter 4. In its broadest use the term is applied to anyone who engages in criminal activity regularly, and in this sense it has been used interchangeably with "career criminal." Indeed, the term *professional killer* is not unknown, but some commentators object to using "professional" in this way (Hagan 1986: 358).

However, a narrower conception of the term *professional criminal* has been quite widely accepted in the criminological literature, including E. H. Sutherland's criminological classic entitled *The Professional Thief* (1937), a first-hand account of the criminal life by the pseudonymous criminal "Chic Conwell." Some of the attributes of professional criminals Sutherland identified include highly developed skills for committing crime; high status in the criminal world; socialization into professional crime values and knowledge through association with others; alliances with other professional criminals, commonly in the form of a mob; and some shared values and professional pride with such associates. Professional criminals attempt to minimize the risk of arrest, prosecution, and imprisonment by carefully planning their crimes, avoiding violence, and putting in the "fix" with corruptible law enforcement and political officials. Among the activities engaged in by professional criminals, according to Sutherland, are theft, picking pockets ("cannons"), shoplifting ("boosting"), switching jewels on inspection and stealing them ("pennyweighting"), hotel burglaries, check forgery ("laying paper"), shakedowns, and short and big "cons."

Of all these activities, the "big con" intersects most fully with white collar crime as a form of "contrepreneurial" crime, and it is this intersection that is of greatest interest to us here. Francis (1988) coined the term *contrepreneurs*—combining "con artist" with entrepreneur—to refer to white collar con artists. The contrepreneur carries out a swindle while appearing to be engaged in a legitimate enterprise.

## Historical Origins of Professional Crime

The origins of professional crime have been traced back to the disintegration of European feudalism during the very late Middle Ages (1350–1550), when a certain proportion of the newly disenfranchised turned to robbery, poaching, banditry, and other outlaw practices (Inciardi 1975). Professional crime in subsequent centuries took on many guises in many places.

In the American tradition, frontier bandits such as Jesse James in the 19th century and bank robbers such as John Dillinger in the 20th century have been regarded as one class of professional criminals. Such criminals have long been romanticed through penny novels, films, and television dramatizations. *The Sting*, a 1973 film featuring Paul Newman and Robert Redford, is one prominent example of an entertainment that portrays professional criminals (in this case, confidence men) in a sympathetic light.

The question of whether professional crime is in decline is a controversial one (Beirne and Messerschmidt 1991; Walker 1981). In his exhaustive study of the historical sources on professional crime, James A. Inciardi (1975) concluded that it entered a decline at least as recently as the 1940s, when increasingly sophisticated crime prevention and detection technology was introduced. Others (see, for example, Staats 1977; King and Chambliss 1984) have argued that professional crime has simply adapted to changing conditions and opportunities; check and credit-card fraud has replaced such activities as safecracking as professional crime activities of choice. It may be that the elaborate types of "big cons" engineered by the legendary Joseph "Yellow Kid" Weil have become less common.

Weil was an elegant, sophisticated man with a formidable knowledge of banking, mining, financing, and other fields, and he would move from city to city representing himself as a successful businessman or a representative of powerful interests. He would establish ties with wealthy individuals and financial institutions, and then proceed to defraud them of large sums of money by enticing them to invest in some phony scheme (Weil and Brannon 1957). Weil claimed that his victims were not only well-heeled but sufficiently greedy to risk making a fast dollar by questionable means.

The old-fashioned big con, then, could be characterized as a form of crime that victimizes people who are predisposed to commit white collar crime. Although Weil's particular style of professional crime may indeed have declined or disappeared, vast amounts of money are still stolen by con artists in the guise of entrepreneurs. Today's white collar contrepreneurs, however, as often as not victimize people with ordinary or modest incomes; of course some contrepreneurial criminals target institutions such as the savings and loans as well.

## The Relation Between Professional Crime and White Collar Crime

Several significant parallels exist between professional criminals and white collar offenders generally. Both are prepared to take risks to make money, both are prepared to violate laws to maximize profit, and both seek to immunize themselves by bribing or financing the campaigns of politicians or becoming informants for law enforcement officials (King and Chambliss 1984). The classic professional criminal, like the white collar offender, relies on skill and planning, rather than direct force or intimidation, to achieve an illegal objective, and both need to convey an aura of respectability and inspire some level of trust to carry out their crimes successfully. In both cases rationalization is important; professional criminals rationalize that legitimate businesspeople are no more honest than they are, and such businesspeople often rationalize that because their competitors are not complying with the law, they shouldn't have to either.

In one sense, professional criminals may feel they can assume a stance of moral superiority over white collar criminals. According to Sutherland's "Chic Conwell,"

> [Con mob members] believe that if a person is going to steal, let him steal from the same point of view that the thief does: do not profess honesty and steal at the same time. Thieves are tolerant of almost everything except hypocrisy. This is why defaulting bankers, embezzlers, etc., are despised strongly by the thief. (Sutherland, 1937: 178)

A similar point was made by Chambliss's informant, the "box man" (safecracker) Harry King:

> Harry had little respect for "square-john society." He saw the straight world as hypocritical and corrupt. Everyone, in Harry's view, was larcenous in their soul and in their deeds, especially those "respectable citizens" like judges, policemen and prison

*officials. The difference between himself and them or, more generally, between professional thieves and them, was that thieves were not hypocrites; they admitted their criminality and were willing to pay the price for it. Indeed, they took pride in it whereas the corrupt officials and business people of the world tried desperately to hide it. (King and Chambliss 1984: 2)*

On the other hand, Sutherland's professional thief also claimed that other professional thieves harbor the hope of getting out of thievery and into a legitimate occupation, and Chambliss's "box man" tired of "rooting and rousting about" and ultimately committed suicide when a "straight" job as a probation counselor failed to come through (Sutherland 1937: 181; King and Chambliss 1984: 2; 140).

What are the differences, if any, between the classic professional criminal and the contrepreneurial white collar criminal? First, there may be a difference in self-identity; the professional criminal may be much more accepting of his outlaw status, whereas contrepreneurial white collar criminals may be more likely to regard themselves primarily as "businesspeople." Second, the professional criminal is more likely to make a deliberate decision to become involved in criminal activities, whereas the contrepreneurial white collar criminal is more likely to drift into fraudulent enterprises. Third, the professional criminal typically attempts a pure theft of money from a vulnerable victim or mark, whereas the contrepreneurial white collar criminal defrauds by giving something of little or no real value in return for money. Contrepreneurial white collar crime in some respects is a true hybrid of elements of classic professional crime and occupational white collar crime, although often there is no practical difference between what professional and contrepreneurial criminals do.

## Fraudulent Businesses: Swindles, Scams, and Rackets

A vast number of businesses and enterprises are in fact swindles, scams, or rackets that annually cost consumers, investors, and other unwitting parties billions of dollars. Although "the operator," as one commentator (Gibney 1978) calls him, has been an enduring figure in U.S. history, current conditions continuously nurture and promote whole new realms for fraudulent activities. Are these activities properly classified as forms of white collar crime?

In some cases the fraudulent activity is more appropriately described as organized crime or professional crime; in other cases a designation of white collar crime is quite clearly justified. Certainly many of the offenders affect the appearance of "white-collar" entrepreneurs or businesspeople, and are so perceived by others. The activities we discuss next, and those who perpetrate them, are commonly designated as white collar crime by the FBI and other law enforcement agencies.

Businesses can be ranged along a continuum extending from the wholly legal and ethical on one end to the blatantly criminal and unscrupulous on the other end. Obviously a good many businesses and enterprises fall somewhere in the grey area between the extremes. Still, a basic premise applies to all businesses: Their success depends significantly on conveying an image of legitimacy and respectability. And, of course, the whole spectrum of enterprises shares the objective of making money. It is sometimes quite difficult, if not impossible, to discriminate clearly between fundamentally legitimate and illegitimate businesses.

**The Fence**  In certain respects, fences illustrate the intersection between legitimate business and outright criminality. Fences buy stolen goods from burglars, thieves, and others who acquire them; they then sell them to consumers or to businesses for resale (Steffensmeier 1986; Klockars 1974). Fences may also play a key role in bankruptcy frauds, in which an apparently legitimate business orders merchandise from suppliers and then sells it through fences, avoiding payment to the suppliers by declaring bankruptcy (Bequai 1978: 39).

Even though fences commit the offense of "receiving stolen property," they typically operate legitimate businesses and are seen (and see themselves) primarily as legitimate businesspeople (Steffensmeier 1986: 21). Although fences are more likely to be classified as professional criminals than as white collar criminals, they do not fit entirely well into either category. Fences have available to them a large number of rationales—for example, "If I didn't buy the stolen goods, someone else would," or "I only make money because conventional businesses and consumers knowingly buy stolen merchandise, if they can get it at a good discount"—which allow them to define themselves primarily as legitimate businesspeople. And legitimate businesses are important customers for them. In some respects the fences' "hot goods" customers are the opposite of the defrauded consumer: They are benefitting at someone else's expense rather than being exploited.

**Fraud**  Fraud appears to have been practiced since the beginnings of recorded history. Laws prohibiting fraud were known in the 4th century B.C. in ancient Greece (Drapkin 1989: 206); an account from this time describes a shipowner attempting to defraud someone by seeking a cash advance for a ship laden with corn, when all along the intent was to scuttle the ship instead of delivering the corn (Clarke 1990: 13). We have clear accounts of consumer fraud (e.g., adulterating food and wine) from the 1st century A.D. in ancient Rome (Green 1990: 209), and we have much evidence that such schemes have been practiced throughout the Western world since then.

In the late 18th century, former magistrate Patrick Colquhoun inveighed against various "sharpers, cheats, and swindlers," including pawnbrokers, auctioneers, merchants who use false weights and measures, and other defrauders, in his *A Treatise on the Police of the Metropolis* (1795, 1969: 110–32). In the late 19th century, Anthony Comstock, a special agent for the Post Office and best known for his "suppression of vice" campaign, published *Frauds Exposed* (1880, 1969), in which he documented numerous consumer frauds, including stock market swindles, phony mining companies, bogus lotteries and contests, and the peddling of worthless merchandise or cures.

In the latter part of the 20th century, Robert S. Rosefsky's *Frauds, Swindles and Rackets* (1973) provided a "red alert" for contemporary consumers, identifying such frauds as "get rich quick" schemes, home improvement rackets, land swindles, and "E-Z" credit offerings. Rosefsky identified assorted other swindles and schemes, including phony charities, long-lost heir searches, magazine subscription rackets, referral schemes, dancing lesson rackets, phony contests, travel deceptions, phony auctions, reducing salon rackets, phony employment agencies, and tax preparation shysters. *Consumer's Research* magazine (1989: 32–33) reported the following as "the top ten scams": prize offers; penny stock; business-to-business fraud; magazine sales; credit repair; precious metals, coins, gems, and gold; travel; art; business ventures; and cellular telephone lottery. Some of these enterprises are described in subsequent sections.

Fraudulent businesses, many of which operate as mail-order businesses, prey upon human vanity, fantasy, loneliness, insecurity, and fear. During hard economic times, when people are desperate for money or savings, get-rich-quick schemes tend to flourish (Bohlen 1994; Kerr 1991a). The elderly, new immigrants, the unemployed, and people with poor credit histories are especially vulnerable to fraud from a variety of sources: contractors promising to make their home safe, people promising to enrich them, firms promising lucrative foreign employment, and companies offering easy loans, second mortgages, or the like (Brenner 1993; Hicks 1993; Sontag 1992; Booth 1993; Nieves 1991; Wald 1992).

Entrepreneurs who are selling basically legitimate products may also fraudulently play on people's vulnerabilites to sell their products. In a New Jersey case, an entrepreneur was charged with 14 counts of consumer fraud for giving newly expectant mothers a gruesome "safety" lecture on the dangers awaiting their infant if they did not purchase his Starlighter Converta Crib, which a regulatory agency had already declared unsafe (Lawrence 1975). Some sellers of burglar alarms may also use "fear accentuation" to mislead potential customers and frighten them into buying an alarm system (Siegel 1978).

Many other products and services are inherently dubious. Consumers are enticed into making payments, which can range from fairly modest to quite substantial, with the misrepresented prospect of obtaining lucrative modeling contracts for their child; selling their musical compositions; publishing their book and having it sold in bookstores; promoting their invention; winning a contest; building up muscles and losing weight; making money from home-assembled products; being identified as an heir of a deceased, unknown relative or of an unclaimed bank account of such a "relative" (usually someone with the same surname but not related); obtaining a loan; meeting a prospective mate; and the like. Most readers of this book have received notices informing them that they have won a prize or enticing them to enter a sweepstakes; these offers are typically misleading at best and could be outright frauds (Sloane 1991b; 1992). A New York entrepreneur pleaded guilty in 1993 to defrauding business owners and executives with highly misleading claims of their selection for listing in *Who's Who in American Executives,* a shoddily produced vanity book (*New York Times* 1993b). Consumers who respond to these enticements typically lose their money and fail to realize their objective, and many may suffer emotional distress as well.

Arguably the single most disturbing form of contrepreneurial fraud involves alleged advocacy and charitable organizations. In 1992, for example, an organization known as United Seniors Association was accused of inducing hundreds of thousands of retirees to contribute millions of dollars on the pretext that the association would lobby to protect their threatened social security payments, even though substantial evidence of either the threat or any such advocacy was lacking (Eckholm

1992). In 1995 the ousted president of United Way of America was convicted (along with two aides) on federal charges of having stolen more than $600,000 from this well-known charitable organization; the money was spent on personal luxuries (Arenson 1995). In other incidents, clothes donated for charitable purposes were being sold abroad for profit, and a shipping company executive was sent to prison for replacing milk powder intended for African famine victims with a cheap product meant for animal use (D. Gonzalez 1991; Hays 1991). Health-charity programs have been accused of benefiting their executives and staffs and the medical establishment, rather than disease victims or the general public (Bennett and DiLorenzo 1994). The pure hypocrisy involved in siphoning off for personal benefit funds intended to assist the vulnerable or to aid the unfortunate is especially evident in these cases.

**Ponzi and Pyramid Schemes**   One of the most famous swindles in U.S. history took place in 1919, when Charles Ponzi, an Italian immigrant, began advertising that he could return very large profits to investors because he had learned how to take advantage of the international currency and postage markets (Kohn 1989: 270–71) The claim was that international postal reply coupons purchased in a poor country such as Italy could be redeemed at a much higher rate in the United States. As word spread of rapid, dramatic profits returned to early Ponzi investors, millions of dollars began to pour in. Ponzi, however, wasn't investing the money; he was spending large amounts of it on himself and paying off early investors with some part of the money pouring in from newer investors. Eventually, of course, the scheme was exposed, many people lost their money, and Ponzi went to prison. But the "Ponzi scheme" itself has proven to be remarkably durable.

In one case that surfaced in the 1980s, a San Diego commodities trader, J. David Dominelli, induced a large number of people to invest a total of $200 million with him, on the claims that the money would be invested in the foreign currency market and that they would receive a 40–50 percent annual return (Bauder 1985). In fact, much of the money went to support Dominelli's lavish lifestyle, and by the time he was finally arrested investors had lost some $80 million. In a somewhat similar case during this period, a recent New York City college graduate, David Bloom, persuaded some 100 individuals to invest $10 million with his Sutton Investing Group (Blum 1988). Bloom used most of the money to buy millions of dollars worth of art, a house in the Hamptons, a $139,000 Aston Martin Volante convertible, and other such luxury items while investors were kept in the dark with phony investment statements.

Many different versions of the Ponzi scheme, sometimes called a pyramid scheme, continue to be perpetrated on whole new generations of naive investors. A large number of fraudulent businesses over the years have enticed people to make investments, purchase dealerships, or buy expensive products on the premise that they will make back their money many times over by bringing in other customers or dealers. In the 1970s this "billion-dollar" industry was called "the nation's No. 1 consumer fraud" (*Time* 1973). In one case, William Penn Patrick, president of the Holiday Magic cosmetics and soap empire, was charged by the SEC with bilking some 80,000 people out of over $250 million. A protégé of Patrick's, Glenn Turner, established the Dare To Be Great Company, which was charged with defrauding thousands of consumers out of their money by inducing them to purchase multilevel distributorships for cosmetics and self-improvement courses; he used the grossly misleading lure that they could earn up to $200,000 a year (Bequai 1978: 60; Rosefsky 1973: 48–52). The cosmetics industry in particular seems to be especially prone to such practices (Springen 1991). Despite recurrent exposés, multilevel distributorship scams continue to surface.

**Home Improvement Frauds** A whole range of home improvement projects, from roofing to basement waterproofing, lend themselves especially well to fraudulent schemes. Some contractors are outright con artists; many others are marginal contractors who mislead customers, do incomplete or shoddy work, and declare bankruptcy or engage in some other subterfuge to avoid settling claims (Bequai 1978; Magnuson and Carper 1978). Energy-related home improvement has been especially prone to abuse. Bequai (1978: 55) cited losses to home improvement fraud totaling some $100 million in the 1970s. A standard approach in these frauds has included gaining entry into homes on false pretexts, such as posing as "inspectors," and then frightening homeowners with claims that, say, their furnace is dangerous or does not meet current pollution emissions standards. One study conducted in the 1970s (Stotland et al. 1980) found some evidence that vigorous prosecution of home repair frauds can have a deterrent effect, but the overall incidence of such fraud (as measured by complaints) has generally risen in recent years.

**Land Sale Frauds** The history of defrauding prospective buyers on land sales is a long one (Paulson 1972). In the 1920s, for example, many people who bought "land" in Florida eventually discovered that their land was underwater; in the 1970s land sale fraud was especially prevalent in the Southwest (Arizona and New Mexico). Losses of billions of dollars are involved; some such swindles have netted $200 million (Bequai 1978: 56; Lindsey 1979).

The basic scheme in these cases is to entice prospective retirees and other investors with attractive brochures of beautiful developments complete with landscaping, golf courses, lakes, and the like. Through the use of high-pressure sales tactics, people are persuaded to pay exorbitant prices for arid desert plots that turn out to be virtually worthless when the promised development plans never materialize. Purchasers are deceived or misled on many other points pertaining to ownership, mortgages, and the like (Snow 1978: 135). In the 1970s in particular, the people running these schemes were able to play upon consumers' fears of inflation by claiming that real estate was the best type of investment in the prevailing economy. These schemes have been carried out by people linked with organized crime, by professional criminals, and by legitimate real estate people who cross the line into white collar crime.

**Travel Scams and Time-Share Vacation Resorts** In a practice that became very widespread in the 1980s, millions of Americans received postcards informing them that they had won a glamorous vacation (to Florida, Hawaii, Las Vegas, or the like) (Pauly 1987). People who responded to such inducements would often be persuaded to pay a fairly substantial "travel club" or "service" fee before receiving their "prize." The "free vacation" would turn out to have so many absurd restrictions that it would be useless to the recipient, who then could often be persuaded to pay additional fees to "upgrade" the arrangements. Recipients often ended up with no vacation, or with one for which they paid a substantial amount of money. Similarly, millions of people receive inducements to buy into time-share vacation plans, a $1-billion-a-year business in the early 1980s (Lyons 1982). Consumers who respond to blatantly misleading announcements about "prizes" that will be awarded if they visit the time-share resorts are subjected to high-pressure sales pitches. Many respondents commit themselves to expensive plans that do not deliver what they promise, and they rarely if ever receive the prizes they have been promised.

**Employment Agency and Education-Related Scams** Unemployed people and individuals hoping to get better jobs have paid fees (sometimes in the thousands of dollars) to "employment agencies" that guarantee them employment, sometimes abroad (Reibstein 1989; Booth 1993). After sending in their money, many clients never hear from the agency again, or they receive sloppily prepared résumés or outdated lists of jobs or corporate contacts. In most cases applicants do not obtain jobs.

Some similar scams involve fraudulent claims relating to education. One variation of this scam involves an "educational consultant" who collects thousands of dollars (from young people in particular) in return for the false promise that the consultant will ensure their placement in a professional (especially medical or dental) school (Bequai 1978: 58). Some correspondence schools or vocationally oriented schools lure students, especially minorities and veterans, with promises of a valid educational or training curriculum that will lead to guaranteed jobs, when in fact the education or training is worthless and no jobs result.

**Telemarketing or "Boiler Room" Scams** In 1989 scam artists using various telemarketing schemes were bilking consumers out of over $1 billion a year (Castro 1989); other estimates put the losses as high as $10 billion. These operations may offer tempting investments (e.g., in rare coins, oil or gas leases, or diamonds), prizes, vitamins, and the like. Even though telemarketers may be placing a call from a shabby little back office, successful ones are able to convey to the recipient of their call an image of a booming, established business enterprise. Some relatively new telemarketing scams include enticements for "cash loans" in which callers are charged $49 for a generic information package on how to apply for bank loans; "one-shot" credit cards, in which callers pay a fee for a card that then turns out to be usable only once; bogus health product promotions, such as water purifiers; and "blind pool" penny stock offerings based on misleading information about new small companies (*Consumer's Research* 1990). The common elements of telemarketing scams are a smooth, polished line to generate trust and interest; persuading the victim to provide a credit card number or to forward payment before they receive anything; the failure to give consumers what they expect; and the difficulty of prosecuting the offenders, who may move around frequently (Holcomb 1986; Meier 1992a).

The "900" numbers have sometimes been used to induce consumers—including children—to make calls for information or services of dubious value (Andrews 1991a; 1991b). Fraud associated with the sale of "penny stocks," which are often sold through telemarketing and call for investments in very small companies that are not listed on stock exchanges, has been estimated to cost investors $2 billion a year (Henriques 1990a). Altogether it seems rather foolhardy either to make investments or purchases of any kind on the basis of unsolicited phone calls, or to provide one's credit card number for such purchases.

**Schemes to Defraud the Wealthy**  Victims of investment scams are not always naive, poorly educated elderly people or naturally gullible parties, as some might imagine; middle-class individuals seeking a high return on their investment can be susceptible, too. Some 6,000 people who invested $350 million in Colonial Realty in the 1980s, for example, lost much of their money when the operation turned out to be fraudulent (Judson 1992). People of means seeking tax shelters—including movie stars, financial columnists, and major bank presidents—are periodically defrauded, as occurred in the celebrated Home-Stake Production Co. case in the 1970s (*Newsweek* 1974). In 1994 a California man was accused of bilking thousands of investors, who mistakenly thought they were investing in tax-sheltered low-income housing projects, out of as much as $130 million (Eaton 1994). The money was in fact never invested, and the investors faced both the loss of their money and possible back taxes.

Even highly sophisticated stock brokerage firms can be vulnerable to investment-related fraud. In the early 1990s a Nigerian grifter who had acquired an understanding of the logistics of high-level trading was able to trade some $1 billion in bonds and notes through major brokerages without putting up a nickel of his own money (Pooley 1993); the embarrassed brokerage houses lost hundreds of thousands of dollars. In another case that is essentially check-kiting on a grand scale, a Long Island car dealer borrowed a staggering $1.75 billion from General Motors for the financing of thousands of cars that did not exist, defrauding the company of several hundred million dollars (Fritsch 1992). That a corporation of this size can be so massively defrauded is surely a sobering realization.

**Respectable Contrepreneurs and High-Stakes Fraud**  The success of contrepreneurs depends significantly on their ability to convey an aura of respectability and trust, and to have credibility with financial institutions and investors. Time after time apparently reputable individuals have used their positions to defraud investors of huge amounts of money.

Samuel Insull and Ivar Krueger were two of the most notorious large-scale swindlers of the first half of the 20th century (Kohn 1989). Insull, a protégé of Thomas Edison, used various fraudulent methods to build up a chain of Midwestern utility companies that then collapsed in 1932, with losses of a billion dollars to investors. Insull was extradited from Turkey and tried several times on various charges, including embezzlement, misuse of the mails to defraud, and bankruptcy law violations, but he was acquitted due to the inadequate laws of the time. Kreuger similarly embezzled and lost through speculation millions of dollars raised by the match-producing companies he controlled.

In the latter half of the 20th century a New Jersey entrepreneur, Robert Vesco, achieved considerable notoriety by misappropriating some $224 million from an international mutual funds company, Investors Overseas Services, over which he had achieved control (Dorman 1975; Herzog 1987). In the face of a federal indictment for illegal campaign contributions to the Nixon campaign, Vesco fled the United States in 1973 to hinder SEC investigation of his activities. In subsequent decades Vesco lived as a fugitive in Central America and the Carribbean, allegedly being involved in bribing the leaders of these countries and financing illegal drug and gun-running operations.

Robert B. Anderson was secretary of the treasury during Dwight Eisenhower's second term in office; between 1957 and 1961 his signature appeared on all U.S. currency. Trained as a lawyer, Anderson enjoyed a distinguished career, serving over the years as Texas tax commissioner, secretary of the navy, deputy secretary of defense, and roving ambassador. In the private sector he had a career as a general counsel for oil and cattle interests and as an international banker. Investors who gave him amounts ranging from $20,000 to over $2 million to invest for them in the early 1980s would appear to have entrusted their money to an individual eminently worthy of such trust (Chambers 1987). Yet in 1987 Anderson, at age 77, was convicted of illegally operating an offshore bank and evading personal income tax. Some of his investors lost several hundred thousand dollars. Although Anderson disputed any criminal intent and blamed his predicament on associates and the distractions of personal problems (his alcoholism, his wife's Alzheimer's disease), he was indicted and pleaded guilty on federal criminal charges. The Anderson case starkly demonstrates that an impressive résumé is no guarantee of personal integrity.

In all of these cases, then, an initial status as a highly successful businessman facilitated fraud on a grand scale.

## Contrepreneurial White Collar Crime, In Sum

We have seen, then, that a vast number of small and middle-sized businesses and enterprises engage in illegal conduct. Although they are not necessarily inherently more or less unethical than major corporations, they contend with different types of pressures and have a different range of opportunities for committing crime. In some cases small businesses are fundamentally fraudulent or criminal operations whose image as a legitimate business is simply a sham. In other cases fundamentally legitimate businesses may engage in sporadic illegalities, sometimes in a desperate effort to survive (Croall 1989: 170). The contrepreneurial enterprise is probably best characterized as one that knowingly and blatantly defrauds consumers while conveying the appearance of a legitimate business.

Some contrepreneurial crime is also committed by individuals who, although they convey a status of respectability and may choose to think of themselves as essentially legitimate businesspeople, nevertheless either deliberately or opportunistically engage in blatant fraud. Although the boundaries separating professional crime, contrepreneurial crime, and traditional forms of corporate or occupational crime are often indistinct, it seems worthwhile to recognize the somewhat different patterns of fraudulent conduct. Contrepreneurial white collar crime, with its combination of legitimate business practices and classical criminal activity, highlights the hybrid nature of much contemporary fraud.

## Avocational Crime and White Collar Crime

ONE CLASS OF illegal activities that is not white collar crime in the strict sense, even though it has a generic relationship to it, can be labeled *avocational crime*. The most common dictionary definition of an avocation is a hobby or occasional occupation. In this context avocational crime refers to occasional economic crimes committed by respectable members of society outside of an occupational context. Geis (1974: 273) characterized avocational crime as follows:

> *(1) The crime is committed by a person who does not think of himself as a criminal; (2) the crime is committed by a person whose major source of income or status is in activities other than crimes; and (3) the crime is deterrable by the prospect of publicly labeling the offender as a criminal.*

Geis's discussion of avocational crime applied the term broadly, to the whole range of white collar crimes, including shoplifting, although here the term will be used more narrowly.

The concept of avocational crime has some similarities with the concepts of occasional property crime, folk crime, and mundane crime. Clinard and Quinney (1973) defined *occasional property crime* as amateur, small-scale property theft or destruction. Ross (1961) used the term *folk crime* to apply to everyday deviance, such as traffic violations, that does not reduce the status of the violator and is generally considered relatively harmless. More recently, Wilson (1983) used the term *folk crime* to apply to violations of fishing conservation laws by New England shellfishers, who avoid the ordinary consequences of law-breaking by violating the letter, but not the intent, of this rather low-priority law. Gibbons's (1983) somewhat related concept of *mundane crime* was applied to commonplace, innocuous, often dull or routine opportunistic forms of lawbreaking with relatively low visibility. Gibbons's examples included underground economy transactions, unreported taxes, workplace crime, long-distance phone calls charged to innocent third parties, and littering.

The preferred use here of the term *avocational crime* over the related terms emphasizes that the illegal activity occurs outside of an occupational context. Even though avocational criminals do not necessarily enjoy a respectable status, it is especially significant that such a high proportion of them do in fact enjoy a respectable status and hold legitimate occupations. Indeed, a respectable status often provides special opportunities for engaging in this type of illegality. The people involved, their motivations, and the consequences of avocational crime are often similar or identical to occupational white collar crime.

Avocational crimes includes evading personal taxes; defrauding of insurance companies; providing false statements in connection with personal loans and obtaining credit, and defaulting on payments of debts; customs evasion; theft of services (e.g., telephone calls, tolls, tickets for travel or entertainment events); theft of copyrighted material (e.g., audiotapes, videotapes personal computer software, printed matter); and the purchasing of stolen ("hot") goods. We could include shoplifting and defrauding of retailers and wholesalers (e.g., rebate and coupon abuse) in this list, but the people who engage in these offenses are less likely to commit white collar offenses. The term *crime hobbyist* that been applied to a collector of fine wines who admitted to switching price tags in wine shops, with the rationale that the prices were inflated and ridiculous (Standing Bear 1994). Improper garbage disposal by householders may well come to be perceived as a significant form of avocational crime as increasing numbers of communities impose stringent recycling and waste disposal rules (Wilson 1991). Altogether, the entire range of illegal activities committed by respectable members of society, for financial advantage or to avoid financial disadvantage, in their roles as citizens, taxpayers, consumers, insured parties, travelers, and the like, can be considered avocational crime.

## Income Tax Evasion

Some scholars of white collar crime (see, for example, Green 1990; Coleman 1989) have classified income tax evasion as a form of occupational or individual white collar crime. But strictly speaking, the obligation to pay income taxes applies to income from whatever sources and is not limited to that from a legitimate occupation. Indeed, it is income that is earned outside of the occupational context—from investments or rental properties, for example—that is most likely to be involved in income tax evasion (Bonsignore et al. 1989: 143).

Federal tax laws require taxpayers to file a timely return, report tax liabilities accurately, and make a timely payment of taxes due; employers are additionally required to withhold the appropriate amount of taxes from their employees' paychecks (Long 1981). Failure to comply with tax law may take different forms, including failure to file and nonreporting of income, underreporting of income, and false or misrepresented claims of deductions.

Tax evasion, which is defined by the Internal Revenue Service (IRS) as an act involving deceit, subterfuge, and concealment, is, of course, illegal. Tax avoidance, on the other hand, is the arrangement of a taxpayer's affairs to minimize tax liability, and it is legal (Carson 1973; Burnham 1989). The growing complexity of tax law makes it increasingly difficult to distinguish clearly between tax evasion and tax avoidance (Long 1981).

Historically, well-off and exceedingly wealthy taxpayers have been much better positioned to engage in tax avoidance than have taxpayers with modest incomes (Stern 1972). Many millionaires or even billionaires have paid only trivial taxes on stupendous incomes by taking advantage of provisions in the tax code that allowed large-scale deductions. In a 1981 congressional hearing it also became evident that the IRS was much more vigorous in its pursuit of tax protesters—those advocating tax evasion—than of tax straddlers—those using illegal tax shelters (Bonsignore et al. 1989: 136–41). By the early 1980s, growing numbers of middle- and upper-income taxpayers were investing in tax shelters, and the IRS increasingly began to crack down on such shelters, which were clearly evasive or outrightly fraudulent (Dentzer 1984). The major federal tax reform of 1986 was largely inspired by growing taxpayer anger at basic inequities in the tax law, although it is far from clear that the reform succeeded in eliminating all the inequities. The tax laws privilege some classes of taxpayers over others and generate some noncompliance among taxpayers who resent perceived inequities.

The income tax has its seminal origins in France in the Middle Ages, when those who did not own land (e.g., artisans, laborers, state officials, and others) had a *taille personelle* imposed on their earned income (Carson 1973). Most of the taxes in the early American colonies took the form of export/import duties and property, poll, and excise taxes, although a "faculty tax" was also levied on arts, trades, and professions.

The American Revolution was precipitated, in part, by the colonists' perception that they were being saddled with unfair taxes. The various excise and property taxes imposed after the Revolutionary War, to retire the war debt, were widely unpopular and even inspired an armed uprising known as the "Whiskey Rebellion" (Long 1981). It wasn't until the Civil War, which generated enormous costs for the government, that a full-fledged, if temporary, income tax was imposed; the cost of wars generally has been a major factor in the development of income tax laws (Long 1981).

With the ratification of the Sixteenth Amendment in 1913, a federal income tax became permanent. Initially the income tax was limited to "lawful" income, but the final version of the amendment reads as follows: "The Congress shall have the power to lay and collect taxes on income, from whatever source derived...." Not surprisingly, only an estimated 10–15 percent of illegally earned income (primarily from gambling or illicit drug sales) is reported (Duke 1983). Case law has established that the Fifth Amendment protection against self-incrimination does not excuse citizens from having to report illegal income.

Originally the Internal Revenue Code was no more than 15 pages long, and only the rich were required to pay income tax. Over time the requirement to pay income taxes came to include almost everyone who has an income, and the tax statute today runs to well over 2,000 pages, plus over 7,000 pages of appended regulations (Long 1981). Income tax (individual and corporate) provides some two-thirds of federal tax revenue, with an additional one-fourth coming from employment taxes; the corporate share of the income tax burden has fallen steadily in this century, especially since World War II (Long 1981). From the beginning there have been interpretive ambiguities about classifying different forms of income and eligibility for various deductions. Corporations and well-off individuals, with access to high-priced lawyers and accountants, have obviously been best positioned to take advantage of these interpretive ambiguities.

Each year the IRS processes some 150 million tax returns and takes in over $1 trillion in taxes, and the United States collects between 80 and 90 percent of what it is owed (Long 1981; Burnham 1989); if there were no cheating (or mistakes), the

IRS has estimated that it would have collected an additional $100 billion in 1990 (Goleman 1991; Smith and Kinsey 1987). The IRS is organized primarily as an enforcement agency, and has a vested interest in claiming it needs a bigger budget and more manpower to be more effective in collecting taxes and identifying cheaters (Long 1981). Some students of income tax claim that noncompliance increased significantly since the early 1970s; others claim that the rate of noncompliance has remained quite stable in recent decades (Duke 1983; Smith and Kinsey 1987; Burnham 1989).

As a broad generalization, the rich and the poor have the best opportunities to cheat on their taxes. The rich are better positioned to use illegal loopholes, offshore accounts, and the like, and may collect and conceal large amounts of cash; the poor also collect a disproportionately higher percentage of their income in cash. Middle-class wage earners are most poorly positioned to cheat on their taxes, regardless of their inclinations, and the largest proportion of income tax comes from those in the broad middle-income category (Duke 1983; Smith 1991).

Nevertheless, tax evasion is practiced by a significant number of middle-class taxpayers. If on the one hand tax liability is strictly speaking an obligation that is independent of occupational status, it is also true that one's occupation may generate opportunities for tax evasion. Self-employed people are probably in the best position to cheat on taxes. The IRS estimates that auto dealers, restaurateurs, and clothing store owners underreport some 40 percent of their taxable income; telemarketers and traveling salespeople 30 percent; doctors, lawyers, barbers, and accountants 20 percent; farmers 18 percent; and real estate operators and insurance agents 16 percent (Smith 1991).

The federal income tax withholding system, instituted during World War II, has been enormously effective as a device for collecting federal taxes. Indeed, because the substantial majority of taxpayers receive refunds after filing their income tax forms, many Americans think of the post-tax period in terms of money they will receive from the government; having a substantial amount of money withheld over the previous year, which they never saw, is psychologically the less painful way to meet their tax obligation. Rather unsurprisingly, an IRS study released in 1991 found that those people who are required to make a lump-sum payment when filing their income tax return are three times as likely to cheat as people who owed the same amount but had it withheld throughout the preceding year (Goleman 1991). Other studies conducted in the 1980s established that people whose incomes had improved dramatically during the previous tax year were more likely to evade taxes than were people under financial strain (Goleman 1991). Clearly there is a significant psychological dimension to tax compliance.

One consistent finding in the tax compliance literature is that fear of detection acts as a deterrent to noncompliance (Klepper and Nagin 1989). The odds of being criminally prosecuted for tax evasion are very slim, as only one tax return in 75,000 is subject to criminal prosecution (Duke 1983). In 1988, for example, only 2,769 taxpayers were indicted on criminal tax charges; due to budget cuts IRS criminal investigations declined some 26 percent during the 1980s (Burnham 1989; Smith 1991). Of those actually convicted of tax crimes, less than half receive a prison sentence (shorter on the average than for other forms of fraud), and 20 percent receive neither prison time nor a fine (Long 1981). Only about 1 percent or so of individual U.S. taxpayers are audited annually, although it has been estimated that some 49 percent of all returns would reveal underreporting of income if audited (Long 1981). Some 70 percent of 1,060,000 individual taxpayers formally audited in 1988 were found liable for additional taxes and penalties, and over a billion dollars in civil penalties were collected, although the average individual civil penalty is quite small (Long 1981; Duke 1983; Burnham 1989).

The enormous strain on finite resources that a criminal prosecution requires, as well as the complexity of the tax laws themselves, means that it is much easier for the IRS to pursue relatively less serious tax frauds and to maintain control over cases that are not referred to the Justice Department for criminal prosecution (Long 1981). It is especially difficult to prove criminal intent for the most common form of tax fraud, the claiming of illegitimate deductions. Still, the overall high rate of compliance of U.S. taxpayers far exceeds that in many other Western developed nations (Burnham 1989). The IRS must also consider a taxpayer backlash, in the form of a potentially catastrophic decline in compliance rates, if it pursues negligent or evasive taxpayers in arbitrary and unfair ways (Duke 1983). Many factors other than fear of detection also enter into compliance. The withholding system has stripped large numbers of taxpayers of good opportunities for significant tax evasion. Other factors include grudging recognition of the need for taxes, patriotism (in a minority of cases producing an eagerness to pay, even overpay, taxes), a basic sense of civic responsibility, and integrity.

Tax cheating has been explained on a number of different levels, although until recently remarkably few serious, empirical studies of factors in taxpayer compliance and noncompliance existed (Duke 1983). The IRS has traditionally emphasized personal dishonesty, which is obviously a factor but hardly the only one. Taxpayers have a large number of rationales for cheating, including the tax codes are unfair, the government wastes the tax money, everyone is doing it, and the like (Maital 1982; Thurman, St. John, and Riggs 1984). Various studies report that many respondents (51 percent) did not regard tax evasion as a serious crime, considering it as much less serious than defrauding an employer and no more serious than stealing a bike (Levi 1987; Maital 1982; Tittle 1980). One recent study of tax compliance suggested that a complex of factors (including opportunity, convenience, and interpretations of the law) is often involved, and that a series of decisions rather than a single one leads to noncompliance (Smith and Kinsey 1987). The tax laws themselves are often complex, onerous, arbitrary, confusing, and illogical, and accordingly promote a certain level of evasion (Duke 1983). Given the relatively low risk of audits and the rather mild sanctions, the real issue may be why so many people do in fact comply with the tax laws (Smith and Kinsey 1987). Authentic corporate compliance with the tax laws appears to be more limited than individual compliance.

One principal response of the IRS to tax evasion has been to target especially prominent Americans for criminal prosecution; the expectation is that the inevitable publicity will have a deterrent effect on ordinary taxpayers. Many eminently respectable citizens—including a former dean of the Harvard Law School, a president of the National City Bank of New York, a chief of police of Providence, Rhode Island, and a vice president of the United States (Spiro Agnew)—have been prosecuted on tax evasion charges (Carson 1973; Cohen and Witcover 1974).

Two widely publicized cases of tax evasion in recent years involved Leona Helmsley, the self-anointed "queen" of the Helmsley hotel empire, and Pete Rose, the former baseball star with the record for the most career hits. Helmsley, the wife of a real estate tycoon with holdings estimated to be worth several billion dollars, was convicted of tax evasion in 1989 in a scheme involving billing the Helmsley businesses for millions of dollars of personal redecorating expenses; she was fined $7.1 million and sentenced to a four-year prison term (Glaberson 1989b). Rose pleaded guilty to filing false income tax returns in 1990; he was sentenced to five months in a federal correctional institution and three months in a community treatment center, and was ordered to pay a $50,000 fine and give 1,000 hours of community service (Smith 1990). In addition to having unusual opportunities to commit tax evasion, both individuals may have had serious personal flaws that led them to do it. Both Helmsley and Rose were characterized as arrogantly assuming that the rules that apply to ordinary citizens did not really apply to them; Helmsley's limitless greed and Rose's obsession with gambling were seen as the principal character flaws that got them into trouble. Even though their occupations (hotel chain owner and baseball star) provided the large income and opportunities for evasion, the tax evasion itself was linked with pursuits in their private life as opposed to business activities.

Income tax evasion, then, is a form of avocational white collar crime. A significant percentage of people who engage in this type of crime are middle- or upper-class businesspeople, professionals, or entrepreneurs. Income tax evasion is committed by people of all types of occupations, or of no occupation (but some income); the scope of opportunities for income tax evasion is often a function of occupation, however, and some occupations provide better opportunities for tax evasion than others. Despite the IRS's best efforts, a conviction for tax evasion seems to have less of a stigmatizing effect than conviction for most comparable economic crimes. The perceived inequities, complexities, and contradictions of the tax laws clearly provide opportunities for evasion and a range of rationales for doing so. The relationship between compliance and noncompliance with income tax laws and other laws specifically applicable in the corporate or occupational setting is worthy of much more substantial investigation.

## Insurance Fraud

Insurance fraud is widely perceived as a growing problem in Western developed nations. Perhaps as many as 20 percent of all insurance claims are fraudulent; false claims principally involve rigged car crashes, auto thefts, slip-and-fall scams, and inflated burglary claims (Bennett 1987: 157). In 1987 the U.S. Chamber of Commerce estimated that 10 percent of automobile or arson claims were fraudulent, with an annual cost in the $15 billion range (Clarke 1990). Up to 40 percent of all auto theft claims may be false—indeed, up to 60 percent of the stolen vehicle reports from a single Long Island, New York, mall were believed to be false—and the annual cost of these claims has been estimated at $6 billion (Kerr 1992a; Sloane 1991a). Some 10 percent—or $1.3 billion—of the annual $13 billion in medical bills relating to vehicle accidents is believed to be paid out for fraudulent or abusive claims (Kerr 1993). Whenever public mass transportation is involved in an accident, fraudulent claims are often forthcoming, including claims from "ghost riders" who were not actually there at the time (Kerr 1993).

Arrests for making such claims are rather uncommon and mostly involve ordinary citizens, including school teachers, grandmothers, and other unlikely parties (Sloane 1991a). In one case in New York City, some 96 ordinary citizens were arrested for participating in an insurance fraud ring that disposed of cars for which phony theft claims were filed with insurance companies (Bennett 1987: 158). Various professionals—including doctors, lawyers, insurance adjusters, and police officers—are involved in facilitating, or even encouraging, false injury, damage, and theft claims (Romano 1992; Kerr 1993). Even though a certain proportion of insurance fraud is carried out by organized crime or professional criminals, and of course some fraudulent claims are made within a legitimate business context (e.g., a failing business is "torched" by the owner, who then collects insurance), much insurance fraud generally is avocational crime committed by respectable, middle- or upper-class members of society.

The enormous expansion of intensely marketed insurance "products" that emphasize the ease of making claims has certainly played a role, as have the inflated values of automobiles and other insured items (Clarke 1990; Kerr 1992a). On the other side of the equation, an erosion of integrity involving "situational morality" is blamed. Insurance companies are perceived as "deep pockets," large corporate entities with massive assets that will hardly be affected by a routine fraud. A spirit of adventure and peer support may accompany such frauds. Many false claims involve relatively minor inflations of actual damages or losses, and such activity—as well as "rate evading" by registering vehicles in neighboring states with lower insurance rates—is not viewed as a significant offense by many people (Sloane 1991a; Romano 1992). The connections between engaging in such frauds in an avocational context and engaging in various forms of corporate or occupational crime demands greater attention.

## False and Fraudulent Actions on Loans, Debts, and Credits

Most Americans take out loans to obtain homes, automobiles, and other major purchases. In recent decades, credit cards have become increasingly pervasive in all manner of consumer purchases. Between 1970 and 1984, for example, credit card purchases in the United States increased by 600 percent, up to some $300 billion annually (Caminer 1985: 746). By the early 1980s, credit card fraud was characterized as the fastest growing crime against business; the rate of fraud was increasing more rapidly than the rate of card use (Caminer 1985).

Consumer debt has also risen exponentially. For installment loans it was up from 2 percent of personal income in the 1940s to 20 percent in the 1980s, or over $660 billion and rising; noninstallment borrowing was at the $100 billion level, or 10 times what it was in 1950. In the 1980s major banks handling credit cards were collectively writing off billions of dollars of debt each year; house foreclosures were rising dramatically, and personal bankruptcies were approaching 800,000 each year (Caminer 1985; Malabre 1987; Stone 1989).

It is not a crime, of course, to become debt-ridden or bankrupt, and it seems clear that the majority of people who are unable to pay off their debts did not take on these obligations with a criminal intent to defraud; in some cases reputable citizens get caught up in desperate situations. A 70-year-old Iowa farmer was sent to prison in 1994, under new sentencing guidelines, because he made false statements about the sale of some livestock in the course of a bankruptcy proceeding (Johnson 1994). But some proportion of debt—and it may be impossible to ascertain how much—is acquired by people who have falsely represented their financial situation and never had the potential to or the intention of repaying those debts. Financial institutions clearly merit some of the blame for the enormous credit losses because recently they have increasingly enticed customers to take out all manner of loans and have made unsolicited offers of credit cards to millions of people.

Effective responses to credit card fraud have proven difficult because state and federal laws, at least into the 1980s, were quite inadequate and enforcement agencies assigned a generally low priority to this type of crime (Caminer 1985). Obviously, a significant amount of credit card fraud occurs when cards are stolen, when professional criminals obtain account numbers, and when merchants make unauthorized charges. But at least some proportion of this fraud or abuse is committed by cardholders themselves, who make false claims pertaining to charges or simply run up charges for which they cannot pay. Because intent is generally difficult to prove, criminal prosecutions are quite uncommon.

## Other Forms of Avocational Crime

Customs evasion is almost surely even less stigmatizing than tax evasion, insurance fraud, and credit fraud. Travelers to foreign countries have long engaged in a battle of wits with customs inspectors in their attempt to bring in foreign purchases (especially jewelry and clothing) without paying duty on it. Customs evaders often come from the highest ranks of society because such people are especially likely to be able to go abroad and make expensive purchases for which they are liable for high duty costs; other customs evaders are ordinary citizens attempting to save money with purchases over the border (*New York Times* 1990). Those caught evading customs are fined several times the cost of the item or items involved.

A good deal of technocrime, discussed in Chapter 6, takes the form of avocational crime, including the theft of services (telephone service, tolls, and the like) and unauthorized copying of copyrighted material (e.g., audiotapes, videotapes, personal computer software, and printed matter)(Levi 1987: 44; Sims 1990a). Some 10–15 percent of the $3 billion in coupons redeemed annually involves fraud; most of these offenders are likely to be women in modest economic circumstances. Professional fences report that their customers include economically comfortable citizens, including judges (Klockars 1974; Steffensmeier 1986). Finally, some frauds are interpersonal frauds in which a relative, a neighbor, or a fellow tenant defrauds others in the settlement of an estate, in an investment scam, or by absconding with rent money that was supposed to go into an escrow account (Daley 1990; Glaberson 1989a; Golden 1990). Although such schemes parallel contrepreneurial and occupational frauds and may involve a violation of trust by someone with "white collar" status, they occur outside an occupational context.

## Avocational Crime, In Sum

Avocational crime, then, is treated here as a form of crime with a marginal relationship to white collar crime. It occurs outside of an occupational context, although of course a great deal of parallel activity such as tax evasion, insurance fraud, and theft of services occurs specifically within such a context. Many who engage in avocational crime have legitimate occupations and a respectable social status, and in this regard avocational offenders are identical with white collar offenders. Some avocational crime is facilitated by occupational status, although it is not wholly dependent on it. Avocational crime also has in common with much corporate and occupational white collar crime the primary objective of maximizing financial advantage or minimizing a financial disadvantage.

Much avocational crime is, on the whole, even less stigmatizing than virtually all forms of white collar crime, at least in part because the primary victims are most typically the government or large corporations, and because the losses appear to be more "abstract" than for other forms of theft or fraud. It has also been given low priority, for the most part, by the criminal justice system, and it receives relatively modest media attention; it may well be understudied by criminologists relative to other forms of crime. The specific nature of the relationship between avocational crime and white collar crime, and how involvement with one influences involvement with the other, merit further study.

# Explaining White Collar Crime: Theories and Accounts

**H**ow do we best explain white collar crime? This straightforward question has inspired a wide range of responses, from a simple human motivation ("greed") to complex structural explanations (e.g., "structural embeddedness" or "contradictions").

Only human beings attempt to explain the behavior of other beings instead of simply responding to it. Attempts to explain criminal behavior and crime—or behavior and activity that deviate in some measurable way from accepted norms—extend far back in history. In modern times a *theory* typically serves as a framework for criminologists' efforts to explain crime. A theory is a formal version of an explanation, then, although it is not necessarily a comprehensive explanation (Vold and Bernard, 1986: 4); it attempts to explain a class of events, whereas an "explanation" might simply attempt to make sense of a specific event (Goode 1994). In the conventional view, a good theory is one that can be tested and fits the evidence provided by research (Williams and McShane, l988: 3).

Perspectives on some phenomenon (such as crime) that direct attention to certain variables and tell us what to look out for are often called theories even though they do not meet the formal criteria for a theory (Goode 1994). Theorizing is not a cumulative enterprise in which new theories simply build upon and extend older theories; rather, it involves competing paradigms, each with quite distinctive assumptions and methodological implications; some paradigms become dominant at particular periods of time (Kuhn 1970). A paradigm is a broader concept than a theory because it incorporates a distinctive methology as well as an explanatory scheme. It is useful to keep this way of thinking about theory in mind in reviewing the different theories.

Previous chapters on the varieties of white collar crime include many references to explanations for such crime, but this chapter provides a much more systematic review of the various applicable theories and perspectives. Given the broad array of activities encompassed by the term *white collar crime*—from individual embezzlement to corporate production of unsafe products—it should be evident that no single theory or explanation fits all white collar crimes. But before proceeding with an examination of some of the specific perspectives on or theories of the causes of white collar crime, it is necessary to identify some of our underlying assumptions and the kinds of questions we should be asking.

## Underlying Assumptions and Points of Departure

EVERY ATTEMPT AT explanation explicitly or implicitly invokes certain metaphysical, ontological, and epistemological assumptions about the ultimate nature of reality and being, and how we come to know and understand our world (Mandelbaum 1987). For example, is reality subjective (in the mind of the observer) or objective (independent of the observer)? Is "causation" simply a human construct, or is it something that can be definitively and objectively established? With regard to human beings, do they have a free will (voluntarism), or is this simply an illusion because all human behavior is instead a function of various internal and external forces (determinism)? Or is some mixture of free will and determinism closest to the truth? Are human beings naturally self-interested and greedy, or naturally socially concerned and altruistic; are we fundamentally rational and guided by reason, or irrational and influenced principally by emotions; or is it simply the case that human nature is endlessly malleable and has no fixed tendencies? Is society itself best thought of as an integrated system bound together by a high level of consensus, or is it more accurately portrayed as a contested terrain of conflicting interest groups, with the more powerful tending to dominate the less powerful? And are the norms and rules that govern human groups rooted in absolute, eternal moral laws, or are they simply products of a particular time and place, and relative to the context in which they were created? These are but a few of the many enduring questions with which social philosophers have grappled through the ages. It is important to understand that almost anything we might say about white collar crime is rooted in our assumptions, whether explicit or implicit, concerning such questions.

The social and behavioral sciences have largely embraced the assumption that much about human activity and existence is explainable, and that it is desirable to produce ever more rigorous, testable explanations. An alternative position is that human activity is more easily interpreted than explained, and that it is endlessly variable or contradictory. Regardless, we have no single, comprehensive explanation of the causes of white collar crime; rather, we have at least provisionally identified some factors that appear to be correlated with or promote such crime.

## What Do We Want to Explain?

A FINANCIER ENGAGES in insider trading; a physician performs unnecessary operations; a corporation dumps toxic wastes illegally; a clerk embezzles money from his employer. At some point we want to explain these actions. But when we are attempting to explain white collar crime, what exactly requires explanation?

The conventional answer is that we must explain criminality, or what it is that makes individuals (or organizations) commit white collar crimes. Such an answer focuses on individual or organizational motivations, and on the forces that promote motivations and lead to the commission of white collar crimes.

A second answer is that we must explain the *crime*, or the event itself. One aspect of this approach addresses the issue of why the incidence of white collar crime varies (among occupations and industries; within occupations and industries; or across time and space). Situational factors that contribute to the generation of white collar crime are especially important on this level of analysis. Criminal behavior has been treated as both an individual (or organizational) propensity and as an event; more sophisticated explanations treat it as a combination of both dimensions. Among the elements that are cited to explain criminal behavior are motivation (the will to deviate); freedom from social constraints (impunity relating to losses); skill (technical ability); and opportunity (the chance to engage in the criminal act) (Sheley 1983). These factors may interact in different ways.

A third answer to the question of what must be explained, one that has received greater emphasis in recent decades, is that *criminalization*—the process whereby particular activities, entities, and individuals come to be defined as criminal—must be explained first (Gibbs 1987). This approach focuses on the origins of white collar crime laws or regulations and on the investigation, prosecution, and adjudication of white collar offenses (Vold and Bernard 1986: 338). The capacity of white collar individuals and organizations to prevent or deflect criminalization of their harmful activities is one of the recurrent themes of this perspective. Because these matters are explored in some depth in Chapters 9, 10, and 11, they will be only briefly treated here, principally in terms of their intersection with causal explanations.

A truly substantial explanation for white collar crime must address each of these matters, and ideally it must explore the variety of interrelationships involved in white collar crime as criminality, as an event (a crime), and as criminalized activity. A second basic issue, originally raised by Sutherland (1940), is whether crime can be explained by a general theory that is applicable to both conventional and white collar crime, or whether white collar crime must be explained by special theories applicable only to this type of crime.

A third basic issue in the explanation of white collar crime is the appropriate explanatory level. In macrolevel explanations the focus is on the conditions within society or the organization that promote white collar crime (i.e., on structural factors). In microlevel explanations the focus is on the offenders and their individual propensities and choices. In mesolevel (or intermediary) explanations, situational factors are examined. Some of the core questions at the various levels include: What type of society or political economy produces the most white collar crime? What type of organization is most likely to promote white collar crime? Which situational factors are most closely associated with white collar crime? Which individual attributes are most fully correlated with involvement in white collar crime? In the sections that follow we will examine some principal efforts to explain white collar criminality, crime, and criminalization.

# Explaining White Collar Criminality

THE MOST BASIC theories of criminality hold that criminals are different, in some fundamental way, from noncriminals; such theories then attempt to identify the nature of the difference. On a sociological level, criminality—the propensity to commit crimes—is shown to vary among different segments of the population or among different organizations. In the sections that follow we explore demonic, biogenetic, psychological, and sociogenic explanations of criminality.

## The Demonic Explanation

The earliest explanation of criminality, which could be called demonic or spiritualistic, does not lend itself to empirical verification (Pfohl 1985; Vold and Bernard 1986). At the core of this explanation was the belief that otherworldly influences caused criminal behavior. Such beliefs significantly influenced the response to crime, which for much of history was largely reactive. Exorcism, trials by ordeal, and penal measures involving corporal and capital punishment to exterminate evil spirits were important parts of this reaction. During the Renaissance (15th through 17th centuries), many thousands of Europeans were charged with witchcraft so that their accusers had reason to confiscate their property (Currie 1968).

Criminologists today are very unlikely to invoke the demonic explanation for criminality, but it is hardly extinct. Some people with fundamentalist religious beliefs continue to equate criminality with sin and otherworldly influences. But these and similar beliefs are not limited to fundamentalists. Richard Quinney (1980), a prominent critical criminologist, has suggested that much that is wrong with our existence today—including, presumably, the rapacious conduct of white collar criminals—reflects a "sacred void" in the face of relentless secular and materialist forces. Even though otherworldly explanations cannot be conclusively proven or disproven, they are still very much with us in some form or another.

## The Biogenetic Explanation

A biogenetic explanation of criminality became especially influential in the 19th century, although its roots could be traced back to much earlier times (Vold and Bernard 1986). At its core was the notion that criminals are inherently different from other people, and in fact look different from them, and it was promoted by Austrian anatomist Franz Joseph Gall's phrenology and Italian criminologist Cesare Lombroso's concept of the "born criminal" as an atavistic (less fully evolved) type. Criminals could be identified by their "primitive" appearance.

The significance of this notion of criminality is that it has persisted in the public imagination long after it was discredited by criminological research. Racist and ethnic elements were often added to the stereotypical conception of the criminal. Because white collar offenders typically do not "look like criminals," jurors and others may be less likely to impute criminality to them.

For much of the 20th century biogenetic explanations of criminality (focusing on factors ranging from body type to brain chemistry) have been discredited or over-shadowed by other forms of explanation. A revival of interest in such explanations since the late 1970s reflects the influences of the emerging field of sociobiology; the widely accepted findings of scientific research that such conditions as schizophrenia, clinical depression, and alcoholism have important biogenetic roots; and a more con-servative political and cultural ambience that is receptive to these kinds of explana-tions (Wilson 1975; Wilson and Herrnstein 1985). Most of the discussion of biogenetic factors applies these factors to certain classes of conventional offenders (Wilson and Herrnstein 1985; Taylor 1984; Jeffery 1990).

Biogenetic explanations have been challenged as having too simplistic a view of crime and of the relationship between biology and human behavior (Katz and Chambliss 1991). The pervasiveness of white collar crime would seem to offer a pow-erful refutation of the proposition that criminality can be generally explained by biogenetic explanations. No legitimate studies have examined the biological makeup of white collar offenders, although C. Ray Jeffery (1990: 339) has suggested that future research might explore the possible role of the brain. To date, there is simply no evidence that biogenetic factors play a role in white collar criminality.

## Psychological Explanations

Criminality has also been explained as a psychological phenomenon. In this approach the focus is on personality, mental processes, the enduring effects of early childhood traumas, and the like. The single most famous psychological explana-tions of human conduct were advanced by Sigmund Freud.

From a Freudian perspective, crime, including white collar crime, can be viewed as a reflection of the eternal conflict between the desires of the individual and the needs of civilization (Freud 1930). In one of his few specific discussions of crime, Freud (1923) suggested that individuals may commit crimes to bring upon them-selves punishment for a preexisting sense of guilt they experience. The fact that at least some white collar offenders have engaged in such self-destructive acts of ille-gality lends this notion some credibility. More specifically, white collar crime in a Freudian approach could be linked with defects in the superego (the conscience), the ego (the balancing voice of reason, or the idealized self), or the id (the aggressive and libidinous innate drives). Many limitations of the Freudian model of the self have been identified, but the core notion of tensions and conflicts among different aspects of the self makes some sense intuitively and can be hypothetically associated in a limited way with white collar criminality.

The variety of psychological theories is very great. Some psychological explana-tions, for example, emphasize cognitive intellectual and moral development, whereas others emphasize the consequences of situational reinforcement. Although such explanations could hypothetically have some relevance in white collar crime cases, they will not be specifically explored here.

Many but not all psychological theories follow the Freudian lead in emphasiz-ing the importance of early childhood experience in shaping adult attitudes and behavior. Whether white collar criminality can be linked to childhood experiences has not been subjected to systematic study. To the extent that one's moral sensibility is shaped by childhood socialization (e.g., early rule-breaking behavior was experienced as rewarding), there may be some connection.

**Personality**  Personality traits are among the most examined of all psychological explanations of white collar crime. Sutherland (1949) specifically repudiated the psychological level of explanation for white collar crime by pointing out that corporate patterns of lawbreaking are independent of specific individual personalities, and that not all divisions of a corporation governed by a white collar criminal with a specific personality will necessarily engage in lawbreaking. Recent students of white collar crime are divided between those who regard personality as a neglible factor (especially for corporate crime) and those who believe it is significant in accounting for why some people commit white collar offenses while others in the same position do not (Coleman 1994; Green 1993; Harris and Hill 1982). Contradictory possibilities exist: On the one hand, corporations may recruit people who are predisposed to go along with corporate crime (organizational conformists); on the other hand, nonconformists might more readily commit white collar crimes against their employers (Coleman 1994: 192–93).

For the most part, the relatively few studies exploring the relevance of personality for involvement in white collar crime have not produced any clear evidence of psychological abnormality, and most white collar offenders appear to fall within the range of normal personality types. A few studies have suggested that white collar offenders are somewhat more likely to display such personality attributes as a tendency toward risk taking and recklessness, ambitiousness and drive, and egocentricity and a hunger for power (Snider 1993; Coleman 1994). Obviously such personality traits can be correlated with legitimate success as well, although we have much still to learn about risk taking as a desirable or undesirable trait (Wheeler 1992).

A psychologist who has worked with white collar offenders has suggested that they are clever, easily frustrated, aloof, and quite creative in rationalizing their illegal conduct (Criddle 1987). One study comparing some 350 incarcerated white collar crime offenders with an equal number of white collar crime executives has reported that the offenders have greater tendencies toward irresponsibility, lack of dependability, and disregard for rules (Collins and Schmidt 1993). It has been speculated that white collar criminals may quite often have an especially pronounced "fear of falling" (or failing) or be less able to defer gratification and exercise self-control (Wheeler 1992; Gottfredson and Hirschi 1990). But most students of white collar crime apparently believe that those who emphasize personality type in explaining white collar crime still have the burden of proving their case.

The appropriate skepticism about the role of personality does not mean that personality is uniformly irrelevant to the understanding of white collar crime. The closely related concepts of character and identity may also have some relevance (Gunkel 1990). Personality is most typically associated with the behavioral characteristics of an individual; character and identity are associated with an individual's nature, and especially his or her moral or ethical qualities. Other things being equal, we would expect that individuals with good "character" (in the sense of moral integrity) are less likely to commit white collar crimes than are those who lack such "character."

The crimes of Adolph Hitler and associates in the Holocaust, and of Richard Nixon and associates in the Watergate Affair, cannot be understood in terms of character and personality alone, but these dimensions may well have played some role (Fest 1970; Woodward and Bernstein 1976). Biographical accounts of such notorious white collar offenders as Michael Milken (securities manipulations), Charles Keating (thrifts fraud), and Leona Helmsley (income tax evasion) identify several personality and character traits, such as obsessions with power and control, narcissism, a sense of superiority, and indifference to conventional rules of conduct, as contributing factors in their criminal conduct (Stewart 1991; Binstein and Bowden 1993; Pierson 1989).

An account of multimillionaire investment banker Martin Siegel's involvement in the Wall Street insider trading crimes of the 1970s refers to his singular insecurity (perhaps rooted in his father's bankruptcy in his youth), his limitless compulsiveness, and his obsession with maintaining an image of breathtaking success (Vise 1987). At the other end of the affluence scale, it seems reasonable to hypothesize that if two low-level employees react quite differently to opportunities to commit illegal acts against an employer, personality or character is one factor in the different responses even though other factors may well be more important. Some white collar crime does indeed seem to be difficult to explain without reference to personality and character.

**Mental Illness, Drug Addiction, and Intellectual Aptitude**   Conventional criminality has been associated with personal pathologies such as mental disorder and substance abuse, and with a lower than average IQ (Wilson and Herrnstein 1985). Are such factors linked to involvement in white collar crime?

Individuals with visible symptoms of mental illness are often precluded from occupying white collar positions of any importance and would thus have few opportunities to commit many types of white collar crime. Of course, in rare occasions some form of psychosis or affective disorder could play a role in the commission of a white collar crime. When an individual holding an important white collar position commits a crime that appears to be at odds with past professional behavior or seems "irrational," mental illness may be blamed. In the fascinating case of a major film studio head who embezzled tens of thousands of dollars, many of his associates insisted that the crime could only be explained in terms of mental or emotional problems (McClintick 1982). To date there is only speculation, but no solid evidence, that illicit drug addiction might play a role in some white collar crime cases (Cowles 1992).

The idea that conventional offenders may have lower IQs than nonoffenders has been challenged on many grounds, including alleged cultural biases of the IQ test and the fact that those caught committing crimes are not necessarily the smarter criminals! People who commit white collar crimes may need above-average intelligence both to qualify for their white collar positions and to carry out often-complex crimes. We do not have an answer to the interesting (and methodologically challenging) question of whether white collar offenders have higher IQs than comparably situated peers who don't break the law.

Altogether, then, there is currently little reason to believe that individualistic factors take us very far in understanding white collar crime.

## Sociogenic Explanations

Some theoretical and empirical work that adopts a sociological framework also addresses the matter of criminality, especially in terms of alleged differences in criminal propensities among members of different social classes or groups. Gottfredson and Hirschi (1990) suggested that levels of self-control, which vary among people, are fundamental factors in people's choices to commit crimes, and that low social control (the inability to defer gratification) is more pronounced among lower-class individuals. People who commit white collar offenses also have low self-control, but in Gottfredson and Hirschi's interpretation, those in the white collar classes typically have more attractive options than lawbreaking, and thus the rate of such crime is relatively low.

Some commentators have argued that the conventional view that criminality is more pronounced among lower-class individuals than among middle- and upper-class individuals is not dictated by theory or supported by empirical observation; others have suggested that much middle-class criminality is for the most part relatively trivial in nature (Goode 1994; Tittle, Villemez, and Smith 1978; Tittle 1983). Still other criminologists, including John Hagan (1989b) and Alex Thio (1988), have developed "structural" or "power" theories of crime, which claim that criminality is more pronounced among the powerful and privileged than among the powerless and underprivileged. In this interpretation, the advantaged have stronger deviant motivations, enjoy greater deviant opportunities, and are subject to weaker social controls. The claim about stronger deviant motivations is based on the contention that the powerful are potently conditioned to aspire to material success, and accordingly they experience relative deprivation much more strongly than do the underprivileged or the powerless.

In a rare study of white collar delinquency—specifically, illegal copying of audio albums, videos, and computer software—Hagan and Kay (1990) found that the presence of power, a positive orientation toward risk taking, and the absence of control (parental, in this case) are correlated with such delinquency. Males from the employer class (i.e., males with a parent who was a business owner) were found to be somewhat more likely than others (e.g., females from the employee class) to engage in illegal copying. Various methodological limitations, and factors such as subjects' access to copying equipment and knowledge of how to operate it, are confounding factors in such a study.

## Organizational Criminality and the Crimes of Organizations

SOCIOLOGICAL THEORIES FOCUS, in particular, on explaining the "behavior" of *social* entities: groups, organizations, and societies. Much white collar crime—especially the most substantial and serious forms, including state-organized and corporate crime—is carried out on a group or organizational level. Organizations, arguably the dominant attribute of modern societies, have been characterized as rational systems with specific goals, as natural systems oriented toward self-survival, and as open systems, of interdependent entities shaped by their external environment (Scott 1992). Organizational theories of crime are often provisional because it is difficult to collect enough relevant data to test them (Shover and Bryant 1993). More systematic study is needed.

## Organizational Responsibility

When we engage in the common practice of referring to organizations (or networks of organizations) as actors, we are not simply speaking of a sum of people and their individual actions; instead we have patterned institutional practices in mind (Gross 1980; Hall 1987). However, even though we may say that the Ford Motor Company produced unsafe cars or the Hooker Chemical Corporation polluted the environment, this practice is somewhat problematic and controversial. In his pioneering study *White Collar Crime* (1949), Sutherland moved back and forth rather freely between discussing the crimes of people of the upper socioeconomic classes and the crimes of corporations. He wrote of white collar crime as a form of "organized" crime, and he wrote of the "criminality of corporations" independent of specific reference to individual executives. In *Corporate Crime* (1980), which is the largest-scale and most prominent study of such crime since Sutherland, Clinard and Yeager specifically defined corporate crime as *organizational crime*. Throughout their study they treated corporations as actors, although of course they recognized that the boundaries between illegal corporate acts and illegal acts carried out by corporate executives for their own benefit can be blurred.

Donald Cressey (1989: 38), a prominent early contributor to the white collar crime literature, criticized his former mentor Sutherland, and Clinard and Yeager as well, for attributing human capabilities to corporations rather than distinguishing them from real people. Even though Sutherland had acknowledged that corporations could not suffer from human psychiatric disorders, he also (somewhat illogically) wrote of corporate criminality as though it occurred independent of the decisions and actions of specific human beings. Cressey insisted that in the final analysis we must recognize that corporations are not people, cannot learn, do not have motivations, and cannot form intent; only individual humans can do these things. For Cressey, causal principles used to explain the criminality of individuals cannot be used to explain the criminality of corporations; statistical correlations between structural variables (such as industry, financial status, and size) and corporate criminality cannot produce causal propositions.

Many students of white collar crime have insisted that a corporation can be regarded as directly responsible for a crime. In one statement of a widely adopted position, Edward Gross (1980) argued that corporations "take on lives of their own"; they develop a need to create orderly markets, and they socialize their executives to respond with criminal actions to circumstances in which profits are threatened. In this view, corporate crime as organizational crime must be explained in terms of organizational factors (Kramer 1982).

In a specific response to Cressey's critique, Braithwaite and Fisse (1990) defended the notion that corporations can take criminal action and can be properly held responsible for such action. They advanced the following arguments: Both individuals and corporations are defined by a mixture of observable and abstracted characteristics; corporations collectively carry out spectacularly complex tasks that no single individual involved can carry out independently, and thus collective decisions are not simply the sum of individual decisions; corporate policies and procedures are the equivalent of corporate intentionality; and although corporations may not have feelings and emotions, they do possess autonomy and thus can properly be held responsible for their decisions. Braithwaite and Fisse (1990) concluded that as a practical matter, modern societies must hold corporations legally responsible for their actions; that if corporations can formulate policy, they can also be affected by punishment; and that if we punish replaceable individuals only, we will not deter corporate crime. Accordingly, they contended, a notion of corporations as capable of committing crimes is both defensible and necessary and complements the individualistic approach to white collar crime.

On the other hand, it must be acknowledged that in a strictly literal sense a corporation cannot act. The decisions and actions of specific human beings set into motion all activities of governmental agencies and corporate entities. Organizational crimes are offenses committed by officers of organizations on behalf of the organization (Finney and LeSieur 1982); individuals are integrated into roles within organizations, and organizations generate patterns of activity (Gross 1980). In this view, individual identity is often subordinated to the demands of the organization. To the extent that the organization trains, indoctrinates, and persuades its members to engage in criminal activities, these crimes can be regarded as crimes of the organization rather than of individuals (Hall 1987). The model of corporate decision making as a product of an organizational process has been contrasted with one model that views the corporation as a rational actor, and with another model emphasizing the individual advantage of corporate executives (Clinard and Yeager 1980: 44). The tension between focusing attention on organizations or individuals can never be fully resolved.

The entire organization is seldom involved in corporate crime, and the majority of personnel do not directly participate (Hall 1987). But it is the organization and its resources that make possible the crimes of even a small number of its officers or employees. Organizations create opportunities for illegal conduct by disproportionately serving affluent, accessible victims, by generating impersonal transactions, by creating and allocating resources, by providing strategic devices to facilitate and cover-up illegalities, and by conditioning the development of new normative prescriptions capable of being violated (Shapiro 1980; Vaughan 1983). Organizations attempt, often with considerable success, to influence the legal environment within which they operate, to enhance the predictability and stability of their economic environment, and to shield themselves from civil and criminal liability (Gross 1980). Furthermore, the following rationalizations for violating regulations or breaking laws are typically generated on the corporate level: The laws or regulations are incomprehensible, excessively complex, too costly, unnecessary, unjustified, and improperly interfere with free enterprise; competitors are violating the laws with impunity; and the violations are economically necessary or even beneficial and do little if any real harm to individuals (Clinard and Yeager 1980; Reichman 1989). The increasing availability and attractiveness of such rationales promote corporate criminality.

## The Various Dimensions of Organizational Criminality

Different levels of organizational analysis are relevant to the understanding of organizational crime. On a social psychological level the organization is viewed as a context or environment that can influence individuals' attitudes and behavior in a criminal direction; on a structural level the organization is viewed as having structural features and social processes (e.g., subunits and specialization) that facilitate the commission of crime; on an ecological level the organization is viewed as part of an environment or interdependent system that has criminogenic tendencies (Scott 1992).

Some organizations are crime-coercive (they literally compel others to commit crimes), whereas others are crime-facilitative (they provide conditions that promote criminal conduct) (Needleman and Needleman 1979). Some industries, or networks of organizations, have been described as inherently criminogenic due to special conditions and industry norms (Clinard and Yeager 1980).

For example, the liquor industry has a three-tiered system of distillers, wholesalers, and retailers; distillers put formidable sales-quota pressures on wholesale distributors, who then engage in price-fixing with each other and kickbacks to retailers, who in turn make illegal deals with distillers and pay bribes to local law enforcers, all in the interest of trying to survive and profit in an inadequately policed industry (Denzin 1977). In the auto industry, manufacturers impose pressures on their dealers to generate high sales volumes, and the resulting low profits induce dealers to enhance profits through fraudulent servicing of cars and fudging on warranties; kickback deals with used-car dealers and manipulating registered sale prices to cut taxes are also characteristic of the industry (Farberman 1975; Leonard and Weber 1970). In the case of the international pharmaceutical industry, a high level of bribery results from fears that products that cost millions of dollars to develop will not be approved for marketing (Braithwaite 1984). In the case of the securities industry, new regulations and pressures to innovate generate new demands for information and transform existing networks and relationships, so that incentives to engage in lawbreaking are no longer effectively held in check by traditional constraints and controls (Reichman 1993). In still other industries (e.g., oil), parallel criminogenic conditions exist.

Organizational crime can be explained in terms of *internal* and *external* factors in the organizational environment. Theories of corporate crime have either attempted to explain why some corporations commit crimes and others do not, or have addressed the apparent overall increase in corporate illegalities at particular periods of time (Shover and Bryant 1993).

Some relevant internal variables include the size of the corporation, the financial performance of the corporation and the degree of its emphasis on profit, the diffusion of responsibility through different divisions and departments, and a corporate sub-culture that promotes loyalty and deference to the interests of the corporation.

On the matter of size, for example, some research has found that the more complex, impersonal, and decentralized character of larger corporations is associated with greater involvement with illegal activity; other research has suggested that larger corporations have the resources and expertise to comply with the law more easily than do smaller corporations (Coleman 1992; Shover and Bryant 1993; Simpson 1993). The preponderance of evidence seems to support the notion that corporations that are doing poorly financially are more likely to engage in illegal activity (Coleman 1992; Shover and Bryant 1993).

According to a study of the nursing home industry, for-profit organizations are more likely to engage in violations of the law than are nonprofit organizations (Jenkins and Braithwaite 1993). When the reward structure of corporations tends to reward short-term success more than it penalizes long-term failure, when middle managers experience relentless pressure from above to maximize profits, and when such managers are shielded from responsibility for at least some of the harmful effects of their decisions, illegal activity is also promoted (Clinard 1983; Ermann and Lundman 1982; Jenkins and Braithwaite 1993). Top management tends to "signal" its expectations rather than giving specific orders to break the law, and middle managers tend to adapt to the prevailing corporate morality that reflects changing corporate needs (Clinard and Yeager 1980: 58; Jackall 1988: 6; Shover and Bryant 1993). Altogether, middle managers believe that these internal factors take precedence over external moral values or expectations in guiding their actions on the job.

Externally, a variety of factors are related to corporate crime, including the economic climate (e.g., a recession), the political environment (e.g., regulatory legislation), the level of industry concentration (i.e., the number of competitors), the style and strength of product distribution networks, product differentiation, and normative traditions within industries (Clinard and Yeager 1980; Simpson 1993; Keane 1993). Corporations are more likely to engage in corporate crime when legitimate opportunities to achieve their goals are blocked but illegitimate opportunities are available, when the local community is relatively tolerant of violations, when regulatory law is weak and ineffective, and when the political or economic climate promotes aggressive pursuit of profit (Braithwaite 1989a; Gunkel and Eitle 1989; Shover and Bryant 1993). Although it would seem logical that increased external pressure to make a profit would encourage a corporation to engage in illegal behavior, existing studies offer only mixed support for this proposition (Simpson 1993).

An organization's location in an "ecosystem" of other similar organizations is another dimension of its external environment (Kunkel 1989). In one interpretation (rooted in a resource dependence model), more-dependent corporations are more likely to engage in misconduct in response to external pressures, especially when alternatives to the misconduct are limited and the organization's structure facilitates such misconduct (Zimmer 1989). In another interpretation, the "structural embeddedness" of financial organizations and corporations within networks that were largely beyond the reach of traditional forms of social control significantly contributed to the large-scale financial crimes of the 1980s (Reichman 1989; Zey 1993). Further, there are various indications that the securities industry is also permeated by low ethical standards or values (Tomasic and Pentony 1989). Altogether, more attention is now being directed toward the network of alliances among organizations, and the criminogenic pressures and opportunities that may arise within these networks.

## Explaining Organizational Crime, In Sum

If on the one hand it is true that organizations are *not* persons and that only actual humans can in the final analysis make decisions and take action, it is also quite evident that once corporate policies, norms, and goals are in place, they produce powerful forces that seem to dictate certain actions, including criminal actions, independent of the particular inclinations of individuals. In the preceding section we have touched on some of the complex of factors that might explain organizational or corporate crime. Adopting extreme positions on either side of the issue—that is, either treating corporations as no different from individuals *or* focusing exclusively on individual decision makers—is likely to produce a distorted view. In some contexts, then, it makes more sense to speak of organizations, in others of individuals, but in either case we should avoid confusing the matter by using ambiguous or inappropriate references.

## Explaining White Collar Crime: Theories and Perspectives

MANY EXPLANATIONS OF white collar crime focus more on the *crime* rather than on criminality. Most (but not all) of these explanations are sociological, and they emphasize differences in circumstances or opportunities over differences among individuals. From this perspective we may wish to explain differences in levels of involvement in white collar crime among different classes of individuals, different professions, different corporate organizations, and different industries.

Sociological theories often emphasize structural factors. A structural perspective in criminology focuses either on social conditions that account for specific forms of criminal behavior, or on how the distribution of power and resources influences how crime is defined and generated (Cullen 1983; Hagan 1939b). Pertinent structural questions include the following: Which forces produce laws that define white collar crime and a justice system that effectively implements and enforces those laws? Which forces produce a set of opportunities for illegal conduct? Which forces promote motivations and rationalizations that are conducive to illegal behavior or activity?

## General Theories of Crime and White Collar Crime Theories

Can the same theories explain both white collar crime and conventional crime, or must different types of crimes be explained by different types of theories? Criminologists have been somewhat divided on this question. E. H. Sutherland was inspired to pursue the study of white collar crime partly because he recognized that the popular criminological theories of his time, which focused on poverty and social pathologies as basic causes of crime, simply did not explain the involvement of upper-class individuals and corporations in illegal conduct. Sutherland (1940) advanced his theory of differential association as a general theory that could account for both conventional and white collar crime. More recent attempts to develop general theories of crime are discussed later in this chapter.

The general theories of crime have been criticized on various grounds, especially for attempting to explain very different types of activities too simplistically and broadly. Although general theories may have some success in accounting for natural and physical phenomena, they are less usefully applied to the enormously variable realm of human activity (Weatherburn 1993). For example, no general theory provides us with a clear basis for explaining variations between conventional and white collar crime rates over time. An alternative perspective, then, is that the explanation of white collar crime requires theories that are fundamentally different from those applied to conventional crime, and that specific types of white collar crime require specific explanatory theories. Perhaps an intermediary position is that only up to a point and on a very high level of generality, some common motivation (i.e., a desire for personal gain) may be shared by the inner-city youth who engages in a mugging and the Wall Street investment banker who engages in insider trading. But this does not take us very far toward understanding the very different patterns of involvement in illegal activities, the complex of circumstances that give rise to illegality, and the distinctive self-concepts and rationalizations of the range of white collar offenders. A theory that claims to explain both juvenile shoplifting and illegal corporate polluting by referring to an identical motivation is not likely to provide us with an especially profound understanding of either type of crime.

## Classical Criminology and Rational Choice

In the late 18th century a variety of influential views of human nature, principles of justice, and economic activity were articulated. In his essay *On Crimes and Punishments (Dei delliti e elle pene)*, published in 1764, the Italian nobleman and economist Cesare Beccaria called for a reformed criminal justice system based on rational, equitable principles toward which rational human beings could orient themselves. (Beirne [1991] has shown that Beccaria's work also incorporated determinist elements.) In *An Introduction to the Principles of Morals and Legislation* (1789), the English philosopher Jeremy Bentham, partially inspired by Beccaria, developed a utilitarian philosophy that incorporated the idea of humans who engage in a calculus to maximize pleasure and minimize pain.

The core notions of humans as capable of making rational choices and of a system of justice with equitable punishments that fit the crime have long been central to the operation of our criminal justice system (Norrie 1986). In 1759 the Scottish moral philosopher and economist Adam Smith wrote *The Theory of Moral Sentiments*, advancing the view of human beings as inherently self-interested actors, who are not immune to the cultivation of moral character. This image has been embraced in some form by mainstream economists through the present era. Of course, many economists today reject the notion of humans as purely rational and recognize the influence of cultural, moral, and psychological factors (Rubinstein 1992; Simon 1987; Sen 1977). In the social sciences one increasingly common view is that human behavior reflects a mixture of rational choice, emotions, and value commitments (Etzioni 1987). Still, the notion of humans as essentially rational and self-interested actors is the dominant view of white collar offenders in the law and in the public consciousness.

The classical assumptions about human nature have recently been embraced (with some qualifications) by neoclassical criminologists and proponents of "rational choice," routine activities, and social control perspectives (Wilson and Herrnstein 1985; Cornish and Clarke 1986; Hirschi 1986; Clarke and Felson 1993). These criminologists essentially see criminal offenders as people who reason and plan strategically, adapt to particular circumstances, and weigh costs and benefits. Individuals who commit crimes are not averse to breaking laws if they see an opportunity they perceive to have both a low likelihood of sanctions and the expectation of personal benefits. Proponents of this perspective do not necessarily deny that other factors—such as constitution (e.g., biogenetic inheritance), development (e.g., family influences), and social context (e.g., labor markets)—limit rationality and play a role in criminal behavior (Cornish and Clarke 1986; Wilson and Herrnstein 1985); but they also believe that rational choices account for a good proportion of criminal conduct. Herman Simon (1976) introduced the concept of "bounded rationality" or "limited rationality" to take into account the fact that choices (of individuals and of organizations) are often based on incomplete (or defective) information and are only "rational" relative to the information available.

Rational choice assumptions would appear to be especially applicable to white collar offenders (Cullen, Maakestad, and Cavender 1987: 344; Bartollas and Dinitz 1989: 114). If we assume that humans have the capability of making rational choices, then those who are better-educated and better positioned in life would seem to have an advantage in considering and acting on various options. It is perhaps paradoxical, then, that those who have prominently promoted the neoclassical and rational choice perspective have focused most of their attention on conventional offenders, not white collar criminals. The principal explanation for this paradox is surely related to the ideological conservatism of most of these scholars, who tend to view conventional crime as the paramount problem.

## A General Theory of Crime and Rational Choice

In their attempt to develop a "general theory" of crime, Hirschi and Gottfredson (1987) advanced the claim that because the behavior of both white collar criminals and conventional criminals can be explained as attempts to satisfy self-interest, there is no justification for crime-specific explanations. Obviously the opportunities for criminality for the white collar worker are different than those of inner-city youths. But Hirschi and Gottfredson regard this as quite irrelevant to the explanation of criminality itself, which relates to the nature of the offense, not to the offender. They claim that white collar crime is relatively rare because people in white collar positions have a set of values and legitimate ways of obtaining gratification that deflect them from criminality; furthermore, on the basis of *Uniform Crime Report* data, the profile of white collar crime offenders on such variables as age, sex, and race are directly comparable with the distributions for conventional offenders.

Conventional theories may have overstated the fundamental motivational differences that distinguish white collar criminality from conventional criminality, but clearly Hirschi and Gottfredson have adopted an exceptionally narrow conception of white collar crime (Reed and Yeager 1991; Steffensmeier 1989). They confuse crimes against organizations with crimes by organizations, quite summarily dismiss the concept of corporate crime, and do not attempt to contend with a range of elite offenses. For them, white collar crime principally means low-level employee embezzlement and marginal types of fraud that are often committed by relatively poor individuals who are not part of the white collar class. Their theory does not clearly explain why most white collar offenders do not commit conventional offenses, or why they commit only certain types of white collar crime (Benson and Moore 1992; Grasmick et al. 1993; Green 1990). Furthermore, a significant proportion of white collar crime involves individuals (i.e., corporate managers) acting rationally in fulfillment of corporate expectations to realize long-term goals; these individuals may be conflicted over violating laws, and in some cases may be putting their own self-interest in jeopardy (Reed and Yeager 1991). Clearly, quite a bit of white collar crime cannot be described in terms of fulfillment of self-gratification.

## Alternative Dimensions of Crime and Choice

There are other approaches to the application of rational choice theory to white collar crime and corporate crime. Paternoster and Simpson (1993) have characterized corporate crime as criminal activity that is rooted in instrumental and strategic choices made by risk-averse managers who weigh various options' perceived costs and benefits (to themselves). These choices involve a broad range of considerations, but the manager's view that laws or rules are unreasonable is one factor that contributes to the choice not to comply. Whatever their preferences may be, individual managers are often subjected to various pressures to act collectively on behalf of the corporation. Of course, this type of rational assessment of risks and benefits in the context of external occupational pressures can be applied to other types of white collar offenders as well.

Although a rational choice and voluntaristic approach to explaining crime is principally associated with a conservative or right-wing perspective, it is a mistake to assume that leftist perspectives are uniformly deterministic. Even Karl Marx assumed that human beings are capable of making choices, particularly the choice to rise up against an oppressive capitalist system (Markovic 1983). Recent neo-Marxist, radical, and critical approaches to crime have tended to emphasize the structural conditions of a capitalist society that promote crime and injustice, but such an approach is not necessarily at odds with voluntaristic, rationalistic assumptions. Some leftist scholars (Gordon 1971; Reiman and Headlee 1981; Young and Matthews 1992a) have argued that crime (white collar and conventional) is at least in part a rational response to the conditions of capitalism. The principal challenge is to transform the political economy so that pressures to make choices harmful to others are reduced or eliminated, and to provide all members of society with more positive alternatives.

A phenomenological or hermeneutic approach to crime also stresses the choices confronting people who engage in crime, although this approach is at odds with the classical assumptions about rationality. Katz (1988), for example, disparaged the traditional sociological emphasis on background factors and treats crime and criminality in terms of emotions and "foreground" factors, including the "moral and sensual attractions" of committing crimes. He suggested that emotional processes parallel to those that entice people into committing robberies and murders may well apply to white collar offenders, although we have too few credible autobiographical accounts to verify this proposition (Katz 1988: 313; 321). At least some white collar offenders may be attracted by the "living sensuality" or emotional thrill of engaging in criminal conduct, especially when they assume risks disproportionate to any prospective payoff. Reichman (1993: 82) suggested that the Drexel Burnham firm, which was at the center of the securities industry crimes of the 1980s, may have created a culture of action, chaos, and control parallel to that of the street criminals and "hardmen" Katz studied. On the other hand, Braithwaite (1992) argued that Katz is mistaken in suggesting that material and economic conditions of a society are irrelevant to understanding another set of emotions—humiliation and rage—that can also inspire criminal behavior.

## Social Control and Bonds

Social control theories adopt assumptions about human nature that are fundamentally at odds with those of most etiological theories. Social control theory reverses the conventional question of why someone engages in criminal behavior and instead asks why someone *doesn't* engage in criminal behavior (Hirschi 1969). The answer to this question is that people with strong bonds (attachment, commitment, involvement, and belief) to conventional institutions (such as the family, the school, and the church) are constrained from engaging in delinquent or criminal conduct. The assumptions of control theory—that a natural inclination toward committing crimes is broadly diffused—would seem to be at odds with Hirschi and Gottfredson's (1989) general theory, which suggests that levels of self-control vary among individuals (Green 1990: 86). These control theory assumptions about human nature are generally compatible with those of rational choice theory, although they are very much at odds with sociological theories that regard human beings as social animals shaped by their environment (Hirschi 1986).

In one test of control theory as applied to white collar crime, Lasley (1988) found that automobile corporation executives with strong corporate attachments and commitments were less likely to report that they had committed white collar offenses against their employers than were peers with weaker such bonds. If social control theory is in fact valid, we would expect that corporate executives with stronger bonds to the corporation are more likely, not less, to engage in corporate crimes on behalf of the corporation.

## Social Process and Learning

We have already noted that Sutherland (1947) promoted a theory of differential association, which views criminal behavior as learned through contact with others with a law-violating orientation; it is applicable to both lower-class and white collar crime. Sutherland formulated a list of nine interrelated propositions on the process and content of learning to be a criminal. In some respects, white collar crime may be better understood by reference to differential association than is true of conventional lower-class crime and delinquency, both because of the broader range of learning options generally available to the white collar offender and the complex nature of the offenses themselves. Modifications of differential association—such as Glaser's (1956) emphasis on differential identification (with a criminal role model) and Akers's (1985) emphasis on reinforcement (conditioning to engage in criminal behavior when it is experienced as rewarding)—can also be applied to the white collar offender.

An overriding limitation of this theoretical approach, however, is that it does not adequately account for structural origins of the illegal patterns of behavior and appears to confuse a process of involvement in criminal behavior with a cause of such behavior (Geis and Goff 1987; Goode 1994). The theory does not address the problem that some white collar crime is quite individualistic (e.g., embezzlement), and that collective forms of white collar crime are committed by individuals who also hold many attitudes that are favorable to obeying laws (Coleman 1994; Goode 1994). Both common sense and empirical evidence support the proposition that a learning process plays a significant role in much white collar crime, but Sutherland's theory hardly provides us with a comprehensive explanation of such crime.

## Interactionism and Labeling

Interactionist (or labeling) perspectives on crime are derived from a symbolic inter-actionist tradition that emphasizes that meaning emanates out of human interaction (Blumer 1969; Mead 1934, 1964). This perspective, which was especially influential in the 1960s and 1970s, has been principally concerned with the process of societal reaction to perceived crime (or the designation of particular individuals as criminals), rather than with the standard etiological question "What made them do it?" (Schur 1971). Nevertheless, seminal concepts such as the "dramatization of evil," "sec-ondary deviance," and "master status" do have some implications for understand-ing patterns of involvement in crime, including white collar crime (Becker 1963; Lemert 1951; Tannenbaum 1938).

The first point relevant to white collar crime is that powerful individuals and organizations are more likely than the powerless to be able to avoid being labeled as deviant or as criminals, or to be able to negotiate more successfully the terms of any effort to so stigmatize them (Schur 1971; Waegel, Ermann, and Horowitz 1981). The very process of being able to shield one's harmful activities from a stigmatizing label might contribute to self-justification and ongoing involvement in such activity (Benson 1990). On the other hand, Lemert's (1951) concept of secondary deviance refers to adaptations that occur after an individual has been labeled a deviant or a criminal; such individuals may adopt a deviant self-image, leading to further devia-tion and criminal activity. In this perspective, the imposition of the criminal label itself is a significant cause of criminal behavior.

The claim that the labeling process itself inspires more criminal behavior than it deters has been challenged on various grounds, and it is difficult to demonstrate empirically (Goode 1994; Mankoff 1971; Wright 1994; Vold and Bernard 1986). White collar offenders who have been processed by the criminal justice system typically have more legitimate options than do conventional offenders and are likely to be able to minimize the full effects of being stigmatized. In a classic study of the effects of legal stigma, Schwartz and Skolnick (1964) found that physicians accused of malpractice were far less likely to suffer harmful consequences to their occupational status than were unskilled workers charged with assault. On the other hand, Benson (1984), in a subsequent study of convicted white collar offenders, found that some offenders (e.g., professionals, such as lawyers, who occupy a position of trust) may suffer significant stigmatizing consequences, whereas others (e.g., business executives) may largely avoid such consequences. Benson (1984; 1990) also found that many convicted white collar offenders are angry at society's attempt to stigmatize them, and he speculates that this anger can translate into less respect for the law.

Erving Goffman (1959; 1963) adopted a theatrical metaphor to explore the ways in which human beings engage in "the presentation of self in everyday life" in a constant process of attempting to manage the impression others have of them. If we follow Goffman, the commission of white collar crime often depends significantly on the offender's success in conveying an image of respectability and trustworthiness—in essence, in playing a role. To the extent that the offender is successful in this regard, opportunities to commit white collar crime are expanded and the likelihood of detection and prosecution minimized. On the other side of this equation, Goffman investigated the means people use to shield themselves from being stigmatized and to manage a stigma that cannot be avoided. This dramaturgic perspective offers one approach to the specific strategies that white collar offenders use to anticipate, deflect, or manage stigma, and these strategies may well be intertwined with their ongoing choices about engaging in white collar crime.

## Neutralization, Rationalization, and Accounts

The interrelated concepts of neutralization, rationalization, and accounts play an especially central role in efforts to make sense of white collar criminality. White collar offenders are not, with few if any real exceptions, classic "outlaw" types—that is, people who are utterly contemptuous of law and conventional standards of proper conduct. White collar criminals most typically conform to most laws and social conventions and are unlikely to identify with or endorse the activities of conventional offenders. How, then, do they become lawbreakers?

One important part of the answer to this question is that they adopt a "vocabulary of motives": excuses, justifications, disclaimers, and denials (Mills 1940; Nichols 1990; Scott and Lyman 1968). Useful distinctions have been made between excuses, which tend to be defensive (e.g., an appeal to accidents) and justifications, which are positive interpretations of actions (e.g., an appeal to higher loyalties)(Scott and Lyman 1968). Another useful dichotomy differentiates between neutralizations, which pertain to future or ongoing behavior, and accounts, which are invoked after the behavior has occurred (Nichols 1990). Despite these distinctions, these and related terms are often used quite interchangeably.

Donald Cressey, in his classic work on embezzlers, *Other People's Money* (1953), assigned central importance to rationalizations in explaining the conduct of white collar offenders. Cressey found that embezzlers were often individuals in positions of trust (e.g., bank clerks) who, when confronted with a nonshareable financial problem, embezzled money while rationalizing that they were only "borrowing" it.

Steven Box (1983) showed that five "techniques of neutralization," which were developed by Sykes and Matza (1957) to demonstrate how juvenile delinquents "drift" between commitments to conventional and delinquent norms and rationalize their illegal activities, are also invoked by corporate officials to rationalize and justify their illegal behavior. First, corporate officials can deny responsibility for any intentional wrongdoing (e.g., in pollution cases) by claiming that the relevant laws are vague or ambiguous, that the incident was an accident, or that other parties made the key decisions. Second, they can deny injury (e.g., in insider trading cases) by rationalizing that their activities have actually been economically beneficial. Third, they can deny the existence of a victim (e.g., in bribery of foreign officials cases) by claiming that no one was really harmed by their activity. Fourth, they can condemn the condemners (e.g., in unsafe workplace cases) by claiming that the laws themselves are an unwarranted interference with free enterprise. And fifth, they can appeal to higher loyalties (e.g., in antitrust cases) by affirming that the needs of their corporation and its stockholders (or their own families) should take precedence over obedience to mere laws. In support of the relevance of such rationalizations, Benson (1985) found that convicted antitrust offenders tended to claim that they were merely following established practices in their business, or that prevailing business conditions left them no choice but to violate the law.

Thus a wide range of white collar offenders, not merely corporate executives, invoke rationalizations in one form or another (Rothman and Gandossy 1982; Ditton 1977). The type of rationale favored tends to vary by offense; tax violators, for example, claim that "everybody does it," whereas defrauders claim that someone else was really to blame (Benson 1985). In the E. F. Hutton check-kiting case, different rationalizations were invoked by executives on different levels of the firm (Nichols 1990).

Rationalizations are especially important in political white collar crime cases, such as Watergate and Iran/Contra, insofar as the perpetrators persuade themselves that "national security" or the long-term national interest requires them to break laws (Wise 1973; Cavender, Jurik, and Cohen 1993). By one interpretation, diffusion of responsibility, "plausible denial," and scapegoating were all elements of a dynamic process of constructing accounts as the Iran/Contra plot unfolded, and these accounts played a role in shaping the direction of the illegal action (Cavender, Jurik, and Cohen 1993). Because rationalizations, neutralizations, and accounts most typically surface after the crimes have been committed, it is not always clear to what extent they facilitated the lawbreaking in the first place, or developed later as attempts to excuse wrongdoing. Still, the mere availability of rationalizations seems to play a role in the commission of many white collar crimes.

**Structural Strain and the Structure of Opportunity**  Emile Durkheim's (1893) original conception of anomie referred to a situation of normlessness (in effect, a break-down of the guidelines for conventional behavior) occurring in circumstances of rapid social change. The insider trading crimes of the 1980s have been linked with an anomic situation that fostered "the unbridled pursuit of pecuniary rewards" (Lilly, Cullen, and Ball 1989: 67).

Robert K. Merton's (1957) revised notion of anomie—one of the most familiar explanations of crime—refers to an enduring situation in a society (such as contem-porary America) in which a generalized goal of material success is promoted, but the means to achieve such success legitimately are not equally distributed. Merton gives the label "innovative" to one class of adaptations that those who lack equal access to legitimate means (i.e., a good education and occupation) use to achieve material success; among such "innovations" is illegal behavior. Although this expla-nation for criminal behavior has most typically been associated with the economi-cally disadvantaged, Merton came to recognize that much white collar crime is not visible or known, and that the 19th-century robber barons and their successors used illegal or unethical "innovations" to realize their economic goals (Merton 1968: 195–98). Merton (1957) had previously noted that the emphasis in science on origi-nality may lead to "innovative" (and unethical or illegal) actions by scientists—including stealing ideas and generating false data—if they are under intense pressure to produce original scientific results.

If "success" is far more heavily emphasized in the higher strata of society, and if its measurement is virtually open-ended in these strata, then Merton's theory of anomie is even more applicable to white collar crime than it is to conventional crime. It has been applied quite specifically ito understanding the "innovative" corporate use of illegal strategies to realize goals that cannot be realized by legitimate means (Keane 1993; Passas 1990; Vaughan 1983). Furthermore, the commission of crimes by privileged segments of society and their broader immunity to prosecution can con-tribute significantly to an anomic climate in society, as less-privileged people become cynical or confused about the prevailing rules (Passas 1990). White collar crime in this sense both reflects and promotes anomie.

Others have produced variants of Merton's theory of anomie (or structural strain). Albert Cohen (1955) formulated status deprivation theory, and Richard Cloward and Lloyd Ohlin (1960) advanced differential opportunity theory. Both of these theories were applied to lower-class juveniles, but some connections with white collar crime can be made.

Status deprivation theory is especially concerned with explaining the nonutili-tarian, malicious, and negativistic character of at least some lower-class delinquency as an alternative way of achieving status. White collar crime tends to be quite uni-formly characterized as utilitarian, instrumental, and goal-oriented toward positive objectives, but surely at least some of it—for example, sabotage and vandalism by dis-gruntled employees—may reflect responses to being deprived of a legitimate status.

Differential opportunity theory contends that the particular form of illegal con-duct, whether it be theft, drug dealing, or gang conflict, is significantly a function of the structure of opportunity. Braithwaite (1992: 86) noted that Cloward and Ohlin neglected the fact that criminals can actively create illegitimate opportunities, and this point is perhaps especially applicable to the powerful and privileged. Some white collar crime may be best understood as a response to a situation in which the attractions of particular illegitimate opportunities, whether preexisting or created, outweigh those of legitimate opportunities.

## Conflict Theory and Criminogenic Societies

CONFLICT THEORY HAS been principally concerned with the process of criminalization. Conflict theory rejects the consensus theory notion of the social world as an organic (or integrated) system. In its so-called "nonpartisan" form, conflict theory is concerned with identifying how the values and interests of different groups are in conflict because the more powerful groups in society are disproportionately able to influence the character and content of the law (Vold and Bernard 1986); in this view, the behavior of the powerless is most likely to be defined as criminal. This theory would seem to offer little by way of explaining white collar crime and criminality, unless we recognize that the "white collar world" is very heterogeneous and that the possession of power is a relative matter. Certainly the values and interests of the various white collar strata are at odds with those who make the laws. The neo-Marxist or radical version of conflict theory, which will be explored next, provides an explanation of the roots of criminal behavior that is at odds with mainstream theories.

### The Structure of Contemporary Capitalist Society and White Collar Crime

The most basic form of structural explanation for white collar crime focuses on the nature of society itself. In particular, a capitalist society has been viewed by some students of white collar crime as a fundamental source of inspiration for such crime. One principal version of conflict theory is Marxist, or neo-Marxist.

Karl Marx and his collaborator Friedrich Engels did not regard crime in any form to be a necessary or inevitable feature of human society (Quinney 1977; Greenberg 1981). Rather, crime is essentially a product of a class society, and of capitalism in particular; to the extent that humans manifest such patterns of behavior, it is capitalism that promotes these tendencies in human beings. The capitalist system dehumanizes people, transforms many objects and dimensions of the human environment into commodities, and promotes "false needs" that generate a significant amount of property crime.

In the Marxist view, the worst crime is committed in the name of capitalism: the systematic exploitation of the working class. In his *The Condition of the Working Class in England* (1845; 1958), Engels contends that the ownership class is in fact guilty of murder because it is fully aware that workers in factories and mines will die violent, premature deaths due to unsafe conditions. The private ownership of capital results in many socially injurious acts that in today's terms can be labeled "crimes of capital" (Michalowski 1985: 314).

But beyond such crimes that are intrinsic to capitalism, Marx and Engels (and their intellectual heirs) have suggested that crime (whether by the rich or the poor) is a rational or inevitable response to an economic system that fosters greed, egoistic or individualistic tendencies, competitiveness, and debasement of humans (Bonger 1916; Coleman 1987; Gordon 1971). Whenever the capitalist system undergoes an economic crisis, the pressures to commit crimes increase (Reiman and Headlee 1981). The alienating and inauthentic dimensions of contemporary capitalism promote complex patterns of collaborative crime between elite organizations and governmental powerholders (Simon and Eitzen 1993). Corporations specifically, operating in an environment of unequal distribution of market power and relentless pressure to increase profit or growth, will violate laws when the potential benefits of doing so outweigh the potential costs (Barnett 1979; 1981b). State regulation of corporate activity is significantly inhibited both by the disproportionate influence of corporations in the making and administration of laws, and by the state's need to foster capital accumulation.

**Limitations of the Marxist Account**   There are two obvious limitations of a structural, Marxist explanation for white collar crime. First, it is not very helpful in explaining either the existence of significant levels of white collar crime in noncapitalist (socialistic) countries or significant variations among different capitalist countries. Second, it is not very helpful in explaining why some individuals (and organizations) within capitalist societies engage in white collar crime while others do not.

On the first point, Braithwaite (1988), among others, has noted that much corrupt and criminal activity equivalent to corporate and occupational crime occurs in socialist countries. In the former Soviet Union, corrupt practices of state bureaucrats could be attributed to "performance pressures" to meet production targets; such pressures are the equivalent of competitive pressures in a capitalist system. But an overemphasis on competitive pressures overlooks the fact that at least some white collar crime is fostered by cooperation (for example, price-fixing among corporations) rather than by competition. Moreover, any attempt to explain white collar crime in terms of the effects of a capitalist system must also acknowledge that capitalist societies today deviate considerably from the classical model of capitalism; for that matter, contemporary socialist societies deviate in varying degrees from the original model as well (Bohm 1982). The United States has, of course, much state regulation of the market and many welfare programs, and socialistic countries have increasingly adopted elements of the free market.

**Capitalism and White Collar Crime, In Sum**   A capitalist political economy, then, is not the only macrolevel structural inspiration for white collar crime. One of the premier lessons of the 20th century has been the corrupting influence of so-called Communist political economies and other economic systems. But many forms of evidence strongly suggest that the capitalistic elements in our society—the privileging of profit and material acquisition, the ruthless competitiveness, the vastly unequal distribution of wealth and power—are a potent force behind much corporate crime, and behind many other forms of white collar crime as well.

The 1980s, the so-called Reagan-Bush era, has been characterized as a celebration of classical American capitalism. In the official rhetoric, such virtues as self-reliance, entrepreneurship, and individual initiative were promoted. But in an alternative critique, a form of "economic wilding"—Charles Derber (1992: 17) defined it as "the morally uninhibited pursuit of money by individuals or businesses at the expense of others"—became rampant. Certainly an epidemic of white collar crime occurred; the S & L fraud and insider trading cases are but two of the more publicized examples. According to Derber, this "individualism run amuck" has parallels with, and impacts on, other forms of "wilding" lower down in the social order, including inner-city violence and pervasive cheating among young people. In a somewhat parallel vein, Rothstein (1992) suggested that the "real looters" of the recent era were not rioting inner-city youths, but the high-level corporate executives who reaped enormous rewards for themselves while causing much economic devastation for workers, consumers, and taxpayers.

Explanations of white collar crime that focus on social attributes as a whole need not be restricted to the organization of the political economy. U.S. society has been described as "criminal" or "criminogenic" on the basis of its modern, urbanized, bureaucratized character, which promotes impersonality and instrumentalism; its competitiveness; and its frontier cultural values, which promote toughness and resistance to authority (Schur 1969; Barron 1981). U.S. society is suffused with contradictions and conflicts pertaining to its religious, ethnic, racial, and gender-related heritage, and its political system celebrates democracy in an environment in which real power is grossly maldistributed. White collar crime must be understood in terms of these structural attributes as well.

## Radical and Critical Perspectives on White Collar Crime

Although contemporary radical thought is often characterized as directly based on Marxist theory, this is not uniformly the case. Reiman (1982), for example, argued that Marxism is materialist insofar as it explains phenomena such as white collar crime as resulting from the organization of material production, whereas radicalism is idealist, at least when it explains something like white collar crime as a function of the intentions of elites. E. H. Sutherland was said to have in his outlook a radical strain that reflected his populist outlook. The radical criminology that developed in the 1970s was significantly influenced by Marxism, but it also sought to explain the crimes of governmental and corporate elites in terms of willful abuses of power within a contemporary American context (Inciardi 1980a; Lynch and Groves 1989). Much of the radical criminological work of this period examined the criminalization process as opposed to the "causes" of crime.

Since the early 1980s, a number of new perspectives emerged within an evolving radical, or critical, criminology (Thomas and O'Maolchatha 1989; Schwartz 1989). These perspectives include left realism, peacemaking criminology, feminist criminology, and postmodernist criminology. Neither the causes of crime in the conventional sense nor white collar crime itself have been important preoccupations of these perspectives; they have been more concerned with how crime is conceived of or constituted, and appropriate responses to it.

*Left realism* has focused on compensating for radical criminology's traditional neglect of conventional crime while offering an alternative to mainstream and ideologically conservative explanations for such crime (Young and Matthews 1992b; Lowman and MacLean 1992). *Peacemaking criminology* has been mainly directed toward promoting a reconciliative alternative to the dominant "war on crime" approach (Pepinsky and Quinney 1991).

An emerging *postmodernist criminology* challenges the strong tendency of conventional criminological perspectives to impose meaning on criminal conduct and events (Pfohl and Gordon 1986; Schwartz and Friedrichs 1994). In a rapidly changing world, theoretical perspectives shaped by the conditions of modernity may no longer be adequate. Constitutive criminology is a new perspective that draws on postmodern thought (among other theoretical traditions) to emphasize the fundamental instability of meaning in a human world in which realities are constantly deconstructed and then reconstructed (Henry and Milovanovic 1991). Crime in this view must be regarded not as something that is caused, but rather as an outcome of processes of interaction involving individuals and groups. As applied specifically to corporate crime, Henry and Milovanovic (1994: 123–24) focus on how middle managers have tended to deflect primary responsibility for their involvement in illegal and unethical corporate practices by engaging in "discursive practices" of denial and finger-pointing. Such discursive practices divide human beings from each other and create opportunities to compartmentalize responsibility and accountability.

Another dimension of a postmodern approach emphasizes the contemporary context within which crime occurs. Postmodernist writers share the premise that the present era represents a fundamental break with the conditions of modernity, although the full scope of this break is a matter of some dispute. The challenge here is to establish connections between such alleged postmodern conditions as the "hyperreal" and the contemporary character of white collar crime. In a discussion of the film *Wall Street* (which dealt with insider trading), Denzin (1990: 37) observed that the film illustrates the commodification (i.e., transformation into commodities) of everything from information to human feelings in "the postmodern moment." Illusions (including the ultimate illusion of money) replace a more substantial dimension of "reality." Wall Street itself, the locus of some of the largest-scale white collar crime, is described in the language of postmodernist analysis as a "a site where a political economy of signs ceaselessly circulates across an imaginary computerized space where nothing is any longer real" (Denzin 1990: 40). Such observations are at least indicative of one form of a postmodernist approach to the understanding of white collar crime, an approach that rejects out of hand any comprehensive or holistic explanation for such crime.

Finally, *feminist criminology* is a critical criminological perspective that offers a particular viewpoint in explaining white collar crime. The white collar world has traditionally been predominantly a male world, and white collar criminals have been mainly white males. The male dominance of the corporations and outside-the-home occupations, especially of the more powerful positions—what Braithwaite (1993a: 225) called "the gendered structure of opportunity"—would seem to be one important factor explaining this discrepancy. But because women have historically been very underrepresented relative to males in almost all categories of crime, other factors (including gendered socialization) that separate the sexes must come into play (Adler 1975; Simon 1975). Official government statistics reveal significant increases in arrests of females for fraud and embezzlement in the late 1980s, but much of this crime (e.g., welfare fraud) is not really white collar crime (Daly 1989; Simon 1990; Walsh and Licatovich 1991).

White collar crime has not been a primary concern of feminist criminology; rather, it has especially focused on exposing the overall patterns of patriarchy and male dominance in the realms pertaining to crime and the legal system. Direct forms of male violence against women (e.g., rape and spouse abuse) have been a major preoccupation of feminist criminology. Nevertheless, Daly (1989) observed not only that women are underrepresented among white collar offenders, but that different motivations (e.g., family financial need) play a more important role in at least some white collar crime by females. Messerschmidt (1993) specifically suggested that corporate crime reflects patriarchal patterns that exclude women from decision-making roles and promote a form of masculinity celebrating aggressive pursuit of material success. It is far from clear, however, that replacing men with women in corporate positions will result in less corporate crime (Snider 1993). The true extent to which gender plays a role in generating white collar crime may not be resolved until women are much more fully represented in the decision-making ranks in the corporate world.

Another dimension of the connection between gender and white collar crime is the provocative claim that in certain respects women are especially vulnerable to being victims of such crime, particularly in its corporate form (Hinch and DeKeseredy 1992; Gerber and Weeks 1992). The thesis here is that women are overrepresented in lower-level corporate jobs in which vulnerability to injury is greater, that they are more likely to be sexually harassed and assaulted on the job, and that at home they disproportionately use harmful pharmaceutical and household-related products. In this account, concerns for women's health and safety are not accorded a high priority in a capitalist, patriarchal society in which women are underrepresented in the corporate decision-making process.

## Explaining Criminalization and White Collar Crime

EXPLAINING CRIMINAL BEHAVIOR and crime has historically been the primary focus of criminology. In the 1960s and 1970s this began to change with the development of theoretical perspectives that focused on criminalization.

Investigations of criminalization pose questions on several levels of analysis. First, how does certain harmful activity come to be defined as criminal, whereas other equally (or more) harmful activity is not defined as criminal? The criminal law is not simply regarded as a given; rather, its particular form and content must be explained. Second, what is the process by which some individuals or organizations that engage in harmful conduct (as defined by some body of law) come to be labeled criminal, whereas others who engage in the same conduct are not labeled criminal? And third, what are the consequences of being so labeled?

In at least one (legalistic) sense, no crime—including white collar crime—exists until and unless there is some formal recognition that a type of activity should be designated a crime. In this sense, then, what we must explain is why certain activity comes to be defined as white collar crime. Conversely, we must explain why other activity, which may be as harmful or more harmful, is not defined as white collar crime. This aspect of criminalization is explored more fully in Chapter 9.

The criminalization process has been directly linked with patterns of engagement in white collar crime. For example, in one interpretation of the perspective of the seminal theorist of capitalism, Adam Smith, white collar crime is a product of lawmaking that interferes with the natural operation of a free market economy (Jesilow 1982a). In this view, such laws will work to the advantage of wealthy corporations, which have the resources to confront and evade regulation more effectively. Thus more white collar crime is to be expected when the market is fixed and has no free competition, when labor is regulated, and when regulatory law is pervasive and unpredictable. The law itself, in this sense, promotes white collar crime, and the public welfare is better served when exploitative activities of corporations and businesses are controlled by a free market—and outraged consumers.

The seminal critic of capitalism, Karl Marx, did not favor criminalization as a response to exploitative and harmful activities of corporations and businesses. For Marx, law by its very form was likely to favor privileged segments of society (Cain and Hunt 1979). Among other functions, it legitimates and shields economic exploitation and harm. In this sense the law helps promote what we call white collar crime. Such crime can be obliterated only by abolishing the private ownership of property and transforming society so that people live in egalitarian, cooperative relationships with each other; in such a society there is simply no need for criminal law.

The failure to criminalize some forms of harmful white collar activity (e.g., "tax avoidance") can help promote such activity, and in this negative way the law promotes white collar crime in the nonlegal sense of the term *crime* (McBarnet 1992). The removal of legal controls can create a whole range of new criminal opportunities. The deregulation of the U.S. savings and loan industry in the early 1980s certainly had this effect and contributed to the staggering losses through fraudulent activities within these institutions (Calavita and Pontell 1990; Pontell and Calavita 1993). Law itself, then, both tolerates some types of harmful white collar activity and produces opportunities for other forms of white collar crime.

## Integrated Theories of White Collar Crime

A NUMBER OF students of white collar crime have attempted to develop integrated theories of such crime that incorporate insights from different theoretical traditions and account for white collar crime on several different levels.

James William Coleman (1987)—who should not be confused with the prominent University of Chicago sociologist James S. Coleman—developed an integrated theory that centers on the coincidence of appropriate motivation and opportunity. A culture characterized by an emphasis on "possessive individualism," competition, and materialism; by a variety of justifying rationalizations; and by an absence of unified restraining influences, generates motivations for lawbreaking. A built-in structure of opportunity renders white collar crime both less vulnerable to legal controls and sanctions (due to the disproportionate power of elites in the formulation and administration of the law) and very open to a variety of attractive possibilities for disregarding or violating the laws that do exist. In the private sector, the attractiveness of illicit opportunities increases as profitability declines; the organizational rhetoric of condemning illegal activity comes into conflict with the conditions (diffusion of responsibility, deniability, and lack of authentic objections) that promote such activity. Various factors—for example, the structure of opportunity, the nature of financial reimbursement, and the occupational subculture—can render some occupations more conducive to illegality than others. Accordingly, white collar crime is most pervasive in societies that have a culture of competition, in organizations that are financially pressured, and in occupations with special opportunities and subcultural values that promote illegality.

John Braithwaite (1989a) based his integrative theory on two traditions: structural Marxist theory (first articulated by Dutch criminologist Willem A. Bonger), which links both white collar and conventional crime with the promotion of egoism in capitalist societies, and differential association theory (first developed by Sutherland), which holds that both white collar and conventional crime are learned relative to differential opportunity. Accordingly, nations with high levels of inequality of wealth and power will have high rates of both white collar and conventional crime because they produce a broad range of illegitimate opportunities that are more rewarding than legitimate opportunities. Organizational crime specifically is a response to relatively more attractive illegitimate opportunities and the subcultural value system that rationalizes taking advantage of them. For Braithwaite, the theoretical challenge is to construct a "tipping point" explanation that predicts when a stake in noncompliance outbalances a stake in conformity with the law. His critical tipping factor is "differential shaming": Conduct is tipped in the direction that avoids the more potent shaming (disapproval), whether it comes from within the organization or from the state. Involvement in white collar criminal conduct can then be understood as a function of relative vulnerability to shaming: Crime flourishes in organizations that shield members from shaming and pressure them to produce; crime is controlled in organizations that take proactive measures to expose law violators to shame. Braithwaite accordingly regarded differential shaming as the missing link integrating two contradictory traditions (subcultural and control).

## An Integrated, Multilevel Approach to Understanding the Looting of the Thrifts

The looting of the S & Ls in America in the 1980s has been described, accurately or not, as the largest-scale white collar crime in our history (Calavita and Pontell 1990). Although it is not possible to say exactly what proportion of the losses were due specifically to criminal activity (as opposed to misjudgments, bad luck, external economic conditions, and the like), by any estimate the losses were in the billions of dollars. Many different explanations have been offered for the failure of the thrifts, ranging from economic determinism to intentional wrongdoing (Zimring and Hawkins 1993). Several different levels of explanation can be applied to the looting of the S & Ls. First we consider the *structural* level.

The thrifts are, to begin with, the creation of a capitalist system. In some respects they are a quintessentially capitalist institution, reflecting Ben Franklin's emphasis on saving and investment; they involve the use of capital (money) to produce more capital. On the other hand, they were traditionally regulated (constrained) in terms of how the money deposited with them could be invested. They were restricted to mortgage loans, and their deposits were insured (up to a point) by the federal government.

In the 1970s and early 1980s S & Ls found themselves under formidable pressure (and often losing money) in competition with newly emerging financial institutions that did not have to operate within the same constraints. In the procapitalist ethos of the Reagan administration, new laws swept away many of the constraints on the ownership and investments of the thrifts. The new deregulated environment created a very broad window of opportunity for unscrupulous individuals to acquire ownership or managerial control of the thrifts, to bring in vastly larger deposits, and either to invest recklessly or engage in outright theft and fraud of the thrift's assets. The political system promoted corrupt dealings between owners of thrifts who made large donations to the campaigns and well-placed political officials, who in turn leaned on regulators to back off from their interference with the operation of these thrifts.

On an *organizational* level, a hierarchical structure within the S & Ls allowed diffusion of responsibility (various forms of "buck passing") or denial of responsibility for misdeeds. Both internal organizational pressure to produce ever-larger profits and organizational subcultural pressure to be loyal to the institution and "part of the team" played roles in putting short-term organizational profits ahead of integrity and other such considerations.

On a *dramaturgic* or situational level, the thrifts often conveyed an image of respectability and trustworthiness, which in varying degrees fooled or deluded investors, regulators, and the media. Much "impression management" was used to inspire confidence in the thrifts.

On an *individualistic* level, some of those at the center of the worst and most fraudulent thrifts appeared to be amoral risk takers, egocentric or sociopathic individuals with delusions of grandeur who were driven to "succeed" and acquire the most conspicuous material symbols of success.

## Explaining White Collar Crime, In Sum

WHITE COLLAR CRIME is clearly a complex, multifaceted phenomenon. No single theory or explanation can comprehensively explain all forms of white collar crime, much less all specific instances of white collar crime. We should always be clear about what it is exactly we are trying to explain: criminality, crime, or criminalization. A portion of this chapter was devoted to theoretical attempts—from

Sutherland to Hirschi and Gottfredson to Braithwaite—to explain all crime, including white collar crime, with a basic principle or proposition about human behavior. But the overarching view adopted here is that the ultimate complexity and diversity of white collar crime precludes the possibility of any single comprehensive theory or explanatory scheme.

We have seen how difficult it is to overcome the methodological barriers to demonstrating conclusively the validity of the competing theories of white collar crime; in some cases the empirical evidence has been contradictory. We also touched on various definitional, conceptual, metaphysical, and typological problems that complicate the challenge of developing viable theoretical explanations.

Even though much theorizing is necessarily interpretive, some theories are more fundamental and more powerful than others. We must recognize the various distinctive levels of theory; some levels are more general than others. Furthermore, some forms of white collar crime are best understood on one level of explanation, others on another level. The individualistic and occupational forms of white collar crime, for example, lend themselves more readily to explanation within the framework of traditional, mainstream theories.

Organizational and corporate forms of white collar crime generate special difficulties. The real challenge is to identify how the macrolevels and microlevels are connected and interact to produce such white collar crime (Vaughan 1992). Numerous factors, ranging from external pressures to organizational position to regulatory patterns of response, may be involved in individual decisions to commit crimes on behalf of organizations. Given the large number of possible variables we cannot easily expect to explain organizational crime with propositions that have the reliability of a scientific law.

So, when all is said and done, need we only invoke the core motivation of "greed" to largely explain white collar crime? The essential thesis of this chapter is that such a simplistic, one-dimensional explanation does not take us very far in understanding either the endlessly complex mixture of factors that may be involved in such crime or the quite different ways of even thinking about what we are trying to explain. Motivation is but one element among many. When we get down to specific cases, different elements may be crucial in one white collar crime case, and only peripheral or essentially irrelevant in another. We must continue to refine our understanding of the interrelationships among criminality, crime, and criminalization as they apply to white collar crime.

# Law and the Social Control of White Collar Crime

**D**O VARIOUS FORMS of white collar crime develop and inspire laws in response to them, or do laws develop that designate certain forms of economic activity as criminal?

The conventional view is that law—formal social control—develops in response to deviant or harmful activity. Some contemporary theoretical perspectives (e.g., conflict theory and labeling theory) have suggested that the opposite is true—that institutions of social control come to define certain activity as deviant or criminal, sometimes quite arbitrarily (Cohen 1985: 6)—and there is considerable evidence to support this contemporary view.

The relationship between law and objectively harmful activities of the white collar strata is complex. This chapter attempts to sort through some of the elements involved in this relationship.

## Social Control and White Collar Crime

FROM THE EARLIEST stages of human history, communities have sought to ensure order through some form of social control. The concept of social control was first introduced in 1901 by E. A. Ross, whose book *Sin and Society* foreshadowed Sutherland's call for greater attention to the crimes of social elites. The term *social control* has been used broadly to refer to all attempts to influence or affect human behavior, and more narrowly to refer to coercive responses to deviant behavior (Black 1984; Cohen 1985; Gibbs 1989; Liska 1992). The conflict perspective has sought to demonstrate that social control is more a function of unequal power than of consensus, and conservatives have invoked the concept to account for social harmony without coercion in U.S. society (Fine 1986; Chunn and Gavigan 1988). Mainstream theorists tend to emphasize both the consensual and the universal character of the primary means of social control, whereas critical theorists tend to emphasize the historically specific ways in which some segments of society impose their will on others.

Even though social control in the form of proscriptions against conventional crimes such as murder, assault, and robbery has existed from at least the time of earliest recorded history, the range of activities defined as white collar crimes have inspired a more limited and typically belated formal response. First, throughout much of history the organization of economic and professional life was far simpler than has been true in modern times, and accordingly the opportunities to defraud, embezzle, or cause harm to others through economic activities have been far more limited. After all, a predominantly agricultural economy of self-sustaining family farms hardly promotes white collar crime. Second, in small, homogeneous communities, people who engage in economic transactions have enduring relationships that include both informal controls and self-serving motivations not to defraud. Third, many of the worst "white collar" offenses in history have been committed in nondemocratic societies by political and economic elites who have not had a strong incentive to impose formal controls on their own predatory practices. Still, it is inaccurate and simplistic to imagine that the legal response to white collar crime is entirely a modern phenomenon.

White collar crime can be seen both as a product of failed social control and as a product of highly successful social control. In the first view it represents the failure of formal and informal institutions of social control to prevent or deter corporations and individuals from engaging in socially harmful conduct. Such external controls have often been either absent or only superficially enforced. In the second view, corporate and other organizational forms of white collar crime may reflect the high level of control over individual human conduct that such entities achieve. Such crime is often a result of conformity to organizational norms.

The call to control crime is quite commonplace, but it is far from self-evident what we should be trying to control (Pepinsky 1980). Any crime control measures entail choices to respond to certain types of activities instead of other activities, and such measures often have some unintended, or harmful, consequences. Traditional criminology has tended to promote various means of extending control over people's lives; critical and peacemaking criminologies have called for diminishing or minimizing such responses. White collar crime, especially in its corporate form, poses some unique challenges and conundrums for proponents of both more social control and less social control. The sections that follow consider the character of the most formal type of social control—law—in its response to white collar crime.

## Formal Law and White Collar Crime

IT IS NECESSARY here to refer again to the debate about the proper meaning of the term *white collar crime.* In the narrower sense it refers to certain violations of the *criminal* law, and from the outset some commentators have insisted that this is the only valid meaning of the term (Tappan 1947; Orland 1980). Sutherland (1940; 1949), however, insisted that the term should be applied more broadly to forms of white collar harm that are not specifically prohibited by the criminal law, but rather by some other form of law (e.g., civil law or administrative law).

Sutherland's basic argument was that because corporations and other elements of the white collar world have too much influence over the criminalization process, the narrower conception of white collar crime allows these powerful segments of society to impose their own limits on our view of crime. Many subsequent students of the phenomenon have adopted some form of Sutherland's argument. An alternative position on corporate activity specifically is that we should distinguish between corporate crime (violations of criminal law) and illegal corporate behavior (violations of civil and administrative law)(Baucus and Dworkin 1991). A third view goes still further and regards white collar crime as the demonstrably harmful practices and activities of elite elements of society, even if the activity violates no state laws or administrative rules (Kauzlarich 1992; Mokhiber 1988; Schwendinger and Schwendinger 1970; Simon and Eitzen 1993). One premise here is that corporate (and governmental) elites in particular are able to prevent, by various means, any formal, legal efforts to respond to some of their most harmful activities. Even when laws attempting to control certain forms of corporate activities are adopted, elite interests often have the power to influence the meaning of the laws (e.g., tax evasion simply becomes tax avoidance)(McBarnet 1992). In this view, law is a terrain of contested meaning.

Much scholarship has been devoted to the challenge of defining the term *law*, which has had many different meanings in the course of Western history (Friedrich 1958). It has been defined as institutionalized social control (Akers and Hawkins 1975: 6), and it may refer to a social institution, a specific legal system, or a particular legal rule. There is no good or perfect definition, only definitions that are more or less useful in some context.

For our purposes, the elements of a useful definition of law as a means of social control directed at white collar crime include the following: Law is formal; it is imperative (a command); it has sanctions (or "teeth"); it is political (governmental); it is administered by government officials; it is an ongoing enterprise; and it is typically quite specific. As a society becomes larger, more complex, and more heterogeneous, the historical tendency is to rely increasingly on law, the most formal type of social control. The application of law has certainly expanded greatly in the response to white collar crime, although the appropriateness of this expansion is the subject of much ongoing debate.

Historically, it has proven more difficult to formulate and apply criminal laws to harms committed in a business or professional context than to conventional forms of harm such as assault and burglary. Unlike most conventional crime, what we call white collar crime typically occurs in the context of legitimate and productive activities, and the proper lines of demarcation between acceptable and unacceptable practices (e.g., effective and fraudulent advertising) are not always clear (Croall 1992).

In the Western, capitalist tradition, the premier philosopher of capitalism, Adam Smith (1776; 1937), argued that the free market, not the legal system, is the best and most efficient means for preventing or minimizing harmful conduct by businesses. One form of white collar criminal law that is logically consistent with Smith's position is antitrust law, which is directed against monopolistic practices that interfere with the operation of a truly competitive free market. Paul Jesilow (1982a) pointed out that Smith had no illusions about the willingness of many businessmen to do harm to consumers; Smith seemed to believe that most laws directed at them would simply be manipulated and evaded by more powerful businessmen, which would lead to more harm rather than less. Some students of white collar crime today argue that there are inherent limitations in the formal legalistic response to crime generally, and to white collar crime in particular, and they call for greater reliance on alternative means of social control (Stone 1975). The concern that laws regulating and restricting business practices are economically counterproductive was especially pronounced during the Reagan era in the 1980s.

Still another related element in the dialogue on social control centers on the appropriate level for responding to white collar crime: Should it be principally at the local, state, national, or international level? The answer to this question significantly depends on the type of white collar crime involved. Low-level frauds, for example, are more likely to require a local response; crimes of nations require some form of international response. White collar crime generally, and in its corporate form especially, is much more likely to call for social control on a national level than is most conventional crime. As "globalization" increases and national boundaries become less and less important for many forms of business, the importance of social control on the international level increases (Michalowski and Kramer 1987). The larger the framework of social control, however, the more difficult it becomes to formulate laws that can be implemented and can garner broad support.

The extent to which social control should be directed toward individuals, groups, organizations, or some combination of these is another issue. Traditionally, social control has focused on the behavior of individuals, but the incidence of corporate white collar crime, in particular, has highlighted the need to control organizations. Still, considerable debate among students of white collar crime centers on what the primary targets for control should be.

## The Historical Origins of White Collar Crime Laws

INVOLVEMENT OF LAW in commercial matters dates from the earliest period of recorded history. According to Drapkin (1989: 16), the first known legal documents were contracts of land sales and other transactions conducted around 2400 B.C. in ancient Mesopotamia. We also have evidence of concern with commercial misconduct in the form of a tablet (dated approximately 2050 B.C.) containing the code of a ruler, Ur-Nammu, that lays out guidelines for a uniform system of weights and measures and prohibits various forms of economic exploitation (Drapkin 1989: 19). Codes from this time also stipulate the punishments imposed on professionals (e.g., surgeons) and builders who caused injury in the performance of their occupational duties (Drapkin 1989: 29). The Old Testament (e.g., Proverbs 11:25; Deuteronomy 25:

13; Leviticus 25: 14) includes proscriptions against deceitful and unfair market practices (Geis 1988: 9; Levine 1980). The classical Greek lawmaker Solon (7th-century B.C.) established laws against embezzling from the state, and the Roman statesman Cicero (1st-century B.C.) discussed the obligations of "insiders" in grain transactions (Drapkin 1989; Vermeule 1983). Such proscriptions and initiatives suggest, at a minimum, a clear recognition in ancient societies of economic crimes that differed from conventional forms of assault and robbery.

The English common law that evolved over hundreds of years (and is an important foundation of American law) addressed occupational offenses less clearly than conventional forms of harm such as homicide and assault. In feudal England (1100–1400) the marketplace was heavily regulated, primarily to protect the interests of the Crown and the nobility (Michalowski 1985). Feudal-period merchants (*pies poudreux*, or "dusty feet") were at a serious disadvantage in a system that regarded profit as dishonorable or sinful (Tigar and Levy 1977; Sheldon and Zweibel 1980). Much control of English merchant activities was informal, but in the late Middle Ages specific laws were enacted to protect consumers; these laws prohibited regrating, engrossing, and forestalling, which were practices entailing either buying up market goods for sale at a profit or buying them up before they reached the market for purposes of driving prices up (Geis 1988: 9). During this period boards and guilds were empowered to establish fair prices (Sheldon and Zweibel 1980: 189). Following the "Black Death" in the 14th century; with its devastating impact on the pool of laborers, new laws were enacted that prohibited giving or receiving of excessive wages, refusing to work at the proper wage level, or refusing to work at all (Bellamy 1973; Chambliss 1964).

With the increasing importance of mercantile activity, new laws were needed. The famous Carrier's case (1473) provided a foundation for the modern law of theft (Hall 1952). Instead of transporting bales of wool from one place to another, the carrier (the defendant in the case) broke open the bales and helped himself to the contents. English laws of the time did not specifically prohibit the use of goods already legally in one's possession for one's own purposes. The court ruled against the carrier, and in doing so established a legal distinction between possession and ownership. This legal distinction was clearly responsive to the needs of an emerging class of merchants and traders, and it provided a precedent for subsequent laws prohibiting employee theft, embezzlement, and related acts.

These acts by employees became a matter of increasing concern to the ownership class, and a series of laws passed in England in the 17th and 18th centuries specifically criminalized such activities (Sharpe 1984: 124). Initially these laws had a somewhat narrow focus, but they became a basis for general laws prohibiting occupational offenses. For example, the Servant Theft Statute (1520), which originally made theft of a master's property a felony, was eventually applied to employees generally; in a similar vein, an embezzlement statute passed in England in 1742, which originally applied only to employees of the Bank of England, became a basis for a general embezzlement statute enacted at the end of the 18th century (Coleman 1989). Altogether, laws specifically addressing harmful commercial practices were relatively few and far between, were sporadically enforced, and seemed to be principally intended to protect the interests of the ownership class (Geis 1988; Michalowski 1985; Snider 1993). The law was not structured to respond effectively to the exploitative and harmful practices of businesses as corporate entities.

In the United States, two essentially contradictory forces relevant to white collar crime laws emerged in the 19th century in response to the country's accelerating transformation into an industrialized, urbanized, mass society. On the one hand, this expanding capitalist economy tended to give entrepreneurs and all manner of economic enterprises a free hand in creating new wealth and a booming economy (Friedman 1977: 52; Hurst 1956: 7–8). On the other hand, the workers, consumers, and investors in this increasingly large and complex society were especially vulnerable to being exploited, defrauded, or harmed by corporations, businesses, and professionals. Toward the end of the 19th century in particular, Congress enacted laws regulating and criminalizing a wide range of business practices. Periodic widespread anger over certain practices—involving, for example, harmful working conditions, dangerous products, fraudulent sales, or environmental damage—led to a series of white collar crime laws (Snider 1993). These legal reform campaigns were sometimes inspired by social critics, by journalistic muckrakers, or by highly publicized "catastrophies," among other factors.

The U.S. Supreme Court has historically waxed and waned in its response to one body of law, regulatory law, which addresses harmful practices of businesses. For example, the Court had originally upheld the body of state regulatory legislation passed in the latter half of the 19th century, but by the end of that century a more conservative Court had shifted to a position favoring the rights of corporations (Hall 1989: 234), a pattern that in some form has continued throughout the 20th century. The historical development of specific bodies of white collar crime law—for example, antitrust law and environmental law—is discussed in subsequent sections. It is worth noting here that the tension between laws that emphasize economic development and those that favor regulating or criminalizing harmful practices is still very much with us.

## Contemporary Legislative Lawmaking and White Collar Crime

LAWMAKING HAS BEEN explained in various ways (Vago 1990). The functionalist perspective regards lawmaking as the crystallization of consensual norms that is necessary for maintaining the basic fabric of the social order and that reflects the failure of other means of social control. An alternative and widely accepted model views lawmaking as an essentially rational, pragmatic process intended to protect members of society from objective harm (as determined by lawmakers). A third view of lawmaking regards it as a process that mediates basic conflicts of interest and values; the uneven distribution of power is a principal determinant of the outcome of the process.

Clearly, no single conception of lawmaking best applies to white collar crime laws. Legislative lawmaking is a complex process that may reflect a variety of influences. Even though it may seem obvious that specific white collar crime laws emerge out of particular historical circumstances and may reflect various mixtures of consensual, rationalistic, and power-based dimensions, most contemporary theories of lawmaking recognize the central role of power, especially in terms of the role of interest groups (Friedman 1977). In a useful study of white collar crime lawmaking, Joachim Savelsberg (1994) attempted to demonstrate that such legislation reflects the activities of lobbying by special interest groups more than the objective needs of society.

An instrumentalist perspective on lawmaking advances the view that in a capitalist society law reflects the elite class's control over the state and is intended to serve the purposes of that class (Quinney 1974). This provocative challenge to a conventional view of law as rooted in democratic consensus is controversial and difficult to reconcile with many laws that appear to work against the immediate interests of major capitalist corporations. An alternative progressive perspective, which has been designated structuralist, recognizes that the state is "relatively autonomous" and is committed to the system's long-term survival rather than to advancing the specific, immediate interests of capitalist elites and entities (Collins 1984; Lynch and Groves 1989). In this account, then, white collar crime law (including corporate crime law) is implemented by the state because it helps sustain the system and "legitimates" the state in the eyes of its citizens. But there may well be tensions among different state officials in terms of their concern with the system's long-term legitimacy or immediate well-being. Calavita and Pontell (1994) suggested that the state has generally been more tolerant of traditional corporate crimes in the manufacturing sector—mainly taking action in response to grassroots political demands—than of financial crimes such as the S & L frauds that enriched individuals at the expense of the economic system.

## The Dialectical Perspective on Lawmaking

William Chambliss advanced a dialectical theory of lawmaking that views it as a process directed toward the resolution of various contradictions, conflicts, and dilemmas confronting society in a particular historical context (Chambliss and Courtless 1992; Chambliss and Seidman 1982). This theory provides useful explanations of laws regulating the meat packing industry in the early 20th century and the more recent antipollution laws. In the dialectical view, conflicts between a public increasingly angry about unhealthful meat (or dangerous forms of pollution) and the short-term economic interests of meatpacking corporations (or corporate polluters)can be resolved by laws that ensure the general public welfare while protecting the long-term economic interests of the larger corporations (Chambliss and Seidman 1982).

It is important to emphasize that corporate and business interests are hardly monolithic. Indeed, the large meatpackers supported the regulatory laws because these laws helped restore public confidence in their product and drove many small competitors (who were unable to meet the new expenses involved) out of business (Poveda 1992; Kolko 1963). The first U.S. laws against water pollution were favored by manufacturing corporations that depended on unclogged rivers for transporting goods (Yeager 1991a). The securities industry has been very supportive of laws directed at practices such as insider trading that promote a loss of trust among investors and potential investors. In general, businesses support laws regarded as promoting a more stable and predictable business environment.

However, when regulatory laws' negative effects on profits outweigh benefits, businesses (especially in the manufacturing segment) tend to oppose these laws. And regulatory laws often give rise to new contradictions. In another illustration of the dialectical model of lawmaking, Kitty Calavita (1990) demonstrated that when laws implemented to sanction employers for hiring cheap immigrant labor threatened U.S. workers, the laws were restructured to accommodate politically influential employers by allowing them to meet superficial paperwork compliance standards while continuing to benefit from the use of cheap immigrant labor. Although the dialectical theory may be more directly applicable to some white collar crime laws than to others, it does provide a general sense of the interrelated factors that guide the ongoing process of lawmaking in this realm.

## The Influence of Business on the Lawmaking Process

Because the evolution of white collar crime law is complex, laws governing economic crimes are likely to be products of various competing constituencies, including formal agencies of social control operating within a particular political context, and thus powerful economic interests do not always prevail (Savelsberg 1987). Nevertheless, business has generally had disproportionate influence over the lawmaking process. The more limited legal response to white collar crime (relative to conventional crime) reflects in part the considerable input businesspeople have in the making and implementation of white collar crime laws; the class of people to whom conventional offenders typically belong has virtually no involvement in the making of conventional criminal law (Croall 1992). The politicians who make the laws often depend on business leaders and corporations—and on the "business class" generally—for financial support for their campaigns, for personal gifts and favors, and for postpolitical career employment or contracts. Quite a number of legislators have become lobbyists (typically for business interests) after leaving office. And responsiveness to at least some business interests is often politically expedient when many of a politician's constituents are dependent on major corporations or are probusiness.

Concern over business influence on the lawmaking process is hardly new. Even Adam Smith, typically considered the most prominent champion of a capitalist economy, issued a warning :

> *The proposal of any new law or regulation of commerce which comes from this order [businessmen] ought never to be adopted till after having been long and carefully examined, not only with the most scrupulous, but with the most suspicious attention. It comes from an order of men whose interest is never the same with that of the public, men who have generally an interest to deceive and even to oppress the public and who accordingly have, upon many occasions, both deceived and oppressed it. (Smith 1776; 1937: 250)*

The business and corporate world does not fully control the lawmaking process. Furthermore, the level of business's political influence has fluctuated, or undergone cycles, in the course of modern U.S. history (Vogel 1989). In the 20th century business has undergone three challenging eras featuring laws regulating various forms of business conduct: the Progressive Era (1900s), when municipal reform groups were among the principal agitators for change; the "New Deal" Era (1930s), when the trade union movement played an especially important role; and the "Great Society" Era (1970s), during which various public interest groups lobbied for new legal initiatives. Vogel (1989) demonstrated that during periods with relatively strong economies (e.g., the 1960s) businesses are vulnerable to more regulation because during such periods higher expectations of business performance tend to develop, and thus businesses cannot credibly claim that they are unable to afford to reform harmful practices. During an economic recession, in contrast, people tend to put a higher priority on jobs than on cracking down on the harmful conduct of business, if the choice comes to that.

Legislators must necessarily be responsive to many constituencies, some of whom are harmed by business practices or are antagonistic toward business generally for any of a variety of reasons. In recent times in particular, relatively well-organized groups (e.g., environmental or consumer groups) have lobbied for laws that criminalize or otherwise penalize corporate and business practices that they view as harmful or threatening. These groups operate as "moral entrepreneurs" that advocate white collar crime laws in the public interest. Although various social movements have promoted new laws throughout U.S. history, the tendency to seek social change through legal reform has intensified since the late 1950s (Handler 1978).

The relative success of the civil rights movement in challenging the legal status of segregation was one important source of inspiration for social movements representing various disadvantaged and beleaguered constituencies. Most of these social movements' law reform initiatives did not focus on white collar crime in the narrower sense, but were directed instead toward imposing more regulation of and greater control over a range of potentially harmful business practices. Even though these social movements, including consumer and environmentalist movements, have sought to influence legislative, judicial, and administrative lawmaking, they have perhaps been most successful in the courts (Handler 1978: 232). Powerful economic interests often have considerable advantages in the legislative and administrative arenas because politicians depend on their support. Reflecting pressure from such interests (as well as conservative ideological commitments), the Republican-dominated Congress passed in March 1995 a series of laws with several intentions: to shift more tort cases to federal jurisdiction; to discourage product-liability lawsuits by imposing responsibility for defendants' legal fees on plaintiffs who lose cases and by sanctioning lawsuits deemed frivolous; to impose limits on punitive damages in tort cases; and to make it more difficult for investors to establish fraud in cases against brokers (Labaton 1995; N. A. Lewis 1995a; 1995b; 1995c).

Finally, various government agencies or entities may actively lobby for white collar crime laws. Such efforts may be inspired either by self-interest, as occurs when an enforcement agency seeks to expand its reach and influence, or by a principled perception of a need for new laws (Lofquist 1993b). The Federal Trade Commission (FTC) was able to expand its regulatory mandate in 1950 by successfully mobilizing various resources to ensure passage of a key piece of antitrust legislation, the Celler-Kefauver Act (Luchansky and Gerber 1993). Legislators, then, can be persuaded to respond to some of the wants and needs of such governmental agencies.

## Alternative Sources and Forms of Law and Lawmaking

THE LEGISLATIVE BRANCH is not the only source of laws, of course. Four alternative sources and forms of law and lawmaking are discussed next.

### The Constitution and Constitutional Law

The U.S. Constitution does not specifically address white collar crime, and the same can be said for the many different state constitutions. Still, the Constitution provides a basic framework for the response to white collar crime through the establishment of a federal court system, its allocation of powers to the different branches of the government, and its imposition of limitations on the exercise of governmental power in the investigation and prosecution of criminal cases (especially in the Bill of Rights). Because a somewhat disproportionate percentage of white collar crime cases are federal cases, the Bill of Rights' protections for those accused of crimes apply directly to these defendants. The Fourteenth Amendment extended "due process" protection to defendants in the far more common state cases.

The Commerce Clause of Article I, Section 8, of the Constitution authorized Congress to make laws regulating commerce between the states, and provided one basis for federal intervention in the affairs of private businesses; at the same time it also became a basis for challenging states' attempts at regulating business activity. The Constitution is, of course, a relatively brief document, and its provisions and amendments include many broad or ambiguous expressions (e.g., "free speech" and "due process") that require specific interpretation. In its celebrated decision in *Marbury v. Madison* (1803), the U.S. Supreme Court established both the supremacy of the Constitution and the Court's own right of judicial review in determining whether laws passed by other bodies were or were not constitutional. Accordingly, a broad body of constitutional law has developed, and some of this law has direct bearing on white collar crime cases.

One of the great paradoxes in constitutional history deserves some mention here. Shortly after the end of the Civil War the Fourteenth Amendment was ratified to ensure that newly emancipated slaves were not for all practical purposes reenslaved by state laws that deprived them of every form of due process. In the latter part of the 19th century former slaves rarely had the financial resources needed to protect themselves by invoking this amendment, but businesses did. Lawyers for wealthy corporations vigorously fought off the federal government's efforts to intervene in some of their unscrupulous business activities by arguing that the corporations' Fourteenth Amendment guarantee of "due process" protection was being violated (Hall 1989). In the 20th century the U.S. Supreme Court has withheld from corporations certain protections, such as the privileges and immunities clause of the Fourteenth Amendment and due process protection of liberty (First 1990: 399). Still, the statutory laws addressing various forms of white collar crime, including the Sherman Antitrust Act, have been especially vulnerable to challenges on the grounds that they are unconstitutionally vague (First 1990: 24). Most of the large body of Supreme Court rulings on constitutional issues affecting conventional offenders has developed since the early 1960s.

The significance of the Constitution in cases of governmental crime is quite obvious. The Watergate Affair can be seen on several levels: as (1) an attempt by the Nixon administration to violate various provisions of the Constitution; (2) a constitutional crisis, when Nixon as head of the executive branch appeared to be prepared to defy the other two branches, Congress and the Supreme Court; and (3) a vindication of the potency of the Constitution, when Nixon finally resigned and political stability was restored (Commager 1974). To the extent that governmental crime in the United States has been less pervasive than in many totalitarian countries, the Constitution can certainly be cited as a fundamental factor.

## Case Law

Law that is a product of appellate court opinions on particular cases has played an important role in the realm of white collar crime for several reasons. Statutory laws pertaining to white collar crime often include ambiguous elements, due to both the difficulty sometimes involved in differentiating between legitimate and illegitimate business practices and the compromises made in response to lobbying by special interests. Defendants in white collar crime cases are often better able to finance a full-scale appeal of criminal convictions than are conventional crime defendants. At the same time, as we noted earlier, public interest groups have often been more successful in the courts than in the legislative arena because the courts (especially the federal courts) are somewhat more insulated from politics and are more open to principled arguments. Since the late 1950s a period of judicial activism has effectively encouraged litigation by a growing number of activist groups, and by the 1970s public interest law firms interested in pursuing test cases before the courts had emerged (Handler 1978: 2). Thus, because the judicial branch is somewhat more autonomous, it is less susceptible to the influence of powerful business and professional interests.

The claim that the courts directly bring about important social change is not uniformly accepted, however (Rosenberg 1991). The counterargument is that change is likely to occur only when court decisions are complemented by social and political forces that are already moving society in that direction. Furthermore, both federal and state appellate court judges are often selected less for their legal brilliance than for their perceived ideological orientation; judges with a conservative orientation have traditionally been regarded as probusiness. During the late 19th century, after World War I, and during the recent Reagan/Bush era, especially large numbers of conservative, probusiness justices were appointed. The U.S. Supreme Court opinion in *Santa Clara v. Southern Pacific Railroad* (1886), which held that a corporation was entitled under the Fourteenth Amendment to the same protections as "natural persons," has been interpreted as a reflection of the subservience of the Court to big business during this period (Horwitz 1992). Of course, in many other cases the courts have upheld statutes regulating and criminalizing certain corporate and business activities.

Some areas of white collar crime law are more fully developed in the case law than in statutory law. For example, the insider trading laws are principally a product of a series of judicial opinions. The courts have also in at least some cases interpreted statutory laws in a manner that extends the scope of the criminal liability of corporations and other white collar actors. A court opinion (as opposed to a specific legislative act) determined that RICO (the Racketeer-Influenced and Corrupt Organizations Act) could be applied to businesspeople and was not restricted to traditional mobsters. These matters are somewhat more fully explored later in this chapter.

In sum, the complex and sometimes ambiguous nature of white collar and corporate crime law has provided the judicial branch, in a legal system with a common law heritage, with especially broad latitude in interpreting and reformulating the law.

## Executive Lawmaking

The executive branch is less directly involved in the making of law than the other two branches of the government, at least in the traditional sense of "lawmaking." Still, this branch contributes to the making of much white collar crime law in its broadest sense. Executive branch personnel have considerable input in the legislative process by providing many experts who testify before legislative committees and assist in the drafting of legislation. The executive branch can use its political clout to lobby for laws it favors, and the chief executive can veto legislation, although the use of this power is somewhat uncommon with respect to criminal law.

Most importantly, the executive branch can be said to "make" law in a very real sense through its control of agencies that investigate, enforce, and prosecute crime. Regardless of what the other two branches of the U.S. government declare to be law, any laws that the executive branch fails to enforce and prosecute in effect do not really "exist." Thus the Reagan administration's lack of interest in enforcing many of the provisions of antitrust law rendered much of the antitrust law "nonexistent" during this period. This executive branch power is especially important with respect to white collar crime, then, because indifference to, and even hostility toward, at least some white collar crime laws has been a recurrent pattern.

The executive branch appoints all federal judges and many state-level judges as well; especially important are Supreme Court justices and appellate court judges. As previously noted, ideological and political factors have historically played a crucial role in such appointments. Accordingly, despite the legislative branch's confirmation powers, the executive branch has considerable discretion in determining which kind of judges will interpret the law, including the laws pertaining to white collar crime. The executive branch also plays the same role in appointing the top people in many of the regulatory agencies, who in turn "make" much of the law that applies to white collar crime in the broadest sense.

The executive branch also has the power to administer penal sanctions, and chief executives on both the federal and the state levels have the power to pardon. Here again, these powers are especially significant for white collar offenders, who have traditionally benefited from correctional classification procedures that most often direct them to minimum-security facilities. White collar offenders have had great advantages in the parole process because they are more likely than conventional offenders to have a social background and demeanor that enables them to make a favorable impression on parole board members. Because of these factors, an executive branch agency, the parole board, often effectively compromises or diminishes the legal sanctions called for by the legislative branch and imposed by the judicial branch. The pardoning power of the chief executive, which might also be said to undercut the legal agenda of the other branches, is also likely to favor the wealthy and influential. The single most notorious use of the pardoning power in recent U.S. history was surely Gerald Ford's pardon of Richard Nixon, during a period when criminal charges relating to the Watergate matter were still under consideration.

In sum, even if the executive branch does not make white collar crime law in the same direct way that the legislative and judicial branches do, in a very real sense the executive branch profoundly influences the form, content, and actual effects of such law. The administrative and regulatory agencies that are formally regarded as a part of the executive branch have sufficient autonomy to be alternatively regarded as "a fourth branch." Their role in white collar crime lawmaking is formidable and is examined in the following section.

## Administrative Law

The regulatory agencies that produce state and federal administrative law are among the less conspicuous sources of law in our legal system. This type of law is of special importance in any discussion of white collar crime insofar as many of the activities commonly classified under that heading are violations of administrative rather than statutory law. There is, however, some dissensus over whether administrative law is really law in the conventional sense, or whether it is more appropriately viewed as a body of rules produced by a special type of governmental entity (Luneburg 1990).

The delegation of broad, policy-making powers to administrative agencies is one of the basic characteristics of contemporary U.S. government (Bryner 1987). As the scope and complexity of matters regulated by the government has expanded, Congress has tended to pass acts that provide only a framework for responding to some problem, and then the appropriate regulatory agency has been authorized to create the detailed, relevant rules (West Publishing 1983: 85). Administrative agency rule making is generally less visible than lawmaking of the official branches of government and is accordingly somewhat vulnerable to abuse. In some cases agencies act with a good deal of autonomy and may formulate rules either on the basis of perceived need or to advance internal agency careers and objectives. On the other hand, administrative agencies may also be very much under the influence of powerful executive or legislative branch officials or corporate interests with whom agency administrators have personal and professional ties.

Agencies produce rules of several different forms, including procedural rules which guide agency organization and operations; interpretative rules, which embody the agency's interpretation of regulatory statutes; and legislative rules, which are specific substantive statutes that the agency has been authorized to enact (West Publishing 1983: 85). Agencies have enjoyed considerable discretion in this rule-making process, although overruling by the courts, new legislative action, or executive branch initatives pose potential constraints.

The history of American administrative law, or rule making, dates from the very first years of the Republic. In 1790 Congress delegated to the president certain legislative powers, such as prescribing rules and regulations to govern trade with Native Americans. In 1813 these powers were extended to other executive branch officials, such as the treasury secretary (Bryner 1987: 10–11). For most of the 19th century and into the first two decades of the 20th century, the use of this power was quite limited. Although administrative law has been challenged periodically by some of its targets and some legal authorities, the Supreme Court has upheld its basic constitutionality.

The peculiar character of administrative agencies in a system of checks and balances has been one source of concern with administrative law. These agencies may be created by and act like the legislative branch, operate as part of the executive branch, and function (at times) like the judicial branch, as in this example:

> [T]he Securities and Exchange Commission is a regulatory agency that formulates laws like a legislature....The commission enforces its rules the way the executive branch of government does—by prosecuting violators.... The commission acts as judge and jury when it conducts adjudicatory hearings to determine violations or prescribe punishments. (West Publishing 1983: 78).

The "New Deal" era of the 1930s produced a great upsurge of regulatory activity and some expansion of administrative law. During this period, concern over improper use of discretionary powers by regulatory agencies led to a number of legislative efforts to impose some constraints on these powers. The 1946 Administrative Procedure Act, the culmination of these efforts, stipulated that regulatory agencies are independent entities in the executive branch, granted aggrieved parties the right to seek judicial review, and distinguished between rule making and adjudication (Bryner 1987: 20–22).

The overriding purpose of the Administrative Procedure Act was to ensure that regulatory agencies would act fairly, with appropriate attention to due process, but it also imposed some limits on judicial powers to rule on or overturn agency actions (West Publishing 1983: 83). The specific parameters of administrative rules and decision-making processes have been an ongoing source of controversy. On the one hand it has been recognized that the regulatory agencies will confront a bewildering variety of situations, not all of which can be clearly anticipated by appropriate laws; in this sense it is regarded as desirable that these agencies are authorized to act with a good measure of bureaucratic discretion. On the other hand, there has also been a historical concern that such agencies will accrue excessive and inappropriate powers that they will use abusively. According to Bryner (1987), even though the regulatory agencies are currently saddled with an ambitious agenda, they have been provided with neither very much guidance nor adequate resources for fully discharging this agenda.

Administrative courts have become an attractive alternative to the traditional courts for the prosecution of some forms of white collar crime. The burden of proof is more modest, no jury is involved, and administrative court judges are especially equipped to settle cases more efficiently; furthermore, the clout of administrative law penalties (including fines of some $1 million a day) has become more formidable. A great deal of regulatory activity never leads to any formal adjudicatory process. Even though the judicial branch has traditionally been reluctant to overrule regulatory agencies, it still represents one ultimate entity for overseeing regulatory agency rule making.

## A Selective Review of Substantive White Collar Crime Lawmaking

IN THE PREVIOUS sections we have reviewed many general principles of white collar crime lawmaking. In this section we consider the specific development of white collar crime law of three significant types: antitrust, occupational health and safety, and environmental damage. We will also examine the controversial application of the RICO (Racketeer-Influenced and Corrupt Organizations) law to white collar crime cases.

### Antitrust Law

In his celebrated *The Wealth of Nations* (1776), Adam Smith articulated the philosophical premises for a capitalist, free-market economy. Smith argued that the entire community benefits when individual entrepreneurs are competing freely with each other because they are motivated to produce the highest-quality goods at the lowest possible price in the interest of enticing consumers to buy their products. In the United States at the end of the 19th century, more than 100 years after the publication of Smith's book, capitalism was booming on a scale probably unimagined by Smith, who lived in a predominantly agricultural society in which craftsmen, not industrial factories, produced most consumer dry goods. One of the ways in which the evolving industrial capitalism distorted Smith's vision was through the growth of immensely rich and powerful corporations that acquired monopolies (or near monopolies) in oil, steel, railroads, and other markets.

In the years following the Civil War the emergence of *trusts* was especially disturbing. Trusts, which were legal entities or holding companies for corporations engaged in the same type of business, were able to fix prices, control production, and organize geographical monopolies for an entire industry (Bohlman, Dundas, and Jentz 1989). The Standard Oil Company, presided over by John D. Rockefeller, was perhaps the most famous and wealthiest of these trusts. It drove small competitors out of business by undercutting their prices, and once its competition was eliminated it could raise prices and rates at will.

Considerable popular sentiment against the big trusts—especially on the part of farmers (who paid exorbitant rates to railroads to transport their goods), small businessmen, and consumers, all of whom suffered from this enormous concentration of economic power—developed during this period (Coleman 1985b). During the years following the Civil War the country suffered through stock market crashes and periods of economic depression blamed at least in part on the maneuvers of the trusts and some members of the economic elite. The national reach of monopolistic corporations and trusts was increasing in an era of rapidly expanded contacts among states. It was in this political and economic environment that the call for national antitrust laws increased greatly.

Antitrust law, broadly defined as law that regulates economic competition, was not an invention of the 19th century. Evidence of efforts by kings to prohibit monopolistic practices in the markets can be found as far back as the 12th century in the Anglo-American common law tradition. From the 15th century through the 18th century, a number of British cases firmly established several fundamental principles of antitrust law: that state-granted monopoly is bad, that cartels harm the public good, that free entry into the markets is good, and that reasonable restraints on marketing practices are desirable and permissible (E. Fox 1990).

In the new American Republic the individual states attempted to prohibit monopolistic practices; these prohibitions were sometimes incorporated into state constitutions, but the increasingly national character of the economy in the 19th century limited the effectiveness of such laws. In a message to Congress in 1888, President Grover Cleveland "warned that trusts, combinations and monopolies were becoming 'the people's master'"(Van Cise 1990). Two years later, in 1890, Congress passed the Sherman Act (named for the senator who introduced it; in Canada, a similar Combines Investigation Act had been passed in 1889). This act, rooted in perceived common law principles that prohibited efforts to "prevent full and free competition," also prohibited combinations that tended to raise the cost to the consumer and actions causing a "restraint in trade" that could lead to monopolies (Van Cise 1990: 986–87). The Sherman Act gave private parties the right to sue for treble damages for violations of the act and gave the state in which such violations occurred the power to criminally prosecute and to seek injunctions (First 1990: 2). Although the initial penalties were a maximum of one year in prison and fines of up to $5,000 per offense for individual offenders only, these penalties were increased in 1974 to a maximum three-year prison sentence (a felony conviction) and fines of $100,000 for individuals and $1 million for corporations.

From the start people have debated the nature of the underlying motivation behind the Sherman Act: whether it was a genuine desire to create an authentic free-market economy for the benefit of consumers and "ordinary people," or whether it was intended to provide a merely symbolic (and somewhat cynical) response to popular hostility toward the trusts but not to threaten the basic structure of a capitalist system that favored major corporations (Coleman 1985b; Peritz 1990). Antitrust law has not been antagonistic to capitalism per se, but rather to grossly abusive practices within the capitalistic system, and it has been tolerant of oligopolies (domination of markets by a small number of major corporations) while opposing outright monopolies (Mensch and Freeman 1990). The rather imprecise language of the Sherman Act has allowed for quite different interpretations of its purpose, ranging from promoting greater economic efficiency to eliminating transfers of wealth from consumers to monopolists (Kauper 1990). The most reasonable interpretation would hold that the Sherman Act reflected a complex mixture of interests and objectives.

In the century following adoption of the Sherman Act a number of new laws—for example, the Clayton Act (1914), the Robinson-Patman Act (1936), and the Celler-Kefauver Act (1950)—were passed to address various perceived limitations of the original antitrust law. The early criminal prosecutions of corporations for violations of the Sherman Act were rather few and far between and rarely successful (Whalley 1990); powerful, wealthy corporations were able to neutralize or challenge various provisions of the Sherman Act and other antitrust laws. Throughout their history the enforcement of these laws has been very uneven and significantly dependent on both the political philosophy of the administration in power and prevailing economic circumstances (Coleman 1985b; Ellis and Wyatt 1992; Gellhorn et al. 1990; Kauper 1990; Jamieson 1994; Peritz 1990; Whalley 1990). In some periods the primary mission of antitrust prosecutions has been to protect consumers; in other periods it has been to protect individuals and business enterprises from arbitrary and unfair economic power used against them. In more recent times, private (or civil) antitrust suits have become much more common.

## Occupational Safety and Health Laws

A great deal of evidence suggests that each year workers by the thousands die prematurely from occupationally related accidents and illnesses, and that workers by the millions are seriously injured or become ill due to occupationally related conditions. At least a significant percentage of these deaths, injuries, and illnesses can be attributed to willful practices of employers, but employers have rarely been held accountable.

Even though protective legislation concerning working conditions (e.g., the length of the working day for children) was first introduced in Great Britain in the early 19th century, very little substantial legal protection for workers existed before 1970. Szasz (1984) largely attributed this absence of laws to industry's mobilization against such legislation, its ability to control access to much of the information necessary for the development of any such laws, and its considerable success in blaming the workers for workplace injuries and illnesses. For much of the 20th century corporate management was able to deflect passage of occupational safety and health laws by creating a network of organizations (such as the National Council for Compensation Insurance) that it claimed addressed the problems arising from such injuries and illnesses (Szasz 1984: 104).

This all began to change in the late 1960s. The relatively healthy economy of the times freed workers to focus on noneconomic issues; a rising work-related injury rate began to receive some attention; and new research was beginning to clearly document the relationship between work-related conditions (e.g., exposure to asbestos) and disease (Szasz 1984: 104–105). Donnelly (1982) claimed that the agitation of rank-and-file workers over the neglect of worker health and safety by employers and labor leaders alike was the decisive factor leading to the Occupational Safety and Health Act of 1970. Labor support was especially important to the two major political parties during this period, and it was therefore politically expedient to support this legislation.

In one interpretation, the legislation was more of a symbolic gesture toward labor than a serious effort to protect workers (Calavita 1983). The affected industries initially attempted to derail implementation of the Act, then adopted defensive strategies to limit the reach of the OSHA agency, and finally launched an aggressive deregulatory campaign against OSHA and similar agencies (Szasz 1984: 106–107).

By the time Ronald Reagan was elected president in 1980, the political and economic climate had changed considerably, and a movement toward deregulation took place. Although the OSHA legislation wasn't repealed, its implementation was much more limited (Calavita 1983). This brief history of one form of corporate crime law demonstrates that such law is responsive to rapidly shifting circumstances and political forces.

## Environmental Protection Laws

The development of laws directed at environmental crimes, and the constraints imposed on such laws, have followed a similar pattern. Harmful environmental practices were for the most part outside the criminal law. The first law to criminalize the dumping of wastes into navigable waters, the Refuse Act of 1899, was passed to protect business interests by ensuring their unobstructed use of waterways. Before the 1960s environmental protection laws were largely responsive to economic interests; they were not inspired by a desire to criminalize pollution practices harmful to citizens generally.

By the late 1960s a set of circumstances favorable to such criminalization had developed (Yeager 1991a). A politically active middle class became increasingly concerned with environmental damage. A series of dramatic environmental disasters, such as oil spills, were featured in the media. New scientific tools had been developed to detect industrial pollution. Finally, organized lobbying could now be directed at the greater concentration of power at the federal level. In one interpretation, an emerging environmentalist movement reflected a shift from industrial to postindustrial values, which emphasize quality of life and environmental protection over accumulation of material wealth and natural-resource exploitation (Hedman 1991).

The Environmental Protection Agency (EPA) was established by executive order in 1970, and throughout the 1970s a series of environmental protection laws were passed, although criminal prosecutions of environmental offenders did not ensue until late in the 1970s, during the Carter administration (Hedman 1991). In 1981 both the EPA and the Justice Department established special criminal enforcement units for environmental crime, and during the 1980s Congress reclassified some environmental crimes from misdemeanors to felonies (Cohen 1992: 1056). Today virtually all environmental statutes include criminal provisions, although they differ on the degree of liability; thus violations of the Clean Air Act, which simply require that the violation was "knowing," are more easily criminally prosecuted than are violations of the Clean Water Act, for which demonstration of willful negligence is required (Cohen 1992: 1067).

In the 1980s criminal prosecutions of environmental offenders rose quite dramatically, despite the conservative Reagan administration's overall aversion to intervening in the conduct of private enterprise. Initially, the Reagan administration attempted to curtail the enforcement of environmental crime laws, but this effort backfired in 1983 with the widely publicized scandal of lax and corrupt EPA practices and the resignation or jailing of top agency officials. The subsequent, somewhat more vigorous response of the Reagan and Bush administrations to environmental crime can be viewed both as a reaction to this scandal and recognition that Americans were becoming increasingly concerned about environmental destruction. A 1990 survey, for example, found that over 70 percent of Americans favored jail terms for deliberate violations of pollution laws (Hedman 1991: 889). Most of the enforcement effort, however, was directed at smaller, less powerful corporations; some 70 percent of those indicted were higher-level executives of such corporations (Cohen 1992: 1074; Adler and Lord 1991).

Despite the increase in criminal prosecutions, in the early 1990s critics could claim that compliance with environmental laws continued to be poor, and that far more vigorous implementation of these laws was needed (Adler and Lord 1991; Hedman 1991; Starr 1991). The sentencing guidelines implemented in the late 1980s called for increased penalties, including longer prison sentences, for environmental offenders, but pickpockets and muggers still faced harsher sentences than did individuals who illegally dumped hundreds of gallons of hazardous waste into the environment (Cohen 1992: 1057; Adler and Lord 1991: 803).

Many constraints have limited full implementation of the environmental laws enacted since the early 1980s, including inadequate budgets, court challenges, interagency jurisdictional conflicts, executive cost-benefit reviews, and "neutral" administrative procedures that are vulnerable to manipulation by corporate interests (Yeager 1991b; Adler and Lord 1991; Starr 1991). Regulatory agencies have often been unwilling or unable, for better or worse, to implement environmental crime laws fully, and judges have been reluctant to impose on environmental offenders the criminal penalties permitted by the law (Adler and Lord 1991; Cohen 1992). On a practical level such offenders have the resources to challenge unfavorable judgments; ideologically, there are concerns about imposing on corporate entities criminal sanctions for actions that may not have been intended, especially on the basis of indirect (vicarious) liability, and environmental harm is not always as easily identifiable and measurable as the harm caused by conventional crime.

A similar pattern of adopting environmental laws that then encountered many constraints occurred in other developed nations such as Australia and Canada (Franklin 1990; Reasons 1991). If anything, these countries have lagged behind the United States; development of environmental law in one Australian state was described as "piecemeal, uneven and reactive to specific episodes" (Franklin 1990: 81). Recognition of the need for new international environmental laws is growing, although it was far from clear in the 1990s that the political will needed to overcome the formidable challenges to such an endeavor was in place (Palmer 1992). Above all, there is and always will be a tension between the objective of providing a safe, clean environment and the economic concerns about the costs (in terms of jobs, prices, and the like) of tough environmental law enforcement.

## The RICO Law

In 1970, as part of the Organized Crime Control Act, Congress enacted a special section on Racketeer-Influenced and Corrupt Organizations (RICO) to provide prosecutors with a more effective weapon for combating organized crime (Poulin 1990). The RICO law prohibits acquisition, operation, or income from an "enterprise" (any individual, associated group, or corporation) through a "pattern" (two or more offenses within a 10-year period) of "racketeering activity" (common-law crimes, including those prohibited by any state, that are punishable by a year or more in prison)(Albanese 1991: 213; Rhodes 1984: 217).

RICO is indisputably a powerful prosecutorial tool because it broadens federal criminal jurisdiction to include violations of state law; allows for important exceptions to the statute of limitations; permits the introduction of a broad range of evidence to demonstrate "criminal association," even if this evidence would normally be excluded from consideration; and provides for substantial forfeiture of property and freezing of assets, including attorney's fees (Poulin 1990). More specifically, individuals convicted under the RICO law face up to 20 years in prison, fines of up to $25,000, forfeiture of any interest in the enterprise involved, and treble civil damages and dissolution of the enterprise itself (Albanese 1991).

RICO was used quite substantially and with considerable (if not uniform) success against organized and syndicated crime figures in the 1970s and 1980s. Unfortunately, those convicted under this law were frequently elderly syndicated crime leaders whose imprisonment led to violent confrontations between would-be successors. Critics have argued that the tough provisions of RICO have inspired an even higher level of crime sydicate infiltration of relatively safe legitimate business, and that in the long run the public may well be even more fully victimized by more sophisticated, larger-scale scams (Albanese 1991).

Other concerns about RICO are especially relevant to white collar crime. First, since its implementation, either the criminal or the civil provisions of RICO have been used most frequently against individuals and groups who do not fit the conventional image of organized criminals, including aggressive unions, anti-abortion protesters, and marijuana growers (Poulin 1990; Brickey 1990). The single most common targets of RICO prosecutions and lawsuits have been white collar offenders involved in some form of commercial or financial fraud or dispute, tax evasion, embezzlement, or bribery (Poulin 1990; Rhodes 1984). Second, the federal courts, including the U.S. Supreme Court, have essentially upheld such broad applications of RICO on the grounds that the statute is couched in language that does not prohibit such applications, and that it is up to Congress to change the law if it believes it is being misapplied (Mansnerus 1989; Mannino 1990). Nevertheless, Chief Justice William Rehnquist has complained bitterly about the burden of dealing with a flood of RICO cases, labeling RICO as "very possibly the single worst piece of legislation on the book" (Poulin 1990: 859; 864).

The "business community" in particular has expressed outrage at being frequent targets of RICO. A New York businessman who underpaid state sales taxes on retail gasoline sales was convicted under RICO, made to forfeit close to $5 million, was liable for a federal fine up to twice that amount, and received a two-year sentence (Poulin 1990). Princeton/Newport Partners, an investment partnership, was indicted on creating false long-term capital gains, with a $13-million tax write-off on false losses, and was forced to liquidate in the face of severe RICO penalties and forfeitures (Labaton 1989c). (The judge in the case imposed brief sentences of three to six months and scaled down a jury forfeiture award from $3.8 million to $1.5 million.) Michael Milken, the insider trader and "Junk Bond King," was charged under RICO and was facing close to $2 billion in fines and forfeitures before he agreed to settle his case (Brickey 1990).

Critics of RICO, especially as applied to white collar offenders, contend that its broad and sweeping language grants the state too much discretionary leeway; that it was never intended that businesspeople would be prosecuted as "racketeers"; that the forfeiture provisions are draconian and punitive and out of proportion to the offenses; that the civil RICO suits are quasi-criminal sanctions that don't adequately differentiate between conduct requiring compensation and conduct requiring condemnation; that defense attorneys are put at a great disadvantage because they can easily be overwhelmed by the government's documentation and cannot effectively advise their clients on outcomes; and that businesspeople may be frightened into making deals to settle their case before trial and may have to liquidate or lose their businesses, with innocent consumers and customers bearing the costs (Rhodes 1984; Tarlow 1988; Brickey 1990; Lynch 1990).

In the early 1990s, business interests and other critics of RICO put pressure on Congress to amend the law to sharply limit its application to white collar crime cases (Labaton 1991). This proposed legislation, which would have protected many of the lawyers, accountants, and investment bankers who played roles in the S & L frauds, never passed in the full House (Holmes 1990). G. Robert Blakey, one of the drafters of the RICO law, suggested that objections to it came from "people who don't like to be held responsible for what they do" (Mansnerus 1989). The ongoing controversy over the RICO law, then, usefully compels us to focus on the relationship between white collar crime and organized crime, and the differences—if any— between "banksters" and "mobsters."

## White Collar Crime Law and the Legal Curriculum

The development of much of white collar crime law is relatively recent, and white collar crime has been an especially dynamic area of law since the 1970s. The latest legal developments pertaining to substantive white collar crimes, and relevant procedural issues as well, are reviewed annually in *American Criminal Law Review*. Attention to white collar crime law has not traditionally been a specific focus of law school curricula and attendant casebooks, although this is beginning to change with the appearance of such books as Harry First's *Business Crime: Cases and Materials* (1990) and Kathleen F. Brickey's *Corporate and White Collar Crime—Cases and Materials* (1990). Of course, selected white collar crime issues have been examined in standard law courses (and accompanying casebooks) concerning such broader matters as corporate law, securities regulations, taxation, and the like. The full-fledged integration of white collar crime law into the legal education curriculum is still in its infancy.

## Civil and Criminal Law and White Collar Crime

THE CIVIL LAW HAS played a much larger role in responding to white collar "crime" than to conventional crime. In principle, civil law cor..erns itself with private, individual harms and objective responsibility, whereas criminal law focuses on public, social harms and morally culpable conduct (Hall 1943). Still, the line of demarcation between the private and the public is often quite blurred, especially when it concerns the harms caused by corporations, businesses, and professionals.

The distinction between a civil law and a criminal law emerged quite clearly in 14th- and 15th-century England; it was very well established by the middle of the 18th century, when the English jurist William Blackstone produced his celebrated commentary on the common law (Mann 1992b: 1803). Subsequent students of law have been somewhat divided between those who emphasize and those who minimize the differences between these branches of the law.

Columbia University law professor John Coffee, Jr. (1992: 1878), who observed that criminal laws are legislative acts whereas the civil law is largely created by judges, identified several other differences between criminal and civil law: (1) The role of intent is greater in criminal law; (2) the criminal law focuses on the creation of risk rather than on actual harm; (3) the criminal law insists on greater evidentiary certainty and is less tolerant of procedural informality; (4) the criminal law relies on public enforcement (although this is tempered by prosecutoiial discretion); and (5) the criminal law involves the deliberate imposition of punishment and the maximization of stigma and censure. Criminal sanctions are intended to express society's outrage over harmful behavior by both punishing morally blameworthy parties and deterring such conduct among others (Spurgeon and Fagan 1981); civil actions focus mainly on compensating an injured party for some measurable harm suffered. Conversely, it is possible to emphasize the similarities between the criminal law and the civil law, or between crimes and torts. Blum-West and Carter (1983) argued that there is an enormous overlap between criminal and civil law in terms of rules of liability, moral judgments, and types of behavior involved.

The distinction between criminal and civil offenses, then, is more a matter of differences in procedural response than of the behavior involved. Furthermore, government prosecutors and administrative agencies initiate civil actions against white collar offenders. Strictly speaking, criminal prosecution is exclusively the prerogative of the government, but in some circumstances (e.g., as provided by the RICO statute) private parties can "prosecute" civilly criminal wrongs and seek severe punitive sanctions (Mann 1992b: 1812). In the view that deemphasizes the differences between civil and criminal law, both types of law require intent and have somewhat parallel rules for establishing culpability (although ordinary negligence is sufficient in tort cases, whereas most state laws require more for establishing criminal liability). Even if moral condemnation is generally greater for crimes than for torts, it is not uniformly so. Contrary to conventional rhetoric, tort sanctions are also often punitive. The public/private interest distinction is artificial because both types of interest are typically involved in criminal and civil tort cases. Blum-West and Carter (1983) accordingly argued that we should not confuse the study of harmful behavior with the study of processes whereby some troublesome behaviors are classified as crime and others as tort.

Even though it is quite widely recognized today that the lines of demarcation between the civil and the criminal law in their responses to white collar offenses have greatly eroded, ongoing debate centers on whether the civil law is encroaching more on criminal law concerns, or whether the criminal law is encroaching on civil and regulatory areas (Coffee 1992: 1875). Those who view the matter of white collar crime primarily in moralistic terms are likely to favor a criminal law approach, which emphasizes the wrongfulness of white collar offenses and their equivalence with conventional crime. Others view the white collar crime issue more pragmatically, with an emphasis on effectively limiting the harmful consequences of such activity, and they are likely to be more favorably disposed toward the civil law approach. Although criminal law has always quite clearly been an instrument of social control, civil law has not been viewed this way traditionally; rather, it has been characterized as a means for compensating injured private parties in an orderly fashion (Mann 1992b). As a practical matter, however, the civil law increasingly fulfills many of the same social control functions as the criminal law, especially when white collar crime is involved.

Because a good deal of publicity about the criminalization of certain corporate practices has appeared since 1970, it may be widely assumed that a general change in emphasis from civil to criminal liability has occurred, at least for corporate crime. This has not been uniformly so, however. Nancy Frank (1983) established that whereas in the latter half of the 19th century criminal statutes were enacted to deal with some of the health and safety problems associated with industrialization, in the 20th century civil penalties were substituted for criminal penalties. Frank observed that this development can be explained in different ways. From a conflict perspective it can be attributed to the power of corporate interests, who are motivated to limit their liability (especially strict liability) for various practices. An alternative explanation attributes this shift to a rational perception that if effective health and safety laws required strict liability, such liability can be more easily reconciled with the tenets of civil law than with those of criminal law. Frank (1983) conceded, however, that it does not follow from such a rationale that the shift to civil liability in fact leads to more efficient enforcement of the health and safety laws.

## Law, Corporations, and the Concept of Criminal Liability

ONE OF THE central issues for a system of criminal law is the imputation of criminal liability or responsibility. Historically, the notion of criminal liability has been principally associated with "natural persons," although originally it seems to have referred to groups rather than individuals and implied an external relationship between the offense and the responsible party rather than a state of mind (Lilly and Ball 1982).

The notion of an individual capable of forming criminal intent, or *mens rea*, developed as a key element in the legal conception of crime; moral responsibility was imputed to the individual. In the modern, Anglo-American tradition, the "natural person" is assumed to be capable of making voluntary choices for which he or she must be held responsible, unless some relevant "excusing condition" (e.g., youth or insanity) is present. A vast wealth of social science and behavioral research over the past hundred years or so has identified the many ways in which human behavior is powerfully influenced—and some would argue is absolutely determined—by factors ranging from genetic inheritance to early childhood experiences to situational peer pressures. (Some of the implications of this research are explored in Chapter 8.)

Individual white collar crime offenders are generally assumed to have willfully and voluntarily engaged in illegal behavior, although they may be better positioned than conventional offenders to invoke excusing conditions. It is perhaps a paradox that disadvantaged members of society, who have limited opportunities and experience many harmful pressures, have more often suffered from the consequences of imputation of criminal liability than have privileged members of society, who have a much wider range of choices. In assessing the level of culpability of individual white collar offenders, some judges and jurors may hold them to a higher standard than conventional offenders, whereas others may empathize more readily with pressures that may have encouraged the criminal conduct. Even though in the final analysis we have no wholly reliable way of establishing to what extent, if any, individual offenders freely choose to break the law, our legal system probably could not function effectively without imputing a basic level of responsibility to criminal offenders.

## Corporate Criminal Liability

The question of whether corporations, as opposed to the individual personnel of corporations, should be held responsible for illegal acts has been a contentious issue in our legal history. Even the appropriate legal meaning of a corporation has been a matter of long-standing, ongoing debate. Alternative views center on whether a corporation is an entity with an existence separate from shareholders and other participants, or simply an aggregation of natural individuals; whether it is an artificial creation of state law or a natural product of private initiative; and whether its activities on the one hand have broad social and political ramifications that justify a substantial body of corporate law, or on the other hand primarily involve private relations between shareholders and managers, with these relations being the proper focus of the law (Millon 1990: 201). The adoption during different historical periods of one or the other of these views has naturally influenced both the form of corporate responsibility for harmful activity and the state's response to such activity.

Corporate criminal liability is largely a 20th-century phenomenon. Under the common-law tradition a corporation could not face criminal charges; until the 15th century, in fact, the law recognized only "natural persons" (Coleman 1982). In the Anglo-American tradition a recognition of "juristic persons" has only gradually emerged since the 11th century, with the breakdown of the hierarchical structure of feudal societies. Churches came to be recognized as entities independent of landowners who built them, towns began to assume distinctive rights and responsibilities, and the notion of "the Crown" was differentiated from the personhood of the monarch (Coleman 1982). The legal construct of a "trust" as a means of holding and passing on land separate from all the restrictions of traditional laws of inheritance and taxation also emerged during the medieval period. New corporations were formed to supervise the exploration and settlement of the colonies. In America, corporations grew rapidly with the establishment of the new republic because states were eager to attract them and shaped their laws in ways that facilitated their charters.

Although legal historians disagree somewhat on this matter, it appears that corporations were held civilly liable, at least up to a point, for the harm they caused since fairly early in their development; the notion of corporate criminal liability developed much more slowly (Belbot 1993; Bernard 1984). One of the seminal roots of corporate civil and criminal liability was the ancient common-law doctrine that masters had legal responsibility for the wrongful acts of their servants (Bernard 1984: 5). Even though there was some early support for the notion that government entities that failed to fulfill mandated duties (e.g., maintaining roads) could be held criminally responsible for such neglect, this notion was not originally applied to private corporations (First 1990: 180).

Through at least the middle of the 18th century, English legal authorities held that private corporations could not form criminal intent and could not be indicted or held directly responsible for crimes, although their members could be (Coffee 1983; Pitt and Groskaufmanis 1990). The doctrine of *ultra vires* held that corporate powers are limited to what is authorized by the corporate charter, and thus the corporation could not be held responsible for executive actions not so authorized (Millon 1990: 209). Accordingly, for much of history, a corporation could avoid liability by denying that harmful acts could be blamed on it because its corporate charter did not authorize them. Conversely, managers of corporations came to recognize that it was in their interest that the corporations—not themselves—assume liability for any harm done (Stone 1975). During the 19th century it became increasingly apparent that the law must more clearly impute liability for the growing range of harms emanating out of corporate growth.

The doctrine of holding corporations criminally responsible did not develop in civil law countries. Among other factors, in the civil law countries the corporation was seen as an aggregate of individuals, precluding the notion of a juristic person; the tradition of judicial interpretation in common law countries, which played a central role in the extension of criminal law liability to corporations, did not exist in civil law countries (Bernard 1984; Lederman 1985). In a parallel vein, Braithwaite and Fisse (1985: 325) noted the paradoxical fact that even though Japan has a collectivist culture, Japanese law emphasizes individual responsibility for organizational crimes, whereas the United States, with an individualistic culture, has law that allows for corporate responsibility for such crime.

In Great Britain and the United States alike, railroads were held criminally responsible for harmful actions in the 19th century, but the notion of corporate criminal intent was not clearly recognized by the U.S. Supreme Court until *New York Central and Hudson River Railroad Co. v. U.S.* (1909), in which the railroad had violated the 1903 Elkins Act prohibiting the granting of rebates in interstate commerce (Coffee 1983; Bernard 1984). The Elkins Act, which amended previous prohibitions on railway rebates, was widely supported by the railroads because it could benefit all of them by deterring selective rate cutting for big shippers (First 1990: 179). One of the provisions of the Elkins Act was that rail executives would not be liable to jail sentences, as it was thought that such liability would inhibit them from testifying against each other. But the New York Central decision paved the way for applying legislative statutes directed at "persons" to corporations as well, so that by 1917, in *State v. Lehigh Valley Railroad Co.,* the Court accepted the long-resisted notion that a corporation could be held directly liable for a criminal charge of manslaughter (Coffee 1983; Parisi 1984).

The criminal liability of a corporation for the actions of its employees, or "agents," has come to be based on two major theories. The *imputation theory* holds that the corporation is liable for the intent and acts of its employees (generally excluding acts intended to benefit the employee only), on any level in the corporate hierarchy; the *identification theory* holds that liability is direct insofar as corporate actors are acting on behalf of the corporation (Parisi 1984; Bernard 1984; Walt and Laufer 1991). On somewhat parallel grounds, corporations have been held criminally liable for the conduct of their subsidiaries; for example, in 1990 the Exxon Corporation was successfully prosecuted for the conduct of a subsidiary, Exxon Shipping Company (Iraola 1995).

The imputation theory, the older and more widely adopted federal criminal law view, is known more specifically as the *respondeat superior* rule (Lederman 1985). This rule, which had originally developed in civil (tort) law, ascribes corporate criminal responsibility when a corporate agent (1) has committed a crime; (2) is acting within the scope of his authority; and (3) has the intent to benefit the corporation (Coffee 1983). To obtain a conviction, a prosecutor need not necessarily identify the specific individuals responsible for the illegal act and need not demonstrate any actual benefit for the corporation from these acts, although as a practical matter it is more difficult to obtain a conviction in the absence of identifiable human culprits and material corporate benefits (Coffee 1983). One study of jurors' assessments of responsibility (in business tort cases) found that jurors preferred to deal with responsibility in terms of individual (as opposed to organizational) actors, but they also believed that corporations should be held to a higher level of responsibility than individuals (Hans and Lofquist 1992). This study found that a complex of factors, including the content of particular cases, influenced jurors' assessments of responsibility.

The *respondeat superior* doctrine, which is a rather controversial expansion of the notion of vicarious (indirect) responsibility, is essentially a product of case law, not statutory law (Lederman 1985). In the case of *U.S. v. Hilton Hotels Corporation* (1972), the U.S. Court of Appeals established that a corporation can be held liable for employees' actions even when such actions are committed contrary to express corporate instructions. The rationale for this principle is to prevent corporations from immunizing themselves from liability by *official* (as opposed to actual) prohibitions on all illegal actions (First 1990: 202–206; Coffee 1983).

The identification theory was advanced by the Model Penal Code and has been adopted by some state legislatures and courts (Friedlander 1990; Walt and Laufer 1991). If the corporation itself is to be held liable, identification theory requires proof of higher authority, specifically when common-law crimes are involved (First 1990: 208; Walt and Laufer 1991: 267). Under this theory, the practical challenge for prosecutors is to establish that the corporate actors who initiated or carried out the illegal activity were at a high enough level in the corporate hierarchy to be said to be acting for the corporation (Benjamin and Bronstein 1987: 279). The corporation is exonerated if a high-level managerial employee took specific steps ("due diligence") to prevent the commission of the illegal activity (Walt and Laufer 1991: 267). It should be emphasized, however, that different states have adopted different criteria for establishing which offenses and which managerial employees are included in the codes.

Some commentators have adopted a third theory of corporate criminal liability, arguing that criminal intent can be imposed on a corporation when a corporate "personality" or "ethos" advances procedures and practices that either promote or fail to prevent illegal activities (Bucy 1991; Fisse 1991; Foerschler 1990; Friedlander 1990). To date this view has not been adopted by lawmaking bodies and courts.

## Corporate Personhood and Corporate Decision Making

Just as modern law in the Anglo-American tradition has assigned criminal responsibility to the corporation, it has also accorded to corporations most if not all of the constitutional rights guaranteed to "natural persons," although of course many corporations are infinitely more powerful than are human individuals (Nader and Mayer 1988). The concept of "corporation" encompasses both vast entities with statelike power and resources and very modest entities that are effectively the alter ego of an individual or a small group of individuals (Flynn 1987). Some commentators call for stripping all corporations, which are goal-directed entities, of rights enjoyed by "natural persons," perhaps by a constitutional amendment (Benjamin and Bronstein 1987; Nader and Mayer 1988). Corporations have rather hypocritically sought formal recognition as "persons" entitled to constitutional protections while seeking to avoid being criminally sanctioned in the manner of "natural persons" (Barrile 1993b). Corporate status as a "juristic person" has significantly benefited corporations even while it has imputed criminal responsibility to them.

The legal paradigms for the treatment of corporations have tended to be divided between a holistic view (the corporation as analogous to a person) and the atomistic view (the corporation as an aggregate of individuals) (Dan-Cohen 1992). Perhaps the most commonly embraced holistic view of the corporation equates it with the classic "economic man," a rational actor that seeks to maximize profit (Metzger and Schwenk 1990; First 1990). Still, it has been argued that such views are wrong insofar as they fail to capture the complex nature of corporations; an alternative view looks to organizational theory to produce a true picture of the dynamics of corporate decision making (Foerschler 1990). The Economics Nobelist Herbert Simon, for example, has long claimed that the rational-actor model does not remotely describe processes of human decision making in complex situations; in particular, the "risky shift" phenomenon suggests that collective corporate decision making may result in less rational and riskier choices than individual corporate actors would make (Metzger and Schwenk 1990). An organizational process model of corporate decision making emphasizes task specialization and the diffusion of responsibility within an organization, as well as "bounded rationality" (search for "good enough" solutions as opposed to ideal solutions) of corporate policy choices. The bureaucratic politics model of such decision making sees individual decisions as leading to coalitions that produce corporate decisions through a process of negotiation (Foerschler 1990; First 1990). Such nonreductionist views of corporate decision making lend support to the position that corporations institutionalize certain practices that render them liable for their criminal acts in ways that cannot be equated either with individual acts or with the sum total of a large number of individual acts.

Foerschler (1990) proposed the following criteria for determining corporate intent: (1) Did a corporate practice or policy violate the law? (2) Was it reasonably forseeable that the corporate practice or policy would result in a corporate agent's violation of the law? (3) Did the corporation adopt a corporate agent's violation of the law? Whether or not we embrace this model for the assignment of corporate criminal liability, we can agree that the law should adapt itself to the realities of corporate decision making.

## The Corporate Criminal Liability Controversy

An enduring controversy concerns the question of whether the imputation of corporate criminal liability is either sensible or just (see, for example, Lederman 1985; Fisse 1983; Note 1979). Arguments against corporate criminal liability often begin with the traditional position that only individual human actors, and not corporate entities, have consciousness and are thus capable of forming criminal intent and acting on such intent (Lederman 1985; Cressey 1989). In this view, the "vicarious" criminal liability ascribed to corporations is deemed inappropriate for the following reasons: The purposes of the criminal law—including incapacitation, deterrence, and rehabilitation—are directed toward individual human beings; vicarious criminal liability wrongly transforms a tool for perpetuating offenses into a criminal actor; vicarious criminal liability injures innocent parties, such as stockholders; vicarious criminal liability unfairly imposes on corporations burdens of resposibility for employee actions that are not imposed on proprietary businesses; and vicarious corporate criminal liability establishes a dangerous precedent for the pernicious notion of vicarious individual liability (Coffee 1983; Lederman 1985; Cressey 1989). It has also been alleged that corporate criminal liability is inefficient because only individuals, and not organizations, can be deterred, and that more flexible civil remedies can be more easily applied to corporate wrongdoing.

Many arguments on the other side of this issue have been offered in support of corporate criminal liability (in conjunction with the individual criminal liability of corporate employees), whether or not one chooses to impute "personhood" to corporations (Walt and Laufer 1991). Some principled and practical rationales for corporate criminal liability include the following: organizational secrecy; the large number of suspects (which makes it difficult to pinpoint blame); corporate profit motive (as when corporations benefit from crime); expendability of personnel (individuals can be fired and replaced); personnel may operate outside the local court's jurisdiction (only the corporation can be held accountable); definition of offenses refers to corporate status; corporate (not individual) negligence is often responsible; corporate intentionality (actions at issue are outcomes of corporate policy); and surrogate liability (personnel may commit offenses on behalf of their corporations at a time when they are exposed to pressures to make profits or conform to illicit corporate practices)(Fisse 1984). Corporations have strong incentives to shift blame for criminal wrongdoing onto one or more individual corporate personnel, who might be titular organization heads, on-site managers, designated oversight directors, or those directly at fault (Braithwaite and Fisse 1985). Only if the corporation itself is liable will it have powerful enough incentives to establish appropriate preventive, disciplinary, and reward policies to minimize executive and employee involvement in criminal conduct. If the corporation is not criminally liable, executives are encouraged to violate or fail to comply with laws in ways that are beneficial to the corporation.

## Law and the Social Control of White Collar Crime, In Sum

IN THIS CHAPTER we have examined some basic propositions about white collar crime and law. First, our ability to generalize broadly about white collar crime laws is severely limited because such a diversity of offenses are involved. Law itself is typically a product of a complex of forces, and no one-dimensional, simplistic explanation of the basis of specific laws is satisfactory. Lawmaking entities enjoy at least some relative autonomy and are not simply tools of special interests, although they tend to be disproportionately responsive to the concerns of such interests. Laws directed at white collar crime may reflect normative or instrumental objectives, or some combination of the two. Further, tensions often exist between short-term needs (e.g., business prosperity) and long-term needs (e.g., the legitimation of the system). In the realm of white collar crime laws the objectives of the state and the business world may well clash, and conflicts often arise among segments of the business or professional communities. Even if powerful private interests are generally unable to dictate what laws should be made, they do disproportionately influence lawmaking. Because many segments of the business or professional communities benefit from the existence, and sometimes from the enforcement, of white collar crime laws made on many different governmental levels, the symbolic purpose of the law may outweigh its practical, formal purpose.

# Policing and Regulating White Collar Crime

**B**Y ANY MEASURE, the proportion of apparent white collar crimes that are officially investigated and lead to enforcement actions is lower than is the case for conventional crime. In the simplest and most colloquial terms, what occurs in the street is more visible and more easily investigated than what occurs "in the suite," behind closed doors. In this chapter we examine the process of policing white collar crime, beginning with the most public form of such policing (by the criminal justice system) and moving to the least official and visible form (self-policing).

Two important ways in which white collar crime differs from conventional crime are the broad range of agencies involved in policing it and the much larger role of institutions and entities other than the formal agencies of the criminal justice system. Much of the policing of white collar crime cases is handled by public regulatory agencies and various private policing agencies or entities. Self-policing, as well, plays a much larger role in the response to white collar crime than it does in the realm of conventional crime. Furthermore, although potential and actual white collar offenders have some influence over the process of policing these crimes, they do not entirely control it. At least in the public sector, policing and regulatory agencies have some degree of autonomy.

## Criminal Justice System Policing: Law Enforcement

HISTORICALLY, WHITE COLLAR crime has not been a principal concern of law enforcement agencies because for many forms of white collar crime the police have lacked jurisdiction, expertise, and/or resources. Even though police involvement with one type of white collar crime, fraud, was substantial in the 19th century (Levi 1987: 120), police involvement with most forms of white collar crime has traditionally been very limited, or at best uneven, although it has increased in more recent years (Stier 1982; Stotland 1982). In some countries (for example, Israel) the police have much broader jurisdictional powers to investigate a wide range of white collar crimes than is the case in the United States (Stotland 1981). White collar crime investigative units have been established in some U.S. big-city police departments and in some state police agencies (Stotland 1982: 70). The police are quite well-positioned to play a key role in the pursuit of certain categories of white collar crime, including consumer frauds, fraudulent insurance claims, local environmental safety violations, and the like.

Many disincentives limit substantial involvement of conventional police forces in white collar crime cases. The principal training of police personnel is oriented toward conventional crime; police officers are more likely to be attracted to the more dramatic forms of street crime than to white collar crime, which typically lacks adrenalin-producing "excitement." White collar crime cases are especially likely to require a greater investment of time than typical conventional crime cases, with a lower probability of a successful resolution. Because the investigation of such crime calls for forms of competence and expertise (e.g., accounting knowledge) that traditional policing agencies often lack, the chances of failure, and of being perceived as incompetent, are therefore considerably higher. Public pressure—and accordingly, pressure from the political leadership—is less likely to be intense for arrests in white collar crime cases than in predatory violence cases. Indeed, political pressure is more likely to be exerted in blocking or derailing white collar crime investigations than in conventional crime cases, and the police can operate effectively against white collar crime only to the extent that they are relatively free of political influence (Stotland 1981). Finally, media images of the consequences of serial murders and other such crimes are more likely to generate powerful and immediate public outrage and fear than are any images relating to most white collar crime.

## State and Federal Enforcement Agencies

Because of the complex, often interjurisdictional character of much white collar crime, federal agencies have played a much larger role in the investigation of this type of crime than have local police agencies. The role of the state police in the investigation of white collar crime has been relatively limited. State police agencies were established in a number of states in the early 20th century in part to restore order in mining communities and other areas of labor unrest (Johnson 1981; Lynch and Groves 1989: 87). In at least some states they apparently operated with a probusiness bias and may have been accessories to corporate crimes against labor.

During the course of the 20th century many other states established their own police forces, the most familiar division of which is the highway patrol. More recently, state police agencies have provided important support services to local police agencies and have investigated crimes occurring outside local jurisdictions, but typically these crimes have not been white collar crimes.

If local, urban police forces are the principal public policing agency responding to street crime, then federal policing agencies make the most substantial response to white collar crime. Altogether, over two dozen separate federal agencies have investigative jurisdiction over white collar crime, including governmental corruption cases (Pence, 1986); the lines of jurisdiction among these agencies are not sharply drawn. Furthermore, the prosecutorial arm of the federal government often engages in quite a bit of investigative inquiry on its own. The principal federal investigative agencies are the Federal Bureau of Investigation (FBI), the Inspector Generals, the U.S. Postal Inspection Service, the U.S. Secret Service, the U.S. Customs Service, and the Internal Revenue Service Criminal Investigative Division.

The federal investigative agencies are charged with bringing the most serious cases—those in which criminal prosecution is warranted—to the attention of the U.S. Department of Justice or one of the 94 U.S. Attorneys with offices in all 50 states and U.S. territories. Only the Department of Justice or one of the U.S. Attorneys can initiate a federal criminal prosecution (Pence 1986: 2).

The Department of Justice has a Criminal Division with several sections that investigate and supervise the prosecution of white collar crime, most notably the Fraud Section and the Public Integrity Section. Some other sections of the Criminal Division, such as the Organized Crime and Racketeering Section, might become involved in white collar crime cases. In addition to the Criminal Division, several other divisions of the Justice Department pursue white collar crime cases, including the Tax Division, the Land and Natural Resources Division, the Antitrust Division, the Civil Rights Division, and the Civil Division.

Other governmental institutions that play a role in the investigation of some form of white collar crime, especially internal governmental corruption, include the General Accounting Office (GAO), which audits executive branch spending; the Merit Systems Protection Board, which investigates and pursues whistle-blower complaints; and the Independent Prosecutor (or Counsel), who investigates and prosecutes criminal acts of high-level governmental officials (Mollenhoff 1988). The Freedom of Information Act, which was passed in 1966 and amended in 1974, has also played a role in uncovering illict governmental activity insofar as it provides a means of access to many governmental records.

## The FBI

The FBI grew from a small, somewhat corrupt Justice Department division into one of the world's largest, most efficient, and most highly regarded policing agencies during the almost 50-year reign (1924–1972) of J. Edgar Hoover. During this entire period, however, white collar crime (with the exception, perhaps, of bank fraud and embezzlement) was not the focus of much of its attention.

Hoover and his associates, who had the typical biases of conservative, white, middle-class males of their time, were principally concerned with highly visible forms of professional crime, such as bank robbery and kidnapping, and the activities of alleged subversives. Hoover was a master of good public relations, and he preferred to allocate FBI resources to crimes that were relatively easy to investigate and most likely to produce impressive enforcement statistics; thus the investigation of complex white collar crimes, for which the outcome is uncertain, was not a top priority

(Poveda 1990: 93). In the final years of the Hoover regime (1970–1972), white collar crime was not even mentioned in the FBI annual reports, although accounting and fraud cases were included under "other criminal investigations" (Poveda 1990: 93). Even though a good deal of information about corrupt and improper dealings of various politicians and businesspeople came to Hoover's attention, he preferred maintaining confidential files on this information for his own purposes over referring it for prosecution. It is widely believed that no president in the later years of Hoover's reign was prepared either to force him to resign or fire him because he was privy to too much damaging information about themselves or their associates.

Following Hoover's death, it came out that the FBI had engaged in various forms of illegal or improper conduct, including the establishment of COINTELPRO, a counterintelligence agency engaged in disrupting domestic dissident groups; illegal entries and burglaries; internal financial corruption; and political misuse of the FBI (Poveda 1990: 65). Rather ironically, Edwin Sutherland was apparently put on an FBI "no contact" list and had difficulty obtaining copies of the *Uniform Crime Report* after he gave a 1938 speech that was critical of the FBI (Geis and Goff 1992). The Hoover FBI, then, took little initiative on white collar crime and even engaged in some activities that could be classified as a cognate form of white collar crime.

Hoover's death in 1972 coincided with declining confidence in traditional institutions such as government and big business and the emergence of the Watergate Affair, and at least partly in response to these developments Hoover's successors as FBI director claimed that they made white collar crime a higher priority of the agency (Poveda 1990; Webster 1980). But FBI claims of allocating greater resources to white collar crime matters have been questioned and largely attributed to reclassifying some of their activities, and the FBI has continued to emphasize embezzlement and low-level fraud cases (Simon and Swart 1984).

The ABSCAM case, involving an FBI "sting" operation in which seven members of Congress were videotaped accepting bribes from "sheiks," was a widely publicized but controversial (on grounds of entrapment) initiative against corruption (Marx 1991). During the Reagan administration (1981–1989), protecting the government and major financial institutions from fraud took precedence over protecting consumers and taxpayers from the harmful activities of corporations and government agencies (Poveda 1990). By the late 1980s and early 1990s, some 1,600 FBI agents were detailed to investigate various forms of white collar and governmental crime, with the S & L frauds and health-care frauds receiving increasing attention.

Even if FBI attention to white collar crime has undeniably increased in recent years, it is quite clear that the incumbent administration's political ideology significantly shapes the extent and scope of the agency's response to this type of crime. Furthermore, the FBI's expertise in investigating such crime is still evolving.

## The Inspectors General

One response to the growth of attention to crime and corruption by and against governmental agencies was the creation (by congressional act in 1978) of Inspectors General to be attached to a variety of government departments and agencies (e.g.,

Housing and Urban Development, the Veteran's Administration, and, as of 1982, the Defense Department).

The Inspectors General have been granted authority to conduct audits and investigations of departments or agencies to which they are attached (Pence 1986: 6). Even though Inspectors General are granted some autonomy and certain powers and are expected to report to the Attorney General and to Congress any internal wrongdoing that comes to their attention, it is far from clear that they are able to root out internal corruption effectively because they are part of the department they are investigating. A review of actions taken on alleged violations of criminal conflict-of-interest statutes by 10 Inspector General offices in 1985 and 1986 revealed that the U.S. Department of Justice prosecuted only two of the 124 alleged violations (U.S. General Accounting Office 1988).

The Inspector General offices are also empowered to ensure that the programs administered by their department are not abused, and in this responsibility they have been more successful, obtaining a significant percentage of convictions resulting in millions of dollars in fines (U.S. President's Council on Integrity and Efficiency 1988). More specifically, Inspectors General have investigated submission of false records by contractors, bribery, and nepotism (Torres 1985). The Office of Inspector General of the Department of Health and Human Services reported that for fiscal year 1990 it obtained 1,310 convictions, imposed 900 sanctions, and garnered $83.1 million in fines, savings, recoveries, settlements, judgments, and restitutions (Office of Investigations 1991). Many of the cases of health-related fraud investigated by this office are resolved with civil penalties and exclusions of those engaged in fraud from the department's programs for a period of time.

## The U.S. Postal Inspection Service

White collar crime is far more likely to involve the use of the U.S. mail than is true of conventional crimes. The U.S. Postal Inspection Service is generally identified as the oldest federal law enforcement agency. Postal "surveyors" were appointed in the colonial postal system, and the inspection service was developed in the early part of the 19th century. In 1872 Congress enacted a mail fraud statute in response to an epidemic of mail swindles that were beyond the jurisdictional reach of local prosecutors.

Since then, the U.S. Postal Inspection Service, which is charged with maintaining the overall security and integrity of the mail system, has played an important role in investigating white collar crimes that involve some use of the mail (Kahn 1973). Among the more common schemes investigated by the U.S. Postal Inspection Service are insurance and banking frauds; land and advance-fee selling swindles; franchise schemes; work-at-home and fraudulent diploma schemes; charity schemes; promotions of fake health cures, beauty devices, fast-working diets, and sex stimulants; and chain letters, lotteries, and solicitations for the sale of advertising specialty items (U.S. Postal Service 1990). Clearly, many of these schemes are at the margins of occupational and professional crime and are accordingly forms of contrepreneurial white collar crime. Mail fraud charges have sometimes been effective in major white collar crime cases involving securities and banking deposits because mail-related evidence may be especially solid. Although the U.S. Postal Service can neither prosecute frauds nor officially mediate disputes concerning frauds, its investigation alone can deter such schemes, and it can refer cases for criminal prosecution.

## The U.S. Secret Service, the U.S. Customs Service, and the U.S. Marshals Service

Even though the Secret Service and the Customs Service are not generally associated with white collar crime, the Secret Service investigates white collar crimes that involve counterfeiting or forgery of any form of federal currency or warranted financial instrument, and the Customs Service investigates cases involving money laundering, falsified import or export documents, illegal product dumping, and foreign corrupt payments (Pence 1986). The specific roles of these agencies in white collar crime cases have been little studied to date.

The U.S. Marshals Service is assigned to various federal justice agencies and has both law-enforcement and court-related duties (Walker 1983: 44). Some 94 marshals and 2,500 deputies work out of 400 offices in the United States and its territories. One of their duties has been to pursue and capture fugitives from federal justice, which traditionally has meant offenders such as bank robbers. In more recent years, however, U.S. marshals have increasingly engaged in the pursuit of white collar crime fugitives (Copetas 1986). A cadre of marshals has been trained in crucial aspects of high finance (e.g., stocks, commodities, international banking, and the like) because their success in capturing high-profile white collar crime fugitives often depends on their successful penetration of a sophisticated, high-finance environment. In some cases major offenders who have fled abroad have been lured, by a ruse involving the prospect of a lucrative deal, to a meeting with an undercover marshal in a location where they can be captured and returned to U.S. jurisdiction.

## The Internal Revenue Service's Criminal Investigative Division

Tax frauds or misrepresentations involving corporations, businesses, and individuals are investigated by the Internal Revenue Service (IRS), and this is a fairly substantial area of white collar crime. Tax audits and investigations may also precipitate investigations of other types of corporate and occupational crime when they uncover evidence of substantial income that cannot be ascribed to legitimate sources. It is virtually a given that financially oriented white collar crimes of all types, including political corruption, generate income that is not reported on tax returns. Sometimes demonstrating that people have illegally evaded taxes is the easiest way to convict those under investigation for other crimes. In one celebrated case in the 1970s, Vice President Spiro Agnew pleaded nolo contendere to one count of tax evasion in a plea bargain arising out of the investigation of his acceptance of bribes.

Even though the IRS's Criminal Investigation Division is small (only 4,000 agents out of a total of 123,000 IRS employees), its agents are widely regarded as particularly smart and capable (Burnham 1989). The IRS's investigative powers are especially broad, reflecting the high priority Congress has assigned to the efficient collection of taxes, and IRS agents can seize evidence much more easily than can FBI or DEA investigators. Businesspeople may be intimidated into cooperating with a criminal investigation when confronted with the prospect of a tax audit (Burnham 1989: 74). The IRS also claims to have the best white collar crime lab in the country (Hershey 1990b). This forensic crime lab has the capability of reconstructing shredded documents, enhancing voices on tapes, and analyzing altered documents, fingerprints, ink, paper, and polygraphs. It has played a role in exposing illegal trading at the Chicago futures market and fraudulent activity at the Bank of Credit and Commerce International (BCCI), among other recent, major white collar crime cases.

The overwhelming majority of tax cases investigated by the IRS are generally disposed of as civil matters; in 1988, for example, only 2,491 tax fraud convictions were obtained, whereas civil penalties were imposed in 23 million cases (Burnham 1989: 79). By some accounts the IRS pursues too many low-level and politically selected cases and not enough major corporate tax-fraud cases (Burnham 1989). Still, the fear or anticipation of an IRS tax-fraud investigation must be a concern of a wide range of white collar offenders.

## Law Enforcement Agencies and White Collar Crime, In Sum

The policing of white collar crime differs from conventional crime policing in a number of ways. The frontline urban and state police play a proportionally much more limited role; a range of federal agencies and other state agencies play a much larger role. Pontell, Calavita, and Tillman (1994: 393) observed that white collar crime policing is generally more proactive than conventional crime policing and requires "tighter coupling" among the different agencies if cases are to be successfully resolved. The investigation of white collar crime tends to be slower, more cumbersome, and less successful than the investigation of conventional street crime because the crimes are often committed by relatively sophisticated people capable of covering their tracks. Victims of white collar crimes are often much more confused than are victims of conventional crime about where to turn for help, and a much larger group of such victims are not even conscious of having been victimized. Organizational victims of white collar crime often prefer to investigate privately rather than going public to some official policing agency due to all the embarrassing publicity that can follow.

The absence of direct, visible illegal actions in white collar crime cases contributes to the difficulties involved in investigating these actions. Public policing actions directed against white collar offenders serve a useful function for corporations and people occupying legitimate occupations by conveying an impression that the laws are enforced in an even-handed manner. In reality, public policing agencies play a fairly limited role in most white collar crime cases.

## The Regulatory System Response

EDWIN SUTHERLAND AND other early students of white collar crime recognized that the dominant legal response to crimes by businesses was regulatory rather than penal (Thomas 1982: 99). Regulatory enforcement occurs in only a very small percentage of the cases in which it could be applied, and it has far less of the moral opprobrium and stigma associated with the criminal justice system. The lines of demarcation among the criminal, civil, and regulatory justice systems are not always sharp, but the regulatory justice system has a lower profile and is less likely to involve an adversarial confrontation between two parties than are the criminal and civil justice systems.

Regulation has been very broadly defined as "any attempt by the government to control the behavior of citizens, corporations or subgovernments," but there is no real consensus on its meaning. Regulation typically involves the imposition of official standards and rules on some form of productive human activity, and it includes an enforcement mechanism and some type of sanctions (Kerwin 1990). It can involve rate-setting, licensing, and financial disclosure requirements, among other things.

A distinction is often made between *economic regulation,* which addresses market relations (e.g., securities, antitrust matters, interstate commerce) and attempts to ensure stability in this realm, and *social* (or protective) *regulation,* which addresses harmful consequences (e.g., to workers, consumers, and citizens) of productive activities (Yeager 1987: 341; Snider 1987: 38). Although significant interaction occurs between these two forms of regulation, the social form in particular has expanded greatly since the early 1970s. Because social or protective regulation is much less likely than economic regulation to serve business interests and involves an inherent conflict between the regulator and the regulated, it met with far more resistance from business interests (Barnett 1990: 228; Szasz 1984). Social regulation typically arises following a crisis, tragedy, or panic over some industrial condition or practice (Snider 1987). In response to public pressure, the government reluctantly develops regulatory agencies and rules, which the affected industry initially resists and then lobbies to limit in scope. Regulatory laws and enforcement practices are often weak at the outset but may become more potent over time.

There is no single theory or model of regulation. One approach views regulation primarily as a rational means of protecting the public interest (Posner 1984; Snider 1987; Frank and Lombness 1988). A second, economic approach to regulation emphasizes a cost/benefit analysis oriented toward efficiency (although this perspective does not necessarily address the important question of how costs and benefits are defined)(Meidinger 1987: 350). A third approach is essentially political; it views regulation primarily in terms of competing interests and the extension of power. Neo-Marxist versions of a political approach to regulation see it as a mechanism for maintaining elites' power and privileges; in this view regulated agencies are dominated by the industries they are supposed to regulate.

## The Origins and Evolution of Regulation

Some form of marketplace regulation was characteristic of even ancient civilizations. Throughout the feudal period in Europe the market was heavily regulated on behalf of the crown. The American experience with regulation has been one of ongoing tension between calls for more and calls for less regulation of a wide range of activities.

Some enthusiasm for congressional intervention in the marketplace existed in the earliest days of the American republic, with the Commerce clause (Article 1, Section 8) of the Constitution providing a basic point of departure for such regulation. Early regulation largely favored commercial and manufacturing interests, and such agencies as the Army Corps of Engineers and the Patent and Trademark Office were mainly intended to promote and encourage economic growth (Kerwin 1990; Hall 1989: 89). Much of the 19th century, however, was dominated by a "laissez faire" economic philosophy and involved little regulation in the modern sense. The Interstate Commerce Commission (ICC), which was established in 1887 to regulate the railroad industry, was the first federal regulatory agency specifically charged with overseeing potentially harmful corporate activity.

During the latter part of the 19th century, various states attempted to regulate not only the railroads but other business activities as well, including insurance agencies and employment practices for women and children (Hall 1989: 197–98). Between 1890 and 1910, most of the states instituted occupational licensing for various occupations in addition to doctors, lawyers, and schoolteachers, who had already been subjected to licensing laws (Hall 1989: 199). Whereas the U.S. Supreme Court had previously upheld state regulatory legislation (as had state courts), in the final 15 years of the 19th century the Court became more conservative, adopted a liberal interpretation of the rights of corporations, and ruled in ways that severely curtailed state regulation (Hall 1989: 233–35). Increasingly during the 19th century an evolving national economy led to a transfer of the primary regulatory responsibility for larger corporations from the states to the federal government, although state governments have continued to play the major role in the regulation of smaller businesses and individual occupations.

Regulatory and deregulatory cycles have occurred throughout U.S. history. The first major period of federal regulatory expansion in the 20th century occurred during the Progressive era (1900–1914), when populist sentiments against the abuses of big business became sufficiently intense to promote significant government intervention in harmful corporate and occupational activities on behalf of the public interest. In reality, however, much of the regulation developed during this period was supported by, and benefited, the newly regulated big businesses. For example, the implementation of the Pure Food and Drug Act (1906) and the regulation of the meat markets after Upton Sinclair's *The Jungle* (1906) exposed the horrendous conditions in meatpacking plants clearly benefited the larger meat producers by promoting consumer confidence in "government-inspected" meat while smaller meatpacking firms that were unable to absorb the added costs of regulation frequently went out of business.

A second major period of regulatory initiatives occurred during the "New Deal" era of the 1930s, at least in part inspired by the belief that the 1929 stock market crash and the economic depression that followed had resulted from unregulated abuses by financiers and major corporations. In an effort to reestablish confidence in failed banks and in the stock market, the Federal Home Loan Bank Board (FHLBB), the Federal Deposit Insurance Corporation (FDIC), the Security and Exchange Commission (SEC), and the National Labor Relations Board (NLRB) were established during this period. These agencies were granted considerable autonomy, although this has hardly made them immune to either political pressures or lobbying by corporate and business interests.

A third major stage of expanding federal regulation began in the relatively affluent "Great Society" era of the 1960s and early 1970s. The predominantly social regulation of this period was responsive to a growing awareness of and organized protest of harmful corporate activities by consumers, environmentalists, and workers (Szasz 1984). The Consumer Product Safety Commission (CPSC), the Environmental Protection Agency (EPA), the Occupational Safety and Health Administration (OSHA), and the Mining Enforcement and Safety Administration were all established between 1970 and 1973. These agencies operate under more direct control of the executive branch than is true of the "New Deal" agencies, and they tend to be more directly responsive to the political agenda of the incumbent administration.

A reasonably high level of consensus on the desirability of government regulation in many new areas eroded in the second half of the 1970s. During this period a deterioration of the economy (including rising inflation and declines in industrial productivity and U.S. competitiveness abroad) enabled critics of government regulation to advance much more effectively the argument that federal regulation had become oppressive and economically harmful.

In 1980 Ronald Reagan ran for president on a platform that was highly critical of a bloated government, and his election was a major factor in the deregulatory era of the 1980s. During this decade regulation was scaled back or severely constrained in many areas (e.g., consumer protection and antitrust), especially when politically dominated agencies were able to act on a discretionary basis (Schechter 1990). The 1980s is now quite widely viewed as a period during which enormous damage to the environment, the workplace, and financial institutions (e.g., the "thrifts") occurred, at least in good part due to excessive deregulation. Some evidence of a new proregulatory cycle surfaced in the 1990s, although each administration must confront countervailing pressures to stimulate economic growth while imposing regulatory constraints.

## The Contemporary Debate on Regulation

The general tendency in an expanding and increasingly complex society is for regulation to grow (Snider 1987; Kagan 1989). Today an ongoing debate centers on the moral rightness, desirability, and expediency of such regulation, whether there is currently too much or too little regulation, and whether specific regulatory statutes, agencies, policies, and actions are or are not defensible. Opponents of regulation have claimed that it is an infringement on the individual's freedom and economic rights; that at least some of the regulated activity (e.g., insider trading) is essentially victimless; that regulation is economically inefficient; and that alternative processes exist for dealing with harmful activities that are organizationally more effective and more efficient than regulation and incorporate greater accountability and due process (Bardach and Kagan 1982; Machan and Johnson 1983; Dorn and Manne 1987). More specifically, governmental regulation has been accused of stifling innovation, accelerating inflation, increasing unemployment, and decreasing international competitiveness. In February 1995, the Republican-dominated House of Representatives approved legislation requiring regulatory agencies to base their rules and actions primarily on economic calculations, as opposed to health-based factors (Cushman 1995). This legislation, which was opposed by the Clinton administration, called for an elaborate system of risk assessments and the justification of financial costs to industries that result from regulatory activity.

The direct costs of regulation have increased exponentially since the early 1970s, and industries and businesses frequently complain about the excessive paperwork and cost ($100 billion in 1980) involved in compliance (Clinard and Yeager 1980: 100; Machan and Johnson 1983: 5; Smith 1983: 95). Social or protective regulation was especially criticized as unreasonable, contradictory, counterproductive, and administered by self-interested regulatory bureaucracies (Bardach and Kagan 1982; Hahn and Hird 1991; Palmer 1978). Shortly before his appointment to the U.S. Supreme Court, Stephen Breyer (1993) published a book arguing that regulators too often applied their rules narrowly in dealing with one problem, thereby worsening another. He called for the establishment of a superregulatory agency to arbitrate competing claims regarding governmental regulatory resources, with the objective of better prioritizing—and reallocating—such resources.

The accurate measurement of the costs and benefits of regulation is complex. Various parties have incentives to inflate costs or conceal benefits, and there is no single way of interpreting either costs or benefits (Bardach and Kagan 1982: 312; Hahn and Hird 1991; Snider 1987). It is especially difficult to measure some long-term benefits of regulation, particularly in matters of health, safety, and environmental protection.

Furthermore, there is no complete consensus on regulatory purposes and goals. A leftist or progressive critique has argued that the principal objective of regulatory agencies in a capitalist society is to maintain broad popular legitimation of the system while promoting corporate accumulation of profits (F. J. Henry 1991; Snider 1987); this is accomplished by adopting regulation that only symbolizes governmental oversight, because regulatory agency effectiveness is severely limited by inadequate budgets and pro-industry regulatory board members who develop specific rules that favor industry interests.

Proponents of regulation contend that it is absolutely necessary in a complex society in which anticompetitive forces with economically undesirable consequences can develop unless the state intervenes, because individuals and communities have neither the necessary information nor the means to protect themselves from a wide range of directly harmful or threatening corporate and business activities (Tolchin and Tolchin 1983). Furthermore, corporations have an uncommon measure of power in shaping perceptions of risks, because the capability of assessing both risk-related information and realistic options for self-protection are not equally distributed in society. Defenders of regulation argue that factors ranging from bad management to declining markets, not the great expansion of federal regulation in the 1970s, were the principal causes of the economic distress of that period (Tolchin and Tolchin 1983: 4).

In this view, businesses actually benefit from federal regulation because without it they would likely face a much greater number of conflicting state regulations and more civil suits from workers, consumers, and citizens. Even if such regulation cannot be shown to "pay" in terms of short-term market efficiency, other interests, such as protecting workers and the environment, should take precedence. Many polls reveal general public support for regulatory protection, especially in health, safety, and environmental matters (Hahn and Hird 1991: 235; Tolchin and Tolchin 1983: 263). Altogether, the pro-regulatory argument holds that this activity prevents and deters much activity that could be labeled white collar crime, and that in its absence much harm occurs.

## The Creation and Operation of Federal Regulatory Agencies

Federal regulatory agencies are created by congressional action, or specifically by an "enabling" statute. Some agencies are structured as executive branch departments, whereas others are set up as relatively independent entities, although it is not clear that the latter structure is less susceptible to political influence than the former (Frank and Lombness 1988: 22).

Regulatory agencies are typically directed by a commission, the members of which are appointed by the president and subject to congressional confirmation. Because they are political appointees, these top agency administrators generally serve only during the term of their presidential sponsor; the managerial personnel below them, however, are more often civil servants who work for the agency over an extended period of time (Snider 1987: 47). The managerial personnel of these agencies may be required to have appropriate technical expertise, although the degree of emphasis on such expertise and the autonomy of the agency vary.

Regulatory agencies have three basic functions: rule making, administration, and adjudication (Frank and Lombness 1988). Congress first delegated the power to make regulatory rules (for trade with Indians) to the president in 1790 and to other executive branch officials in 1813 (Bryner 1987: 10). In 1911 (in *U.S. v. Grimaud*) the U.S. Supreme Court upheld the constitutionality of regulatory agency rule making (challenged on the claim that legislative powers cannot be delegated), ruling that the agencies are simply filling in the details of legislative laws (Frank and Lombness 1988: 30). Since that time rather extensive rule making by various regulatory agencies has been promoted by other Supreme Court decisions and has been generally accepted, although not without recurrent challenges and complaints (Bryner 1987: 24).

Regulatory rule making has been supported on the grounds that it allows for more flexible responses to developing circumstances and often requires specialized scientific or technical knowledge that resides in regulatory agencies. It also frees the Congress of the enormous burden of passing thousands of rules, and it diminishes the political consequences of unpopular or contested rules (Clinard and Yeager 1980: 76). On the other hand, the legislative oversight process for regulatory rule making has become quite cumbersome, and it has been recognized that the rule-making process can be distorted by many political or other inappropriate considerations (Clinard and Yeager 1980; Bryner 1987). Industry and business lobbying groups, for example, often succeed in delaying for many years the implementation of new rules they find threatening to their interests.

In recent years federal regulatory agencies have been issuing as many as 7,000 rules and regulations annually, as compared with some 300 public laws enacted annually by Congress (Bryner 1987: 10). Many of these regulatory rules are relatively minor. In contrast to criminal laws, regulatory rules are likely to be more ambiguous, tend to focus on the risk (not the occurrence) of harm, and are geared toward strict liability, not criminal intent.

The investigatory process of regulatory agencies typically involves a mixture of reactive and proactive strategies; more visible offenses (especially those involving formal complaints) generally take priority over the more complex, costly proactive investigations in which agencies take the initiative (Frank 1984b; Frank and Lombness 1988). Violations come to the attention of regulatory agencies from many sources, including consumer complaints, government investigations, congressional committee investigations, business competitors, the media, and employees (Clinard and Yeager 1980: 81–83).

When it is determined that hearings are appropriate, regulatory agencies can act quite informally in many circumstances without observing due-process guidelines. A fairly large body of law, codified in a basic way by the Administrative Procedure Act (APA) in 1946, governs formal agency proceedings (Moore, Magaldi, and Gray 1987: 120). Agency hearings most typically take the form of quasi-criminal proceedings and are less formal than regular court hearings and trials (Metzger et al. 1986: 36). Such hearings are presided over by an administrative judge or hearing examiner, who is independent of agency personnel. Defendants can have attorneys, but they are not entitled to a jury trial. Administrative judges and hearing examiners are empowered to impose various orders or sanctions on defendants, including cease-and-desist orders (equivalent to injunctions); special orders (e.g., directives intended to correct past conduct, or product recalls); consent orders (negotiations regarding certain actions); summary orders (e.g., prevention of the sale of food); and license suspension or revocation (Clinard and Yeager 1980: 94; Frank and Lombness 1988).

Administrative agencies can impose some direct sanctions or civil fines. Cases may also be referred for criminal action or may lead to civil suits. Appeals from hearing decisions must first go through an internal agency appeal process and only then are eligible for appellate court review, although appellate courts have typically been reluctant to overturn agency decisions (Metzger et al. 1986: 37). When agency decisions are overturned, the basis for such reversals is likely to be a determination that the decision was fundamentally arbitrary, capricious, or discriminatory; was not based on substantial evidence; violated applicable constitutional safeguards; or exceeded the statutory authority of the agency.

## The Regulatory Agency's Philosophy: Compliance Versus Deterrence

Regulatory enforcement and decision-making styles vary greatly in terms of regulatory philosophy, regulatory officials' assessments of compliance and noncompliance, and the actions officials take when they identify violations (Frank and Lombness 1988; Kagan 1989). Many cases are dropped because it is impractical to pursue them further; cases that are pursued may be dealt with by administrative action, civil action, or referral for criminal prosecution (Clinard and Yeager 1980: 94). In the 1970s in particular, federal regulatory agencies seemed more willing to support the application of criminal sanctions (Thomas 1982).

Regulatory personnel on all levels may be considered antagonists by the regulated and may act quite autonomously. A study by Frank (1984a) found that threats and assaults against regulatory inspectors were not so uncommon; in this respect regulatory inspectors may have more in common with traditional enforcement agents than is generally thought to be the case. On all levels, a vigorous enforcement approach to regulatory violations typically encounters both practical and philosophical constraints.

Regulatory agencies, then, confront a basic choice between emphasizing compliance (persuasion and cooperation) or deterrence (prosecution and punishment) (Braithwaite, Walker, and Grabosky 1987; Gunningham 1987). In one conceptual scheme, regulatory agencies extend along a continuum from particularistic nonenforcers (who engage in cooperative fostering of self-regulation) to rulebook enforcers (who emphasize command and control)(Braithwaite, Walker, and Grabosky 1987). In another scheme, four regulatory agency policing styles have been characterized as service, watchman, legalistic, and free agent (Frank 1984b). The first two styles favor persuasion; the service style displays greater proactive initiative and technical competence than the watchman style, which is industry-dominated and reactive; the legalistic and free agent styles are prosecutorial, but the legalistic is more mechanistic and formal, whereas and the free agent style is more informal and autonomous.

Traditionally, most regulatory personnel have probably thought of themselves less as a police force and more as governmental agents who seek to gain voluntary compliance with regulatory standards (Conklin 1977: 127; Frank and Lombness 1988: 89). Regulatory agencies typically adopt some mixture of cooperative and punitive approaches (Barnett 1990; Braithwaite, Walker, and Grabosky 1987; Kagan 1989). Informality and bargaining—and a norm of accommodation—take precedence over the strict implementation of legal rules for most regulatory agencies (Hawkins and Thomas 1983; Gunningham 1987). Still, the degree to which cooperative versus punitive strategies should be adopted has been heatedly debated.

Many different interacting factors shape regulatory enforcement styles. These factors include the technical, economic, and legal problems encountered in regulatory implementation; features of the "task environment" (e.g., detectability); and the political environment of the regulatory agency (Kagan 1989). Regulatory laws vary considerably, for example, in their stringency and specificity and the objectives they are promoting. The regulatory task environment takes into account such concrete factors as the visibility of violations, the size and sophistication of the regulated enterprises, the costs of compliance, and the seriousness of risks of harm. Specific regulatory agencies often develop different strategies for different corporations, based on their perception of whether the corporation is basically good or bad (Scholz 1984: 387). According to Kagan and Scholz (1983), regulatory personnel tend to categorize corporate offenders as amoral calculators, who break laws to maximize profit; political citizens, who disagree on principle with regulatory rules or laws; and the organizationally incompetent, whose lawbreaking is a product of mismanagement and incompetence. Circumstances (such as an industrial catastrophe), corporate pressures, and cultural values also influence an agency's orientation toward implementation of regulatory rules (Meidinger 1987; Reichman 1992). Clearly, then, a complex of factors shape regulatory agency philosophy and policy choices.

## Criticisms of Regulatory Agencies

Politics is often a potent element in the regulatory agency appointment process, at least on the higher levels of agency staffing. Perhaps unsurprisingly, the ideological commitments of agency administrators apparently have important impacts on agency policies and practices.

Harold Barnett's (1990) study of Environmental Protection Agency actions regarding the "Superfund" for environmental cleanup during the 1980s demonstrated that its enforcement was heavily affected by changes in the political environment. President Reagan's first EPA administrator, Anne Burford, was a conservative strongly committed to the deregulatory agenda. In 1983 a major scandal developed upon revelations that rather than being used for its intended purpose, the Superfund was being conserved to reduce the federal deficit, and that the EPA had established excessively accommodative relations with corporations involved in toxic waste disposal. Burford was compelled to resign, and her successors adopted a more proregulatory policy. Barnett (1990; 1993) concluded that this proregulatory (enforcement first) approach was much more effective in terms of quantitative and qualitative enforcement outcome measures, although it continued to encounter formidable industry resistance.

If on the one hand regulatory agencies have been criticized as too responsive to a political agenda, they have also been criticized on the grounds that they are run by appointed bureaucrats with too much power, too little competence, and too little accountability (Bryner 1987). On the competence issue, it has been claimed that because government salaries cannot generally compete effectively with private sector salaries, regulatory agencies (especially in lower-level jobs) disproportionately attract individuals with mediocre qualifications. Industry representatives claim that this leads to inefficient—even absurd—overregulation, whereas critics of industry claim that regulatory personnel are too easily misled and tend to underregulate. In one illustration of the latter concern, modestly compensated government accountants, accustomed to auditing rather straightforward home mortgages, were grossly misled and manipulated by the savings and loan fraudsters of the 1980s, resulting in losses in the billions of dollars.

It is commonly conceded that regulatory agencies are greatly understaffed and underfunded, given their responsibilities. Public pressure for agency action is small relative to that for conventional crime, and business interests have traditionally lobbied for various limitations on agency powers and budgets (Conklin 1977; Clinard and Yeager 1980). OSHA, for example, has several hundred inspectors with responsibilities relating to several million businesses; the SEC has an annual budget in the tens of millions of dollars to police financial transactions in the hundreds of billions of dollars. These agencies increasingly rely on computers to uncover illegal activities (Reichman 1987), but this use of computer technology raises concern about excessive government intrusion and invasions of privacy.

Even though small businesses may indeed be intimidated by government regulatory agencies, there is good reason to believe that the larger corporations often have an advantage over regulatory agencies. In view of the enormous economic consequences of many regulatory actions, the potential, and the reality, of corruption are ever-present on all levels. Corruption may be direct or indirect, ranging from outright bribes to prospects of postgovernment-service jobs with lucrative salaries (Conklin 1977: 123; Snider 1987: 47). The meat industry provides the salaries for inspectors, and this arrangement—however cost-effective for the government—is obviously conducive to corruption (Coleman 1989: 163). Regulatory personnel may also be compromised by their subservience to powerful political officials, who may in turn put pressure on them on behalf of corporate and individual benefactors. This pattern was exemplified in the "Keating Five" case involving five prominent U.S. senators who pressured thrift regulators on behalf of Charles Keating, the head of a major thrift who had donated heavily to their political campaigns.

## Agency Capture

The concept of agency capture has been one part of the critique of regulatory agencies, although there has been considerable disagreement on whether it is appropriately applied to contemporary regulatory agencies (Freitag 1983; Braithwaite 1985a; Snider 1987).

There is no single definition of the agency capture concept, and it has been variously applied to situations when little disruption of industry profits occurs; when the level of regulation is minimal and acceptable to industry; and when enforcement of regulatory law is lenient (Frank and Lombness 1988: 101). More specifically, suspicions of agency capture occur when regulatory agency officials with a pro-industry bias are appointed (or when such officials can anticipate lucrative private-industry careers following their government service), and when various forms of inducement or influence (political or psychological) are evident.

A study of nine federal regulatory agencies during 1970–1975 found that more than half the agencies' appointees had worked in the industry they were now charged with regulating (Conklin 1977: 123). In contrast, a subsequent study found that only a small percentage (under 10 percent) of the regulatory commissioners came from the regulated industry, and that even then they were likely to be representatives of smaller businesses (Freitag 1983). (This study also conceded that three times as many commissioners leave government service to go into the regulated industry.) Other observers (see, for example, Ayres and Braithwaite 1991) have argued that agency capture—signified by close and cooperative relationships with regulated industries—cannot simply be equated with corruption and does not necessarily lead to corruption.

Some of the typical criteria for identifying agency capture have been criticized. Industry interests are not necessarily unified or in conflict with public interests, although nonindustry interests may not be adequately represented within regulatory agencies (Clinard and Yeager 1980: 108; Frank and Lombness 1988: 102). Regulatory agency policies that may appear to signify "capture" may instead reflect a distaste for confrontation and a view of social welfare shared by the regulators and the regulated alike (Ayres and Braithwaite 1991: 471).

Despite such reservations about the notion of agency capture, regulatory agencies (e.g., the EPA and the FDIC) have in various instances been coopted by the industries or businesses they are supposed to be regulating, and some of these cases are cited elsewhere in this text. Since at least the 1970s a number of policies and strategies have been adopted to minimize the chances of agency capture, including prohibiting entry into regulated industries for a significant period of time after regulatory agency service, limiting agency discretion with more specific statutes, and professionalizing agency personnel (Frank and Lombness 1988: 113–17). Such measures may have diminished but have not eliminated the problem of agency capture.

## Other Factors in Regulatory Response

Beyond the specific problem of agency capture, other factors affect the regulatory response to corporations. In a study of the EPA, Yeager (1987) found evidence of a strong structural bias in the regulatory process that favors larger, more powerful corporations. This bias exists because only the larger corporations are likely to have the resources to afford technical and legal experts who can challenge and negotiate with agency experts, and only the larger corporations can easily absorb (with their large volume of production) the formidable costs of compliance with regulatory requirements. Regulatory agency inspectors tend to regard larger corporations as more responsible and less prone to violations than small corporations (Lynxwiler, Shover, and Clelland 1983). As a practical matter, cases brought against large corporations are more complex and time-consuming and are likely to confront the formidable political clout of such corporations (Snider 1987). The important implication of Yeager's (1987) analysis is that the regulatory system reflects, reproduces, or reinforces social inequalities of wealth and power, the structural bias toward large corporations leads to underestimations of the level of violations committed by such corporations in official sanctioning data.

Altogether, regulatory agencies often find themselves contending with countervailing proregulatory and antiregulatory forces, and as a matter of survival they may have to steer a middle course between these forces (Hawkins and Thomas 1983). A complex of factors, ranging from political pressures to professional pride to personal greed, are involved in the regulatory process.

## Prominent Regulatory Agencies and Their Functions

In the sections that follow we briefly examine the origins and functions of five important federal regulatory agencies: the FDA, the FTC, the SEC, the EPA, and the OSHA.

**Food and Drug Administration (FDA)**   The Food and Drug Administration, which is presently a part of the Health and Human Services Department, has its seminal origins in the Food and Drug Act of 1906, which mandated public protection from hazardous (adulterated or mislabeled) foods, drugs, cosmetics, and medical devices (*Congressional Quarterly* 1990). The FDA, originally the Federal Bureau of Chemistry empowered to administer the 1906 act, was given considerably broader powers following a dramatic incident in 1937, when more than 100 people died after taking a dose of an alleged cure-all medication, elixir of sulfanilamide (Clinard and Yeager

1980: 77–78). Another equally dramatic incident in the early 1960s—the discovery that pregnant women who had taken the drug thalidomide gave birth to grossly deformed infants—led to still further legislation that strengthened the FDA.

The FDA today regulates, inspects, monitors, tests, and develops guidelines for a wide range of foods, drugs, cosmetics, and medical devices. In many cases the manufacturer actually conducts the tests, and the FDA has no direct control over this testing process (Coleman 1989: 159). Its field inspectors are authorized to inspect any plant that produces products falling under the jurisdiction of the agency. It can respond to perceived violations of its rules with a regulatory (warning) letter, a recall order, an injunction against further manufacture or distribution, a citation threatening criminal action unless appropriate information is provided, direct seizure of prohibited goods, and/or recommendations for the imposition of civil monetary penalties or the initation of criminal prosecution.

The FDA's effectiveness has been inhibited over the years both by its focus on small companies rather than on powerful, major corporations and by corruption in the form of FDA generic drug reviewers' acceptance of bribes from drug companies. The FDA has been criticized on the one hand for holding up approval of experimental drugs for the treatment of AIDS, and on the other hand for not requiring adequate testing of new medical devices. In 1995 some Republican members of Congress promoted proposals to eliminate the FDA or to shift the drug approval process to private entities (A. Lewis 1995).

**Federal Trade Commission (FTC)**   The Federal Trade Commission was created as an independent agency in 1914 (*Congressional Quarterly* 1990). It was originally created as the federal government's principal weapon against the trusts, but during its existence it has also been empowered to contend with unfair and deceptive business practices (including deceptive advertising) that defraud consumers. The FTC is empowered to issue trade regulation rules, which in their final form have the force of law, and it has broad powers to require businesses to produce various forms of information. Its overall charge—to prevent unfair competition and anticompetitive mergers—is so broad that it has stimulated considerable debate and litigation over the proper interpretation of its mandate (Coleman 1989: 158). The commission issues advisory opinions to businesses that inquire about the potential liability of some of their planned practices.

The FTC can initiate adjudicative proceedings against businesses that have engaged in practices prohibited by the agency's rules and can seek civil penalties or injuctions against businesses, although it is often able to simply negotiate a consent order calling for the cessation of the prohibited practice. The FTC has been attacked by consumer advocates for its relatively feeble and inefficient protection of consumers and by various business and professional groups for its perceived interference with their legitimate operations (Clinard and Yeager 1980: 77). Unsurprisingly, the Reagan administration cut the FTC's budget quite dramatically and scaled back on its surveillance and enforcement practices, especially in connection with corporate mergers. More recently the agency has endeavored to restore its overall credibility.

**The Securities and Exchange Commission (SEC)** The Security and Exchange Commission was established in 1934 as one governmental response to the massive stock manipulations and frauds that were an important factor in the famous 1929 stock market crash (Seligman 1982; Shapiro 1984). The agency got off to a fairly strong beginning under its first three chairmen, Joseph P. Kennedy (father of President Kennedy), James M. Landis (a former Harvard Law dean), and William O. Douglas (subsequently a celebrated and controversial U.S. Supreme Court Associate Justice for 37 years). It has headquarters in Washington, D.C., and today has branch offices in 15 U.S. cities.

The SEC, which is an independent regulatory agency composed of five commissioners, was given broad responsibilities to regulate and police the securities markets (Shapiro 1984). Some of these responsibilities, authorized by federal securities legislation, include serving as a repository and examiner for registration statements filed by companies planning to sell stock to the general public; providing information on securities to investors; advising on some bankruptcy reorganizations; and, especially, investigating and initiating action when federal securities laws are violated and frauds are committed.

The specific methods used by SEC staff attorneys to investigate securities matters, and the complex of factors involved in their decision-making process on responding to cases, have been exhaustively explored in Susan Shapiro's pioneering *Wayward Capitalists: Targets of the Securities and Exchange Commission* (1984). One important finding was that the SEC rarely refers cases for criminal prosecution (only six out of 100 parties investigated ultimately find themselves in criminal court), preferring instead to resolve cases by various other means (Shapiro 1984; Shapiro 1985). The SEC's enforcement powers are limited; it does not, for example, have legal access to evidence developed in grand jury inquiries into securities cases, and it must go to court and have a judge authorize any restraining orders or injunctions it seeks to impose (Eichenwald 1990c). But people in the securities business credit the SEC with playing a very important role in restoring a good measure of investor confidence in the market.

The SEC has been criticized by some as unnecessary; others have regarded it as insufficiently vigilant and aggressive (Herman 1985). In the many decades of its existence the SEC has clearly gone through periods of lethargy and relatively limited effectiveness (Seligman 1982; Shapiro 1984). Its funding and staffing has always been somewhat limited in view of its responsibilities for policing security markets involving literally hundreds of billions of dollars. Its responses to conglomerate mergers, to corporate governance, and to the policing of exchange self-regulation of member finances and operations have in particular been criticized, and during the early years of the Reagan administration it was seen as retreating from its traditional role as protector of investors (Seligman 1982; Kerwin 1990). In the late 1980s the SEC became somewhat more visible during a period of great growth of corporate takeovers, when a selective crackdown on insider trading cases was one major agency response (Kerwin 1990; Nash 1986). With economic deregulation came calls for broader enforcement powers for the SEC (Pitt and Shapiro 1990). In the 1990s the SEC remains quite conspicuous in the policing of various forms of financial crime, although by 1994 it was contending with some calls in Congress for cutting its funding (Henriques 1994).

**Environmental Protection Agency (EPA)**　The Environmental Protection Agency was established in 1970 as an independent executive branch agency headed by an administrator appointed by the president (*Congressional Quarterly* 1990). The establishment of this agency was clearly a response to growing public concern with harm to the environment that rose sharply after a dramatic oil spill off the coast of Santa Barbara, California, early in 1969.

The EPA has mandated responsibilities to set standards and monitor practices relating to air quality, water quality, and the disposal of various forms of hazardous waste. It has been an especially large, visible, and controversial agency, attacked both by environmentalists who complain that it hasn't been sufficiently aggressive in protecting the environment and by business interests who complain that it imposes unreasonable costs and enforces unnecessary regulations. The EPA promotes voluntary compliance with environmental protection standards and encourages state and local initiatives in environmental matters. If polluters do not respond to orders to cease harmful activities, the agency can initiate informal negotiations, and if these efforts are unsuccessful it can initiate civil proceedings. The EPA also has a criminal investigation unit that can initiate criminal prosecution for willful environmental criminals. Civil penalties may include revocation of licenses and permits and substantial fines. In the rather rare criminal cases, imprisonment can be imposed in addition to fines.

Although the EPA's reach expanded quite significantly during the 1970s, in the early years of the Reagan administration it was the subject of a previously mentioned scandal involving lax enforcement of environmental regulations and corrupt dealings with regulated industries. Rita Lavelle, a political appointee who headed the "Superfund" environmental cleanup program, was convicted on criminal charges of perjury and sentenced to six months in prison. The evidence demonstrated that Lavelle and some of her associates in the EPA were more concerned with accommodating the administration's corporate supporters and maintaining positive ties with potential future employers in regulated industries than with fulfilling the EPA's mandate. In response to public concern and congressional pressure, the EPA became somewhat more vigilant in subsequent years.

**Occupational Safety and Health Administration (OSHA)**　The Occupational Safety and Health Administration, established as a Labor Department agency in 1970, has been one of the most controversial federal regulatory agencies (*Congressional Quarterly* 1990). The OSHA, which was created in response to a growing concern over unsafe and hazardous workplace conditions, was authorized to develop and enforce procedures and standards for workplace health and safety, and to compensate for limitations of alternative remedies such as Workman's Compensation, civil tort suits, and criminal prosecutions. The Occupational Safety and Health Act that established the OSHA also gave states the option of developing their own enforcement plans, and as of 1992 some 23 states had federally approved plans (Frank 1993). At least some of these states (e.g., California) have agencies that pursue cases much more aggressively than does the federal agency (Brill 1992: 67). Occupational health and safety standards in states that have not developed their own plans are enforced by the federal agency.

Some commentators have argued that the OSHA was created primarily as a symbolic concession to labor forces, rather than as a consequence of a serious governmental commitment to improving workplace conditions (Donnelly 1982; Calavita 1983). The agency has jurisdiction over most employers, although in 1976 most small businesses were exempted from OSHA's record-keeping requirements. In addition to developing protective standards and overseeing employer record keeping, the OSHA is empowered to conduct workplace inspections (typically without advance notice) and issue citations for violations; it can recommend (to the Occupational Safety and Health Review Commission) the imposition of monetary civil penalties (up to $10,000 per violation) and jail terms (up to six months per violation).

The OSHA has been vigorously criticized by the business community for formulating and enforcing rules and regulations that are both unnecessary and enormously costly to employers. But it is far from clear that the OSHA has either imposed real burdens on businesses or significantly improved workplace health conditions. Calavita (1983) argued that the Reagan administration's attempt to debilitate the OSHA must be understood primarily as an ideological and symbolic effort to put labor on the defensive. Although the Reagan administration was originally committed to abolishing the OSHA, it instead only succeeded in imposing some significant constraints on its operation (Frank 1993).

During the 1980s, the OSHA was criticized for failing to take adequate steps against hazardous workplace conditions, and from a progressive point of view it was virtually criminally negligent in failing to enforce regulations (Brill 1992). In the 1980s the OSHA principally relied on inspections rather than on vigorous enforcement, and it concentrated more on worker safety than on health hazards (Viscusi 1986). Regulating direct, visible safety hazards that cause physical injury has in fact proven much easier than addressing unsafe conditions that may cause health problems over an extended period of time (Frank 1993). In a study of workplace injuries and OSHA inspections for nearly 7,000 manufacturing plants, Gray and Scholz (1993) found a 22 percent decline in injuries in the years following the imposition of post-inspection penalties. In response to criticisms of its performance during the Reagan era, subsequent administrations initiated tougher actions against various employers with unsafe practices, and Clinton's secretary of labor, Robert Reich, professed a strong commitment to beefing up the OSHA (Noble 1994).

**Consumer Product Safety Commission**  This agency was established in 1972, at the height of the consumer movement, when an estimated 20 million Americans a year were being injured while using consumer products (*Congressional Quarterly* 1990). The agency, which originally had five commissioners, was given the responsibility of protecting the public from dangerous products, assisting in the evaluation of products, setting standards, and sponsoring investigations of the causes of, and means of prevention for, product-related deaths, illnesses, and injuries. The agency is expected to monitor the enforcement of consumer product standards. Although it is empowered to impose civil fines, it is much more likely to negotiate consent agreements with producers of dangerous or defective products. It can order bans on products or demand that they be redesigned. Although the agency was accorded considerable autonomy to minimize the chances of "capture," from the outset administrations antagonistic to its mission have attempted to impose constraints on it. During the Reagan administration the CPSC experienced drastic budget cuts and massive staff reductions and went into a state of virtual paralysis. In the 1990s there appears to be some revival of support for this agency.

## The Regulatory System, In Sum

We have devoted considerable attention to the regulatory system because it represents a principal form of response to a range of the most important white collar crimes broadly defined. Of course, disagreement will persist over whether the activities overseen by the regulatory agencies are properly seen as a form of crime or as mere technicalities. The debate over whether the regulatory system is essentially oppressive and counterproductive, or instead a means of deflecting serious and substantial crimes from the more visible, accountable criminal justice system, is sure to continue as well. The questions concerning what the guiding philosophy of the regulatory system should be, and what the nature of its relations with the other systems of justice should be, are likely to assume greater importance in future scholarly dialogue on white collar crime.

## Private Policing of White Collar Crime

IN RECENT YEARS it has come to be recognized that policing is carried out by a very broad range of agencies and institutions, many of which are essentially private. Private policing as such has a long history. Many of the functions of modern police forces were once carried out by employees and servants of the powerful and privileged. Throughout much of the modern history of private police forces, they may have been used more often as an instrument whereby corporations committed crimes (e.g., against employees) than as a means of ferreting out and pursuing white collar crime cases, especially at the higher executive levels.

Since World War II private policing has grown exponentially (Shearing and Stenning 1987: 9). Some important interconnections exist between public and private police, and the lines of demarcation between them cannot always be easily drawn (Marx 1987: 172–73). Public and private police may join forces in criminal investigations (as when the FBI and IBM Security collaborated on a computer-secrets theft case); private police may be hired to investigate crimes that public police do not have time to investigate (as happened in a counterfeit handbag case); public police investigations may be subsidized by private entities (as occurred in a case involving pirating of copyrighted material); some investigative units may be public/private hybrids (as is the case with the Law Enforcement Intelligence Unit, a private organization of public police); and much intermixing of public and private policing personnel occurs (for example, many private policing agencies are headed by retired public police)(Marx 1987). All such interrelationships are especially pronounced in the white collar crime realm.

The private security industry is a vast, multibillion dollar enterprise. In the 1980s it had twice as many employees as public policing agencies in the United States, and over $20 billion a year was being expended on private security (Timm and Christian 1991: 10). Of course, a great deal of this massive private security effort is devoted to the physical protection of business assets—from fire, burglary, and shoplifting, among other threats—and has nothing to do with white collar crime. But a certain proportion of such private policing focuses on external or internal frauds or embezzlements by employees and outside parties alike. Only a small proportion of private policing is directed at the illegal or improper activities of the corporate executives who typically hire and control private police. Indeed, security departments of major corporations may be confronted with the ethical and practical dilemma of responding to the discovery that their employer is suppressing research findings of injurious effects from their product or is engaging in some other form of illegal or harmful conduct (Nalla and Newman 1990: 126). It is likely that more often than not internal security departments do not report to some external enforcement agency any high-level corporate wrongdoing that comes to their attention.

When it comes to business, executives are socialized to think more in terms of "loss" than of crime (Stenning 1988); they are oriented toward preventing loss and using resources efficiently to maximize profit. Whenever possible, they prefer to avoid formally invoking the notion of "crime" because criminalization typically generates many costs and complications. One security executive in a very large corporation asserted that only one out of 10 frauds within the company is likely to come to the attention of the security department (Cunningham et al. 1991: 28). Many middle-level executives and managers fear that reports of fraud and other employee illegalities in their department will reflect poorly on them, and they prefer to handle these matters directly.

In recent years especially, private security firms that specialize in the pursuit of white collar criminals have proliferated (Lohr 1992a); the various financial scandals of the 1980s were a boon for such investigators. Perhaps the most prominent of these investigative firms is Kroll Associates of New York, which received considerable publicity for locating Saddam Hussein's assets in bank accounts and corporate investments around the world (Byron 1991). Kroll Associates, which is typically hired by law firms or insurance companies attempting to investigate suspected white collar crime, has also undertaken hundreds of "due diligence" reports (seeking possible fraud and other improprieties) for investment banking houses anticipating the sale of a corporation's bonds or stocks. Intertect, another such firm, has 46 employees and major contracts with the federal government, banks, and other businesses (Shuger 1992). Still another private investigator, Jay Rowe, specializes in investigating defense contractors suspected of defrauding the government.

In 1993 the Association of Certified Fraud Examiners, founded some five years earlier, was claiming a membership of 10,000 antifraud professionals in the United States and abroad (Wells 1993b). It plays a role in the training of private investigators

(Lohr 1992a). Several universities now offer courses on fraud examination, or "fraud auditing." Because antifraud investigations typically require months of painstaking examination of mounds of financial documents, these investigators use computers and data banks instead of the tools of traditional private eyes. Many of their private business clients, hoping to be spared embarrassment and possible lawsuits, want investigators to produce evidence that will prompt financial restitution rather than a criminal indictment. In a parallel vein, private insurance company fraud units have become an important factor in the response to insurance-related fraud (Ghezzi 1983). Because such special investigation units (SIU) often use investigative procedures that would render evidence inadmissible in courts, such cases rarely go to court.

Private police, then, are often constrained from responding to apparent criminality in the same way as public police might, and they may be called in either because businesses do not want to involve the police or have yet to be successful in the case. According to a private investigator who specializes in white collar crime cases, the client's principal objective is often limited to locating and recovering stolen funds (Grant and Wolf 1988: 20). Although recovery rather than revenge or "administering justice" is also a primary objective for some victims of conventional crime, it appears to be a more important factor in white collar cases. Furthermore, businesses are often reluctant to press charges against an insider (especially a top executive) who has defrauded the company due to concerns about bad publicity, possible declines in the company's stock value, and embarrassment about their own misplaced trust (Grant and Wolf 1988: 39). Accordingly, private policing in a corporate or business setting is often directed toward concealing rather than broadly exposing white collar crime.

## The Role of Lawyers and Accountants in Policing White Collar Crime

IN COMMENTING ON the massive fraud committed over a period of years by Charles Keating's Lincoln Savings and Loan, Federal Judge Stanley Sporkin asked:

> Where...were the outside accountants and attorneys when these transactions were effectuated? What is difficult to understand is that with all the professional talent involved (both accounting and legal), why at least one professional would not have blown the whistle to stop the overreaching that took place in this case. (Monse 1992: 4–5)

The question of the "policing" obligations of professionals such as lawyers and accountants is considered here.

### Lawyers and Professional Ethics

Lawyers are typically thought of principally in terms of their obligation to defend clients against investigations and adjudications. But are there circumstances in which a lawyer is obliged to play a "policing" role? This is a complicated and contentious issue.

As a general rule a lawyer is prohibited from misrepresenting facts, knowingly offering false evidence, or furthering a fraud (Gerson 1992; Hughes 1993). American Bar Association (ABA) canons on a lawyer's ethical obligations when he or she discovers that a client has perpetrated a fraud are quite confusing, however, and appear to prohibit an attorney's participation in client misconduct while simultaneously discouraging the attorney's investigation of client activities (Belbot 1991: 158; Monse 1992: 3). ABA rules of professional conduct adopted in the 1980s require lawyers to call on clients to rectify ongoing frauds they become aware of and to inform affected parties if clients fail to do so, unless a privileged lawyer-client communication is involved or disclosure would be detrimental to the client's interests (Steinberg 1991: 3). It is difficult to conceive of a situation, however, in which these two constraints could not be said to be applicable. When a specially appointed ABA commission recommended extending the obligation of lawyers to reveal to legal authorities a client's acts whenever either substantial financial harm was possible or the lawyer's services had been used to further some fraud, the ABA rejected the recommendation (Belbot 1991: 160). It instead adopted the rule that lawyers could report their clients' activities to prevent future crimes involving death or substantial bodily harm, a circumstance that would not likely arise in a clear-cut manner in the white collar crime realm.

Rules that require lawyers to be "stool pigeons" against their clients have been attacked as unfair and harmful (Frankel 1992). One basic objection to requiring attorneys to "police" their clients, especially white collar crime defendants, is based on the complexity of laws, rules, and regulations, which may make it difficult for clients to clearly discriminate between legal and illegal actions (Belbot 1991: 156). If clients know that under some circumstances their lawyer will report them and testify against them, they may withhold information a lawyer needs to mount an effective defense.

The ABA rules can also be viewed as intended to shield lawyers from liability rather than to protect the broader public from fraudulent activity. These rules hold that when a corporate board or high-level management insists on committing fraudulent and illegal activity, counsel should resign from representation; however, the specific obligations of counsel following such resignation are less clear. In the celebrated OPM Leasing case involving a massive fraud of business clients who were leasing computer services, the original lawyers did not in any way inform successor counsel that their client was engaged in an ongoing fraud; their actions are certainly controversial (Steinberg 1991: 21). Altogether the actions of lawyers in some of the major recent white collar frauds have provided little basis for confidence that lawyers will protect the public from being defrauded by their clients.

In more recent years, however, government prosecutors have more aggressively pursued the position that lawyers who advised clients engaged in ongoing massive frauds are themselves responsible. The dramatic losses involved in the savings and loan castastrophe of the 1980s were an important source of inspiration for this policy and brought some of the ethical issues of legal representation into sharp focus (Monse 1992). In early 1992 the federal government sued a leading New York law firm (Kaye, Scholer, Fierman, Hays and Handler) and its former managing partner for $275 million and sought to freeze their assets over their representation of Charles Keating, the convicted head of a savings and loan institution guilty of large-scale frauds (Labaton 1992a; Hughes 1993). The government's argument was that the lawyers involved both improperly advised the savings and loan company that some of its investments were permissible and were guilty of conflicts of interest. The lawyers repeatedly misled thrift examiners and engaged in obstructionist tactics for a savings and loan operation whose losses will ultimately cost the taxpayers some $2 billion. The government's position is that a lawyer's obligations to a client are compromised if the client is supported in some way by taxpayer money, and that a bank examination should not be equated with an adversarial proceeding (Labaton 1992b; Gerson 1992; Hughes 1993).

Recently the courts have been divided concerning counsel's disclosure obligations, and in most jurisdictions today lawyers do not have a specific obligation to "blow the whistle" on their clients (Steinberg 1991). Furthermore, after a sharply divided U.S. Supreme Court in 1994 ruled against the long-standing practice of permitting investors to file "aiding and abetting" accusations against lawyers representing securities defrauders, the lawyers for one group of defrauded investors simply accused the defendant's lawyers of direct complicity (Henriques 1994). The outrage over the size and scope of the savings and loan losses has generated a call for a greater responsibility on the part of professionals—accountants as well as lawyers—to "police" their clients under certain circumstances, or themselves face charges and various penalties for their direct or implicit involvement in the clients' wrongful conduct.

## Accountants and Auditing Responsibilities

Accountants also face conflicts in their obligations to clients and as discoverers of fraudulent activities. Accountants are, of course, sometimes brought in by management specifically when it suspects embezzlement or internal fraud, or when such matters as suspicious insurance claims arise. This type of investigative auditing is known as forensic accounting, and it has become an increasingly common specialty (Bologna and Lindquist 1987; Kleinfeld 1990; Wells 1992).

Accountants are much more commonly brought in by corporations and businesses to conduct audits certifying the soundness and accuracy of financial statements and reports. Annual audits are in fact required by the SEC for all companies traded on the stock market (Wells 1993a). Inevitably accountants become aware of fraudulent misrepresentations in such statements and reports; most typically they have quietly dropped such accounts or deliberately overlooked these misrepresentations. When accountants produce reports certifying the soundness and accuracy of these business financial statements, they can wittingly or unwittingly become parties to an ongoing fraud because investors, regulators, and others may take actions premised on the accountants' (or auditors') certification.

The legal liability to third parties of auditors that have been negligent or active participants in the production of misleading financial statements is rooted in common law principles and the securities acts (Elliott and Willingham 1980: 13). The traditional standard has been that auditors are responsible for detecting managerial misrepresentations that would produce misleading financial statements, *if* such errors are detected by generally accepted auditing practices (Elliott and Willingham 1980: 11). In the case of the savings & loan crisis, Richard Breeden (1991), chairman of the SEC, argued that the accounting standards widely applied to the S & Ls were inherently defective and produced a very misleading picture of the thrifts' assets and liabilities. Part of the problem, then, lies with the standards, but clearly the S & L losses also involved outright fraud and misrepresentation by any standards.

In response to increasing criticism of their profession, the chief regulatory body for accountants asserted in 1988 that accountants have a responsibility to look actively for financial fraud inside companies they audited (Berg 1988). This body, the American Institute of Certified Public Accountants, has nevertheless emphasized that accountants cannot be expected to uncover all instances of fraud, and it voted overwhelmingly in 1992 to maintain the policy of prohibiting members from volunteering confidential client information to government agencies (McCarroll 1992). Thus accountants are required to inform managerial authorities but not outside entities, of any fraud they have discovered (Elliott and Willingham 1980: 20).

As is true for lawyers, the obligation of client confidentiality has taken precedence over other considerations. Of course, the fact that auditors are investigating possible improper and illegal activities by those who pay for their services is a built-in conflict of interest (Wells 1993a). Accounting professionals generally adhere to the position that the corporate management prepares and must assume basic responsibility for financial statements, and that accountants or auditors merely issue opinions based on information provided to them (Jennings, Reckers, and Kneer 1991). Increasingly, however, government agencies are investigating the criminal and civil liability of accountants in long-running frauds of corporations and businesses they have audited (Wells 1993a). As of 1992, accounting firms were facing some 4,000 liability suits and more than $15 billion in damages—primarily in S & L cases—and members of Congress were calling for legislation requiring accountants to blow the whistle on lawbreaking clients (McCarroll 1992; Wells 1993a). Accountants, then, face increasing pressure to "police" their clients more proactively.

## Self-Regulation: Internal Controls and Professional Associations

THE NOTION OF self-regulation, or private policing directed at one's own company or professional peers, is something that generally distinguishes white collar crime from conventional crime; that is, conventional criminals are not typically expected to police or regulate their own illegal conduct. In some respects organized crime and crime syndicates may be said to engage in periodic self-policing when they act against fellow criminals who violate their rules. Informers in the whole range of conventional crime cases are "policing" their criminal associates, although often with wholly selfish motives. (We discussed whistleblowers who report transgressions to public agencies and the media in Chapter 1.) But only in the corporate and legitimate occupational realm do we find official, internal enforcers of codes or laws pertaining to the conduct of employers and employees.

Self-regulation is important because government does not even begin to have either the resources or the expertise to police or regulate fully all the activities of corporations, retail businesses, professionals, and legitimate white collar and blue collar entrepreneurs. On the one hand many corporate crimes are instigated or inspired by the highest levels of authority in the corporation, and obviously these executives are unlikely to encourage any investigation of such activity (Clinard 1983). On various levels, however, corporate executives may cultivate "concerted" or "strategic" ignorance of certain specific, culpable actions as a way of protecting themselves (and the corporation as a whole) from criminal charges (Katz 1980a). White collar crime lawyers advise top executives to avoid involving themselves too directly in internal investigations—when allegations of corporate wrongdoing arise—as a way of minimizing the executives' exposure in any subsequent prosecution (Magnuson 1992). Thus in many circumstances the chief executives of corporations either discourage self-policing or distance themselves from any self-policing inquiries.

On the other hand, Braithwaite and Fisse (1987: 322) pointed out that, contrary to what we might expect, corporations often expend resources to police themselves because (1) they are not uniformly indifferent to an ethical obligation to do so; (2) they have a powerful self-interest in maintaining a good public reputation; and (3) they want whenever possible to preempt the imposition of the less palatable alternative of governmental regulation. Braithwaite and Fisse contended that self-policing can be much more thorough and effective—can involve more substantial resources and broader access—than external policing and may be able to impose tough internal sanctions. But because the willingness of corporations to police themselves cannot always be depended on, they favored *enforced* self-regulation, a policy proposal addressed in Chapter 12.

## Self-Regulation in Financial Firms

In-house policing units have been established in many major financial firms. In the 1950s a prominent stock brokerage was suspended by the SEC for 30 days for failing to adequately supervise brokers, who defrauded clients. Since that time stock brokerage and investment banking firms have hired compliance officers who are responsible for monitoring the firm's activities and ensuring that its personnel comply with pertinent laws and regulations (Cowan 1991). Throughout much of this period compliance officers occupied a fairly modest status within their firm, especially insofar as they were not involved in directly generating income for the firm, but the various scandals and investment banking house collapses of the late 1980s and early 1990s inspired a new appreciation of the potential benefits of a strongly backed compliance staff. Because the compliance officer is an employee of the firm, however, keeping the firm out of trouble may take precedence over protecting customers and clients.

## Self-Regulation and the Professions

Self-regulation has played an important role in the professions and has in fact been one of the hallmarks of professionalism (Moore 1970; Abel 1988b: 218). Because of the historical tendency to assume that only professionals have the specialized knowledge needed to judge the professional behavior of their peers, the state has often deferred to peer judgments. Although criminal prosecution is always the prerogative of the state, crimes committed in their occupational capacities by such professionals as physicians and lawyers may be recognizable as such only by fellow professionals.

Even though professional associations such as the American Medical Association (AMA) and the American Bar Association (ABA) have no formal disciplinary powers beyond expulsion from association membership, such professional associations and their state affiliates formulate codes of conduct, form committees or boards to evaluate allegations of professional misconduct, and are empowered to revoke licenses and the right to practice. Professional associations have traditionally been much more concerned with promoting the economic and other interests of the profession than with vigorously policing misconduct of professionals.

State and federal laws often prohibit aggressive legal actions against physicians for many forms of professional misconduct (Brinkley 1985). States typically delegate licensing and disciplining powers to a state board of examiners that is heavily influenced by medical societies through recommendations for membership and suggestions for standards of practice (Bene 1991: 918). Although at least half the states have laws requiring state medical associations to report disciplinary actions to state boards, they apparently rarely do so (Brinkley 1985: B6). State medical boards or agencies tend to be understaffed and underfinanced, and any actions taken against physicians are likely to be complicated, expensive, and time-consuming. Board members, fearful of lawsuits, rarely invoke their powers against fellow physicians for alleged professional misconduct. In many states in a given year no physician is stripped of a medical license; in other states this sanction is imposed on no more than a handful of physicians (Brinkley 1985).

The term *professional misconduct* is quite vague and indefinite and may encompass anything from gross malpractice to deceptive claims to fee-splitting to improper sexual advances (Flaster 1983: 164). Despite some recent increase in concern with medical crime and incompetence (not always so easily separated), the evidence suggests that a system of control that heavily relies on peer review has been exceptionally feeble.

In the case of the legal profession, until well into the 20th century professional discipline was principally a matter of informal peer control (Abel 1988b: 219). Although the ABA promulgated around the turn of the century ethical rules that have been subjected to much revision and refinement over the years, the ABA seems to have been much less concerned with their actual enforcement. Furthermore, clients have either lacked the necessary knowledge to institute formal complaints against their attorneys or have been beneficiaries of their misconduct (Abel 1988b: 219). Complaints made against lawyers most typically involve false advertising, fee abuse, neglect, misappropriation, and lack of communication; these complaints, then, range from specifically criminal actions to professional malpractice or incompetence (Schneyer 1991a: 126).

As is the case for physicians, only a few lawyers each year are subjected to professional disciplinary action, and an average of only 30 lawyers a year are disbarred in the United States (Bene 1991). In fact, only about 1 percent of those accused of misconduct are actually suspended from practice or disbarred (Abel 1988b: 220). The targets of such disciplinary action are most often solo practioners, some of whose flagrantly unethical or illegal actions have always been an embarrassment to the profession. The disproportionate disciplining of solo practioners is significant given the fact that an increasingly large percentage of lawyers now practice within large law firms (Schneyer 1991b). There clearly are, then, many limitations on the existing self-policing practices of the legal profession.

Self-regulation or self-policing has the obvious advantages of economic efficiency and (in principle) appropriate expertise. Businesses and professions have found it advantageous to control themselves, but history suggests that such self-regulation or self-policing is unlikely to be extensive or effective unless formidable external pressures compel businesses and professions to take this responsibility more seriously.

## Policing and Regulating White Collar Crime, In Sum

THE POLICING AND regulating of white collar crime produces many challenges and complications that are less likely to arise in response to conventional crime. In particular, the number of different agencies and institutions centrally involved in this process is greater, as is the role of self-policing. The evolution of the current cumbersome and decentralized manner of policing and regulating white collar crime into something more efficient and effective is likely to be one of the important challenges facing the justice system in the 21st century.

# Prosecuting, Defending, and Adjudicating White Collar Crime

**O**NLY A SMALL PERCENTAGE of white collar crimes are prosecuted and adjudicated by the criminal justice system. This relatively low level of formal processing reflects class biases inherent in our system, the greater resources available to people accused of white collar offenses, the complexity and costliness of prosecuting such cases, and the existence of alternative forms of response deemed more efficient or appropriate.

Still, at least some white collar crime cases do end up in the criminal courts. The state's needs—to maintain or enhance its status as legitimate and deserving of compliance and to uphold the claim that in a democratic society the law applies equally to rich and poor—lead to selective prosecution of white collar crime cases. Some segments of the corporate and white collar community benefit from prosecution of especially flagrant white collar crimes because it reinforces the notion that such crimes are principally the actions of a few "bad apples." Accordingly, attention is deflected from some of the structural sources and the pervasiveness of white collar crime. Indeed, the failure to respond more effectively to conventional crime has been labeled a "Pyrrhic defeat" that deflects public anger from the far more substantial harms committed by corporate and governmental criminals (Reiman 1995). Still, criminal justice system personnel have some autonomy and may pursue white collar crime cases on behalf of their own values, interests, and goals.

## Prosecution at the Local, State, and Federal Levels

### Local Prosecutors

The prosecutor, a key figure in the American criminal justice system, has formidable discretionary power over which criminal cases will be prosecuted and which specific charges will be pursued. Local prosecutors have traditionally directed most of their time and attention to the broad range of conventional crime cases, including assaults, thefts, burglaries, robberies, and the like. This pattern is a consequence of a number of factors. Local police agencies deal principally with these types of cases and refer them to prosecutors for further action; victims of such crimes are especially likely to report their cases to the criminal justice system; the voters, who elect and reelect district attorneys or chief prosecutors, are especially concerned with seeing conventional criminal offenders convicted and behind bars; and prosecutors have been socialized and trained, for the most part, to think of crime in conventional terms.

It has long been argued—by Sutherland and many others—that businesspeople and corporations are well-positioned to use their influence to avoid prosecution for their crimes. But until quite recently relatively little has been known about the local prosecution of white collar crime cases. A number of studies of local prosecutors, principally by Michael L. Benson, Francis T. Cullen, and William J. Maakestad (1990a; 1990b; 1992; 1993), have cast some light on the attitudes and actions of local prosecutors in response to white collar crime.

The relatively low level of attention to white collar crime by local prosecutors results from several factors. First, local prosecutors do not typically regard such crime as especially serious; in one survey, less than 4 percent of urban prosecutors considered corporate crime a "very serious" problem, and half did not regard it as at all serious (Benson, Cullen, and Maakestad 1990a). Second, corporate and finance crime cases in particular require very large expenditures of time and special investigative skills, involve greater difficulties in establishing criminal intent, and pose problems in obtaining appropriate witness or victim cooperation (Benson, Cullen, and Maakestad 1993; Cullen, Maakestad, and Cavender 1987; Markham 1991). These cases may require sifting through masses of dull and difficult-to-understand records (Schudson, Onellion, and Hochstedler 1984). A decision to prosecute a corporation requires a major commitment of finite resources. As a practical matter, a more substantial local prosecutorial response would require more sharing of information, automation, computer networks, and regional laboratories (Benson, Cullen, and Maakestad 1993). Accordingly, the local prosecution of corporate crime is significantly a function of the level of resources and expertise available to a local prosecutor's office (Benson, Cullen, and Maakestad 1992).

Third, prosecutors can rationalize their failure to take on corporate crime cases on the basis that such cases are the responsibility of various state or federal agencies, and to the extent that these agencies are pursuing a case, local prosecutors are far less likely to get involved (Benson, Cullen, and Maakestad 1993). Fourth, local prosecutors may be reluctant to antagonize powerful business interests (Gurney 1985: 621). The evidence suggests that whenever economic crime units (ECUs) have been established as a device for more effectively prosecuting white collar crime, the units place protecting the property interests of corporations and other organizations ahead of protecting individual citizens from corporate wrongdoing and harm (Gurney 1985: 622–23). Furthermore, many local prosecutors eventually go into private practice and thus become dependent on local businesses and corporations as clients and sources of income.

Despite such obstacles and rationales, some criminal prosecutions of corporations occur. In one study, almost 70 percent of the urban prosecutors and some 35 percent of the rural prosecutors surveyed had prosecuted at least one corporate offense in 1988 (Benson, Cullen, and Maakestad 1990a: 364–65). Of the urban prosecutors surveyed, some 41 percent reported prosecuting consumer frauds; about 30 percent had prosecuted insurance fraud, false claims, and environmental offenses; about 22 percent had prosecuted securities frauds; and about 16 percent had prosecuted tax fraud and illegal payments cases (Benson, Cullen, and Maakestad 1990a: 365). However, no more than one case in each of these categories (and in some cases, none) had been prosecuted in the year in question.

Since the 1970s local prosecutors have apparently become more concerned about white collar crime, probably as a reflection of greater public concern and because of changes in law and federal policy that extend both prosecutorial powers and local jurisdiction in such cases (Benson, Cullen, and Maakestad 1990a). In the 1990s, for example, local prosecutors were more actively pursuing environmental crime cases and were more willing to proceed with only circumstantial evidence (Rebovich and Nixon 1994). In one survey, local prosecutors claimed idealistic motivations for their pursuit of white collar crime cases (Benson, Cullen, and Maakestad 1990b: 6). Prosecution is most likely in cases in which physical harm to human beings or substantial economic harm has occurred, and in cases involving multiple offenses or large numbers of victims (Benson, Cullen, and Maakestad 1993; Cullen, Maakestad, and Cavender 1987; Gurney 1985; Schudson, Onellion, and Hochstedler 1984). Criminal prosecution may be inspired in these cases by authentic moral outrage, a desire to educate the public, and the hope of deterring such conduct by signaling a willingness to prosecute (Benson, Cullen, and Maakestad 1993; Schudson, Onellion, and Hochstedler 1984; Cullen, Maakestad, and Cavender 1987). One study found that county prosecutors were most likely to take action in cases involving individual defendants, organizational victims, and multiple victims (Gurney 1985); the author suggests this is so because it is easier to prove cases with multiple (as opposed to individual) victims, because organizational victims can augment the investigative resources of the prosecutor's task force, and because individual defendants are easier to prosecute than are organizations. In the case of organizations, prosecutors are confronted with the intimidating task of sorting through masses of accumulated records; the relevant records of individuals are likely to be less complex and more manageable.

Economically depressed communities are apparently less willing to prosecute corporate and business crimes if jobs may be lost as a consequence (Benson, Cullen, and Maakestad 1992). However, some types of white collar offenders may be more vulnerable during periods of economic distress. For example, Arnold and Hagan (1992) found that solo practitioner lawyers who engage in professional misconduct are more likely to be prosecuted during a recession, perhaps in part because they are easy targets for frustration and anger during such a time. Conversely, economically stable and prosperous communities are more likely to have the resources to prosecute sophisticated business crime and are less likely to be tolerant of harmful corporate conduct.

Although obtaining a conviction is normally the primary criterion for measuring prosecutorial success, other worthwhile goals can be accomplished when corporations are prosecuted, even if they are not convicted. To the extent that the public is outraged by corporate crimes, prosecutors can reap favorable publicity (and better prospects of reelection) by prosecuting these cases.

## The Pinto Case and the BCCI Case

We now consider two well-publicized exceptions to the general reluctance of local prosecutors to take on large and powerful corporate entities. In 1978 the part-time Elkhart County (Indiana) prosecutor, Michael Consentino (a conservative Republican), sought and got an indictment against the Ford Motor Company on the grounds that criminal negligence in the design of its Pinto (in which the gas tank was unprotected in the rear of the car) was the principal cause of the death of three teenage girls (Cullen, Maakestad, and Cavender 1987). The prosecutor attributed Ford's acquittal in this case to the enormous legal resources available to the corporation and its attendant ability to keep much of the critical evidence out of the trial (Kramer 1985: 3–4). Although this prosecutor, an elected official with a private practice on the side, had some justifiable concerns about the negative reactions of his conservative constituents and clients to this indictment, he claimed that his perception of Ford's very real responsibility for the tragedy motivated him to pursue the case.

In the BCCI case, Manhattan district attorney Robert Morgenthau, one of the pioneers in vigorously pursuing white collar crime cases in the 1990s, took the initiative in prosecuting this international bank on charges involving billions of dollars of bribery and fraud when the U.S. Department of Justice refrained from aggressively pursuing the matter (Brenner 1992). In December 1991, Morgenthau's office managed to obtain BCCI's guilty plea to numerous charges of racketeering, fraud, and larceny leading to the forfeiture of $550 million in assets and payment of a $10-million fine. The far larger resources of Morgenthau's office, compared with Consentino's, may well have played a role in the different outcomes of these cases.

## State Attorney Generals

Even though state attorney generals have greater resources to pursue significant white collar crime cases than do local and county prosecutors, their resources have remained limited; in the 1970s about half the states did not have consumer fraud units (Coleman 1989: 169). Although more recently some 80 percent of state attorney generals surveyed indicated that they had the jurisdiction to investigate and prosecute white collar crime cases, the defendants were overwhelmingly individuals or individuals doing business as an organization (Ayers and Frank 1987). Fraudulent transactions were the most common white collar crimes handled, followed by theft or embezzlement in a white collar setting. Slightly less than half the white collar crime cases were disposed of by a criminal prosecution; the remainder of the cases were dropped or handled by civil or administrative procedures. Even though the state attorney generals in this survey were quite willing to use tough criminal sanctions against certain classes of white collar offenders, they believed that corporate crime should be prosecuted on the federal level. In the relatively few cases in which state prosecutors pursued corporations, they often did so in a cooperative venture with local and federal prosecutors in a process known as "cross designation" (Schudson, Onellion, and Hochstedler 1984: 139). More typically, when corporate crime had to be handled on the state level, a civil or administrative approach, rather than the use of criminal sanctions, was preferred.

State attorney generals identified several key factors in the decision to prosecute, including the amount of money involved, the number of victims, their belief in the guilt of the accused, and the likelihood of prosecutorial success, as opposed to political or public relations considerations (Ayers and Frank 1987). The overall hardening of state attorney generals toward white collar offenders may well reflect shifting public sentiments, and these state prosecutors are surely aware of the public relations aspects of prosecuting certain highly visible white collar crime cases. On the one hand, state attorney generals have the resources to handle certain types of white collar crime cases that local prosecutors may lack; on the other hand, they typically contend that complex corporate crimes should be pursued at the federal level.

## Federal Prosecutors

Virtually by default, then, federal prosecutors have assumed the primary responsibility for pursuing major white collar crime cases. The 94 U.S. attorneys in the United States, one for each federal judicial district, are appointed by the president (with the considerable input of U.S. senators) and are in charge of major federal prosecutions. With only a few conspicuous exceptions, U.S. attorneys did not focus on white collar crime prosecutions until the 1970s, when the pace of federal prosecutions of white collar crime cases increased quite dramatically (Katz 1980a). During this period, for example, the U.S. Attorney's office for the Eastern District of New York began prosecuting a series of powerful local politicians for such crimes as double-billing, tax evasion, embezzlement, kickbacks, and extortion (Katz 1980a: 163–64). It also prosecuted corporations and corporate executives for charges involving adulterated food, bribery, negligent handling of hazardous products, and illegal campaign contributions, and it greatly increased the frequency of its prosecutions of defrauders of government agencies and programs, including the Small Business Administration and Medicaid.

Many other U.S. attorney's offices independently pursued white collar crime cases much more vigorously during this period and established special sections to handle consumer fraud or environmental protection. U.S. attorneys also took considerable initiative in pursuing novel cases to promote a broader application of existing white collar crime laws, which were full of gaps (Katz 1980a: 170). For example, wire fraud statutes were used to obtain indictments for a corporation accused of bribing a foreign official, and pollution laws were used as a basis for criminally prosecuting corporate executives.

In the shifting public attitudes promoted by the exposure of the Watergate Affair in the early 1970s, ambitious federal prosecutors found it increasingly appealing to pursue white collar cases, and this policy shift became somewhat institutionalized in the 1980s (Coffee 1988b; Katz 1980a). (Ironically, the U.S. Justice Department and its highest officials or former officials became targets of allegations of complicity in political white collar crime during the Watergate period, and former Attorney General John Mitchell was convicted and imprisoned on such charges.) At a Senate Judiciary Committee hearing in 1986, the Justice Department claimed dramatic increases in white collar crime prosecutions and the development of specialized expertise and prosecutorial units within the department (Committee on the Judiciary 1987: 26; 36). Other data generated by the FBI indicated a decline in white collar crime convictions between 1983 and 1986 (Caringella-MacDonald 1990: 97).

During the 1980s two conservative Republican administrations adopted a conception of white collar crime that deemphasized many major forms of corporate crime and emphasized relatively low-level frauds and individual white collar crime cases. President Reagan's attorney general, Edwin Meese, overruled the recommendation of Justice Department prosecutors that criminal indictments be sought against executives of the E. F. Hutton company in a case in which billions of dollars of check-kiting occurred as a matter of company policy; Meese made similar decisions in two other cases involving major pharmaceutical corporations, Eli Lilly and Company and SmithKline Beckman Corporation (Stewart 1987: 348–49). Only after 1987 and in response to the unfolding S & L scandal did federal prosecutors regard banking crimes as worthy of their serious attention (Green 1991: S161).

In the 1990s various critics alleged that the Justice Department had failed either to pursue information brought to its attention years earlier concerning the involvement of BCCI in large-scale money laundering, massive fraud, and other illegal activities or to investigate CIA complicity in a scheme by an Atlanta bank to illegally funnel arms funding to Iraq's Saddam Hussein (Baquet 1991; Safire 1993). The finding of a federal bankruptcy court judge that in the 1980s the Justice Department defrauded a private company, Inslaw, out of some legal software, is especially disturbing (Richardson 1991). The moral bankruptcy of the Justice Department itself has been a serious concern.

Throughout the 1980s and into the 1990s, then, the conservative Republican Reagan and Bush administrations showed little commitment to prosecuting all forms of white collar crime. Still, relatively autonomous U.S. attorneys generated some momentum in this realm, vigorously pursuing some of the S & L fraud cases, insider trading cases, and criminal corruption cases directed at high-level government officials and politicians. The application of RICO (Racketeer-Influenced and Corrupt Organizations Act) to white collar crime cases and emerging federal sentencing guidelines were among the new arsenal of potent prosecutorial weapons. Recognizing that only the federal government has the resources and manpower to pursue major, complex white collar crime cases, the Clinton administration took office with a commitment to pursue white collar crime cases more vigorously.

The various federal agencies are one source of referrals for federal criminal prosecution. Even though a great deal of evidence of white collar crime activity comes to the attention of the Internal Revenue Service, the Environmental Protection Agency, and the Securities and Exchange Commission, these agencies are not always eager to refer cases to the Justice Department because in one sense any such referral is an admission of failure on their part; once the Justice Department takes on a case, the regulatory agency loses control of it. In addition, the SEC, to consider one example, is conscious of the need to meet higher standards of proof in criminal cases and is often skeptical that criminal prosecution will result in the most satisfactory resolution of a case involving securities (Shapiro 1985). Thus only a small proportion of cases of alleged wrongdoing that come to the attention of regulatory agencies are handled by federal prosecutors.

Federal prosecutors are also authorized to bring civil proceedings against white collar offenders. The use of civil proceedings, either in place of or in conjunction with criminal proceedings, is far more common in white collar crime than in conventional crime cases, and "consent decrees," which are essentially negotiated compromises between the prosecutor and the indicted party, are especially common (Mokhiber 1988: 5, 8; Mann 1992b), in part because of the obvious fact that white collar offenders have far greater financial assets than conventional offenders. The ongoing tendency to regard white collar cases as primarily civil matters plays a role, but from a tactical point of view a prosecutor may choose civil proceedings instead of criminal proceedings because the burden of proof is considerably lower and because the complexities of establishing criminal liability are especially daunting (Green 1991: S179). Because monetary penalties are often imposed in white collar crime cases, a prosecutor may have a much better chance of successfully resolving a civil case that imposes civil penalties equivalent to (if not exceeding) any applicable criminal sanction. The role of civil suits in white collar crime cases is more fully explored later in this chapter.

## The Prosecution of Antitrust Cases

Violations of antitrust law are one form of white collar crime that exemplifies the need for federal prosecution. The prosecution of antitrust cases, directed at various anticompetitive business practices, has been highly selective and especially influenced by the political ideology of the incumbent administration (Clinard and Yeager 1980). Corporate antitrust cases tend to be large and complicated, stretching across various jurisdictions and lasting an extended period of time. Antitrust cases initiated by the Federal Trade Commission are more likely to be settled by negotiation and agreement, whereas the Department of Justice's Antitrust Division tends to be more enforcement-oriented (Jamieson 1994).

Donald Scott (1989) studied Department of Justice criminal prosecutions of collusive trade agreements (price-fixing) between 1946 and 1970. Most complaints of price-fixing originated in the private sector, often from competing businesses disadvantaged by the collusion, but disgruntled corporate employees also played an important role as informants. Most of these complaints were not pursued because of inadequate cooperation from complainants, the absence of clear evidence of illegality, the jurisdiction of some other agency, or a determination that a private or informal settlement was warranted. The decision to move forward with a criminal prosecution following subsequent investigation of such a complaint involved a substantial commitment of personnel and resources; an average price-fixing case required 21 months to investigate and 23 months to litigate. Scott found that Antitrust Division heads differed in their preference for relying on criminal (as opposed to civil) proceedings for these corporate collusion cases.

After an initial investigation of a substantive complaint and the circulation of evidentiary memos, the determination to prosecute is based on the quality of the evidence, the amount of interstate commerce and the size of the parties involved, and the likely impact of such prosecution on the department's reputation. Almost 70 percent of the criminal cases pursued were settled with a nolo contendere plea; the principal sanction was a fairly modest fine (approximtely $5,000 before 1955, subsequently raised to approximately $50,000). Prison sentences in such cases were rare.

Once federal prosecutors begin to turn on the heat in price-fixing cases, conspirators tend to be eager to cooperate by testifying against associates to minimize their own exposure to sanctions. A 1974 revision of the Sherman Act that provided for felony provisions in antitrust cases led to fewer cases, less plea bargaining, and more acquittals. By 1978 the Antitrust Division had shifted its attention away from major price-fixing conspiracies toward bid-rigging involving government contracts. The Justice Department of the Reagan administration clearly did not consider antitrust cases one of its higher priorities; indeed, it dropped a major antitrust case against IBM that had been initiated by a previous administration. During the Clinton administration the Justice Department pursued a larger number of antitrust cases but suffered a surprising setback in February 1995, when Judge Stanley Sporkin rejected its planned antitrust settlement with Microsoft (the software giant) on the grounds that the agreement was too easy on the company (Andrews 1995). Whether prosecutors or judges ought to have final say on such agreements was a matter of some debate.

## The Prosecution of Environmental Crime

Throughout most of our history, the parties responsible for myriad types of environmental destruction were not subjected to criminal prosecution, although private parties have traditionally initiated civil suits against corporations and other entities whose polluting activities caused harm. The Rivers and Harbors Act (1899), considered the first congressional expression of intent to criminalize polluting activity, did not lead to any serious, measurable prosecutorial activity against environmental criminals for the first seven decades of the 20th century (Starr 1991). In the late 1960s and early 1970s an environmentalist movement emerged, reflecting a shift from industrial values promoting exploitation of natural resources to postindustrial values favoring environmental protection (Hedman 1991). For most of the 1970s a wave of new laws and the newly established Environmental Protection Agency were the principal legal system manifestations of this value shift. Still, little actual criminal prosecution of environmental offenders occurred.

During the relatively conservative Nixon and Ford administrations, the EPA resisted referring environmental cases to the Department of Justice for criminal prosecution; only 25 federal criminal cases were prosecuted on environmental charges during all of the 1970s (DiMento 1993: 135). Only during the Carter administration (1977–1981) did criminal prosecutions increase. During the 1980s the level of criminal investigatory and prosecutorial resources directed toward environmental crime expanded considerably, despite the conservative Reagan administration; by 1985 up to 50 cases a year were being referred to the Department of Justice for criminal action (DiMento 1993: 135). This expansion reflected autonomous momentum against such crime, fueled in part by considerable public outrage over revelations in 1983 of corrupt dealings between high-level EPA officials and corporate polluters.

In the early 1990s high-level government officials were claiming a substantial increase in their commitment to pursue criminal prosecution of environmental crime cases (Thornburgh 1991a; Strock 1991). Skeptics have argued that Department of Justice prosecutions of environmental criminals had leveled off by 1990, that criminal sanctions were still relatively light compared with other crimes, and that overall compliance with environmental laws continued to be poor (Adler and Lord 1991). Furthermore, until 1984 no large corporation had been prosecuted for violations of federal environmental laws, and between 1984 and 1990 only 6 percent of the corporations prosecuted under these laws were Fortune 500 companies, even though an estimated two-thirds of them were breaking the laws (Adler and Lord 1991: 795–96). Despite some modest increases in prosecutions, fines, and prison sentences for individual corporate executives, there has been a systematic reluctance to imprison environmental offenders or to fine corporate environmental offenders more than a fraction (1–5 percent) of the statutory maximum for these offenses. There has in fact been a historical reluctance to prosecute corporate environmental crime cases in the first place.

Various commentators have called for substantially more resources, interagency coordination, more autonomous EPA enforcement authority, earlier discrimination between civil and criminal cases, better inducements for voluntary compliance, and refinements of existing legislation (Adler and Lord 1991; Marella 1992; Starr 1991). Altogether, support for more vigorous prosecution of environmental crimes is growing.

## Special Prosecutors (Independent Counsel)

Cases of governmental crime or political white collar crime are inherently problematic for prosecutors, who may be accused of either conducting vendettas against political enemies or failing to prosecute fully political allies or superiors. Special prosecutors (or independent counsels) have sometimes been appointed in politically sensitive cases (e.g., in the Teapot Dome case in the 1920s and in connection with a tax scandal in the early 1950s) to act free of direct supervision by the administration in power (Harriger 1992).

The Watergate Affair illustrated the potential problems involved in prosecuting governmental and political white collar crime (Silverstein 1988). The Justice Department officials originally investigating the Watergate break-in had to report to President Nixon, who was himself deeply involved in covering it up. Under great public pressure in 1973, Nixon appointed a special prosecutor, Archibald Cox, but when Cox attempted to subpoena incriminating White House tapes later that year, Nixon fired him (or persuaded the solicitor general to fire him after the attorney general and his deputy resigned rather than doing so). This "Saturday Night Massacre" was a key factor in Nixon's ultimate resignation in 1974. The next two Watergate Special Prosecutors, Leon Jaworski and Henry Ruth, directed the case through the conviction and imprisonment of some of the key conspirators, even though neither sought an indictment against Nixon himself.

The office of special prosecutor was formally created by the Ethics in Government Act of 1978; some further amendment of the office resulted from the Independent Counsel Reauthorization Act of 1987 (Laughlin 1989: 800). The formal creation of the special prosecutor's office was clearly a response to (some would say an overreaction to) the Watergate Affair and its investigation (Nolan 1990: 14). It was intended to address the obvious, inherent potential for a conflict of interest when a Justice Department, with its various ties to other divisions of the executive branch, is faced with prosecuting criminal allegations against powerful people in that branch. Originally the attorney general's office was regarded as a relatively neutral source of legal policy; over time it became increasingly politicized, although attorney generals have varied considerably in terms of the extent to which they have played a neutral or politically partisan role (Baker 1992; Clayton 1992; Rogovin and Rogovin 1993).

Under the Independent Counsel Reauthorization Act, the attorney general of the United States, after receiving allegations of illegalities by one of the high government officials covered by the act, must within a certain period of time either determine that there is no substance to the allegations or notify the special division of the Court of Appeals for the District of Columbia, which is then authorized to appoint and oversee a special (or independent) prosecutor. In *Morrison v. Olson* [108 S. Ct. 2597 (1988)], the U.S. Supreme Court ruled that this office was not a violation of the Constitution's separation of powers doctrine (Laughlin 1989); no increase in congressional power at the expense of executive power is involved.

During the Reagan administration, numerous high-level members of the executive branch were alleged to have committed illegal acts related to their office, and in 1986 a special prosecutor, Lawrence Walsh, was appointed to pursue the first national political scandal since Watergate: the Iran-Contra Affair (Spencer 1993). Over the course of a seven-year investigation, 14 people were charged with criminal offenses (primarily withholding information from Congress) and 11 pleaded guilty or were convicted—although the convictions of two central figures, Admiral John Poindexter and Colonel Oliver North, were overturned on appeal (Johnston 1991; 1994). Poindexter and North had given testimony under immunity to a congressional hearing, and the Appeals Court found that this testimony tainted their criminal trial.

The objective of successfully prosecuting those involved in governmental crime cannot always be reconciled with the legislative branch's insistence on publicly probing major political scandals; the final report of the special prosecutor concluded that President Reagan, Vice President Bush, and Attorney General Meese all participated in some way in covering up the scandal.

A special prosecutor was also appointed in 1992 to investigate the Bush administration's handling of a billion-dollar bank fraud case involving illegal loans to Iraq, and a special counsel was appointed in 1994 to investigate the Clintons' Whitewater investments (Sciolino 1992; Turque 1994). In the latter case the appointment was not made under the independent counsel law, which had expired in 1992; Congress reinstated it in 1994 (Rosenbaum 1994). This law had been widely criticized, and not only by targets of these prosecutors (Nolan 1990; Smith 1992). Yale University law professor Stephen L. Carter (1988), for example, claimed that it was both unnecessary (insofar as ordinary federal prosecutors experience formidable pressures to pursue the appropriate cases, and Congress has adequate powers to pursue executive branch miscreants) and unfair (insofar as the appointment of a special prosecutor virtually presupposes that a prosecution must result). Still, in the final analysis Congress and the president seemed to agree that an independent counsel law was necessary.

## The Role of the Grand Jury in White Collar Crime Cases

THE GRAND JURY is more important in white collar crime cases than in conventional cases because a grand jury indictment is constitutionally required in the federal system, in which a higher proportion of white collar crime cases are prosecuted. Many state courts have eliminated grand juries.

In principle, one of the traditional rationales for grand jury indictments—to act as a buffer against vindictive, improper prosecution—is especially applicable in certain classes of white collar crime cases. A grand jury ideally acts as a check on politically motivated prosecution; it may also be more appropriate for a grand jury of anonymous citizens to return indictments in sensitive cases involving the powerful than for a politically vulnerable prosecutor to seek an indictment in such cases.

A second rationale for grand juries in white collar crime cases emphasizes the secrecy of the inquiry. Ideally, allegations about illegal activities by reputable organizations and individuals should be examined behind closed doors; if these allegations are wholly unsupported, the profoundly damaging publicity of a public inquiry is avoided. Finally, special grand juries are sometimes empaneled to investigate major ongoing criminal enterprises, including various forms of governmental or business crime, and the broad subpoena powers of a grand jury enable it to conduct such investigations especially thoroughly.

Critics of the grand jury commonly argue that it is manipulated by prosecutors who are able to use its broad subpoena powers to go after vulnerable targets (Magnuson 1992). People granted immunity can be compelled to testify, although if they are only granted "use" immunity they may still be vulnerable to prosecution so long as their immunized testimony is not used. The secrecy of the grand jury is not infrequently violated, and prosecutors have sometimes been accused of leaking evidence and testimony that emerged in grand jury hearings as a means of putting pressure on their targets. Finally, special grand juries may be seen as instruments that vindictive prosecutors can use to harass and persecute selected groups or organizations.

The grand jury, then, is an important element of white collar crime cases. The accused in such cases is especially concerned with avoiding indictment, and defense lawyers have attempted to challenge the traditional, strict constraints on their participation in grand jury hearings (First 1990: 435). On the prosecutorial side, the subpoena powers of the grand jury may be essential for gathering evidence in complex cases in which a mass of documents and many witnesses are involved. Still, prosecutors are often ambivalent about grand juries, finding them useful in certain situations and cumbersome in others.

## Defending White Collar Criminals

IT IS COMMONLY assumed that one of the main differences between defendants in conventional crime cases and defendants in white collar crime cases is that the latter can afford private lawyers and accordingly get a much better defense. This is typically true, but not uniformly so. In one study of federal white collar crime defendants, 57 percent retained private counsel, as opposed to only 16 percent of a comparable sample of conventional defendants (Weisburd et al. 1991: 100). But these figures also mean that over 40 percent of white collar crime defendants do not retain private counsel. The likelihood of obtaining a private lawyer varied by type of case; all of the antitrust defendants and only 34 percent of the bank embezzlement defendants retained private counsel.

Defendants with private counsel usually have an advantage, but not always. An indigent defendant in a criminal case who is represented by a highly experienced (if overworked) public defender could conceivably get a better defense than a white collar defendant with modest means who hires a lawyer with relatively little experience in such cases. On the upper end of the scale, of course, wealthy white collar crime defendants and corporate defendants can hire the best available legal counsel, which likely gives them a significant advantage but does not guarantee a favorable result. In his highly publicized securities fraud case, Michael Milken hired a team of some of the best lawyers in the country. Despite legal bills of $1 million a month or more in the final years of his case, Milken ended up with a $600 million fine and a 10-year prison sentence, although this sentence was subsequently reduced substantially (Labaton 1990a; Stewart 1993).

White collar crime defense work has become a fully recognized (if still somewhat uncommon) legal practice specialty. Defense lawyers tend to be somewhat divided between those who adopt a conciliatory, cooperative strategy with prosecutors and those who attempt to intimidate them by threatening all-out legal combat (Lewis 1992). Some practical, written guides to white collar crime defense provide advice on strategies for controlling case information and minimizing client criminal liability (Bailey and Rothblatt 1984; Lawless 1988; Magnuson 1992). Although the general rule is to avoid commenting to the media in high-profile cases, a proactive public relations campaign may be adopted as part of the defense strategy (Kasinof 1991; Magnuson 1992). Regardless, the overall objective is to minimize damage at every stage of the criminal justice procedure.

The major study of the white collar crime bar is Kenneth Mann's *Defending White-Collar Crime: A Portrait of Attorneys at Work* (1985), which studied all defense lawyers who handled white collar crime cases in the Southern District of New York between 1974 and 1978. White collar crime defense was apparently the fastest growing specialty in the legal profession during this period. Many of the lawyers who chose this specialty were graduates of elite law schools who had gained firsthand experience with white collar crime cases by serving as assistant U.S. attorneys. They were drawn to the specialty of defense counsel because it is quite lucrative (up to $300 an hour at that time), allows for solo practice or affiliation with a small firm (as opposed to a large organization), and often produces intrinsically fascinating cases with complex issues and high stakes. The specific kinds of cases handled by these lawyers include securities fraud, tax fraud, embezzlement, corruption, bribery, conspiracy to defraud, criminal regulatory violations, antitrust violations, and bankruptcy fraud.

According to Mann's study, much earlier involvement in the case is one of the primary differences between white collar crime defense work and conventional crime defense work. Because a major objective of these defenses is to control information, defense lawyers seek to ascertain what the prosecution knows and try to keep harmful evidence from being revealed. Clients and other potential witnesses are instructed to refrain from disclosing anything that does not have to be disclosed. White collar crime lawyers often employ investigators to learn as much as possible about the case, beyond even what the prosecutors may know, hoping to be in a position to dissuade the government from even seeking an indictment. Because white collar crime prosecutions require such a large commitment of government time and resources, the prosecution may be receptive to a well-informed argument that it will not be able to obtain a conviction or that the client has not really violated laws.

Alternatively, defense lawyers may seek to head off an indictment in exchange for the client's cooperation with the prosecutors. A defense lawyer's previous experience as a prosecutor or a regulatory agency lawyer is often especially useful at this stage, both in terms of finely honed skills as a negotiator and personal connections with the prosecutors in the case. If the client is indicted anyway, defense lawyers are likely to explore the best possible deal in return for a guilty plea, emphasizing that the government will expend formidable resources if it is to mount a successful prosecution. If the case in fact goes to trial, at every possible step white collar defense lawyers attempt to exploit their superior financial resources to challenge the prosecution's case, and they may also attempt to take advantage of the greater ambiguity of the pertinent white collar crime laws and the great complexity of white collar cases generally.

At the sentencing stage, white collar crime attorneys usually play a much larger role than conventional crime defense lawyers because defendants typically have many credible accomplishments to counterbalance their illegal acts. Again, defense lawyers may emphasize the ambiguous nature of the offense and the often more diffuse character of responsibility or blameworthiness in these cases. Michael Milken's lawyers orchestrated a letter-writing campaign by numerous prominent people attesting to Milken's good character and deeds, and they argued that at most he had committed technical violations on behalf of some clients in the context of overwhelmingly legitimate business dealings (Stewart 1991).

Finally, white collar crime lawyers play an important role at the appeal stage because the complexity of many white collar crime cases may generate a wider range of options for appealing a conviction. If a client has financial means, a lawyer can devote a great deal of time to the appeal process.

White collar crime defense lawyers can find themselves caught in the middle of various ethical conundrums. One concern is the source of lawyers' fees. In at least some white collar crime cases there is reason to suspect that the fees come from illegally obtained funds. In the Watergate case, paper bags filled with huge amounts of cash were delivered anonymously to one of the defense lawyers for defending the original "burglars." This money was subsequently shown to have been raised by the White House as part of the "hush money" for inducing the original defendants not to implicate the Committee to Reelect the President (Doyle 1977); the lawyer involved never faced criminal charges.

White collar crime lawyers are now more vulnerable concerning the source of their fees. Section 1957 of the Money Laundering Control Act (1986) makes lawyers liable for criminal prosecution if they deposit client fees in excess of $10,000 that they know to come from criminally derived sources (Mann 1985; Lawless 1988: 42). White collar criminal defense lawyers must now ensure that they obtain their fees without putting themselves in legal jeopardy.

In corporate crime cases, the question of whether the corporation counsel represents the corporation or individual executives may arise (Clinard and Yeager 1980: 282). When counsel's primary responsibility is to the corporation, then individual executives may find that corporate counsel attempts to shift blame for the illegality to them personally as a way of shielding the corporation from criminal liability. It is not unethical for corporations to employ defense lawyers to represent accused corporate executives (Clinard and Yeager 1980: 283), but it may not be possible to represent accused executives collectively because their individual interests may be at odds.

In white collar crime cases in which lawyers become aware that their clients are involved in an ongoing illegal enterprise or have made deliberately false statements in judicial proceedings, the role of criminal defense lawyers is beset with ethical conflicts. On the one hand, a lawyer has an ethical obligation to neither knowingly stand by while new crimes are committed nor be party to a deliberate misrepresentation to the court. On the other hand, criminal defense lawyers have argued that they cannot properly represent clients if those clients must constantly fear that their attorney will incriminate them (Mann 1985). This important issue is explored more fully in Chapter 10.

## Adjudicating White Collar Crime: Plea Bargaining and Trial

THE GREAT MAJORITY of conventional criminal cases in most jurisdictions are resolved by plea bargaining. In some jurisdictions well over 90 percent of the indictments for crimes are disposed of in this way. As noted earlier, the process of negotiation in white collar crime cases is much more intense before charges are filed;

indeed, formal charging of a white collar client is more likely to be regarded as a failure than is true in conventional crime cases (Mann 1985: 10).

When the defense's arguments against charging fail, however, a strong incentive exists to plead guilty because of the low likelihood of winning cases for which such arguments have failed. Given the larger measure of resources that typically must be devoted to successfully prosecuting white collar crime cases, it makes sense that prosecutors will principally pursue formal charges only in cases in which formidable evidence for conviction exists. An analysis of sentencing data for 1,597 white collar crime cases in seven federal courts suggests that in complex cases the accused can often avoid punishment or incarceration if they are willing to plead guilty and cooperate with the efficient processing of their case (Albonetti 1994). White collar defendants are especially likely to be intimidated by the prospect of a prison sentence and may resist pleading guilty if such a sentence is involved. Michael Milken strongly resisted a negotiated plea because of his unwillingness to contemplate going to prison (Kornbluth 1992; Stewart 1993). By the time he finally entered into plea negotiations, he had lost much of his original negotiating leverage, and thus he received a stiff prison sentence (reduced because of his postconviction "cooperation" in other cases). On the other hand, John McNamara, a Long Island car dealer who admitted defrauding General Motors out of $436 million, was allowed to keep almost $2 million in assets and remain in business, and was likely to avoid imprisonment when he agreed early on to plead guilty and testify against former local officials, who were subsequently acquitted of bribery charges (Marks 1995).

White collar crime defendants might be expected to have greater confidence in their lawyers than would be true of conventional crime defendants, and the lawyers themselves are more likely to have economic incentives to take white collar (as opposed to conventional) crime cases to trial. From a strategic point of view, the white collar crime defense may believe that in court it can exploit ambiguities in the law, the complex or problematic nature of the evidence, and the defendant's respectable appearance and reputable standing in the community more effectively than would be true in a conventional crime case. The prosecutor may resist making plea bargaining arrangements in the relatively few white collar crime cases in which formal charges are filed, both because of the greater visibility of the case and the prosecutor's confidence that the evidence will support the charges. Altogether, there appears to be somewhat less cooperative negotiation and somewhat more adversarial confrontation in white collar crime cases as compared to conventional crime cases.

The percentage of all white collar crime cases that advance to criminal proceedings is small. According to one study of white collar crime defendants in federal cases, 20 percent of these defendants pleaded not guilty and went to trial (Weisburd et al. 1991: 114). In many jurisdictions no more than 5 percent of conventional crime defendants go to trial; thus white collar crime defendants are approximately four times more likely to go to trial than are conventional crime defendants. In the study just cited, securities fraud and bribery cases (28 percent and 25 percent respectively) were the most likely white collar crime cases to go to trial, whereas a far smaller percentage of bank embezzlement and antitrust cases (7 percent and 13 percent) went to trial.

When the state widens the net and seeks more indictments against more individuals, defendants apparently become intimidated and are more likely to plead guilty. In 1985 and 1986, for example, only 10–20 percent of the individuals indicted in environmental crime cases engaged in plea bargaining; when the rate of indictments increased substantially in 1987, the percentage of cases settled by plea bargaining rose to 40 percent (Adler and Lord 1991: 797).

## The Role of the Trial Jury

TWO ISSUES THAT have been raised in the ongoing controversy concerning trial juries center on their representativeness (or possible biases) and their competence. On the issue of representativeness, neither conventional crime defendants (e.g., muggers) nor high-status white collar crime defendants (e.g., corporate executives) are likely to face juries literally made up of their peers. Are typical jurors more likely or less likely to be favorably disposed toward corporate and occupational crime defendants? Some evidence suggests that in criminal cases jurors are more likely to hold corporations more blameworthy than individual executives for wrongdoing (Hans 1989: 197). On the other hand, in other circumstances, especially in civil liability cases, jurors resist holding corporations responsible for harmful consequences that they believe individual plaintiffs should have anticipated; thus, with rare exceptions, juries have refused to hold tobacco companies responsible for the harmful consequences of smoking.

In the case of individual defendants, a well-heeled defense may be able to pay for a study to provide profiles of the types of people likely to be sympathetic and unsympathetic to the defendant. In the 1974 trial of John Mitchell and Maurice Stans (former cabinet officers and high officials for the campaign to reelect President Nixon, who were accused of accepting an illegal $200,000 campaign donation from fugitive financier Robert Vesco), a public relations firm conducted a survey to produce such profiles (Zeisel and Diamond 1976); Mitchell and Stans were in fact acquitted.

A body of research strongly suggests that jurors are most likely to be sympathetic toward people like themselves. Some research has established that higher status, better-educated, and older males are more likely than others to be selected as jury forepersons (Wrightsman 1991: 291). If it is also true that forepersons with such personal attributes tend to exercise some influence over other jurors, then middle-class white collar crime defendants might be expected to have a marginal advantage with juries because jurors generally (and more influential jurors in particular) may see defendants as more similar to themselves than would be the case with defendants in conventional crime cases. The types of crimes for which white collar crime defendants are charged—income tax evasion is a classic example—may not seem to jurors so remote from things they have done themselves or could imagine doing, especially compared to the alleged crimes of inner-city muggers. The white collar crime defendant typically does not "look like a criminal." Indeed, Maurice Stans's lawyer specifically asked the jury: "Does my client look like a criminal?" Perhaps the jury perception that Stans did not look like a criminal played a role in his acquittal.

Of course, it is also true that elite white collar offenders may inspire deep-seated resentment on the part of jurors. In a mock jury study involving 160 undergraduates, highly esteemed medical specialists were found to be especially vulnerable to jurors' negative bias in very serious criminal cases (involving homicide charges), but in more moderate criminal cases (involving Medicaid fraud) their status seemed to work in their favor (Rosoff 1989). The effects of jurors' bias, then, are not simple, and prestige may work either for or against white collar crime defendants.

The second basic question about trial juries concerns their competence. Judge Jerome Frank once claimed that a jury applies law it doesn't understand to facts it can't get straight (Vidmar 1989: 1). To the extent that there is any truth to this sweeping claim, it is more likely to apply to complex white collar cases than to conventional crime cases. Even though considerable research suggests that in most cases juries perform quite competently and are able to focus on the legally relevant evidence as opposed to extralegal factors (Hans 1989), this finding must be qualified somewhat for criminal and civil white collar cases.

A study of very lengthy federal trials (which often involve complex criminal charges or civil claims against corporations) found that jurors for such cases were more likely to be unemployed and less likely to be college-educated than average jurors (Hans 1989: 190); gainfully employed, well-educated people have more reason to try to avoid serving in these burdensome cases. A number of studies of complex criminal and civil cases involving corporations or high-level frauds found that jurors could not accurately remember important scientific, medical, and economic information, reacted more to witnesses' personal attributes than to their testimony, and misunderstood the judge's instructions (Hans 1989: 187; Hans and Vidmar 1986; Institute for Civil Justice 1992: 26). Jurors in cases against corporations must evaluate collective responsibility, which is a more complicated concept than individual responsibility (Hans 1989: 186). For those reasons many defendants choose a bench trial (before a judge only) over a jury trial, especially if they are offering a "technical" defense that a judge might be able to appreciate more objectively.

Overall, the evidence does not suggest that juries are either significantly more or less likely than judges to acquit white collar crime defendants (Levi 1987). One commentator has suggested that juries in federal cases are more likely to convict than juries in state cases, because in the former cases prosecutors get both the first and last word (Magnuson 1992: 156). Far more remains to be learned about the role of juries in white collar crime cases.

## Judges and the Sentencing of White Collar Criminals

THE JUDGE IS the principal officer of the court. Aristotle equated the judge with "living justice." One of the great 20th-century associate justices of the U.S. Supreme Court, Benjamin Cardozo (1921: 17), said that "in the long run, there is no guarantee of justice except the personality of the judge." If in conventional crime cases judges typically deal with defendants who are very different from themselves and have committed offenses quite removed from their own patterns of behavior, this is not necessarily the case with white collar crime cases. Judges presiding over these cases often confront special challenges. The trial is likely to take longer, and testimony and evidence will more often be dry and tedious. Given the greater complexity of the law, the more ambiguous elements of intent and culpability, and the greater sophistication of defense lawyers involved in white collar crime cases, judges are more vulnerable to error.

## Sentencing

Two beliefs about the judicial sentencing of white collar offenders have been widely adopted over the years. One belief is that white collar offenders are treated more leniently at the sentencing stage than are conventional offenders; the other is that the sentencing decision is quite idiosyncratic and haphazard (Clinard and Yeager 1980: 286–287).

Many methodological problems are involved in comparing conventional and white collar crime sentences, including inconsistency in defining such crimes, the variable socioeconomic status of white collar crime defendants, and different patterns of processing (e.g., white collar crime cases are far more likely to be federal as opposed to state cases)(Hagan and Nagel 1982). Nevertheless, there can be no question that traditionally the harshest sentences have been imposed on conventional offenders such as murderers, rapists, muggers, and burglars. Sentencing leniency may be offered in exchange for testimony and evidence necessary for other convictions. Because such cooperation is more important in complex white collar crime cases than in conventional crime cases, sentencing disparity favoring the white collar defendants results (Nagel and Hagan 1982). It is worth noting that the harshest of all sentences, the death penalty, has never been imposed on a convicted white collar offender in the United States.

Judges have been reluctant to impose tough sentences on businesspeople, apparently believing that they are generally well-intentioned even if they have somehow broken the law (Conklin 1977). Judges may believe that the shame of criminal prosecution is punishment enough for many such offenders; they often allow businesspeople to remain in the community, where they can resume productive activity and can generate income to make restitution to victims; they may take into account the older age and poorer health of some white collar crime defendants; they may consider the perceived suffering of families, employees, or other dependants; they may be persuaded by the defendant's articulate expression of contrition, good past record, and absence of directly threatening attributes; and they may perceive that the offense itself may have been illegal without being fundamentally immoral, and that the defendant is the scapegoat for an organizational misdeed (Clinard and Yeager 1980; Mokhiber 1988; Wheeler, Mann, and Sarat 1988).

Two major factors in any sentencing decision are the seriousness of the offense and the record of the accused. A basic paradox confronting judges in white collar crime cases is the contradiction between a serious offense (most typically involving substantial financial harm) and a defendant who is a respected member of the community, has never before been in trouble with the law, belongs to various worthwhile community organizations, has a good family life, and so forth (Wheeler, Mann, and Sarat 1988).

On some level, judges are also more likely to experience some sense of empathy—apparently more as a function of identification with common values, rather than from similar background—with defendants in white collar crime cases than in cases involving conventional criminals (Croall 1992: 121). On the other hand, because some judges are conscious of their empathy for such offenders, they may lean over backwards to avoid being biased in their favor. They sometimes will consider white collar defendants as more culpable than conventional defendants because they expect more of people with a respectable and trusted status, like themselves.

White collar crime offenders are more likely to be fined or put on probation than are conventional offenders (Weisburd et al. 1991). Further, community service sentences are more common in white collar crime cases (Mokhiber 1988: 28). Such sentences imposed on wealthy financiers convicted of securities-related crimes and tax frauds have included running a computer camp, setting up a homeless shelter, and teaching golf to handicapped youths (Lyne 1993). Indeed, a new specialized service identifies community organizations willing to provide such community service assignments to convicted white collar offenders.

Much evidence from government reports and scholarly studies supports the argument that white collar criminals are considerably less likely to go to prison than are conventional offenders, and that the prison sentences they receive are of shorter duration (Reiman 1990). In one study of a federal district in the 1970s, defendants convicted of white collar crimes had a 36 percent chance of going to prison, whereas those convicted of nonviolent conventional offenses stood a 53 percent chance and those convicted of violent offenses had an 80 percent chance of imprisonment; Federal Bureau of Prison statistics for 1986 revealed that the average time served for robbery, larceny/theft, and burglary was 46.5, 18.3, and 17.9 months, respectively, whereas for fraud, embezzlement, and income tax evasion it was 13.6, 11.4, and 10.3 months, respectively (Reiman 1990: 104–105). In a federal courthouse in New York during one week in 1973, an entrepreneur who engineered a massive stock swindle resulting in losses of $200 million to the investing public received a nine-month prison sentence, whereas a laborer convicted of possession of $5,000 worth of stolen drugstore goods received a four-year prison sentence (Bazell 1973; Reiman 1990: 98). A study of white collar offenders guilty of Medicaid fraud in California found that they were less likely to be incarcerated and were generally accorded more leniency than were similarly charged non-white collar offenders, whose offenses involved less money (Tillman and Pontell 1992). No corporate executives ever went to prison in some of the most notorious corporate crime cases, including the Ford Pinto case and the Hooker Chemical Love Canal case, and in the Film Recovery Systems case involving the death of a worker exposed to cyanide, the prison sentences imposed by the judge were set aside on appeal (Barrile 1993a). Indeed, corporate offenders and white collar criminals generally are more likely to obtain reversals of convictions on appeal than are conventional offenders.

## Explaining Disparities Among Sentences for White Collar Offenders

Not surprisingly, some types of white collar offenses elicit harsher sentences than others. Judges are especially tough on people who violate a public trust, although a violation of any occupational trust is typically considered a serious matter as well (Croall 1992: 116; Hagan and Nagel 1982). In a study of white collar offenders processed in a federal court, individuals convicted of crimes such as mail fraud or fraud against a government agency received sentences equivalent in seriousness to conventional crime sentences, whereas most white collar offenders (e.g., those convicted of price-fixing) received more lenient treatment (Hagan and Nagel 1982).

Considerable variation also exists among white collar offenses in the likelihood of receiving probation or fines. In one study, 90 percent of the bank embezzlers, but only 50 percent of antitrust offenders, received probation; 100 percent of the antitrust offenders, but only 15 percent of bank embezzlers, received fines (Weisburd et al. 1991: 150–51; 158). Most fines are fairly modest and reflect the offender's perceived ability to pay. White collar offenders who have victimized the government are most likely to be fined. Only about 12 percent of the white collar crime offenders were ordered to pay restitution (a proportion roughly equivalent to that for conventional crimes), mostly in cases (such as bank embezzlement) in which the level of harm was quite small (Weisburd et. al. 1991: 159).

Finally, the likelihood of a prison sentence depends significantly on the type of white collar crime involved. In a study of federal white collar crime defendants, Weisburd et al. (1991: 130) found that 20 percent of antitrust violators went to prison (generally for short terms), whereas two-thirds of the security fraud offenders received prison sentences. It is clear from these data that it is difficult to generalize about the sentences imposed on individuals classified as white collar offenders.

The influence of a person's class on white collar crime has been much disputed; part of the difficulty is a lack of consensus on the appropriate meaning of "class" (Benson 1989). Studies conducted by Wheeler, Weisburd, and Bode (1982) and Weisburd et al. (1991) produced the surprising finding that higher-status white collar crime offenders received severer sentences than lower-status white collar crime offenders. The explanation for such a counterintuitive finding may well be that the very small number of high-status offenders who get to the formal sentencing stage in a criminal justice proceeding are vulnerable to tough sentences because their offenses are quite substantial and their visibility is quite high.

Hagan and Parker (1985) concluded that higher-level corporate executives were less likely than subordinate managers to be indicted, tried, and ultimately sentenced for white collar crimes because the law makes it more difficult to establish criminal culpability for higher-level executives. Giving tough sentences for high-level offenders who are actually indicted, tried, and convicted, aided by attendant high levels of publicity, allows a judge to send a very direct message to offenders' peers; the 10-year prison sentence imposed on Michael Milken is one example of such a sentence.

A certain percentage of judges are especially outraged when a privileged, powerful member of society engages in illegal actions. Hagan and Parker's study was conducted after the Watergate Affair, and at least some judges may have been responding to a heightened public concern with the crimes of the privileged and powerful. Indeed, in another study of federal sentencing practices during this period, white collar offenders were more likely to receive prison sentences in the post-Watergate period than before, although the sentences were on the average shorter (Hagan and Palloni 1986).

Despite the occasional case of a high-level offender receiving a stiff sentence, it is far from clear that such offenders are uniformly at a disadvantage. A study by Benson and Walker (1988) did not lend support to the finding that higher-status offenders get tougher sentences. Rather, Wheeler and colleagues' (1982) findings may result from the fact that this study was conducted in urban federal districts with an especially high volume of white collar crime cases presided over by liberal judges. In an analysis of 1,597 white collar crime cases in federal courts, Albonetti (1994) concluded that offenders of higher social status were generally more likely to avoid punishment than were those of lower social status, although this outcome appears to be related more to the complexity of their cases (which provides them with bargaining leverage) than to a class bias operating in their favor.

The principal study on the sentencing of white collar criminals is *Sitting in Judgment* (1988) by Stanton Wheeler, Kenneth Mann, and Austin Sarat, based on interviews with 51 federal judges. The kinds of white collar crimes these federal judges most typically adjudicated included bribery, income tax fraud, mail and wire fraud, price-fixing, false claims and statements, and bank embezzlement. Even though judges often considered the sentencing of white collar offenders to be especially complicated, Wheeler, Mann, and Sarat (1988) indentified an "informal common law" of sentencing for white collar crime offenses. The federal judges generally agreed that harm, blameworthiness, and consequence are the three basic factors involved in sentencing in these cases. More specifically, judges believed that they must assess the level and nature of the harm caused by the defendant's actions, the individual's culpability in the illegal activity, and the actual consequences for both the defendant and the community of any sanctions imposed. They also tended to agree on the importance of considering the totality of circumstances and factors in a case, as opposed to basing sentences on the formal charges alone. But even if there was fairly broad agreement on general principles, it does not follow that the judges agreed how exactly to resolve contradictions among equally valid principles, or how much weight should be given to each case's numerous factors in arriving at an appropriate sentence.

## Sentencing Organizational Offenders

Organizational offenders represent only a small proportion of criminal defendants. During one four-year period (1984–1987), only 1,569 organizational defendants out of a total of 200,000 criminal defendants (less than 1 percent) went to trial in the U.S. district courts (Parker 1989: 521); organizational defendants typically represent an even smaller proportion of the caseload in state and local courts. Furthermore, most of these organizations are not the major corporations that have been the focus of so much attention in corporate crime studies. Of the 1,283 corporations (82 percent of the organizational defendants) actually convicted of federal crimes during 1984–1987, only 10 percent had annual sales exceeding $1 million or more than 50 employees, and fewer than 3 percent offered public stock (Cohen 1989: 606). The offenses for which organizations (overwhelmingly business corporations) are sentenced are fraud, antitrust, environmental, national defense-related, tax, and other offenses (including monetary, food and drug-related, racketeering, and property), in approximately that order (U.S. Sentencing Commission 1990: 91).

Because no centralized source of data on corporate crime exists, assessing criminal sentences for organizational crime is difficult. One study that sampled 288 corporate offenders (or 30 percent of those convicted of federal crimes during 1984–1987, excluding antitrust cases) found that 89 percent were fined, 16 percent were ordered to pay restitution, and 19 percent were ordered to make civil or other types of payments (Cohen 1989: 610). The average fine for organizations that were sanctioned was a little over $50,000; restitution and other such sanctions, when imposed, averaged approximately $250,000 (Cohen 1989: 611). Some 30 percent of the organizations were put on probation for a period averaging a little over 40 months; only 1 percent were ordered to perform community service, and about 6.5 percent received some form of suspension of licensure (Cohen 1989: 615).

The seriousness of a fine as a criminal sanction is meaningful only in relation to the harm caused and the resources of the organization fined. The average fine imposed on organizations totaled only 76 percent of the harm caused (which means that for every $1 of harm caused, the organization would pay only 76 cents, in addidition to any other sanctions such as restitution) (Cohen 1989: 658). Furthermore, corporate organizations that caused the largest amount of harm ended up paying fines that were a considerably lower percentage of the cost of the harm caused than did corporate organizations that caused more modest monetary harm. Because most of these organizations ultimately incorporate these fines into their business expenses, any punitive or deterrent effect is seriously diluted.

In many cases corporations evade payment of their fines (Mokhiber 1988: 32). Even Exxon's enormous criminal fine of $100 million, paid in conjunction with a $1.1 billion civil settlement concerning the *Valdez* oil spill in Alaska, was dismissed by the corporate chairman as something that "will not curtail any of our plans," and indeed Exxon stock rose dramatically after the announcement of this settlement (Adler and Lord 1991: 784). Much evidence suggests, then, that the principal criminal sanction imposed on organizations has had limited punitive or deterrent impact.

## Sentencing Guidelines and White Collar Offenders

The adoption of federal and state sentencing guidelines was one of the most significant developments in criminal justice in the 1980s. The Sentencing Reform Act of 1984 (one part of the Comprehensive Crime Control Act of that year) marked the formal adoption of federal sentencing guidelines; these guidelines went into effect on November 1, 1987 (Hutchison and Yellen 1991: 1–2). A U.S. Sentencing Commission was created to oversee the production, implementation, and revision of the guidelines. Congress's official objective in forming the commission and endorsing the guidelines was to create a more honest, more uniform, and fairer sentencing scheme. The U.S. Supreme Court upheld the constitutionality of the guidelines and the Sentencing Commission in *Mistretta v. United States* (488 U.S. 361 1989).

The sentencing guidelines appear to have constrained judicial discretion in sentencing (despite allowing for some "departures" that must be justified) and have increased the average amount of time spent in prison without clearly reducing disparity among sentences imposed on comparable offenders (Heaney 1991). The adoption of federal sentencing guidelines increased the fines and jail sentences for white collar crime offenders (e.g., those guilty of environmental crimes), but as of the early 1990s such offenders were still only receiving a fraction of the maximum sentences allowable (Adler and Lord 1991: 802). Indeed, under the sentencing guidelines pickpockets and muggers faced higher fines and longer jail sentences than did environmental criminals whose dumping of hundreds of gallons of hazardous waste caused some $40,000 in damage and resulted in the hospitalization of 12 people (Adler and Lord 1991: 803). Two factors built into the sentencing guidelines—previous criminal record and the use of direct violence—inevitably favor white collar offenders because such factors are far more likely to be present in conventional crime than in white collar crime cases.

Judges generally believe that they should have greater flexibility in tailoring sentences to fit specific offenders and circumstances. This might be especially true in white collar crime cases, in which complex and contradictory factors are often involved. "Sentencing consultants" have profited by deciphering the sentencing guidelines judges use and then assisting well-heeled defendants (such as Leona Helmsley) in formulating appeals to have their sentences reduced (Zagorin 1993). Some 100 sentencing consultancy firms have formed a National Association of Sentencing Advocates.

The sentencing guidelines were formulated principally with individual violators of the federal criminal code in mind. Two dimensions of white collar crime that posed particular challenges for the Sentencing Commission are regulatory offenses and organizational offenders. The initial guidelines identified and addressed the most significant regulatory offenses (Hutchinson and Yellen 1991: 11); other technical violations, some of which have serious consequences, were addressed in a separate system.

As of the end of 1990, corporate defendants were involved in a mere 1 percent of the federal sentencing proceedings; only 50 corporations were actually sentenced in that year (Chaset and Weintraub 1992: 41). This number has the potential to increase substantially, and of course corporations are involved in some of the most important cases. Due to the complexities involved in the sentencing of organizations, the original sentencing guidelines provided only a framework for fines of antitrust offenders (Parker 1989: 514).

After several years of study and hearings, the U.S. Sentencing Commission promulgated sentencing guidelines for organizations in 1991. Even though the common law tradition provided little guidance for the sentencing of corporations, the Sentencing Commission has insisted that the goals and purposes applied to "natural persons," including deterrence, punishment, and restitution, can be applied to organizations (Chaset and Weintraub 1992; U.S. Sentencing Commission 1988; 1989). The practical effect of the commission's organizational sentencing guidelines is to increase the size of fines and eliminate some of the sentences formerly available to judges in such cases. However, the guidelines included organizational probation as one important, if controversial, sentencing option (Lofquist 1993a). Due to a firestorm of protest from influential corporations, the commission had retreated from the 1989 draft version's call for huge fines (Etzioni 1993). In the early stages of the guidelines' implementation, it was far from clear that more organizations would in fact face stiffer sentences, and that such sentences would not be deflected and circumvented at various stages.

## Sentencing White Collar Offenders, In Sum

White collar offenders are far less likely to find themselves standing before a judge awaiting sentencing than are conventional offenders. Of the relatively few such offenders who have ended up in this situation, many have undoubtedly received sentences that are lenient relative to the great harm they have caused.

Clearly, few broad generalizations can be made about the sentencing of white collar offenders. A small proportion of the highly visible, major white collar offenders may receive fairly harsh sentences. Relatively lower-level white collar offenders who have defrauded identifiable victims typically receive harsher sentences than do high-level corporate executives. Judges in these cases often find themselves wrestling with pronounced complexities involving the offense, the attributes of the offender, the likely consequences of the sentence, and various purposes of imposing sanctions in the first place. Further, these complexities of major white collar crimes, especially corporate forms, make it more difficult for judges to ascertain the appropriate degree of culpability. Some of the objectives of traditional criminal sentencing, including incapacitation and rehabilitation, are viewed as either irrelevant or inappropriate in many white collar crime cases. The large and ongoing debate on the appropriate sanctions for such crime, especially corporate crime, is sufficiently important to warrant a separate discussion in Chapter 12 of this text.

## White Collar Criminals in the Correctional System

INDIVIDUAL WHITE COLLAR offenders are relatively rarely sent to prison. When such offenders are incarcerated, they are almost always sent to minimum security prisons, where the conditions are quite different from those in the maximum security prisons filled with conventional offenders. These prisons—Allenwood in Pennsylvania and Lompoc in California are two examples—have sometimes been characterized as "country clubs" or "Club Fed." Although they look more like a campus than a fortress, have a scenic setting, contain fairly extensive recreational facilities, and lack prison cells (Lounsberry 1991), the inmates are not at liberty to leave the grounds, must accept banal work assignments, are quartered with other inmates in small cubicles or dormitories, and have limited choices concerning food and other

amenities. Thus even though such incarceration is likely to be experienced as punitive, it is substantially less punitive than the experience of the typical conventional
career criminal in a maximum-security prison such as Attica or Leavenworth.

The assumption that white collar offenders who have lived in comfortable (or
even lavish) circumstances and have enjoyed a respectable (or even prestigious)
status suffer more from both the material deprivations and shame of imprisonment
than do conventional, lower-class offenders has not been well studied. Benson and
Cullen (1988) cast some doubt on the validity of this "special sensitivity" thesis in
their study of a small sample of 14 white collar offenders who had been incarcerated.
Their interviews revealed that these offenders had adjusted remarkably well to their
prison experience and seemed to be quite free of emotional problems rooted in this
experience. Benson and Cullen suggested that individuals with more education,
greater family ties, and noncriminal identities may adapt better to prison than do
individuals without these advantages. Furthermore, white collar offenders are more
likely than conventional offenders to have had experience adapting to the expectations of a formal organization, and accordingly they may more easily conform to
prison rules and regulations. One of the participants in this study, who did time in a
federal prison, put it this way:

> Once you're past the first initial period, it's really not so bad. I mean sitting in
> prison, I got all the food, three square meals a day. I really have no problems, no
> worries....Yeah, it's punishment, but its effect as punishment is gone after the first
> few days. I mean you're afraid of going to prison till you get to prison, and once
> you're in prison, you really don't want to go back to prison, but once you're there
> for a couple of months, you just kind of get into it. You live. You're there. You
> survive....(Benson and Cullen 1988: 209)

Such an account may, of course, be bravado, and it may be atypical; caution is
warranted for drawing any conclusions from such a limited sample. But this study
suggests that conventional wisdom about the impact of the prison system on white
collar offenders may be wrong, and that conventional lower-class offenders may
suffer as much or even more. Indeed, by some accounts, a certain proportion of white
collar offenders may actually have years added to their lives by being compelled in
prison to eat a healthier and more balanced diet and to exercise regularly.

Still, no one should doubt that white collar offenders experience significant
humiliation and dramatically changed conditions in their daily lives when they are
incarcerated. Michael Milken, who had spent the latter part of the 1980s as a billionaire and one of the most powerful financiers in America, had to share a small
dormitory room with several other men at Pleasanton Federal Penitentiary and was
assigned such tasks as cleaning bathrooms, mopping floors, tidying up the trash area,
and scouring rust off signs (Kornbluth 1992: 344). Dennis Levine (1991a: 49), one
of the key figures in the 1980s insider trading cases, described a humiliating strip
search, assignment to a small cubicle with a soiled mattress and a mafioso cellmate,
his initial job scrubbing toilets and urinals (for 11 cents an hour), and the poor prison
food that greeted him at Lewisburg, a federal prison camp.

Once white collar offenders leave prison, many return either to similar jobs or
to lucrative new challenges (Clinard and Yeager 1980: 296). The overall conse-

quences of conviction and imprisonment for a white collar offense vary, of course. Benson (1984) found that professionals and public-sector employees were more likely to suffer "a fall from grace" (a loss of occupational status) than were private businesspeople.

In general, however, the options available to white collar offenders who have served time are broader than those available to conventional crime "ex-cons." At least some of them may once again become involved in illegal or ethically questionable business activities. Dennis Levine was back in business as a financial advisor in New York City and living in a Park Avenue condominium not long after his release from prison; "60 Minutes" aired a segment claiming that he was engaged in unethical dealings that cost two businessmen, who had hired him to assist them in obtaining major loans, a substantial amount of money (Reibstein 1991). In other cases, however, the experience of incarceration may have a redemptive effect. After Michael Fury, a real estate lawyer, spent 18 months in a federal penitentiary for bank fraud, he became an ordained Protestant minister (Steinberg 1993a). Even though the impact of incarceration varies for conventional offenders as well, they are less likely to have the personal resources and connections that many white collar offenders enjoy.

## Civil Suits

MUCH OF THE recent response to what is broadly classified as white collar crime has taken the form of civil (or private) lawsuits, and such suits (as well as the threat of such suits) continue to be a principal mechanism for attempting to control and punish white collar crim. It is unclear ˉ ʰether a traditional public/private distinction in law makes sense in a contemporary environment in which profit-making corporations make decisions that impose serious risks on the general public (Bender 1990: 864). Nevertheless, civil lawsuits seeking millions of dollars from white collar offenders, who often have substantial assets, have become more common (Institute for Civil Justice 1992). Such suits may occur in conjunction with criminal prosecution; alterntively, white collar offenders (especially corporations) may avoid criminal prosecution and sanctions by agreeing to make a civil settlement of claims against them.

Civil lawsuits initiated by private parties against corporations, businesspeople, or professionals who have been responsible for some form of harm (e.g., workplace injury and malpractice) have often faced a formidable challenge, because defendants typically have the resources to mount a powerful defense and the laws governing liability are somewhat narrowly interpreted. Private parties can be intimidated by the fact that civil cases can take years to resolve. Early in the 20th century industrial accidents were claiming an estimated 35,000 lives annually and causing some 2 million injuries, but only a small fraction of these incidents resulted in lawsuits, and most victims were poorly (if at all) compensated (Lieberman 1983: 38); at the end of the century only a very small proportion of victims are filing suit (Conlin 1991) because the obstacles to the successful pursuit of such suits are still considerable.

The civil lawsuits most directly relevant to white collar crime are tort cases, in which compensation (and sometimes punitive damages) is sought in response to some injury, damage, or loss (Sherman 1987). Despite the various obstacles, the number of tort lawsuits increased measurably in the past several decades, especially in the federal courts, although not all commentators agree that the overall rate of litigation has increased (Friedman 1984: 283; Institute for Civil Justice 1992: 15; Lieberman 1983; Lindsey 1986). As of 1990, close to half a million tort cases, involving expenditures of tens of billions of dollars, were being filed annually in state courts (Conlin 1991: 114; Institute for Civil Justice 1992: 51).

Even though most of these suits concerned matters usually unrelated to white collar crime (e.g., automobile accidents), many other lawsuits involved such crime in the broad sense. For example, malpractice suits against physicians increased from 1 per 100 doctors in 1960 to 18 per 100 doctors in 1985; settlements rose from $60 million in 1980 to over $5 billion a mere six years later (Hiatt 1991: 42). The increase in product liability lawsuits was also especially pronounced (Friedman 1984). In particular, there has been an increase in complex litigation involving multiple parties and causes of action, novel legal theories, and difficult technical evidence (Institute for Civil Justice 1992: 25). In part this increase can be attributed to a movement in tort jurisprudence since the 1960s away from contract principles that imposed more responsibility on plaintiffs, and toward principles such as "enterprise liability," a form of strict liability that imposed more responsibility on manufacturers, professionals, and other potential defendants and displayed a greater concern with compensating injured parties (Hall 1989: 297; Huber 1988: 149; Croley and Hanson 1991: 1; Sherman 1987: 431).

Targets of tort lawsuits—from manufacturers facing product liability claims to physicians facing malpractice suits—have frequently complained of a "civil liability crisis" or "litigation explosion" directed at them; the many harmful consequences that result include plant closings, product discontinuances, abandoned medical practices, and price increases (Institute for Civil Justice 1992; Waren 1988: 14). Some real estate developers, alleged polluters, public servants, and other parties who have been opposed by citizens groups have initiated their own civil lawsuits—Strategic Lawsuits Against Public Participation, or SLAPPS—to discourage these citizens groups from pursuing actions against them (Bishop 1991). This emerging legal tactic could become yet another obstacle to citizens groups mobilizing against corporate crime.

Others have persuasively taken issue with people who blame the tort crisis on lawsuit-happy litigants, greedy lawyers, irresponsible juries, and bleeding-heart judges. Syracuse University law professor Leslie Bender (1990) argued that the liability crisis is caused by corporate violence, corporate irresponsibility, and the relentless forces that place corporate profits ahead of all other considerations, not by tort law itself or victims of corporate torts. In the same spirit, UCLA law professor Richard Abel (1988a) asserted that the crisis is injuries, not liability, and that only a small minority (16 percent, according to one ABA study) of people who report being victims of torts even consulted lawyers; an even smaller percentage of these victims successfully pursued cases and recovered damages. Jethro K. Lieberman (1983: 49), a critic of the American legal system, noted that the social costs of product-related injuries may exceed $10 billion annually, even though fewer than 1 percent of the injured parties filed suit.

In this view, then, tort liability provides an important incentive for safer practices on the part of businesses and professionals, compensates the injured, and informs consumers about dangerous goods and services (Abel 1988a: 36–37; Bender 1990; Swartz 1987). A study conducted by a Harvard Medical School professor and some colleagues produced some solid evidence that medical malpractice suits indeed have a deterrent effect in terms of reducing negligent injuries (Hiatt 1991). In 1992 a bill that would have made it more difficult for consumers to sue manufacturers over defective products was defeated in the U.S. Senate (Meier 1992d). Thus a favorable view of tort litigation or lawsuits need not be restricted to the lawyers who make a living off such suits.

Despite recent legislative and jurisprudential reforms that aided plaintiffs in tort cases, wealthy corporate defendants still have a considerable overall advantage in such lawsuits (Bender 1990), and it is far from clear that plaintiffs will benefit from recent reforms indefinitely. With respect to product liability, for which the economic stakes are especially large, the evidence suggests that since the mid-1980s the courts have reverted to favoring defendants, and conservative scholars were calling for a return to principles of contract and negligence (Labaton 1989c; Croley and Hanson 1991). Since the mid-1980s, legislation in various states has imposed caps on awards (especially for punitive damages), time limits for the filing of cases, and in some cases restrictions on contingency fees (Institute for Civil Justice 1992: 18). Although in recent years the U.S. Supreme Court has expressed some discomfort with multi-million dollar punitive damage awards, in a 1993 decision it once again declined to place a meaningful constitutional limit on such awards (Greenhouse 1993). In the case in question, the Court conceded that a $10 million punitive civil judgment against TXO Corporation, which had sought through a frivolous lawsuit to deprive another company (Alliance Resources, Inc.) of oil and natural gas royalties, was substantial; it also concluded that the size of the potential loss to the plaintiff, the wealth of the defendant, and the fraudulent conduct of the defendant all justified such an award.

Recent research does not support claims by business and professional interests that the punitive awards imposed on them were unjust. One 1990 study found that punitive awards were made in less than 5 percent of civil cases, less than 9 percent of product liability cases, and less than 3 percent of medical malpractice suits (Conlin 1991: 116). Another study found that during a recent 25-year period, only 355 product liability cases against corporations resulted in punitive damage awards (Rustad and Koenig 1991). Furthermore, the substantial majority of product liablity and medical malpractice cases are won by the defendants, not the plaintiffs (Conlin 1991). The percentage of medical malpractice and product liability cases won by plaintiffs dropped precipitously between 1989 and 1992 (from 48 percent to 31 percent, and from 59 percent to 41 percent, respectively), and the size of awards leveled off (Perez-Pena 1994). In sum, even if civil lawsuits have increasingly been directed at corporate criminals and white collar professional criminals, corporations and professionals still retain the overall advantage in these lawsuits.

## Citizen Suits and Class Action Suits

"Citizen suits" and large-scale class action civil suits against major corporations have become far more common following a liberalization of federal rules in 1966 and congressional implementation of federal citizen suits (Lieberman 1983: 17; Simon 1991: 30).

Citizen suits allow private parties who have been injured or threatened (e.g., by some environmentally harmful corporate action) to petition the court to enjoin the harmful activity, and under some statutes to seek assessments of civil fines payable to the U.S. Treasury (Simon 1991). Environmentalist groups initiated several such suits after 1982 in response to their frustration with the Environmental Protection Agency's indifference concerning enforcement actions.

Class action lawsuits, in contrast, involve a group of directly injured parties seeking compensation (and possible punitive damages) from an organizational harm-doer. When a major corporation (or even the government) is charged with some form of harmful conduct, individual plaintiffs are typically at a formidable disadvantage due to the much more limited resources at their disposal. When a large group of victims of the same harmful conduct join together in a class action against some major organizational entity, their collective resources can be formidable. First-class lawyers are often prepared to devote much time and effort, on a contingency basis (i.e., taking a significant percentage of the monetary award if they win, and nothing if they lose), to a case in which they may ultimately recover millions of dollars in fees.

Major recent class action lawsuits against corporations include the Agent Orange case against Dow Chemical and the U.S. government, the asbestos case against the Manville Corporation, and the Dalkon shield case against the A. H. Robins Corporation (Brodeur 1985; Perry and Dawson 1985; Schuck 1986). Although some of these lawsuits resulted in judgments in favor of the plaintiffs for hundreds of millions or even billions of dollars, the lawyers involved may have been the primary beneficiaries (Labaton 1989b; Rosenberg 1986). Several of these corporations, including Manville and A. H. Robins, filed for bankruptcy to limit their financial liability (Delaney 1989; Sobol 1991). Distribution of the damage awards often takes years and may result in as little as several thousand dollars for each individual plaintiff. The formidable costs and frustrations involved in these cases are generating considerable pressure to reform the law, use alternatives to adjudication, and resolve claims more efficiently and equitably (Bovbjerg and Metzloff 1991; McGovern 1991; Galen 1992). It seems likely that civil law responses to white collar crime will undergo various changes in the years ahead.

## Collateral Civil Suits

The federal government (especially its regulatory agencies) often finds it more practical or efficient to pursue corporate wrongdoers and some classes of white collar criminals through civil suits, either in conjunction with or in place of criminal prosecution. Major environmental damage cases (such as the Exxon *Valdez* oil spill) and insider trading cases (such as the Ivan Boesky and Michael Milken cases) have involved civil law settlements of hundreds of millions of dollars.

The government and its agents have traditionally been legally shielded from many kinds of civil lawsuits, largely on the premise that government operations would be seriously hampered if such lawsuits were permitted. Still, in recent years the courts have permitted some civil suits against government officials, and citizen groups, consumer interest groups, and corporate or business interests have initiated suits against federal regulatory agencies on the grounds that the agencies either do not effectively enforce regulatory laws or enforce them too liberally (Coleman 1989: 175).

Clearly, various types of civil lawsuits continue to play critical roles both in the response to some white collar crime (especially its corporate form) and in the efforts of corporate and professional interests to limit government intrusion into their affairs. Although their effects are difficult to measure, the surfeit of expensive, well-publicized civil lawsuits has impressed on many corporations and other white collar enterprises the need to avoid harmful practices. On the other hand, a civil lawsuit does not have the equivalent moral force and stigmatizing effect of a criminal prosecution, and white collar offenders can more easily rationalize their harmful actions when the major sanctions against them are civil lawsuits.

## Prosecuting and Adjudicating White Collar Crime, In Sum

WE SAW IN this chapter that many different agencies and entities respond to white collar crime, and that this response is far less concentrated and centralized than is true for conventional crime. Furthermore, there is far less consensus on the most appropriate means of responding to white collar crime, and there are many constraints or inhibitions on any such responses that do not generally apply to conventional crime. Despite all of the recent initiatives against white collar crime, for the most part it is still less likely to be investigated, to be subjected to enforcement or prosecution, or to result in harsh sanctions than is conventional crime. The development of increasingly effective criminal justice and alternative responses to white collar crime will be one of the major challenges for our legal system in the years ahead.

# Responding to the Challenge
# of White Collar Crime

**N**O ONE SHOULD have illusions about the immensity of the challenge of responding effectively to the problem of white collar crime in all its guises. There are many dilemmas and quandaries, and no obvious or easy answers. Achieving a consensus on the guiding principles, legal and otherwise, that should underlie our response to white collar crime is generally more difficult than is the case for conventional crime. The practical problems of gathering the facts of white collar crimes and marshalling the resources to address these crimes are also much more formidable.

This text has attempted to provide a "mapping" of the white collar crime terrain. It has addressed some of the formidable problems in conceptualizing and studying white collar crime. It has identified the extraordinary range of activities that can either be characterized as forms of white collar crime or are associated with it. And it has described some of the massive economic, physical, social, and psychological harm caused by white collar crime. What, then, can be done about it?

## Raising Consciousness of White Collar Crime

**THE FIRST STEP** in any program for a more effective response to white collar crime calls for an elevated level of consciousness of it. A persistent thesis in the white collar crime literature is that the response to such crime is more limited and less severe than the response to conventional crime. This text has suggested many reasons for a more attenuated response, and it has cited some evidence for a growing appreciation of the seriousness of white collar crime. The challenge is to cultivate this appreciation, and to do so in a way rooted more in reality than in rhetoric.

Despite a considerable expansion of interest in white collar crime within criminology and criminal justice, it continues to be somewhat slighted in the educational curriculum, especially in criminal justice programs (Wright and Friedrichs 1991).

There is a need, then, to promote more extensive treatment of white collar crime within the academic realm. Ideally, primary and secondary school teachers would have some formal exposure to the study of white collar crime, so that they could then provide a more balanced and well-informed representation of the crime problem to their students.

Criminologists or criminal justicians could play a role in fostering broader attention to white collar crime in the media by engaging in "newsmaking criminology" (Barak 1994). Grassroots organizations can continue to play a larger role in responding to corporate crime, as is evident in the environmental movement directed at corporate pollution (Cable and Benson 1993). The more the seriousness and the many harmful consequences of white collar crime is understood, the more effective any specific response to it is likely to be.

## Policy Options for Responding to White Collar Crime

In Chapter 8 we discussed such matters as the nature of reality, human nature, and the nature of the moral and social order because our assumptions on these matters significantly influence how we tend to explain white collar crime. The same is true, of course, about the choices we make for responding to such crime.

White collar crimes inspire an especially broad range of responses, from outrage to pragmatism to apathy. Apathy toward such crime is probably more widespread than it is for conventional crime, especially when people do not consider themselves to be affected by the crime. A cynical form of resignation to such crime is likely in people who regard humans as naturally corrupt. People who believe the state should not intervene at all in many activities defined as forms of white collar crime can even get defensive. Others view white collar crime as a reflection of regulatory overreach; such "crime" is largely an artifact of law (Reynolds 1985).

White collar crime differs in a fundamental way from conventional crime, because it is closely associated with productive, desirable activities. There is a concern that excessively restrictive and punitive responses toward such crime (especially in its corporate form) will deter such productive activities more than it will prohibited activities. Some conservative critics claim that governmental action and new laws adopted as responses to such problems as the savings and loan failures cause more harm than they resolve (Rowlett 1993; Shackelford 1993). Thus a basic tension exists between strategies that are interventionist and those that are noninterventionist. Fisse and French (1985) suggested that a pragmatic, "incrementalist" approach, with a mixture of laws, regulation, and negotiation, could serve as a middle ground.

Responses to white collar crime may be directed toward structural, organizational, or individualistic levels; that is, they may address fundamental conditions in the social structure, organizational factors, or individual orientations that promote white collar crime. Likewise, responses to white collar crime may address social control (e.g., legal reform), opportunity structures (e.g., occupational conditions), or cognitive states (e.g., motivations).

Responses to white collar crime may be essentially normative, utilitarian, or coercive; that is, they may attempt to persuade (normative), they may appeal to reason or offer practical inducements (utilitarian), or they may rely on threats of intervention and punishment (coercive). Similarly, responses to white collar crime may be essentially preventive (keeping the criminal activity from occurring in the first place), regulatory (operant while the criminal activity is in progress), or retaliatory (put into effect after the criminal activity has occurred). Rationales for responding formally to white collar crime include retribution (revenge), incapacitation, deterrence, and rehabilitation.

Responses to white collar crime range from very informal to highly formal; that is, they may rely on public opinion and shaming, self-policing, private negotiations, citizens group boycotts, civil lawsuits, administrative regulation, or the criminal justice system.

The most effective and enduring solutions to white collar crime are structural, normative, and preventive. Virtually all serious students of white collar crime and corruption recognize that coercive, retaliatory responses that emphasize investigation, enforcement, adjudication, and punishment will always have limited effectiveness, especially because only a small percentage of offenders can be identified, prosecuted, and penalized. Furthermore, reactive (especially retaliatory) responses to white collar crime will most often take effect only after grievous, often irreparable harm has occurred. Nevertheless, potent arguments have been advanced that favor a coercive, punitive response to white collar crime.

Structural, normative, and preventive strategies must operate on several different levels. First, they must attempt to diminish (if not eliminate) motivations for committing white collar crimes. Second, they must attempt to transform the ethical and normative climate that helps promote such crime. Third, they must attempt to diminish the conditions that provide opportunities for such crime.

## Responding to White Collar Crime as a Moral Issue

MORAL OUTRAGE IS one very understandable response to white collar crime. That large and powerful corporations would knowingly flout the law and endanger the lives of employees, customers, and citizens, or defraud them, is outrageous. That well-educated or affluent professionals, entrepreneurs, and retailers would engage in such activities is outrageous. That some crimes appear to be driven by pure greed—which is more likely to be the case with white collar crime than with other crimes—is outrageous.

Even if moral outrage at white collar crime is justifiable and perhaps necessary, it is less clear that social policies fueled primarily by such outrage are the most effective ways of responding to it (Fisse and French 1985: 4). One of the tensions in the ongoing debate about the appropriate social policy response to white collar crime pits those who believe that moral idealism should provide the point of departure against those who believe that practical realism should be the primary basis of social policy. Social policies based principally on moral outrage can have unintended harmful consequences for innocent parties. The conundrums and contradictions in formulating justifiable and effective social policy responses are especially pronounced with respect to white collar crime. We should be wary of policy proposals that are either excessively sanctimonious and self-righteous or excessively faint-hearted and "practical."

## Moral Appeals

In the popular imagination, at least, white collar crime reflects immoral (and unethical) choices. Are moral appeals, then, a feasible means of promoting higher levels of compliance with the laws governing white collar crime, or are they utterly idealistic?

In a study of the use of moral appeals (through the mass media) to promote taxpayer compliance, Mason and Mason (1992: 382–83) identified several advantages relative to alternative approaches: They are relatively inexpensive; they may reach some of the many potential offenders who will not be dissuaded by enforcement efforts and sanctions; and they are politically appealing because they are less alienating than conventional enforcement efforts. But can such an approach have a measurable impact? In an oft-cited early study, Schwartz and Orleans (1967) found that moral appeals were more effective than threats; a subsequent replication by McGraw and Scholz (1991) found that moral appeals did not affect behavior, even if they influenced what people say about cheating. Mason and Mason (1992) found some evidence that media appeals that induce taxpayers to focus on the fairness (or unfairness) of their conduct have some potential for success. The research on this question, then, has produced somewhat contradictory findings.

## Business Ethics Courses in the Curriculum

One response to the perception of an ethics crisis in U.S. business was the much wider introduction of business ethics courses. The call for business ethics in the curriculum was first heeded in the 1950s, although it has only partially been realized (Weber 1990). Between the early 1970s and early 1980s the number of business ethics courses in U.S. educational institutions increased fivefold, and the call for strong ethics programs intensified during the 1980s (Pitch 1983; Palmer 1986). By the late 1980s, over 90 percent of U.S. business schools offered some form of business ethics studies; on the undergraduate level, autonomous business ethics courses were less common, as fewer than 10 percent of business programs required such a course for their majors (Hoffman 1989: 46). Ideally, these business ethics courses promote values that put integrity and concern with the well-being of others ahead of personal or corporate enrichment and advantage.

Unfortunately, it is far from clear that integrating business ethics into the curriculum will measurably elevate the ethical behavior of businesspeople. One view is that by the time students get to business or professional school, their ethical mindsets are quite fully developed; put another way, ethical conduct is a matter of early training and character formation (Levin 1989; Hutcheson 1990). A more optimistic view indicates that whereas some 25 percent of MBA students are fundamentally indifferent to ethical concerns, and some 25 percent are deeply committed to such concerns, the remaining 50 percent are not locked into either position and thus may be reached by business ethics education (Wilkes 1989). A review of several studies suggested that any improvements in students' ethical awareness and reasoning after formal exposure to business ethics courses was apparently short-lived (Weber 1990). The contextual forces at work within a business or organization are likely to be more potent than exposure to one or more business ethics courses.

## Business Ethics Within the Business World

Business ethics has become a big business itself. Some people consider the notion of "business ethics" to be an oxymoron. An ongoing debate concerns business's principal ethical obligation: Is it maximizing the financial return to owners (shareholders), or the broader social responsibility to promote society's well-being (Madsen and Shafritz 1990)? But businesses (especially larger corporations) have become conscious of a need to at least appear concerned with ethical conduct (although some internal ethical issues—for example, those regarding employee layoffs, drug screening tests, and performance evaluations—do not involve white collar crime in the conventional sense).

Historically, corporations have lacked a formal mechanism for guiding and monitoring ethical decision making. A small minority of major corporations (less than 15 percent, as of the late 1980s) have established ethics committees, ethical ombudsmen, and ethics judiciary boards; the defense industry is a leader in implementing corporate ethics programs (Hoffman 1989: 47; I. Ross 1992: 195–96). More broadly, businesses have established compliance programs that include a code of ethics, a compliance office (with a full-time director), and mechanisms for processing inquiries and complaints about questionable corporate activities. Only a minority— perhaps 25 percent—of major corporations have specific ethics training programs for employees.

A code of ethics is the single most common element of corporate ethics programs, and as of the early 1990s some 90 percent of Fortune 500 corporations, and about half of all other companies, had some such code (Metzger, Dalton, and Hill 1993). However, these codes mainly emphasize the corporation's legal responsibilities so that it can minimize its legal exposure in the event of unethical actions by its employees. Of course, another important objective of these ethics codes and programs is to discourage unethical (and illegal) behavior against the corporation itself.

The success of any program incorporating a code of conduct significantly depends on the extent to which the targeted parties are consulted on and help formulate the codes, rather than simply having the codes imposed upon them (Findlay and Stewart 1992). Even though corporate ethics programs are generally intended to reach individual consciences, the recognition that an organization's ethical ambience is a key element of corporate crime requires programs that address ethics collectively, rather than individually. The implementation of such programs always raises the question of whether they represent a serious commitment to ethical corporate conduct or are instead a form of "window-dressing" intended to curry favorable public opinion (Young 1981). Even if the commitment to ethical conduct is sincere, it is hardly self-evident that ethical considerations will prevail over a corporation's financial interests. Some studies have even suggested that pressures to reach profit-related goals were actually greater, and federal agency citations more numerous, for companies with ethical codes than for those without such codes (Clinard 1990; Metzger, Dalton, and Hill 1993). Unless there are specific incentives to reward ethical behavior, conduct codes are unlikely to have any positive effect:

> As long as you have a business culture that puts people in impossible situations— "your division has to grow 7 percent in the next year or else we're going to be No. 2 in the field and if we are, you're going to be job-hunting"—you're going to have people shipping inferior goods, juggling the books, bribing when they have to, trampling workers beneath them and generally conducting themselves in the time-honored tradition. Results, and only results, count. (Gary Edwards, in Wilkes 1989: 24).

Some observers hope that over time more corporations will adopt the view that "good ethics is good business." Even though corporations that foster a morally defensible internal environment appear to enjoy some long-term benefits due to enhanced employee morale and loyalty (Etzioni 1988b: 239; Metzger, Dalton, and Hill 1993), it would clearly be a mistake to rely on corporations to embrace voluntarily morally superior ethical standards.

The preceding discussion has been limited to corporations, but of course issues of immoral and unethical conduct apply to all types of businesses, professions, and occupations. The corporate environment may produce more intense pressures to behave unethically and more opportunities to rationalize ethical misconduct than other settings, and the harmful consequences of unethical conduct carried out on behalf of a corporation are likely to be especially far-reaching. Still, the ethical lapses of corporations are hardly unique to the business world.

## Shaming as a Response to White Collar Crime

A moralistic or normative response to white collar crime is ideally preventive, but it may come about as a reaction to such crime. John Braithwaite (1989c; 1993a; 1993b) reintroduced the ancient notion of "shaming" into the ongoing dialogue concerning responses to crime generally. In his view, one of the reasons why punishment has largely failed to reduce the crime rate is that it has been "uncoupled" from its moral roots: shame (Braithwaite 1989c: 61). Thus for individuals and corporations alike, shaming from without (e.g., by state agencies) and from within (e.g., by corporate colleagues) is a normative form of social control that has the potential to be far more effective than other forms of social control (especially coercive ones).

White collar individuals and corporations are concerned with their reputations, perhaps both as a function of self-esteem or corporate pride and for economic reasons. An evolving societal consensus on the criminality of actions such as environmental damage has made those responsible for such crimes even more vulnerable to shaming today than in the recent past (Braithwaite 1993a). Shaming, which takes the form of adverse publicity and identification as a wrongdoer, focuses on this concern.

In Braithwaite's (1989c; 1993a) view, the shaming process should be reintegrative (promotes reintegration of the shamed individual or organization back into the community) rather than stigmatizing (excludes and pushes the offender away from the community and into further crime and deviance). Ideally it is carried out by the peer community of the offending individual or organization. Reintegrative shaming emphasizes that certain deeds and actions may be evil, but that individuals (and organizations) are not typically beyond redemption. The effectiveness of such a strategy, however, tends to presuppose a rather high level of consensus on the perceived shamefulness of white collar crimes, and this assumption has been challenged (Uggen 1993). Individual white collar and corporate offenders are also especially likely to rationalize their illegal activity, and to characterize attempts to shame them as unjustifiable forms of persecution..

## Securing Compliance and Sanctioning White Collar Crime

WHAT ARE THE best ways to secure compliance with laws, regulations, and rules directed at minimizing the harm done by corporations, entrepreneurs, and professionals? Ongoing debates in the realm of white collar crime center on the circumstances under which intervention does and does not make sense, and the degree to which coercive and noncoercive means of inducing compliance should be used.

A variety of *specific* sanctions can be used to respond to white collar crime. The term *sanction* is most commonly equated with punishment, but strictly speaking sanctions may be positive or negative.

*Positive sanctions* include grants, bounties, fees, tax credits, loan guarantees, prizes or rewards, favorable administrative consideration, praise, inducements, incentives, indulgences, and compensatory power (Freiburg 1987: 229; Grabosky 1993: 4; Smith and Stalans 1991). Positive sanctions are not commonly used by the criminal law; when they are used, they are mainly intended to induce cooperation in a criminal prosecution or to encourage whistleblowers to come forward.

In 1986 Congress updated the False Claims Act of the Civil War era, thereby lifting the award ceiling and enabling whistleblowers to sue employers for damages (I. Ross 1992: 138–41). This has proven very effective. Between 1986 and mid-1992, for example, 450 such private suits were directed at corporations (principally defense contractors). In one case involving a major defense contractor, the Singer Company, a former employee was awarded $7.7 million for revealing fraudulent overcharges in the tens of millions of dollars. Inevitably there is some concern that such whistleblowers may be overrewarded or may even lie to obtain a large award.

Positive sanctions can be directed toward potential lawbreakers as well (Friedland 1989; Grabosky 1993). In a study of regulation of nursing homes, Makkai and Braithwaite (1993) found that the use of praise (for positive accomplishments) by nursing home inspectors helped improve levels of compliance with regulatory standards. A review of research on tax compliance by Smith and Stalans (1991) found that positive incentives (such as respectful treatment and praise) were more likely to produce compliance than were material inducements (e.g., monetary rewards).

Such findings are consistent with a basic axiom of 20th-century psychology: that rewarding good behavior is generally more effective than punishing bad behavior.

Positive incentives can have many advantages: They increase freedom of choice; they are more likely to be perceived as legitimate and are less likely to be alienating; they can facilitate learning of desired behavior; they can induce necessary cooperation and assistance from third parties; and they can foster collective pride in an organization (Freiburg 1987; Grabosky 1993: 11–16; I. Ross 1992). On the other hand, such incentives can be manipulative and paternalistic (as when they appear to offer bribes to engage in morally proper conduct), can foster a climate of distrust within an organization, and can be costly as well as vulnerable to fraud (Grabosky 1993: 17–20; 33). The challenge with positive incentives, then, is to apply them whenever they are more effective than negative sanctions, are cost-effective, and do not have corrupting effects.

A wide range of *negative sanctions* are more commonly applied to crime, including white collar crime. In the case of individual offenders, negative sanctions may range from imprisonment to fines to occupational disqualification; in the case of organizations they may range from loss of charter to fines to adverse publicity. Although negative sanctions are most readily associated with the criminal law, they may also be applied through civil and administrative law, and by nongovernmental systems of social control as well. Negative civil sanctions include damages, divestiture orders, restitution, compensation, confiscation, injunctions, warnings, cease and desist orders, licensure revocation, suspension, cancellation, and fines (Freiburg 1987: 224). At least some sanctions may have a mixture of positive and negative elements. For example, a requirement of community service or restitution is a form of punishment for the perpetrator, but it directly benefits the community or the victims of white collar crimes.

## Law and the Coercive Response to White Collar Crime

A TRADITIONAL BIAS, especially on the part of legislators, lawyers, and police officers, holds that *law* is the best way to control and respond to harmful behavior. But law is ultimately coercive insofar as it it backed up by the threat of force. Although law is ordinarily thought of principally in terms of its effectiveness in preventing or deterring harmful activity, it has other important objectives, including expressing societal anger and imposing justice (Hedman 1991).

The use of the *criminal* law in response to the activity known as white collar crime is generally more open to dispute than it is with respect to conventional crime. On one side of the argument are people who favor broader application of the criminal law to harmful corporate and occupational activities by using a more prosecutorial and punitive approach; on the other side are people who favor decriminalizing some currently recognized forms of white collar crime and relying less on invoking the criminal law in response to other offenses.

Since the 1970s the criminal law has in fact been more broadly applied to corporate wrongdoing such as worker safety violations, toxic dumping, and environmental pollution. Coffee (1991) argued that this trend unnecessarily entangles individuals and corporations who have not consciously chosen to do harm in a criminal process. Goldstein (1992) suggested that the label "criminal" can lose some of its stigmatizing power if it is too readily applied to individuals (or organizations) not considered criminal by the general public.

In his influential *Where the Law Ends* (1975), Christopher Stone adopted the thesis that the effectiveness of the law in responding to corporate crime has inherent limitations. The law was originally developed to deal with individuals, not organizations. A built-in "time lag" in the application of the law is not well-suited to addressing or preventing ongoing harm. The more threatening the law becomes to corporations, the more incentive such organizations have either to contest the law (making its implementation especially costly) or to withdraw from productive activity. Because corporations have many means of either shielding themselves from or minimizing the impact of efforts to control them by law, we should explore all available alternatives to the criminal law.

## Civil Suits and Penalties

Because the costs associated with the use of the criminal law are especially high, prosecutors have begun relying more and more on civil law for going after corporate offenders, especially in cases in which the harm appears to have been unintentional (Frank 1984b; Frank and Lynch 1992; Mann 1992b). Of course, many other factors can influence a prosecutor's decision to pursue criminal or civil action, including the specific amount of harm associated with the offense, the gain to the offender, the continuation of violations after regulatory agency notifications, the strength of the evidence, and the offender's degree of cooperation and compliance (Cohen 1992: 1070).

The use of civil procedures allows prosecutors to avoid meeting the criminal law's stringent standards for establishing proof and culpability; at the same time, the severity of judgments that can be imposed in civil proceedings is comparable to or exceeds criminal penalties. Furthermore, collecting a substantial civil judgment is far more economical than imposing prison sentences. At present, substantial overlap exists between civil and criminal proceedings and sanctions (Cohen 1992); one response to this situation is a call for more systematic coordination of civil and criminal sanctions, especially as applied to corporations (Yellen and Mayer 1992). One suggestion is that criminal sanctions could be lessened in cases in which civil penalties are especially punitive.

Private parties who have been injured by white collar offenders have always had the option of a civil lawsuit, but as a practical matter they have often lacked the necessary financial resources. Historically, it has been especially intimidating for injured private parties to take on large corporations, but in the second half of the 20th century *class action lawsuits* (see Chapter 11) have been permitted in certain cases and have become a significant device for responding to some forms of white collar crime. In these suits a large class of plaintiffs—many thousands, in some cases—join together in a lawsuit, and an attorney or law firm takes the case on a contingency basis, collecting a significant percentage of any successful judgment but nothing in lost cases. In the last quarter of the 20th century, major class action civil suits included the Agent Orange case against Dow Chemical, other chemical companies, and the U.S. government; the abestos case against the Manville Corporation; and the Dalkon shield case against the A. H. Robins Corporation (Brodeur 1985; Perry and Dawson 1985; Schuck 1986). Although the plaintiffs won huge judgments in each of these cases, some commentators insisted that the lawyers were the primary bene-ficiaries, and individual plaintiffs had to wait years for relatively modest settlements (Labaton 1989b; Rosenberg 1986). Furthermore, some of the corporations (e.g., the Manville Corporation and the A. H. Robins Corporation) filed for bankruptcy as a strategic move to limit their ultimate financial liability (Delaney 1989; Sobol 1991). The corporations involved seem to consider these lawsuits primarily as a cost of doing business rather than as a response to their criminal actions.

Historically, corporations have often found it less costly to contend with civil lawsuits than to limit profits by fully complying with the law or correcting the haz-ards they created (Frank and Lynch 1992). Thus it is difficult to state a general prin-ciple concerning the relative effectiveness of civil suits as a deterrent to corporate crime, or to ascertain whether they result in more or less substantial punishment for offending corporations.

## Cooperative Versus Punitive Approaches to Corporate Crime

An ongoing, fairly vigorous debate centers on whether a response to white collar crime (the corporate form in particular) that relies on invoking the criminal law as punishment is more appropriate and effective than a cooperative regulatory response that attempts to avoid using criminal sanctions. Serious students of corporate crime generally agree that corporations are guided by self-interest and will mostly resist efforts to impose regulations on them, and that some mixture of strategies is required to minimize the harm they do (Pearce and Tombs 1991). The debate, however, cen-ters principally on the extent to which cooperative and punitive measures should be emphasized.

The so-called compliance approach favors cooperative strategies and is very much rooted in the assumption that a cooperative strategy is both a practical neces-sity and a more effective way of limiting the harm of corporate activities. At least some proponents of this approach disavow policy advocacy and consider their work a reflection of the realities of regulatory enforcement practices (Hawkins 1990). Whether or not specific policy endorsements are involved, the reality, in this view, is that punitive approaches are both costly and risky and deflect regulatory personnel from their primary mission of inspecting corporate operations and inducing corpo-rations to abandon or diminish harmful practices (Hawkins 1990). Compliance advo-cates consider punitive approaches to be based on false assumptions about how corporations operate (e.g., by purely rational calculations), and punitive sanctions are most likely to affect relatively low-level corporation managers.

Proponents of the compliance approach cite considerable evidence indicating that corporate-related harmful practices have in fact declined over time, particularly in countries such as Great Britain that have emphasized a cooperative approach over a punitive strategy (Hawkins 1990). The pragmatic argument here is that enforcement resources should be allocated in the most efficient possible manner and should have as their primary objective the reduction of harmful corporate activity (Gray and Scholz 1991). Proponents of a punitive approach are accused, then, of ignoring empirical evidence and the realities of regulatory enforcement practices. Another reality, in this view, is that the harsh application of punitive sanctions to corporations inspires a corporate backlash against regulation generally, with broadly harmful consequences (Hawkins 1990; Hawkins 1991). In sum, persuasion works better than coercion.

In contrast, some citizens' advocates such as Ralph Nader, some mainstream criminologists, and progressive criminologists in particular argue that the criminalization of harmful corporate activity is long overdue, and that the imposition of tough, punitive sanctions is either an essential component or the only strategy that is likely to have an impact on corporate crime (Clinard 1979; Clinard 1990; Pearce and Tombs 1990; Snider 1993). In the progressive criminologists' view, the capitalist mode of production inevitably promotes violations of law, and as a result regulatory violations are widespread for all types of corporations (Pearce and Tombs 1990: 425). Furthermore, recent corporate takeovers and merger activity have put severe pressures on management to place short-term profits ahead of health and safety concerns (Pearce and Tombs 1991). This approach holds that although a broad range of regulatory strategies (including preventive strategies) should be used, only the early, strict, and consistent enforcement of criminal law, with punitive sanctions for serious violations, can be effective against the immense power of corporations.

Snider (1993: 165) asserted that the legal system has been "incredibly forgiving" when it comes to corporate crime. Furthermore, Snider (1993: 157) contended that the cooperative approach may be costlier than the punitive approach if it requires more regulatory personnel. Above all, the compliance approach enables corporations to evade or reduce their responsibility for a range of enormously harmful endeavors. Pearce and Tombs (1990: 436) argued that "if corporations wish to engage in business and so make profits, they must be forced to accept a far greater proportion of the real costs of their activity."

The position taken here is that the law, the criminal law in particular, must continue to be one central feature of the response to white collar crime. It is the only mechanism of social control that can adequately express appropriate moral outrage at the most serious white collar crimes: corporate and occupational crimes. The relatively recent extension of a criminal law response to environmental crimes is justifiable and even necessary during a period when the harmful consequences of such offenses become ever more evident. On the other hand, a certain irony exists when progressive criminologists, who are generally antagonistic toward the capitalist state, call for stronger state action.

The objectives and effectiveness of the criminal law require dispassionate evaluation. Traditionally, the principal objectives of such law have been retribution, incapacitation, deterrence, and rehabilitation. We consider some of the issues involved in the realization of these objectives in the following sections.

## "Just Deserts" and Corporate Crime

DISILLUSIONMENT WITH THE notion that the criminal justice system can rehabilitate people became much more widespread in the 1970s. Likewise, people continued to question whether the existing penal system effectively deters crime, either on the individual or corporate level. Some students of criminal justice policy concluded that if the system could not be depended on either to rehabilitate or deter offenders, it should instead ensure that offenders receive the penalty they deserve. This "just deserts" approach is associated with the ancient rationale of retribution for wrongdoing, and is more specifically rooted in principles articulated by the late 18th- and early 19th-century German philosophers Immanuel Kant and G. W. F. Hegel.

Although retribution is typically regarded as the pursuit of pure revenge, it has also been advocated in principled terms relating to legitimating the demands and obligations of citizenship and the need to realize justice through social harmony (Schlegel 1988a: 618). A recent version of "just deserts" emphasizes the element of "public reprobation" for wrongdoing over the earlier notion of restoring a balance of justice. Schlegel (1988a; 1990) contended that the application of this model to corporations has been largely neglected, and that such an application is both justifiable and effective. Sanctions for corporate crime must be sufficiently severe to convey the appropriate level of social condemnation. In this view, such punishment not only plays a crucial role in deterring crime, but powerfully endorses and revives important values as well. Schlegel held that principles of just deserts, if correctly applied, fulfill the basic requirements of justice.

The "just deserts" approach as applied to corporations has been challenged on a number of grounds. In *Not Just Deserts: A Republican Theory of Criminal Justice*, John Braithwaite and Phillip Pettit (1990: 182) argued that the punitive response built into this model will in practice mete out harsher sanctions to conventional offenders than to corporate offenders. Further, no government has the enormous resources needed to enforce the law and administer punishments to corporations according to the "just deserts" formula; rather, its regulators are necessarily constrained by pragmatism (Braithwaite and Pettit 1990: 190–91). Braithwaite (1982b) argued that such a model inevitably results in injustices: Corporations are punished unjustly for the deeds of individual or small groups of corporate officers and employees acting against the interests of the corporation, and employees and stockholders are punished for corporate acts undertaken without their endorsement and against their interest. Altogether, some commentators regard the problem of establishing culpability and levels of harm as much more difficult whenever corporate crime is involved, and it is more difficult as well to measure the justice of punishments that affect many people as opposed to individuals (Croall 1992: 148; Mann 1992a: 568). A "just deserts" approach has the potential, then, of expanding rather than reducing the scope of injustice.

## Deterrence and White Collar Crime

EVEN THOUGH DETERRENCE of crime is surely one of the central objectives of the criminal justice system, little consensus exists on how and whether legal sanctions have a deterrent effect. Indeed, various criminologists have come down on opposite sides of this issue, and the evidence to support deterrence is equivocal (Simpson and Koper 1992: 349; Wright 1994). The concept of deterrence has been used in different ways, sometimes quite broadly; the deliberate decision to refrain from engaging in illegal activity out of fear of legal sanctions is the conception adopted here (Moore 1987: 381).

The deterrent effect of sanctions has been long recognized to be a function of their certainty, severity, celerity, and uniformity; the first factor, certainty, is the most important (Simpson and Koper 1992: 347). An increasingly sophisticated contemporary literature on deterrence distinguishes between *actual* (objective) and *perceptual* (subjective) deterrence—that is, between the real probabilities of being sanctioned and the perceived likelihood of being punished; the subjective perception is the more important (Wright 1994). The research literature also suggests that *formal* sanctions are less deterrent than *informal* ones, although an important interactive effect occurs when formal sanctions trigger subsequent informal sanctions (Simpson and Koper 1992: 347; Wright 1994). A traditional distinction has been made between *general deterrence*, in which potential offenders (i.e., the general public) are persuaded to refrain from illegal actions by the use of legal sanctions, and *specific deterrence*, in which punished offenders are dissuaded from the commission of further offenses after they have had legal sanctions imposed on them.

The nature of deterrence is clearly complex. Most of us have both avoided punishment for some past wrongdoing and have had some sort of punishment imposed upon us for other wrongdoing. As Stafford and Warr (1993) pointed out, most people are likely to have had a mixture of direct and indirect experiences with both punishment and its avoidance. These researchers have therefore proposed a reconceptualization of general and specific deterrence, with general deterrence referring to the deterrent effect of *indirect* experience with punishment and punishment avoidance, and with special deterrence referring to the deterrent effect of *direct* experience with the same.

Any theory of deterrence adopts, in some form, the classical criminological model of human beings as rational creatures capable of making a calculated, cost-benefit analysis of prospective criminal activity (Simpson and Koper 1992: 357). Our criminal law essentially adopts this model, although a mass of social and behavioral science research has either cast serious doubt on its validity or identified many factors that compromise and limit rational choice. Although some crime may well be deterred on either a general or specific level, clearly a great deal of crime is not deterred by the threat of criminal sanctions.

William Chambliss (1967) made a distinction between *instrumental crimes* (e.g., theft) and *expressive crimes* (e.g., substance abuse). Because instrumental crimes are directed toward material gain whereas expressive crimes are directed toward the satisfaction of some enticement, emotional need, or compulsion, Chambliss posited that it should be easier to deter instrumental as opposed to expressive crimes; not all students of deterrence have agreed (see, for example, Andenaes 1974). The alternative view holds that the extent to which one offense is linked to either subcultural support or moral condemnation is more relevant to deterrence than whether the offense is instrumental or expressive.

White collar crime is typically viewed as a quintessentially instrumental (or rational) crime, and accordingly proponents of Chambliss's view would expect white collar crime to be more amenable to deterrence than many forms of conventional crime (Simpson and Koper 1992). Furthermore, as Braithwaite and Geis (1982) observed, white collar offenders should logically be more deterrable than conventional offenders because their illegal activity is less likely to be an integrated part of their lifestyle, they have more to lose materially, they are more likely to look to the future, and they are more likely to be concerned about their reputation. In adopting one version of this perspective, Bene (1991), argued that attorneys in particular should be susceptible to deterrence by appropriate fines because they often commit economic crimes; they are sophisticated, intelligent, and attuned to cost/benefit analysis; they are somewhat risk-aversive (to preserve the investment in their careers); and they are relatively well-off and stand to lose much if caught committing a crime.

Such arguments make good logical sense, but it is difficult (if not impossible) to demonstrate conclusively that the threat of criminal sanctions deters white collar crime. Clearly, given the pervasiveness of such crime, a great deal of it has not been deterred. Furthermore, the perceived improbability of detection and punishment of white collar offenders surely compromises any deterrent effect.

Deterrence has traditionally been thought of in terms of individuals, not organizations; can corporations be deterred from criminal conduct? Corporations, as collective, goal-oriented enterprises, are commonly assumed to be more rational than traditional individual offenders, and accordingly they should be more deterrable. Braithwaite and Geis (1982) identified some of the differences between conventional crime and corporate crime that are relevant to the question of whether corporations can be deterred and even rehabilitated. On the one hand, corporate crime is more difficult to detect and corporate offenders are more difficult to convict; on the other hand, corporate offenders are more capable of being apprehended, deterred, incapacitated, and rehabilitated. Some evidence suggests that the imposition of more severe sanctions can inhibit corporations from reoffending (Simpson and Koper 1992: 360). Logically, corporations should be more responsive than individuals to any scheme that diminishes the likelihood that crime will pay.

This rather optimistic view of the potential for deterring corporations has been questioned, primarily on the basis that because corporate decision making is guided by a complex of factors relating to economic pressures, particular opportunities, and the need to survive, it does not simply take the form of rational calculations based on maximizing profit (Moore 1987; Simpson and Koper 1992; Stone 1975). Furthermore, as a practical matter the legal system can impose only very limited controls on corporations, although it occasionally prosecutes corporate executives. Moore (1987) pointed out that corporations are especially well-positioned to lobby against legislation regulating or criminalizing their activities and to engage in evasive actions such as filing for bankruptcy, shifting operations to less-regulated environments, and dumping unsafe products abroad.

Braithwaite has subsequently qualified his earlier optimism about deterring corporations. In a study that claimed to be the first quantitative measure of perceptual deviance on the corporate level, Braithwaite and Makkai (1991) found partial support for certainty of detection as a predictor of corporate compliance with laws, but they found no support for an effect related to the certainty or severity of sanctions. According to this study, top management may be guided more by self-interest than by rational determinations of the corporation's interest; may have professional loyalties that override corporate loyalty; won't necessarily make rational decisions in any case; and may not even have control over middle-management personnel who actually violate laws. Decisions of top corporate managers may be driven more by emotions such as envy and pride than by dispassionate consideration of possible sanctions. Despite acknowledging that we have much to learn about how managers differentiate between personal and corporate vulnerability to sanctions and how reputational and economic sanctions have different effects, Braithwaite and Makkai (1991) concluded that deterrence works better on the corporate than on the individual level.

Altogether, we still lack an even remotely adequate base of knowledge and understanding of how the complex of factors involved in corporate behavior interact, and just which policies actually deter corporate illegality (Simpson and Koper 1992). In sum, the challenges of deterring corporate crime are especially complex and formidable.

## Rehabilitation, Probation, and Enforced Self-Regulation

REHABILITATION IS THE most recent rationale for penal responses to crime. The overriding objective of rehabilitation is to transform an offender from a lawbreaker into a constructive, law-abiding citizen. A basic question is whether penal institutions are capable of promoting rehabilitation of individuals. The recent conventional wisdom has been that if rehabilitation in fact occurs within a correctional institution, it is more likely to have occurred in spite of (rather than because of) that institution because many aspects of such institutions tend to work against the rehabilitative objective. A 1970s critique claiming there was little clear evidence of the effectiveness of rehabilitative programs became quite influential, and the rehabilitative objective came to be largely overshadowed by other penal objectives, including retribution, incapacitation, and deterrence.

The rehabilitation of white collar crime offenders involves some paradoxes. One important component of rehabilitative programs has been to provide convicted offenders with the education and job training they need to be able to support themselves by legitimate activities. This aspect of rehabilitation is generally less relevant for individual white collar offenders; indeed, their educational credentials and job skills were often instrumental in putting them in a position to commit white collar crimes in the first place. In some cases white collar offenders are barred from returning to their original profession following release from prison, but the correctional system is rather unlikely to have the resources to provide these offenders with vocational preparation for an alternative career. To the extent that white collar offenders become rehabilitated in prison, such rehabilitation is much more likely to be a result of the old notion of "expiation" for their sins—that is, a personal realization of the wrongfulness of their conduct and a willful repudiation of such conduct in the future—than a function of formal rehabilition programs. In some cases counseling and group therapy might play a role, but successful reintegration of a law-abiding citizen into mainstream society is more likely to result from factors external to the correctional process, such as whether the offender has a supportive family and good job prospects. Finally, any "rehabilitation" of organizations such as corporations must necessarily take place outside of correctional institutions.

## Probation

Probation has typically been regarded as more appropriate for individual white collar offenders than for conventional offenders (Weisburd et al. 1991). The reasons are obvious. The white collar offender is very unlikely to be viewed as a direct physical threat to the community (the single least controversial rationale for incarcerating someone) and is much more likely to be viewed as capable of remaining in the community as a constructive, gainfully employed citizen. However, probation as a response to individual white collar crimes may be regarded as excessively lenient, and it may leave offenders in a position to continue engaging in harmful conduct.

The notion of probation for organizations is a recent one, dating from the early 1970s (Lofquist 1993a). It was first imposed in *U.S. v. Atlantic Richfield Co.* (1971), apparently as a result of a judge's confusion about the precedents concerning non-monetary sanctions (Lofquist 1993b). Subsequent attempts to apply it to corporations were vigorously challenged in the courts, which conceded that corporations could refuse to be subjected to such probation and could choose instead to pay a fine or meet other provisions of their sentences. In the early 1990s the U.S. Sentencing Commission formally established organizational probation as an option, partly as a concession to sentencing commissioners who favored tougher penalties for organizations and were unhappy with the scaling down of the fine schedule in response to business and political lobbying (Lofquist 1993a; 1993b). The original purpose of organizational probation was to ensure that the corporation in question remained in compliance with the laws and followed through on orders to pay fines and restitution; now it can be applied more proactively to intervene in and attempt to transform organizational operations. Organizational probation is still too new to have been widely applied, and its effectiveness as a means of rehabilitating corporate criminals has not yet been evaluated. There is some reason to believe that it will be more widely used in the future, especially if its availability gives prosecutors added incentive to pursue corporate crime cases.

## Enforced Self-Regulation

For many years John Braithwaite (1982b; 1990; 1993c) has advocated *enforced* self-regulation by corporations. A basic premise for Braithwaite's call for self-regulation is that as a practical matter the state cannot effectively inspect and regulate vast numbers of corporations; indeed, corporate inspectors are often better trained and better qualified than government inspectors. Furthermore, corporations typically have "multiple selves"; that is, at least some corporate executives are concerned with responsible, ethical behavior and the long-term reputation of the corporation, and we should attempt to reach these parties. Even though some corporations are not capable of effectively regulating themselves, some are prepared to support compliance programs fully (Braithwaite and Fisse 1987: 225). All of the preceding principles are especially applicable to the growing number of transnational corporations.

Braithwaite contended that although corporations cannot typically be expected to adopt self-regulation on an entirely voluntary basis, they will be responsive to *enforced* self-regulation. In this scheme a corporate compliance director would be required to report to a relevant regulatory agency and would be criminally liable for failing to do so (Braithwaite 1982b: 1470). Among the perceived advantages of this enforced self-regulation model are the following: Rules would be tailored to specific companies and could be adjusted more easily for changing conditions; rules and regulations could be more innovative, comprehensive, and consistent, and companies would be more committed to rules they helped formulate and more willing to assume more of the costs associated with their enforcement; offenders would be more easily caught, more effectively sanctioned by corporate discipline, and more easily prosecuted by the government when necessary. Altogether, in Braithwaite's view, corporations would have a formidable incentive to comply, as opposed to engaging in a costly, time-consuming, and embarrassing attempt to counter an enforced investigation and prosecution.

Braithwaite acknowledged that critics can raise many objections to his enforced self-regulation model—principally that corporations are capable of preempting and severely limiting meaningful regulation—but he argued that the enforcement component successfully counters such objections. Furthermore, Braithwaite (1993c) cited some empirical evidence supporting the self-regulation model: that some transnational pharmaceutical corporations adhere to higher standards than are required in many of the countries in which they operate..

Ideally, enforced self-regulation operates preventively. A related notion proposed by Metzger and Schwenk (1990) calls for the adoption of the ancient device of a "devil's advocate" (used by the Catholic church in canonization procedures) as an element of corporate probation. The objective here is to cultivate an internal critique (and exposure) mechanism within corporate organizations. Such a strategy could conceivably be imposed on companies guilty of repeated, serious offenses and would probably be most appropriate for large, diversified corporations. Metzger and Schwenk (1990) seemed to believe that such a strategy would be both less intrusive and less costly than alternatives (e.g., corporate restructuring) that might be imposed after a corporate conviction.

Alternatively, the courts could require a corporation (or an entire industry) to prepare a report identifying reasons for an offense, those responsible for it, and specific measures to be taken to address the problem (Braithwaite 1993c: 17–18; French 1989). Although at least one version of this approach allows corporations a "first free bite" (by shifting attention away from their initial offense), and even though it imposes a greater burden on the justice system, this approach replaces reliance on industry standards (which may be too low) with reliance on the adequacy of the corporation's response.

## Fines, Restitution, and Community Service

WHITE COLLAR CRIMES are mainly thought of as a form of economic crime, and economic sanctions have been especially commonly imposed on convicted offenders. These economic sanctions can take different forms, including the forfeiture of assets (or illegal profits) and mandatory restitution to victims. Most typically, economic sanctions take the form of criminal or civil *fines*, especially in corporate crime cases, in part because corporations per se obviously cannot be incarcerated (Cohen 1991). The use of fines (as opposed to imprisoning corporate executives) has traditionally been strongly favored by conservatives, who argue that considerations of economic efficiency should be paramount (Romano 1991). If one adopts the premise that a corporation (or any business, for that matter) is essentially an economic institution, then it follows that it should be most responsive to appropriate economic sanctions.

Fines can be punitive, can deter lawbreaking, and can even be rehabilitative if they enable the corporation, business, or individual offender to pay for the harm done and compensate victims. Although fines are likely to be cost-efficient for the justice system, some basic policy choices must be made. When criminal acts are carried out through a corporation and fines are imposed, who should be the targets of the fines: the corporation, the managers and employees who are directly responsible, or both? Questions of deterrence and of fairness are involved in the choices here.

Many additional issues are involved in imposing fines, including the challenge of setting the appropriate amount and determining whether the fine should be based on losses to society or gains to offenders (First 1990: 356–57). Conservative economists generally favor the first choice, even allowing corporations to profit from their illegal activity so long as they pay identifiable costs; they also tend to believe that the threat of excessive fines against corporations may inhibit managers from undertaking some activities that in the long run might prove to be socially beneficial (Macey 1991). On a more practical level, an excessive fine may be so high that it may be uncollectable, may ruin the business, and may well inspire a political backlash. Excessive fines may also seem to strip the punishment of corporations of any serious moral component by treating the issue as a purely economic one. On the other hand, too low a fine may be treated as a "cost of business" and is unlikely to have any significant deterrent effect.

### Sentencing Guidelines for Fines

The U.S. Sentencing Commission's attempts to establish guidelines for fines took into account various factors, including the amount of loss the offense caused (sometimes diffuse and difficult to calculate); the offense "multiple" (difficulty of detecting and prosecuting, to ensure that the fine is both a deterrent and a just punishment); and the enforcement costs involved (Cohen 1992). These factors are added together to produce a total monetary sanction (which may be broken down into restitution, forfeitures, and fines). The Sentencing Guidelines for Organizations generally called for significantly higher fines than those traditionally imposed, and they reflected a dramatic increase in the size of fines for organizations since the mid-1980s (Cohen 1991; 1992). The growing recent trend of imposing punitive civil fines that are equivalent to or larger than criminal fines (Mann 1992b) has generated some controversy over whether prosecutors are using civil sanctions inappropriately—that is, imposing "criminal" penalties without having to meet the rigorous evidentiary standards of the criminal court.

Are fines truly effective and equitable, or are they indeed mainly treated as a cost of doing business? Metzger and Schwenk (1990: 328) argued that fines are likely to have little effect on the managers who make the crime-related decisions; corporations may indemnify agents for any individually imposed fines resulting from illegal activity taken on behalf of corporations (Stone 1989: 218). The costs of fines imposed on the corporation can be largely (if not wholly) passed on to customers or shareholders. And one of the many ironies involved in the imposition of fines is that precisely those shareholders who know the corporation will be fined are least likely to experience a punitive loss because they will have sold their shares before stock values drop.

Various alternatives to traditional fines have been proposed, including equity fines, installment fines, pass-through fines, and superadded liability (Metzger and Schwenk 1990). Of these alternatives, equity fines (or stock dilution) are regarded as an especially interesting alternative. Equity fines call for convicted corporations to issue equity securities (special shares) and place them with a state-run victim compensation board, which in turn can liquidate these securities when they can realize a maximum return (Coffee 1981a). Such fines avoid the limitations imposed by the corporation's current cash assets, potentially allow for a more powerful deterrent effect because they threaten future earnings, and limit harm mainly to corporate owners (and shareholders) and spare consumers and other wholly innocent parties.

In the case of individual white collar crime offenders, fines alone (unaccompanied by prison sentences) have been justified on various grounds. In addition to saving the taxpayers the cost of imprisoning such offenders, many people view fines as both most appropriate for economic crimes not involving direct violence and more effective than alternatives in preventing recidivism (Bene 1991: 937). Of course, fines may also be regarded as insufficiently punitive and fundamentally inequitable because conventional offenders are much more likely to serve time in prison. Furthermore, even when a substantial fine is imposed, it does not necessarily follow that it will actually be collected. Thus even though the federal courts imposed large fines on the S & L defrauders, as of June 1992 only a fraction (less than 5 percent) of the hundreds of millions of dollars in fines had been collected (Pizzo and Muolo 1993: 26); some individuals ordered to pay fines or restitution of hundreds of thousands of dollars paid nothing by claiming bankruptcy.

## Restitution

White collar offenders, particularly business organizations or corporations, are especially well-positioned to make restitution to victims and to pay compensation for the losses they have caused. On the one hand, restitution or compensation can be especially appealing because it is constructive and economically efficient (i.e., the offender, not the taxpayer, pays for losses attributable to the illegal activity). On the other hand, restitution and compensation in the absence of more direct criminal sanctions can overemphasize the economic aspects of white collar crime.

## Community Service

Finally, both individual and organizational offenders may be required to perform community service to pay for their offenses (First 1990; Fisse 1985). Again, the most appealing dimension of this sanction is that a direct, positive benefit accrues to the community without significant costs. Physicians and lawyers can be compelled to donate their professional services to clinics serving underprivileged populations; businesses can be directed to undertake community cleanup and neighborhood enhancement projects; corporations can be required to establish programs that provide goods and services to needy organizations. Any such community service orders must be closely monitored, however, to ensure that the convicted offender, whether an individual, business, or corporation, does not transform the community service into a public relations coup. Further, such a sanction, especially if it is the only sanction imposed, may allow the offender to rationalize that something other than a crime was involved.

## Occupational Disqualification

LOSS OF LICENSE or occupational disqualification can be a fairly drastic penalty for an individual. It is punitive, is intended to be a deterrent, and is also incapacitative (insofar as it deprives convicted offenders of opportunities for committing their occupationally related crimes).

Some commentators consider occupational disqualification to be a particularly appropriate sanction for executives convicted in corporate crime cases because it avoids some of the practical limitations of other sanctions (McDermott 1982). In this view, disqualification is the direct equivalent of a substantial fine for convicted executives who either cannot afford to pay direct fines or who could be indemnified by their corporate employer; it is especially likely to have both specific and general deterrent effects, and it should prevent individual executives from continuing illegal activities within the corporation.

If occupational disqualification of corporate executives is to be effective, it must be administered from outside the corporation because corporations may be reluctant to disqualify their own executives (Coffee 1980). The corporation is likely to be more concerned with maintaining employee morale and fulfilling corporate objectives, and it may fear what disqualified executives can reveal about the corporation's misconduct. On the other hand, even if executives are disqualified by an outside entity, the corporation may simply replace them and resume its pattern of misconduct. Disqualified executives blocked from legitimate professional employment may be sufficiently desperate or embittered to resort to other forms of illegal activity.

Despite such reservations, occupational disqualification has a place in the arsenal of sanctions for white collar crime, whether it is permanent or imposed for a specified period of time. Even though several of those convicted in the celebrated insider trading cases of the 1980s were permanently banned from the securities industry (Stewart 1991), such a penalty did not necessarily preclude their involvement in other types of business opportunities. For physicians and lawyers, however, loss of license or disbarment can have especially devastating consequences; thus such sanctions are relatively rare events in these professions, at least partly because of a reluctance to impose a penalty seen as having such potentially draconian consequences.

## Incarceration

COMPARED TO CONVENTIONAL offenders, relatively few white collar criminals are sent to prison. Corporations, of course, cannot be imprisoned, although corporate executives can be. A standard joke in the white collar crime literature is that many corporations have a "vice president in charge of going to prison." In this view, certain executives will be designated as accountable if the corporation is found guilty of illegal actions, and these executives will "take the fall" for the corporation.

The imprisonment of white collar crime offenders is quite controversial. Some arguments in favor of incarceration include the following: (1) Because white collar offenses typically involve a high level of intent, calculation, and rationality and are typically committed over an extended period of time, the purely punitive dimension of prison is especially deserved; (2) the prospect of prison, perhaps more than any other sanction, is feared by white collar offenders, and thus it has a powerful deterrent effect on both convicted and prospective offenders alike; (3) the scope of harm caused by white collar offenders is often great enough to merit so serious a punishment as incarceration; (4) it is simply unfair (and an inspiration for cynicism) to send conventional offenders to prison in large numbers without imposing the same sanction on white collar offenders who have caused equivalent or greater harm, typically with less excuse for doing so; and (5) the victims of white collar crimes, especially those who have suffered direct losses and injuries, may expect or demand imprisonment for convicted offenders.

Conversely, the various arguments advanced against the use of imprisonment in white collar crime cases include the following: (1) the "rehabilitation" dimension of imprisonment, which is one rationale for its existence, simply does not apply to white collar offenders, who are not in need of rehabilitative training; (2) the humiliation and loss of status and position suffered by white collar offenders are on the average substantially greater than those sustained by conventional offenders, and imprisonment is a gratuitous, additional punishment; (3) it is wasteful to put people in prison, especially highly competent business executives, professionals, and other skilled and well-educated people who could be making constructive contributions in the larger society; (4) white collar offenders are not "dangerous" in the direct, predatory sense, and accordingly they need not be incarcerated; and, (5) it is more beneficial to victims of white collar crimes to require offenders to earn money legally outside prison and make restitution, which also saves taxpayers the costs of incarceration.

Thus the "rational" arguments against imprisoning white collar offenders are many. But if it is indeed true that corporate executives (and most other white collar offenders) fear imprisonment most, then incarceration is probably necessary in at least some cases (Clinard 1979; 1990). Ultimately, any defensible theory of justice demands imprisonment for at least some white collar offenders so long as we apply this sanction to conventional offenders as well.

## Organizational Reform and Corporate Dissolution

SOME OF THE most harmful white collar crime is committed by or through an organization; large corporations are especially noteworthy in this respect. One ongoing debate centers on whether we should punish only the culpable individual executives within an organization or the organization itself. In the case of corporate crime, it is generally very difficult to identify the guilty party and to ascertain whether illegal acts were committed to benefit the corporation as a whole, some specific division within the corporation, or individual corporate executives (Braithwaite 1982b; Stone 1989: 216). Crimes committed on behalf of the corporation typically occur without either the participation or the endorsement of many of the corporation's employees or stockowners.

Prosecutors may sometimes determine that both the organization and some of its executives are appropriate targets (Stone 1989: 217). Many principled and practical reasons have been advanced for prosecuting organizations as well as individual executives. The organization must be deterred from future crimes (Saltzburg 1991) and is better able to compensate victims of its crimes than are individual executives. Prosecutors can often secure more effective cooperation when they have the option of prosecuting both the organization and individual executives.

One view holds that if much of the most significant white collar crime is organizational or corporate in form, then preventive efforts must be directed toward the organizational structure. Numerous proposals have been advanced to reform or transform corporations to make them more accountable and less likely to engage in harmful and illegal actions, including imposing on corporations a legal obligation to report activities that may cause death, injury, or loss; requiring corporations to institute effective compliance programs; redefining the rights of corporations to prevent them from using purely individual rights to protect themselves; limiting corporate ownership and control over the media; mandating that corporations' misdeeds be publicized and promoting more direct consumer pressure on corporations; freeing lawmaking bodies from corporate PAC control; strengthening whistleblower laws to protect those within corporations who expose harmful and illegal practices; requiring that a percentage of fines be used to support independent corporate watchdogs; mandating public directors or worker representatives for corporate boards; compelling corporations to undertake socially beneficial projects using their special skills; requiring corporations to make restitution to their victims; discouraging investments in criminally recidivist corporations, and prohibiting criminal companies from receiving government grants, licenses, or contracts; decreasing the size of corporations; and requiring federal (as opposed to state) chartering of corporations, to allow for more potent federal oversight and to close up loopholes in some state chartering standards (Clinard and Yeager 1980; Mokhiber 1988; Clinard 1990; Coleman 1994). This list of proposed reforms is extensive but hardly exhaustive, and it provides some sense of the broad range of possibilities for change.

All corporate reform proposals are inevitably controversial on ideological grounds; that is, they are seen by some as unacceptable and economically destructive forms of intervention in the free-market system. For example, conservative critics of the federal chartering proposal fear a movement toward public ownership of corporations and an increase in the cost of doing business. Among progressives, however, reform proposals are largely regarded as delusions because they can always be coopted or counteracted by powerful corporations, and because structural transformation of the capitalist system and nationalization of corporations are necessary if corporate crime is to be addressed in any substantial way (Barnett 1981a; Young 1981). By any criteria, the reform proposals face formidable practical barriers. It remains difficult to demonstrate that such measures, when implemented, can be truly effective in preventing or limiting corporate crime. Even if it can be agreed that the overriding objective in addressing white collar crime on the organizational level is to diminish (or even eliminate) both organizational pressures and opportunities to commit illegalities, there are clearly many very different opinions on how this should be accomplished.

Perhaps the most extreme sanction that can be imposed on a corporation is "capitalist punishment," or the forced dissolution ("death sentence") of the corporation (Coffee 1981a; Schwartz and Ellison 1982; Mokhiber 1988). Such a sanction would seem to be justified for corporations involved in massively harmful activities over some extended period of time. As a practical matter, however, this penalty is widely regarded as too extreme and too harmful to too many innocent parties (e.g., workers, stockholders, suppliers). It is also obviously the case that the "execution" of a corporation is not the same as the execution of a "natural person" insofar as a corporation cannot suffer pain directly, and the key personnel of the corporation can hypothetically regroup after a dissolution and seek to reestablish the corporation with a new name and a new charter in a new location. Some major corporations have in fact dissolved following revelations of their involvement in large-scale financial crime, either as a consequence of their internal corruption and frauds, fines and bad publicity from criminal prosecution, or both. The Equity Funding Corporation (insurance fraud), the American Continental Corporation (thrift and real estate fraud), and Drexel Burnham (insider trading) are but three examples of multimillion dollar corporations or financial entities that collapsed largely due to their involvement in white collar crime.

## Responding to Residual Forms of White Collar Crime

THE COMMON CONCEPTUAL dichotomy between individual/occupational white collar crime and organizational/corporate white collar crime has been shown to be a simplification of an increasingly complex reality. This text has identified a number of hybrid and marginal forms of white collar crime that do not neatly fit into commonly recognized categories. These "residual" forms of white collar crime include state/corporate crime, finance crime, technocrime, enterprise crime, contrepreneurial crime, and avocational crime. Although the responses to these forms of crime incorporate many of the elements of the more general responses to white collar crime we have discussed, they may also require some unique features as well. Deterrence of state/corporate crime, for example, requires a very independent (and aggressive) free press, potent laws supporting open access to information about state/corporate transactions, formidable restrictions on relationships and employment patterns between those in the private and public sectors, and autonomous private- and public-sector investigative/prosecutorial entities. Ultimately, however, a transformation of the political economy may be necessary to challenge this type of crime seriously.

Finance crime, which includes large-scale fraud within thrift institutions and securities markets manipulations, reflects in important ways the shortcomings of a capitalist, free-enterprise system. Such a system both promotes values (e.g., insatiable materialism) and creates opportunities (e.g., inadequate regulatory oversight) that foster this type of crime. Short of transforming the system, an effective response to this type of crime requires strong deterrent sanctions, political campaign financing reforms, and exceptionally sophisticated and proactive regulation and investigation.

Technocrime, the whole range of illegal activities carried out through the use of high technology, is very likely to increase almost exponentially in a society in which high technology becomes ever more pervasive. Because the current movement toward dependence on such technology in a wide range of settings is unlikely to be reversed, we face the formidable challenge of ensuring that technologically sophisticated security measures keep ahead of emerging new opportunities for committing technocrimes. Because high technology can create new and more efficient modes of investigation and surveillance, one of the potential dangers intrinsic to high-tech surveillance by government agencies is intrusion into citizens' privacy and other forms of abuse.

Enterprise crime, which refers to cooperative and interrelated enterprises involving traditional organized crime mobs and "legitimate" businesses, compels us to recognize that the distinctions among types of crimes, and between legitimate and illegitimate businesses, are eroding (Calavita and Pontell 1993). An expansive application of such prosecutorial tools as RICO (Racketeer-Influenced and Corrupt Organizations Act) is one element of the response to this type of crime. Sophisticated forensic accounting and investigative specialists capable of untangling complex networks of corruption are needed in this realm. Insofar as enterprise crime is becoming increasingly global, an effective response is likely to depend on high levels of international cooperation.

Contrepreneurial crime is a term used to characterize the vast range of "scams" that have the outward appearance of legitimate businesses but that in varying degrees defraud people by deceit. One approach to responding to this type of crime involves greatly enhancing consumer awareness and strengthening consumer protection laws and investigatory agencies. Such crime tends to thrive in a society that assigns greater importance to unregulated free enterprise than to accountability and integrity.

Finally, avocational crime refers to illegal activities such as tax evasion and insurance fraud that involve a high proportion of the same parties involved in white collar crime but occur outside an occupational or organizational setting. The problem of moral integrity is regarded as especially pertinent for this type of crime, and accordingly various strategies that enhance such integrity are particularly applicable. Although investigatory methods can always be refined and made more proactive, investigation is likely to inspire considerable resistance and antagonism. Again, the values of a capitalist system that tends to reward individualism and materialism at the expense of commitment to the well-being of others and of the community generally play a central role.

## Controlling State Crime and Governmental Crime

GOVERNMENTAL CRIME HAS been treated here as a cognate form of white collar crime. Such crime, especially when it is committed at the highest levels of government, is extraordinarily difficult to control because those who are committing the crimes also often have disproportionate power to shield themselves from criminal investigation and prosecution. We must confront the basic paradox that even though we depend on governmental entities and agencies to control white collar crime, the state, its agencies, and politicians generally are the sources of some of the most serious and harmful crime. When a state comes to be viewed as fundamentally criminal and corrupt, the ultimate response may be a popular uprising or a coup by disenchanted groups. In nondemocratic societies this may be the only real option for challenging state crime.

Ideally, international tribunals would have both the jurisdiction and the means to mount an effective response to state crime. It seems unlikely that an international prosecutorial regime will be established in the forseeable future, although there may be some hope for enhanced international cooperation in response to human rights violations (Molina 1995).

Much of the response to state crime continues to rely on an international free press and various international organizations for monitoring state crime and corruption and generating pressure for action through exposure and shaming. Historically, high-level state criminals have had to answer directly for their crimes to an international court only following their military defeat and capture, as did the surviving Nazi leadership brought to trial at Nuremberg after World War II. Some commentators suggest that abolishing the state itself would be the best way to reduce or eliminate state crime, but the enduring anarchist dream of living in a world without states is highly unlikely to be realized (Martin 1995). It remains to be seen whether an international entity that can prevent or punish state crime without itself perpetrating gross abuses of power will emerge in the 21st century.

In democratic societies, citizens expect that a system of checks and balances and a free press will expose and effectively respond to state and governmental crime. Decentralization of power is one approach to diminishing the opportunities for at least some forms of governmental crime. The existing means of financing political campaigns are widely recognized to promote corrupt arrangements between public officials and corporations or other entities that donate money to their campaigns. Even though campaign financing reforms have been undertaken periodically, they have hardly eliminated the problem of corrupt public officials. At present, corporate PACs (large sums of campaign money raised and donated by corporations) are a central factor in corrupting the political process, even if direct payoffs for specific favors can rarely be demonstrated (Clawson, Neustadtl, and Scott 1992). The "revolving door" syndrome—in which people first move from the private sector into governmental regulatory positions in which they wield considerable influence over private-sector activities, and then leave public office to return to lucrative positions in the industry or business they once regulated—is an obvious source of corruption. Despite laws and presidential directives intended to minimize this syndrome, it continues to be a problem. On all levels of governmental work, from the very top down to police officers and municipal repair crews, a disparity exists between the relative power or illegal opportunities of government employees and their legal compensation.

## Structural Transformation as a Response to White Collar Crime

IN ONE FATALISTIC view, human nature is inherently corrupt, and thus no form of human intervention can obliterate the basic impulses that contribute to the commission of white collar crimes. In a more optimistic view, a substantial reduction of white collar crime requires a transformation of society's political, economic, and cultural structure. James William Coleman (1994) considered a fundamental repudiation of the "culture of competition" and a restructuring of social and economic relationships to be necessary if we are to diminish markedly the scope of white collar crime.

David Simon and D. Stanley Eitzen (1993) contended that a transformation of our society into an "economic democracy" is the only appropriate response to elite deviance and all the interrelated problems of a modern capitalist society. A progressive political and economic transformation requires nationalization of certain industries, fundamental tax reform, income redistribution, and sound ecological policies. In this view, a society organized according to the general principles of democratic socialism is much more likely both to foster a genuine sense of community and concern and to discourage selfish and predatory conduct. The opportunities for large-scale private enterprises to engage in various forms of exploitative and harmful activity would be greatly curtailed. Organizational and individual energy would be channeled into cooperative and productive endeavors.

Those who contend that a structural transformation is necessary if white collar crime (especially in its elite and corporate forms) is to be curtailed in a substantial and enduring way are surely correct on some level. All smaller scale reforms—that is, new laws, different sanctions, and innovative educational programs—are likely to have only limited effect, if past experience is any guide. Still, some limitations of structural transformation must be acknowledged. First, it may be viewed as utopian and somewhat out of touch with reality, insofar as relatively little support for such a transformation in the United States is apparent. Second, structural transformations undertaken out of progressive aspirations have all too often led to corrupt, totalitarian societies, especially in the 20th century; the recently collapsed Soviet Union is a prominent example. Third, any political and economic transformation that is to realize progressive goals must be accompanied by a cultural transformation that redirects human values and priorities. Those who call for a democratic socialist system often underestimate the importance of such cultural transformation.

A growing perception of the expansion of white collar as a serious issue can be linked with both an emerging crisis of confidence and a legitimacy crisis (Friedrichs 1980a; 1981). A crisis of confidence reflects erosion of confidence in the leadership class (e.g., politicians and businesspeople); a legitimacy crisis reflects loss of faith in the system itself. Polls and "anecdotal" sources provide significant evidence of a crisis of confidence in the leadership class, which can be seen at least partly as a response to revelations of illegal conduct and partly as an erosion of trust that makes such allegations more credible. Although we have not experienced a full-scale legitimacy crisis (as occurred in eastern European countries and the former Soviet Union), the United States has experienced at least some elements of such a crisis. Some erosion of faith in the system can contribute to the perception that the system is the source of corrupt and illegal activities; it can also increase the cynicism that facilitates the commission of white collar crimes. Accordingly, a structural, long-term response to the problem of white collar crime requires both a mitigation of the crisis of confidence and the development of a system that is more fully considered legitimate and worthy of respect and compliance.

## Responding to the Challenge of White Collar Crime, In Sum

IT IS SURELY foolish and naive to harbor the illusion that there is an easy solution to the problem of white collar crime. Even though moral indignation and a fair measure of outrage are often justified and can be productive up to a point, such emotional responses must be tempered with a measure of pragmatism. Severe condemnation and harsh, selectively applied penal measures are necessary elements in the response to white collar crime, as are all strategies that maximize voluntary compliance. This chapter has identified a range of responses to white collar crime that fall between harsh penal measures and noninterventionist inducements for compliance.

In response to the corporate form of white collar crime, John Braithwaite (1990) called for an "enforcement pyramid" based on the following premises: Although corporate actors are driven by contradictory commitments (including a desire to comply with law), at least some will comply with the law only when it is economically rational for them to do so; neither a strategy based entirely on persuasion (which is relatively cheap but vulnerable to exploitation) nor one based entirely on coercion (which is costly and likely to promote ill will and organized resistance) is likely to foster optimal levels of compliance. Furthermore, in complex, rapidly changing industries, regulators are especially dependent on cooperation from knowledgeable experts within the corporations. Thus the most effective strategy, in this view, is one that mixes persuasion with punishment. It begins by initiating the least coercive form of control and moves on to increasingly coercive forms of control as needed. (Accordingly, the sequence of the "enforcement pyramid" is persuasion, warning letter, civil penalty, criminal penalty, license suspension, license revocation. A parallel regulatory strategy pyramid includes self-regulation, enforced self-regulation, command regulation with discretionary punishment, command regulation with nondiscretionary punishment.)

Braithwaite has also been a proponent of "tripartism," a regulatory policy that fosters the participation of nongovernmental organizations (e.g., public interest groups) in the regulatory process (Ayres and Braithwaite 1991). Such an approach decentralizes some of the power that tends to accumulate within governmental regulatory agencies and is responsive to the dilemma of "who will guard the guards." The overriding objective of the strategy is to foster a culture that promotes trust and offers incentives to refrain from cheating or engaging in illegal conduct. As a practical matter, more substantial training of enforcement personnel, greater funding, and a better reward structure are needed. Prosecutors and judges need more options and resources if they are to take effective action against white collar offenders. Responding to white collar crime should be a higher priority. Still, we must not ignore the evidence that suggests that we cannot and should not rely excessively on responses rooted in a coercive criminal justice system.

How can we resolve the tensions between the pragmatist and progressive, the realist and idealist, approaches to white collar crime? This is not an easy dilemma to resolve. The position adopted here could be described as progressive pluralism, which calls for moving against white collar crime on two tracks simultaneously. On the one hand, we must generate a much broader consciousness of the harm caused by white collar crime. Only with a much more widespread consciousness of this harm is it possible to undertake the structural and cultural transformation necessary as a precondition for substantially reducing the scope of white collar crime. At the same time, we must address the immediate challenge of white collar crime with an appropriate mixture of punishment and persuasion, a wide range of demonstrably effective sanctions, and any authentic means of promoting self-regulation.

Much of our knowledge of white collar crime is somewhat parochial and lacks a comparative or international perspective; Punch (1991) observed that the literature on white collar crime is disproportionately American. As the business environment becomes ever more global, business crime will increasingly take advantage of the gaps and shortcomings of national laws and of very limited international control structures. Accordingly, international organizations such as the United Nations and cooperative international responses to the major forms of white collar crime will become more important (Michalowski and Kramer 1987; Braithwaite 1993c). At least some efforts to realize new international controls—for example, the creation of a "new world order"—may simply serve to extend the interests of powerful nations and transnational corporations (Chomsky 1993). But any efforts to develop authentically effective international responses to white collar crime will draw upon more systematic study of the different national styles of responding to such crime, the particular context within which these styles exist, and their relative successes.

Altogether, it is clear that white collar crime must be addressed on many different levels. Surely it merits a higher priority than it has been historically accorded by society at large, the justice system, and the criminal justice curriculum. Ultimately, an effective response to white collar crime requires basic transformations in the structure of the capitalist political economy, the character of corporations and businesses, and the ethics of professions and individuals alike.

## A Concluding Note: Trusted Criminals and White Collar Crime in the 21st Century

AS WE MOVE into the 21st century, white collar crime in the broadest sense endures as a major threat to our physical and financial well-being. The proposition that white collar crime is a complex phenomenon has been a guiding premise of this book. We have rejected one-dimensional, simplistic, and dogmatic proclamations about white collar crime; instead we have emphasized the multiple dimensions of such crime and have recognized that it generates difficult public policy conundrums.

Accordingly, we endeavored to "map" the whole terrain of white collar crime. The book began with a consideration of how white collar crime has been "discovered" both as a concept and a social phenomenon. Next we examined the special challenges involved in studying white collar crime, the different methods for doing so, the matter of public perceptions of white collar crime, the means of measuring it and assessing its costs, and the nature of white collar crime victimization. The next five chapters explored in some depth what we currently know about a variety of white collar crimes, including corporate and occupational crime, cognate forms of white collar crime such as governmental crime, and hybrid or marginal forms of white collar crime such as state-corporate crime, finance crime, technocrime, enterprise crime, contrepreneurial crime, and avocational crime. The interrelationships among these different forms of white collar crime are many and varied. Following the chapters that focused on types of white collar crime, we reviewed the broad range of theories and explanations for white collar crime. The final part of the book identified and described in some detail the social control of what we call white collar crime by law and other means, the many agents empowered to investigate and police such crime, and the different processes for adjudicating it. This final chapter has attempted to assess the specific options available to us in our response to the formidable challenge of white collar crime.

The study of white collar crime inevitably raises some large questions that are unlikely to ever be fully resolved. Whether we should consider the many activities that involve some significant level of measurable harm but are not proscribed by the criminal law to be white collar *crime* is a matter of ongoing dispute. From the author's point of view, the designation is justified for financially driven forms of intentional or negligent harm perpetrated by upper- and middle-class institutions and individuals in an occupational context; the low-level thefts and minor frauds of poorer (below middle-class) people are probably better regarded as forms of occupational crime that do not meet the criteria of *white collar* crime. The crimes of large and powerful organizations such as corporations are especially pernicious. In a complex world of diminishing resources and increasing interdependency, the notion that corporations are devoid of social responsibility—and are justified in being exclusively oriented toward maximizing profit—is likely to become increasingly intolerable. But the response to white collar crime occurs in a dynamic political environment of countervailing forces pitting progressive reforms against conservative restraints. In the mid-1990s in the United States, for example, we saw both executive branch initiatives to reinvigorate regulatory agencies such as OSHA and legislative branch initiatives to limit the liability of corporations, the securities industry, and professionals in lawsuits claiming physical or financial harm from their activities. In this era, concern with conventional crime and violence, the welfare system, and high taxes continue to overshadow public indignation over white collar crime, although a generally high level of disenchantment with the political establishment also existed. As we move into the postmodern world of the 21st century, the ongoing revolutionary transformations in computerization and telecommunications will create broad new opportunities for white collar crime, and such crime will increasingly take on a global character. The challenge of responding effectively to such crime is likely to intensify.

Note: The vast majority of references listed below are cited in the text. A number of other sources that provided some background insights or information are also listed.

ABADINSKY, H. (1981; 1985) *Organized crime*. Boston: Allyn & Bacon.

ABEL, R. L. (1988a) "The crisis is injuries, not liability." Pp. 31–41 in W. Olson (Ed.) *New directions in liability law*. New York: The Academy of Political Science.

ABEL, R. L. (1988b) "United States: The contradictions of professionalism." Pp. 186–243 in R. L. Abel and P. S. C. Lewis (Eds.) *Lawyers in society: The common law world*. Berkeley: University of California Press.

ADAMS, J. R. (1990) *The big fix: Inside the S & L scandal*. New York: Wiley.

ADAMS, J. R. and FRANTZ, D. (1992) *A full-service bank: How BCCI stole billions around the world*. New York: Pocket Books.

ADAMS, W. and BROCK, J. W. (1989) *Dangerous pursuits—Mergers and acquisitions in the age of Wall Street*. New York: Pantheon Books.

ADELSON, A. (1988) "U.S. indicts Rockwell on billing." *New York Times* (April 2): A1.

ADKINS, L. (1982) "The high cost of employee theft." *Dun's Business Month* 120: 66–76.

ADLER, F. (1975) *Sisters in crime*. New York: McGraw-Hill.

ADLER, R. W. and LORD, C. (1991). "Environmental crimes: Raising the stakes. *The George Washington Law Review* 59: 781–861.

AGEE, P. (1988) "Remarks: The role of the CIA, anti-communism and the U.S." Institute for Media Analysis, Harvard University, November 11–13.

AKERS, R. L. (1985) *Deviant behavior: A social learning approach*. 3rd ed. Belmont, CA: Wadsworth.

AKERS, R. L. and HAWKINS, R. (1975). *Law and control in society*. Englewood Cliffs, NJ: Prentice-Hall.

ALATAS, S. H. (1990) *Corruption: Its nature, causes and functions*. Aldershot, UK: Avebury.

ALBANESE, J. S. (1982) "What Lockheed and La Cosa Nostra have in common: The effect of ideology on criminal justice policy." *Crime & Delinquency* 28: 211–232.

ALBANESE, J. S. (1991) "Organized crime: The mafia myth." Pp. 201–218 in J. F. Sheley (Ed.) *Criminology: A contemporary handbook*. Belmont, CA: Wadsworth.

ALBINI, J. L. (1971) *The American mafia: Genesis of a legend*. New York: Irvington.

ALBONETTI, C. A. (1994) "The symbolic punishment of white-collar offenders." Pp. 269–282 in G. S. Bridges and M. A. Myers (Eds.) *Inequality, crime, and social control.* Boulder, CO: Westview Press.

ALLEN, H. E., FRIDAY, P. C., ROEBUCK, J. B., and SAGARIN, E. (1981) *Crime and punishment.* New York: Free Press.

ALSCHULER, A. W. (1991) "Ancient law and the punishment of corporations: Of frankpledge and deodand." *Boston University Law Review* 71: 307–313.

ALTER, J. (1989) "Two reporters you don't want on your tail." *Newsweek* (April 24): 71.

ALTHEIDE, D. L. (1976) *Creating reality: How TV news distorts events.* Beverly Hills, CA: Sage.

ALTHEIDE, D. L., ADLER, P. A., ADLER, P., and ALTHEIDE, D. A. (1978) "The social meaning of employee theft." Pp. 90–124 in J. Johnson and J. Douglas (Eds.) *Crime at the top: Deviance in business and the professions.* Philadelphia: Lippincott.

ALTHEIDE, D. L. and SNOW, R. P. (1991) *Media worlds in the postjournalist era.* Hawthorne, NY: Aldine de Gruyter.

ALTMAN, L. (1994) "Researcher falsified data in breast cancer study." *New York Times* (March 14): A1.

ANDENAES, J. (1974) *Punishment and deterrence.* Ann Arbor: University of Michigan Press.

ANDERSON, A. G. (1979) *The business of organized crime: A cosa nostra family.* Stanford, CA: Hoover Institution Press.

ANDERSON, J. and ROBINSON, P. (1992) "Isn't it time to clean up Medicare?" *Parade* (November 8): 8, 10.

ANDERSON, M. (1992) *Imposters in the temple.* New York: Simon & Schuster.

ANDREW, C. and GORDIEVSKY, O. (1990) *KGB—The inside story.* New York: HarperCollins.

ANDREWS, E. L. (1991a) "F.C.C. takes steps to combat abuses on '900' numbers." *New York Times* (March 15): A1.

ANDREWS, E. L. (1991b) "F.C.C. wins accord on '900' numbers." *New York Times* (May 9): A1.

ANDREWS, E. L. (1991c) "Phone service theft at companies surges." *New York Times* (August 27): D1.

ANDREWS, E. L. (1995) "Judge in the Microsoft case is willing to test the limits." *New York Times* (February 21): D1.

ANECHIARICO, F. (1990) "Remembering corruption." *Corruption and Reform* 5: 109–124.

ANONYMOUS. (1971) "Criminal deviancy in a small business: Superior TV." Pp. 198–207 in H. T. Buckner (Ed.) *Deviance, reality and change.* New York: Random House.

ANSPACH, D. F. (1990) "Door to door mutual funds: The legal taking of other people's money." A Paper Presented at the Annual Meeting of the American Society of Criminology (Baltimore), November.

APPLEBOME, P. (1989) "Bakker sentenced to 45 years for fraud in his TV ministry." *New York Times* (October 25): A1.

APPLEBOME, P. (1993a) "G.M. is held liable over fuel tanks in pick-up trucks." *New York Times* (February 5): A1.

APPLEBOME, P. (1993b) "Alabama governor found guilty of ethics charges and is ousted." *New York Times* (April 23): A1.

ARENDT, H. (1963) *Eichmann in Jerusalem—A report on the banality of evil.* New York: Viking Press.

ARENSON, K. W. (1995) "Former United Way chief guilty in theft of more than $600,000." *New York Times* (April 4): A1.

ARNOLD, B. L. and HAGAN, J. (1992) "Careers of misconduct: The structure of prosecuted professional deviance among lawyers." *American Sociological Review* 57: 771–780.

ASHMAN, C. R. (1973) *The finest judges money can buy.* Los Angeles: Nash Publishing.

ASSOCIATED PRESS. (1987) "Inspector sees danger in meats." *Scranton Times* (May 16): 1.

ASSOCIATED PRESS. (1988) "U.S. says big meatpacker cheated workers." *New York Times* (April 2): A10.

ASSOCIATED PRESS. (1990) "Bethlehem Steel fined $1 million on Benzene." *New York Times* (April 6): B4.

ASSOCIATED PRESS. (1991) "Oil firms face trial on price fixing." *The Scranton Times* (June 3): A1.

ATWELL, B. L. (1991) "Product liability and preemption: A judicial framework." *Buffalo Law Review* 39: 181–230.

AUBERT, V. (1952) "White collar crime and social structure." *American Journal of Sociology* 58: 263–271.

AUERBACH, J. S. (1976) *Unequal justice—Lawyers and social change in modern America.* New York: Oxford University Press.

AYERS, K. and FRANK, J. (1987). "Deciding to prosecute white collar crime: A national survey of state attorneys general." *Justice Quarterly* 4 (September): 425–440.

AYRES, I. and BRAITHWAITE, J. (1991) "Tripartism: Regulatory capture and empowerment." *Law & Social Inquiry* 16: 435–496.

BAIDA, P. (1990) *Poor Richard's legacy: American business values from Benjamin Franklin to Donald Trump.* New York: Morrow.

BAILEY, F. L. and ROTHBLATT, H. B. (1984). *Defending business and white collar crimes: Federal and state.* 2nd ed. Rochester, NY: The Lawyers Cooperative Publishing Company.

BAKER, N. C. (1992) *Conflicting loyalties: Law and politics in the attorney general's office, 1789–1990.* Lawrence: University of Kansas Press.

BAKER, W. E. and FAULKNER, R. R. (1993) "The social organization of conspiracy: Illegal networks in the heavy electrical equipment industry." *American Sociological Review* 58: 837–860.

BALL, D. (1970) "The problematics of respectability." Pp. 326–371 in J. D. Douglas (Ed.) *Deviance and respectability: The social construction of moral meanings.* New York: Basic Books.

BALL, H. V. and FRIEDMAN, L. M. (1965) "The use of criminal sanctions in the enforcement of economic legislation." *Stanford Law Review* 17: 197–223.

BAQUET, D. (1991) "Handling of B.C.C.I. case arouses deep suspicions." *New York Times* (September 6): A1 +.

BARAK, G. (1990) "Crime, criminology, and human rights: Towards an understanding of state criminality." *The Journal of Human Justice* 2: 11–28.

BARAK, G. (1991) *Crimes by the capitalist state—An introduction to state criminality.* Albany: SUNY Press.

BARAK, G. (1994) *Media, process and the social construction of crime.* New York: Garland Publishing Co.

BARAK, G. and BOHM, R. M. (1989) "The crimes of the homeless or the crime of homelessness? On the dialectics of criminalization, decriminalization, and victimization." *Contemporary Crises: Law, Crime and Social Policy* 13: 275–288.

BARBER, B. (1983) *The logic and limits of trust.* New Brunswick, NJ: Rutgers University Press.

BARBROOK, A. T. (1987) "Campaign finance in American state elections." *Corruption and Reform* 2: 17–40.

BARDACH, E. and KAGAN, R. A. (1982) *Going by the book: The problem of regulatory unreasonableness.* Philadelphia: Temple University Press.

BARKER, A. (1994) "The upturned stone: Political scandals and their investigation process in twenty democracies." *Crime, Law & Social Change* 21: 337–373.

BARKER, T. and CARTER, D. L. (Eds.) (1986) *Police deviance.* Cincinnati: Pilgrimage.

BARLOW, H. D. (1993) "From fiddle factors to networks of collusion: Charting the waters of small business crime." *Crime, Law and Social Change* 20: 319–337.

BARLOW, M. H., BARLOW, D. E., and CHIRICOS, T. G. (1995) "Economic conditions and ideologies of crime in the media: A content analysis of crime news." *Crime & Delinquency* 41: 3–19.

BARNET, R. J. and MULLER, R. E. (1974) *Global reach: The power of the multinational corporations.* New York: Simon & Schuster.

BARNETT, H. C. (1979) "Wealth, crime, and capital accumulation." *Contemporary Crises* 3: 171–186.

BARNETT, H. C. (1981a) "Review of *Corporate Crime.*" *The Insurgent Sociologist* 11: 107–111.

BARNETT, H. C. (1981b) "Corporate capitalism, corporate crime." *Crime & Delinquency* 27: 4–23.

BARNETT, H. C. (1982) "The production of corporate crime in corporate capitalism." Pp. 157–171 in P. Wickman and T. Dailey (Eds.) *White-collar and economic crime.* Lexington, MA: Lexington.

BARNETT, H. C. (1986) "Industry culture and industry economy: Correlates of tax compliance in Sweden." *Criminology* 24: 553–574.

BARNETT, H. C. (1990) "Political environments and implementation failures: The case of Superfund enforcement." *Law & Policy* 12: 225–246.

BARNETT, H. C. (1993) "Crimes against the environment: Superfund enforcement at last." *The Annals* 525: 119–133.

BARRETT, A. (1994) "Insider trading." *Business Week* (December 12): 70–82.

BARRETT, P. R. (1990) "U.S. finds it tough to establish crimes in savings & loan mess." *The Wall Street Journal* (June 26): 1.

BARRILE, L. (1993a) "Determining criminal responsibility of corporations." A Paper Presented at the Annual Meeting of the American Society of Criminology, San Francisco, November.

BARRILE, L. (1993b). "A soul to damn and a body to kick: Imprisoning corporate criminals." *Humanity & Society* 17: 176–196.

BARRON, J. (1989) "Unnecessary surgery." *New York Times Magazine* (April 16): 25–46.

BARRON, M. (1981) "The criminogenic society: Social values and deviance." Pp. 136–152 in A. S. Blumberg (Ed.) *Current perspectives on criminal behavior.* 2nd ed. New York: Knopf.

BARTLETT, S. (1990) "Getting a mental grip on the dimensions of the savings disaster." *New York Times* (June 10): 4/1.

BARTLETT, S. (1991) "Salomon's errant cowboy." *New York Times* (August 25): E1.

BARTOLLAS, C. and S. DINITZ (1989). *Introduction to criminology.* New York: Harper & Row.

BASLER, B. (1982) "As traffic anarchy increases, so does concern of citizens." *New York Times* (December 5): 1.

BASLER, B. (1987) "'Bad Guys' Wear Pin Stripes." *New York Times* (January 27): D1.

BAUCUS, M. S. and DWORKIN, T. M. (1991) "What is corporate crime? It is not illegal corporate behavior." *Law & Policy Review* 13: 231–244.

BAUDER, D. C. (1985) *Captain Money and the Golden Girl.* San Diego: Harcourt Brace Jovanovich.

BAZELL, R. (1973) "Trades a short jail term for $6 M." *New York Post* (November 19): 2.

BEATY, J. and GWYNNE, S. C. (1991) "The dirtiest bank of all." *Time* (July 29): 42–47.

BEATY, J. and HORNIK, R. (1989) "A torrent of dirty dollars." *Time* (December 18): 50–56.

BECCARIA, C. (1764; 1819) *On crimes and punishments.* Philadelphia: Philip H. Nicklin.

BECKER, H. L. (1963) *Outsiders: Studies in the sociology of deviance.* New York: Free Press.

BECKER, T. L. and MURRAY, V. G. (Eds.) (1971) *Government lawlessness in America.* New York: Oxford University Press.

BECKWITH, D. (1987) "The high price of friendship." *Time* (December 28): 23.

BEHAR, R. (1989) "Fear and cover-ups in the IRS." *Time* (August 7): 40.

BEHAR, R. (1990) "Catch us if you can." *Time* (March 26): 60.

BEHAR, R. (1991) "The thriving cult of greed and power." *Time* (May 6): 50–57.

BEHAR, R. (1992) "A lawyer's precipitous fall from grace." *Time* (March 16): 52.

BEHRENS, J. C. (1977). *The typewriter guerrillas: Closeups of 20 top investigative reporters.* Chicago: Nelson Hall.

BEIRNE, P. (1991) "Inventing criminology: The "science of man" in Cesare Beccaria's *Dei Delitti E Delle Pene* (1764)." *Criminology* 29: 777–820.

BEIRNE, P. and MESSERSCHMIDT, J. (1991). *Criminology.* San Diego: Harcourt Brace Jovanovich.

BELBOT, B. A. (1991) "Whistleblowing and lawyers." *Journal of Contemporary Criminal Justice* 7: 154–166.

BELBOT, B. A. (1993) "Corporate criminal liability." Pp. 211–238 in M. B. Blankenship (Ed.) *Understanding corporate criminality*. New York: Garland Publishing Co.

BELL, D. (1962) "Crime as an American way of life: A queer ladder of social mobility." Pp. 127–150 in *The end of ideology*. New York: Free Press.

BELL, R. (1992) *Impure science—Fraud, science, and political influence in scientific research*. New York: Wiley.

BELLAMY, J. (1973) *Crime and public order in England in the later middle ages*. London: Routledge & Kegan Paul.

BELLINI, J. (1986) *High tech holocaust*. London: David & Charles.

BENDER, L. (1990) "Feminist (re)torts: Thoughts on the liability crisis, mass torts, power, and responsibilities." *Duke Law Journal* (September): 848–912.

BENE, S. G. (1991) "Why not fine attorneys? An economic approach to lawyer disciplinary sanctions." *Stanford Law Review* 43: 864–941.

BENEKOS, P. J. and HAGAN, F. E. (1990) "Fixing the thrifts: Prosecution and regulation in the great savings and loan scandal." A Paper Presented at the Annual Meeting of the Academy of Criminal Justice Sciences, Denver, March.

BENJAMIN, M. and BRONSTEIN, D. A. (1987) "Moral and criminal responsibility and corporate persons." Pp. 277–282 in W. J. Samuels and A. J. Miller (Eds.) *Corporations and society: Power and responsibility*. New York: Greenwood Press.

BENNETT, G. (1987) *Crimewarps—The future of crime in America*. Garden City, NY: Anchor Press.

BENNETT, J. T. and DILORENZO, T. J. (1994) *Unhealthy charities: Hazardous to your health*. New York: Basic Books.

BENOIT, P. and HAUSMAN, C. (1991) "Honoring copyrights should be a matter of simple decency." *Chronicle of Higher Education* (May 1): B2.

BENSON, M. L. (1984) "The fall from grace: Loss of occupational status as a consequence of conviction for a white collar crime." *Criminology* 22: 573–595.

BENSON, M. L. (1985) "Denying the guilty mind: Accounting for involvement in white-collar crime." *Criminology* 23: 583–608.

BENSON, M. L. (1989) "The influence of class position on the formal and informal sanctioning of white-collar offenders." *The Sociological Quarterly* 30: 465–479.

BENSON, M. L. (1990) "Emotions and adjudication: Status degradation among white-collar criminals." *Justice Quarterly* 7: 515–528.

BENSON, M. L. and CULLEN, F. T., (1988) "The special sensitivity of white-collar offenders to prisons: A critique and research agenda." *Journal of Criminal Justice* 16(3): 207–216.

BENSON, M. L., CULLEN, F. T., and MAAKESTAD, W. J. (1990a) "Local prosecutors and corporate crime." *Crime & Delinquency* 36: 356–372.

BENSON, M. L., CULLEN, F. T., and MAAKESTAD, W. J. (1990b) "The social movement against corporate crime: Assessing the role of local prosecutors." A Paper Presented at the Annual Meeting of the Academy of Criminal Justice Sciences, Denver, March

BENSON, M. L., CULLEN, F. T., and MAAKESTAD, W. J. (1990c) "The prosecution of corporate crime." A Paper Presented at the Annual Meeting of the American Society of Criminology Baltimore, November.

BENSON, M. L., CULLEN, F. T., and MAAKESTAD, W. J. (1992) "Community context and the prosecution of corporate crime." Pp. 269–288 in K. Schlegel and D. Weisburd (Eds.) *White collar crime reconsidered*. Boston: Northeastern University Press.

BENSON, M. L., CULLEN, F. T., and MAAKESTAD, W. J. (1993) "Local prosecutors and corporate crime." *NIJ Research in Brief* (January): 1–7.

BENSON, M. L., MAAKESTAD, W. J., CULLEN, F. T., and GEIS, G. (1988) "District attorneys and corporate crime: Surveying the prosecutorial gatekeepers." *Criminology* 26: 505–518.

BENSON, M. L. and MOORE, E. (1992) "Are white-collar and common offenders the same? An empirical and theoretical critique of a recently proposed general theory of crime." *Journal of Research in Crime & Delinquency* 29: 251–272.

BENSON, M. L. and WALKER, E. (1988) "Sentencing the white-collar offender." *American Sociological Review* 53: 294–302.

BENTHAM, J. (1789; 1948) *An introduction to the principles of morals and legislation.* New York: Macmillan.

BEQUAI, A. (1978) *White collar crime: A 20th century crisis.* Lexington, MA: Heath.

BEQUAI, A. (1987) *Technocrimes.* Lexington, MA: Lexington.

BERG, E. N. (1988) "Auditors must search for fraud under new rule." *New York Times* (February 10): 1A.

BERG, E. N. (1989) "The lapses by Lincoln's auditors." *New York Times* (December 28): Business/1.

BERG, E. N. (1991) "$415 million settlement and pensions." *New York Times* (December 3): D1.

BERGER, J. (1992) "New York school safety chief is accused of improprieties." *New York Times* (July 4): A1.

BERGER, P. and LUCKMANN, T. (1966) *The social construction of reality.* New York: Anchor Press.

BERLE, A. A. and MEANS, G. C. (1932) *The modern corporation and private property.* New York: Commerce Clearing House.

BERMAN, H. J. (1966). *Soviet criminal law and procedure.* Cambridge, MA: Harvard University Press.

BERNARD, T. J. (1984) "The historical development of corporate criminal liability." *Criminology* 22 (February): 3–18.

BERNSTEIN, C. and WOODWARD, B. (1975) *All the president's men.* New York: Warner.

BETZ, M. and O'CONNELL, L. (1983) "Changing doctor-patient relationships and the rise in concern for accountability." *Social Problems* 31: 84–95.

BINSTEIN, M. and BOWDEN, C. (1993) *Trust me: Charles Keating and the missing billions.* New York: Random House.

BIRCH, J. W. (1983) "Reflections on police corruption." *Criminal Justice Ethics* 2: 2–9.

BIRENBAUM, A. (1977) "Medicine, social change, and deviant behavior." Pp. 139–154 in E. Sagarin (Ed.) *Deviance and social change.* Beverly Hills, CA: Sage.

BISHOP, K. (1991) "Developers and others use new tool to quell protests by private citizens." *New York Times* (April 26): B9.

BLACK, D. (1984) "Social control as a dependent variable." Pp. 1–36 in D. Black (Ed.) *Toward a general theory of social control.* Volume I. Orlando, FL: Academic Press.

BLOCH, H. A. and GEIS, G. (1962; 1970) *Man, crime and society.* New York: Random House.

BLOCK, A. A. and CHAMBLISS, W. J. (1981) *Organizing crime.* Amsterdam: Elsevier.

BLOCK, A. A. and SCARPITTI, F. (1985) *Poisoning for profit: The mafia and toxic waste in America.* New York: Morrow.

BLOOM, M. T. (1970) *The trouble with lawyers.* New York: Pocket Books.

BLUM, D. (1988) "Rich kid, poor kid." *New York* (February 22): 48–55.

BLUMBERG, A. (1967) "The practice of law as a confidence game: Organizational cooptation of a profession." *Law & Society Review* 1: 15–39.

BLUMBERG, P. (1989) *The predatory society: Deception in the American marketplace.* New York: Oxford University Press.

BLUMENTHAL, R. (1992) "22 are charged with faking or inflating insurance damage claims." *New York Times* (December 22): B1.

BLUMER, H. (1969) *Symbolic interaction: Perspective and method.* Englewood Cliffs, NJ: Prentice-Hall.

BLUM-WEST, S. and CARTER, T. J. (1983) "Bringing white-collar crime back in: An examination of crimes and torts." *Social Problems* 30: 545–554.

BOCK, G. (1988) "'The Chairman' and his board." *Time* (May 30): 45.

BOGDANOVICH, W. (1992) *The great white lie: Dishonesty, waste, and incompetence in the medical community.* New York: Simon & Schuster.

BOHLEN, C. (1994) "A new Russia: Now thrive the swindlers." *New York Times* (March 17): A1.

BOHLMAN, H. M., DUNDAS, M. J., and JENTZ, G. A. (1989) *The legal environment of business*. St. Paul: West Publishing Co.

BOHM, R. M. (1982) "Capitalism, socialism and crime." Pp. 49–60 in H. E. Pepinsky (Ed.) *Rethinking criminology*. Beverly Hills, CA: Sage.

BOIES, J. L. (1989) "Money, business, and the state: Material interests, Fortune 500 corporations, and the size of political action committees." *American Sociological Review* 54: 821–833.

BOLOGNA, G. J. and LINDQUIST, R. J. (1987). *Fraud auditing and forensic accounting*. New York: Wiley.

BONGER, W. A. (1916) *Criminality and economic conditions*. Boston: Little, Brown.

BONN, R. (1990) "Is white collar crime countable?" A Paper Presented at the Annual Meeting of the American Society of Criminology, Baltimore, November.

BONNER, R. (1987) *Waltzing with a dictator*. New York: Times Books.

BONSIGNORE, J. J., KATSH, E., D'ERRICO, P., PIPKIN, R. M., ARONS, S., and RIFKIN, J. (1989) *Before the law*. 4th ed. Boston: Houghton Mifflin.

BOONE, L. E. (Ed.)(1992) *Quotable business*. New York: Random House.

BOONE, M. (1989) *Capital crime—Black infant mortality in America*. Newbury Park, CA: Sage.

BOOTH, C. (1993) "Nice work if you can get it." *Time* (March 8): 57.

BORKIN, J. (1978) *The crime and punishment of I.G. Farben*. New York: Free Press.

BOVBJERG, R. and METZLOFF, T. B. (Eds.) (1991) "Medical malpractice: Lessons for reform." *Law & Contemporary Problems* 54: 1–223.

BOX, S. (1983) *Power, crime and mystification*. London: Tavistock.

BOYE, M. W. (1991) *Self-reported employee theft and counterproductivity as a function of employee turnover antecedents*. Ph.D. Dissertation, DePaul University.

BRADY, J. (1983) "Arson, urban economy, and organized crime: The case of Boston." *Social Problems* 31: 1–27.

BRADY, K. (1984) *Ida Tarbell: Portrait of a muckraker*. New York: Seaview.

BRAITHWAITE, J. (1982a) "Paradoxes of class bias in criminological research." Pp. 61–84 in H. E. Pepinsky (Ed.) *Rethinking criminology*. Beverly Hills, CA: Sage.

BRAITHWAITE, J. (1982b) "Enforced self-regulation: A new strategy for corporate crime control." *Michigan Law Review* 80: 1466–1507.

BRAITHWAITE, J. (1984) *Corporate crime in the pharmaceutical industry*. London: Routledge & Paul Kegan.

BRAITHWAITE, J. (1985a) "White collar crime." Pp. 1–25 in R.H. Turner, and J.F. Short, Jr. (Eds.) *Annual Review of Sociology*. Palo Alto, CA: Annual Reviews, Inc.

BRAITHWAITE, J. (1985b) *To punish or persuade: The enforcement of coal mine safety*. Albany: SUNY Press.

BRAITHWAITE, J. (1987) "From bodgies and widgies to J. R. Ewing: Beyond folk devils in media depiction of crime." Pp. 55–72 in S. Yeo (Ed.) *Media effects on attitudes to crime*. Sydney: Institute of Criminology/Sydney University Law School.

BRAITHWAITE, J. (1988) "White-collar crime, competition, and capitalism: Comment on Coleman." *American Journal of Sociology* 94: 627–632.

BRAITHWAITE, J. (1989a) "Criminological theory and organizational crime." *Justice Quarterly* 6: 333–358.

BRAITHWAITE, J. (1989b) "The state of criminology: Theoretical decay or renaissance." Pp. 155–166 in W. S. Laufer and F. Adler (Eds.) *Advances in criminological theory*. Volume 2. New Brunswick, NJ: Transaction.

BRAITHWAITE, J. (1989c) *Crime, shame and reintegration*. New York: Cambridge University Press.

BRAITHWAITE, J. (1989d) "Getting on with the job of understanding organizational deviance." A Paper Presented at the Workshop on Organizational Deviance, Harvard Business School, March 8–10.

BRAITHWAITE, J. (1990) "Convergences in models of regulatory strategy." *Current Issues in Criminal Justice* 2: 59–66.

BRAITHWAITE, J. (1992) "Poverty, power and white-collar crime: Sutherland and the paradoxes of criminological theory." Pp. 78–107 in K. Schlegel and D. Weisburd (Eds.) *White-collar crime reconsidered*. Boston: Northeastern University Press.

BRAITHWAITE, J. (1993a) "Shame and modernity." *The British Journal of Criminology* 33: 1–18.

BRAITHWAITE, J. (1993b) "Pride in criminological dissensus." *Law & Social Inquiry* 18: 501–512.

BRAITHWAITE, J. (1993c) "Transnational regulation of the pharmaceutical industry." *The Annals* 525: 12–30.

BRAITHWAITE, J. and FISSE, B. (1985). "Varieties of responsibility and organizational crime." *Law & Policy* 7: 315–343.

BRAITHWAITE, J. and FISSE, B. (1987). "Self-regulation and the control of corporate crime." Pp. 221–246 in C. Shearing and P. C. Stenning (Eds.) *Private policing*. Newbury Park, CA: Sage.

BRAITHWAITE, J. and FISSE, B. (1990) "On the plausibility of corporate crime theory." Pp. 15–38 in W. S. Laufer and F. Adler (Eds.) *Advances in criminological theory*. Volume 2. New Brunswick, NJ: Transaction.

BRAITHWAITE, J. and GEIS, G. (1982) "On theory and action for corporate crime control." *Crime & Delinquency* 28: 292–314.

BRAITHWAITE, J. and MAKKAI, T. (1991) "Testing an expected utility model of corporate deterrence." *Law & Society Review* 25: 7–39.

BRAITHWAITE, J. and PETTIT, P. (1990) *Not just deserts—A republican theory of criminal justice*. Oxford: Clarendon Press.

BRAITHWAITE, J., WALKER, J., and GRABOSKY, P. (1987) "An enforcement taxonomy of regulatory agencies." *Law & Policy* 9 (July): 315–343.

BRANDT, A. M. (1990) "The cigarette, risk, and American culture." *Daedalus* 119: 155–176.

BRECHER, J. (1974) *Strike!* Greenwich, CT: Fawcett Books.

BREEDEN, R. C. (1991) "Thumbs on the scale: The role that accounting practices played in the savings and loan crisis." *Fordham Law Review* 59: 571–591.

BRENNER, E. (1993) "Protecting elderly residents from predatory contractors." *New York Times* (May 23): Bus./1.

BRENNER, M. (1992). "How they broke the bank." *Vanity Fair* (April): 169–267.

BREWTON, P. (1992) *The mafia, the CIA, and George Bush*. New York: Shapolsky Publishers.

BREYER, S. (1993) *Breaking the vicious circle*. Cambridge, MA: Harvard University Press.

BRICKEY, K. F. (1990a) "RICO forfeitures as 'excessive fines' or 'cruel and unusual punishments.'" *Villanova Law Review* 35: 905–928.

BRICKEY, K. F. (1990b) *Corporate and white-collar crime: Cases and materials*. Boston: Little, Brown.

BRILL, H. (1992) "Government breaks the law: The sabotaging of the Occupational Safety and Health Act." *Social Justice* 19: 63–81.

BRINKLEY, J. (1985) "Medical discipline laws: Confusion reigns." *New York Times* (September 3): A1.

BRINKLEY, J. (1988) "Other Reagan officials accused of improprieties." *New York Times* (March 28): A8.

BROBECK, S. and AVERYT, A. (1983) *The product safety book*. New York: Dutton.

BRODEUR, P. (1985) *Outrageous misconduct: The asbestos industry on trial*. New York: Pantheon Books.

BROMBERG, C. (1991) "In defense of hackers." *New York Times Magazine* (April 21): 45–49.

BROOKS, J. (1987) *The takeover game*. New York: Dutton.

BROWN, D. (1971) *Bury my heart at Wounded Knee*. New York: Holt, Rinehart & Winston.

BROWN, S. E. (1982) "Hidden assaults and the tobacco industry." A Paper Presented at the Annual Meeting of the American Society of Criminology, Toronto, November.

BROWNING, F. and GERASSI, J. (1980) *The American way of crime*. New York: Putnam.

BROWNLEE, S. and ROBERTS, S. V. (1994) "Should cigarettes be outlawed?" *U.S. News and World Report* (April 18): 32–38.

BROWNSTEIN, R. (1981) "The toxic tragedy." Pp. 1–59 in R. Nader, R. Brownstein, and J. Richard (Eds.) *Who's poisoning America—Corporate polluters and their victims in the chemical age*. San Francisco: Sierra Club Books.

BRYNER, G. C. (1987) *Bureaucratic discretion: Law and policy in federal regulatory agencies*. New York: Pergamon Press.

BUCY, P. (1991) "Corporate ethos: A standard for imposing corporate criminal liability." *Minnesota Law Review* 75: 1095–1184.

BUDER, L. (1987) "18 arrested in illegal use of cellular phones." *New York Times* (March 27): A1.

BUDER, L. (1989) "Two on board face charges about hiring." *New York Times* (December 2): 29.

BUREAU OF JUSTICE STATISTICS (1985) *Electronic fund transfer fraud*. Washington, DC: U.S. Department of Justice.

BURNHAM, D. (1989) *A law onto itself—The IRS and the abuse of power*. New York: Random House.

BURROUGH, B. and HELYAR, J. (1989) *Barbarians at the gate: The fall of RJR Nabisco*. New York: Harper & Row.

BURT, D. (1982) *Abuse of trust: A report on Ralph Nader's network*. Chicago: Regnery Gateway.

BYRON, C. (1990) "Drexel's fall." *New York* (March 19): 31–40.

BYRON, C. (1991) "High spy: Jules Kroll's modern gumshoes are on a roll." *New York* (May 13): 70–84.

BYRON, C. (1992) "Strike it rich." *New York* (February 17): 21–22.

BYRON, C. (1994) "Dial S for suckers." *New York* (March 7): 46–52.

CABLE, S. and BENSON, M. (1993) "Acting locally: Environmental injustice and the emergence of grass-roots environmental organizations." *Social Problems* 40: 464–477.

CAIN, M. and HUNT, A. (1979) *Marx and Engels on law*. London: Academic Press.

CALAVITA, K. (1983) "The demise of the occupational safety and health administration: A case study in symbolic interaction." *Social Problems* 30: 437–448.

CALAVITA, K. (1990) "Employer sactions violations: Toward a dialectical model of white-collar crime." *Law & Society Review* 24: 1041–1069.

CALAVITA, K. and PONTELL, H. N. (1990) "'Heads I win, tails you lose': Deregulation, crime, and crisis in the savings and loan industry." *Crime & Delinquency* 36: 309–341.

CALAVITA, K. and PONTELL, H. N. (1993) "Savings and loan fraud as organized crime: Towards a conceptual typology of corporate illegality." *Criminology* 31: 519–548.

CALAVITA, K. and PONTELL, H. N. (1994) "The state and white-collar crime: Saving the savings and loans." *Law & Society Review* 28: 297–324.

CAMINER, B. (1985) "Credit card fraud: The neglected crime." *Journal of Criminal Law and Criminology* 76: 746–763.

CANBY, V. (1989) "My hero may be your stoolie." *New York Times* (August 27): II:1.

CAPLOWITZ, D. (1967) *The poor pay more*. New York: Free Press.

CARBONELL-CATILO, A. (1986) "The Philippines: The politics of plunder." *Corruption and Reform* 1: 235–243.

CARDOZO, B. N. (1921) *Nature of the judicial process*. New Haven, CT: Yale University Press.

CARINGELLA-MACDONALD, S. (1990) "State crises and the crackdown on crime under Reagan." *Contemporary Crises* 4: 91–118.

CARLIN, J. E. (1966) *Lawyers' ethics: A survey of the New York bar*. New York: Russell Sage.

CARLSON, M. (1989a) "$1 billion worth of influence." *Time* (November 6): 27–28.

CARLSON, M. (1989b) "A legal bank robbery." *Time* (November 27): 29.

CARLSON, M. (1990a) "Money talks." *Time* (April 9): 18–20.

CARLSON, M. (1990b) "Seven sorry senators." *Time* (January 8): 48–50.

CARPENTER, D. S. and FELONI, J. (1989) *The fall of the House of Hutton*. New York: Holt, Rinehart & Winston.

CARPENTER, T. (1989) *Missing beauty*. New York: Zebra Books.

CARROLL, R., PINE, S., CLINE, C., and KLEINHAUS, B. (1974) "Judged seriousness of Watergate-related crimes." *Journal of Psychology* 86: 235–239.

CARSON, G. (1973) "The income tax and how it grew." *American Heritage* 25: 4 + .

CARSON, R. (1962) *Silent spring.* Boston: Houghton Mifflin.

CARTER, S. L. (1988) "Comment: The indepedent counsel mess." *Harvard Law Review* 102: 105–142.

CASEY, J. (1985) "Corporate crime and the state: Canada in the 1980s." Pp. 100–111 in T. Fleming (Ed.) *The new criminologies in Canada: Crime, state and control.* Toronto: Oxford University Press.

CASTRO, J. (1986) "Roaring into tax reform." *Time* (November 10): 74.

CASTRO, J. (1987) "Of loose lips and stock tips." *Time* (November 30): 63.

CASTRO, J. (1989) "Reach out and rob someone." *Time* (April 3): 38–39.

CAVENDER, G., JURIK, N. C., and COHEN, A. K. (1993) "The baffling case of the smoking gun: The social ecology of political accounts in the Iran-Contra affair." *Social Problems* 40: 152–166.

CAVICCHIA, J. (1992) "The prospects for an international criminal court in the 1990s." *Dickinson Journal of International Law* 10: 223–261.

CENTER FOR RESEARCH ON CRIMINAL JUSTICE. (1977) *The iron fist and the velvet glove— An analysis of the U.S. police.* 2nd ed. Berkeley, CA: Center for Research on Criminal Justice.

CHALK, F. and JONASSOHN, K. (1990) *The history and sociology of genocide—Analyses and case studies.* New Haven, CT: Yale University Press.

CHALMERS, D. (1959) "The muckrakers and the growth of corporate power: A study in constructive journalism." *American Journal of Economics and Sociology* (April): 295–311.

CHAMBERS, M. (1987) "From treasury secretary to guilt in a fraud." *New York Times* (June 16): A1.

CHAMBLISS, W. J. (1964) "A sociological account of the law of vagrancy." *Social Problems* 12: 46–67.

CHAMBLISS, W. J. (1967) "Types of deviance and the effectiveness of legal sanctions." *Wisconsin Law Review* (Summer): 703–714.

CHAMBLISS, W. J. (1981) "The criminalization of conduct." Pp. 45–64 in H. L. Ross (Ed.) *Law and deviance.* Beverly Hills, CA: Sage.

CHAMBLISS, W. J. (1988a) *On the take—From petty crooks to presidents.* 2nd ed. Bloomington: Indiana University Press.

CHAMBLISS, W. J. (1988b) *Exploring criminology.* New York: Macmillan.

CHAMBLISS, W. J. (1989) "State–organized crime." *Criminology* 27: 183–208.

CHAMBLISS, W. J. and COURTLESS, T. F. (1992) *Criminal law, criminology, and criminal justice.* Pacific Grove, CA: Brooks/Cole.

CHAMBLISS, W. J. and SEIDMAN, R. (1982) *Law, order, and power.* 2nd ed. Reading, MA: Addison-Wesley.

CHASE, S. and SCHLINK, F. J. (1927) *Your money's worth.* New York: Macmillan.

CHASET, A. J. and WEINTRAUB, B. B. (1992) "New guidelines for sentencing corporations." *Trial* (April): 41–44.

CHAVEZ, L. (1982) "Toxic waste entrepreneur." *New York Times* (May 27): D1.

CHEN, L-C. (1989) *An introduction to contemporary international law.* New Haven, CT: Yale University Press.

CHEVIGNY, P. (1969) *Police power—Police abuse in New York City.* New York: Vintage.

CHIDESTER, D. (1988) *Salvation and suicide: An interpretation of Jim Jones, the People's Temple and Jonestown.* Bloomington: Indiana University Press.

CHOMSKY, N. (1991) *Media control—The spectacular achievements of propaganda.* Westfield, NJ: Open Magazine.

CHOMSKY, N. (1993) "World order and its rules: Variations on some theories." *Journal of Law & Society* 20: 145–165.

CHOMSKY, N. and HERMAN, E. (1979) *The Washington connection and third world facism.* Nottingham: Spokesman.

CHUNN, D. E. and GAVIGAN, S. A. M. (1988) "Social control: Analytical tool or analytical quagmire?" *Contemporary Crises* 12: 125–144.

CHURCH, G. J. (1994) "It's a jungle out there." *Time* (March 28): 27–29.

CHURCHILL, W. and VANDER WALL, J. (1990) *The Cointelpro papers—Documents from the FBI's secret wars against domestic dissent.* Boston: South End Press.

CLARK, J. P. and HOLLINGER, R. (1977) "On the feasibility of empirical studies of white collar crime." Pp. 139–158 in R. F. Meier (Ed.) *Theory in criminology—Contemporary views.* Beverly Hills, CA: Sage.

CLARK, J. P. and HOLLINGER, R. C. (1983) *Theft by employees in work organizations.* Washington, DC: National Institute of Justice.

CLARKE, L. (1988) "Explaining choices among technological risks." *Social Problems* 35: 22–35.

CLARKE, L. (1989) *Acceptable risk? Making decisions in a toxic environment.* Berkeley: University of California Press.

CLARKE, M. (1990) *Business crime—Its nature and control.* New York: St. Martin's Press.

CLARKE, R. V. and FELSON, M. (1993) "Introduction: Criminology, routine activity and rational choice." Pp. 1–14 in R. V. Clarke and M. Felson (Eds.) *Routine activity and rational choice.* New Brunswick, NJ: Transaction.

CLAWSON, D., NEUSTADL, A., and SCOTT, D. (1992) *Money talks: Corporate PACs and political influence.* New York: Basic Books.

CLAYTON, C. W. (1992) *The politics of justice: The attorney general and the making of legal policy.* Armonk, NY: M. E. Sharpe.

CLINARD, M. B. (1952) *The black market: A study of white collar crime.* New York: Holt, Rinehart & Winston.

CLINARD, M. B. (1983) *Corporate ethics and crime: The role of the middle manager.* Beverly Hills, CA: Sage.

CLINARD, M. B. (1990) *Corporate corruption: The abuse of power.* New York: Praeger.

CLINARD, M. B. and QUINNEY, R. (1967; 1973) *Criminal behavior systems: A typology.* New York: Holt, Rinehart & Winston.

CLINARD, M. B. and YEAGER, P. C. (1978) "Corporate crime—Issues in research." *Criminology* 16: 255–272.

CLINARD, M. B. and YEAGER, P. C. (1980) *Corporate crime.* New York: Free Press.

CLINARD, M. B. , YEAGER, P., BRISSETTE, J., PETRASHEK, D., and HARRIS, E. (1979) *Illegal corporate behavior.* Washington, DC: U.S. Department of Justice.

CLINES, F. X. (1993) "An unfettered Milken has lessons to teach." *New York Times* (October 16): A1.

CLOWARD, R. A. and OHLIN, L. E. (1960) *Delinquency and opportunity: A theory of delinquent gangs.* Glencoe, IL: Free Press.

COFFEE, J. C., JR. (1980) "Corporate crime and punishment: A non–Chicago view of the economics of criminal sanctions." *American Criminal Law Review* 17: 419–476.

COFFEE, J. C., JR. (1981a) "'No soul to damn; no body to kick': An unscandalized inquiry into the problem of corporate punishment." *Michigan Law Review* 79: 386–459.

COFFEE, J. C., JR. (1981b) "From tort to crime: Some reflections on the criminalization of fiduciary breaches and the problematic line between law and ethics." *American Criminal Law Review* 19: 117–172.

COFFEE, J. C., JR. (1983) "Corporate criminal responsibility." Pp. 253–264 in S. Kadish (Ed.) *Encyclopedia of crime and justice.* New York: Free Press .

COFFEE, J. C., JR. (1988a) "Hush!: The criminal status of confidential information after *McNally* and *Carpenter* and the enduring problem of overcriminalization." *American Criminal Law Review* 26: 121–154.

COFFEE, J. C., JR. (1988b) Statement on prosecuting white collar crime. *Proceedings of Symposium 87: White Collar/Institutional Crime—Its measurement and analysis.* Sacramento, CA: Department of Justice, Bureau of Criminal Statistics and Special Services.

COFFEE, J. C., JR. (1991) "Does 'unlawful' mean 'criminal'?: Reflections on the disappearing tort/crime distinction in American law." *Boston University Law Review* 71: 193–245.

COFFEE, J. C., JR. (1992) "Paradigms lost: The blurring of the criminal and civil law models—and what can be done about it." *Yale Law Review* 101: 1875–1892.

COHEN, A. K. (1955) *Delinquent boys: The culture of the gang.* New York: Free Press.

COHEN, A. K. (1990) "Criminal actors: Natural persons and collectivities." Pp. 101–125 in School of Justice Studies (Arizona State University). *New directions in the study of justice, law and social control.* New York: Plenum.

COHEN, A. K., LINDESMITH, A., and SCHUESSLER, K. (Eds.) (1956). *The Sutherland papers.* Bloomington: Indiana University Press.

COHEN, D. A. (1988) *Pillars of salt: The transformation of New England crime literature, 1674–1860.* Brandeis University. Ph.D. Dissertation.

COHEN, M. A. (1989) "Corporate crime and punishment: A study of social harm and sentencing practices in the federal courts, 1984–1987." *American Criminal Law Review* 26: 605–662.

COHEN, M. A. (1991) "Corporate crime and punishment: An update on sentencing practices in the federal courts, 1988–1990." *Boston University Law Review* 71: 249–279.

COHEN, M. A. (1992) "Environmental crime and punishment: Legal/economic theory and empirical evidence on enforcement of federal environmental statutues." *The Journal of Criminal Law and Criminology* 82: 1054–1108.

COHEN, R. (1990) "In books, greed is out, the environment is in." *New York Times* (April 25):

COHEN, R. W. and WITCOVER, J. (1974) *A heartbeat away: The investigation and resignation of Vice President Spiro Agnew.* New York: Bantam Books.

COHEN, S. (1985) *Visions of social control—Crime, punishment, and classification.* Oxford: Polity Press.

COHEN, S. (1993) "Human rights and the crimes of the state: The culture of denial." *Australian & New Zealand Journal of Criminology* 26: 97–115.

COLE, D. (1983) *The attitudes of manufacturing executives to offenses against the environment.* Adelaide: Social and Ecological Assessment.

COLEMAN, J. S. (1974) *Power and the structure of society.* New York: Norton.

COLEMAN, J. S. (1982) "Power and the structure of society." Pp. 36–52 in M. D. Ermann and R. J. Lundman (Eds.) *Corporate and governmental deviance: Problems of organizational behavior in contemporary society.* 2nd ed. New York: Oxford University Press.

COLEMAN, J. W. (1985a; 1989; 1994) *The criminal elite.* New York: St. Martin's Press.

COLEMAN, J. W. (1985b) "Law and power: The Sherman Antitrust Act and its enforcement in the petroleum industry." *Social Problems* 32: 264–274.

COLEMAN, J. W. (1987) "Toward an integrated theory of white-collar crime." *American Journal of Sociology* 93: 406–439.

COLEMAN, J. W. (1988) "Competition and the structure of industrial society: Reply to Braithwaite." *American Journal of Sociology* 94: 632–636.

COLEMAN, J. W. (1992) "The theory of white-collar crime: From Sutherland to the 1990s." Pp. 53–77 in K. Schlegel and D. Weisburd (Eds.) *White-collar crime reconsidered.* Boston: Northeastern University Press.

COLINO, S. (1990) "Felony 101." *Student Lawyer* (October): 32–37.

COLLINS, H. (1984) *Marxism and law.* New York: Oxford University Press.

COLLINS, J. M. and SCHMIDT, F. L. (1993) "Personality, integrity and white collar crime: A construct validity study." *Personnel Psychology* 46: 295–311.

COLLISON, M. N. (1990) "Survey at Rutgers suggests that cheating may be on the rise at larger universities." *Chronicle of Higher Education* (October 24): A30.

COLQUHOUN, P. (1795; 1969) *A treatise on the police of the metropolis.* Montclair, NJ: Patterson Smith.

COMMAGER, H. S. (1974) "The constitution is alive and well." *New York Times* (August 11): Op ed page.

COMMITTEE on FEDERAL REGULATION OF SECURITIES. (1987) "Report of the task force on regulation of insider trading." Pp. 212–227 in H. L. Pitt, (Ed.) *Insider trading—Counselling and compliance.* Clifton, NJ: Prentice-Hall Law & Business.

COMMITTEE ON THE JUDICIARY, U.S. SENATE. (1987) *Oversight of the problem of white collar crime: Hearings.* Washington, DC: U.S. Government Printing Office.

COMSTOCK, A. (1880; 1969) *Frauds exposed*. Montclair, NJ: Patterson Smith.

*CONGRESSIONAL QUARTERLY.* (1990) *Federal regulatory directory*. 6th ed. Washington, DC: Congressional Quarterly.

CONKLIN, J. E. (1977) *"Illegal but not criminal": Business crime in America*. Englewood Cliffs, NJ: Prentice-Hall .

CONLIN, R. B. (1991) "'Litigation explosion': Tempest in a teapot." *Trial* (November): 114–118.

CONLY, C. (1990) *Organizing for computer-crime investigation and prosecution*. Washington, DC: National Institute of Justice Reports.

CONLY, C. and MCEWEN, J. T. (1990) *Computer crime*. Washington, DC: National Institute of Justice Reports.

*CONSUMERS'S RESEARCH.* (1989) "The top ten scams." *Consumer's Research* (June): 32–33.

*CONSUMER'S RESEARCH.* (1990) "Telephone scams for the 1990s." *Consumer's Research* (May): 29–31.

CONYERS, J., Jr. (1990) "RICO reform: A second windfall for S & L crooks." *New York Times* (July 9): A17.

COOKSON, P. W. and PERSELL, C. H. (1985) *Preparing for power—America's elite boarding schools*. New York: Basic Books.

COOPER, M. H. (1987) "Corporate take-overs." *Editorial Research Reports*. Washington, DC: Congressional Quarterly, Inc.

COPETAS, C. (1986) "White-collar manhunt." *New York Times Magazine* (June 8): 45–46, 75–80.

CORNISH, D. and CLARKE, R. V. (1986) *The reasoning criminal: Rational choice perspectives on offending*. New York: Springer-Verlag.

*CORRUPTION AND REFORM.* (1986) "Corruption and reform: An editorial essay." *Corruption and Reform* 1: 3–11.

COTTAM, M. and MARENIN, O. (1989) "Predicting the past: Reagan administration assistance to police forces in Central America." *Justice Quarterly* 6: 589–618.

COTTLE, T. J. (1994) "When you stop, you die: The human toll of unemployment." Pp. 75–81 in J. Skolnick and E. Currie (Eds.) *Crisis in American institutions*. 9th ed. New York: HarperCollins.

COWAN, A. L. (1991) "Compliance officer's day in the sun." *New York Times* (October 20): 10F.

COWAN, A. L. (1992) "Big law and auditing firms to pay millions in S & L suit." *New York Times* (March 31): A1.

COWLES, E. L. (1992) "Is the boardroom immune? An assessment of drug use on employment-related financial crime." A Paper Presented at the Annual Meeting of the American Society of Criminology, New Orleans, November.

COWLEY, G. (1988) "Science and the cigarette." *Newsweek* (January 23): 60.

COWLEY, G. (1989) "Kicking a deadly habit." *Newsweek* (January 23): 60.

COWLEY, G. (1990) "Secondhand smoke: Some grim news." *Newsweek* (June 11): 59.

COX NEWS SERVICE. (1990) "FBI official tells of 'triage' in prosecuting S & Ls." *Scranton Times* (May 12): B8.

CRAY, E. (1972) *The enemy in the streets*. New York: Doubleday.

CRESSEY, D. R. (1953) *Other people's money*. Glencoe, IL: Free Press.

CRESSEY, D. R. (1969) *Theft of the nation*. New York: Harper & Row.

CRESSEY, D. R. (1980) "Management fraud, controls, and criminological theory." Pp. 117–147 in R. K. Elliott and J. T. Willingham (Eds.) *Management fraud: Detection and deterrence*. New York: Petrocelli.

CRESSEY, D. R. (1989) "The poverty of theory in corporate crime research." Pp. 31–55 in W. S. Laufer and F. Adler (Eds.) *Advances in criminological theory*. Volume 1. New Brunswick, NJ: Transaction.

CRIDDLE, W. (1987) "They can't see there's a victim." *New York Times* (February 22): E3.

CROALL, H. (1989) "Who is the white collar criminal? *British Journal of Criminology* 29: 157–173.

CROALL, H. (1992) *White collar crime*. Buckingham: Open University Press.

CROLEY, S. P. and HANSON, J. D. (1991) "What liability crisis: An alternative explanation for recent events in products liability." *Yale Journal of Regulation* 8: 1–112.

CROVITZ, L. G. (1987) "Crime, the Constitution, and the Iran-Contra affair." *Commentary* (October): 23–30.

CULLEN, F. T. (1983) *Rethinking crime and deviance theory.* Totowa, NJ: Rowman & Allenheld.

CULLEN, F. T. and BENSON, M. L. (1993) "White collar crime: Holding a mirror to the core." *Journal of Criminal Justice Education* 4: 325–348.

CULLEN, F. T., CLARK, G., LINK, B., MATHERS, R., NIEDOSPIAL, J., and SHEAHAN, M. (1985) "Dissecting white-collar crime: Offense type and punitiveness." *International Journal of Comparative and Applied Criminal Justice* 9: 16–27.

CULLEN, F. T., LINK, B. G., and POLANZI, C. W. (1982) "The seriousness of crime revisited: Have attitudes toward white-collar crime changed?" *Criminology* 20: 83–102.

CULLEN, F. T., MAAKESTAD, W. J., and CAVENDER, G. (1987) *Corporate crime under attack: The Ford Pinto case and beyond.* Cincinnati: Anderson.

CULLEN, F. T., MATHERS, R., CLARK, G., and CULLEN, J. (1983) "Public support for punishing white-collar criminals: Blaming the victim revisited?" *Journal of Criminal Justice* 11: 481–493.

CUNNINGHAM, W. C., STRAUCHER, J. J., and VAN METER, C. W. (1991) *Private security trends—1970 to 2000.* Boston: Butterworth-Heineman.

CURRA, J. (1994) *Understanding social deviance—From the near side to the outer limits.* New York: HarperCollins.

CURRAN, D. J. and RENZETTI, C. (1990) *Social problems: Society in crisis.* 2nd ed. Boston: Allyn & Bacon.

CURRENT BIOGRAPHY YEARBOOK. (1986) "Ralph Nader." Pp. 402– 405 in *Current biography yearbook.* New York: H. W. Wilson.

CURRIE, E. P. (1968) "Crimes without criminals: Witchcraft and its control in Renaissance Europe." *Law & Society Review* 3: 7–32.

CURRIE, E. and SKOLNICK, J. (1988) *America's problems.* 2nd ed. Glenview, IL: Scott, Foresman.

CUSHMAN, J. H. (1986) "U.S. says Lockheed overcharged by hundreds of millions on plane." *New York Times* (August 28): A1.

CUSHMAN, J. H. (1990) "United and Boeing held at fault in deaths on jet." *New York Times* (April 11): A14.

CUSHMAN, J. H. (1991) "Federal regulation growing as a Quayle panel fights it." *New York Times* (December 24): 1A.

CUSHMAN, J. H. (1993) "Paul, Weiss law firm to pay U.S. $45 million." *New York Times* (September 29): D1.

CUSHMAN, J. H. (1995) "House approves a new standard for regulations." *New York Times* (March 1): A1.

DALEY, S. (1990) "$1.7 million in rent strike disappears." *New York Times* (February 27): B1.

DALY, K. (1989) "Gender and varieties of white-collar crime." *Criminology* 27: 769–793.

DAN-COHEN, M. (1992) "Responsibility and the boundaries of the self." *Harvard Law Review* 105: 959–1011.

DAVIDSON, A. (1990) *In the wake of the Exxon Valdez.* San Francisco: Sierra Club Books.

DAVIDSON, B. (1961) *The African slave trade.* Boston: Little, Brown .

DAVIS, M. S. (1989) *The perceived seriousness and incidence of ethical misconduct in academic science.* Ph.D. dissertation, Ohio State University.

DELAMARTER, R. T. (1976) *Big blue—IBM's use and abuse of power.* New York: Dodd, Mead.

DELANEY, K. J. (1989) "Power, intercorporate networks, and 'strategic bankruptcy.'" *Law & Society Review* 23: 643–666.

DELANEY, K. J. (1992) *Strategic bankruptcy.* Berkeley: University of California Press.

DELANEY, K. J. (1994) "The organizational construction of the 'bottom line.'" *Social Problems* 41: 497–518.

DELOUGHRY, T. J. (1991) "Up to 300 institutions may be cut by U.S. from loan programs." *Chronicle of Higher Education* (May 22): A1 + .

DEMARIS, O. (1974) *Dirty business: The corporate–political–money–power game.* New York: Harper's Magazine Press.

DENTZER, S. (1984) "How Americans beat the tax man." *Newsweek* (April 16): 56–60.

DENZIN, N. K. (1977) "Notes on the criminogenic hypothesis: A case study of the American liquor industry." *American Sociological Review* 42: 905–920.

DENZIN, N. K. (1990) "Reading 'Wall Street': Postmodern contradictions in the American social structure." Pp. 31–44 in B. B. Turner (Ed.) *Theories of modernity and postmodernity.* London: Sage.

DEPALMA, A. (1991) "A college acts in desperation and dies playing the lender." *New York Times* (April 17): A1 +.

DEPALMA, A. (1992a) "House inquiry is expanded into research overcharges." *New York Times* (January 20): B8.

DEPALMA, A. (1992b) "In trial, M.I.T. to defend trading student aid data." *New York Times* (June 24): A17.

DEPALMA, A. (1992c) "M.I.T. ruled guilty in antitrust case." *New York Times* (September 3): A1 +.

DEPARLE, J. (1990) "'Robin Hud' given a stiff sentence." *New York Times* (June 23): A6.

DERBER, C. (1992) *Money, murder, and the American dream.* Boston: Faber & Faber.

DERBER, C., SCHWARTZ, W. A., and MAGRASS, Y. (1990) *Power in the highest degrees— Professionals and the rise of a new Mandarin order.* New York: Oxford.

DEXTER, L. A. (1970) *Elite and specialized interviewing.* Evanston, IL: Northwestern University Press.

DIAMOND, S. (1986) "NASA wasted billions, federal audits disclose." *New York Times* (April 23): A1.

DIMENTO, J. F. (1993) "Criminal enforcement of environmental law." *The Annals* 525: 134–146.

DINITZ, S. (1982) "Multidisciplinary approaches to white-collar crime." Pp. 129–152 in H. Edelhertz and T. D. Overcast (Eds.) *White-collar crime: An agenda for research.* Lexington, MA: Lexington.

DIRKS, R. L. and GROSS, L. (1974) *The great Wall Street scandal.* New York: McGraw-Hill.

DITTON, J. (1977) *Part–time crime: An ethnography of fiddling and pilferage.* London: Macmillan.

DOMINICK, J. (1978) "Crime and law enforcement in the media." Pp. 105–128 in C. Winick (Ed.) *Deviance and the mass media.* Newbury Park: Sage.

DONG, E. (1991) "Confronting scientific fraud." *Chronicle of Higher Education* (October 9): A50.

DONNELLY, P. G. (1982) "The origins of the occupational safety and health act of 1970." *Social Problems* 30: 13–25.

DORMAN, M. (1975) *Vesco—The infernal money-making machine.* New York: Berkeley.

DORN, J. A. and MANNE, H. G. (Eds.)(1987) *Economic liberties and the judiciary.* Fairfax, VA: George Mason University Press.

DOUGLAS, J. D. (1992) "Betraying scientific truth." *Society* (November/December): 76–82.

DOUGLAS, J. D. and JOHNSON, J. M. (Eds.) (1977) *Official deviance.* Philadelphia: Lippincott.

DOUGLAS, M. (1990) "Risk as a forensic resource." *Daedalus* 119: 1–16.

DOWIE, M. (1977) "Pinto madness." *Mother Jones* (September/October): 18–32.

DOWNIE, L. (1976) *The new muckrakers.* Washington, DC: New Republic Book Co.

DOYLE, E. J. (1977) *Not above the law—The battles of Watergate prosecutors Cox and Jaworski.* New York: Morrow.

DRAPER, E. (1984) "Risk by choice? Knowledge and power in the hazardous workplace." *Contemporary Sociology* 13: 688–691.

DRAPER, T. (1991) *A very thin line: The Iran-Contra affairs.* New York: Farrar, Straus & Giroux.

DRAPKIN, I. (1989) *Crime and punishment in the ancient world.* Lexington, MA: Lexington.

DRISCOLL, D. J. (1989) "The development of human rights in international law." Pp. 41–56 in W. Laquer and B. Rubin (Eds.) *The human rights reader.* Rev. ed. New York: New American Library.

DUKE, S. (1983) "Economic crime: Tax offenses." Pp. 683–688 in S. Kadish (Ed.) *Encyclopedia of crime and justice.* New York: Macmillan and Free Press.

DURHAM, A. M. (1988) "Crime seriousness and punitive severity: An assessment of social attitudes." *Justice Quarterly* 5: 132–153.

DURKHEIM, E. (1893; 1933) *Division of labor in society*. New York: Macmillan.

DURKHEIM, E. (1912; 1965) *The elementary forms of the religious life*. New York: Free Press.

DZEICH, B. W. and WEINER, L. (1984) *The lecherous professor—Sexual harassment on campus*. Boston: Beacon Press.

EATON, L. (1994) "U.S. says man bilked investors of $130 million." *New York Times* (May 18): D1.

ECKHOLM, E. (1992) "Alarmed by fund raiser, the elderly give millions." *New York Times* (November 12): A1.

EDELHERTZ, H. (1970) *The nature, impact and prosecution of white collar crime*. Washington, DC: National Institute for Law Enforcement and Criminal Justice.

EDSALL, T. B. (1988) *Power and money*. New York: Norton.

EGAN, T. (1990) "If the Exxon Valdez spill is a crime, whose is it?" *New York Times* (February 11): 6.

EICHENWALD, K. (1990a) "Milken set to pay a $600 million fine in Wall Street fraud." *New York Times* (April 21): A1.

EICHENWALD, K. (1990b) "Milken defends 'junk bonds' as he enters his guilty plea." *New York Times* (April 25): A1.

EICHENWALD, K. (1990c) "S.E.C. complains about its limits." *New York Times* (April 30): 2D.

EICHENWALD, K. (1991) "Judge who gave Milken 10 years backs a parole after he serves 3." *New York Times* (February 20): A1.

EICHENWALD, K. (1992) "Two sued by S.E.C. in bidding scandal at Salomon Bros." *New York Times* (December 3): A1.

EICHENWALD, K. (1993a) "Prudential agrees to a settlement in securities fraud." *New York Times* (October 22): A1.

EICHENWALD, K. (1993b) "New cloud over Prudential Bache." *New York Times* (December 17): D1.

EICHENWALD, K. (1993c) "Millions for us, pennies for you." *New York Times* (December 19): Sect. 3: 1, 12.

EICHENWALD, K. (1994a) "An inquiry broadens at Prudential." *New York Times* (May 16): D1.

EICHENWALD, K. (1994b) "He told. He suffered. Now he's a hero." *New York Times* (May 29): 3/1.

EICHLER, N. (1989) *The thrift debacle*. Berkeley: University of California Press.

EINSTADTER, W. (1992) "Asymmetries of control: Surveillance, intrusion, and corporate theft of privacy." *Justice Quarterly* 9: 285–298.

EITZEN, D. S. and TIMMER, D. A. (1989) "The politics of crime rates." Pp. 39–44 in D. A. Timmer and D. S. Eitzen (Eds.) *Crime in the streets and crime in the suites*. Boston: Allyn & Bacon.

ELIAS, R. (1986) *The politics of victimization—Victims, victimology and human rights*. New York: Oxford University Press.

ELLIOTT, R. K. and WILLINGHAM, J. J. (1980) *Management fraud: Detection and deterrence*. New York: Petrocelli Books.

ELLIS, P. J. and WYATT, J. R. (1992) "Antitrust violations." *American Criminal Law Review* 29: 175–193.

ELMER–DEWITT, P. (1994) "Nabbing the pirates of cyberspace." *Time* (June 13): 62–63.

EMERY, F. (1994) *Watergate*. New York: Times Books.

ENGELBERG, S. (1989) "Boeing expected to plead guilty in Pentagon case." *New York Times* (January 9): A1.

ENGELBERG, S. (1994) "In immigration labyrinth, corruption comes easily." *New York Times* (September 12): A1.

ENGELS, F. (1845; 1958) *The condition of the working class in England*. Translated by W. O. Henderson & W. H. Chaldner. Stanford, CA: Stanford University Press.

ERIKSON, K. (1976) *Everything in its path: Destruction of community in the Buffalo Creek flood*. New York: Touchstone.

ERMANN, D. and LUNDMAN, R. (1982) *Corporate deviance.* New York: Holt, Rinehart & Winston.

ETZIONI, A. (1987) "How rational are we?" *Sociological Forum* 2: 1–20.

ETZIONI, A. (1988a) *Capital corruption—The new attack on American democracy.* New Brunswick, NJ: Transaction Books.

ETZIONI, A. (1988b) *The moral dimension: Toward a new economics.* New York: Free Press .

ETZIONI, A. (1993) "The U.S. sentencing commission on corporate crime: A critique." *The Annals* 525: 147–156.

EVANS, P. B. and SCHNEIDER, S. A. (1981) "The political economy of the corporation." Pp. 216–241 in S. G. McNall (Ed.) *Political economy—A critique of American society.* Glenview, IL: Scott, Foresman.

EVANS, S. S. and LUNDMAN, R. J. (1983) "Newspaper coverage of corporate price-fixing." *Criminology* 21: 529–541.

EVANS, T. D., CULLEN, F. T., and DUBECK, P. J. (1993) "Public perception of corporate crime." Pp. 85–114 in M. B. Blankenship (Ed.) *Understanding corporate criminality.* New York: Garland Publishing Co.

EVEREST, L. (1985) *Behind the poison cloud—Union Carbide's Bhopal massacre.* Chicago: Banner Press.

FABRIKANT, G. (1994) "Time aide in accord to pay fine." *New York Times* (May 13): D1.

FALK, R., KOLKO, G., and LIFTON, R. J. (Eds.) (1971) *Crimes of war.* New York: Vintage.

FALUDI, S. C. (1990) "Safeway LBO yields vast profits but exacts a heavy human toll." *Wall Street Journal* (May 16): 1 + .

FARBERMAN, H. A. (1975) "A criminogenic market structure: The automobile industry." *The Sociological Quarterly* 16: 438–457.

FARNSWORTH, C. (1989) "Wrongdoing at the IRS." *New York Times* (July 29): D1.

FATTAH, E. (Ed.) (1986) *From crime policy to victim policy—Reorienting the justice system.* New York: St. Martin's Press.

FEDER, B. J. (1982) "Manville submits bankruptcy filing to halt lawsuits." *New York Times* (August 27): 1 + .

FEDER, B. J. (1990) "G.E. agrees to pay $16.1 million fine for Pentagon fraud." *New York Times* (July 27): A1.

FELSTINER, W. L. F. and SIEGELMAN, P. (1989) "Neoclassical difficulties: Tort and deterrence for latent injuries." *Law & Policy* 11: 309–329.

FENDRICH, R. P. (1992) "Bush's antitrust lawyers attack philanthropy." *Wall Street Journal* (July 27): A13.

FEST, J. (1970) *The faces of the Third Reich.* New York: Ace.

FIJNAUT, C. (1990) "Organized crime: A comparison between the United States of America and Western Europe." *British Journal of Criminology* 30: 321–340.

FINDLAY, M. and STEWART, A. (1992) "Implementing corruption prevention strategies through codes of conduct." *Corruption and Reform* 7: 67–85.

FINE, B. (1986) "What is social about social control?" *Contemporary Crises* 10: 321–327.

FINEMAN, H. and COHN, B. (1994) "Troubled waters." *Newsweek* (January 17): 14–15.

FINNEY, H. C. and LESIEUR, H. R. (1982) "A contingency theory of organizational crime." Pp. 255–299 in S. B. Bacharach (Ed.) *Research in the sociology of organizations.* Volume 1. Greenwich, CT: JAI Press.

FIRST, H. (1990) *Business crime—Cases and materials.* Westbury, NY: Foundation Press.

FISHER, L. (1992a) "Accusation of fraud at Sears." *New York Times* (June 12): D1.

FISHER, L. (1992b) "Sears auto centers to halt commissions." *New York Times* (June 23): D1.

FISSE, B. (1983) "Reconstructing corporate criminal law: Deterrence, retribution, fault and sanctions." *Southern California Law Review* 56: 1141–1246.

FISSE, B. (1984) "The duality of corporate and individual criminal liability" Pp. 41–68 in E. Hochstedler (Ed.) *Corporations as criminals.* Beverly Hills, CA: Sage.

FISSE, B. (1985) "Sanctions against corporations: The limitations of fines and the enterprise of creating alternatives." Pp. 137–157 in B. Fisse and P. A. French (Eds.) *Corrigible corporations and unruly law.* San Antonio, TX: Trinity University Press.

FISSE, B. (1991) "Corporate criminal responsibility." *Criminal Law Journal* 15: 166–174.

FISSE, B. and FRENCH, P. A. (1985) *Corrigible corporations and unruly law.* San Antonio, TX: Trinity University Press.

FLASTER, D. J. (1983) *Malpractice: A guide to the legal rights of patients and doctors.* New York: Scribner.

FLIGSTEIN, N. and BRANTLEY, P. (1992) "Bank control, owner control, or organizational dynamics: Who controls the large modern corporation?" *American Journal of Sociology* 98: 280–307.

FLOOD, J. (1988) "All cretans are liars: The fight against corporate crime." *Law & Society Review* 21: 811–815.

FLYNN, J. J. (1987) "The jurisprudence of corporate personhood: The misuses of a legal concept." Pp. 131–160 in W. J. Samuels and A. S. Miller (Eds.) *Corporations and society—Power and responsibility.* New York: Greenwood Press.

FOERSCHLER, A. (1990) "Corporate criminal intent: Toward a better understanding of corporate misconduct." *California Law Review* 78: 1287–1311.

FOX, E. (1990) "The Sherman Antitrust Act and the world." *Antitrust Law Journal* 59: 109–118.

FOX, S. (1984) *The mirror makers.* New York: Vintage.

FOX, S. (1989) *Blood and power—Organized crime in twentieth century America.* New York: Morrow.

FRANCIS, D. B. (1987) *Computer crime.* New York: Dutton.

FRANCIS, D. (1988) *Contrepreneurs.* Toronto: Macmillan of Canada.

FRANK, J., CULLEN, F. T., TRAVIS, L., and BORNTRAGER, J. L. (1989) "Sanctioning corporate crime: How do business executives and the public compare?" *American Journal of Criminal Justice* 13: 139–169.

FRANK, N. (1980) "Unintended murder and corporate risk-taking: Defining the concept of justificability." *Journal of Criminal Justice* 16: 17–24.

FRANK, N. (1983) "From criminal to civil penalties in the history of health and safety laws." *Social Problems* 30: 532–544.

FRANK, N. (1984a) "Assaults against inspectors: The dangers of enforcing corporate crime." *Law & Policy* 6: 361–378.

FRANK, N. (1984b) "Policing corporate crime: A typology of enforcement styles." *Justice Quarterly* 1: 235–252.

FRANK, N. (1993) "Maiming and killing: Occupational health crimes." *Annals* 525: 107–118.

FRANK, N. and LOMBNESS, M. (1988) *Controlling corporate illegality.* Cincinnati: Anderson.

FRANK, N. and LYNCH, M. J. (1992) *Corporate crime, corporate violence: A primer.* New York: Harrow & Heston.

FRANKEL, M. E. (1992) "Lawyers can't be stool pigeons." *New York Times* (March 14): 15a.

FRANKLIN, N. (1990) "Environmental pollution control—The limits of the criminal law." *Current Issues in Criminal Justice* 2: 81–94.

FRANTZ, D. (1987) *Levine & Co.—Wall Street's insider trading scandal.* New York: Avon Books.

FRANTZ, D. (1994) "Reports describe widespread abuse in farm program." *New York Times* (October 3): A1.

FREEDMAN, S. G. (1982) "The town Manville built has mixed feelings." *New York Times* (September 1): B1.

FREIBURG, A. (1987) "Reconceptualizing sanctions." *Criminology* 25: 223–256.

FREIDSON, E. (1970) *Professional dominance.* New York: Atherton Press.

FREIDSON, E. (1986) *Professional powers.* Chicago: University of Chicago Press.

FREITAG, P. J. (1975) "The cabinet and big business: A study of interlocks." *Social Problems* 23: 137–152.

FREITAG, P. J. (1983) "The myth of corporate capture: Regulatory commissions in the United States." *Social Problems* 30 (April): 480–491.

FRENCH, P. A. (1979) "The corporation as a moral person." *American Philosophical Quarterly* 16: 207–215.

FRENCH, P. A. (1989) "Enforced corporate responsive adjustments." *Legal Studies Forum* 13: 115–134.

FREUD, S. (1923) *The ego and the id.* London: Hogarth Press.

FREUD, S. (1930) *Civilization and its discontents*. London: Hogarth Press.

FREUDENBURG, W. R. and PASTOR, S. K. (1992) "Public responses to technological risks: Toward a sociological perspective." *Sociological Quarterly* 33: 389–412.

FREUDENHEIM, M. (1989) "Exposing the F.D.A." *New York Times* (September 10): Sect. 3, 1.

FREUDENHEIM, M. (1993) "U.S. subpoenas blood-test files in new health care fraud inquiry." *New York Times* (August 28): A1.

FRIDAY, C. and HAMMER, J. (1989) "Penny-stock scam." *Newsweek* (May 1): 51.

FRIED, J. J. (1991) "Uniysys settles U.S. fraud case for $190 million." *Philadelphia Inquirer* (September 7): 7D.

FRIEDLAND, M. L. (1989) *Sanctions and rewards in the legal system—A multidisciplinary approach*. Toronto: University of Toronto Press.

FRIEDLAND, M. L. (Ed.) (1990) *Securing compliance: Seven case studies*. Toronto: University of Toronto Press.

FRIEDLANDER, S. L. (1990) "Using prior corporate convictions to impeach." *California Law Review* 78: 1313–1339.

FRIEDMAN, L. M. (1977) *Law and society—An introduction*. Englewood Cliffs, NJ: Prentice-Hall .

FRIEDMAN, L. M. (1984) *American law*. New York: Norton.

FRIEDMAN, L. M. (1993) *Crime and punishment in American history*. New York: Basic Books.

FRIEDRICH, C. J. (1958) *The philosophy of law in historical perspective*. Chicago: University of Chicago Press.

FRIEDRICH, O. (1987) "Where there's smoke." *Time* (February 27): 22–23.

FRIEDRICHS, D. O. (1980a) "The legitimacy crisis in the United States: A conceptual analysis." *Social Problems* 27: 540–555.

FRIEDRICHS, D. O. (1980b) "Radical criminology in the United States: An interpretive understanding." Pp. 35–60 in J. A. Inciardi (Ed.) *Radical criminology: The coming crises*. Beverly Hills, CA: Sage.

FRIEDRICHS, D. O. (1981) "The crisis of confidence and criminal justice." *The Justice Reporter* 1: 1–6.

FRIEDRICHS, D. O. (1983) "Victimology: A consideration of the radical critique." *Crime & Delinquency* 29: 283–294.

FRIEDRICHS, D. O. (1985) "The nuclear arms issue and the field of criminal justice." *The Justice Professional* 1: 5–9.

FRIEDRICHS, D. O. (1992) "White collar crime and the definitional quagmire: A provisional solution." *Journal of Human Justice* 3: 5–21.

FRIEDRICHS, D. O. (1995) "State crime or governmental crime: making sense of the conceptual confusion." Pp. 53–79 in J. T. Ross (Ed.) *Controlling State Crime: An Introduction*. New York: Garland Publishing Co.

FRITSCH, J. (1992) "Prosecutors depict vast fraud scheme by L. I. car dealer." *New York Times* (April 16): B1.

FURSTENBERG, F. (1972) "Fear of crime and its effects on citizen behavior." Pp. 52–65 in A. Biderman (Ed.) *Crime and justice*. New York: Justice Institute.

FYFE, J. (1988) "Police use of deadly force." *Justice Quarterly* 5: 165–205.

GALBRAITH, J. K. (1986) "A classic case of euphoric insanity." *New York Times* (November 23): E/3.

GALEN, M. (1992) "Guilty!" *Business Week* (April 13): 60–65.

GALLIHER, J. F. (1979) "Government research funding and purchased virtue: Some examples from criminology." *Crime and Social Justice* (Spring/Summer): 44–50.

GAMBETTA, D., (Ed.) (1988) *Trust: Making and breaking cooperative relations*. New York: Basil Blackwell.

GANS, H. J. (1979) *Deciding what's news—A study of CBS Evening News, NBC Nightly News, Newsweek and Time*. New York: Pantheon Books.

GANZINI, L., MCFARLAND, B., and BLOOM, J. (1990) "Victims of fraud: Comparing victims of white collar and violent crime." *Bulletin of the American Academy of Psychiatry and Law* 18: 55–63.

GARDINER, J. A. (1986) "Controlling official corruption and fraud: Bureaucratic incentives and disincentives." *Corruption and Reform* 1: 33–50.

GARFINKEL, H. (1956) "Conditions of successful degradation ceremonies." *American Journal of Sociology* 61: 420–424.

GARMENT, S. (1992) *Scandal—The culture of mistrust in American politics.* New York: Doubleday.

GEIS, G. (1967) "White collar crime: The heavy electrical equipment antitrust cases of 1961." Pp. 139–151 in M. Clinard and R. Quinney (Eds.) *Criminal behavior systems: A typology.* New York: Holt, Rinehart & Winston.

GEIS, G. (1974) "Avocational crime." Pp. 272–298 in D. Glaser (Ed.) *Handbook of criminology.* New York: Rand McNally.

GEIS, G. (1984) "White collar crime and corporate crime." Pp. 132–166 in R. Meier (Ed.) *Major forms of crime.* Beverly Hills, CA: Sage.

GEIS, G. (1987) "Edwin H. Sutherland's white collar crime in America: An essay in historical criminology." Pp. 1–31 in L. Knafla (Ed.) *Criminal justice history.* Volume 7. Westport, CT: Meckler.

GEIS, G. (1988) "From Deuteronomy to deniability: A historical perlustration on white-collar crime." *Justice Quarterly* 5: 7–32.

GEIS, G. (1992) "White-collar crime: What is it?" Pp. 31–52 in K. Schlegel and D. Weisburd (Eds.) *White-collar crime reconsidered.* Boston: Northeastern University Press.

GEIS, G. (1993) "The evolution of the study of corporate crime." Pp. 3–28 in M. Blankenship (Ed.) *Understanding corporate criminality.* New York: Garland Publishing Co.

GEIS, G. and GOFF, C. (1982) "Edwin H. Sutherland: A biographical and analytical commentary." Pp. 3–21 in P. Wickman and T. Dailey (Eds.) *White collar and economic crime.* Lexington, MA: Heath.

GEIS, G. and GOFF, C. (1987) "Edwin H. Sutherland's white-collar crime in America: An essay in historical criminology." Pp. 1–31 in L. Knafla (Ed.) *Criminal justice history.* Volume 7. Westport, CT: Meckler.

GEIS, G. and GOFF, C. (1992) "Lifting the cover from undercover operations: J. Edgar Hoover and some of the other criminologists." *Crime, Law & Social Change* 18: 91–104.

GEIS, G. and MEIER, R. F. (Eds.) (1977) *White-collar crime.* New York: Free Press.

GEIS, G., PONTELL, H. N., and JESILOW, P. (1988) "Medicaid Fraud." Pp. 17–39 in J. E. Scott and T. Hirschi (Eds.) *Controversial issues in crime and justice.* Beverly Hills, CA: Sage.

GEIS, G. and STOTLAND, E., (Eds.) (1980) *White collar crime: Theory and research.* Beverly Hills, CA: Sage.

GELB, R. L. (1977) *White collar crime: The need for a counter-offensive.* International Association of Chiefs of Police. Hackensack, NJ: National Council on Crime and Delinquency.

GELLHORN, E., JAMES, C. A., POGUE, R., and SIMS, J. (1990) "Has antitrust outgrown dual enforcement? A proposal for rationalization." *The Antitrust Bulletin* 35: 695–744.

GERBER, J. and FRITSCH, E. J. (1993) "On the relationship between white-collar crime and political sociology." *Teaching Sociology* 21: 130–139.

GERBER, J. and SHORT, J. F., JR. (1986) "Publicity and the control of corporate behavior: The case of infant formula." *Deviant Behavior* 7: 195–216.

GERBER, J. and WEEKS, S. L. (1992) "Women as victims of corporate crime: A call for research on a neglected topic." *Deviant Behavior* 13: 325–347.

GERSON, S. M. (1992) "When lawyers must disclose." *New York Times* (April 9): 25A.

GERTH, J. (1981) "Embezzling case at Wells Fargo: Keys are computers and volume." *New York Times* (February 23): A1.

GERTH, J. (1985) "Dynamics deferral of U.S. income tax." *New York Times* (February 1): D1.

GERTH, J. (1988) "$69 million award in Ashland case." *New York Times* (June 14): D1.

GERTH, J. (1990a) "Misuse of savings bailout reported in Texas purchase." *New York Times* (July 8): A1.

GERTH, J. (1990b) "Panel is told how subsidies profited in savings institution." *New York Times* (July 10): A1.

GERTH, J. (1990c) "A one-time aide to Bush shows a lobbyist's magic." *New York Times* (July 15): A1.

GERTH, J. (1990d) "Insolvent bank bought cheaply with help of former Bush aide." *New York Times* (July 22): A1.

GHEZZI, S. G. (1983) "A private network of social control: Insurance investigation unit." *Social Problems* 30: 521–531.

GIBBONS, D. C. (1979) *The criminological enterprise—Theories and perspectives.* Englewood Cliffs, NJ: Prentice-Hall .

GIBBONS, D. C. (1983) "Mundane crime." *Crime & Delinquency* 29: 213–228.

GIBBS, J. P. (1987) "The state of criminological theory." *Criminology* 25: 821–840.

GIBBS, J. P. (1989) *Control: Sociology's central notion.* Champaign: University of Illinois Press.

GIBNEY, F. (1978) "What's an operator?" Pp. 9–22 in J. M. Johnson and J. D. Douglas, (Eds.) *Crime at the top: Deviance in business and the professions.* Philadelphia: Lippincott.

GILSON, R. J. (1987) "The outside view of inside trading." *New York Times* (February 8): A23.

GITLIN, T. (1980) *The whole world is watching.* Berkeley: University of California Press.

GITLIN, T. (1983) *Inside prime time.* New York: Pantheon Books.

GIULIANI, R. (1990) Interview: "From Milken to the Mafia." *Barron's* (November 26): 12–13; 24; 26.

GLABERSON, W. (1987) "Wall Street informer admits his guilt in insider trading." *New York Times* (February 18): A1.

GLABERSON, W. (1989a) "Millions, and friends' trust, vanish in Brooklyn betrayal." *New York Times* (November 21): B1.

GLABERSON, W. (1989b) "Helmsley gets 4-year term for tax fraud." *New York Times* (December 13): B1.

GLABERSON, W. (1990) "Court says job hazards may be a crime." *New York Times* (October 17): B1.

GLASER, D. (1956) "Criminality theories and behavioral images." *American Journal of Sociology* 61: 433–444.

GLASER, K. and POSSONY, S. T. (1979) *Victims of politics—The state of human rights.* New York: Columbia University Press.

GLAZER, M. P. and GLAZER, P. M. (1989) *The whistleblowers.* New York: Basic Books.

GLICK, B. (1990) "Preface." *The Cointelpro papers.* Boston: South End Press.

GOFF, C. and NASON-CLARKE, N. (1989) "The seriousness of crime in Fredericton, New Brunswick: Perceptions toward white-collar crime." *Canadian Journal of Criminology* 31: 19–34.

GOFF, C. and REASONS, C. E. (1978) *Corporate crime in Canada: A critical analysis of anti-combines legislation.* Scarborough, Ontario: Prentice-Hall of Canada.

GOFFMAN, E. (1959) *The presentation of self in everyday life.* New York: Doubleday.

GOFFMAN, E. (1963) *Stigma: Notes on the management of spoiled identity.* Englewood Cliffs, NJ: Prentice-Hall .

GOLD, A. R. (1988) "Ocean Spray Company indicted as a polluter." *New York Times* (January 29): A1.

GOLD, A. R. (1990) "State is called New York's no. 1 polluter." *New York Times* (March 3): A25.

GOLDEN, T. (1990) "After seeming so nice, she's indicted for fraud." *New York Times* (December 3): B3.

GOLDSTEIN, A. S. (1992) "White-collar crime and civil sanctions." *Yale Law Journal* 101: 1795–1874.

GOLDSTEIN, H. (1975) *Police corruption.* Washington, DC: Police Foundation.

GOLEMAN, D. (1991) "Tax tip: If it's lump sum, cheating is more likely." *New York Times* (April 13): 6.

GONZALEZ, D. (1991) "Clothing gifts to charities may not reach needy." *New York Times* (May 7): B4.

GONZALEZ, J. (1991) "Senatorial privilege?" *New York Daily News* (September 24): C3.

GOODE, E. (1994) *Deviant behavior*. 4th ed. Englewood Cliffs, NJ: Prentice-Hall.

GORDON, D. M. (1971) "Class and the economics of crime." *The Review of Radical Political Economics* 3: 51–72.

GORDON, J. S. (1991) "Understanding the S & L mess." *American Heritage* (February/March): 49–68.

GORMAN, C. (1990) "This is a rescue?" *Time* (March 11): 58–59.

GOTTFREDSON, M. R. and HIRSCHI, T. (1990) *A general theory of crime*. Stanford, CA: Stanford University Press.

GOTTLIEB, M. (1986) "Court orders disbarring of Cohn, citing misconduct in four cases." *New York Times* (June 24): A1.

GRABER, D. (1980) *Crime news and the public*. New York: Praeger.

GRABOSKY, P. N. (1990) "Professional advisers and white collar illegality: Toward explaining and excusing professional failure." *University of New South Wales Law Journal* 13: 73–90.

GRABOSKY, P. N. (1993) *Rewards and incentives as regulatory instruments*. Canberra, Australia: Australian National University.

GRABOSKY, P. N., BRAITHWAITE, J., and WILSON, P. R. (1987) "The myth of community tolerance toward white collar crime." *Australian and New Zealand Journal of Criminology* 20: 33–44.

GRABOSKY, P. and WILSON, P. R. (1989) *Journalism and justice: How crime is reported*. Sydney: Pluto Press.

GRANT, A. and WOLF, M. J. (1988) *Platinum crime*. New York: Pocket Books.

GRASMICK, H. G., TITTLE, C. R., BURSIK, R. J., and ARNEKEV, B. J. (1993) "Testing the core empirical implications of Gottfredson and Hirschi's general theory of crime." *Journal of Research in Crime & Delinquency* 30: 5–24.

GRAY, W. B. and SCHOLZ, J. T. (1991) "Analyzing the equity and efficiency of OSHA enforcement." *Law & Policy* 13: 185–210.

GRAY, W. B. and SCHOLZ, J. T. (1993) "Does regulatory enforcement work? A panel analysis of OSHA enforcement." *Law & Society Review* 27: 177–214.

GREEN, B. A. (1991) "After the fall: The criminal law enforcement response to the S & L crisis." *Fordham Law Review* 59: S155–192.

GREEN, G. S. (1985) "General deterrence and television cable crime: A field experiment in social control." *Criminology* 23: 629–646.

GREEN, G. S. (1990) *Occupational crime*. Chicago: Nelson Hall.

GREEN, G. S. (1993) "Reflections on the study of white-collar criminal careers." A Paper Presented at the Annual Meeting of the American Society of Criminology, Phoenix, October.

GREEN, M. J. (1975) *The other government—The unseen power of Washington lawyers*. New York: Grossman.

GREEN, M. J. (1984) *Who runs Congress?* New York: Dell.

GREENBERG, D. (1981) *Crime and capitalism*. Palo Alto, CA: Mayfield Publishing Co.

GREENHOUSE, L. (1986) "House approves measure to make computer crime a federal crime." *New York Times* (June 4): A1.

GREENHOUSE, L. (1993) "Justices again reject limit on punitive damages." *New York Times* (June 26): A8.

GREENWALD, C. (1980) *Banks are dangerous to your wealth*. Englewood Cliffs, NJ: Prentice-Hall .

GREENWALD, J. (1990) "Predator's fall." *Time* (February 26): 46.

GREENWALD, J. (1993) " A matter of honor." *Time* (June 21): 33–34.

GRISANTI, M. L. (1989) "The Caesarean epidemic." *New York* (February 20): 55–61.

GRISHAM, J. (1991) *The firm*. New York: Dell.

GROSS, E. (1978) "Organizational crime: A theoretical perspective." Pp. 55–85 in N. Denzin (Ed.) *Studies in symbolic interaction*. Volume 1. Greenwich, CT: JAI Press.

GROSS, E. (1980) "Organization structure and organizational crime." Pp. 52–76 in G. Geis and E. Stotland (Eds.) *White-collar crime: Theory and research*. Beverly Hills, CA: Sage.

GROTZNER, C. (1973) "Organized crime and the businessman." Pp. 105–119 in J. E. Conklin, (Ed.) *The crime establishment*. Englewood Cliffs, NJ: Prentice-Hall.

GULLEY, B. and REESE, M. E. (1980) *Breaking cover*. New York: Warner.

GUNKEL, S. E. (1990) "Rethinking the guilty mind: Identity salience and white collar crime." A Paper Presented at the Annual Meeting of the American Society of Criminology, Baltimore, November.

GUNKEL, S. E. and EITLE, D. J. (1989) "Local state structure and corporate crime." A Paper Presented at the Annual Meeting of the American Society of Criminology, Reno, November.

GUNNINGHAM, N. (1987) "Negotiated non-compliance: A case study of regulatory failure." *Law & Policy* 9 (January): 69–93.

GURNEY, J. N. (1985) "Factors influencing the decision to prosecute economic crime." *Criminology* 23: 609–628.

HAGAN, F. (1986) *Introduction to criminology*. Chicago: Nelson Hall.

HAGAN, F. (1992) "From HUD to Iran-Contra: Crime during the Reagan Administration." A Paper Presented at the Annual Meeting of the American Society of Criminology, New Orleans, November.

HAGAN, F. and BENEKOS, P. S. (1991) "The great savings and loan scandal: An analysis of the biggest financial fraud in American history." *Journal of Security Administration* 14: 41–64.

HAGAN, J. (1983) *Victims before the law: The organizational dominance of criminal law*. Toronto: Buttersworth.

HAGAN, J. (1987) "White collar and corporate crime." Pp. 320–336 in R. Linden (Ed.) *Criminology: A Canadian perspective*. Toronto: Holt, Rinehart & Winston.

HAGAN, J. (1989a) "Why is there so little criminal justice theory? Neglected macro- and micro-level links between organization and power." *Journal of Research in Crime and Delinquency* 26: 116–135.

HAGAN, J. (1989b) *Structural criminology*. New Brunswick, NJ: Rutgers University Press.

HAGAN, J. and KAY, F. (1990) "Gender and delinquency in white-collar families: A power-control perspective." *Crime & Delinquency* 36: 391–407.

HAGAN, J. and NAGEL, I. H. (1982) "White-collar crime, white-collar time: The sentencing of white-collar offenders in the Southern District of New York." *American Criminal Law Review* 20: 259–289.

HAGAN, J. and PALLONI, A. (1986) "'Club Fed' and the sentencing of white-collar offenders before and after Watergate." *Criminology* 24: 603–622.

HAGAN, J. and PARKER, P. (1985) "White-collar crime and punishment." *American Sociological Review* 50: 302–316.

HAGEDORN, A. and BARRETT, P. M. (1990) "One lawyer's fraudulent dealings." *Wall Street Journal* (July 17): B6.

HAHN, R. W. and HIRD, J. A. (1991) "The costs and benefits of regulation: Review and synthesis." *Yale Journal of Regulation* 8: 233–278.

HALBROOKS, C. (1990) "It can happen here." *Newsweek* (November 26): 10.

HALL, J. (1943) "Interrelations of criminal law and torts." *Columbia Law Review* 43: 753–779; 967–1001.

HALL, J. (1952) *Theft, law and society*. 2nd ed. Indianapolis: Bobbs–Merrill.

HALL, K. L. (1989) *The magic mirror—Law in American history*. New York: Oxford University Press.

HALL, R. H. (1987) *Organizations—Structures, processes and outcomes*. Englewood Cliffs, NJ: Prentice-Hall .

HALLER, M. H. (1990) "Illegal enterprise: A theoretical and historical interpretation." *Criminology* 28: 207–231.

HALLORAN, R. (1987) "U.S. hints at Hutton indictment in money scheme." *New York Times* (October 11): 29.

HALPIN, B. (1988) "Plot to sell uninspected meat alleged." *Scranton Times* (March 30): 1.

HAMILTON, W. H. (1931) "The ancient maxim of caveat emptor." *Yale Law Journal* 40: 1133–1187.

HAMMER, J. (1990) "Fear in the backroom." *Newsweek* (September 24): 64.

HANDLER, J. F. (1978) *Social movements and the legal system: A theory of law reform and social change.* New York: Academic Press.

HANLEY, R. (1990) "Eastman Kodak admits violations of anti-pollution laws." *New York Times* (April 6): B4.

HANS, V. (1989) "The jury's response to business and corporate wrongdoing." *Law and Contemporary Problems* 52: 177–201.

HANS, V. and VIDMAR, N. (1986) *Judging the jury.* New York: Plenum.

HANS, V. P. and LOFQUIST, W. S. (1992) "Jurors judgments of business liability in tort cases: Implications for the litigation explosion." *Law & Society Review* 26: 85–116.

HARDING, R. (1983) "Nuclear energy and the destiny of mankind—Some criminological perspectives." *Australian and New Zealand Journal of Criminology* 16: 81–92.

HARFF, B. and GURR, T. R. (1989) "Victims of the state: Genocides, politicides, and group repression since 1945." *International Review of Victimology* 1: 23–41.

HARMER, R. M. (1975) *American medical avarice.* New York: Abelard Schuman.

HARRIGER, K. (1992) *Independent justice: The federal special prosecutor in American politics.* Lawrence: University of Kansas Press.

HARRIS, A. R. and HILL, G. (1982) "The social psychology of deviance: Toward a reconciliation with social structure." Pp. 161–186 in R. Turner and J. A. Short, Jr.(Eds.) *Annual review in sociology.* Palo Alto, CA: Annual Reviews.

HARRIS, A. R. (1991) "Race, class, and crime." Pp. 95–120 in J. Sheley (Ed.) *Criminology: A contemporary handbook.* Belmont, CA: Wadsworth.

HARRIS, J. (1974) "The Marxist conception of violence." *Philosophy & Public Affairs* 3: 192–220.

HARTJEN, C. (1974) *Crime and criminalization.* New York: Praeger.

HARTUNG, F. (1950) "White collar offenses in the wholesale meat industry in Detroit." *American Journal of Sociology* 56: 25–32.

HARTUNG, F. (1953) "Common and discrete values." *Journal of Social Psychology* 38: 3–27.

HASS, N. (1994) "New games, new rules." *Newsweek* (March 14): 43.

HAUBER, A. R., TOONVLIET, L. C., and WILLEMSE, A. M. (1988) "The perceived seriousness of white collar crime and conventional crime." *Corruption and Reform* 3: 41–64.

HAWKINS, K. (1984) *Environment and enforcement: Regulation and the social definition of pollution.* New York: Oxford University Press.

HAWKINS, K. (1989) "FATCATS" and prosecution in a regulatory agency: A footnote on the social construction of risk." *Law & Policy* 11: 370–391.

HAWKINS, K. (1990) "Compliance strategy, prosecution policy and Aunt Sally." *British Journal of Criminology* 30: 444–466.

HAWKINS, K. (1991) "Enforcing regulations: More of the same from Pearce and Tombs." *British Journal of Criminology* 31: 427–430.

HAWKINS, K. and THOMAS, J. M. (1983) "Perspectives on regulation: Law, discretion, and bureaucratic behavior." *Law & Policy* 5 (January): 35–74.

HAYES, P. (1987) *Industry and ideology—I. G. Farben in the Nazi era.* Cambridge: Cambridge University Press.

HAYES, T. C. (1990a) "Former savings executive sentenced to 30 years in jail." *New York Times* (April 6): D1.

HAYES, T. C. (1990b) "Sick savings units riddled by fraud, FBI head asserts." *New York Times* (April 12): A1.

HAYS, C. L. (1991) "Executive gets top sentence in famine fraud." *New York Times* (October 13): 39.

HEANEY, G. W. (1991) "The reality of sentencing guidelines: No end to disparity." *American Criminal Law Review* 28: 161–232.

HEDMAN, S. (1991) "Expressive functions of criminal sanctions in environmental law." *The George Washington Law Review* 59: 889–899.

HEEREN, J. W. and SHICHOR, D. (1993) "Faculty malfeasance: Understanding academic deviance." *Sociological Inquiry* 63: 49–63.

HEIDENHEIMER, A. J. (1977) "Definitions, conceptions and criteria of corruption." Pp. 19–26 in J. Douglas and J. M. Johnson (Eds.) *Official deviance.* Philadelphia: Lippincott.

HEILBRONER, R. C. (1975) "None of your business." *New York Review of Books* (March 20): 6–10.

HENDERSON, J. H. and SIMON, D. R. (1994) *Crimes of the criminal justice system.* Cincinnati: Anderson.

HENRIQUES, D. B. (1990a) "The latest penny-stock shuffle." *New York Times* (April 1): Business/1.

HENRIQUES, D. B. (1990b) "A paradoxical anti-takeover bill." *New York Times* (April 8): 15.

HENRIQUES, D. B. (1991a) "In world markets, loose regulation." *New York Times* (July 23): D1.

HENRIQUES, D. B. (1991b) "Free-wheeling treasuries market is at turning point with Congress." *New York Times* (September 3): A1.

HENRIQUES, D. B. (1992a) "A new insider trading case hits major business figures." *New York Times* (June 5): A1.

HENRIQUES, D. B. (1992b) "Falsifying corporate data becomes fraud of the 90's." *New York Times* (September 21): A1.

HENRIQUES, D. B. (1993) "Evidence mounts of rigged bidding in milk industry." *New York Times* (May 23): A1.

HENRIQUES, D. B. (1994a) "Towers investors try aggressive new legal tack." *New York Times* (June 10): D1.

HENRIQUES, D. A. (1994b) "Republicans may curb S.E.C. and fraud suits by investors." *New York Times* (December 12): A1.

HENRY, F. J. (1991) "Corporate violence: Government regulation and the possibilities of reform." *Free Inquiry in Creative Sociology* 19 (November): 145–153.

HENRY, S. (1978) *The hidden economy: The context and control of borderline crime.* London: Martin Robertson.

HENRY, S. (1991) "The informal economy: A crime of omission by the state." Pp. 253–272 in G. Barak (Ed.) *Crimes by the capitalist state.* Albany: SUNY Press.

HENRY, S. and MILOVANOVIC, D. (1991) "Constitutive criminology: The maturation of critical criminology." *Criminology* 29: 293–316.

HENRY, S. and MILOVANOVIC, D. (1994) "The constitution of constitutive criminology: A postmodern approach to criminological theory." Pp. 110–133 in D. Nelkin (Ed.) *The futures of criminology.* London: Sage.

HENSLIN, J. M. (1968) "Trust and the cab driver." Pp. 138–158 in M. Truzzi, (Ed.) *Sociology and everyday life.* Englewood Cliffs, NJ: Prentice-Hall .

HERLING, J. (1962) *The great price conspiracy: The story of the antitrust violations in the electrical industry.* Washington, DC: Robert B. Luce.

HERMAN, E. S. (1982) *The real terror network—Terrorism in fact and propaganda.* Boston: South End Press.

HERMAN, E. S. (1985) Review essay: "The transformation of Wall Street." *ABF Research Journal* (Summer): 691–697.

HERSHEY, R. D., JR. (1984) "Panel says U.S. can trim costs by $424 billion." *New York Times* (January 13): A1.

HERSHEY, R. D., JR. (1990a) "Thrift office will open its cases." *New York Times* (July 6): D1 + .

HERSHEY, R. D., JR. (1990b) "Tax sleuths turn to technology." *New York Times* (March 23): D1.

HERSHEY, R. D., JR. (1994a) "I.R.S. finds fraud grows as more file by computer." *New York Times* (February 21): A1.

HERSHEY, R. D., JR. (1994b) "I.R.S. staff is cited in snoopings." *New York Times* (July 19): D1.

HERZOG, A. (1987) *Vesco.* New York: Doubleday.

HEYDEBRAND, W. (1990) "Government litigation and national policymaking: From Roosevelt to Reagan." *Law & Society Review* 24: 477–495.

HIATT, H. (1991) "Patients, doctors, and lawyers: Resolving the malpractice crisis." *Bulletin— The American Academy of Arts & Sciences* 44: 41–50.

HICKEY, N. (1981) "Is television doing its investigative reporting job?" Pp. 166–170 in B. Cole (Ed.) *Television today: A close-up view.* New York: Oxford University Press.

HICKS, J. P. (1993) "Home-repair schemes victimizing the elderly." *New York Times* (February 17): B3.

HICKS, K. M. (1994) *Surviving the Dalkon shield IUD: Women v. the pharmaceutical industry.* New York: Teachers College Press.

HILBERG, R. (1961) *The destruction of the European Jews.* Chicago: Quadrangle.

HILBERG, R. (1980) "The anatomy of the Holocaust." Pp. 85–102 in H. Friedlander and S. Milton (Eds.) *The Holocaust: Ideology, bureaucracy and genocide.* New York: Kraus International Publications.

HILLS, S. L. (1980) *Demystifying social deviance.* New York: McGraw-Hill.

HILLS, S. L. (1982) "Crime and deviance on a college campus: The privilege of class." *Humanity & Society* 6: 257–266.

HILLS, S. L. (1987) *Corporate violence.* Totowa, NJ: Rowman & Littlefield.

HILTS, P. J. (1989) "F.D.A. acts to limit food health claims." *New York Times* (December 15): D17.

HILTS, P. J. (1992a) "Maker of implants balked at tests, its records show." *New York Times* (January 8): A1.

HILTS, P. J. (1992b) "Top manufacturer of gel implants replaces its chief." *New York Times* (February 11): A1.

HILTS, P. J. (1993a) "Manufacturer admits selling untested devices for heart." *New York Times* (October 16): A1.

HILTS, P. J. (1993b) "Misconduct in science is not rare, a survey finds." *New York Times* (November 12): A22.

HINCH, R. and DeKESEREDY, W. (1992) "Corporate violence and women's health at home and in the the workplace." In B. Bolaria and H. Dickinson (Eds.) *The sociology of health care in Canada.* 2nd ed. Toronto: Harcourt Brace Jovanovich.

HIRSCHI, T. (1969) *Causes of delinquency.* Berkeley: University of California Press.

HIRSCHI, T. (1986) "On the compatibility of rational choice and social control theories of crime." Pp. 105–118 in D. B. Cornish and R. V. Clarke (Eds.) *The reasoning criminal—Rational choice perspectives on offending.* New York: Springer-Verlag.

HIRSCHI, T. and GOTTFREDSON, M. (1987) "Causes of white-collar crime." *Criminology* 5: 949–974.

HIRSCHI, T. and GOTTFREDSON, M. (1989) "The significance of white-collar crime for a general theory of crime." *Criminology* 27: 359–371.

HOCHSTEDLER, E. (1984) *Corporations as criminals.* Beverly Hills, CA: Sage.

HODSON, R. and SULLIVAN, T. A. (1990) *The social organization of work.* Belmont, CA: Wadsworth.

HOFFMAN, W. M. (1989) "The cost of a corporate conscience." *Business and Society Review* 69: 46–47.

HOLCOMB, B. (1986) "Inside the boiler room." *New York* (August 4): 38–41.

HOLLINGER, R. C. and LANZA–KADUCE, L. (1988) "The process of criminalization: The case of computer crime laws." *Criminology* 26: 101–126.

HOLLINGER, R. C., SLORA, K. B., and TERRIS, W. (1992) "Deviance in the fast-food restaurant: Correlates of employee theft, altruism, and counterproductivity." *Deviant Behavior* 13: 155–184.

HOLMES, S. A. (1990) "Congress to take new look at racketeering law." *New York Times* (September 14): B18.

HOLUBA, J. (1987) "Chrysler is accused of hiding mileage on cars sold as new." *New York Times* (June 25): A1.

HOPE, K. R. (1987) "Administrative corruption and administrative reform in developing states." *Corruption and Reform* 2: 127–147.

HORNING, D. (1983) "Employee theft." Pp. 698–704, in S. Kadish (Ed.) *Encyclopedia of crime and justice.* New York: Macmillan and Free Press.

HORNING, D. (1970) ' blue-collar theft: Conceptions of property, attitudes toward pilfering, and work norms in a modern industrial plant." Pp. 46–64 in E. O. Smigel and H. L. Ross (Eds.) *Crimes against bureaucracy*. New York: Van Nostrand Reinhold.

HORWITZ, M. J. (1992) *The transformation of American law, 1870–1960: The crisis of legal orthodoxy*. New York: Oxford University Press.

HOWARD, L. and ZEMAN, N. (1991) "Computerland." *Newsweek* (April 8): 8.

HUBER, P. (1988) "Tort reform by contract." Pp. 174–185 in W. Olson (Ed.) *New directions in liability law*. New York: The Academy of Political Science.

HUBER, P. (1990) "Pathological science in court." *Daedalus* 119: 97–118.

HUGHES, E. C. (1964) "Good people and dirty work." Pp. 23–36 in H. S. Becker (Ed.) *The other side: Perspectives on deviance*. New York: Free Press .

HUGHES, J. A. (1993) "Law firm Kaye, Scholer, Lincoln S & L and the OTS." *Notre Dame Journal of Law, Ethics & Public Policy* 7: 177–222.

HUME, E. (1990) "Why the press blew the S & L scandal." *New York Times* (May 24): A25.

HUMPHRIES, D. (1981) "Serious crime, news coverage and ideology: Crime coverage in a metropolitan paper." *Crime & Delinquency* 27: 191–205.

HUNTINGTON, S. (1968) *Political order in changing societies*. New Haven, CT: Yale University Press.

HURST, J. W. (1956) *Law and the conditions of freedom in the nineteenth century United States*. Madison: University of Wisconsin Press.

HUTCHESON, M. (1990) "Teaching the right thing." *NYU Alumni Magazine* (Fall): 12–15.

HUTCHISON, T. W. and YELLEN, D. (1991) *Federal sentencing law and practice—1991 supplement*. St. Paul, MN: West Publishing Co.

HUTTER, B. M. and LLOYD-BOSTOCK, S. (1990) "The power of accidents: The social and psychological impact of accidents and the enforcement of safety regulations." *British Journal of Criminology* 30: 409–422.

IANNI, F. A. and REUSS-IANNI, E. (1972) *A family business*. New York: New American Library.

ICAHN, C. (1986) "Confessions of a raider." *Newsweek* (October 20): 51–55.

INCIARDI, J. A. (1975) *Careers in crime*. Chicago: Rand McNally.

INCIARDI, J. A. (1980a) *Radical criminology: The coming crises*. Beverly Hills, CA: Sage.

INCIARDI, J. A. (1980b) "Youths, drugs and street crime." Pp. 175–204 in F. Scarpitti and S. Datesman (Eds.) *Drugs and youth culture*. Beverly Hills, CA: Sage.

INSTITUTE FOR CIVIL JUSTICE. (1992) *Annual report*. Santa Monica, CA: Rand.

*INTERNATIONAL SOCIAL SCIENCE JOURNAL*. (1992) "The Americas: 1492–1992." *International Social Science Journal* 134: 457–606.

IRACOLA, R. (1995) "Criminal liability of a parent company for the conduct of its subsidiary: The spillover of the Exxon Valdez." *Criminal Law Bulletin* 31: 3–18.

ISAACSON, W. (1983) "The winds of reform." *Time* (March 7): 12–30.

ISEMAN, F. (1986) "Let corporate takeovers keep rolling." *New York Times* (December 1): A21.

JACHCEL, E. (1981) *Towards a criminological analysis of the origins of capital*. Ph.D. Dissertation, University of Sheffield.

JACK, R. and JACK, D. C. (1992) *Moral vision and professional decisions: The changing moral values of women and men lawyers*. New York: Cambridge University Press.

JACKALL, R. (1988) *Moral mazes: The world of corporate managers*. New York: Oxford University Press.

JACKSON, B. (1988) *Honest graft*. New York: Knopf.

JACKSON, D. D. (1974) *Judges*. New York: Atheneum.

JACKSON, J. H. (1983) "International law." Pp. 247–251 in *The guide to American law*. Volume 6. St. Paul, MN: West Publishing Co.

JACKSON, P. G. (1990) "Sources of Data" Pp. 21–56 in L. Kempf (Ed.) *Measurement issues in criminology*. New York: Springer-Verlag.

JACOBS, J. and DOPKEEN, L. (1990) "Risking the qualitative study of risk." *Qualitative Sociology* 13: 169–182.

JACOBY, T. (1988) "Going after dissidents." *Newsweek* (February 8): 29.

JAMIESON, K. M. (1994) *The organization of corporate crime*. Thousand Oaks, CA: Sage.

JASCHIK, S. (1990) "As probe of tuition ends its first year, colleges are confused, cautious." *Chronicle of Higher Education* (August 15): A1 + .

JEFFERY, C. R. (1990) *Criminology—An interdisciplinary approach*. Englewood Cliffs, NJ: Prentice-Hall .

JEFFREYS-JONES, R. (1989) *The CIA and American democracy*. New Haven CT: Yale University Press.

JENKINS, A. and BRAITHWAITE, J. (1993) "Profits, pressure, and corporate law-breaking." *Crime, Law & Social Change* 20: 221–232.

JENKINS, P. (1988) "Whose terrorists? Libya and state criminality." *Contemporary Crises* 12: 5–24.

JENKINS, P. (1993) "The C.T.A. case: A study in political corruption." *Crime, Law and Social Change* 20: 329–351.

JENNINGS, B., CALLAHAN, D., and WOLF, S. M. (1987) "The professions: Public interest and common goals." *Hastings Center Report* (February): 3–10.

JENNINGS, M., RECKERS, P. M. J., and KNEER, D. (1991) "The auditor's dilemma: The incongruous judicial notions of the auditing profession and actual auditor practice." *American Business Law Journal* 29: 89–122.

JENSEN, G. and BROWNFIELD, D. (1986) "Gender, lifestyles and victimization: Beyond routine activities." *Violence and Victims* 1: 85–99.

JESILOW, P. (1982a) "Adam Smith and white-collar crime." *Criminology* 20: 319–328.

JESILOW, P. (1982b) *Deterring automobile repair fraud: A field experiment*. Unpublished Ph.D. dissertation, University of California, Irvine.

JESILOW, P., KLEMPNER, E., and CHIAO, V. (1992) "Reporting consumer and major fraud: A survey of complainants." Pp. 149–168 in K. Schlegel and D. Weisburd (Eds.) *White collar crime reconsidered*. Boston: Northeastern University Press.

JESILOW, P., PONTELL, H. N., and GEIS, G. (1985) "Medical criminals: Physicians and white collar crime." *Justice Quarterly* 2: 149–166.

JESILOW, P., PONTELL, H. N., and GEIS, G. (1987) "Physician immunity from prosecution and punishment for medical program fraud." Pp. 7–22 in W. B. Groves and G. R. Newman (Eds.) *Punishment and privilege*. New York: Harrow & Heston.

JESILOW, P., PONTELL, H. N., and GEIS, G. (1992) *Prescription for profit—How doctors defraud Medicaid*. Berkeley: University of California Press.

JOHNSON, D. (1994) "A farmer, 70, saw no choice; nor did the sentencing judge." *New York Times* (July 20): A1.

JOHNSON, D. R. (1981) *American law enforcement: A history*. St. Louis: Forum Press.

JOHNSON, H. (1991) *Sleepwalking through history: America in the Reagan years*. New York: Norton.

JOHNSON, L. K. (1985) *A season of inquiry: The Senate intelligence investigation*. Lexington: University Press of Kentucky.

JOHNSON, M. (1986) *Takeover—The new Wall Street warriors*. New York: Belvedere Books/Arbor House.

JOHNSTON, D. (1989) "Hastings ousted as Senate vote convicts judge." *New York Times* (October 21): A1.

JOHNSTON, D. (1990) "100 possible cases of savings fraud given U.S. priority." *New York Times* (July 7): A1.

JOHNSTON, D. (1991) "Judge in Iran-Contra trial drops case against North after prosecutor gives up." *New York Times* (September 17): A1.

JOHNSTON, D. (1994) "Reagan had role in arms scandal, prosecutor says." *New York Times* (January 19): A1.

JOHNSTON, D. (1995) "Concluding that Cisneros lied, Reno urges a special prosecutor." *New York Times* (March 15): A1.

JONES, K. (1993) "Wal-Mart's pricing on drugstore items is held to be illegal." *New York Times* (October 13): A1.

JOSEPHSON, M. (1934) *The robber barons—The great American capitalists.* New York: Harcourt, Brace & World.

JOYNSON, R. B. (1994) "Fallible judgments." *Society* (March/April): 45–52.

JUDSON, G. (1992) "Real estate empire was built on illusion." *New York Times* (March 9): A1.

KAGAN, R. A. (1989) "Editor's introduction: Understanding regulatory enforcement." *Law & Policy* 11: 89–119.

KAGAN, R. A. and SCHOLZ, J. T. (1983) "The criminology of the corporation and regulatory enforcement strategies." In K. Hawkins and J. Thomas (Eds.) *Enforcing regulation.* Boston: Kluwer–Nijhoff Publishers.

KAHN, E. J., JR. (1973) *Fraud—The United States Postal Inspection Service and some of the fools and knaves it has known.* New York: Harper & Row.

KAHN, P. W. (1987) "From Nuremberg to the Hague: The United States position in *Nicaragua v. United States* and the development of international law." *Yale Journal of International Law* 12: 1–62.

KALETTE, D. (1990) "Dangerous lessons." *USA Today* (November 29): 1A +.

KANE, E. J. (1989) *The S & L insurance mess: How did it happen?* Washington, DC: The Urban Institute Press.

KARMEN, A. (1990) *Crime victims—An introduction to victimology.* 2nd ed. Pacific Grove, CA: Brooks/Cole.

KASINOF, J. (1991) "The chutzpah defense." *New York* (November 11): 38–44.

KATZ, J. (1979) "Concerted ignorance: The social construction of cover-up." *Urban Life* 8: 295–316.

KATZ, J. (1980a) "Concerted ignorance: The social psychology of cover-up." Pp. 149–170 in R. K. Elliott and J. J. Willingham (Eds.) *Management fraud: Detection and deterrence.* New York: Petercelli.

KATZ, J. (1980b) "The social movement against white-collar crime." Pp. 161–184 in E. Bittner and S. Messinger (Eds.) *Criminology review yearbook.* Volume 2. Beverly Hills, CA: Sage.

KATZ, J. (1988) *Seductions of crime: Moral and sensual attractions of doing evil.* New York: Basic Books.

KATZ, J. and CHAMBLISS, W. J. (1991) "Biology and crime." Pp. 244–271 in J. Sheley (Ed.) *Criminology: A contemporary handbook.* Belmont, CA: Wadsworth.

KAUPER, T. E. (1990) "The justice department and the antitrust laws: Law enforcer or regulator?" *The Antitrust Bulletin* 35: 83–122.

KAUZLARICH, D. (1992) "Epistemological barriers to the study of harms: A sociology of criminology." A Paper Presented at the Annual Meeting of the American Society of Criminology, New Orleans, November.

KAUZLARICH, D. and KRAMER, R. C. (1993) "State-corporate crime in the U.S. nuclear weapons production complex." *Journal of Human Justice* 5: 4–25.

KAUZLARICH, D., KRAMER, R. C., and SMITH, B. (1992) "Towards the study of governmental crime: Nuclear weapons, foreign intervention, and international law." *Humanity & Society* 16: 543–563.

KEAN, P. (1994) "Temps perdus." *Lingua Franca* (April): 49–53.

KEANE, C. (1993) "The impact of financial performance on frequency of corporate crime: A latent variable test of strain theory." *Canadian Journal of Criminology* (July): 293–308.

KELLY, R. J. (1986) *Organized crime—A global perspective.* Totowa, NJ: Rowman & Littlefield.

KEMPE, F. (1990) *Divorcing the dictator—America's bungled affair with Noriega.* New York: Putnam.

KEMPF, K. L., ARSHADI, N., and EYSSELL, J. H. (1992) "Its insider trading but the offenders are really outsiders." *Journal of Crime & Justice* 15: 111–137.

KERR, P. (1991a) "Hard times prove fecund for swindlers." *New York Times* (June 7): B1.

KERR, P. (1991b) "Mental hospital chains accused of much cheating on insurance." *New York Times* (November 24): A1.

KERR, P. (1991c) "Vast amount of fraud discovered in worker's compensation system." *New York Times* (December 29): A1.

KERR, P. (1992a) "Blatant fraud pushing up the cost of car insurance." *New York Times* (February 6): A1.

KERR, P. (1992b) "Centers for head injury accused of earning millions for neglect." *New York Times* (March 16): A1.

KERR, P. (1992c) "Insurers faulted on policy switch." *New York Times* (April 22): A1.

KERR, P. (1993) "'Ghost riders' are target of an insurance sting." *New York Times* (August 18): A1.

KERRY, J. (1990) "Where is the S & L money?" *New York Times* (June 1): A29.

KERWIN, C. (1990) "Introduction." *Federal Regulatory Directory.* 6th ed. Washington, DC: Congressional Quarterly.

KILBORN, P. T. (1986a) "Big Trader to pay U.S. $100 million for insider abuses." *New York Times* (November 15): A1.

KILBORN, P. T. (1986b) "Inquiry on abuses on inside trading expected to grow." *New York Times* (November 17): A1 + .

KING, H. and CHAMBLISS, W. J. (1984) *Harry King—A professional thief's journey.* New York: Wiley.

KLEIN, J. (1990) "It's a wonderful life." *New York* (April 23): 19–20.

KLEINFELD, N. R. (1978) "The myriad faces of fraud on the phone " *New York Times* (March 27): D1.

KLEINFELD, N. R. (1990) "Looking into accounting's heart of darkness." *New York Times* (April 15): 12E.

KLEINFELD, N. R. (1992) "Telling on clients." *New York Times* (March 5): 13d.

KLEPPER, S. and NAGIN, D. (1989) "Tax compliance and perception of risk of detection and criminal prosecution." *Law & Society Review* 23: 209–240.

KLOCKARS, C. (1974) *The professional fence.* New York: Free Press.

KLOCKARS, C. (1977) "White collar crime." Pp. 220–258 in E. Sagarin and F. Montanino (Eds.) *Deviants: Voluntary actors in a hostile world.* Morristown, NJ: General Learning Press.

KLOCKARS, C. (1980) "The Dirty Harry problem." *Annals* 452: 33–47.

KLONOSKI, R. J. (1986) "The moral responsibilities of stockholders." *Journal of Business Ethics* 5: 385–390.

KLOPFENSTEIN, B. (1989) "The diffusion of the VCR in the United States." Pp. 21–40 in M. R. Levy (Ed.) *The VCR age.* Newbury Park, CA: Sage.

KNAPP COMMISSION (1973) *Report on police corruption.* New York: George Braziller.

KNIGHT–RIDDER NEWSPAPERS. (1990a) "Insurance fraud probed." *Scranton Tribune* (June 11): 1.

KNIGHT–RIDDER NEWSPAPERS. (1990b) "Doctors costing patients billions." *Scranton Times* (June 21): 1.

KNIGHTLY, P., EVANS, H., POTTER, E., and WALLACE, M. (1979) *Suffer the children: The story of Thalidomide.* New York: Viking Press.

KOEPP, S. (1986) "Money was the only way." *Time* (December 1): 50–51.

KOEPP, S. (1988a) "Fraud, fraud, fraud." *Time* (August 15): 28–29.

KOEPP, S. (1988b) "Tobacco's first loss." *Time* (June 27): 48–50.

KOHN, G. (1989) *Encyclopedia of American scandal.* New York: Facts on File.

KOLKO, G. (1962) *Wealth and power in America.* New York: Praeger.

KOLKO, G. (1963) *The triumph of conservatism.* New York: Free Press.

KORNBLUTH, J. (1992) *Highly confident: The crime and punishment of Michael Milken.* New York: Morrow.

KRAMER, L. (1989) Reports from the Holocaust. New York: St. Martin's Press.

KRAMER, R. C. (1982) "Corporate crime: An organizational perspective." Pp. 75–94 in P. Wickman and T. Dailey (Eds.) *White-collar and economic crime.* Toronto: Lexington Books.

KRAMER, R. C. (1984) "Corporate criminality: The development of an idea." Pp. 13–38 in E. Hochstedler (Ed.) *Corporations as criminals.* Beverly Hills, CA: Sage.

KRAMER, R. C. (1985) "Pinto prosecutor interviews." *ACJS White Paper.* Omaha, NE: Academy of Criminal Justice Sciences.

KRAMER, R. C. (1989) "Criminologists and the social movement against corporate crime." *Social Justice* 16:146-164.

KRAMER, R. C. (1992) "The space shuttle Challenger explosion: A case study of state-corporate crime." Pp. 214-243 in K. Schlegel and D. Weisburd (Eds.) *White collar crime reconsidered.* Boston: Northeastern University Press.

KRAMER, R. C. and MICHALOWSKI, R. J. (1990) "State-corporate crime." A Paper Presented at the Annual Meeting of the American Society of Criminology (Baltimore), November 7-12.

KRAUSS, C. (1994) "12 police officers charged in drug corruption sweep: Bratton sees more arrests." *New York Times* (April 16): A1.

KRIMERMAN, L. I. and PERRY, L. (Eds.) (1966) *Patterns of anarchy.* New York: Anchor Press.

KRUTTSCHNITT, C. (1985) "Are businesses treated differently? A comparison of the individual victim and the corporate victim in the criminal courtroom." *Sociological Inquiry* 55: 225-238.

KUHN, T. (1970) *The structure of scientific revolutions.* 2nd ed. Chicago: University of Chicago Press.

KUNEN, J. S. (1994) *Reckless disregard—Corporate greed, government indifference, and the Kentucky school bus crash.* New York: Simon & Schuster.

KUNKEL, K. R. (1989) *A structural approach to illegal corporate activity: The auto-producers, mail-order houses, meat-packers, and movie-makers from 1890-1950.* University of Missouri–Columbia. Ph.D. dissertation.

KUZMA, S. M. (1988) "Criminal liability for misconduct in scientific research." *University of Michigan Journal of Law Reform* 25: 357-421.

KWITNY, J. (1979) *Vicious circles—The Mafia in the marketplace.* New York: Norton.

LABATON, S. (1988) "Drexel concedes guilt on trading; to pay $650 million." *New York Times* (December 22): A1.

LABATON, S. (1989a) "Does an assault on nature make Exxon a criminal?" *New York Times* (April 23): 4/1.

LABATON, S. (1989b) "Five years after settlement, Agent Orange war lives on." *New York Times* (May 8): 1d.

LABATON, S. (1989c) "Uncertain future for RICO cases." *New York Times* (November 13): D2.

LABATON, S. (1989d) "Product liability's quiet revolution." *New York Times* (November 27): D2.

LABATON, S. (1990a) "Defiance didn't help defendants, it seems." *New York Times* (April 25): D8.

LABATON, S. (1990b) "Fraud uncovered in property sales in savings rescue." *New York Times* (June 21): A1.

LABATON, S. (1990c) "The bitter fight over the Manville Trust." *New York Times* (July 8): 3/1.

LABATON, S. (1990d) "Corporate crime and punishment." *New York Times* (October 1): D2.

LABATON, S. (1991) "Congress moves on price-fixing." *New York Times* (May 16): D2.

LABATON, S. (1992a) "U.S. moves to freeze assets at law firm for S & L role." *New York Times* (March 3): A1.

LABATON, S. (1992b) "Telling on clients." *New York Times* (March 5): D13.

LABATON, S. (1992c) "400 million bargain for Ernst." *New York Times* (November 25): D1.

LABATON, S. (1993) "Ex-official convicted in HUD scandal." *New York Times* (October 27): A8.

LABATON, S. (1994a) "Plea is accepted in B.C.C.I. scandal." *New York Times* (July 9): A1.

LABATON, S. (1994b) "A Clinton friend admits mail fraud and tax evasion." *New York Times* (December 7): A1.

LABATON, S. (1995) "GOP preparing bill to overhaul negligence law." *New York Times* (February 19): A1.

LABEFF, E., CLARK, R. E., HAINES, V., and DIEKHOFF, G. M. (1990) "Situational ethics and college student cheating." *Sociological Inquiry* 60: 190-198.

LAFOLLETTE, M. C. (1992) *Stealing into print: Fraud, plagiarism, and misconduct in scientific publishing.* Berkeley: University of California Press.

LAMB, D. (1987) *The Africans.* New York: Vintage.

LANDA, R. (1991) "The poor pay more." *New York Daily News* (April 15): C5.

LANE, R. A. (1953) "Why businessmen violate the law." *Journal of Criminal Law, Criminology and Police Science* 44: 151–165.

LANGWORTHY, R. and LATESSA, E. (1989) "Criminal justice education: A national assessment." *The Justice Professional* 4:172–187.

LANZA–KADUCE, L. (1980) "Deviance among professionals: The case of unnecessary surgery." *Deviant Behavior* 1: 333–359.

LASH, J., GILLMAN, K., and SHERIDAN, D. (1984) *A season of spoils: The Reagan administration's attack on the environment.* New York: Pantheon Books.

LASLEY, J. R. (1988) "Toward a control theory of white-collar offending." *Journal of Quantitative Criminology* 4: 347–362.

LAUB, J. H. (1983) *Criminology in the making: An oral history.* Boston: Northeastern University Press.

LAUGHLIN, P. F. (1989) "Ethics in Government Act." *American Criminal Law Review* 26: 789–805.

LAWLESS, J. (1988) "The white-collar defendant." *Trial* 24: 42–47.

LAWRENCE, S. (1975) "He sold fear to new mothers." *New York Post* (June 26): 4.

LEAPE, L. L. (1989) "Unnecessary operations." *Health Services Research* 24: 351–408.

LEARY, W. E. (1993) "Companies accused of overcharging for drugs developed with U.S. aid." *New York Times* (January 26): C6.

LEDERMAN, E. (1985) "Criminal law, perpetrator and corporation: Rethinking a complex triangle." *Journal of Criminal Law and Criminology* 76: 285–341.

LEMERT, E. (1951) *Social pathology.* New York: McGraw-Hill.

LEONARD, W. and WEBER, M. G. (1970) "Automakers and dealers: A study of criminogenic market forces." *Law & Society Review* 4: 407–424.

LESLIE, C. (1989) "An ivy league cartel." *Newsweek* (August 27): 65.

LEVI, M. (1987) *Regulating fraud—White-collar crime and the criminal process.* London: Tavistock.

LEVI, M. (1991) "Public, business, and victim perceptions of white-collar crime and criminal justice." A Paper Presented at the International Law & Society Conference, Amsterdam, June.

LEVI, M. (1992) "White-collar crime victimization." Pp. 169–194 in K. Schlegel and D. Weisburd (Ed.) *White collar crime reconsidered.* Boston: Northeastern University Press.

LEVIN, M. (1989) "Ethics courses: Useless." *New York Times* (November 25): A23.

LEVIN, N. (1973) *The Holocaust—The destruction of European Jewry, 1933–1945.* New York: Schocken.

LEVINE, A. (1980) *The enterprise of Jewish law: Aspects of Jewish business ethics.* New York: Yeshiva University Press.

LEVINE, D. (1991a) "The insider." *New York* (September 16): 38–49.

LEVINE, D. H. (1991b) *Inside out—An insider's account of Wall Street.* New York: Putnam.

LEVINE, R. (1988) "Hertz concedes it overcharged for car repairs." *New York Times* (January 26): A1.

LEVY, B. (1968) "Cops in the ghetto: A problem in the police system." Pp. 347–358 in L. H. Masotti and D. R. Bowen (Eds.) *Riots and rebellion: Civil violence in the urban community.* Beverly Hills, CA: Sage.

LEVY, C. J. (1993) "Store founder pleads guilty in fraud case." *New York Times* (July 23): B1.

LEWIS, A. (1995) "Reform or wreck?" *New York Times* (January 27): Op ed.

LEWIS, H. W. (1990) *Technological risk.* New York: Norton.

LEWIS, M. (1989) *Liar's poker.* New York: Penguin Books.

LEWIS, N. A. (1992) "A lawyer beloved of the famous and troubled." *New York Times* (October 16): B18.

LEWIS, N. A. (1994) "U.S. drug industry is battling image for price gouging." *New York Times* (March 7): A1.

LEWIS, N. A. (1995a) "House approves a major change in legal system." *New York Times* (March 8): A1.

LEWIS, N. A. (1995b) "House passes bill that would limit suits of investors." *New York Times* (March 9): A1.

LEWIS, N. A. (1995c) "House debates bill to limit damages on civil suits." *New York Times* (March 10): A1.

LEWIS, P. H. (1994) "Student accused of running network for pirated software." *New York Times* (April 9): A1.

LIAZOS, A. (1972) "The poverty of the sociology of deviance: Nuts, sluts, and preverts." *Social Problems* 20: 103–120.

LICHTER, S. R., LICHTER, L. S., and ROTHMAN, S. (1991) *Watching America*. New York: Prentice-Hall.

LIEBERMAN, J. K. (1972) *How the government breaks the law*. New York: Penguin Books.

LIEBERMAN, J. K. (1983) *The litigious society*. New York: Basic Books.

LILLY, J. R. and BALL, R. A. (1982) "A critical analysis of the changing concept of criminal responsibility." *Criminology* 20: 169–184.

LILLY, J. R., CULLEN, F. T., and BALL, R. A. (1989) *Criminological theory: Context and consequences*. Newbury Park, CA: Sage.

LINDSEY, R. B. (1986) "Businesses change ways in fear of lawsuits." *New York Times* (November 18): 1A.

LINDSEY, R. B. (1979) "Swindlers in Arizona said to make millions." *New York Times* (May 21): A1.

LING, E, (1991) *Fraud and social change: Whistle-blowing and white-collar crime in a major corporation*. Ph.D. dissertation, The Ohio State University.

LISKA, A. (1992) "Social control." Pp. 1819–1823 in E. Borgatta (Ed.) *Encyclopedia of Sociology*. Volume 4. New York: Macmillan.

LOEB, V. (1991) "Philippines locked in corruption grip." *Philadelphia Inquirer* (July 29): A1.

LOFQUIST, W. S. (1993a) "Organizational probation and the U.S. Sentencing Commission." *Annals of the American Academy of Political & Social Science* 525: 157–169.

LOFQUIST, W. S. (1993b) "Legislating organizational probation: State capacity, business power, and corporate crime control." *Law & Society Review* 27: 741–784.

LOGAN, G. J. (1988) "Profile: Better business bureau." *Consumer's Research*. September: 29–31.

LOGUE, J. (1988) "Conclusion." Pp. 254–265 in A. Markovits and M. Silverstein, (Eds.) *The politics of scandal: Power and process in liberal democracies*. New York: Holmes & Meier.

LOGUE, J. (1994) "When they close the factory gates: How Big Steel scrapped a community." Pp. 50–57 in J. H. Skolnick and E. Currie (Eds.) *Crisis in American institutions*. 9th ed. New York: HarperCollins.

LOHR, S. (1991) "At the end of a twisted trail, piggy bank for a favored few." *New York Times* (August 12): A1.

LOHR, S. (1992a) "A new breed of Sam Spade trails crooks' hidden assets." *New York Times* (February 20): A1.

LOHR, S. (1992b) "Indictment charges Clifford took bribes." *New York Times* (July 30): A1.

LONG, S. B. (1981) "Social control in the civil law: The case of income tax enforcement." Pp. 181–214 in H. Laurence Ross (Ed.) *Law and deviance*. Beverly Hills, CA: Sage.

LONG, S. B. and SWINGEN, J. A (1991) "Taxpayer compliance: Setting new agendas for research." *Law & Society Review* 25: 637–689.

LONGMIRE, D. R. (1982) "The new criminologist's access to research support: Open arenas or closed doors?" Pp. 19–34 in H. E. Pepinsky (Ed.) *Rethinking criminology*. Beverly Hills, CA: Sage.

LOUNSBERRY, E. (1991) "Federal prison at Allenwood becomes known as Club Fed." *The Sunday Times* (Scranton), (September 15): 16.

LOWMAN, J. and MACLEAN, B. (1992) *Realist criminology: Crime control and policing in the 1990s*. Toronto: University of Toronto Press.

LUBAN, D. (1987) "The legacies of Nuremberg." *Social Research* 54: 779–830.

LUBASCH, A. H. (1989) "Ex-official is charged in theft of $1 million from New York City." *New York Times* (June 9): A9.

LUCHANSKY, B. and GERBER, J. (1993) "Constructing state autonomy: The Federal Trade Commission and the Celler-Kefauver Act." *Sociological Perspectives* 36: 217–240.

LUECK, T. J. (1993) "20 New York schools to lose U.S. grants." *New York Times* (October 21): B3.

LUHMANN, N. (1979) *Trust and power.* Chicester: Wiley.

LUNDBERG, F. (1968) *The rich and the super-rich: A study in the power of money today.* New York: Lyle Stuart.

LUNEBURG, W. V. (1990) "State and federal administrative law." *Administrative Law Review* 42: 113–120.

LUPSHA, P. A. (1986) "Organized crime in the United States." Pp. 32–57 in R. J. Kelly (Ed.) *Organized crime—A global perspective.* Totowa, NJ: Rowman & Littlefield.

LYNCH, G. (1990) "How useful is civil RICO in the enforcement of criminal law?" *Villanova Law Review* 35: 929–948.

LYNCH, G. and MISSAL, M. J. (1987) "Recent civil and criminal prosecutions of insider trading violations." Pp. 20–64 in H. L. Pitt (Ed.) *Insider trading—Counselling and compliance.* Clifton, NJ: Prentice-Hall Law & Business.

LYNCH, M. J. and GROVES, W. B. (1989) *A primer in radical criminology.* 2nd ed. New York: Harrow & Heston.

LYNCH, M. J., NALLA, M. K., and MILLER, K. W. (1989) "Cross-cultural perceptions of deviance: The case of Bhopal." *Journal of Research on Crime and Delinquency* 26: 7–35.

LYNE, B. (1993) "Giving the bad guys a shot at redemption." *New York Times* (March 28): F29.

LYNXWILER, J., SHOVER, N., and CLELLAND, D. J. (1983) "The organization and impact of inspector discretion in a regulatory bureaucracy." *Social Problems* 30: 435–436.

LYONS, R. D. (1982) "Time-sharing resorts under inquiry." *New York Times* (May 30): 37.

MAAS, P. (1973) *Serpico.* New York: Bantam Books.

MACEY, J. (1991) "Agency theory and the criminal liability of organizations." *Boston University Law Review* 71: 315–340.

MACHAN, T. R. and M. B. JOHNSON (Eds.)(1983) *Rights and regulation: Ethical, political and economic issues.* Cambridge, MA: Ballinger.

MACNAMARA, D. E. J. (1991) "The victimization of whistle-blowers in the public and private sectors." Pp. 121–133 in R. J. Kelly and D. E. J. MacNamara (Eds.) *Perspectives on deviance: Domination, degradation and denigration.* Cincinnati: Anderson.

MADSEN, A. (1984) *60 Minutes.* New York: Dodd, Mead.

MADSEN, P. and SHAFRITZ, J. M. (Eds.) (1990) *Essentials of business ethics.* New York: Penguin Books.

MAGLEBY, D. and NELSON, C. J. (1990) *The money chase—Congressional campaign/finance reform.* Washington, DC: Brookings Institute.

MAGNUSON, E. (1988a) "It's lovely at the top." *Time* (April 11): 25–26.

MAGNUSON, E. (1988b) "The Pentagon up for sale." *Time* (June 27): 16–18.

MAGNUSON, R. J. (1992) *The white-collar crime explosion: How to protect yourself and your company from prosecution.* New York: MacGraw-Hill.

MAGNUSON, W. G. and CARPER, J. (1978) "Caveat emptor." Pp. 23–43 in J. M. Johnson and J. D. Douglas (Eds.) *Crime at the top: Deviance in business and the professions.* Philadelphia: J. B. Lippincott.

MAHONEY, P. G. (1990) "Securities regulation by enforcement: An international perspective." *Yale Journal on Regulation* 7: 305–320.

MAITAL, S. (1982) "The tax evasion virus." *Psychology Today* (March): 74–78.

MAKIN, J. (1986) "Business ethics." *Public Opinion* (November/ December): 4–6; 57.

MAKINSON, L. (1990) *Open secrets—The dollar power of PACS in Congress.* Washington, DC: Congressional Quarterly.

MAKKAI, T. and BRAITHWAITE, J. (1993) "Praise, pride and corporate compliance." *International Journal of the Sociology of Law* 21: 73–91.

MAKKAI, T. and BRAITHWAITE, J. (1994) "Reintegrative shaming and compliance with regulatory standards." *Criminology* 32: 361–386.

MALABRE, A. L., Jr. (1987) *Beyond our means.* New York: Vintage.

MALEC, K. and GARDINER, J. (1987) "Measurement issues in the study of official corruption: A Chicago example." *Corruption and Reform* 2: 267–278.

MALLON, T. (1989) *Stolen words—Forays into the origins and ravages of plagiarism.* New York: Ticknor & Fields.

MANDEL, E. (1983) "Joint-stock company." Pp. 241–244 in T. Bottomore (Ed.) *A dictionary of Marxist thought.* Cambridge, MA: Harvard University Press.

MANDELBAUM, M. (1987) *Purpose and necessity in social theory.* Baltimore: The Johns Hopkins University Press.

MANES, S. and ANDREWS, P. (1994) *Gates.* New York: Touchstone Books.

MANKOFF, M. (1971) "Societal reaction and career deviance: A critical analysis." *Sociological Quarterly* 12: 204–218.

MANN, K. (1985) *Defending white collar crime.* New Haven, CT: Yale University Press.

MANN, K. (1987) "Procedure rules and information control: Gaining leverage over white collar crime." Pp. 332–351 in K. Schlegel and D. Weisburd (Eds.) *White collar crime reconsidered.* Boston: Northeastern University Press.

MANN, K. (1992a) "White collar crime and the poverty of the criminal law." *Law & Social Inquiry* 17: 561–572.

MANN, K. (1992b) "Punitive civil sanctions: The middle ground between criminal and civil law." *Yale Law Review* 101: 1795–1874.

MANNHEIM, H. (1965) *Comparative criminology.* London: Routledge & Kegan Paul.

MANNINO, E. F. (1990) "Less corn and more hell: The application of RICO to financial institutions." *Villanova Law Review* 35: 883–904.

MANSNERUS, L. (1988) "Smoking becomes 'deviant behavior.'" *New York Times* (April 24): E/1+.

MANSNERUS, L. (1989) "As racketeering law expands, so does pressure to rein it in." *New York Times* (March 12): E4.

MANSON, D. A. (1986) "Tracking offenders: White-collar crime." *Special reports.* Washington, DC: Bureau of Justice Statistics.

MARELLA, V. J. (1992) "The Department of Justice prosecutive guidelines in environmental cases involving voluntary disclosure—A leap forward or a leap of faith?" *American Criminal Law Review* 29: 1179–1196.

MARGOLICK, D. (1991) "Missing lawyer: Robin Hood or $25 million thief?" *New York Times* (January 22): B1.

MARGOLICK, D. (1992) "Till debt do us part." *New York Times Magazine* (December 16): 46+.

MARKHAM, J. W. (1991) "Manipulation of commodity futures prices—The unprosecutable crime." *Yale Journal on Regulation* 8: 281–378.

MARKOFF, J. (1992) "Though illegal, copied software is now common." *New York Times* (July 27): A1.

MARKOVIC, M. (1983) "Human nature." Pp. 214–217 in T. Bottomore (Ed.) *A dictionary of Marxist thought.* Cambridge, MA: Harvard University Press.

MARKOVITS, A. and SILVERSTEIN, M. (Eds.)(1988) *The politics of scandal: Power and process in liberal democracies.* New York: Holmes & Meier.

MARKS, F. R. and CATHCART, D. (1986) "Discipline within the legal profession." Pp. 62–102 in M. Davis and F. A. Elliston (Eds.) *Ethics and the legal profession.* Buffalo, NY: Prometheus Books.

MARKS, P. (1995) "Dealer's plea in G. M. fraud may be bargain of his life." *New York Times* (January 20): A10.

MARKUSEN, E. (1992) "Genocide and modern war." Pp. 117–148 in M. Dobkowski and I. Wallimann (Eds.) *Genocide in our time.* Ann Arbor, MI: Pierian Press.

MARS, G. (1982) *Cheats at work—An anthology of workplace crime.* London: Unwin.

MARSH, H. C. (1991) "A comparative analysis of crime coverage in newspapers in the United States and other countries from 1960–1989: A review of the literature." *Journal of Criminal Justice* 19: 67–79.

MARSHALL, J. (1976) *The power to probe.* New York: Random House.

MARTIN, B. (1995) "Eliminating state crime by abolishing the state." Pp. 389–417 in J. I. Ross (Ed.) *Controlling state crime.* New York: Garland Publishing Co.

MARTINSON, R. (1974) "What works? Questions and answers about prison reform." *The Public Interest* 35: 22–54.

MARTZ, L. (1986) "Deaver's deals." *Newsweek* (May 5): 18–20.

MARTZ, L. (1987) "New doubts about Meese and the Contra inquiry." *Newsweek* (April 20): 29–30.

MARTZ, L. (1990a) "Bonfire of the S & Ls." *Newsweek* (May 21): 20–25.

MARTZ, L. (1990b) "S & Ls: Blaming the media." *Newsweek* (June 25): 42.

MARX, G. (1987) "The interweaving of public and private police in undercover work." Pp. 172–193 in C. D. Shearing and P. C. Stenning (Eds.) *Private policing.* Newbury Park, CA: Sage.

MARX, G. (1988) *Undercover—Police surveillance in America.* Berkeley: University of California Press.

MARX, G. (1991) "When the guards guard themselves: Undercover tactics turned inward." *Policing and Society* 1: 1–22.

MARX, K. (1867) *Capital.* Volume 1. Hamburg: Otto Meissner.

MASON, L. and MASON, R. (1992) "A moral appeal for taxpayer compliance: The case of a mass media campaign." *Law & Policy* 14: 381–399.

MAYER, M. (1984) *The money bazaar—Understanding the banking revolution around us.* New York: Dutton.

MAYER, M. (1990) *The greatest-ever bank robbery.* New York: Scribner.

MAYER, M. (1994) *Stealing the market—How the giant brokerage firms, with help from the SEC, stole the stock market from investors.* New York: Basic Books.

MCBARNET, D. (1992) "Legitimate rackets: Tax evasion, tax avoidance, and the boundaries of legality." *The Journal of Human Justice* 3: 56–74.

MCCABE, D. L. (1992) "The influence of situational ethics on cheating among college students." *Sociological Inquiry* 62: 365–374.

MCCAGHY, C. H. and CERNKOVICH, S. A. (1987) *Crime in American society.* 2nd ed. New York: Macmillan.

MCCARROLL, T. (1992) "Who's counting?" *Time* (April 13): 48–50.

MCCARTHY, J., LADIMER, I., and SIREFMAN, J. P. (1989) *Managing faculty disputes.* San Francisco: Jossey-Bass.

MCCLEARY, R., O'NEIL, M. J., EPPERLEIN, T., JONES, C., and GRAY, R. H. (1981) "The effect of legal education and work experience on perceptions of crime seriousness." *Social Problems* 28: 276–289.

MCCLINTICK, D. (1982) *Indecent exposure.* New York: Dell.

MCCORMICK, A. E. (1977) "Rule enforcement and moral indignation: Some obervations on the effects of criminal antitrust convictions upon societal reaction processes." *Social Problems* 25: 30–39.

MCDERMOTT, M. F. (1982) "Occupational disqualification of corporate executives: An innovative condition of probation." *Journal of Criminal Law and Criminology* 73: 604–641.

MCEWEN, T. (1990a) "The growing threat of computer crime." *Detective* (Summer): 6–11.

MCEWEN, T. (1990b) *Dedicated computer crime units.* Washington, DC: National Institute of Justice.

MCFADDEN, R. D. (1987) "Judge sent poisoned candy: Man he sentenced arrested." *New York Times* (February 21): A1.

MCFARLAND, A. S. (1984) *Common cause: Lobbying in the public interest.* Chatham, NJ: Chatham House.

MCGOVERN, F. E. (Ed.)(1990) "Claims resolution facilities and the mass settlement of mass torts." *Law and Contemporary Problems* 53 (Autumn): 1–205.

MCGRAW, K. M. and SCHOLZ, J. T. (1991) "Appeals to civic virtue versus attention to self-interest: Effects on tax compliance." *Law & Society Review* 25: 471–478.

MCGUIRE, M. V. and EDELHERTZ, H. (1980) "Consumer abuse of older Americans: Victimization and remedial action in two metropolitan areas." Pp. 266–292 in G. Geis and E. Stotland (Eds.) *White-collar crime: Theory and research.* Beverly Hills, CA: Sage.

MCMILLEN, T. (1992) *Out of bounds*. New York: Simon & Schuster.

MCMULLAN, J. L. (1982) "Criminal organization in sixteenth and seventeenth century London." *Social Problems* 29: 311-323.

MCSHANE, M. D. and WILLIAMS, F. P. III (1992) "Radical victimology: A critique of the concept of victim in traditional victimology." *Crime & Delinquency* 38: 258-271.

MEAD, G. H. (1934; 1964) *Mind, self and society: From the standpoint of a social behaviorist.* Chicago: University of Chicago Press.

MEDARD, J. F. (1986) "Public corruption in Africa: A comparative perspective." *Corruption and Reform* 1: 115-131.

MEEKER, J. W., DOMBRINK, J., and PONTELL, H. N. (1987) "White collar and organized crimes: Questions of seriousness and policy." *Justice Quarterly* 4: 73-98.

MEIDINGER, E. (1987) "Regulatory culture: A theoretical outline." *Law & Policy* 9: 349-386.

MEIER, B. (1990) "Study finds frequent cheating at the gas pump." *New York Times* (April 27): A13.

MEIER, B. (1992a) "Sharing of credit card numbers by merchants brings new fears of fraud." *New York Times* (March 28): 50.

MEIER, B. (1992b) "Bronco accidents pose new questions for Ford on safety." *New York Times* (June 15): A1.

MEIER, B. (1992c) "Crazy Eddie's insane odyssey." *New York Times* (July 19): 3/1.

MEIER, B. (1992d) "Bill to curb consumer lawsuits falls short." *New York Times* (September 13): E3.

MEIER, B. (1992e) "Data show G.M. knew for years of risk in pickup trucks' design." *New York Times* (November 17): A1.

MEIER, B. (1993) "Courtroom drama pits G.M. against a former engineer." *New York Times* (January 19): D1.

MEIER, R. F., (1986) Review essay: White collar crime books. *Criminology* 24: 415-420.

MEIER, R. F. and SHORT, J. F., JR. (1982) "The consequences of white-collar crime." Pp. 23-50 in H. Edelhertz and T. D. Overcast (Eds.) *White-collar crime: An agenda for research.* Lexington, MA: Lexington Books.

MEIER, R. F. and SHORT, J. F., JR., (1985) "Crime as hazard: Perceptions of risk and seriousness." *Criminology* 23: 389-399.

MENDELSOHN, R. S. (1979) *Confessions of a medical heretic.* New York: Warner Books.

MENDELSON, M. A. (1974) *Tender loving greed.* New York: Random House.

MENSCH, E. and FREEMAN, A. (1990) "Efficiency and image: Advertising as an antitrust issue." *Duke Law Journal* 20: 321-373.

MERTON, R. K. (1957) "Social theory and anomie." *American Sociological Review* 3: 672-682.

MERTON, R. K. (1968) *Social theory and social structure.* New York: Free Press.

MESSERSCHMIDT, J. (1993) *Masculinities and crime: Reconceptualization of theory.* Lanham, MD: Rowman & Littlefield.

METZGER, M., DALTON, D. R., and HILL, J. W. (1993) "The organization of ethics and the ethics of organizations: The case for expanded organizational ethics audits." *Business Ethics Quarterly* 3: 27-43.

METZGER, M. B., MALLOR, J. P., BARNES, T. B., and PHILLIPS, M. J. (1986) *Business law and the regulatory environment: Concepts and cases.* 6th ed. Homewood, IL: Irwin.

METZGER, M. B. and SCHWENK, C. R. (1990) "Decision-making models, devil's advocacy, and the control of corporate crime." *American Business Law Journal* 28: 323-377.

MEYER, M. (1995) "Stop! Cyberthief!" *Newsweek* (February 6): 36-38.

MICHAELS, J. W. and MIETHE, T. D. (1989) "Applying theories of deviance to academic cheating." *Social Science Quarterly* 70: 870-885.

MICHALOWSKI, R. J. (1985) *Order, law and crime.* New York: Random House.

MICHALOWSKI, R. J. and KRAMER, R. C. (1987) "The space between the laws: The problem of corporate crime in a transnational context." *Social Problems* 34: 34-53.

MICHALOWSKI, R. and PFUHL, E. H. (1991) "Technology, property and law: The case of computer crime." *Crime, Law and Social Change* 15: 255-275.

MIETHE, T. D. (1982) "Public consensus on crime seriousness." *Criminology* 20: 516-526.

MIETHE, T. D. (1984) "Types of consensus in public evaluations of crime: An illustration of strategies for measuring consensus." *Journal of Criminal Law and Criminology* 75: 459–473.

MIETHE, T. D. and ROTHSCHILD, J. (1994) "Whistleblowing and the control of organizational misconduct." *Sociological Inquiry* 64: 322–347.

MILGRAM, S. (1963) "Behavioral Study of Obedience." *Journal of Abnormal and Social Psychology* 67: 371–378.

MILLER, A. G. (1986) *The obedience experiments: A case study of controversy in social science.* Westport, CT: Praeger.

MILLER, G. (1981) *It's a living.* New York: St. Martin's Press.

MILLER, N. (1992) *Stealing from America: A history of corruption from Jamestown to Reagan.* New York: Paragon House.

MILLON, D. (1990) "Theories of the corporation." *Duke Law Journal* 20: 201–262.

MILLS, C. W. (1940) "Situated actions and vocabularies of motives." *American Sociological Review* 5: 904–913.

MILLS, C. W. (1943) "The professional ideology of social pathologists." *American Journal of Sociology* 49: 165–180.

MILLS, C. W. (1956) *The power elite.* New York: Oxford University Press.

MINDELL, E. (1987) *Unsafe at any meal.* New York: Warner Books.

MINTZ, B. (1985) *The power structure of American business.* Chicago: University of Chicago Press.

MINTZ, B. and SCHWARTZ, M. (1981) "The structure of intercorporate unity in American business." *Social Problems* 29: 87–103.

MINTZ, M. (1985) *At any cost: Corporate greed, women, and the Dalkon shield.* New York: Pantheon Books.

MINTZ, M. (1993) "The plight of the whistleblower." *Village Voice* (February 9): 31–38.

MINTZ, M. and COHEN, J. S. (1971) *America, Inc.* New York: Dell.

MINTZ, M. and COHEN, J. S. (1976) *Power, Inc.* New York: Viking Press.

MITFORD, J. (1963) *The American way of death.* New York: Simon & Schuster.

MIZRUCHI, M. S. (1982) *The American corporate network, 1904–1974.* Beverly Hills, CA: Sage.

MOFFAT, M. (1989) *Coming of age in New Jersey—College and American culture.* New Brunswick, NJ: Rutgers University Press.

MOHR, C. (1983) "Spare parts for arms can cost an arm and a leg." *New York Times* (November 20): E7.

MOKHIBER, R. (1988) *Corporate crime and violence—Big business power and the abuse of the public trust.* San Francisco: Sierra Club Books.

MOLINA, L. (1995) "Can states commit crimes? The limits of international law." Pp. 349–388 in J. I. Ross (Ed.) *Controlling state crime.* New York: Garland Publishing Co.

MOLLENHOFF, C. R. (1988) "Essential institutions to combat fraud and corruption in government operations." *Corruption and Reform* 3: 125–134.

MONAGHAN, P. (1991) "Sociologists' close-up look at big-time basketball depicts a world in which players' academic goals are subverted." *Chronicle of Higher Education* (February 6): A31.

MONSE, M. D. (1992) "Ethical issues in representing thrifts." *Buffalo Law Review* 40: 1–64.

MOONEY, C. J. (1992) "Critics question higher education's commitment and effectivness in dealing with plagiarism." *Chronicle of Higher Education* (February 12): A13; A18.

MOORE, C. A. (1987) "Taming the giant corporation? Some cautionary remarks on the deterrability of corporate crime." *Crime & Delinquency* 33: 379–402.

MOORE, E. and MILLS, M. (1990) "The neglected victims and unexamined costs of white-collar crime." *Crime and Delinquency* 36: 408–418.

MOORE, G. A., MAGALDI, A. M., and GRAY, J. A. (1987) *The legal environment of business: A contextual approach.* Cincinnati: Southwestern Publishing.

MOORE, W. E. (1970) *The professions: Roles and rules.* New York: Russell Sage.

MORAN, J. A., PARELLA, M. A., and DAKAKE, N. (1988) *White collar crime study.* Kingston, RI: Governor's Justice Commission.

MORAN, W. B. (1985) *Investigative methods for white-collar crime*. Port Townsend, WA: Loompanics.

MORASH, M. and HALE, D. (1987) "Unusual crime or crime as unusual? Images of corruption at the interstate commerce commission." Pp. 129–149 in T. S. Bynum (Ed.) *Organized crime in America*. Monsey, NY: CT Press.

MORGENTHAU, T. (1989) "The S & L scandal's biggest blowout." *Newsweek* (November 6): 35–36.

MRKVICKA, E. F. (1989) *The bank book*. New York: Harper & Row.

MUELLER, G. O. W. and ADLER, F. (1985) *Outlaws of the ocean*. New York: Hearst Maritime Books.

*MULTINATIONAL MONITOR*. (1993) "Cheating the public." *Multinational Monitor* (January/February): 3.

MUNDY, L. (1992) "The fixers—How they may have tampered with your pay." *Lingua Franca* (November/December): 1; 28–33.

MUNDY, L. (1993) "The dirty dozen—Academia's skankiest funders." *Lingua Franca* (March/April): 1; 24–31.

MUTTERPERL, M. H. and MCGOVERN, M. G. (1991) "Federal criminal enforcement of intellectual property rights." *White-collar Crime Reporter* 5: 1–10.

MYERS, G. (1907) *History of the great American fortunes*. New York: The Modern Library.

MYERS, S. L. (1992) "To cabbies, inspection is fear, passing is a living." *New York Times* (July 23): B3.

NADER, R. (1965) *Unsafe at any speed: The designed-in dangers of the American automobile*. New York: Grossman.

NADER, R. and GREEN, M. J. (1972) "Crime in the suites: Coddling the corporations." *New Republic* (April 29): 17–21.

NADER, R. and MAYER, C. J. (1988) "Corporations are not persons." *New York Times* (April 4): 31.

NAGEL, I. and HAGAN, J. (1982) "The sentencing of white-collar criminals in federal courts: A socio-legal exploration of disparity." *Michigan Law Review* 80: 1427–1465.

NALLA, M. and NEWMAN, G. (1990) *A primer in private security*. New York: Harrow & Heston.

NASAR, S. (1994) "Fallen bond trader sees himself as an outsider and a scapegoat." *New York Times* (June 5): A1.

NASH, D. T. (1987) *Medical mayhem*. New York: Walker.

NASH, N. C. (1986) "Suddenly, a sleepy SEC is wide awake." *New York Times* (November 23): 5E.

NASH, N. C. (1989a) "Savings regulators see fraud by head of failed institution." *New York Times* (November 1): A1.

NASH, N. C. (1989b) "Savings executive won't testify and blames regulators for woes." *New York Times* (November 22): A1.

NASH, N. C. (1989c) "Collapse of Lincoln Savings leaves scars for rich, poor and the faithful." *New York Times* (November 30): A22.

NASH, N. C. (1990a) "Losses at savings and loan in 1989 were the biggest ever." *New York Times* (March 27): A1.

NASH, N. C. (1990b) "Bush promising quicker pursuit in savings case." *New York Times* (June 23): A1.

NASH, N. C. (1990c) "Savings agency considers suit against Bush's son and others." *New York Times* (July 11): A1.

NASH, N. C. (1990d) "Greenspan's Lincoln Savings regret." *New York Times* (November 20): D1.

NASH, N. C. and SHENON, P. (1989) "Figure in savings debacle: Victim or villain?" *New York Times* (November 9): A1.

NATIONAL ADVISORY COMMISSION ON CIVIL DISORDERS. (1968) *Report*. New York: Bantam Books.

NATIONAL HEART SAVERS ASSOCIATION. (1990) "The poisoning of America." (Advertisement) *New York Times* (April 4): A21.

NECKEL, S. (1989) "Power and legitimacy in political scandal: Comments on a theoretical framework for the study of political scandals." *Corruption and Reform* 4: 147–158.

NEEDLEMAN, M. L. and NEEDLEMAN, C. (1979) "Organizational crime: Two models of criminogenesis." *The Sociological Quarterly* 20: 517–528.

NEELY, R. (1986) *Judicial jeopardy: When business collides with the courts.* New York: Addison-Wesley.

NELKIN, D. and BROWN, M. (1984) *Workers at risk—Voices from the workplace.* Chicago: University of Chicago Press.

NELLI, H. S. (1986) "Overview," Pp. 1–9 in R. J. Kelly (Ed.) *Organized crime—A global perspective.* Totowa, NJ: Rowman & Littlefield.

NEWFIELD, J. and BARRETT, W. (1988) *City for sale—Ed Koch and the betrayal of New York.* New York: Harper & Row.

NEWMAN, D. J. (1958a) "White-collar crime: An overview and analysis." *Law and Contemporary Problems* 23: 228–232.

NEWMAN, D. J. (1958b) "Public attitudes toward a form of white-collar crime." *Social Problems* 4: 228–232.

NEWMAN, G. (1976) *Comparative deviance: Perceptions and law in six cultures.* New York: Elsevier.

NEWPORT, J. P., JR. (1989) "LBOs—Greed, good business—or both?" *New York Times* (January 2): G6 + .

*NEWSWEEK.* (1974) "A star-spangled swindle." *Newsweek* (July 8): 56–57.

*NEWSWEEK.* (1989) "Hey Ma, get me a lawyer!" *Newsweek* (October 30): 10.

*NEW YORK TIMES.* (1987) *The Tower commission report.* New York: Bantam Books.

*NEW YORK TIMES.* (1990) "Canadians cross falls for U.S. prices." *New York Times* (April 15): 23.

*NEW YORK TIMES.* (1991) "Electronics fraud victims seek Congress's aid." *New York Times* (June 24): A11.

*NEW YORK TIMES.* (1993a) "The M.I.T. case: Time to back off." *New York Times* (September 27): A16.

*NEW YORK TIMES.* (1993b) "Entrepreneur pleads guilty in mail fraud." *New York Times* (March 4): B7.

NEW YORK STATE ORGANIZED CRIME TASK FORCE. (1988) *Corruption and racketeering in the New York City construction industry.* Ithaca, NY: ILR Press.

NICHOLS, L. T. (1990) "Reconceptualizing social accounts: An agenda for theory building and empirical research." *Current Perspectives in Social Theory* 10: 113–144.

NICHOLS, L. T. (1991) "'Whistleblower' or 'renegade': Definitional contests in an official inquiry." *Symbolic Interaction* 14: 395–414.

NICHOLSON, C. K. (1990) "Computer viruses: Information age vulnerability and the technopath." *American Criminal Law Review* 27: 525–543.

NICKLIN, J. L. (1991) "Many colleges learn the hard way they are vulnerable to embezzlement by employees and need strict procedures." *Chronicle of Higher Education* (April 10): A25–26.

NICKLIN, J. L. (1993) "Mississippi college contends its president embezzled $3 million." *Chronicle of Higher Education* (September 1): A42.

NIEVES, E. (1991) "Region's quick-cash frauds snare desperate consumers." *New York Times* (February 6): A1.

NOBLE, B. P. (1991) "Price-fixing and other charges roil a once-placid market." *New York Times* (July 28): D5.

NOBLE, B. P. (1994) "Breathing new life into OSHA." *New York Times* (January 23): F25.

NOLAN, B. (1990) "Removing conflicts from the administration of justice: Conflicts of interest and independent counsels under the Ethics in Government Act." *Georgetown Law Journal* 79: 1–80.

NOONAN, J. T., JR. (1984) *Bribes.* Berkeley: University of California Press.

NORRIE, A. (1986) "Practical reasoning and criminal responsibility: A jurisprudential approach." Pp. 217–230 in D. B. Cornish and R. V. Clarke (Eds.) *The reasoning criminal*. New York: Springer-Verlag.

NORRIS, F. (1990) "Sales are halted at 2 'junk' funds." *New York Times* (November 9): D1.

NOTE. (1979) "Developments in the law—Corporate crime: Regulating corporate behavior through criminal sanctions." *Harvard Law Review* 92: 1365–1375.

NUSSBAUM, B. (1990) *Good intentions*. New York: Penguin Books.

O'CONNELL, M. E. (1992) "International law." Pp. 980–984 in E. F. Borgatta and M. L. Borgatta (Eds.) *Encyclopedia of Sociology*. New York: Macmillan.

OFFICE OF INVESTIGATIONS, Department of Health and Human Services (1991) *1990 Inspector General's annual report*. Washington, DC.

OLSON, W. K. (1991) *The litigation explosion*. New York: Truman-Talley.

ORESKES, M. (1987) "The corruption scandals: What went wrong and the impact on the system." *New York Times* (March 23): B4.

ORLAND, L. (1980) "Reflections on corporate crime: Law in search of theory and scholarship." *American Criminal Law Review* 17: 501–520.

OSTLING, R. N. (1992) "The tuition game." *Time* (November 9): 60 + .

OSTROVSKY, V. and HOY, C. (1990) *By way of deception*. New York: St. Martin's Press.

PACE, D. F. (1991) *Concepts of vice, narcotics, and organized crime*. 3rd ed. Englewood Cliffs, NJ: Prentice-Hall.

PADGETT, T. (1989) "Big trouble in the pits." *Newsweek* (August 14): 36.

PALERMO, P. F. (1978) *Lincoln Steffens*. Boston: Twayne.

PALMER, G. (1992) "New ways to make international environmental law." *The American Journal of International Law* 86: 259–283.

PALMER, J. (1978) "The rising risks of regulation." *Time* (November 27): 85; 87.

PALMER, R. E. (1986) "Let's be bullish on ethics." *New York Times* (June 21): A31.

PAPKE, D. R. (1987) *Framing the criminal: Crime, cultural work and the loss of critical perspective*. Hamden, CT: Archon.

PARISI, N. (1984) "Theories of corporate criminal liability." Pp. 41–68 in E. Hochstedler (Ed.) *Corporations as criminals*. Beverly Hills, CA: Sage.

PARKER, D. B. (1980) "Computer-related white-collar crime." Pp. 199–200 in G. Geis and E. Stotland (Eds.) *White-collar crime: Theory and research*. Beverly Hills, CA: Sage.

PARKER, J. S. (1982) "Social control and the legal profession." Pp. 197–230 in P. Wickman and T. Dailey (Eds.) *White-collar and economic crime*. Lexington, MA: Lexington Books.

PARKER, J. S. (1989) "Criminal sentencing policy for organizations: The unifying approach for optimal penalties." *American Criminal Law Review* 26: 513–604.

PASSAS, N. (1990) "Anomie and corporate deviance." *Contemporary Crises* 4: 157–178.

PASSAS, N. (1993) "Structural sources of international crime: Policy lessons from the BCCI affair." *Crime, Law & Social Change* 20: 293–309.

PASSELL, P. (1995) "How much for a life? Try $3 million to $5 million." *New York Times* (January 29): E3.

PATERNOSTER, R. and SIMPSON, S. (1993) "A rational choice theory of corporate crime." Pp. 37–58 in R. V. Clarke and M. Felson (Eds.) *Routine activity and rational choice*. New Brunswick, NJ: Transaction.

PATTERSON, M. J. and RUSSELL, R. H. (1986) *Behind the lives: Case studies in investigative reporting*. New York: Columbia University Press.

PAULSON, M. C. (1972) *The great land hustle*. Chicago: Regnery.

PAULY, D. (1987) "Travel scams: A costly trip." *Newsweek* (April 27): 48–49.

PEAR, R. (1990) "I.R.S. investigating foreign companies over units in U.S." *New York Times* (February 18): A1.

PEAR, R. (1991a) "In Bush presidency, the regulators ride again." *New York Times* (April 6): E3.

PEAR, R. (1991b) "Study says fees are often higher when doctor has stake in clinic." *New York Times* (August 9): A1.

PEAR, R. (1991c) "Federal auditors report rise in abuses in medical billing." *New York Times* (December 20): A1.

PEAR, R. (1992a) "U.S. seeks millions back in charges." *New York Times* (January 13): A1 +.

PEAR, R. (1992b) "U.S. says hospitals demand physicians pay for referrals." *New York Times* (September 28): A1.

PEAR, R. (1992c) "Top infant–formula makers charged by U.S. over pricing." *New York Times* (December 12): A1.

PEAR, R. and ECKHOLM, E. (1991) "When healers are entrepreneurs: A debate over costs and ethics." *New York Times* (June 2): A1.

PEARCE, F. (1976) *Crimes of the powerful.* London: Pluto Press.

PEARCE, F. and TOMBS, S. (1989) "Bhopal: Union Carbide and the hubris of the capitalist technology." *Social Justice* 16: 116–144.

PEARCE, F. and TOMBS, S. (1990) "Ideology, hegemony, and empiricism: Compliance theories of regulation." *British Journal of Criminology* 30: 423–443.

PEARCE, F. and TOMBS, S. (1991) "Policing corporate 'skid rows': A reply to Hawkins." *British Journal of Criminology* 31: 415–426.

PENCE, L. L. (1986) "The federal enforcers: An overview of the prosecutors and investigators." Pp. 1–50 in L. L. Pence, G. A. Feffer, and E. C. Hoffman III (Eds.) *White collar crime manual.* Washington, DC: Federal Publications.

PENNSYLVANIA CRIME COMMISSION. (1980) *A decade of organized crime.* St. David's, PA: Pennsylvania Crime Commission.

PENNSYLVANIA CRIME COMMISSION. (1991) *Organized crime—Report.* Harrisburg, PA: Commonwealth of Pennsylvania.

PEPINSKY, H. E. (1974) "From white collar crime to exploitation: Redefinition of a field." *Journal of Criminal Law and Criminology* 65: 225–233.

PEPINSKY, H. E. (1980) *Crime control strategies.* New York: Oxford University Press.

PEPINSKY, H. E. (1986) "A sociology of justice." *Annual Review of Sociology* 12: 93–108.

PEPINSKY, H. E. and QUINNEY, R. (Eds.)(1991) *Criminology as peacemaking.* Bloomington: Indiana University Press.

PEREZ–PENA, R. (1993) "Investigator asks: Did Lockheed clean house?" *New York Times* (September 8): B9.

PEREZ–PENA, R. (1994) "U.S. juries grow tougher on plaintiffs in lawsuits." *New York Times* (June 17): A1.

PERITZ, R. J. (1990) "A counter–history of antitrust law." *Duke Law Journal* 20: 263–320.

PERROW, C. (1984) *Normal accidents—Living with high-risk technologies.* New York: Basic Books.

PERRUCCI, C., PERRUCCI, R., TARG, D. B., and TARG, H. R. (1988) *Plant closings: International context and social costs.* New York: Aldine de Gruyter.

PERRUCCI, R., ANDERSON, R. M., SCHENDEL, D. E. and TRACHTMAN, L. E. (1980) "Whistle–blowing: The professionals' resistance to organizational authority." *Social Problems* 28: 149–164.

PERRY, S. and DAWSON, J. (1985) *Nightmare: Women and the Dalkon shield.* New York: Macmillan.

PETERSON, B. (1989) "U.S. accuses 46 of major fraud in commodities." *San Francisco Chronicle* (August 3): 1.

PETERSON, M. J. (1989) "An historical perspective on the incidence of piracy." Pp. 41–60 in E. Ellen (Ed.) *Piracy at sea.* Paris: International Maritime Bureau.

PETZINGER, T. (1987) *Oil & honor: The Texaco-Pennzoil wars.* New York: Berkley Books.

PFOHL, S. (1985) *Images of deviance and social control.* New York: McGraw-Hill.

PFOHL, S. and GORDON, A. (1986) "Criminological displacements: A sociological deconstruction." *Social Problems* 33: 94–113.

PFOST, D. R. (1991) "Reagan's Nicaraguan policy: A case study of political deviance and crime." *Crime & Social Justice* 27: 66–87.

PFUHL, E. (1987) "Computer abuse: Problems of instrumental control." *Deviant Behavior* 8: 113–130.

PIERSON, R. (1989) *The queen of mean: The unauthorized biography of Leona Helmsley.* New York: Bantam Books.

PILZER, P. Z. with DEITZ, R. (1989) *Other people's money*. New York: Simon & Schuster.

PITCH, T. (1983) "Business ethics new appeal." *New York Times* (December 11): 3.

PITT, H. L. (1987) *Insider trading—Counselling and compliance*. Clifton, NJ: Prentice-Hall Law & Business.

PITT, H. L. and GROSKAUFMANIS, K. (1990) "Minimizing corporate, civil and criminal liability: A second look at corporate codes of conduct." *The Georgetown Law Review* 78: 1559–1654.

PITT, H. L. and SHAPIRO, K. L. (1990) "Securities regulation by enforcement: A look ahead at the next decade." *Yale Journal of Regulation* 7: 149–304.

PIZZO, S. (1990) "The real culprits in the thrift scam." *New York Times* (April 2): A17.

PIZZO, S., FRICKER, M., and MUOLO, P. (1991) *Insider job: The looting of America's savings and loans*. New York: Harper Perennial.

PIZZO, S. P. and MUOLO, P. (1993) "Take the money and run." *New York Times Magazine* (May 9): 26; 56–62.

PLATT, A. and COOPER, L. (1974) *Policing America*. Englewood Cliffs, NJ: Prentice-Hall .

PONTELL, H. N. and CALAVITA, K. (1992) "Bilking bankers and bad debts: White-collar crime and the savings and loan crisis." Pp. 195–213 in K. Schlegel and D. Weisburd (Eds.) *White-collar crime reconsidered*. Boston: Northeastern University Press.

PONTELL, H. N. and CALAVITA, K. (1993) "White-collar crime in the savings and loan scandal." *Annals* 525: 31–45.

PONTELL, H. N., CALAVITA, K., and TILLMAN, R. (1994) "Corporate crime and criminal justice system capacity: Government response to financial institution fraud." *Justice Quarterly* 11: 383–410.

PONTELL, H. N., GRANITE, D., KEENAN, C., and GEIS, G. (1985) "Seriousness of crimes: A survey of the nation's chiefs of police." *Journal of Criminal Justice* 13: 1–13.

PONTELL, H. N., JESILOW, P. D., and GEIS, G. (1982) "Policing physicians: Practioner fraud and abuse in a government medical program." *Social Problems* 30: 117–125.

PONTELL, H. N., JESILOW, P. D., GEIS, G., and O'BRIEN, M. J. (1985) "A demographic portrait of physicians sanctioned by the federal government for fraud and abuse against Medicare and Medicaid." *Medical Care* 23: 1028–1031.

POOLEY, E. (1993) "Scamming Wall Street." *New York Times* (June 7): 28–36.

POSNER, R. (1984) "Theories of economic regulation." Pp. 240–250 in A. I. Ogus and C. G. Veljanovski (Eds.) *Readings in the economics of law and regulation*. Oxford: Clarendon Press.

POTTS, M., KOCHAN, N., and WHITTINGTON, R. (1992) *Dirty Money: BCCI—The inside story of the world's sleaziest bank*. Washington, DC: National Press Books.

POULIN, A. B. (1990) "RICO: Something for everyone." *Villanova Law Review* 35: 853–864.

POVEDA, T. G. (1990) *Lawlessness and reform: The FBI in transition*. Pacific Grove, CA: Brooks/Cole.

POVEDA, T. G. (1992) "White-collar crime and the Justice Department: The institutionalization of a concept." *Crime, Law and Social Change* 17: 235–252.

POVEDA, T. G. (1994) *Rethinking white-collar crime*. Westport, CT: Praeger.

POWELL, B. (1986a) "The case for asbestos." *Newsweek* (September 29): 40–42.

POWELL, B. (1986b) "Can corporate America cope?" *Newsweek* (November 17): 64–65.

PRADOS, J. (1986) *Presidents' secret wars: CIA and Pentagon covert operations from World War II through Iranscam*. New York: Morrow.

PRESIDENT'S COMMISSION ON LAW ENFORCEMENT AND ADMINISTRATION OF JUSTICE. (1967) *The challenge of crime in a free society*. Washington, DC U.S. Government Printing Office.

PRESIDENT'S COMMISSION ON LAW ENFORCEMENT AND ADMINISTRATION OF JUSTICE. (1967) *Task force report: Organized crime*. Washington, DC: U.S. Government Printing Office.

PRESIDENT'S COMMISSION ON ORGANIZED CRIME. (1987) *The Impact: Organized crime today*. Washington, DC: U.S. Government Printing Office.

PRESS, C. (1981) *The political cartoon*. London: Associated Press.

PRIEST, G. L. (1990) "The new legal structure of risk control." *Daedalus* 119: 207–228.

PUNCH, M. (1991) "Tough or tame? The contextuality of tackling business crime in three societies." *Corruption and Reform* 6: 211–235.

QUINN, J. B. (1994) "Here we go again." *Newsweek* (February 7): 28–30.

QUINN, M. (1990) "Don't aim that pack at us." *Time* (January 29): 60.

QUINNEY, R. (1963) "Occupational structure and criminal behavior: Prescription violations by retail pharmacists." *Social Problems* 11: 179–185.

QUINNEY, R. (1964) "The study of white collar crime: Toward a reorientation in theory and research." *Journal of Criminal Law, Criminology and Police Science* 55: 208–214.

QUINNEY, R. (1974) *Critique of legal order.* Boston: Little, Brown .

QUINNEY, R. (1977) *Class, state and crime.* New York: David McKay.

QUINNEY, R. (1979) *Criminology.* 2nd ed. Boston: Little, Brown .

QUINNEY, R. (1980) *Providence: The reconstruction of social and moral order.* New York: Longman.

QUINT, M. (1990) "New estimate in savings bailout says cost could be $500 billion." *New York Times* (April 7): 1.

QUINT, M. (1994) "Mischief under the Travelers umbrella." *New York Times* (May 1): 3/4.

RAMIREZ, A. (1992) "5 are indicted in computer credit theft." *New York Times* (July 9): A14.

RANDALL, D. M. (1987) "The portrayal of corporate crime in network television newscasts." *Journalism Quarterly* 64: 150–153.

RANDALL, D. M., LEE-SAMMONS, L., and HAGNER, P. R. (1988) "Common versus elite crime coverage in network news." *Social Science Quarterly* 69: 910–929.

RANELAGH, J. (1986) *The agency—The rise and decline of the CIA.* New York: Simon & Schuster.

RAPOPORT, R. (1975) "Dr. Nork will see you now." *New Times* (May 1): 27–33.

RASHKE, R. (1986) *The killing of Karen Silkwood.* Boston: Houghton Mifflin.

RAWLINGS, P. (1992) *Drunks, whores, and idle apprentices: Criminal biographies of the eighteenth century.* New York: Routledge.

REASONS, C. E. (1991) "Crimes against the environment: Some theoretical and practical concerns." *The Criminal Law Quarterly* 34: 86–105.

REASONS, C. E., BRAY, B., and CHAPPELL, D. (1989) "Ideology, ethics, and the business of law: Varying perceptions of the ethics of the legal profession." *Legal Studies Forum* 13: 171–188.

REASONS, C. E. and CHAPPELL, D. (1987) "Continental capitalism and crooked lawyering." *Crime & Social Justice* 26: 38–59.

REASONS, C. E. and PERDUE, W. D. (1981) *The ideology of social problems.* Sherman Oaks, CA: Alfred Publishing Co.

REBOVICH, D. and NIXON, R. T. (1994) *Environmental crime prosecution: Results of a national survey.* Washington, DC: National Institute of Justice.

REED, G. E. and YEAGER, P. C. (1991) "Organizational offending and neoclassical criminology: A challenge to Gottfredson and Hirschi's general theory of crime." A Paper Presented at the Annual Meeting of the American Society of Criminology, San Francisco, November.

REED, J. P. (1979) "Watergate attitudes and white collar crime: A longitudinal look at impact in a student population." *International Journal of Comparative and Applied Criminal Justice* 3: 67–77.

REED, J. P. and REED, R. E. (1975) "Doctor, lawyer, indian chief: Old rhymes and new on white-collar crime." *International Journal of Criminology & Penology* 3: 279–293.

REGENSTEIN, L. (1986) *How to survive in America the poisoned.* Washington, DC: Acropolis Books Ltd.

REIBSTEIN, L. (1989) "Employment agency scams." *Newsweek* (February 20): 40.

REIBSTEIN, L. (1991) "Hail felons well met." *Newsweek* (October 7): 44–45.

REICH, R. B. (1983) *The next American frontier.* New York: Times Books.

REICH, R. B. (1989) "America pays the price." *New York Times* (January 29): 32–40.

REICHMAN, N. (1986) Review of James W. Coleman, *The Criminal Elite. Contemporary Sociology* 15: 379–380.

REICHMAN, N. (1987) "Computer matching: Toward computerized systems of regulation." *Law & Policy* 9: 387–413.

REICHMAN, N. (1989) "Breaking confidences: Organizational influences on insider trading." *The Sociological Quarterly* 30: 185–204.

REICHMAN, N. (1991) "Regulating risky business: Dilemmas in security regulation." *Law & Policy* 13: 263–295.

REICHMAN, N. (1992) "Moving backstage: Uncovering the role of compliance practices in shaping regulatory policy." Pp. 244–268 in K. Schlegel and David Weisburd (Eds.) *White-collar crime reconsidered.* Boston: Northeastern University Press.

REICHMAN, N. (1993) "Insider trading." Pp. 55–96 in M. Tonry and A. J. Reiss, Jr. (Eds.) *Beyond the law—Crime in complex organizations.* Chicago: University of Chicago Press.

REIMAN, J. H. (1982) "Marxist explanations and radical misinterpretations: A reply to Greenberg and Humphries." *Crime & Delinquency* 28: 610–617.

REIMAN, J. H. (1990; 1995) *The rich get richer and the poor get prison.* Boston: Allyn & Bacon.

REIMAN, J. H. and HEADLEE, S. (1981) "Marxism and criminal justice policy." *Crime & Delinquency* 27: 24–47.

REINERTSEN, R. and BRONSON, R. J. (1990) "Informant is a dirty word." Pp. 99–104 in J. Gilbert (Ed.) *Criminal investigation.* Columbus, OH: Merrill Publishing Co.

REISS, A. J., Jr. (1971) *The police and the public.* New Haven, CT: Yale University Press.

REISS, A. J., JR. and BIDERMAN, A. (1980) *Data sources on white-collar law breaking.* Washington, DC: U.S. Government Printing Office.

RETTIG, S. and PASSAMANICK, B. (1959) "Changes in moral values over three decades." *Social Problems* 6: 320–328.

REUTER, P. (1993) "The cartage industry in New York." Pp. 149–202 in M. Tonry and A. J. Reiss (Eds.) *Beyond the law—Crime in complex organizations.* Chicago: University of Chicago Press.

REUTERS (1990) "Sanford Weill's wife named as unwitting stock tipper." *New York Times* (May 18): D15.

REYNOLDS, M. (1985) *Crime by choice: An economic analysis.* Dallas, TX: The Fisher Institute.

RHODES, R. P. (1984) *Organized crime—Crime control vs. civil liberties.* New York: Random House.

RICHARDSON, E. L. (1991) "A high-tech Watergate." *New York Times* (October 21): A17.

ROBB, C. (1990) *White-collar crime in modern England: Financial fraud and business morality, 1845–1929.* Ph.D. dissertation, Northwestern University.

ROBB, G. (1992) *White-collar crime in modern England: Financial fraud and business morality, 1845–1929.* Cambridge, UK: Cambridge University Press.

ROBERG, R. R. and KUYKENDALL, J. (1993) *Police and society.* Belmont, CA: Wadsworth.

ROEBUCK, J. and WEEBER, S. C. (1978) *Political crime in the United States.* New York: Praeger.

ROGOVIN, M. and ROGOVIN, W. M. (1993) "The office of attorney general: 'Not properly political.'" *The Journal of Law & Politics* 9: 317–328.

ROMANO, J. (1992) "A state crackdown on insurance fraud." *New York Times* (December 27): 13/1.

ROMANO, R. (1991) "Comment: Organization theory and the criminal liability of organizations." *Boston University Law Review* 71: 377–382.

ROSE-ACKERMAN, S. (1978) *Corruption—A study in political economy.* New York: Academic Press.

ROSEFSKY, R. S. (1973) *Frauds, swindles and rackets.* Chicago: Follett.

ROSENBAUM, D. E. (1990a) "How capital ignored alarms on savings." *New York Times* (June 6): A1.

ROSENBAUM, D. E. (1990b) "Southwest to get economic benefits in savings bailout." *New York Times* (June 25): A1.

ROSENBAUM, D. E. (1994) "Clinton may gain as counsel bill clears Congress." *New York Times* (June 22): A1.

ROSENBERG, D. (1986) "The dusting of America: A story of asbestos—Carnage, cover-up and litigation." *Harvard Law Review* 99: 1693–1706.

ROSENBERG, G. H. (1991) *The hollow hope: Can courts bring about social change?* Chicago: University of Chicago Press.

ROSENBLATT, R. (1994) "How do tobacco executives live with themselves?" *New York Times Magazine* (March 20): 34 + .

ROSENTHAL, E. (1990) "Health insurers say rising fraud is costing them tens of billions." *New York Times* (July 5): A1.

ROSENTHAL, E. (1993) "Drug companies' profits finance more promotion than research." *New York Times* (February 21): A1.

ROSHIER, B. (1973) "The selection of crime news by the press." Pp. 28–39 in S. Cohen and J. Young (Eds.) *The manufacture of news.* Beverly Hills, CA: Sage.

ROSOFF, S. M. (1989) "Physicians as criminal defendants: Specialty, sanctions, and status liability." *Law and Human Behavior* 15: 231–235.

ROSS, E. A. (1901; 1922) *Social control.* New York: Macmillan.

ROSS, E. A. (1907; 1973) *Sin and society: An analysis of latter day iniquity.* New York: Harper & Row.

ROSS, H. L. (1961) "Traffic law violation: A folk crime." *Social Problems* 8: 231–241.

ROSS, I. (1992) *Shady business: Confronting corporate corruption.* New York: The Twentieth Century Fund.

ROSS, J. I. (1992) "Towards a conceptual clarity of police criminality." University of Lethbridge. Unpublished ms.

ROSS, J. I. (Ed.) (1995) *Controlling state crime.* New York: Garland Publishing, Inc.

ROSS, S. (1988) *Fall from grace: Sex, scandal and corruption in American politics from 1702 to the present.* New York: Ballantine Books.

ROSSI, P., WAITE, E., BOSE, C., and BERK, R. (1974) "The seriousness of crimes: Normative structure and individual differences." *American Sociological Review* 39: 224–237.

ROSSIDES, D. (1990) "A dialectical discussion on the nature of disciplines and disciplinarity: The synthesis." *Social Epistemology* 4: 229–258.

ROTHMAN, M. L. and GANDOSSY, R. P. (1982) "Sad tales: The accounts of white-collar defendants and the decision to sanction." *Pacific Sociological Review* 25: 449–473.

ROTHMAN, R. (1978) *Inequality and stratification in the United States.* Englewood Cliffs, NJ: Prentice-Hall .

ROTHSTEIN, R. (1992) "Who are the real looters?" *Dissent* (Fall): 429–430.

ROWAN, R. (1986) "The 50 biggest Mafia bosses." *Fortune* (November 10): 24–38.

ROWLETT, J. R. (1993) "The chilling effect of the Financial Institutions Reform Recovery and Enforcement Act of 1989 and the Bank Fraud Prosecution Act of 1990: Has Congress gone too far?" *Journal of Criminal Law* 20: 239–262.

RUBIN, B. (1987) *Modern dictator—Third world coup makers, strongmen, and populist tyrants.* New York: McGraw-Hill.

RUBINSTEIN, D. (1992) "Structural explanation in sociology: The egalitarian imperative." *The American Sociologist* 23: 5–19.

RUSCHMANN, P. A. (1981) Review of corporate crime. *Journal of Criminal Justice* 9: 253–255.

RUSSELL, G. (1986a) "The fall of a Wall Street superstar." *Time* (November 24): 71–74.

RUSSELL, G. (1986b) "Going after the crooks." *Newsweek* (December 1): 46–56.

RUSTAD, M. and KOENIG, T. (1991) "Demystifying punitive damages in product liability." A Paper Presented at the International Conference on Law and Society, Amsterdam, June.

SACK, K. (1993) "26 states and Fleet settle suit." *New York Times* (February 9): D1.

SAFIRE, W. (1993) "Justice in contempt." *New York Times* (February 11): A31.

SALE, K. (1977) "The world behind Watergate," Pp. 240–252 in G. Geis and R. F. Meier (Eds.) *White-collar crime: Offenses in business, politics, and the professions.* New York: Free Press.

SALE, K. (1990) *The conquest of paradise.* New York: Knopf.

SALTZBURG, S. A. (1991) "The control of criminal conduct in organizations." *Boston University Law Review* 71: 421–453.

SAMPSON, A. (1973) *The sovereign state of ITT*. Greenwich, CT: Fawcett.

SAMUELS, W. J. (1987) "The idea of the corporation as a person: On the normative significance of judicial language." Pp. 113–129 in W. J. Samuels and A. S. Miller (Eds.) *Corporations and society—Power and responsibility*. New York: Greenwood Press.

SAMUELSON, R. T. (1987) "Corporate socialism." *Newsweek* (December 28): 42.

SAMUELSON, R. T. (1991) "The boss as welfare cheat." *Newsweek* (November 11): 55.

SANDERS, J. (1989) "Firm risk management in the face of product liability rules." *Law & Policy* 11: 253–280.

SANDERS, W. B. (1974) *The sociologist as detective: An introduction to research methods*. New York: Praeger.

SAPOLSKY, H. M. (1990) "The politics of risk." *Daedalus* 119: 83–96.

SARASOHN, J. (1993) *Science on trial: The whistleblower, the accuser and the Nobel laureate*. New York: St. Martin's Press.

SARGENT, N. (1990) "Law, ideology and social change: An analysis of the role of law in the construction of corporate crime." *The Journal of Human Justice* (Spring): 97–116.

SAVELSBERG, J. S. (1987) "The making of criminal law norms in welfare states: Economic crime in West Germany." *Law & Society Review* 21: 529–562.

SAVELSBERG, J. (1994) *Constructing white-collar crime: Rationalities, communication, power*. Philadelphia: University of Pennsylvania Press.

SCHECHTER, R. E. (1990) "A retrospective on the Reagan FTC: Musings on the role of an administrative agency." *Administrative Law Review* (Fall): 489–517.

SCHELL, J. (1982) *The fate of the earth*. New York: Avon Books.

SCHELLING, T. C. (1973) "Economic analysis and organized crime." Pp. 75–104 in J. F. Conklin (Ed.) *The crime establishment*. Englewood Cliffs, NJ: Prentice-Hall .

SCHEMO, D. J. (1993) "Software maker accused of using virus to compel client to pay bill." *New York Times* (November 23): A1.

SCHEPPELE, K. L. (1988) *Legal secrets: Equality and efficiency in common law*. Chicago: University of Chicago Press.

SCHERZER, M. (1987) "Insurance." Pp. 185–200 in H. L. Dalton, S. Burns, and Yale AIDS Law Project. *AIDS and the law*. New Haven, CT: Yale University Press.

SCHJOLBERG, S. and PARKER, D. B. (1983) "Computer crime." Pp. 218–223 in S. Kadish (Ed.) *The encyclopedia of crime and justice*. New York: Macmillan and Free Press.

SCHLEGEL, K. (1988a) "Desert, retribution, and corporate criminality." *Justice Quarterly* 5: 615–634.

SCHLEGEL, K. (1988b) Review essay: "Research on white-collar crime: Overcoming a crisis of legitimacy." *Criminal Justice Review* 13: 69–77.

SCHLEGEL, K. (1990) *Just deserts for corporate criminals*. Boston: Northeastern University Press.

SCHLESINGER, A., JR. and BRUNS, R. (1975) *Congress investigates*. New York: Chelsea House.

SCHMIDT, W. E. (1987) "For Jim and Tammy Bakker, excess wiped out a rapid climb to success." *New York Times* (May 16): A8.

SCHNEIDER, K. (1991a) "Coal company admits safety test fraud." *New York Times* (January 19): A14.

SCHNEIDER, K. (1991b) "Exxon to admit criminal count, pay a $100 million fine in spill." *New York Times* (March 3): A13.

SCHNEIDER, K. (1994) "Exxon is ordered to pay $5 billion for Alaska spill." *New York Times* (September 17): A1.

SCHNEIDER, M. W. (1982) "Criminal enforcement of federal water pollution laws in an era of deregulation." *The Journal of Criminal Law and Criminology* 73: 642–674.

SCHNEIDER, V. W. and WIERSEMA, B. (1990) "Limits and use of the Uniform Crime Reports." Pp. 21–48, in D. L. Mackenzie, P. J. Baunach, and R. R. Roberg (Eds.) *Measuring crime: Large-scale, long-range efforts*. Albany: SUNY Press.

SCHNEYER, T. (1991a) "Professional discipline in 2050: A look back." *Fordham Law Review* 60: 125–131.

SCHNEYER, T. (1991b) "Professional discipline in law firms." *Cornell Law Review* 77: 1–46.

SCHOLZ, J. T. (1984) "Voluntary compliance and regulatory enforcement." *Law & Policy* (October): 385–404.

SCHRAGER, L. S. and SHORT, J. F., JR. (1977) "Toward a sociology of organizational crime." *Social Problems* 25: 407–419.

SCHRAGER, L. S. and J. F. SHORT, JR. (1980) "How serious a crime? Perceptions of organizational and common crimes." Pp. 14–31 in G. Geis and E. Stotland (Eds.) *White collar crime*. Beverly Hills, CA: Sage.

SCHUCK, P. H. (1986) *Agent orange on trial: Mass toxic disasters in the court*. Cambridge, MA: Harvard University Press.

SCHUDSON, C. B., ONELLION, A. P., and HOCHSTEDLER, E. (1984) "Nailing an omelet to the wall: Prosecuting nursing home homicide." Pp. 131–145 in E. Hochstedler (Ed.) *Corporations as criminals*. Beverly Hills, CA: Sage.

SCHUR, E. M. (1969) *Our criminal society*. Englewood Cliffs, NJ: Prentice-Hall .

SCHUR, E. M. (1971) *Labeling deviant behavior—Its sociological implications*. New York: Harper & Row.

SCHWARTZ, M. (1987) *The structure of power in America: The corporate elite as a ruling class*. New York: Holmes & Meier.

SCHWARTZ, M. D. (1989) "The undercutting edge in critical criminology." *The Critical Criminologist* 1: 1–5.

SCHWARTZ, M. D. and ELLISON, C. (1982) "Criminal sanctions for corporate misbehavior." *Humanity & Society* 6: 267–293.

SCHWARTZ, M. D. and FRIEDRICHS, D. O. (1994) "Postmodern thought and criminological discontent: New metaphors for understanding violence." *Criminology* 32: 201–226.

SCHWARTZ, R. D. and ORLEANS, S. (1967) "On legal sanctions." *University of Chicago Law Review* 34: 274–290.

SCHWARTZ, R. D. and SKOLNICK, J. H. (1964) "Two studies of legal stigma." Pp. 103–118 in H. S. Becker (Ed.) *The other side*. New York: Free Press.

SCHWEITZER, M. (1990) "Insurance insolvencies: Next mega-crisis?" *New York Times* (June 8): A31.

SCHWENDINGER, H. and SCHWENDINGER, J. (1970) "Defenders of order or guardians of human rights?" *Issues in Criminology* 5: 123–137.

SCIOLINO, E. (1992) "Attorney general names prosecutor in Iraq loans case." *New York Times* (October 17): A1.

SCOTT, D. W. (1989) "Policing corporate collusion." *Criminology* 27: 559–587.

SCOTT, J. C. and AL-THAKEB, F. (1977) "The public's perceptions of crime: A comparative analysis of Scandinavia, Western Europe, the Middle East, and the United States." Pp. 78–88 in C. Huff (Ed.) *Contemporary corrections*. Beverly Hills, CA: Sage.

SCOTT, M. B. and LYMAN, S. (1968) "Accounts." *American Sociological Review* 22: 664–670.

SCOTT, W. J. (1988) "Competing paradigms in the assessment of latent disorders: The case of agent orange." *Social Problems* 35: 145–161.

SCOTT, W. R. (1992) *Organizations: Rational, natural and open systems*. Englewood Cliffs, NJ: Prentice-Hall .

SELIGMAN, J. (1982) *The transformation of Wall Street: A history of the Securities and Exchange Commission and modern corporate finance*. Boston: Houghton Mifflin.

SELKE, W. and PEPINSKY, H. E. (1984) "The politics of police reporting in Indianapolis, 1948–1978." *Law and Human Behavior* 6: 327–342.

SELLIN, T. and WOLFGANG, M. E. (1964) *The measurement of delinquency*. New York: Wiley.

SEN, A. (1977) "Rational fools: A critique of the behavioral foundations of economic theory." *Philosophy and Public Affairs* 6: 316–345.

SESSIONS, W. S. (1991) "Computer crime—An escalating crime trend." *FBI Law Enforcement Bulletin* (February): 12–15.

SETHI, S. P. (1982) *Up against the corporate wall*. Englewood Cliffs, NJ: Prentice-Hall .

SEXTON, J. (1994) "New York police often lie under oath, report says." *New York Times* (April 22): A1.

SHACKELFORD, D. B. (1993) "Commentary: The savings and loan crisis." *Law & Policy* 15: 195–198.

SHAPIRO, S. P. (1980) *Thinking about white collar crime: Matters of conceptualization and research.* Washington, DC.: U.S. Department of Justice.

SHAPIRO, S. P. (1983) "The new moral entrepreneurs: Corporate crime crusaders." *Contemporary Sociology* 12: 304–307.

SHAPIRO, S. P. (1984) *Wayward capitalists: Targets of the Securities and Exchange Commission.* New Haven, CT: Yale University Press.

SHAPIRO, S. P. (1985) "The road not taken: The elusive path to criminal prosecution for white-collar offenders. *Law & Society Review* 19: 179–217.

SHAPIRO, S. P. (1987) "The social control of impersonal trust." *American Journal of Sociology* 93: 623–658.

SHAPIRO, S. P. (1990) "Collaring the crime, not the criminal: Reconsidering the concept of white-collar crime." *American Sociological Review* 55: 346–365.

SHARPE, J. A. (1984) *Crime in early modern England: 1550–1750.* London: Longman.

SHATZ, M. S. (1971) *The essential works of anarchism.* New York: Bantam Books.

SHEAK, R. (1990) "Corporate and state attacks on the material conditions of the working class." *Humanity & Society* 14: 105–127.

SHEARING, C. D. and STENNING, P. C. (1987) *Private policing.* Newbury Park, CA: Sage.

SHEFF, D. (1994) *Game over—How Nintendo conquered the world.* New York: Vintage.

SHELDON, J. A. and ZWEIBEL, G. T. (1980) "Historical developments of consumer fraud law." Pp. 185–202 in E. Bittner and S. Messinger (Eds.) *Criminology review yearbook.* Beverly Hills, CA: Sage.

SHELEY, J. F. (1983) "Critical elements of criminal behavior explanation." *The Sociological Quarterly* 24: 161–186.

SHELEY, J. F. (1991) "Conflict and criminal law." Pp. 21–40 in J. F. Sheley (Ed.) *Criminology: A contemporary handbook.* Belmont, CA: Wadsworth.

SHENK, J. F. and KLAUS, P. A. (1984) "The economic cost of crime to victims." *Special Report.* U.S. Department of Justice: Bureau of Justice Statistics.

SHEPARD, C. E. (1989) *Forgiven—The rise and fall of Jim Bakker and the PTL ministry.* New York: Atlantic Monthly.

SHERIZEN, S. (1978) "Social creation of crime news." Pp. 203–224 in C. Winick (Ed.) *Deviance and mass media.* Newbury Park, CA: Sage.

SHERMAN, H. L., JR. (1987) "Torts." Pp. 418–431, in R. L. Janosik (Ed.) *Encyclopedia of the American judicial system.* New York: Scribner.

SHERMAN, L. W. (Ed.)(1974) *Police corruption: A sociological perspective.* Garden City, NY: Doubleday.

SHERMAN, L. W.(1978a) *The quality of police education.* San Francisco: Jossey-Bass.

SHERMAN, L. W. (1978b) *Scandal and reform: Controlling police corruption.* Berkeley: University of California Press.

SHERMAN, L. W. and LANGWORTHY, R. (1979) "Measuring homicide by police officers." *Journal of Criminal Law and Criminology* 4: 546–560.

SHICHOR, D. (1989) "Corporate deviance and corporate victimization: A review and some elaboration." *International Review of Victimology* 1: 67–88.

SHILTS, R. (1987) *And the band played on—Politics, people, and the AIDS epidemic.* New York: St. Martin's Press.

SHORT, J. F., JR. (1984) "The social fabric of risk: Toward the social transformation of risk analysis." *American Sociological Review* 49: 711–725.

SHORT, J. F., JR. (1989) "Editor's introduction: Toward a sociolegal paradigm of risk." *Law & Policy* 11: 241–252.

SHORT, J. F., JR. (1990) "Hazards, risks and enterprise: Approaches to science, law, and social policy." *Law & Society Review* 24: 179–198.

SHOVER, N. and BRYANT, K. M. (1993) "Theoretical explanations of corporate crime." Pp. 141–176 in M. B. Blankenship (Ed.) *Understanding corporate criminality.* New York: Garland Publishing Co.

SHOVER, N., CLELLAND, D. A., and LYNXWILER, J. (1986) *Enforcement of negotiation: Constructing a regulatory bureaucracy.* Albany: SUNY Press.

SHOVER, N., FOX, G. L., and MILLS, M. (1991) *Victimization by white collar crime and institutional delegitimation*. University of Tennessee, unpublished ms.

SHOVER, N., FOX, G. L., and MILLS, M. (1994) "Long-term consequences of victimization by white-collar crime." *Justice Quarterly* 11: 75–98.

SHRIVER, R. F. (1989) *Computer crime techniques prevention*. Rolling Meadows, IL: Bankers Publishing Co.

SHUGER, S. (1992) "Public eye." *New York Times Magazine* (September 3): 57; 74–87.

SIEBER, U. (1986) *The international handbook on computer crime—Computer-related economic crime and the infringement of privacy*. Chichester: Wiley.

SIEGEL, G. C. (1978) "Cashing in on crime: A study of the burglar alarm business." Pp. 69–89 in J. M. Johnson and J. D. Douglas (Eds.) *Crime at the top: Deviance in business and the professions*. Philadelphia: Lippincott.

SIEH, E. W. (1993) "Employee theft: An examination of Gerald Mars and an explanation based on equity theory." Pp. 95–111 in F. Adler and W. S. Laufer (Eds.) *New directions in criminological theory*. Volume 4. New Brunswick, NJ: Transaction.

SILK, L. (1990) "The true cost of the bailout." *New Youk Times* (June 1): D2.

SILVERMAN, M., REE, P. R., and LYDECKER, M. (1982) *Prescriptions for death: The drugging of the third world*. Berkeley: University of California Press.

SILVERSTEIN, M. (1988) "Watergate and the American political system." Pp. 15–37 in A. Markovits and M. Silverstein, (Eds.) *The politics of scandal: Power and process in liberal democracies*. New York: Holmes & Meier.

SIMON, D. (1988) "White-collar crime and its future." *Justice Quarterly* 5: 155–160.

SIMON, D. and EITZEN, D. S. (1993) *Elite deviance*. Boston: Allyn & Bacon.

SIMON, D. R. and SWART, S. L. (1984) "The Justice department focuses on white-collar crime: Promises and pitfalls." *Crime & Delinquency* 30: 91–106.

SIMON, H. (1976) *Administrative behavior*. 3rd ed. New York: Free Press.

SIMON, H. (1979) "Rational decision-making in business organizations." *American Economic Review* 69: 493–513.

SIMON, H. (1987) "Rationality in psychology and economics." In R. Hogarth and M. Reder (Eds.) *Rational choice*. Chicago: University of Chicago Press.

SIMON, J. F. (1991) "Citizen suits for environmental enforcement." *Trial* (September): 30–33.

SIMON, R. J. (1975) *Women and crime*. Lexington, MA: Lexington Books.

SIMON, R. J. (1990) "Women and crime revisited." *Criminal Justice Research Bulletin* 5: 1–11.

SIMPSON, S. S. (1993) "Strategy, structure and corporate crime: The historical context of anti-competitive behavior." Pp. 71–94 in F. Adler and W. S. Laufer (Eds.) *New directions in criminological theory*. Volume 4. New Brunswick, NJ: Transaction.

SIMPSON, S. S., HARRIS, A. R., and MATTSON, B. A. (1993) "Measuring corporate crime." Pp. 115–140 in M. B. Blankenship (Ed.) *Understanding corporate criminality*. New York: Garland Publishing Co.

SIMPSON, S. S. and C. S. KOPER (1992) "Deterring corporate crime." *Criminology* 30: 347–376.

SIMS, C. (1989) "Phone call thieves hitting corporate switchboards." *New York Times* (December 11): D1.

SIMS, C. (1990a) "Phone fraud: It's still a big problem on campus." *New York Times* (January 3): B6.

SIMS, C. (1990b) "U.S. accuses 2 Nynex companies of overcharging and fines them." *New York Times* (February 8): A1.

SIMS, C. (1992a) "G.E. whistleblower is awarded $13.4 million." *New York Times* (December 5): A 35.

SIMS, C. (1992b) "Company to pay $110 million in health-claims fraud suit." *New York Times* (December 19): A1.

SIMS, C. (1993) "Keating convicted of U.S. charges." *New York Times* (January 7): D1.

SINCLAIR, U. (1906; 1960) *The jungle*. New York: New American Library.

SKLAR, J. N. (1964; 1986) *Legalism: Law, morals, and political trials*. Cambridge, MA: Harvard University Press.

SKOLNICK, J. H. (1969) *The politics of protest*. New York: Ballantine Books.

SLOANE, L. (1991a) "Rising fraud worrying car insurers." *New York Times* (November 16): 48.

SLOANE, L. (1991b) "Beware postcards bearing gifts and 900 numbers." *New York Times* (December 14): A12.

SLOANE, L. (1992) "How an '800' call can cost $15.60." *New York Times* (March 28): 52.

SMIGEL, E. O. (1970) "Public attitudes toward stealing as related to the size of the victim organization." Pp. 15–28 in E. Smigel and H. L. Ross (Eds.) *Crimes against bureaucracy.* New York: Van Nostrand Reinhold.

SMITH, A. (1759; 1976) *The theory of moral sentiments.* Oxford: Clarendon Press.

SMITH, A. (1776; 1937) *An inquiry into the nature and causes of the wealth of nations.* (E. Canaan, ed.) New York: Modern Library.

SMITH, C. (1990) "Rose sentenced to 5 months for filing false tax returns." *New York Times* (July 20): A1.

SMITH, D. C., JR. (1978) "Organized crime and entrepreneurship." *International Journal of Criminology and Penology* 6: 161–177.

SMITH, D. C., JR. (1980) "Paragons, pariahs, and pirates: A spectrum-based theory of enterprise." *Crime & Delinquency* 26: 358–386.

SMITH, D. C., JR. (1982) "White-collar crime, organized crime, and the business establishment: Resolving a crisis in criminological theory." Pp. 23–38 in P. Wickman and T. Dailey (Eds.) *White-collar and economic crime.* Lexington, MA: Lexington Books.

SMITH, G. K. (1992) "The independent counsel in the Iran/Contra affair: Why Gordon Liddy went to jail and Oliver North went to Disneyworld." *American Criminal Law Review* 29: 1261–1299.

SMITH, J. C. (1983) "The process of adjudication and regulation, a comparison." Pp. 78–91 in T. R. Machan and M. B. Johnson (Eds.) *Rights and regulation: Ethical, political and economic issues.* Cambridge, MA: Ballinger.

SMITH, K. W. and KINSEY, K. A. (1987) "Understanding taxpayers' behavior: A conceptual framework with implications for research." *Law & Society Review* 21: 639–663.

SMITH, K. W. and STALANS, L. J. (1991) "Encouraging tax compliance with positive incentives: A conceptual framework and research directions." *Law & Policy* 13: 35–53.

SMITH, M. (1991) "Who cheats on their income taxes." *Money* (April): 101–108.

SNIDER, L. (1987) "Towards a political economy of reform, regulation, and corporate crime." *Law & Policy* 9: 37–68.

SNIDER, L. (1990) "Cooperative models and corporate crime: Panacea or cop-out?" *Crime & Delinquency* 36: 373–389.

SNIDER, L. (1993) *Bad business—Corporate crime in Canada.* Scarborough, Ontario: Nelson Canada.

SNIZEK, W. E. (1974) "Deviant behavior among blue-collar workers-employees: Work-norm violation in the factory." Pp. 67–74, in C. D. Bryant (Ed.) *Deviant behavior—Occupational and organizational bases.* Chicago: Rand McNally.

SNOW, R. P. (1978) "The golden fleece: Arizona land fraud." Pp. 133–150 in J. Johnson and J. D. Douglas (Eds.) *Crime at the top.* Philadelphia: Lippincott.

SOBLE, R. J. and DALLOS, R. E. (1974) *The impossible dream: The Equity funding story.* New York: Putnam.

SOBOL, R. B. (1991) *Bending the law: The story of the Dalkon shield bankruptcy.* Chicago: University of Chicago Press.

SOEKEN, K. L. and SOEKEN, D. R. (1987) "A survey of whistleblowers: Their stressors and coping strategies." Pp. 537–548 in Senate Committee on Governmental Affairs, *Hearings* on S. 508 Before Subcommittee on Federal Services, Post Office, and Civil Service, 100th Congress, 1st Session, July 20 and 31.

SOLOMON, A. M. (1989) "The risks were too good to pass up." *New York Times Book Review* (October 29): 27–28.

SOLOMON, J. (1992) "Mickey's secret life." *Newsweek* (August 31): 70–72.

SOLOMON, J. (1993) "Brave new directors." *Newsweek* (March 1): 59–60.

SONTAG, D. (1992) "Immigrants swindle their own, prey on trust." *New York Times* (August 25): B1.

SPARKS, A. (1990) *The mind of South Africa.* New York: Knopf.

SPENCER, J. W. and TRICHE, E. (1994) "Media constructions of risk and safety: Differential framings of hazard events." *Sociological Inquiry* 64: 199–213.

SPENCER, S. (1993) "Lawrence Walsh's last battle." *New York Times Magazine* (July 4): 11 + .

SPERBER, M. (1990) *College sports, Inc.* New York: Holt.

SPRINGEN, K. (1991) "A slippery pyramid?" *Newsweek* (July 22): 39.

SPURGEON, W. A. and FAGAN, T. P. (1981) "Criminal liability for life—Endangering corporate conduct." *The Journal of Criminal Law and Criminology* 72: 400–433.

STAATS, G. R. (1977) "Changing conceptualizations of professional criminals: Implications for criminology theory." *Criminology* 15: 49–65.

STAFFORD, M. C. and WARR, M. (1993) "A reconceptualization of general and specific deterrence." *Journal of Research in Crime and Delinquency* 30: 123–135.

STALLINGS, R. A. (1990) "Media discourse and the social construction of risk." *Social Problems* 37: 80–97.

STANDING BEAR, Z. G. (1994) "Crime as a hobby: Taking an 'involuntary discount' on expensive wines." *Deviant Behavior* 15: 111–124.

STARR, J. W. (1991) "Turbulent times at Justice and EPA: The origins of environmental criminal prosecutions and the work that remains." *The George Washington Law Review* 59: 900–915.

STEFFENS, L. (1904) *The shame of the cities.* New York: McClure, Phillips.

STEFFENSMEIER, D. (1986) *The fence.* Totowa, NJ: Rowman & Littlefield.

STEFFENSMEIER, D. (1989) "On the causes of 'white-collar' crime: An assessment of Hirschi and Gottfredson's claims." *Criminology* 27: 345–358.

STEIER, R. (1993) "The price isn't always right." *New York Post* (February 26): 3.

STEIN, B. (1994) "Should sleazy stockbrokers get off on a technicality?" *New York* (March 14): 22–27.

STEINBERG, A. (1972) *The bosses.* New York: Macmillan.

STEINBERG, J. (1993a) "Risen from a 'Living Cemetery'." *New York Times* (March 29): B1.

STEINBERG, J. (1993b) "Connecticut store owner sentenced for tax fraud." *New York Times* (October 21): B1.

STEINBERG, M. I. (1991) "Attorney liability for client fraud." *Columbia Business Law Review* 1: 11–26.

STENNING, P. (1988) "Corporate policing: Some recent trends." Pp. 37–45 in *Business and crime: A consultation.* Windsor, Great Britain: Centre for Criminological & Sociolegal Studies, University of Sheffield.

STERN, G. M. (1976) *The Buffalo Creek disaster.* New York: Vintage.

STERN, P. M. (1972) *The rape of the taxpayer.* New York: Vintage.

STERN, P. M. (1980) *Lawyers on trial.* New York: Time Books.

STERN, P. M. (1988) *The best Congress money can buy.* New York: Pantheon Books.

STERNBERG, W. and HARRISON, M. C. (1989) *Feeding frenzy.* New York: Holt.

STERNGOLD, J. (1990) *Burning down the house—How greed, deceit, and bitter revenge destroyed E. F. Hutton.* New York: Summit Books.

STEVENSON, R. W. (1990a) "Lockheed fined $1 million as polluter." *New York Times* (February 17): A10.

STEVENSON, R. W. (1990b) "How one savings institution came apart." *New York Times* (June 12): A1.

STEVENSON, R. W. (1991a) "Keating's trial begins with emotion flaring." *New York Times* (August 3): A35.

STEVENSON, R. W. (1991b) "U.S. accuses G.E. of fraud in Israeli deal." *New York Times* (August 15): A1.

STEVENSON, R. W. (1992a) "Keating is sentenced to 10 years for defrauding S & L customers." *New York Times* (April 11): A1.

STEVENSON, R. W. (1992b) "Pentagon disciplines G. E. unit." *New York Times* (June 3): D1.

STEVENSON, R. W. (1992c) "U.S. judge orders $7.5 million award to whistle-blower." *New York Times* (July 15): A1.

STEVENSON, R. W. (1992d) "G.E. guilty plea in U.S. aid to Israel." *New York Times* (July 23): D1.

STEWART, J. B. (1987) *The prosecutors.* New York: Touchstone Books.

STEWART, J. B. (1991) *Den of thieves.* New York: Simon & Schuster.

STEWART, J. B. (1993) "Michael Milken's biggest deal." *The New Yorker* (March 8): 58–71.

STIER, E. H. (1982) "The interrelationships among remedies for white-collar criminal behavior." Pp. 153–174 in H. Edelhertz and T. D. Overcast (Eds.) *White collar crime—An agenda for research.* Lexington, MA: Lexington.

STOHL, M. and LOPEZ, G. A. (Eds.) (1984) *The state as terrorist: The dynamics of governmental violence and repression.* Westport, CT: Greenwood Press.

STONE, C. (1975) *Where the law ends.* New York: Harper.

STONE, C. (1989) "Choice of target and other law enforcement variables." Pp. 203–223 in M. L. Friedland (Ed.) *Sanctions and rewards in the legal system: A multidisciplinary approach.* Toronto: University of Toronto.

STONE, M. (1986) "Insiders." *New York* (July 28): 26–34.

STOTLAND, E. (1977) "White collar criminals." *Journal of Social Issues* 33: 179–195.

STOTLAND, E. (1981) "Can white-collar crime investigators be protected from improper pressures? The case of Israel." *Journal of Criminal Justice* 9: 265–288.

STOTLAND, E. (1982) "The role of law enforcement in the fight against white-collar crime." Pp. 69–98 in H. Edelhertz and T. D. Overcast (Eds.) *White collar crime—An agenda for research.* Lexington, MA: Lexington.

STOTLAND, E., BRINTNALL, M., L'HEUREUX, A., and ASHMORE, E. (1980) "Do convictions deter home repair fraud?" Pp. 252– 265 in G. Geis and E. Stotland (Eds.) *White collar crime—Theory and research.* Beverly Hills, CA: Sage.

STROCK, J. M. (1991) "Environmental enforcement priorities for the 1990s." *The George Washington Law Review* 59: 916–937.

STRUM, C. (1991) "Trend in Hudson County." *New York Times* (December 19): B7.

STULLER, J. (1989) "Computer cops and robbers." *Across the Board* (June): 13–19.

SULLIVAN, R. (1990) "Voting-machines lobbyist says official sought bribe." *New York Times* (April 4): B3.

SULSKI, J. (1990) "Crackdown on crime is raising question of computer rights." *Chicago Tribune* (November 18): 17–18.

SURETTE, R. (1992) *Media, crime, and criminal justice: Images and realities.* Pacific Grove, CA: Brooks/Cole.

SUTHERLAND, E. H. (1924) *Criminology.* Philadelphia: Lippincott.

SUTHERLAND, E. H. (1937) *The professional thief.* Chicago: University of Chicago Press.

SUTHERLAND, E. H. (1940) "White-collar criminality." *American Sociological Review* 5:1–12.

SUTHERLAND, E. H. (1945) "Is 'white-collar crime' crime?" *American Sociological Review* 10: 132–139.

SUTHERLAND, E. H. (1947) *Criminology.* 4th ed. Philadelphia: Lippincott.

SUTHERLAND, E. H. (1949) *White collar crime.* New York: Holt, Rinehart & Winston.

SUTTON, A. and WILD R., (1985) "Small business: White-collar villains or victims?" *International Journal of the Sociology of Law* 13: 247–259.

SWANSON, W. and SCHULTZ, G. (1982) *Prime rip.* Englewood Cliffs, NJ: Prentice-Hall.

SWARTZ, E. M. (1987) "Product liability and the captive consumers." *Case and Comment* (November–December): 3–6.

SYKES, C. J. (1988) *Profscam: Professors and the demise of higher education.* Washington, DC: Regnery Gateway.

SYKES, G. M. and MATZA, D. (1957) "Techniques of neutralization: A theory of delinquency." *American Sociological Review* 22: 664–670.

SZASZ, A. (1984) "Industrial resistance to occupational safety and health legislation, 1971–1981." *Social Problems* 32: 103–116.

SZASZ, A. (1986a) "The process and significance of political scandals: A comparison of Watergate and the 'Sewergate' episode at the Environmental Protection Agency." *Social Problems* 33: 202–217.

SZASZ, A. (1986b) "Corporations, organized crime, and the disposal of hazardous waste: An examination of the making of a criminogenic regulatory structure." *Criminology* 24: 1–28.

SZOCKYJ, E. (1990) "From Wall Street to Main Street: Defining insider trading as a social problem." A Paper Presented at the Annual Meeting of the American Society of Criminology, Baltimore, November.

SZOCKYJ, E. (1993) *The law and insider trading: In search of a level playing field.* Buffalo, NY: Hein.

TABOR, M. B. W. and RAMIREZ, A. (1992) "Computer savvy, with an attitude." *New York Times* (July 23): B1.

TAGER, M. (1988) "Corruption and party machines in New York City." *Corruption and Reform* 3: 25–39.

TANNENBAUM, F. (1938) *Crime and the community.* New York: Columbia University Press.

TAPPAN, P. (1947) "Who is the criminal?" *American Sociological Review* 12: 96–102.

TARBELL, I. (1904; 1925) *History of the Standard Oil Co.* New York: Macmillan.

TARLOW, B. (1988) "RICO forfeiture of business." *Trial* (September): 52–55.

TAYLOR, L. (1984) *Born to crime—The genetic causes of criminal behavior.* Westport, CT: Greenwood Press.

TAYLOR, S. (1983) "Ethics and the law: A case history." *New York Times Magazine* (January 9): 31–33; 46–49.

TAYLOR, S. (1985) "Criminal lawyers and lawyers who turn criminal." *New York Times* (March 19): A17.

TAYLOR, T. (1970) *Nuremberg and Vietnam: An American Tragedy.* New York: Bantam Books.

TEUBER, A. (1990) "Justifying risk." *Daedalus* 119: 235–254.

THIO, A. (1973) "Class bias in the sociology of deviance." *The American Sociologist* 8: 1–12.

THIO, A. (1988) *Deviant behavior.* 3rd ed. Harper & Row.

THOMAS, J. M. (1982) "The regulatory role in the containment of corporate illegality." Pp. 99–127 in H. E. Edelhertz and T. D. Overcast (Eds.) *White-collar crime: An agenda for research.* Lexington, MA: Lexington.

THOMAS, J. and O'MAOLCHATHA, A. (1989) "Reassessing the critical metaphor: An optimistic revisionist view." *Justice Quarterly* 6: 143–172.

THOMAS, L. M. (1993) *Vessels of evil—American slavery and the Holocaust.* Philadelphia: Temple University Press.

THOMAS, R. (1990) "Feast of the S & L vultures." *Newsweek* (July 30): 40.

THOMAS, R. (1994) "Forget about the experts." *Newsweek* (October 31): 42.

THOMMA, S. (1994) "Rostenkowski indicted on 17 counts." *Philadelphia Inquirer* (June 1): 1.

THOMPSON, D. F. (1987) *Political ethics and public office.* Cambridge, MA: Harvard University Press.

THOMPSON, M. W. (1990) *Feeding the beast—How Wedtech became the most corrupt little company in America.* New York: Scribner.

THORNBURGH, R. (1991a) "Criminal enforcement of environmental laws—A national priority." *The George Washington Law Review* 59: 775–780.

THORNBURGH, R. (1991b) "Foreword: Sixth annual survey of white collar crime." *American Criminal Law Review* 28: 383–391.

THORNBURGH, R. (1990) "Money laundering." *Vital Speeches of the Day* 56: 578–580.

THURMAN, Q., ST. JOHN, C. and RIGGS, L. (1984) "Neutralization and tax evasion: How effective would a moral appeal be in improving compliance to tax laws?" *Law & Policy* 6: 309–327.

TIDWELL, G. L. (1993) *Anatomy of a fraud.* New York: Wiley.

TIGAR, M. and LEVY, M. R. (1977) *Law and the rise of capitalism.* New York: Monthly Review Press.

TILLMAN, R. (1994) "Politicians and bankers: The political origins of two local banking crises." *Crime, Law & Social Change* 21: 319–335.

TILLMAN, R. and PONTELL, H. N. (1992) "Is justice 'collar-blind'? Punishing Medicaid provider fraud." *Criminology* 30: 547–574.

TILLY, C. (1985) "War making and state making as organized crime." Pp. 169–191 in P. B. Evans, D. Rueschmeyer, and T. Skocpol (Eds.) *Bringing the state back in.* Cambridge: Cambridge University Press.

*TIME.* (1973) "Battling the biggest fraud." *Time* (July 16): 51.

TIMM, H. W. and CHRISTIAN, K. E. (1991) *Introduction to private security.* Pacific Grove, CA: Brooks/Cole.

TITTLE, C. R. (1980) *Sanctions and social deviance.* New York: Praeger.

TITTLE, C. R. (1983) "Social class and criminal behavior: A critique of the theoretical foundations." *Social Forces* 62: 334–373.

TITTLE, C. R., VILLEMEZ, W. J., and SMITH, D. A. (1978) "The myth of social class and criminality: An empirical assessment of the empirical evidence." *American Sociological Review* 43: 643–656.

TITUS, R. M., HEINZELMANN, F., and BOYLE, J. M. (1995) "Victimization of persons by fraud." *Crime & Delinquency* 41: 54–72.

TOBIAS, A. (1990) "Not a sure thing." *Time* (October 22): 48–50.

TOLCHIN, M. (1984) "One enlists in the campaign against waste." *New York Times* (February 28): A14.

TOLCHIN, S. J. and TOLCHIN, M. (1983) *Dismantling America—The rush to deregulate.* Boston: Houghton Mifflin.

TOMASIC, R. and PENTONY, B. (1989) "Insider trading and business ethics." *Legal Studies Forum* 13: 151–170.

TOMASSON, R. E. (1991) "Nintendo to pay $25 million in rebates on price fixing." *New York Times* (April 11): D1.

TONRY, M. and REISS, A. J., JR. (1993) *Beyond the law—Crime in complex organizations.* Chicago: University of Chicago Press.

TORRES, D. A. (1985) *Handbook of federal police and investigative agencies.* Westport, CT: Greenwood Press.

TRACY, P. E. and FOX, J. A. (1989) "A field experiment on insurance fraud in auto body repair." *Criminology* 27: 589–603.

TRAUB, J. (1988) "Into the mouths of babes." *New York Times Magazine* (July 24): 18–20; 51.

TRAUB, J. (1990) *Too good to be true: The outlandish story of Wedtech.* New York: Doubleday.

TROST, C. (1984) *Elements of risk—The chemical industry and its threat to America.* New York: Times Books.

TRUELL, P. and GURWIN, L. (1992) *False profits: The inside story of BCCI, the world's most corrupt financial empire.* New York: Houghton Mifflin.

TUCHMAN, G. (1978) *Making news: A study in the construction of reality.* New York: Free Press.

TURK, A. (1982) *Political criminality.* Beverly Hills, CA: Sage.

TURNER, D. F. (1990) "The virtues and problems of antitrust law." *The Antitrust Bulletin* 35: 297–310.

TURQUE, B. (1994) "Wading into Whitewater." *Newsweek* (January 31): 42.

TYLER, G. (1981) "The crime corporation." Pp. 273–290 in A. S. Blumberg (Ed.) *Current perspectives on criminal behavior.* New York: Knopf.

UGGEN, C. (1993) "Reintegrating Braithwaite: Shame and consensus in criminological theory." *Law & Social Inquiry* 18: 481–499.

U.S. CONGRESS, HOUSE SUBCOMMITTEE ON ENERGY AND POWER AND HOUSE SUBCOMMITTEE ON CRIME. (1979) *White collar crime in the oil industry.* Washington, DC U.S. Government Printing Office.

U.S. DEPARTMENT OF JUSTICE. (1989) *White collar crime: A report to the public.* Washington, DC: U.S. Government Printing Office.

U.S. GENERAL ACCOUNTING OFFICE. (1988) *Ethics enforcement: Results of conflict of interest investigations.* Washington, DC: U.S. Government Printing Office.

U.S. HOUSE OF REPRESENTATIVES, SUBCOMMITTEE ON CRIME. (1986; 1987) E. F. Hutton mail and wire fraud: *Report* of the subcommittee of the committee on the judiciary. Washington, DC: U.S. Government Printing Office.

U.S. POSTAL SERVICE. (1990) *The postal inspection service.* Washington, DC: U.S. Postal Service.

U.S. PRESIDENT'S COUNCIL ON INTEGRITY AND EFFICIENCY, COMMITTEE ON INVESTIGATIONS AND LAW ENFORCEMENT. (1988) *Report.* Washington, DC: U.S. Government Printing Office.

U.S. SENATE. (1987) *Hearings* before the committee on the judiciary: Oversight of the problem of white collar crime. Washington, DC: U.S. Government Printing Office.

U.S. SENTENCING COMMISSION. (1988) *Discussion materials on organizational sanctions.* Washington, DC: U.S. Sentencing Commission.

U.S. SENTENCING COMMISSION. (1989) *Preliminary draft: Sentencing guidelines for organizational defendants.* Washington, DC: U.S. Sentencing Commission.

U.S. SENTENCING COMMISSION. (1990) *Annual Report.* Washington, DC: U.S. Sentencing Commission.

USEEM, M. (1983) *The inner circle: Large corporations and the rise of business political activity in the U.S. and U.K.* New York: Oxford University Press.

VAGO, S. (1990) *Law and society: An introduction.* 3rd ed. Englewood Cliffs, NJ: Prentice-Hall.

VAN CISE, J. G. (1990) "Antitrust past–present–future." *The Antitrust Bulletin* 35: 985–1008.

VAN DUYNE, P. C. (1993) "Organized crime and business crime enterprises in the Netherlands." *Crime, Law and Social Change* 19: 103–142.

VAN VOORST, B. (1993) "Toxic dumps: The lawyers' money pit." *Time* (September 13): 63–64.

VARETTE, S. E., MEREDITH, C., ROBINSON, R. B., HOFFMAN, D., and ABT ASSOCIATES OF CANADA. (1985) *Research on white collar crime: Exploring the issues.* Ottawa: Ministry of Justice.

VAUGHAN, D. (1980) "Crime between organizations: Implications for victimology." Pp. 77–97 in G. Geis and E. Stotland (Eds.) *White collar crime: Theory and research.* Beverly Hills, CA: Sage.

VAUGHAN, D. (1981) "Recent developments in white-collar crime theory and research." Pp. 135–147, in I. L. Barak-Glantz and C. R. Huff (Eds.) *The mad, the bad and the different: Essays in honor of Simon Dinitz.* Lexington, MA: Lexington.

VAUGHAN, D. (1983) *Controlling unlawful corporate behavior.* Chicago: University of Chicago Press.

VAUGHAN, D. (1989) "Regulating risk: Implications of the Challenger accident." *Law & Policy* 11: 330–349.

VAUGHAN, D. (1992) "The macro–micro connection in white collar crime theory." Pp. 124–148 in K. Schlegel and D. Weisburd (Eds.) *White collar crime reconsidered.* Boston: Northeastern University Press.

VERMEULE, C. (1983) "Crime and punishment in antiquity." *Harvard Magazine* (November/December): 64–70.

VIDMAR, N. J. (1989) "Foreword—Empirical research and the issue of jury competence." *Law and Contemporary Problems* 52: 1–8.

VILLA, J. K. (1988) *Banking crimes.* New York: Clark Boardman.

VISCUSI, W. K. (1983) *Risk by choice: Regulating health and safety in the workplace.* Cambridge, MA: Harvard University Press.

VISCUSI, W. K. (1986) "The structure and enforcement of job safety regulation." *Law and Contemporary Problems* 49: 127–150.

VISE, D. A. (1987) "One of the markets best and brightest is caught." *The Washington Post* (March 2): 6–7.

VITIELLO, J. (1992) "The new world order—From fraud and force to business as usual in the global free market: The up-to-date evidence." *Crime, Law and Social Change* 17: 253–266.

VOGEL, D. (1986) *National styles of regulation: Environmental policy in Great Britain and the United States.* Ithaca, NY: Cornell University Press.

VOGEL, D. (1989) *Fluctuating fortunes.* New York: Basic Books.

VOHRA, N. K. (1994) "Downsizing sweeps the industry." Pp. C75–C77, in *Industry surveys.* New York: Standard & Poor.

VOLD, G. B. (1958) *Theoretical criminology.* New York: Oxford University Press.

VOLD, G. B. and BERNARD, T. J. (1986) *Theoretical criminology.* 3rd ed. New York: Oxford University Press.

VON HOFFMAN, N. (1988) *Citizen Cohn.* New York: Doubleday.

WACHSMAN, H. F. (1989) "Doctors who maim and kill." *New York Times* (August 25): A29.

WACHSMAN, H. F. (1990) "Trial lawyers as S & L bounty hunters." *New York Times* (June 21): A23.

WAEGEL, W. B., ERMANN, M. D., and HOROWITZ, A. M. (1981) "Organizational responses to the imputation of deviance." *Sociological Quarterly* 22: 43–55.

WAGNER, C. F. (1979) *The CPA and computer fraud.* Toronto: Lexington.

WALD, M. L. (1988) "Using liability law to put tobacco on trial." *New York Times* (February 14): F 11.

WALD, M. L. (1990a) "Whistleblowers in atomic plants to be aided." *New York Times* (March 11): A28.

WALD, M. L. (1990b) "I.R.S. seeks $7 billion in case with Exxon." *New York Times* (August 7): D4.

WALD, M. L. (1992) "Credit fraud a growing menace, survey finds." *New York Times* (July 8): C13.

WALDMAN, M. (1990) *Who robbed America? A citizen's guide to the savings & loan scandal.* New York: Random House.

WALDMAN, S. (1989) "The HUD Rip-off." *Newsweek* (August 7): 16–22.

WALKER, A. (1981) "Sociology and professional crime." Pp. 153–178 in A. S. Blumberg (Ed.) *Current perspectives on criminal behavior.* New York: Knopf.

WALKER, S. (1980) *Popular justice—A history of American criminal justice.* New York: Oxford University Press.

WALKER, S. (1983) *The police in America.* New York: McGraw-Hill.

WALKLATE, S. (1989) *Victimology: The victim and the criminal justice process.* London: Unwin Hyman.

WALLACE, M., SAFER, M., RATHER, D., and REASONER, H. (1980) *60 Minutes verbatim.* New York: Arno.

WALSH, M. F. and SCHRAM, D. D. (1980) "The victim of white-collar crime: Accuser or accused?" Pp. 32–51 in G. Geis and E. Stotland (Eds.) *White collar crime: Theory and research.* Beverly Hills, CA: Sage.

WALSH, W. F. and LICATOVICH, B. (1991) "Analysis of female corporate criminality." A Paper Presented at the Annual Meeting of the Academy of Criminal Justice Sciences Meeting. Pittsburgh, March.

WALT, S. and LAUFER, W. S. (1991) "Why personhood doesn't matter: Corporate criminal liability and sanctions." *American Journal of Criminal Law* 18: 263–287.

WALZER, M. (1977) *Just and unjust wars: A moral argument.* New York: Basic Books.

WAREN, W. T. (1988) "The product liability dilemma." *State Legislatures* (April): 12–16.

WARR, M. (1980) "The accuracy of public beliefs about crime." *Social Forces* 59: 456–470.

WARR, M. (1989) "What is the perceived seriousness of crimes?" *Criminology* 27: 795–821.

WASIK, M. (1991) *Crime and the computer.* Oxford: Clarendon Press.

WATSON, R. (1986) "How to spend a billion." *Newsweek* (March 26): 34–38.

WAYNE, L. (1989a) "Where were the accountants?" *New York Times* (March 12): 3/1.

WAYNE, L. (1989b) "Showdown at 'Gunbelt' Savings." *New York Times* (March 12): B1.

WAYNE, L. (1994) "A side deal and a wizard's undoing." *New York Times* (May 15): D1.

WEATHERBURN, D. (1993) "On the quest for a general theory." *Australian and New Zealand Journal of Criminology* 26: 35–46.

WEBB, T. (1990) "Light sentences in S & L cases blasted." *Scranton Times* (July 19): 5.

WEBER, J. (1990) "Measuring the impact of teaching ethics to future managers: A review, assessment and recommendation." *Journal of Business Ethics* 9: 1183–1190.

WEBSTER, W. H. (1980) "An examination of FBI theory and methodology regarding white-collar crime investigation and prevention." *American Criminal Law Review* (Winter): 275–286.

WEIL, J. R. and BRANNON, W. T. (1957) *"Yellow Kid" Weil—Con man.* New York: Pyramid.

WEINER, E. (1990) "Eastern Airlines indicted in scheme over maintenance." *New York Times* (July 26): A1.

WEIR, D. and NOYES, D. (1983) *Raising hell—How the Center for Investigative Reporting gets the story.* Reading, MA: Addison-Wesley.

WEISBURD, D., CHAYET, E. F., and WARING, E. J. (1990) "White-collar crime and criminal careers: Some preliminary findings." *Crime & Delinquency* 36: 342–355.

WEISBURD, D., WHEELER, S., WARING, E. J., and BODE, N. (1991) *Crimes of the middle class.* New Haven, CT: Yale University Press.

WELLS, J. T. (1992) *Fraud examination: Investigative and audit procedures.* New York: Quorum Books.

WELLS, J. T. (1993a) "Accountancy and white-collar crime." *Annals* 525: 83–94.

WELLS, J. T. (1993b) "From the chairman." *The White Paper* 7: 1.

WEST PUBLISHING (1983) *The guide to American law.* St. Paul, MN: West Publishing Co.

WHALLEY, J. L. (1990) "Crime and punishment—Criminal antitrust enforcement in the 1990s." *Antitrust Law Journal* 59: 151–160.

WHEELER, S. (1976) "Trends and problems in the sociological study of crime." *Social Problems* 23: 525–534.

WHEELER, S. (1983) "White collar crime: History of an idea." Pp. 1652–1656 in S. Kadish (Ed.) *Encyclopedia of crime and justice.* New York: Macmillan and Free Press.

WHEELER, S. (1992) "The problem of white-collar motivation." Pp. 108–123 in K. Schlegel and D. Weisburd (Eds.) *White-collar crime reconsidered.* Boston: Northeastern University Press.

WHEELER, S., MANN, K., and SARAT, A. (1988) *Sitting in judgment: The sentencing of white-collar criminals.* New Haven, CT: Yale University Press.

WHEELER, S., WEISBURD, D., and BODE, N. (1982) "Sentencing the white-collar offender: Rhetoric and reality." *American Sociological Review* 47: 641–659.

WHEELER, S., WEISBURD, D., WARING, E., and BODE, N. (1988) "White collar crimes and criminals." *American Criminal Law Review* 25: 331–358.

WHITE, D. M. and AVERSON, R. (1979) *The celluloid weapon.* Boston: Beacon Press.

WHITE, E. M. (1993) "Too many campuses want to sweep student plagiarism under the rug." *The Chronicle of Higher Education* (February 24): A44.

WHITE, L. (1983) *Human debris: The injured worker in America.* New York: Putnam.

*White-collar Crime Reporter.* (1990) "Court limits scope of insider trading cases." *White Collar Crime Reporter* 4: 1–4.

WHITESIDE, T. (1972) *The investigation of Ralph Nader: General Motors vs. one determined man.* New York: Pocket Books.

WHITFORD, W. C. (1989) "Critical empiricism." *Law and Social Inquiry* 14: 61–67.

WILDAVSKY, A. and DAKE, K. (1990) "Theories of risk perception: Who fears what and why?" *Daedalus* 119: 41–60.

WILKES, P. (1989) "The tough job of teaching ethics." *New York Times* (January 22): E1, 24.

WILLIAMS, E. (1966) *Capitalism and slavery.* New York: Capricorn.

WILLIAMS, F. P. and MCSHANE, M. D. (1988) *Criminological theory.* Englewood Cliffs, NJ: Prentice-Hall.

WILLIAMS, K. (1989) "Researching the powerful: Problems and possibilities of social research." *Contemporary Crises* 13: 253–274.

WILLIAMS, R. (1987) *Political corruption in Africa.* Aldershot: Gower.

WILLIAMS, W. (1985) "White-collar crime: Booming again." *New York Times* (June 9): 3, 1+.

WILMSEN, S. K. (1991) *Silverado—Neal Bush and the savings & loan scandal.* Washington, DC: National Press Books.

WILSON, E. D. (1975) *Sociobiology.* Cambridge, MA: Harvard University Press.

WILSON, J. Q. (1961) "The economy of patronage." *Journal of Political Economy* 69: 369–380.

WILSON, J. Q. (1966) "Corruption: The shame of the states." *The Public Interest* 2: 28–38.

WILSON, J. Q. (1983) *Thinking about crime.* New York: Basic Books.

WILSON, J. Q. and HERRNSTEIN, R. J. (1985) *Crime and human nature.* New York: Simon & Schuster.

WILSON, M. (1983) "Folk crime: Patterns of accommodation." *Deviant Behavior* 4: 123–140.

WILSON, N. K. (1991) "Recycling offenses, the routine ground of everyday activities, and Durkheimian functionality in crime." A Paper Presented at the Annual Meeting of the Academy of Criminal Justice Sciences, Nashville, March.

WINANS, R. F. (1986) *Trading secrets.* New York: St. Martin's Press.

WINERIP, M. (1994) "Billions for school are lost in fraud, waste and abuse." *New York Times* (February 2): A1 + .

WISE, D. (1973) *The politics of lying.* New York: Vintage.

WISE, D. (1976) *The American police state—The government against the people.* New York: Random House.

WISE, E. N. (1989) "International crimes and domestic criminal law." *DePaul Law Review* 38: 923–966.

WOLD, G. and SHRIVER, R. F. (1989) *Computer crime techniques prevention.* Rolling Meadows, IL: Bankers Publishing Co.

WOLFF, R. P. (1976) *In defense of anarchism.* New York: Harper Torchbooks.

WOLFGANG, M. E., FIGLIO, R. M., and THORNBERRY, T. P. (1978) *Evaluating criminology.* New York: Elsevier.

WOLFGANG, M., FIGLIO, R., TRACY, P., and SINGER, S. (1985) *The national survey of crime severity.* Washington, DC: U.S. Government Printing Office.

WOOD, C. (1993) "A prophet of doom." *MacLean's* (March 15): 24 + .

WOODBURY, R. (1990) "If the loot's there, he'll find it." *Time* (May 21): 67.

WOODWARD, B. and BERNSTEIN, C. (1977) *The final days.* New York: Avon Books.

WRIGHT, J. (1979) *On a clear day you can see General Motors.* New York: Avon Books.

WRIGHT, J. P., CULLEN, F. T., and BLANKENSHIP, M. B. (1995) "The social construction of corporate violence: Media coverage of the Imperial Food Products fire." *Crime & Delinquency* 41: 20–36.

WRIGHT, R. A. (1994) *In defense of prisons.* Westport, CT: Greenwood Press.

WRIGHT, R. A. and FRIEDRICHS, D. O. (1991) "White collar crime in the criminal justice curriculum." *Journal of Criminal Justice Education* 2: 95–119.

WRIGHTSMAN, L. (1991) *Psychology and the social system.* 2nd ed. Pacific Grove, CA: Brooks/Cole.

WYMAN, D. S. (1984) *The abandonment of the Jews—America and the Holocaust, 1941–1945.* New York: Pantheon Books.

YARNOLD, B. (1995) "A new role for the International Court of Justice: Adjudicator of international and state transnational crimes." Pp. 317–347 in J. I. Ross (Ed.) *Controlling state crime.* New York: Garland Publishing Co.

YEAGER, P. C. (1987) "Structural bias in regulatory law enforcement: The case of the U.S. Environmental Protection Agency." *Social Problems* 34: 330–344.

YEAGER, P. (1991a) *The limits of law: The public regulation of private pollution.* Cambridge: Cambridge University Press.

YEAGER, P. (1991b) "Law, crime and inequality: The regulatory state." A Paper Presented at the Annual Meeting of the American Society of Criminology, San Francisco, November.

YEAGER, P. C. and KRAM, K. E. (1990) "Fielding hot topics in cool settings: The study of corporate ethics." *Qualitative Sociology* 13: 127–148.

YELLEN, D. and MAYER, C. J. (1992) "Coordinating sanctions for corporate misconduct: Civil or criminal punishment?" *American Criminal Law Review* 29: 961–1024.

YOUNG, J. and MATTHEWS, R. (1992a) "Questioning left realism." Pp. 1–18 in R. Matthews and J. Young (Eds.) *Issues in realist criminology.* London: Sage.

YOUNG, J. and MATTHEWS, R. (1992b) *Rethinking criminology: The realist debate.* London: Sage.

YOUNG, M. (1991) *The Vietnam wars: 1945–1990.* New York: HarperPerennial.

YOUNG, T. R. (1981) "Corporate crime: A critique of the Clinard Report." *Contemporary Crises* 5: 323–335.

ZAGORIN, A. (1993) "Get out of jail, not quite free." *Time* (May 24): 50.

ZEISEL, H. and DIAMOND, S. (1976) "The jury selection in the Mitchell-Stans conspiracy trial." *ABF Research Journal* 1: 151–174.

ZEITLIN, L. (1971) "A little larceny can do a lot for employee morale." *Psychology Today* 5: 22 +.

ZERUBAVEL, E. (1991) *The fine line: Making distinctions in everyday life*. New York: Free Press.

ZEY, M. (1993) *Banking on fraud: Drexel, junk bonds, and buyouts*. New York: Aldine de Gruyter.

ZIETZ, D. (1981) *Women who embezzle or defraud: A study of convicted felons*. New York: Praeger.

ZILINSKAS, R. (1995) "State crimes against the environment." Pp. 235–281 in J. I. Ross (Ed.) *Controlling state crime*. New York: Garland Publishing Co.

ZIMMER, C. R. (1989) *Resource dependence, differential association, and corporate misconduct*. The University of North Carolina at Chapel Hill, Ph.D. dissertation.

ZIMRING, F. (1987) "Problems and means of measuring white collar crime." Office of the Attorney General: Symposium '87: *White collar/Institutional crime*. California Department of Justice.

ZIMRING, F. E. and HAWKINS, G. (1993) "Crime, justice and the savings and loan crisis." Pp. 247–292, in M. Tonry and A. J. Reiss, Jr. (Ed.) *Beyond the law—Crime in complex organizations*. Chicago: University of Chicago Press.

ZUCKERMAN, H. (1977) "Deviant behavior and social control in science." Pp. 87–138 in E. Sagarin (Ed.) *Deviance and social change*. Beverly Hills, CA: Sage.